KEATING'S
GENERAL HISTORY
OF
IRELAND.

Translated from the original Irish, with many curious Amendments
taken from the Psalters of Tara and Cashel, &c.,

BY DERMOD O'CONNOR, Esq.

BRIAN BOIROIHME, KING OF MUNSTER.

DUBLIN:
JAMES DUFFY, SONS, & CO.,
15, WELLINGTON QUAY:
AND 14, PATERNOSTER ROW, LONDON.

[188-]

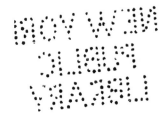

PATTISON JOLLY,
STEAM-PRESS PRINTER,
22. ESSEX-ST. WEST, DUBLIN.

TO THE

MOST NOBLE AND PUISSANT LORD,

WILLIAM O'BRYEN,

EARL AND BARON OF INCHIQUIN, AND BARON OF BURREN, IN THE COUNTY
OF CLARE, IN THE KINGDOM OF IRELAND.

MY LORD,

The following General History of Ireland humbly addresses your Lordship for protection ; a History deduced, with great fidelity, from the most early accounts of time, and abounding with relations of the most memorable events and heroic exploits of the ancient Irish, among whom the royal ancestors of your Lordship have filled the throne of Ireland for twenty-nine successions, (as appears from the subsequent genealogy of your Lordship's most illustrious house,) and with signal bravery have repelled the invasions of foreign enemies, and gave a fresh supply of life and vigour to the cause of their expiring country.

Were the translation of this work proportionable to the dignity of its subject, it might naturally hope for countenance from your Lordship, whose noble and warlike progenitors shine with unrivalled lustre through many pages of this collection ; which I humbly request your Lordship to look upon with an eye of favour, not only as it delivers down to posterity an unexceptionable account of your Lordship's most noble family, but as a most sacred refuge for the following history, from the censures of illiterate and unjust men, who insolently attempt to vilify and traduce the lineal descendants of the great MILESIANS, (a martial, a learned, and generous race,) as a nation ignorant, mean-spirited, and superstitious.

It has ever been the distinguishing practice of your Lordship's most noble family not only to preserve inviolable the genealogies of your own renowned line, but to express a just veneration and regard for the public records and annals of your native country, which I declare openly to the world, are faithfully translated in this history, without fraud or falsehood ; and therefore I am farther encouraged to inscribe my labours to your Lordship's name and patronage.

And never, may it please your Lordship, was any man more ambitious of proper means to publish to after ages the antiquity and grandeur of your Lordship's extraction, which flows in a direct line from the brave GADELIANS, the great founders of the Irish name; and Providence has at last gratified the passionate desire I have always had, of paying my due respects to your Lordship, though I despair of paying my just acknowledgments; and though I was never able to produce any thing of my own, worthy of your Lordship's view, yet that misfortune is relieved by the present opportunity of offering a translation of the genuine and venerable antiquities and monuments of Ireland to your Lordship's candid approbation.

To pray for the prosperity and continuance of your Lordship's illustrious life, and that your noble line may for ever flourish, as a security for the blessing of peace and liberty to their country, as it is my duty, so my Lord, it is my ambition to appear upon all occasions,

Your Lordship's most obedient,

and most devoted humble servant,

DERMOD O'CONNOR

THE PEDIGREE

OF THE

RIGHT HON. WILLIAM O'BRYEN,

EARL OF INCHIQUIN,

TO KING MILESIUS, OF SPAIN.

WILLIAM O'BRYEN, the fourth earl of Inchiquin, married to Lady Anne Hamilton, eldest daughter and coheir to George Hamilton, earl of Orkney; son of

William O'Bryen, third earl of Inchiquin, married Mary, daughter to Sir Ed. Villiers, knt., and sister to the earl of Jersey; son of

William O'Bryen, second earl of Inchiquin, married Lady Margaret Boyle, daughter to Roger Boyle, first earl of Orrery; son of

Morough O'Bryen, fifth lord baron of Inchiquin, created first earl of Inchiquin married Elizabeth, daughter of Sir Wm. St. Leger, knt., lord president of Munster, son of

Dermod O'Bryen, fourth lord baron of Inchiquin, married Ellen, daughter of Sir Edmond FitzGerald, of Ballimaloe, knt.; son of

Morough O'Bryen, third lord baron of Inchiquin, married Margaret daughter of Sir Thos. Cusiack., knt., lord chancellor, and one of the lord justices of Ireland; son of

Morough O'Bryen, second lord baron of Inchiquin, married to Mable, daughter of Christ. Nugent, lord baron of Delvin; son of

Dermod O'Bryen, first lord baron of Inchiquin, married to Lady Margaret, daughter to Donough, second earl of Thomond; son of

Morough O'Bryen, fourth son to the last prince of Thomond, married to Eleanor, daughter of Thos. FitzGerald, called Knight of Valley; son of

Turlough O'Bryen, prince of Limerick and Thomond, married to Joan Fitz Maurice, daughter to lord Fitz Maurice, alias Vulgo Balbus, lord baron of Kerry and Lixnaw; son of

Teige an Condaig O'Bryen, married to Annabella Bourk, daughter to Ulic William; son of

Turlough O'Bryen, married to Slany, daughter to Loghlen Ladir Macnamara ; son of

Bryen Cathaneny O'Bryen, married to Slanyin Macnamara ; son of

Mabon O'Bryen, married to the daughter of the prince of Leinster, of
the lineal descent of Dairy Barrach, son of Cathaoir More, monarch
of Ireland; son of

Muiriertagh O'Brien, married to Sarah; daughter to O'Kennedy ,
son of

Turlough O'Bryen, married to Aurina, daughter to Daniel More
Macarty ; son of

Teige O'Bryen, married to Fynwola, daughter to Kennedy ; son of

Connor na Suidini O'Bryen, married to More Macnamara ; son of

Donogh Cairbreagh O'Bryen, married to Sarah, the daughter of
Donough O'Kennedy ; son of

Daniel More O'Brien (vixit temp. Henrici II.), king of Cashel and
Limerick 30 years, married to Orlacam, daughter to Mac Morough ;
son of

Turlough O'Bryen, king of Munster 5 years, married to Nariait,
daughter to O'Fogherta ; son of

Dermod O'Bryen, king of Munster 4 years, married Sarah, daughter
of Teig Macarty ; son of

Turlough O'Bryen, ruled as monarch of Ireland 12 years, married
More, daughter of O'Heyne ; son of

Teige O'Bryen, married to More, the king of Leinster's daughter ;
son of

Bryen Boiromh, monarch of Ireland 12 years. He was slain in the
great battle of Clontarf, and was married to Gormfhlath, daughter
to Morough Mac Flinn ; son of

Kennedy, king of Munster 18 years, married to Beibhion, the daughter of Archadh, son of Morough, lord of West Conacht ; son of

Lorcan, king of Thomond 6 years ; son of

Laghtna, king of Thomond 3 years ; son of

Corc, king of Munster 17 years ; son of

Anluan, prince of Munster ; son of

Mahon (vixit circa septimum sæculm post nat. Christi) ; son of

Turlough, king of Munster 36 years ; son of

Cathal, king of Thomond 7 years ; son of

Aodh Caomh, king of Thomond 41 years ; son of

Conall, prince of Thomond ; son of

Eochaidh Baldearg, king of Munster 29 years ; son of

Carthan Fionn, king of Thomond 45 years ; son of

Bloid, king of Thomond 16 years ; son of

Cas, king of Thomond 16 years ; son of

Conall Eachluath, king of Munster 13 years ; son of

Luighaidh Mean, king of Munster 27 years ; son of

Aongus Cinaithreach, king of Munster 30 years ; son of

Fearchorb, king of Munster 16 years ; son of

Modh Chorb, king of Munster 27 years ; son of

Cormac Cas, king of Munster 12 years ; son of

Oilioll Olum, king of Munster 27 years; son of
Eogan More, king of Munster 15 years; son of
Modha Neid, king of Munster 23 years; son of
Deary, prince of Munster; son of
Deirgthine, half king of Munster 13 years; son of
Eana Munchaoin, half king of Munster 10 years; son of
Luigheach More, king of Munster 2 years; son of
Modhafeibhis, prince of Munster; son of
Muireach, king of Munster 17 years; son of
Eochaidh Garbh, king of Munster 36 years; son of
Duach Donn Dalta Deagha, monarch of Ireland 10 years; son of
Cairbre Cuisgleathan, king of Munster 28 years; son of
Luighaidh Laighne, monarch of Ireland 5 years; son of
Jonadhmhar, monarch of Ireland 3 years; son of
Niadh Seadhamhuin, monarch of Ireland 7 years; son of
Adamhar, monarch of Ireland 5 years; son of
Fearchorb, monarch of Ireland 11 years; son of
Modhchorb, monarch of Ireland 7 years; son of
Cobhthaig Caomh, king of Munster 29 years; son of
Reachta Righdhearg, monarch 20 years; son of
Lughaidh Laighe, monarch 7 years; son of
Eochaidh, monarch 7 years; son of
Oilioll Fionn, monarch 9 years; son of
Art, monarch 6 years; son of
Luighaidh Lamhdhearg, monarch 7 years; son of
Eochaidh.Vairceas, monarch 12 years; son of
Luighaidh Jardhoinn, monarch 9 years; son of
Eadhna Dearg, monarch 12 years; son of
Duach Fionn, monarch 5 years; son of
Seadhna Jonaraice, monarch 20 years; son of
Breasrigh, monarch 9 years; son of
Art Imleach, monarch 22 years; son of
Elim, monarch 1 year; son of
Rotheachta, monarch 7 years; son of
Roane, prince of Ireland; son of
Failbhe, king of Munster 26 years; son of
Cas Cead Chaigneach, king of Munster 36 years; son of
Aildergoid, monarch 7 years; son of
Muinneamhoin, monarch 5 years; son of
Casclothacht, king of Munster 13 years; son of
Irereorda, prince of Ireland; son of
Rotheachta, monarch 25 years; son of
Glas; son of
Nuagatt Deaghlamh; son of
Rosa, prince of Ireland; son of
Eochaidh Faobharglas, monarch 20 years; son of
Conmaol, monarch 30 years; son of
Heber Fionn, half monarch of Ireland one year; son of
Milesius, king of Spain

THE LIFE

OF

THE REV. JEOFFRY KEATING, D.D

VERY little information can be obtained at present of the early years of the Rev. J. Keating, till his departure to Spain, where he studied in the college of Salamanca for twenty-three years. On the return of this memorable divine, he was received with singular respect by all ranks of his countrymen, and his native parish, Tybrud, conferred on him, which he afterwards resigned to the Rev. Eugene Duhy. This Duhy, like a second Moses, prayed with uplifted hands, whilst our Rev. author fought the enemy of the souls and the character of his countrymen, for many years, which reflects infinite honour on his memory, and renders the Irish nation for ever indebted to him. He appeared always cheerful and pleasing, and the fervent zeal of his soul suffered no moment of his life to pass unemployed in the service of his God, but was either praying, preaching, or writing; his amiable conversation was ever blended with edifying examples and instruction; his shining virtues charmed and captivated the minds of the worthy and benevolent, insomuch that many of the Protestant religion contributed to erect a parish chapel for him, which still remains in the same yard with their own church. His zealous discharge of his sacerdotal duties endangered his life; a lady, kept by a gentleman, was excommunicated by him; furious with rage, this wicked man threatened the life of our author, who, in order to avoid the effects of his malice, was obliged to conceal himself in the wood of Aharla, situated between the mountain Gaßte and the town of Tipperary. During his concealment there, he wrote the history of Ireland.

Of the writers which Ireland has produced, none was more disinterested than our Rev. author. Although perfectly skilled in the English language, he chose the Irish, the language of his country, not only for his history, but for his numerous valuable 'works, which still exist, and are superior to it. Labouring from no lucrative view, he cheerfully bestowed his productions to confirm and edify his countrymen.

In the following verses the Irish language is thus described by him:—

> As milis an teanga an Ghaoidhilge,
> Guth gan, chabhair, choigchriche,
> Glor glo, gling, gasda,
> Seimh, suairc, sult-bhlasda.

            Cia Eabhra teanga as seannda,
            Cia Laidion is leaghanta,
            Uatha uirthe nior frith ling,
            Tuairem focail do chomaoin.

In English:

            The Irish is a language completely sweet,
         In aid of which no foreign e'er did meet;
         A copious, free, keen, and extending voice,
         And mellifluent, brief; for mirth most choice.
         Although the Hebrew language be the first,
         And that, for learning, Latin be the best,
         Yet still, from them, the Irish ne'er was found
         One word to borrow, to make its proper sound.

The following inscription, in raised letters, is placed over the door of the church of Tybrud, where those venerable divines, the Rev. Eugene Duhy and the Rev. J. Keating, are interred.

I I–I S   ✠   Maria
                                                  I Ꝑ R

ORATE, proaiabg P. Eugenij : Duhy vic. de Tybrud : et P. Doct. Galf. kearing huig sacelli Fundatoru : necno etprooibg alijs Ta sacerd. quam Laicis quoru corpa. in eod. jacet sa. Aᵒ Doni 1644.

The foregoing inscription is thus plainly expressed.

Orate pro animabus Parochi Eugenii Duhy, Vicarii de Tubrud, et Divinitatis Doctoris Galfridii Keating, hujus Sacelli Fundatorum; nec non et pro omnibus aliis, tam Sacerdotibus quam Laicis, quorum Corpora in eodem jacent Sacello. Anno Domini 1644.

In English:

Pray for the souls of the Priest Eugenius Duhy, Vicar of Tybrud,* and of Jeoffry Keating, D.D., Founders of this Chapel; and also for all others, both Priests and Laity, whose Bodies lie in the same Chapel. In the year of our Lord 1644.

On our author the following epitaph also has been written:

            In one urn in Tybrud, hid from mortal eye,
            A poet, prophet, and a priest doth lie;
            All these, and more than in one man could be,
            Cocentered were in famous Jeoffry.

THE

TRANSLATOR'S PREFACE.

NOTWITHSTANDING the great length of the original preface of DR. KEATING, I am obliged to detain the reader by a short account of this translation, the induce ments that led to it, and the objections made against it.

The genuine merit of the following history is so far from being questioned by the learned Irish, that the nobility and gentry of the kingdom have preserved it as an invaluable collection of antiquity, and the author has said so much in its vindication, that I submit it to the impartial and judicious, only desiring it might be read with that degree of candour which justly belongs to a subject that runs through so many dark and unlearned ages. This chronicle of Ireland is not offered to the world as an infallible record, perfectly free from errors and mistakes, for it is impossible that the true origin of any kingdom or people in the world can be discovered at this remote distance; and it is certain that the histories of all nations, the higher they are traced, the more they are encumbered with fictions, and often with relations utterly incredible. But does it follow that the whole of these accounts is nothing but fable, because some matters are recorded which carry an air of falsehood? If this rule be admitted, no history or chronicle in the world, except the inspired writings, would escape; for human compositions, notwithstanding all imaginable care, can never claim a right to infallibility.

It is well known that a translation of Dr. Keating's history has been often attempted, but without success; nor did the design miscarry from any discouragements it met with, but being a work of great expense, and written in a difficult and mysterious language, it did not come to maturity before this time, to the great disappointment of the nobility and gentry of the kingdom, who had the original in that esteem, that they thought it justly deserved a translation, and resolved to support it. It was some years ago when I entertained the first thoughts of this undertaking, and I communicated myself to Dr. Anthony Raymond of Dublin, who approved of my design, and promised to assist me in it: but some misfortunes falling upon his own private affairs, I desisted from prosecuting my resolution at that time. When I arrived in England I could have no prospect, in a strange country, of encouragement to publish so chargeable a work, but was again solicited, by the importunity of friends, to resume my design of a translation, to offer it to the world by way of subscription; I undertook the work and finished it, and have met with encouragement beyond my expectation. The most noble personages in the kingdom of Ireland, for birth, quality, and learning, have done me the honour of their names, which is an evidence of the high esteem they entertained of the original, and that they judged it so far from being an old insipid legend of fables, that they valued it as the choicest collection of ancient records that possibly can be recovered from the ruins of time, to support the honour of their ancestors, and to give the world a just idea of the dignity of the country where they were born.

There is an author, who has concealed his name, that has, with great ignorance and envy, attempted to explode and ridicule the labours of the great Dr. Keating, and to stigmatize the following history as a fictitious and romantic composition. He has likewise bestowed some flowers of his oratory in representing the weakness of my abilities, and my incapacity for the work I had undertaken. Wha relates to myself, being entirely personal, and weak, insignificant scandal, is below the concern of the reader and my own, and therefore I shall only in this place, answer an objection or two, wherein he has aspersed the character of my author, and vindicate the reputation of this history, whose intrinsic worth, in the opinion of men of learning, is placed beyond the reach of his malice, though among the injudicious, and before the publishing of this translation. his spleen had in some measure the effect he desired, and in a small degree prejudiced me in my subscriptions.

The prefacer to the Memoirs of the Marquis of Clanricarde promises the world. In his pompous title-page, a learned dissertation, wherein was inserted a digression containing several curious observations concerning the antiquities of Ireland And he has fulfilled his word so far as to labour in the proof that there are no res, antiquities in the kingdom of Ireland; that their records are not genuine. but the invention of bards or druids, who, in the times of ignorance and superstition, imposed upon the world; and that the chronicle of Dr. Keating is a collection from those spurious and romantic compositions, whose authority he knew to be invalid, and to whose testimony he never gave any real belief. But the insolence of this censure appears, not only by destroying in one breath the evidence of all the national chronicles of Ireland, but as it proceeds from a person who never had in his possession one of those ancient records, which, if he had, his ignorance and want of skill in the language made him incapable to understand. It is certain that the abilities of this prefacer in the Irish tongue extend no farther than the knowledge of a school-boy, and a small acquaintance with the modern characters of that language; and the utmost of his learning consists only in turning over some fabulous tracts, of a late date, such as Bruighean Chaorthuin, Eachtra an Ghiolla Dheachair, Cath Fionntragh. &c., which, by the way, was the true reason, why he never performed his promise to the world, of publishing a history of Ireland from the ancient records, for he was sensible his ignorance of the original Irish language rendered him incapable to fulfil it; and therefore it is no wonder that he has traduced those venerable antiquities, as false and incredible fictions, having no other way to make a tolerable excuse to those persons whom, for many years, he put in expectation of an Irish history. I confess I have, in one sense, done him an irreparable damage. by publishing this translation, because he can no longer impose upon his friends, by amusing them with a history of Ireland, and consequently he must be sensibly affected by the discontinuance of the many favours he has received upon the merits of that prospect. However it must always be esteemed a malicious and ungenerous practice, for a man to throw aspersions upon the public records of a nation, upon whose character he has been supported for many years, and upon whose authority he laid a scheme for his future subsistence.

It is with great confidence asserted, by this prefacer, that there is no such person in this age, as an antiquary, throughout the kingdom of Ireland when it is most evident, and I call upon thousands to attest it, that there are numbers of them, whose employment it is to transcribe the ancient chronicles. and to instruct the youth in the proper language of the country; and his malice is equally conspicuous where he says, that the only remaining copy of Dr. Keating's history is in the hands of the Baron of Cathir, since it is unquestionably certain, that many copies have been transcribed, and the manuscripts are preserved in several hands, and scattered through most parts of the kingdom.

Dr. Lloyd, it seems, we are told with great triumph, in his catalogue of Irish manuscripts he found in Trinity College, Dublin, makes no mention of the Psalters of Cashel and Tara; from whence it is inferred, that there are no such records, and consequently to pretend to quote them is an imposition and an abuse upon mankind. In answer to this charge it must be observed, that Dr. Lloyd was a professed stranger to the old manuscripts of that kingdom, as he generously confesses in his Archæologia Britannica; and it is well known that there is a large folio, in fine vellum, fairly written some hundred years ago, in Ballimore, in the county of Meath, which contains one historical transcript of those Psalters, the Book of Ardmagh, and other valuable antiquities. This choice record is now preserved in Trinity College, which I had the favour of perusing, and I kept it in my custody for six months. I take this opportunity to express my gratitude to the learned Dr. Anthony Raymond, of Trim, for the favour he did me in entering into a bond of a thousand pounds, as security for my restoring this ancient manuscript after my perusal of it.

What this prefacer observes, concerning a translation of Dr. Keating's history, by the procurement of the Right Honourable the Earl of Orrery, grandfather to the present earl, is true in fact, and I confess that this chronicle was translated by Timothy Roe O'Connor, the father of Conn O'Connor, lately deceased; but the reflection made upon it, that the earl suppressed this translation, out of justice to the world, which he resolved not to abuse with lies and fables, is a charge as false and malicious. For the true reason why that noble lord refused to let that translation come abroad, was to enhance the value of it, and to make his manuscript the greater curiosity, which would have lost much of its esteem if it had been printed and published.

Thus far have I followed and detected the ignorance and peevishness of this writer, whose envy and disappointments have carried him into manifold errors, and into the lowest of personal reflections. But I leave him to be corrected by the torment of his own mind, and the contempt of his former friends, who, justly sensible of his ungenerous proceedings, his invincible malice, and his notorious want of capacity, have banished him their acquaintance, as an infamous renegade and wicked libeller upon the glory and honour of his native country.

For want of a more convenient opportunity, and because the following information came too late to be inserted in the body of the history, the account I have received shall be communicated in this place.

There has been a dispute among learned men, whether the ancient kings of Ireland, of the Milesian race, wore crowns of gold, after the manner of other nations. We are informed by Hector Boetius, in his second and tenth book, that the kings of Scotland, from the time of Feargus to the reign of Achaius, used a plain crown of gold, militaris valli forma, "in the form of a military trench;" and it is more than probable that in this practice they followed the Irish monarchs, from whom they derived their descent and customs. And this conjecture is still rendered more reasonable by a golden cap, supposed to be a provincial crown. that was found in the year 1692, in the county of Tipperary, at a place called Barnanely by the Irish, and by the English, the Devil's Bit; it was discovered about ten feet under ground, by some workmen that were digging up turf for firing. This cap or crown weighs about five ounces; the border and the head is raised in chase-work and it seems to bear some resemblance to the close crown of the eastern empire, which was composed of the helmet together with a diadem, as the learned Selden observes in his Titles of Honour, Part I. chap. 8.

Some of the antiquarians of Ireland have imagined, that this was the crown worn by some provincial kings, under the command of Bryen Boiroimhe, who beat the Danes in so many battles; others are rather inclined to believe that it belonged to the Irish monarchs, before the planting of Christianity in that kingdom; and they give this reason, because it is not adorned with a cross, which was the common ensign of Christian princes. However, it is a valuable piece of curiosity, and would unavoidably have been melted down, had it not been preserved by Joseph Comerford, Esq., a curious gentleman, descended from a younger brother of Comerford, in the county of Stafford, who attended King John in his expedition into Ireland, and there married the niece of Hugo de Lacy, a great favourite of that king; ever since which time the family has flourished in that country, and were formerly barons of Danganmore. This gentleman being rendered incapable, by reason of his religion, to purchase lands in his own country, has bought the marquisate of Anglure, with a good estate upon the river Aule in Champaigne, which he has settled in default of issue from himself, upon his brother Captain Luke Comerford, an officer of great esteem in the French service and his heirs male, and in default of such issue, upon his kinsman Sir John Comerford (a major-general, and colonel of a regiment of foot, in the service of the king of Spain), and his male issue. Sir George Skiddy, a near relation to Mr. Comerford, has likewise acquired a good estate in France. This gentleman is a great-grandson to Sir George Skiddy, formerly of Waterford, and of Skiddy's Castle in the county of Cork, is a knight of the military order of St. Lewis, and colonel of foot.

DR. KEATING'S PREFACE

WHOEVER undertakes to write the history of any nation or kingdom, ought to give a true and impartial account, not only of the country and the laws, but also of the customs and manners of the people; and therefore, having undertaken to deduce the history of Ireland from the most distant ages, I think myself obliged to remove beforehand, those false and injurious representations which have been published concerning the ancient Irish, who for above these three thousand years have inhabited this kingdom, as well as what relates to the old English who have been settled here ever since the reign of King Henry II.

The English historians, who have since that time wrote about the affairs of Ireland, have industriously sought occasion to lessen the reputation of both; as appears by Giraldus Cambrensis, Spencer, Stanihurst, Morrison, Campion, and others who, when they write of Ireland, seem to imitate the beetle, which, when enlivened by the influence of the summer heats, flies abroad, and passes over the delightful fields, neglectful of the sweet blossoms or fragrant flowers that are in its way, till at last, directed by its sordid inclination, it settles upon some nauseous excrement. Thus the above-mentioned authors proceed when they write of this kingdom: what was worthy or commendable in the Irish nobility and gentry they pass over. They take no notice of their piety, learning, and courage, of their charitable disposition to build churches and religious houses, or of the great privileges and endowments they conferred and settled upon them: they omit to speak of the protection and encouragement they gave to their historiographers, and to other men of learning, to whom their liberality was so abounding, that they not only relieved the indigency of those who made their applications to them, but made public invitations to find an opportunity to bestow gratifications upon persons of merit and desert. They forget to mention their virtues and commendable actions; but, in their accounts of this kingdom, these authors dwell upon the manners of the lower and baser sort of people, relate idle and fabulous stories, invented on purpose to amuse the vulgar and ignorant, and pass over all that might be said with justice, to the honour of the nobility and gentry of this nation.

It is certain that the old Irish, before the English invasion, were a generous and brave people, as appears particularly by the trouble they gave the Romans, and by the assistance they afforded the Scots, and by obliging the Britons to erect a wall of a vast extent between England and Scotland, to defend themselves from the terrible incursions of the Scotch and Irish; and though the Romans were obliged to keep up an army of 52,000 foot and 300 horse, to preserve the boundaries and to secure the limits of their conquests, and likewise had in constant pay a body of 28,000 foot and 1300 horse, to protect the sea-coasts and other parts of the country from the hostilities of the Scots and Picts, yet the bravery of the ancient Irish broke through their lines and fortifications, and often defeated the whole power of the Roman army, and carried off immense booty from the inhabitants, as Samuel Daniel, an English historian, in his chronicle expressly testifies.

Cormac Mac Cuillenan, king of Munster, and archbishop of Cashel, gives an account in his Psalter, that the irresistible valour of the Irish and Picts compelled the Britons three several times to give up, as a sacrifice, the chief commander of the Romans, in order to stop the fury of their arms and obtain their friendship. Nor is it to be forgotten into what miseries and distress the Britons were reduced by the Irish, in the reign of Vortigern, who found himself obliged to retain Hengist, and his German auxiliaries, to defend him from their incursions; as the same English annalist particularly asserts. The same author relates that the Romans, who called themselves the conquerors of the world, were forced to erect fourteen strong garrisons, to protect them from the hostilities of the Scots and Picts, who harassed them with continual inroads, and cut off numbers of their legionary soldiers, notwithstanding they were assisted by the whole power of the Britons, from the time of Julius Cæsar to the reign of Valentinian, the third emperor of that name, which consisted of the space of 500 years. The Romans lost the command of Britain in the year of our redemption 441; before which time it was, that the contest happened between Theodosius and Maximus, which obliged the latter to transport with him a considerable number of Britons, into that part of France called Armorica or Little Britain; the natives of that country he expelled, and fixed the Britons in their possessions, whose posterity are known in that place to this day.

There are authors in being of some antiquity, who are very solicitous to blemish the character of the ancient Irish; particularly Strabo, who in his fourth book asserts, that they were cannibals, and lived upon human flesh. In answer to this opprobrious charge, it is to be observed, that Strabo had no opportunities to inform himself of the disposition and manners of the Irish; nor is there any chronicle relating to that nation, which gives the least encouragement to this opinion, or any instance of this practice to be found in the ancient records, except of a lady, whose name was Eithne, daughter to a king of Leinster, that was nursed in the country of Deisies, in the province of Munster, whose fosterers fed her with the flesh of children, in order to make her the sooner ripe for matrimonial embraces. But the reason of this, it must be observed, was to accomplish a prediction, which foretold that the fosterers of this lady should be fixed in the possession of large territories by the prince who was to be her husband, who proved to be Aongus Mac Nadfaoich, king of Munster, as will be taken notice of in the body of the following history.

But is this candid, to pronounce upon the manners of a whole nation from one example? and if such barbarity was consistent with the general disposition of the people, is it not strange, that this instance of Eithne should stand by itself upon record, which it would have been impertinent to mention, if the body of the old Irish concurred in this savage practice? The testimony of this author, therefore, is not to be regarded, who asserts, that the eating of human flesh was a custom in this nation, which is impossible to be proved but from one single instance; and even this action was committed in the times of paganism and idolatry, and upon a particular occasion. The authority of Strabo is well known by the learned not to be sacred, nor will this aspersion affect the humanity of the ancient Irish among sober and impartial judges.

Never was any nation under heaven so traduced by malice and ignorance as the ancient Irish. Among other falsehoods and absurdities, Solinus, in his twenty-first chapter asserts, that there are no bees in the island, that the male children receive the first food they eat from the point of a sword, and scandalously relates, that the Irish wash their faces with the blood of their enemies whom they slew in battle; and these facts are positively laid down, without evidence or quotation, and with no other design, than to stigmatise a nation be hated to all posterity.

Pomponius Mela, a writer of the same authority, speaking in his third book of the ancient Irish, gives them the character of a people* "ignorant of all virtues." Other writers might be produced, who fixed the same false imputation upon the Irish, without the least certainty; which made the judicious Camden, when he spoke of the manners of the Irish, express himself thus, with great truth and integrity; "We only mention the names of these writers, for we have no witnesses to depend upon, worthy of credit or belief."† The same Camden refutes expressly one of the falsehoods of Solinus, who asserted, that there were no bees in Ireland; where he says, "So great is the multitude of bees in that country, that they are to be found, not only in hives, but in the hollow places of trees, and of the earth."‡ The English writers particularly, have never failed to exert their malice against the Irish, and represent them as a base and servile people. I shall here mention some remarkable instances of their falsehoods, as they have transcribed them from that ignorant and malicious writer, Giraldus Cambrensis, the great patron of these mercenary and sordid historians. This positive writer asserts, with an air of certainty, that the kingdom of Ireland paid tribute and chiefry to King Arthur, who obliged them to this acknowledgment of subjection in the city of Leon, in the year of our Lord 519; as Campion observes in the second chapter of the second book of his Chronicle, where he says, that one Giollamara was king of Ireland at that time. Notwithstanding the author of the Policronicon, and other English writers of a later date, make mention of Gio lamara, king of Ireland, yet I challenge the malice and industry of the most inveterate of our enemies, to find, in the antiquities of Ireland, that there ever was a king of that name, unless they are deceived by the analogy of the sound, and intend Murthough More Mac Arca, who was monarch of the Island in king Arthur's time, and sent six of his brothers into Scotland, one of whom, Feargus More Mac Arca, afterwards became king, and raised himself to the sovereignty of that country. It is certain that King Arthur himself fell by the sword of the Scots and Picts; and of equal credit it is, that the Feargus above-mentioned was the first king of the Scots; though Hector Boetius, a fabulous writer, labours to evince the contrary, and to prove, that twenty-nine kings sat upon the throne of that kingdom before Feargus wore the crown. He relates likewise, with the same certainty, that Feargus, the son of Fearagher, king of Ireland, was the first king of the Scottish race; which is an assertion without support, for never was there a monarch of Ireland of the name of Fearagher; and therefore Feargus Mac Fearagher was not king of Scotland, as Hector Boetius confidently lays down. It is certain that Murtough More, king of Ireland, was pleased that his brother, Feargus Mac Arca, should wear the crown of Scotland, but upon condition to pay homage to Murtough, who in the annals of Ireland is called rex Scotorum, king of the Scots; to intimate that he possessed the sovereignty over the two kingdoms of Scotland and Ireland, and therefore was a prince of more superior note than to submit or confess himself a tributary to king Arthur.

Speed, in his Chronicle, with greater justice observes, that the king of Ireland owned no manner of chiefry or tribute to King Arthur, but that both princes engaged in a league offensive and defensive against all their enemies. This he calls jus belli socialis, the right of a social war, in the same manner as the treaty

* Omnium virtutem ignari.
† Horum quæ commemoramus, dignos fide testes non habemus.
‡ Apum est tanta multitudo, ut non solum alvearibus sed etiam in arborum et terræ cavernis reperiantur

B

concluded between the king of Spain and the emperor; not that it was intended as if the emperor was to pay a tribute to the king of Spain, or the king of Spain was under any acknowledgments of chiefry to him, but they were mutually bound to support one another against all attempts. The same friendship and stipulation was established between King Arthur and Murtough; they were equally obliged to defend each other, but under no testimonies of submission on either side. And the truth of this equality between the two kings is abundantly confirmed by the testimony of Nubigensis, who, in the twenty-sixth chapter of the second book of his history has this expression, concerning the kingdom of Ireland;[*] "Ireland never lay under a foreign power." And Cambrensis himself agrees with this opinion, in his forty-sixth chapter, where he thus speaks to the same purpose.[†] "Ireland from the beginning remained free from the incursion of foreign nations." From whence it is evident, that neither King Arthur, nor any other power, received tribute, or any servile acknowledgment, from the kingdom of Ireland, until they submitted to King Henry II. Nor is it to be supposed, that the Britons could lay claim to any authority over this island, since the hardy Romans could never make her tributary; so far from that, that instead of losing her liberty, she not only preserved her own freedom, but was a safeguard and protection to other nations, and a scourge to the Romans and other oppressors, wherever she displayed her banners.

The learned Camden gives this testimony in his Britannia,[‡] "When the Romans had extended their empire on all sides, many, no doubt, out of Spain, France and Britain, removed into Ireland, in order to avoid the most unjust yoke of the Romans." From this evidence it is to be collected, not only that the Romans never extended their conquests into Ireland, but that the miserable people of the neighbouring countries found a refuge from the oppressions of the Romans among the invincible Irish, who were never subdued. Whoever so much envies the glory of the ancient Irish, as to assert that they were under the power of the Romans, let him have recourse to the same judicious writer, who says,[‖] "It will be the utmost difficulty to make me believe, that the country of Ireland was at any time under the dominion of the Romans."

Cambrensis (an inexhaustible fund of falsehood) injuriously relates, in his ninth chapter, that the Irish men succeeded in their brother's bed, and married the women who had been before married to their brothers, and that tithes were never paid to the clergy in Ireland, till the arrival of Cardinal John Papirion from Rome; which will appear to be a forgery, and an imposition upon mankind, not only in the body of this history, but in this preliminary vindication now before us. The same author, speaking in his seventh chapter of the natural curiosities of Ireland, writes, that there is a fountain in the province of Munster, which instantly makes the hair of the head gray when it is dipped into it; and that there is another fountain in Ulster, of a quite contrary quality, that upon wetting it restores the hair to its genuine colour; though upon a survey there are now no footsteps, not even in the traditions of the people, remaining of such wells, nor were they in the days of Cambrensis, who imposes upon the world with his fabulous rarities, and amuses his readers at the expense of his own credit and veracity. Equally worthy of belief is what he relates in his twenty-second chapter, that when the gentlemen of Ireland, who had been at variance, were willing to become friends, they used the custom of kissing the relics of

---

[*] Hibernia nunquam subjacuit externæ ditioni.
[†] Hibernia ab initio ab omni alienarum gentium incursu libera permansit.
[‡] Cum suum Romani imperium undique propagassent, multi proculdubio ex Hispania, Gallia et Britannia hic se receperunt, ut iniquissimo Romanorum jugo colla subducerent.
[‖] Ego animum vix inducere possum ut hanc regionem in Romanorum potestatem aliquando concessisse credam.

saints in the presence o a bishop, as a solemn testimony of their reconciliation but what follows is monstrous and incredible, that they took a draught of each other's blood. This is boldly asserted, with his usual effrontery, and without proof or foundation; for if this practice had been received among the Irish, how should the professed antiquaries and historians of the kingdom be silent and take no notice of it, who were bound to record such a custom, if it had been used, unde, no less penalty, than for the omission to be degraded and deprived of their patrimonies? So that this romantic writer is to be stripped of the character of a true historian, and to be placed among the vain authors of fables. In his tenth chapter he entertains us with a notorious falsehood, and gives a character of the Irish that they are a penurious and poor-spirited people; his expression is,* "The Irish are an inhospitable people." But Stanihurst gives a quite contrary testimony, and sufficiently confutes this scandal: his words are,† "The Irish are the most hospitable men, nor can you oblige them more than by visiting them frequently, at their own houses, of your own accord, and without invitation."

This Cambrensis has perverted a fact of great consequence in the Irish history where he asserts positively that it was the queen of Meath who ran away from her husband with Dearmud Nangall, king of Leinster; but the universal testimony of the Irish antiquaries is against him upon this subject, who agree unanimously that that lascivious lady was the wife of Tiernan O'Rourke, king of Briefny; that her name was Dearbhurgill, and that she was daughter to Murrough Mac Floin, king of Meath. He writes that the rivers Suir, Feoir, and Bearow, flow out of the mountain of Sliabh Bladhma, which is a manifest falsehood easy to be disproved; for it is evident that the Bearow rises out of the east point of Sliabh Bladhma, and that the Suir and Feoir proceed out of the east point of Mount Aildium, otherwise called Sliabh Bearnain, in the territory of Cuirnin. He abuses the world, in the twenty-fifth chapter of his history, by saying, that the ceremony of inauguration, in making kings of the family of O'Donill, was performed in this manner: all the inhabitants of the country were assembled upon a high hill; here they killed a white mare, whose flesh they boiled in a great cauldron, in the middle of a field, when it was sufficiently boiled the king was to sup up the broth with his mouth, and eat the flesh out of his hands, without the assistance of a knife or any other instrument, but with his teeth only; then he divided the rest of the flesh among the assembly, and afterwards bathed himself in the broth. This is a fiction not to be paralleled, compounded of ignorance and malice, and directly opposite to the testimony of the Irish antiquaries, who have delivered to us an express description of this ceremony. These writers inform us that the Irish kings of the line of O'Donill, sat upon the summit of a hill, surrounded with the principal nobility and gentry of their country; one of the chief of them, advancing towards him, presented him with a straight white wand, and upon the delivery of it he used this form: — "Receive, O king, the command of thine own country, and distribute justice impartially among thy subjects." The ceremony of the rod was attended with an excellent moral; for it was straight and white, to recommend uprightness in judgment, and to intimate that a prince should rule with clean and unspotted hands, should keep them white, and never stain them with the blood of his people. So that the confidence of Cambrensis is the more astonishing, who conceals so rational and laudable a custom, and introduces in the room of it a savage and abominable practice, that has no foundation in truth or in history, but is the effect of inveterate malice, which urges him on into absurdities and monstrous

---

* Est autem gens hæc gens inhospita.
† Sunt sane homines hospitalissimi, neque illis ·"·a in re magnis gratificari potes quam vel sponte a~ voluntate eorum domus frequentare,

relations, which derive more blemishes upon the character of his history th: n upon the ancient Irish, whom at all hazards he resolves to traduce. It is certain that that royal family has produced persons of the first order for religion and piety, and many of this illustrious line have retired from the world, and ended their days in privacy and devout contemplations, particularly St. Columba, whose memory among the Irish will be ever sacred. Nor is it to be supposed, that the nobility of Ireland, who were a polite and civilised people, would permit the kings of O'Donill to make use of this abominable custom, had they been so disposed; and it is unjust to charge this family with such a savage inclination, since they were princes of strict piety and exemplary virtue, and abhorred a ceremony so odious, which was inconsistent with the religion they professed, and savoured so strongly of pagan superstition. This, therefore, is another falsehood of Cambrensis, which ought to destroy his credit for ever among lovers of truth, and brand on him an indelible mark of infamy to all posterity.

There is one Spencer, a writer of a chronicle, who, in the thirty-third page of his history, asserts, with great injustice, that Eigfrid, king of the Protombi, and Edgar, king of England, exercised a civil jurisdiction over the kingdom of Ireland; but he brings no evidence to support this opinion, and as it opposes the authentic records of the kingdom, it must be manifestly false: besides it is well known, that the English authors themselves are forced to confess that the Saxons destroyed all the public monuments and chronicles of that nation, and defaced or melted down all the coins before their own time, with a design that there should no certain memorial remain of the transactions of former ages. And Daniel agrees, that the principal part of the British antiquaries are lost, as Gildas complains in the fourth part of his history.

I remember that Rider, a Latin lexicographer, in treating of the word Brigaine, is of opinion, that Britannia does not receive its derivation from Brutus, because it should then with more propriety be called Brutia or Brutica; and this etymology would scarce have escaped the observation of Julius Cæsar, Cornelius Tacitus, Diodorus Siculus, the learned Beda, or other writers, who have had occasion frequently to relate the transactions of Britain, and yet make no mention of this derivation. Spencer, therefore, should rather have searched into the name of his own country, and attempted to clear some dark and incredible passages in the English history, than to take upon him to write of the affairs of Ireland, which it was impossible he could ever come to the knowledge of. But what is most surprising in this audacious writer, is, that he should undertake to fix the genealogies of many of the gentry of Ireland, and to pretend to derive them originally from an English extraction. He particularly takes notice of seven families of note in this kingdom, the families of Mac Mahon, Swynies, Shyhies, Macnamaras, Cavanaghs, Tuathallaghs, and Byrns; and says, that from Ursa, Fitz Ursula, or Bears (sirnames that are in England), descended the Mac Mahons of Ulster, and that Beare and Mahon are of the same signification; and consequently, that the Mac Mahons aforesaid are derived from that house in England.

My answer to this assertion is, that it is as reasonable, by the etymology of the word, that the Mac Mahons of Thumond, or the O'Mohunys of Cairbry, should descend from thence, as the Mac Mahons of Ulster. And since it is certain that those of Thumond or Cairbry did not descend from thence, it may be concluded that the Mac Mahons of Ulster are not descended from the house of Ursa, or Fitz Ursula, in England, but are lineally derived from Colla da Chrioch, son of Eochaidh Dubhlein, son of Cairbre Liffeachair, monarch of Ireland, of the royal line of Heremon.

The Swynies, he would likewise persuade his readers, are originally of an English descent, and are derived from a house called Swyn in that kingdom, but this assertion has no more foundation than the former, for it may be questioned whether there ever was such a family in England, and there is not an antiquary in Ireland but knows, and can demonstrate that the Swynies are a genuine branch of the race of Heremon.

The family of the Shyhies this writer pronounces of an English extraction; but this is a falsehood so easily evinced, that it appears, by their successive genealogies, that they are lineal descendants from Colla Uais; and that Shighagh Mac Faghduin, Mac Allasdruim, Mac Donill (from whom descended the Mac Donills of Scotland and Ireland), was the great ancestor to whom the Mac Shyhies owe their original.

With the same freedom and ignorance he deduces the family of the Macnamaras from a house in England called Mortumer; but there is no manner of analogy in the sound to prove this opinion, and it is certain, that this family are the genuine offspring of a person called Cumara, from whom they were distinguished by the title of Clan (which signifies the children of) Macnamara. The proper sirname of this tribe is Siol Aodha, that is the issue of Aodha, and they came originally from Caisin, Mac Caiss, Mac Conilleaghluath, of the posterity of Eivir, or Hiberus.

This confident author attempts to prove that the sirnames of the Byrns, of the Tuathallaghs, and the Cavanaghs, were first brought out of Britain into Ireland. But the evidence is very inconclusive by which he supports this conjecture; for he is deceived by the similitude of the sound, which made him believe that these names were derived from words in the British language; for instance, the word Brin, he says, is the same as woody in English; but supposing this to be true, yet the family of the Byrns are not derived from the word Brin, but from a person whose name was Branmuit. The word Toll, he says, signifies hilly, by which means the Tuathallaghs from thence must derive their name, as he affirms. But notwithstanding Toll and Hilly we allow to be the same, yet Toll and Tuathall are vastly different. Besides it is well known, that the ancient family of the Tuathallaghs is descended from a person whose name was Tuathall, and therefore this supposition of Spencer is false and ill-grounded. This writer is equally absurd in his conjecture relating to the family of the Cavanaghs. The word Cavanagh, he says, signifies strength or strong, and from hence he declares that the family of the Cavanaghs are derived; but he should have considered likewise, that the word Cavan signifies a person of a mild and good-natured disposition, and the tribe of the Cavanaghs descended lineally from Daniel Cavanagh, Mac Dermod ne Ngall, to whom this name of distinction was given, because he had his education in a place called Cillcaovan, in the lower part of the province of Leinster; which tribe, according to their sirname, are derived of the same race with the Cinsalaghs. But that they are of an English extraction is so far from being true, that they are originally Irish, as expressly appears by their genealogies; and are derived from Charles the Great, king of Ireland. It is surprising to me how Spencer could advance such falsehoods, as carry with them their own confutation. He was a writer that was unable to make himself acquainted with the Irish affairs, as being a stranger to the language; and besides, being of a poetical genius, he allowed himself an unbounded licence in his compositions It was the business of his profession to advance poetical fictions, and clothe them with fine insinuating language, in order to amuse his readers without improving them, and to recommend his fables to the world, when he designed to conceal, or found he could not come at the truth.

Stanihurst is likewise justly to be censured, for his misrepresentations in relating the affairs of Ireland. He asserts that the country of Meath was the division that anciently fell to Slainge, Mac Dala, Mac Loigh; but this is falsely advanced, because an ancient treatise, called Leabhar Gabhala, or the Book of Conquests, observes that the country of Meath, in the time of Slainge, consisted but of one territory, that lies in the neighbourhood of Visneagh, and did not extend farther till the time of Tuathal Teachtmhar. He says, likewise, that the river of Slainge, that passes through the middle of the province of Leinster, and runs to Wexford, received its name from that Slainge ! and therefore it appears to him, that the country of Meath was the division he obtained from his brethren ; and for a reason equally invalid, he declares, that Dumha Slainge (otherwise called Dion Riogh, situated upon the bank of the Bearow, between Catharlagh and Laghlin, upon the west side of that river), had that name from the Slainge above-mentioned, whose mansion-house he asserts it was, and the place where he died. But these notions are the genuine offspring of his own brain ; for he was ignorant of the antiquities of Ireland, he had no opportunities of consulting the ancient records, and therefore he must be a stranger to the concerns and the transactions of the kingdom.

For will any man persuade me, that this writer made a strict search and inquiry into the chronicles of that nation, when he says, that Rossmacruin lies in the province of Munster ?   And so utterly unacquainted was he with the division of the kingdom, that he positively asserts that Meath was a province, when Cambrensis (whose ignorance or malice carried him into notorious falsehoods) never gives it that appellation, but agrees so far with the public chronicles, as to call it only a division of the country taken out of the other provinces. This Stanihurst with great confidence divides the kingdom of Ireland into two parts, the one inhabited by English, the other possessed by English and Irish ; and with uncommon effrontery asserts, that the meanest Fingallian in Ireland would esteem it a corruption of his blood to marry his daughter into the best families among the Irish.   The words he uses in his chronicle are,[*] "The meanest Cuillineach, that lives in the English province, would not give his daughter in marriage to the most noble prince among the Irish."   But where is the fidelity of this author, when it is evident, that many noblemen of the first quality, who are originally of English extraction, have married into Irish noble families, without any diminution of their honour, or blemish to their posterity.   Among many instances that might be offered, it will be sufficient to mention the Earl of Kildare, who married into the family of Mac Carty Reogh and O'Neill, and by that means is related to many gentry in the kingdom ; the Earl of Ormond contracted into the family of O'Bryen and Mac Gully Patrick; the Earl of Desmond is allied to the tribe of Mac Carthy More, and the Earl of Conacht to the family of O'Rourke ; not to speak particularly of viscounts, barons, and gentlemen of English descent, and as nobly extracted as any Cuillineach in Fingall, who have not disdained to marry among the original Irish, and upon all occasions to cultivate an alliance with them.

But in order the more effectually to invalidate the testimony of Stanihurst, that false historian, it must be observed, that he was the most improper to write a chronicle of Ireland, because he was overrun with prejudice, and set to work by persons who naturally abhorred an Irishman, and urged him on to misrepresent them, at all adventures, as a worthless and ignominous people.   This author was a renegado from his own country, as well as from integrity and truth, and with the first air which he drew in England, where he received his education, he conceived an inflexible aversion to the Irish, which he discovered upon his return, when he undertook, without any abilities or proper materials, to write the history of Ireland.   This doughty performance he was big with for some years, and

---

[*] Culinorum omnium ultimus qui in Anglia provincia habitat, filiam suam nobilissimo principi Hibernorum in matrimonium non daret.

by the help of spleen and ill-nature, was at last delivered of, to the great joy of his English patrons, who bought him off from his honesty with large bribes, and are much more industrious to stigmatise the Irish, than to deliver the memorials of their own nation uncorrupt to posterity. As one notorious instance of the hatred this author bore to the people of Ireland, he remarks, that the Cuillineachs of Fingall were highly to blame for not expelling the Irish language out of that part of the country, when they drove out the inhabitants, and forced them to look out for new settlements; and the more to express his virulency he observes, that notwithstanding the great encomiums bestowed upon the Irish language, whoever makes himself acquainted with it will soon discover the rudeness and incivility of those who speak it. What can be the design of these reflections, but to intimate, that the English, when they got the sovereignty of the kingdom into their hands, ought to have extirpated the Irish race, and, like Pagan conquerors, have rooted out the very name and language from off the earth? Whatever people carry their arms into another country, and subdue it, if they are Christians, are contented with the submission of the inhabitants, and with transplanting colonies of their own country among the natives: but the practice of the Pagans was, after they had reduced a country to obedience, to extirpate the native possessors, and compel them to look out for new abodes in foreign countries. Thus, according to the barbarity of this author, ought the English to have carried on their conquests, to have shaken hands with the principles of humanity and religion, and put all the Irish to the sword. A conqueror, who has any sentiments of Christianity within him, never suppresses the language of the nation he overcomes; and in this manner the English were treated by William of Normandy. When he made a conquest of that kingdom, he permitted the people to retain their language, by which means it is continued by the inhabitants with some alterations to this day: but Hengist the Saxon, when by the success of his arms he became formidable in England, compelled the inhabitants to forsake the country, and transplanted people of his own in their room; by which means the native language was extirpated, and the new colonies introduced another of their own. This Pagan conqueror acted consistent with the cruel sentiments of Stanihurst, who laments that the Irish language was not banished the island; which could not have been done unless the inhabitants who used it had been expelled, which had been an act so barbarous and wicked, that no politician but Stanihurst would have suggested it, and no conqueror unless a Pagan would have put it in execution. Such, therefore, we perceive, was the irreconcilable hatred of this writer to the nation of the Irish, that the principles of humanity and religion, and law of nature and nations, are to be violated, to destroy the native Irish, and in the general massacre the people and the language are to be rooted out.

This writer, among other reflections, condemns the judges for their methods of administering justice, and censures the physicians of Ireland as unskilful, and of the meanest capacity in their profession. Those aspersions are unpardonable in one who had not the least knowledge of the Irish language, and by consequence must be a stranger to the method they used in their judicial proceedings; he must be ignorant of the laws and customs of the country, nor is he able to form a judgment of the abilities of one profession of men in it. This was the case of Stanihurst, who neither was able to read or understand the Irish tongue, and might with great justice be compared to a blind man, who finds fault with the colour of a piece of cloth, when it is impossible he should have an idea of colours, or know the difference between black and blue. The same improper judge is this writer, to pronounce sentence upon the arts and sciences, the laws and customs of the Irish, when he understood not a word in the language, could not read their books, nor converse with the learned professors in their own tongue.

Equally to be exploded is the testimony of this writer, when he passes a censure upon the musicians of Ireland, and contemns them as ignorant of that divine art, and strangers to that harmony which belongs to it. With what face could Stanihurst assert this falsehood, who had no notion of music, of harmony, or distinction of sounds, and no capacity to judge of the notes and excellency of that art But malice and prejudice have betrayed him into ignorance to all impartial judges; for it is well known to all who have conversed in the least with the ancient chronicles of Ireland, that no people in the world had a better taste of music, and took more delight or employed more of their time in the pleasures of it. Their laws, their systems of physic, and other sciences, were poetical compositions, and set to music, which was always esteemed the most polite part of learning among them. This author, therefore, is rash and ignorant in his censures, when he traduces the Irish as a rude and unharmonious nation, when their genius peculiarly inclined them to music, in which they became excellent proficients, and improved the art to a wonderful advantage. I admire that he had not upon this occasion consulted Giraldus Cambrensis, who gives a different character of the Irish, and particularly applauds them for their accomplishments in music. In the nineteenth chapter of his history he has this expression:[*] " I find the commendable diligence of that nation to be particularly employed in musical instruments, with which they are incomparably furnished above any other nation that I have seen." But Stanihurst overlooks whatever tends to raise the character of the Irish, and throws scandal and invective in an abundant manner, and even in his spleen exceeds the falsehoods of Cambrensis himself, who had more modesty than to oppose truth so notoriously evident as that the Irish are naturally lovers of music, and have a polite taste of that art. The same author bestows a great encomium upon the Irish music in the same chapter:[†] " The melody is completed and rendered agreeable by so sweet a swiftness, by so unequal a parity of sound, by so disagreeing a concord." From these citations, taken from a writer who renounced all partiality in favour of the Irish, it appears that what Stanihurst advances concerning the Irish music is the effect of his malice; and of the same certainty with the character which he gives of the musicians of Ireland, whom he calls a set of blind harpers; whereas, if he had inquired at the time when he wrote his romantic history, he would have found, that for one musician that was blind there were twenty who had their perfect sight, and could see clearly into the malice of his rotten heart, when he undertook to vilify and traduce the Irish, and represent them in the blackest colours to posterity.

It ought to be observed in this place, that Stanihurst was, for three unanswerable reasons, utterly unqualified to write a chronicle; and therefore he had no right to the title of an historian, nor ought by men of learning to be esteemed as such. In the first place, he was so young when he undertook this work that his years would not allow him to read and examine the ancient chronicles of the kingdom, or to arrive at the least knowledge of the genealogies of the people whose history he proposed to write. Secondly, if his years would have permitted him to peruse the public records of the kingdom, he had not the least acquaintance with the Irish language, in which all the memorable transactions and the pedigrees of the inhabitants were originally written. And thirdly, he had renounced that impartiality which is essentially necessary to an historian; for, being a person of an ambitious nature, and solicitous of applause, those who urged him on to engage in his design courted him with large gifts and promises

---

[*] In musicis solum instrumentis commendabilem invenio gentis istius diligentiam, in quibus præ omni natione quam vidimus incomparabiliter est instructa.

[†] Tam suavi velocitate, tam dispari paritate, tam discordi concordia, consona redditur et completur melodia.—

st advancement, upon condition he would blacken the Irish nation; so that his integrity was corrupted by bribes, and therefore he was disabled, unless he would betray his trust and disappoint his patrons, to write the truth, and be just in his representations. It is certain that Stanihurst was faithful to those who employed him, and the history which he drew up fully answered their expectations; but he lived to repent the injustice he had been guilty of, and when afterwards he entered into holy orders, he promised, by a formal recantation, publicly to revoke all the falsehoods he had recorded in that work; and for that purpose, as I am credibly informed, a writing was drawn up, in order to be printed in Ireland, and laid before the world; but if it was ever published, I could never find a copy of it, and, therefore, am apt to believe that it was by some means or other utterly suppressed. If this recantation had seen the light, among infinite mistakes that would have been corrected, his history, I am persuaded, would have been purged of this ignorant blunder, where he says that the Irish when they are fighting cry out, Pharo, Pharo, Pharo, which word, with great stupidity, he imagines, is derived from Pharaoh, king of Egypt; whereas the word is the same with Faire, Faire, which in the English signifies Watch, Watch, and imports as much as is intended by the French, who cry out Garde, Garde, when they apprehend their friend, whom they value, is in imminent danger.

Doctor Hanmer likewise, in his chronicle, has been guilty of great mistakes. He asserts that one Bartolinus was the commander of the Milesians when they first came into Ireland. Partholanus is the name he means in this place; and it is evident by the Irish chronicles that there was more than the distance of 700 years between the coming of Partholanus and the landing of the Milesians in Ireland. Partholanus discovered the coasts 300 years after Noah's flood, and it was 1080 years after the Flood when the sons of Milesius set foot upon the Irish shore. And, as the great Camden justly observes, more regard is to be paid to the old records of the kingdom than to the testimony of Hanmer, whose authority is far from being infallible. "Detur sua antiquitate venia," was the saying of that learned antiquary, whose opinion it was, that the antiquities of Ireland are much more valuable, and of more authority, than those of any other nation in the world. When he speaks of Ireland, in his Britannia, he has this expression:[*] "This island was not without reason called the ancient Ogygia by Plutarch;" and the reason he gives is,[†] "for they begin their histories from the most profound memory of antiquity, so that the antiquity of all other nations, in respect of them, is mere novelty." From whence it may be reasonably concluded that the public chronicles of Ireland are of uncontested authority, and sufficient to overthrow the testimony of Hanmer, or any modern writer whatsoever.

There are some writers who expressly assert that Froto, king of Denmark, was king of Ireland at the time when Christ was born; and among the rest Hanmer gives into this opinion. But this assertion has no foundation, for the ancient records of the kingdom observe that Criomthan Niadhnar was the monarch of the island at the birth of Christ; and Hanmer, who was an Englishman, and never saw nor understood the chronicles of Ireland, could never know what particular prince had the sovereignty of the island at that time; and no wonder, when it was out of his power to discover who was the king of Britain at so great a distance of time as the birth of Christ. Daniel, Gildas, Rider, and many other authors, who have attempted to write the history of Britain, confess that they can come to no certainty concerning the transactions of that king-

[*] Non immerito hæc insula Ogygia pervetiqua a Plutarcho dicta fuit.
[†] A profundissima enim antiquitatis memoria historias suas auspicantur, adeo ut præ illis cæteris omnium gentium antiquitas sit novitas.

...om before the arrival of the Saxons and Normans; which gave occasion to the learned Camden to observe, that he could not absolutely determine so much as from whence the country of Britain received its name, and therefore is contented to give us his conjecture among other writers. From hence I infer, that if Hanmer, and other English historians, found it impossible to discover who reigned in the kingdom of Britain at the distance of so many ages as the birth of Christ, it is presumption and ignorance in him to assume a right of asserting, positively, that Froto, the king of Denmark, was the monarch of Ireland when our Saviour first appeared in the world: it was impossible for him to arrive at any knowledge of the Irish affairs, and therefore what he says is no more than conjecture, and his authority of no account.

Nor is this writer to be less censured, for declaring, that St. Patrick had no right to be called the Irish apostle; that he was not the first who planted the Christian faith in the kingdom of Ireland, neither was he the first who discovered St. Patrick's cave in the island of purgatory. These actions he ignorantly ascribes to another Patrick, an abbot, who lived in the year of Christ, 850. But there is no foundation in truth for this assertion; and to prove this, the words of St. Cæsarius, who lived 600 years after the birth of Christ, and 150 before Patrick the abbot was born, are of great consequence: this author in the thirty-eighth chapter of his book, entitled, Liber Dialogorum, has this expression;* "Whoever doubts of purgatory, let him go to Scotland, and he will no longer question the pains of purgatory." From hence it evidently appears that St. Patrick's cave, in the island of purgatory, could not be originally discovered by the abbot above mentioned, but by St. Patrick, who is justly called the apostle of the Irish; for to say otherwise would be to confess, that Patrick the abbot found this cave 250 years before he was born; since it is evident, that Cæsarius speaks expressly of Patrick's purgatory 250 years before that abbot lived, and, consequently, that cave received its name from St. Patrick, the apostle of the Irish. Besides the ancient records and traditions of the kingdom agree unanimously, that St. Patrick, originally found out the cave in the island of purgatory, which is authority of sufficient weight to overrule the opinion of Hanmer, who, from his aversion to the Irish, advanced this falsehood, and that the Irish might have the least title to favour in that cave.

Another observation of equal credit is made by this author in his twenty-fourth page, where he declares, that Fionn Mac Cumhaill was originally of British extraction. In this assertion he is opposed by the ancient records of Ireland, which pronounce him of Irish descent; that he came from Nuadha Neacht, king of Leinster, who sprang from the royal line of Heremon, son of Milesius, king of Spain. With the same falsehood he asserts, that the Irish authors make mention of one Giollamarra, that was king of Ireland, who he says was son to the king of Thumond. I shall content myself with what has been already said with regard to this fiction, and take no further notice of it, since it carries its own confutation. The account he gives, in his chronicles, of the battle of Fionn Tragha, I suppose was designed to ridicule the authority of the Irish records, and to persuade the world that their testimony ought to be esteemed of no weight, since it is evident to the meanest capacity, that the battle of Fionn Tragha, though it be related in some of the chronicles of Ireland, yet is no more than a poetical fiction, designed to entertain and divert the reader, and not related as a matter of fact; which answer is sufficient to destroy the credit of what he writes of some other transactions which he has recorded, particularly wha. he speaks of Fiana Eirionn, &c.

* Qui di purgatorio dubitat Scotiam pergat, et amplius de pœnis purgatorii non dubitabit.

Among other notorious falsehoods of this author, he asserts, that Slainge, the son of Dela, the son of Loich, was king of Ireland thirty years; but this is contradicted by our authentic chronicles, which determine that one year was the whole extent of his reign. Nor is he to be believed, when he declares that the archbishop of Canterbury exercised a jurisdiction over the clergy of Ireland, from the time of Augustine the monk; since the chronicles of Ireland observe expressly, that the archbishop of Canterbury never claimed any authority over the Irish clergy till the reign of William the Conqueror; and even then he did not pretend to a power that extended farther than the clergy of Dublin, Wexford, Waterford, and Cork, who descended originally from the Danes, and were called Normans, from their affection to the people of Normandy, and put themselves under the jurisdiction of the archbishop of Canterbury, out of an inflexible aversion to the Irish, and to introduce a foreign power among them. Besides, there is good authority to believe that that part of the clergy acknowledged no subjection to the see of Canterbury, but during the government of three archbishops, Rodolph, Lanfranc, and Anselm: so that what Hanmer advances in this place, that the Irish clergy were under the archiepiscopal see of Canterbury, from the time of Augustine the monk, is a falsehood as ignorant as malicious, and deserves no credit

Nor is he to be believed, when he writes that Morough, the son of Coghlan, was king of Ireland in the year of our redemption 1060; for it is evident beyond denial, that Roderick O'Connor was the monarch of the island at that time, which was four years before the English landed upon the coasts. He likewise asserts that Comhghall, the abbot of Beannchuir, was born in Great Britain, which is entirely a fiction of his own; for it appears, in the account of his life, that he was born at a place, in the province of Ulster, called Dail na Ruighe, and that he descended from the family of the Dail na Ruighes in that country.: but this writer had a design in making this abbot of British extraction, which must be detected; for it must be observed, that the pious Comhghall was the founder of the abbey of Beannchuir, in the province of Ulster, which was the mother of all the monasteries in Europe. The same religious person raised a monastery in Wales, near West Chester, called Bangor; so that if this doughty historian could persuade the world, that Comhghall was of a British descent, whatever foundations he laid, and structures he erected, would contribute to the glory of the English nation, and the Irish would be robbed of the honour of them. The same inveterate enemy of the Irish asserts farther, that Farsa Faolan, and Ultan, were illegitimate children of the king of Leinster; but this is a malicious perversion of fact, for the chronicles of Ireland speak expressly, that they were the sons of Aodh Beanin, king of Munster. Were I to enumerate all the errors arising either from malice or ignorance, which Hanmer has committed in his chronicle, I should enlarge this preface to an improper length, and weary the patience of the reader, who, by these instances, may judge of the capacity of this author, and his qualifications for an historian. and therefore I shall cease to pursue him any farther.

John Barclay, speaking of the country of Ireland, has these words:* "They build slight houses of the height of a man, which are in common for themselves and their cattle." But this writer imitates the sordid disposition of the beetle, who stoops to excrements for his diet, and neglects the fragrant flowers, and a more delicate nourishment. In like manner Barclay describes the mean and contemptible abodes of the lowest of people, and passes over in silence the stately palaces, and magnificent structures, erected from time to time by the nobility and gentry of Ireland, equal to, if not surpassing, in grandeur and expense, the

* Fragiles domos ad altitudinem hominis excitant sibi et pecoribus communes.

most costly and splendid fabrics of the neighbouring nations. This partiality is sufficient to overthrow the testimony of this author, among learned judges, and to invalidate his evidence, when he attempts to derive a scandal and reproach upon the state and magnificence of the ancient Irish.

Morison has given himself wonderful diversion, and fancies he delightfully entertains his reader, by writing in a ludicrous manner of the customs and manners of the Irish; but notwithstanding his fluency of style in the English language, his pen contradicted his knowledge, and he was sensible, that under a humorous way of expressing he disguised the truth, and imposed fables in the room of it. Such a writer is not worthy the name of an historian, who attempts to give an account of the inhabitants of any country, and yet conceals whatever is praiseworthy and honourable relating to them; and with the most abusive partiality records only what gives them a mean and despicable character, and tends to reproach and lessen them in the eyes of posterity. This author had conceived the utmost prejudice, and a most cordial detestation of the Irish, and was urged on to write by professed enemies to the glory of that nation; and therefore it is not to be wondered that he describes them as a base and contemptible people. It were an easy matter, were it consistent with the rules of true history, to rake among the dregs of any nation, and enlarge upon the rudeness and incivilities of their manners; but this is not the business of an historian, who sinks beneath his proper character, when he stoops to such low arts, and prostitutes his pen upon so insignificant a subject. Take a survey of the obstinate and unruly temper of the common people in Scotland, the ungovernable disposition of the English populace, the proud and insolent peasants in France, and the lordly mechanics of Flanders, the vanity and pride of a poor Spaniard, and boorishness of the Germans; go into Italy, and inquire into the most learned and polite parts of Europe, and it would swell volumes to describe the rude manners and customs of the meaner sort, though it is below the dignity of an historian to take notice of them, since it discovers the malice and partiality of the writer, and tends rather to corrupt than to improve mankind. Whoever attempts to treat in general of the manners of a country, and describes only the disposition of the uncivilized populace, without giving an account of the nobility and gentry, ought not to retain the name of an historian, but of a libeller and pamphleteer, who conceals the truth, to oblige the party that employ him, which was the case of Morison, Campion, and some others.

Nor is the learned Camden free from the imputation of partiality, when he speaks of the inhabitants of Ireland. He asserts, that it is a custom in that country, that the priests, with their wives and children, have their dwelling in the churches consecrated to divine use, where they feast, and riot, and play upon music; by which means those holy places are desecrated, and used to profane purposes. In answer to this charge, it must be observed, that this irreligious custom was introduced after the reformation, by Henry VIII. king of England; nor has it been practised for many ages, but in the most uncivilized part of the kingdom, and by a sort of clergy, who pretend to be exempt from the authority of ecclesiastical superiors, and placed beyond the reach of church discipline. Giraldus Cambrensis has given a satisfactory account of the piety and devotion of the Irish clergy, and sufficiently refutes this falsehood of Camden. The expression he makes use of is this:[*] "If any dedicate themselves to religion, they govern themselves with a religious austerity, in watching and praying, and mortifying themselves by fasting." And the same author, in his twenty-seventh chapter, speaking particularly of the Irish clergy, gives

---

[*] Si qui religioni se consecrant, religiosa quædam austeritate se continent, vigilando, orando, et jejuniis se macarando.

them this character;* "The clergy are sufficiently commendable for their religion, and, among other virtues that are perspicuous in them, their chastity is most eminently distinguished." From whence the partiality of Camden appears, by charging the whole body of the Irish clergy with that indecent and profane custom. Stanihurst, who was never partial in favour of the Irish, has this expression in his history of Ireland, written in the year 1584;† "The people of Ireland, for the most part, are of a very religious disposition;" so that this practice could not be justly charged upon the clergy of Ireland, but upon such of them as denied the authority of their superiors, and indulged themselves in many rude and unjustifiable actions, without control or restraint.

This English antiquary asserts farther, that the people of Ireland made no account of matrimony, except such as lived in cities, and in the civilized part of the kingdom. This is an accusation, not only false and invidious, and highly reflecting upon the nobility and gentry, who are natives of the island, but upon the English, who have settled and obtained possessions in the country I confess, indeed, that some of the meaner sort are of a wild and untractable nature; and, like the populace in all parts of the world, are ungovernable in their appetites, and not to be restrained by any laws, either civil or ecclesiastical. It is an unpardonable instance of partiality, therefore, in Camden, to condemn the whole body of the Irish nobility and gentry, who live in the country, remote from towns and cities, as if they wildly followed the rules of lust, without any respect to matrimonial contracts; since it is evident, that a few only of the baser sort are guilty of this abominable practice, and indulge themselves in such bestial liberties It is barbarity for a whole nation to be aspersed for the guilt of a few, and those the very dregs of the people. I pay a great respect in other cases to the memory of Camden, and confess the value of his writings, but I cannot acquit him of prejudice, in laying this savage custom to the whole nation of Ireland, who are, generally speaking, a polite and virtuous people, and just to their matrimonial engagements; and deserve not to suffer, for the sake of a few, who, like the vulgar in all countries, allow themselves unchristian freedoms, and fly in the face of the laws which attempt to correct them. With regard to what is charged upon the Irish by other writers, that they very religiously observe their matrimonial contracts for the space of a year, and think they may lawfully dissolve them, it is sufficient to reply, that this opinion prevailed only among the rude and unpolished part of the people, who despised the discipline of the Church, and denied the authority of their ecclesiastical superiors.

Campion, in the sixth chapter of the first book of his history, with great injustice remarks upon the Irish, that they are so weak in their judgments, as to believe implicitly whatever is declared to them by their spiritual guides, whom they obey without reserve, and who have it in their power to impose upon and lead them which way they please ; and to support this charge he relates a fabulous story to this effect. "There was," says he, " a very covetous prelate in Ireland, who had the art to impose upon his people, and make them believe whatever he pleased, however monstrous and incredible. This bishop, upon a time, wanted a sum of money, and in order to obtain it from his congregation, he tells them, that some years ago St. Patrick and St. Peter had a very violent contest about an Irish Golloglach, that St. Patrick designed to introduce into heaven ; but St. Peter opposed him, and in his passion struck St. Patrick with his key, and broke his head, so that he desired their contribution : by which means the people were prevailed upon to part with their money, and the bishop obtained his

---

* Est autem clerus satis religione commendabilis, et inter varias quibus præizcet virtutes, castitas prærogativa præeminet.

† Hibernici etiam magna ex parte sunt religionis summe colentes.

purpose." This is. the story related by Campion, who, like an actor upon the stage imposes upon the world with fictions that could not possibly have any foundation in nature. For can it be supposed, that a Christian of the meanest capacity would believe, that St. Patrick, who died above a thousand years ago, and St. Peter, should quarrel and come to blows, and that St. Patrick should have his head broke with St. Peter's key; as if the key had been made of iron, which every body knows to be nothing material, but implies only a power of binding and loosing? Besides, this fabulous writer, to show his accomplishments, confesses, in his epistle prefixed, that he spent but ten weeks in compiling his history of Ireland; which is sufficient to convince impartial judges of the merits of his performance, and how impossible it was in so short a time to provide matter for the work; or if the materials were ready to his hand, to dispose them into method and form, and to judge of the truth of facts, which in his hurry he wrote at all adventures, and insolently calls his book the History of Ireland.

There was an English priest, whose name was Good, that taught a school in Limerick, in the year of Christ 1566, and upon the strictest survey and inquiry gives this account of the people of Ireland.[*] "They are a people robust and of great agility of body, of a stout and magnanimous disposition, of a sharp and warlike genius, prodigal of life, patient of labour, of cold, and of hunger. of an amorous inclination, exceeding kind and hospitable to strangers, constant in their love, implacable to their enemies, easy to believe, impatient of reproach and injury." And Stanihurst gives them the following character :[†] "In labour the most patient of mankind, and seldom despairing under the greatest difficulties."

One John Davis, an English author, takes upon him to censure the laws and usages of Ireland, particularly he remarks how unjust the customs are, that the brother of a deceased person should succeed in the inheritance of the estate before the son; that the estate of a family should be divided equally among the brothers, and that the law will accept of a satisfaction in money and cattle from the murderer when a person is killed. In answer to the complaint of this writer, it must be observed, that the laws and customs of countries generally differ, and are variable in their own nature, as the exigency of affairs requires; and likewise that these three customs were not originally admitted into the body of Irish laws, but were introduced when the natives fell into civil dissensions among themselves in every part of the kingdom, so that they were killing and plundering one another, with the utmost cruelty, without mercy or distinction; for which reason, the nobility and gentry of the island, who were best acquainted with the Irish laws and constitutions, wisely considered what fatal consequences might follow, and with great prudence thought fit to establish the three customs abovementioned. First, they thought proper that the estate should descend to the brother, in order that every family might be supplied with an able and experienced commander, to defend them and lead them into the field: for if the son was to succeed in the command of his deceased father, it must sometimes unavoidably happen, that he will be an infant, or of too raw years to defend the family from the attempts of their enemies. Secondly, the custom of dividing estates among the brothers could not well be avoided in Ireland, for otherwise the rent of every country would be insufficient to pay the number of soldiers that was necessary for its defence; but when the lands were divided, the brother who had the least lot, would be as able to defend his country as the chieftain

---

[*] Gens hæc corpore valida, et imprimis agilis, animo fortis, et elata, ingenio acris et bellicosa, vitæ prodiga, laboris et frigoris et inediæ patiens venori indulgens hospitibus, perbenigna, amore constans, inimico implacabilis, credulitate levis, contumelia et injuriæ impatiens.

[†] In laboris ex omni hominum genere patientissimi, in rerum angustiis raro fracti.

himself: and thirdly, it was necessary that money or cattle should be admitted as satisfaction for a person killed; because if the murderer could find means to escape into the next country, he avoided the hands of justice, and it was impossible to punish him; and therefore the law ordained, that the friends of the deceased should receive satisfaction from the relations of the murderer, which was a sum of money, or a number of cattle; for it would have been injustice, if the relations, who were not accessary to the fact, should answer it with their lives, if the principal was not to be found. So that it was not candid in Davis to reflect upon the Irish laws for those customs; the two former of which the Irish constitution could not possibly subsist without, and they were absolutely necessary to the support of the public peace; the last, I am informed, is now practised in England, and therefore Davis might have looked at home, and first have reformed the laws of his own country, before he attemped to censure and reflect upon the inoffensive customs of the Irish.

The learned Camden, while he writes of Ireland, has this expression :* "These noblemen have their lawyers, whom they call Brehons; their historians, who describe their exploits; their physicians, their poets, whom they call bards, and musicians, and all of a certain and several family; that is, the Brehons are of one tribe and name, their historians of another, and so of the rest, who instruct their children and relations in their several arts and professions; and they are always their successors, to whom they leave the estates and revenues assigned them." From this testimony of Camden it appears, that the Irish instituted a proper method to preserve and improve the liberal arts and sciences; for they appointed a suitable maintenance and provision for every person, who excelled in the art which he particularly professed; and the artist so distinguished, had authority and jurisdiction over the several members of the same art or profession, and was principally esteemed, and more honourably provided for by the patron that retained him. So that these salaries and revenues, being settled upon the learned professors, occasioned an emulation, and provoked the industry of all the youth in the kingdom; who, encouraged by the rewards annexed, endeavoured with the utmost application to arrive at perfection in their several studies. And this establishment among the Irish, preserved the state of learning and art in a flourishing condition; insomuch, that the neighbouring nations were supplied with professors from thence, who instructed the youth, and propagated their knowledge over the greatest part of the western world. And the nobility and gentry of Ireland did not only confer a handsome maintenance and support upon their learned professors, but it was established by the laws, that the land and patrimonies belonging to them should be esteemed sacred, and not to be violated, and they were allowed as a refuge and asylum to all who fled thither for sanctuary. So that when many fierce wars fell out between the English and Irish, the learned and their scholars were exempt from plunder and military executions, and never felt the calamities of war.

Whoever reads the sixth chapter of the sixth book of the Commentaries of Julius Cæsar, will find, that their sages and men of learning, who went from other parts of Europe to teach in France, were indulged in the same privileges, which perhaps were originally copied from the practice of the Irish This introduction would be too tedious and prolix, should I particularly reflect upon all the malicious and ignorant falsehoods related by English writers, in what they call their histories of Ireland; for most of them are so monstrous

* Habent enim hi magnates suos juridicos quos Brehones vocant; suos historicos qui es gestas descrbunt: medicos, poetas, quos bardos vocant, et citharædos, et certæ et singulæ familiæ; scilicet, Brehoni unius stirpis et nominis, historici alterius, et sic de cæteris, qui suos liberos, sive cognatos, in sua qualibet arte erudiunt; et semper successores habent quibus singulis sua prædia assignata sunt.

and incredible, that they carry with them their own confutation; and ought farther to be considered, that whatever these writers deliver, in disparise of the Irish nation, has no other authority, than the bare relation of persons, who bore an inflexible hatred to the Irish name, and were ignorant of the transactions of that kingdom, by reason of their unskilfulness in the language, and by consequence must unavoidably be mistaken, and impose falsehoods upon the world

Camden, who bears the principal character among these historians; is very blind information to support what he observes of the affairs of Ireland. He has not taken the least notice of the conquest of the Tuatha de Danans, who held the sovereignty of the island 197 years; and erroneously fixes the first invasion of Ireland to be that of Cæsar, which the public chronicles of the kingdom never mention under the name of conquest, though they give a particular account of it: so that the design of this English antiquary could be no less than to throw a blemish upon the Irish, both ancient and modern.   Besides, it must be observed, that this writer had but a very shor time to search into the chronicles of Ireland; he continued in the country but the space of a year and a half, and then returned to England: his history, when he left Ireland, was so far from being finished, that a year would not serve to complete it, and he was obliged to leave it to the care of his companion, whose name was Bertram Verdon, who was as unacquainted with the genuine chronicles of Ireland as himself.   Upon the whole, it is left to all impartial judges to consider, whether I have unjustly censured Cambrensis, an I the English authors, who followed his steps, and copied his falsehoods; and to pronounce impartially, whether my history does not stand upon a better foot of credit, than any relations of theirs, which they received only by tradition, and recorded upon that authority only.   And it cannot be improper upon this occasion, to observe, that, with regard to myself, I am a person of an advanced age, and have acquired a more valuable experience, by understanding the public chronicles and ancient authors in their original language, than they (being of other countries, of minor years, and not having time to digest, or capacity to understand the ancient records) could possibly arrive at.   It is not from a principle of love or aversion, nor that I am moved by the importunity of friends, or the strong influence of rewards, that I undertook to write the following history of Ireland, but was urged on by reflecting, that so noble a country as the king dom of Ireland, and so worthy and generous a people who possessed it, ought not to be abused by fabulous relations, or have their memories buried in oblivion, without being transmitted, and the antiquity and names of the inhabitants recorded with honour to posterity; and I humbly conceive that my history should the rather take place, because I trace the antiquity of the Irish much higher, and with better authority than other writers, and give a particular account of the most ancient Irish, the Gadelians: and if any one should suppose that I bestow too large encomiums upon that brave and illustrious tribe, or speak with partiality of their exploits, let it be considered that I have no temptation to be unjust, being myself originally of an English extraction.

I have observed, that every modern historian, who has undertaken to write of Ireland, commends the country, but despises the people; which so far raised my resentment and indignation, that I set out in this untrodden path, and resolved to vindicate so brave a people from such scandalous abuses, by searching into original records, and from thence compiling a true and impartial history.   It grieved me to see a nation hunted down by ignorance and malice, and recorded as the scum and refuse of mankind, when upon a strict inquiry they have made as good a figure, and have signalised themselves in as commendable a manner to posterity, as any people in Europe   The valour and unshaken bravery of the old Irish, and particularly their fixed constancy in the Christian religion, and the Catholic faith, ought to be honourably mentioned, as a proper standard and example for ages that follow. I have no occasion to speak particularly of the number of saints and holy persons that this island has produced, exceeding in proportion any country in Europe; all histories allow that Ireland was the established seat of learning, that annually afforded numbers of professors, who were sent to cultivate and improve the neighbouring nations of France, Italy, Germany, Flanders, England and Scotland; as appears abundantly from the preface before the book that treats of the lives of St. Patrick, Columba, and Bridget, that is written in English.

If it be objected, that the chronicles of Ireland are liable to suspicion, and may be justly questioned, let it be observed in reply, that no people in the world took more care to preserve the authority of their public records. and to deliver them uncorrupt to posterity. The chronicles of the kingdom were solemnly purged and examined every three years, in the royal house of Tara, in the presence of the nobility and clergy, and in a full assembly of the most learned and eminent antiquaries in the country: and to prove this, the undernamed books of the first note, that are to be seen at this day, are indisputable authorities: the book of Ardmach, the Psalter of Cashel, written by the holy Cormac Mac Cuillenan, king of Munster and archbishop of Cashel; the book entitled Leabhar na huachhugabhala; the book called Leabhar chluana hianach, Psalter na rann, Leabhar glindaloch, Leabhar nagceart, written by St. Beningus; Vighir chiarain, written in Cluain mac naies; Leabhar buidhe, or The yellow book of Moling; the black book of Molaige, and Fionntan a laoghis. The particular titles and contents of many ancient books are as follow: Leabhar gabhala. signified, The book of conquests; Eehabhar na geoigeadh, The book of provincial acts; Reim riogradh, otherwise called The roll of the kings; The book of ages, the book called Leabhar comhsiorgachta, or An account of the people who lived in the same age; The book of antiquity, the book called Coranmach, or of Etymologies; the book called Uracept, that was written by the leared Cionn Fola; the book called The visions of Columba, written by Dallan Forguill, soon after the death of that saint; An account why the woods, the hills, the rivers and lakes in the kingdom, were distinguished by the names they bear, The pedigrees of women, and many others

The treatises that are to be seen at this day in the Irish language, contain particular relations of all the memorable battles and transactions that happened in Ireland from the first account of time, and give an account of the genealogies of the principal families in the island; and the authority of these public records cannot be questioned, when it is considered that there were above two hundred chroniclers and antiquaries, whose business was to preserve and record all actions and affairs of consequence relating to the public; they had revenues and salaries settled upon them for their maintenance, and to support the dignity of their character; their annals and histories were submitted to the examination and censure of the nobility, clergy and gentry, who were most eminent for learning, and assembled for that very purpose, which is evidence sufficient to evince their authority, and to procure them, upon the account of what has been mentioned, a superior esteem to the antiquities of any other nation, except the Jewish, throughout the world.

Nor are we to omit in this place to observe, that the chronicles of Ireland receive an additional value from this consideration, that they were never suppressed by the tyranny and invasion of any foreign power; for though the Danes occasioned great troubles in the kingdom of Ireland for many ages yet the number of these public registerers, whose office was to enter upon record the affairs of the kingdom, were so many. that the Danes could not easily destroy them un, though it must be confessed that some of the chronicles of those times did actually perish. No other country in Europe, that I know of, can justly boast of the same advantage ; for though the Romans, the Gauls, the Goths. Saxons, Saracens, Moors, and Danes generally were careful to suppress the public records in their respective incursions, yet it was impossible that the antiquities of Ireland should be involved in the same fate, because copies of them were lodged in so many hands, and there were so many antiquaries to take care of them. And this Cambrensis, in his forty-sixth chapter sufficiently confirms; his words are,* " Ireland, from the beginning, was free from the incursions of other nations ; by which is intended, that Ireland was never so far under the yoke of any foreign power, as to confess itself conquered, or that the public antiquities of the king-dom were suppressed, which is a privilege that no other nation in Europe can justly pretend to

I have taken the liberty, in the following history, upon good grounds, to change the number of years that are applied to the reigns of some of the pagan Irish kings, and have varied from the account I have met with in some of the annals of the kingdom; and the reason is, because I cannot reconcile the time allotted them, to any chronology since the creation to the birth of Christ ; besides, there must be mistakes which no history can consist with, particularly with regard to the reign of Siorna Saogalach, who, if we are directed by the ancient annals of the kings, reigned monarch of the island 250 years. The chronicles assert, that Siorna when he began to reign, was fifty years old : so that if I had relied wholly upon the authority of the old records, this king would have lived 300 years, which is utterly incredible ; for this reason I thought it proper to allow him a reign of twenty-one years, which I collected from an old verse, that expressly declares his reign to be of no longer a date. Cobhthach Caolmbreac is said, in the ancient records, to be king of Ireland fifty years, yet it is impossible reasonably to allow him any more than thirty ; for it must be considered, that Moriat, the daughter of Scoriat, king of Concaduibhne, fell in love with Maoine, otherwise called Labhra Loingseach, a youth and a stranger that was entertained in her father's house : she was at that time very young and after she was married she bore him many children ; so that if the length of fifty years was properly the reign of Cobhthach, it would follow that Moriat was sixty years of age when she bore those children to Labhra Loingseach, which is scarcely possible to suppose ; for which reason the reign of Cobhthach must be shortened, and reduced to the space of thirty years. For other reasons of equal force with these mentioned, I have changed the date of the reign of some other kings in the times of paganism, but I may venture to acquit the public antiquaries and original chronicles from being blamed for these mistakes : they certainly are with greater justice to be imputed to the ignorance of some transcribers, who copied their works, and were incapable to mend those defects.

It must be lamented, that the Irish, since the English got possession of the kingdom, have omitted the ancient and laudable custom of purging and examining into their chronicles ; and the reason seems to be because the public antiquaries and historians desisted from their employments, their privileges being destroyed, and their estates seized and alienated, so that there was no encouragement for men of learning to pursue their studies, or a competent maintenance to support them. The nobility and gentry of the kingdom withdrew their contributions, and there arose so many violent quarrels and disputes among the Irish and English, that the kingdom was often in confusion, and so embroiled, that the antiquaries had neither encouragement nor protection to carry on the business of their profession.

✝ Hibernia ab initio ab omni alienarum gentium incursu libera permansit.

It will not seem strange that the chronology in the following history may in some cases be imperfect and defective, if it be observed what disagreement there is among authors, in their computation of time from Adam to the birth of Christ; insomuch, that the most learned chronologers in the world have differed in their accounts, as will abundantly appear by taking a survey of some of th most distinguished in that study, who are as follow :—

Amongst the Hebrews.	YEARS.	Amongst the Greeks.	YEARS.	Amongst the Latins.	YEARS
Paul Sedecholin counts,	3518	Metrodorus	5000	St. Hierom	394
The Talmundistes	3784	Eusebius	5199	St. Augustin	5376
The new Rabbins	3760	Theophilus	5476	Isidorus	5270
Rabbi Nassson	3740			Orosius	5199
Rabbi Moses Germaldist.	4580			Beda	3952
Josephus	4192			Alphonsus	5957

These are authors of principal note for chronological computations, and it is easy to observe the notorious variations there are in their several accounts, so that it is not to be wondered at, if the Irish chronicles differ in that point; yet, were I to decide this controversy I think it would be the most plausible standard to allow 4052 years between Adam and the birth of Christ. My design therefore, is to follow the computation that comes nearest to the account I have mentioned, with regard to the reign of the Irish monarchs, petty princes, and chieftains of the island, and the public concerns and transactions of the kingdom.

If it should seem surprising, that the following history is diversified with so many quotations out of ancient poetry, to prove several matters of fact advanced, and to adjust the chronology of the Irish history ; it must be considered, particularly, that the authors of the Irish chronicles composed their work generally in verse, that their records might be the less subject to corruption and change, that the obscurity of the style might be a defence to them, and that the youths, who were instructed in that profession, might be the better able to commit them to memory. The Irish compositions in verse, or dann, that were of principal note, were called in the Irish language Psalter na Teamhrach, which was always preserved in the custody of the chief antiquaries of the kings of Ireland; the Psalter of Cashel was written by Cormac Mac Cuilleanan; and as the word psalm in English, and duain or dann in the Irish, are of the same signification so a psalter (in Latin psalterium) is a book that contains many particula poems; and since most of the authentic records of Ireland are composed in dann or in verse, I shall receive them as the principal testimonies to consult in compiling the following history : for notwithstanding that some of the chronicles of Ireland differ from those poetical records in some cases, yet the testimony of the annals that were written in verse, is not for that reason invalid, because all the public chronicles, as well in verse as in prose, were submitted to a solemn correction and purgation, and therefore it is reasonable they should be esteemed of equal authority.

I have often heard it pronounced impossible, that the genealogy of any person could be lineally traced so high as Adam; but this seeming difficulty will vanish, by observing that it was easy for the Irish to keep exact pedigrees from the time of Gadelas. The Irish were furnished with a learned body of men, called druids or soothsayers, whose peculiar office it was to take a strict account of the several genealogies, and to record the most memorable transactions that happened in the kingdom; it will appear by the course of this history, that these priests or druids were sufficiently accomplished for this business; particularly that Niul, the father of Gadelas, obtained all his riches and honour upon the account of his learning and exquisite art, from whom were derived not only the streams of learning and knowledge, but a sufficient skill to adjust the pedigrees of families, and to transmit them uncorrupt to after ages.

I shall instance in this place, an example taken from a Welsh author, whose name was Asherus, where he gives the pedigree of one of the kings of Britain, and traces it as high as Adam, which I mention as an evidence of the possibility of the thing, and to take off the wonder how the Irish could be masters of such an art, or depend upon the certainty of it.

Elfred, the son of Neulrof, son of Egbert, son of Ethalmund, son of Ewan, son of Indild, son of Corenred, son of Ceulavald, son of Chatwin, son of Elianlem, son of Cinriffe, son of Creda, son of Cerdy, son of Ellisa, son of John, son of Brond, son of Verdon, son of Frealde, son of Frealse, son of Fradawoulfe, son of Cread, son of Cruturaz, son of Bean, son of Seldouin, son of Hewnor, son of Heremon, son of Hatra, son of Hinula, son of Berdatrius, son of Japhet, son of Noah.

Upon the whole, I am persuaded, that whoever consults this history with candour, and with such proportion of allowance as seems due to the obscure and unfrequented track I have pursued, may find satisfaction; and if he will farther give himself the trouble of searching into the ancient chronicles of Ireland, he will be convinced, that I have been just and faithful in the use I have made of them; but if it should so unfortunately happen, that my labours should be despised and the following history be esteemed of no value, I must confess, that it exceeded my abilities to give another account, for I did my best. I take my leave, therefore, and ask pardon of the reader, if I have in any case led him out of his way; assuring him, that the mistake was not the effect of malice in me but because I wanted skill to direct him better.

JEOFFRY KEATING.

GENERAL HISTORY OF IRELAND

FROM THE FIRST INHABITING THEREOF.

THE first name of IRELAND, which we meet with, was Inis na bhfiodhbhuidhe, which signifies a woody isle ; and was so called by a messenger, that was sent thither by Nion, the son of Pelus, to discover this isle, who, finding it all covered with wood, except the plain of Moynealta, gave it that name. This plain was so called from the number of fowl which came there to bask themselves in the sun. It is now called Clountarffe ; where Brian Boiromhe, monarch of Ireland, with his Irish army, gave the last total defeat to the Danes. This monarch, with one of his sons and grandsons, had the hard fate to be slain. The Irish, notwithstanding, gained a most signal victory ; and by it freed themselves from the continual troubles and incursions of the Danish forces, as shall be hereafter mentioned.

2. Ireland was also called Crioch na bhfuineadhach, which is to say, the neighbouring country, as it stood in the neighbourhood of one of the three parts of the world that was then inhabited.

3. Its third name was Inis alga, that is, the noble island ; and this name they enjoyed in the time of the Firbolgs, an ancient colony of people, who were settled here before the Scythians or Gadelians, of whom, in the pursuit of this history, we shall take particular notice.

4. The next name appropriated to this island, was Eire, i. e., Ireland ; so called from the word Æria, a name by which formerly Crete, now Candia, was called. Egypt from whence the Gadelians came, was called by that name : and the same author is of opinion, that the isle of Crete was called Æria, because the Gadelians remained there, after the time when Sru, the son of Easru, with all the Gadelians, were banished out of Egypt. Most of the ancient

D

authors, however, are of opinion, that it took the name of Eire, from a queen of the Tuatha de Danans, (a colony, so called from their great skill in necromancy, of whom some were so famous as to be styled gods,) whose name was Eire, and the wife of Mac Greine, who was king of this isle when the sons of Milesius first invaded it.

5. Fodhla was the fifth name it received from another queen of the same colony, so called, who was the wife of Mac Ceacht.

6. It was after this called Banba, from the name of a third queen of the same colony, who was wife to Mac Coill. These three queens were three sisters, and married to three brothers; amongst whom there was an agreement, that each brother should alternatively take his year of government, and that, during the year of his reign, the isle should be called after the name of his queen. And if you find it more frequently called Eire than Fodhla or Banba, it was by reason that the husband to queen Eire, from whom the island was called Ireland, happened to be king at the time it was conquered by the sons of Milesius.

7. From the colony of the Tuatha de Danans before mentioned it received, after this, the name of Inis fail; from a stone that was brought by them to Ireland, called Lia fail, and by some, the fatal stone. Hector Boethius, in his history of Scotland, calls it Saxum fatale. This was esteemed an enchanted stone, and in great veneration for its admirable virtue, which was, to make a terrible noise, resembling thunder, to be heard at a great distance, when any of the royal race of the Scythians should seat themselves upon this stone to be crowned, as it was then the custom, upon the decease of the former king; but, if the person elected was not of the royal blood of Scythia, not the least emotion or noise proceeded from the stone. But all idols and diabolical charms lost their force and virtue upon the birth of our Saviour, and such was the fate of this stone.

All the monarchs of Ireland, upon their succession, were crowned on this stone, until Fergus, son of Earca, (the first king of Scotland of the Scythian race,) sent to his brother Mortough, then king of Ireland, to desire that he would please to send him that stone to Scotland, that he might be crowned theron king of that nation; believing that the crown would be more firmly fixed to him and his posterity, by the innate virtue there was in that extraordinary stone. The king of Ireland complied with his request; and, about the year of Christ 513, Fergus upon it received the crown of Scotland. This stone was kept with great care at the abbey of Scone, in Scotland; and it was customary for the kings of that country to be crowned thereon, until King Edward I. of England had it brought from Scotland. It is now placed under the coronation chair, in Westminster Abbey; of which we shall speak more fully hereafter, as well as of the prophecy which attended it.

8. The sons of Milesius were designing to land on this island, when, appearing in sight of Wexford, the forementioned Tuatha de Danans assembled together, and, by their magical enchantments, made the isle appear no bigger than a hog's back; whereupon they gave it the name Muicinis, that is, the hog's isle.

9. Its ninth appellation it received likewise from the sons of Milesius, who named it Scotia, from their mother's name, Scota, who was the daughter of Pharaoh Nectonebus, king of Egypt; or perhaps from themselves, they being originally of the Scythian race.

10. It was also, by these sons of Milesius, called Hibernia; some say from a river in Spain called Iberus; but as others conjecture, from Heber the son of Milesius; though the holy Charles Mac Cuillenan is of opinion, that it was so called from the Greek word Hiber, which may signify Insula occidentalis, or the western island.

11. Ptolemeus calls this isle Juernia, Solinus names it Juerna, Claudian styles it Jerna, and Eustathius, Verna: and it is the general opinion, that these authors, not perfectly understanding the derivation of the word, varied it according to the particular seuse of each.

12. Diodorus Siculus, supposed to aim only as the others did, at the signification of the word, gave it the twelfth name, Irin.

13. It was likewise called Fonn no fearon Ir, that is Irlandia, or the land of Ir; from Ir, who was the first of the sons of Milesius that was buried in this isle, from whence the island received that name; Jrlandia signifying, in the Irish language, the land of Ir. And that thus it obtained this name, we have reason to believe, because it is particularly mentioned in the book of Ardmach, that this island was called Ireo, which is as much as to say the grave of Ir.

14. Plutarch calls it Ogygia, which signifies in Latin, Insula perantiqua, that is, the most ancient isle, which is a very suitable name to Ireland; it plainly appearing, from the ancient annals of the kingdom, preserved by the antiquaries, and impartially transmitted by them to posterity, that several ages have past since it was first inhabited, which shall be more fully explained in the course of this history.

THE FIRST DIVISION OF IRELAND

Partholanus, originally a Scythian, came from Greece, and first invaded this island, about three hundred years after the Deluge.

He soon divided the country into four parts ; allotting an equal share to each of his four sons.   To Er, he gave all the land from Oileach Neid, in the north of Ulster, to Dublin, in Leinster. From thence to a part of Munster called the island of Barrimore, he assigned to his son Orua.   From thence to Athcliath Meuruidhe. near Galway, he bestowed on his son Fearon.   From that place backwards to the before-mentioned Oileach Neid, he gave to the possession of his fourth son, Fergna.

THE SECOND DIVISION OF IRELAND.

Beothach, Simon, and Britan, the sons of Nimedius, being the three chief commanders, divided Ireland into three parts, which they shared amongst them.   All the land from Toirinis, in the north of Conacht, to the river Boyne, in Leinster, was given to the possession of Beothach.   To Simon's share fell all from thence to the meeting of the three streams near Cork, in Munster ; and Britan enjoyed all the remainder, round to the forementioned Toirinis, in Conacht.

THE THIRD DIVISION OF IRELAND.

This country was divided into five parts, by the five sons of Dela, (the son of Loich, named Firbolgs,) which at this time are called the five provinces of Ireland.   Cambrensis confirms this, in the account he gives of this country, in these words : *
"Into five almost equal parts this country was anciently divided viz., the two provinces of Munster, (Desmond southward, and Thoumond towards the north.) Leinster, Ulster. and Conacht." The five commanders of the Firbolgs, who governed those five provinces, were, Slainge, Seangann, Gann, Geanann, and Rughraidhe.   Slainge possessed the province of Leinster, from Drocheda to a place called Comarna dtri nuisgeadh, which signifies the meeting of the three streams : Gann presided over the province of Eachach Abhradhruadh, which began at the meeting of the three streams, and extended to Bealach Conglais : Seangann governed the province of Conrigh Daire, from Bealach Conglais to Limerick : Geanann had for his share the province of Conacht, from Limerick to Drobhaois ; and Rughraidhe. for

* In quinque enim portiones fere æquales antiquitus hæc regio divisa fuit ; videlicet, in Momoniam duplicem, borealem et australem Lageniam, Ultoniam, et Conaciam.

his, the province of Ulster, from Droohaois to Drocheda aforesaid.

Some historians perhaps may imagine, that Ireland was divided into three equal parts, between the sons of Cearmody Milbheoil of the Tuatha de Danans; but this can hardly be supposed, because we have grounds to believe that these princes governed alternately, and reigned annually, in their turns, over the whole island. And this appears, from the reasons that are given above, why Ireland was more frequently called by the name of Eire than of Fodhla or Banba.

THE FOURTH DIVISION OF IRELAND, BY THE SONS OF MILESIUS, KING OF SPAIN.

I am sensible that some antiquaries are of opinion, that Ireland was divided between Eabhear-Fionn, and Ereamhon, called Heremon, in this manner : the whole country from Dublin and Galway southward, to Eabhear-Fionn, or Heberus-Fionn; and the rest, that lay northward, to Ereamhon; and Eisger Reada was agreed to be the boundary between the two kingdoms. But it is certain, that Ireland was never thus divided; for the two provinces of Munster, at that time called Deisiol Eirionn, that is, the south of Ireland, were given to Eabhear-Fionn; the provinces of Conacht and Leinster, to Ereamhon; and the province of Ulster to Eabhear, the son of Ir, their brother's son. The Spanish nobility, and military forces, that came over in this expedition, were likewise divided between these three princes, who severally received them as subjects, and took them as the supports and ornaments of their new kingdoms.

THE FIFTH DIVISION OF IRELAND, BY CEARMNA AND SOBHAIRCE.

These two princes were of the posterity of Ir, and divided the island between them : Sobhairce possessed all the country from Drocheda to Limerick northward : and Cearmna had, for his share, the whole territory southward. Each of them built a royal palace in his own kingdom, and called it by his own name; the northern seat was called Dun Sobhairce, and the southern, Dun Mac Patrick, which is in Curcies country to this day.

THE SIXTH DIVISION OF IRELAND, BY UGAINE THE GREAT.

Ugaine, who was called the Great, divided Ireland into twenty-five parts, and allotted shares to each of his twenty five children; as we shall have occasion to mention more particularly in the progress of this history.

THE SEVENTH DIVISION OF IRELAND, BETWEEN CONN, CALLED OF THE
HUNDRED BATTLES, AND EOGAN MOR, THAT IS, EUGENIUS THE GREAT.

Con, and Eogan Mor, who had the title likewise of Mogha
Nuagatt, or the strong labourer, divided the island equally
between them : all the country northwards from Dublin and
Galway, belonged to Conn ; and from thence southward, to
Eogan Mor ; Eisgir Reada was the limits of their several king
doms.   From this division, the north part of the country wa·
called Leath Coinn, that is Conn's share ; and the south, Leath
Mogha, that is, the share of Mogha ; by which distinctions those
two parts of the kingdom are known by those names to this
time.

The seven divisions of the island, which I have mentioned,
are related faithfully, in a chronological order, from the ancient
annals of the kingdom, where the revolutions that happened in
the government are recorded.   I shall now look back to the
division of the country since the time of the Firbolgs, and their
first arrival in Ireland ; because the island, to this very day, is
divided into the same five provinces, which are still called by the
same names.   There was a stone erected at Visneagh, in Meath,
as the centre where the several provinces met, which remained
till Tuathall Teachtmhar ascended the Irish throne, and cut off
a part from each province, where he built a royal palace for the
monarchs of the island, and appointed this territory as a support
and revenue to the house of Tara.   This tract of the country is
now called the county of Meath and Westmeath ; as will appear
hereafter, when I come to the history of Tuathall's reign.

THE PARTICULAR DIVISIONS OF MEATH.

Before I treat of the Irish provinces, I shall first describe the
particular divisions of Meath, because it was the royal seat of
the kings of Ireland, and a standing revenue for the support of
the house of Tara; a territory, as the records of the kingdom inform us, exempt from all taxes, laws, and contributions, and
independent of all the monarchs and princes of the island, as
will be observed hereafter in its proper place.   Meath, from east
to west, contained eighteen tracts of land, thirty towns in each
tract, twelve plough-lands in every town, sixty acres in every
plough-land; so that every tract contained 360 plough-lands
which, in the whole, by that computation, makes up 6480 plough-
lands in all Meath.

There are two reasons to be given, why this part of the island
was called Meath ; the first, because the parcel of land, that was

separated from every province by Tuathall Teachtmhar, to make this tract, was called, in Irish, Meidhe gach Coigeadh, that is, the neck of each province, for the word Meidhe signifies a neck; from whence it came afterwards, by corruption, to be called Meath, though among the ancient Irish it still retains its proper name of Conde na Meidhe. Others derive the name from Midhe, a son of Bratha, son of Deaghatha, who was the principal druid or high priest to the royal family of Neimhidh or Nemedius. This druid was the first that kindled a fire in the island, after the arrival of these foreigners, who for this signal service rewarded him with a tract of land near Visneach, the place where the fire was first kindled; which tract, from the name of the druid, was called Midhe. The whole extent of Meath was no more at first than this small territory, till the munificence of Tuathall Teachtmhar enlarged its bounds.

THE BOUNDARIES OF MEATH, AS THEY WERE IMPROVED BY TUATHALL TEACHTMHAR.

The river Shannon, it is observed, runs west of Dublin, to the river Abhain Righe, and so westward to Cluanconrach, to the French mills' ford, to Cumar Cluana Hioraird, to Tochar Carbre, to Cranaigh Geisille, to Druim Cullin, to Biorra, to Abhain Carra northwards, and so to Loch Ribh. All the islands upon the Shannon, as far as Lochbodearg, belong to Meath; and from thence to Athlone, to Sgairbh Vachtarach, to Cumar, to Lin Cluana Heodhais, to Loch da Ean, to Magh Cnoghbha, to Duibhir, Atha an Doill, on the mountain Sliabh Fuaid; from thence to Magh an Chosnamhaidh, in a place called Cill Isleibhe; so to Snamh Eagnachair, to Cumar, and to the river Liffee, as an old bard thus elegantly describes it.

> From Lochbodearg to Biorra, from thence to the seaside,
> To Cumar Cluana Hioraird, and to Cumar Cluana Hoirde
> The poets celebrate, in lasting verse,
> The thirteen tracts in Meath: fair Breagmhuigh
> Has five well known in the records of fame.
> O fertile Meath, and most delightful Breag,
> Your praise for ever shall adorn my song;
> Whose fat'ning soil along the Shannon's side
> Extends, till in the ocean's rugged waves
> Her streams are lost: northward, the tract of Meath
> Reaches to Teabhtha, for heroes famed;
> And so to Carbre, marked for men of war;
> And thence to Casan Breag, a place renowned
> For noble blood, and troops that never fled,
> And men of learning faithful to the truth.

Meath was afterwards divided by Aodha Oirudighe, monarch of Ireland, between the two sons of Dinnis, the son of Daniel, who had been king of the island before him ; their names were Connor and Olioll : he gave the west of Meath to one of them ; and the east, wherein was the royal seat of Tara, to the other.

THE DIVISIONS OF CONACHT.

The province of Conacht, from Limerick to Drobhaois, contained 900 towns or villages and thirty territories, thirty towns in each territory, twelve plough-lands in every town, and 120 acres in every plough-land ; so that there are 1008 plough-lands in the whole province. It received its name, as some suppose, from a trial of necromancy between Cithneallach and Conn, two druids of the Tuatha de Danans : the prize fell to Conn, who, by his magical skill, covered the whole country of Conacht with snow ; Connsneachta signifying the snow of Conn, from whence it obtained the name of Conacht. Others derive the word from Conn iachta, that is, the children of Conn (iocht signifying children ;) because Eochaidh Moighmheadhoin and his posterity, who were descendants from Prince Conn, inhabited that part of the island ; which may be a reason why the country was called Conacht. The province of Conacht was afterwards divided by Eochaidh Feidlioch, between three petty princes : from Fidheach to Limerick, to Fidheach, the son of Feig ; from Galway to Dubh, to Drobhaois, he settled upon Eochaidh Alath, jorrus Domhnan ; from Galway to Limerick, upon Tinne, the son of Connrach, he bestowed Magh Gainibh, and the old lands of Taoidean, from Fidheeuh to Teamhair Bhrotha niadh ; and Cruachan was the royal seat of the three princes.

THE DIVISIONS OF ULSTER.

The province of Ulster, from Drobhaois to Inbher Colpa, contains thirty-six territories, 900 towns or villages, and 12,960 plough-lands are in the whole province. It was called Uladh, that is, Ulster, from the word Ollsaith, which implies land abounding with plenty of fish of all kinds, and the other necessaries of life ; for the word Oll signifies great, and Saith signifies wealth, as the poet long ago observed in the following verses :

Ceadaoin doluigh Judais tar ord ; ar'lorg deamhain diodhuil gharg, Ceadaoin do ghabh saint um shaith Ceadoin do bhraith Josa ard.

Wednesday the traitor Judas. for his guide Made choice of Catan and the fiends below ; When, blinded with desire of wealth, that day He basely sold his master

Or perhaps the province received its name from Ollamh Fodhla, which the poet intimates in these verses,

Ollamh Fodhla Feochair Ghoil uaide do hai nmhiagh Ulladh,
Jar bhirfeas Teamhrach na dtreabh as leis ar dtus do hoirneadh.

> From Ollamh Fodhla, Ulster had its name,
> A wise and valiant prince, who first assembled
> The royal parliament of Tara.

There were two royal seats in the province of Ulster, Emhaii Mhacha and Oileach Neidh.

THE DIVISIONS OF LEINSTER.

The province of Leinster, from Inbher Colpa, now called Drocheda, to the meeting of the three streams in the bounds of Munster, consists of thirty-one territories, which contain 930 towns or villages, and 11,760 plough-lands. The province received its name from Laighin, that is, the long spears, which were the weapons the Gauls made use of, when they invaded the island under Labhra Loing seach, when first they came on shore in this part of the kingdom, which afterwards was called Laighin that is a spear. These foreigners slew, in Dinrigh, Cobhthach Caolmbreace, monarch of Ireland, with one of these weapons, which gave occasion to these lines of the poet,

Da chead ar f hithid cead Gall go Laighnibh leathna leo anall,
Ona Laighnibh Sin gan oil diobh Rohaimnnigheadh Laigion.

> From the broad spears of the invading Gauls
> The province had its name.

The royal seats that were in Leinster where the kings of the country kept their court were Dinrigh and the Naas.

OF THE PROVINCE OF EOCHAIDH ABHRADHRUADH.

The province of Eochadh Abhradhruadh, reaching from Cork to Limerick eastward, and so to the meeting of the three streams, contains thirty-five territories, in which are 12,600 plough-lands. It is called east Munster; and the two royal seats, where the kings of the province kept their court, were Dungcrott and Duu-jasy.

OF THE PROVINCE OF CONRIGH MACDAIRI.

This province, extending from Bealach Congiais, by the counties of Cork and Limerick, to the west of Ireland, contained thirty-five territories, in which were 1050 towns or villages; there were 12,600 plough-lands in all the west of Munster; the two palaces where the princes of the province gave audience, were Dunclaire and Duneochairmhaghe. The two divisions of Munster were governed by two families, that descended from Dairine and Deirgthene, till the reign of Oilioll Ollum, who was of the posterity of Deirgthene. This prince after he had banished Macon, who was of the line of Dairine, out of the island, assumed the government of both provinces, and settled the succession upon two of his own issue; under this restriction, that the posterity of his two sons, Eogan Mor and Cormac Cas, should succeed alternately; that is the eldest of these princes was to reign during his life, but upon his demise, his son was not to inherit, but his brother, if alive, or the next heir of his family, and then the crown was to return again; and this limitation was observed for many ages, without any dispute or quarrel between the two houses. The four royal seats, that I have mentioned, were the places where the kings of Munster resided, till the time of Corc, son of Luidh-lheach, who governed that province; and in his reign it was that Cashel was first discovered, after this manner. The place, which is now called Carrick Patrick, where the royal palace of Cashel was built, was originally covered with woods, and called Ciothdhruim, being wholly desert and uninhabited, and used only as a pasture for beasts. It so happened that two herdsmen, Ciolarn and Durdre, the one belonging to the king of Ely, the other to the king of Muscrie Tire, which we call Ormond, drove their herds into the wood to feed; and, when they had continued there for some time, upon a certain evening, they discovered a most beautiful person, who, advancing toward them, began to sing with a soft and melodious voice; and then, walking solemnly about, he consecrated, as it were, that spot of land whereon the palace of Cashel was built, prophesying aloud of the coming of St. Patrick, soon after which he vanished. The herdsmen, surprised at so unusual a sight, when they came to their homes, related what they had seen, till at length it reached the court of Corc, son of Luighdheach, king of Munster. This prince, from a sense of religion, repaired immediately to Ciothdhruim, afterwards called Cashel, and built there a most stately palace, calling it Lios na Laochruidhe, which he made the seat of his residence. He received the taxes and revenues of his kingdom upon Carraic Patrick, that is Patrick's rock, but then called Caisiol, or Cios oil; for Cais signifies rent, and Oil, in Irish, is a rock or stone; and, therefore the king of Munster receiving his rents and taxes upon that stone, by joining the words cais and oil, this royal palace came afterwards to be called Cashel.

When Oilioll Ollum governed the two provinces of Munster, be divided them into five parts, called in general the province of Munster. Thumond, which is the first part, extends in length from ᵀeim congouloin to Slighe dhala, called Bealach mor, in Ossery, the breadth of it is from Sliabh Eachtighe to Sliabh Eibhlinne. All the country from Sliabh Eachtighe to Limerick belonged originally to the province of Conacht, till Luighuidh Mean, who descended from Cormac Cas, made a conquest of it by his sword, and added it to the province of Munster. This tract was called Grabh Fhearou Luigheadh, that is, the lands of Luigheadh. This country, to Dailgeais, was exempt from all tributes and taxes, and paid no revenue to any of the kings of Ireland. The second division called Urmhumha, that is, Ormond, extends in length from Gabhran to Cnamhchoill near Tipperary and its breadth is from a place called Bearnan Eile to Oilead Vibaric. The third part called Meadhon Mummhoin, or middle Munster, reaches in length from Cnamhchoill to Luachæir dheaghadh. The fourth part is distinguished by the name of Jarmhumhoin, that is, west Munster; and its length is from Luachaird-neaghadh westward to the main ocean, and its breadth from Glenrouchty to the Shannon. The last division, called Ceasmhumhain, or south Munster, extends in length from Sliabh Caoin southward to the sea. The two provinces of Munster are called, in the Irish language, Da Coigeadh Mumhan, from the word Mumho, which signifies great or of large extent; because they include a greater tract of land than any other province in the whole island. · For though I have mentioned, that the province of Ulster contained thirty-six territories, yet it consisted but of thirty-three, till the kingdom was divided into provinces, then it was that Carbre Niadhnar, king of Leinster bestowed all the country from Loch an Choigeadh to the sea, upon Connor, the king of Ulster; and, contrary to the practice of latter ages, added it to his province as a reward for obtaining his daughter in marriage; as will be more particularly observed in the course of this history.

In the whole kingdom of Ireland were 185 territories, or tracts of land, containing 5550 towns, in which were 66,000 ploughlands, according to the land measure of the ancient Irish, which was much larger than what was observed in England; for one acre in Ireland would make two or three acres of the English, as they are now computed.

OF THE ARCHBISHOPRICS AND BISHOPRICS IN IRELAND.

There are four archbishops in the kingdom of Ireland ; the archbishop of Ardmach, primate of the whole kingdom, the archbishop of Dublin, the archbishop of Cashel, and the archbishop of Tuam.   Under the primate is the bishop of Meath, called by Camden, the bishop of Aolna Mirion, from a large stone that stands in Visneath, by the name of Aolna Mirion.   This stone was the boundary of the five provinces of Ireland, before a part was taken from each province to form the country of Meath ; and because it was erected as a land-mark, to distinguish the limits of each province, it was called Aolna Mirion ; for the word Mir, or Mir ion, signifies, in the Irish language, a share or part of a thing, and Aol signifies a stone : it was likewise styled Clock-na-Gooi-geadh, or the provincial stone, because it was fixed centre at the meeting of the five provinces.   Under the jurisdiction of the primate are also the bishop of Dunda Leithghlas, the bishop of Clocher or Louth, the bishop of Rathboth or Rapho, the bishop of Rathbuck, the bishop of Dailniachair, and the bishop of Derry.

The archbishop of Dublin has under him, the bishop of Glendaloch, the bishop of Fearns o Fearna, the bishop of Ossery, the bishop of Leithghlin, and the bishop of Kildare.

The following bishops are under the government of the archbishop of Cashel : the bishop of Killaloe, the bishop of Limerick, the bishop of Iniscatha, the bishop of Kilfenore, the bishop of Emly, the bishop of Roscre, the bishop of Waterford, the bishop of Lismore, the bishop of Cloine or Cluain uam aigh, the bishop of Cork, the bishop of Rosscarbry, and the bishop of Ardfeart.

The jurisdiction of the archbishop of Tuam extends over the bishop of Kill Mach Duach, the bishop of Maigheo or Mayo, the bishop of Anaochduin, the bishop of Cill iarthair, the bishop of Roscomon, the bishop of Cluainfeart, the bishop of Achoury, the bishop of Cillaluidh, the bishop of Conaine, the bishop of Cill Mac Duacht, the bishop of Cill monuach, and the bishop of Eplin.   The archiepiscopal sees were first erected in the year of Christ 1152, according to Camden ; from whom I have given an account of many bishoprics, that are now no where to be found, either because they are wholly abolished, or united to other sees ; as the bishoprics of Lismore and Waterford are now but one diocess, and the sees of Cork and Cluain are under one bishop.

THE SITUATION OF IRELAND

The kingdom of Ireland is bounded by Spain on the south-west, and by France on the south-east ; England lies due east, Scotland north east, and the main ocean due west of it. The island is observed by Maginus, in notes upon Ptolomy, to resemble the form of an egg, situated between 51 and 55 degrees of latitude : according to the same author, the longest day, in the southeast part of the kingdom, is sixteen hours and three quarters, and in the north, full eighteen hours. The length of the island is computed from a place called Carn ui Neid, in the south, to Cloch and Stacain, in Ulster ; and the breadth from Inbher Mor to Hiarus Domhnonn. It is not the proper business of this history to describe particularly the cities, towns, harbours, and creeks of the kingdom of Ireland, because Camden in his new chronicle has given a full account of them ; and they will fall under consideration, as far as is necessary, when we come to speak of the invasion of this island by the English.

AN ACCOUNT OF THE FIRST INHABITANTS OF IRELAND, EXTRACTED FROM THE MOST ANCIENT MANUSCRIPTS OF THE KINGDOM.

To give a regular account of the first inhabitants of Ireland, I am obliged to begin at the creation of the world ; but it is not to be expected, that at the distance of so many thousand years, I should omit taking notice of some remarkable passages, which may be censured as fabulous, and it would be severe treatment to judge of the value of this history, by the credibility of such relations ; however, the ancient manuscripts of the kingdom are the guides I shall chiefly follow. It is impossible for me to have other lights, which, how obscure soever, are to be regarded for their antiquity, and to be used with candour, considering the superstition and ignorance of those dark ages.

Adam, the first of human race, was created upon the sixth day of the age of the world ; and when he lived fifteen years he begat Cain, and his sister Colmana ; thirty years after his creation he begat Abel, and Delbora his sister ; and when he was a hundred and thirty years old he begat Seth ; according to the computation of the Welsh in the Polichronicon.

THE GENEALOGY OF NOAH TO ADAM, AND THE DISTANCE OF TIME FROM ADAM TO THE DELUGE.

Noah was the son of Lamech, son of Methuselah, son of Enoch, son of Mahalaleel, son of Enos, son of Seth, son of

Adam, the great ancestor of mankind, whose descendants inhabited the earth till the general deluge, when the whole posterity were reduced to the small number of Noah's family. The distance of time, from Adam to the Flood, was sixteen hundred and fifty-six years; as the poet observes in the following distich.

> Cead aimser an bheatha bhin-otha Adhamh go Dilion,
> Se bliadhna caogad radhnglc ar se cheaduibh ar mhile.

> From the sixth day, when Adam first was form'd,
> Till God's avenging wrath drown'd all the world,
> Was fifty-six and sixteen hundred years.

Another author of great antiquity agrees with this account. His verse is rough, according to the poetry of those times, and may thus be expressed in English.

> Six hundred and a thousand years,
> And fifty-six, it plain appears,
> Was all the time the world had stood
> From the Creation to the Flood.

The age of Noah, and of his forefathers, is thus computed. Noah lived 950 years, Lamech 777, Methuselah 969, Enoch 369, Iared 962, Mahalaleel 895, Cainan 910, Enos 905, Seth 912, and Adam 930 years.

THE DIVISION OF THE WORLD BETWEEN THE SONS OF NOAH.

The wicked Cain, by the murder of his righteous brother, did not only derive a curse upon his own head, but his posterity were also marked by God with a brand of infamy; insomuch, that the descendants of Seth were expressly forbidden to contract any friendship or alliance with them, and were commanded to avoid them, as persons abandoned by Heaven, and wholly out of the care of Divine providence. But this injunction was soon disobeyed by the family of Seth, who married promiscuously into that cursed line; and, by their sins, brought down the vengeance of God upon their own heads, and upon all the inhabitants of the earth, by a general deluge, the family of Noah only excepted. This man found favour in the sight of God; who, for his piety and obedience to his commands, preserved him and his children in that dreadful visitation. He with his wife Cobha, and his three sons, Shem, Ham, and Japhet, with their three wives, Olla, Olvia, and Olibana, survived the drowning of the world; which was afterwards divided into three parts, by Noah, the monarch of the universe, and bestowed upon his three sons : to Shem he gave Asia, to Ham Africa, and Europe to Japhet. This division of the whole earth is thus recorded by an ancient poet.

> Sem do ghabh an Asia ait, Cam ghon acloin an Afraic,
> Japhet sa mhic asiad do ghabh an Eoruip.

> Shem over Asia did the scepter bear,
> Ham governed Africa for heat severe,
> And Japhet ruled in Europe's cooler air.

AN ACCOUNT OF THE POSTERITY OF THE THREE SONS OF NOAH, FROM WHOM DESCENDED THE 72 FAMILIES THAT ATTEMPTED THE BUILDING OF THE TOWER OF BABEL.

Shem was the father of twenty-seven sons, from whom came Arphaxed, Assur, and Persuir, and from them descended the nation of the Hebrews. Ham had thirty sons, and Japhet had fifteen. The posterity of Japhet inhabited most of the northern countries of Asia, and all Europe ; Magog, one of the sons of Japhet, was the great ancestor of the Scythians, and the severa. families that invaded the kingdom of Ireland after the Flood, before the Milesians made a conquest of the island ; and this will more fully appear in the body of this history.

OF THE FIRST INVASION OF IRELAND BEFORE THE FLOOD

It has been a general complaint of historians, that, in searching into the beginning of kingdoms, and discovering the first inhabitants of countries, they are always perplexed with insuperable difficulties ; and the higher they pursue their inquiries, and the nearer they come to the origin of a nation, the more obscure and involved are the antiquities of it ; and all, at last, ends in romantic and fabulous relations, that are scarce worthy of a place in historical writings. But yet, all authors, for want of better information, and for the sake of method, are obliged to mention the accounts they meet with, how uncertain or incredible soever ; and it is for the same reason that I shall transcribe what is observed by the old antiquaries, concerning the first invasion of Ireland before the Flood ; not that I would be thought to give credit to such chimerical traditions, or would impose them upon the belief of others, but I shall offer them faithfully, as they are recorded in the most ancient manuscripts that treat of the first inhabitants of this kingdom.

Various are the pinions concerning the first mortal that set a foot upon this island.   We are told by some, that three of the daughters of Cain arrived here several hundred years before the Deluge ; and the old poet gives us this account.

Tri hingiona chaidhin Chain mar aon ar Seth mac Adhamh,
Ad chonaire an Banba ar uus ar meabhair liom aniomthus.

The three fair daughters of the cursed Cain,
With Seth, the son of Adam, first beheld
The isle of Banba.

The White book, which in the Irish is called Leabhar Ihroma sneachta, informs us that the eldest of these sisters was called Banba, who gave a name to the whole kingdom. After them we are told that three men and fifty women arrived in the island ; one of them was called Ladhra, from whom was derived the name of Ardladhan. These people lived forty years in the country, and at last they all died of a certain distemper, in a week's time ; from their death, it is said, that the island was uninhabited for the space of 200 years, till the world was drowned.

We are told by others, that the first who set foot upon the island were three fishermen, that were driven thither by a storm from the coast of Spain. They were pleased with the discovery they had made, and resolved to settle in the country; but they agreed first to go back for their wives, and in their return were unfortunately drowned by the waters of the Deluge, at a place called Tuath Inbhir. The names of these three fishermen were Capa, Laighne, and Luasat ; and for this tradition we have the authority of the poet, who says,

Capa, Laighne ar Luasat ghrinn, bhadar bliadhain ria ndilion,
For Inis Banba na mban, bhadar go calma comhlann.

Twelve months before the Flood, the noble isle
Of Banba first was seen, by Capa, Laighne,
And Luasat, men of strength, and fit for war.

Others again are of opinion, that Ceasar, the daughter of Bith, was the first who came into the island before the Deluge. The poet speaks thus, to the same purpose.

Ceasar inghion Bheatha bhuain dalta Sabhuill mac aionuaill,
An chead bhean chalma do chinn, an Inis Banba ria ndilion.

Ceasar, daughter of the good Beatha,
Nursed by the careful hand of Sabhuill,

Was the first woman, in the list of fame,
That set a foot on Banba's rugged shore
Before the world was drowned.

The manuscripts of Ireland, though not credited by their antiquaries, give this account of Ceasar's first coming into this island. When Noah was building the Ark, to preserve himself and his family from the Deluge, Bith, the father of Ceasar, sent to him to desire an apartment for himself and his daughter, to save them from the approaching danger. Noah, having no authority from Heaven to receive them into the Ark, denied his request. Upon this repulse, Bith Fiontan, the husband of Ceasar, and Ladhra, her brother, consulted among themselves what measures they should take in this extremity; but, coming to no resolution, Ceasar thought it proper to apply to an idol, and know how they could secure themselves and their families from the Flood, which, by the preaching of Noah, they found would drown the whole world. They consented unanimously to this advice (and as the Devil ever attempted to ape and imitate Almighty God) the oracle enjoined them to build a ship in the form of the Ark that Noah was preparing, and that when they had laid in provisions for a long voyage, they should commit themselves to the mercy of the waves; but the idol had no knowledge of the time when the rain should begin to descend upon the earth: they immediately applied themselves to the work, and with great labour and application at length fitted out the vessel, and put to sea. The persons that went on board in this manner were Bith, Ladhra, and Fiontan, with their wives Ceasar, Barran, and Balbha, and fifty of the most beautiful women that would venture along with them. These raw sailors, for want of skill in navigation, were tossed and driven from sea to sea, for the space of seven years and a quarter, till they arrived at last upon the western coast of Ireland, and landed a a place called Dun na mbarc, in the barony of Corchadu ibhne as we may observe in the following verses :—

As ann ghabhadar port ag Dun na mbarc an bhanntracht,
Agcuil Ceasrach agcoch charin acuig deag dia siathruin.

The trembling fair now unknown climes explore,
And sea-sick land upon the western shore
Of Ireland, in Ceasara's wood.

They came into the island forty days before the waters began to overspread the earth. Another old poet gives the same

E

account of these adventures, with this additional circumstance
that they began their voyage from an eastern part of the world.

> Do luig anoir Ceasar, inghion Bheatha an bhear
> Gona caogad inghion agus gonadh triar fear.

> Ceasar, the fair daughter of Beatha,
> Sailed from the east, with fifty women more
> Attended by these men for valour famed.

When the ship came close to the shore of Dun na mbare, on
the western part of the island, the first that set foot upon the
land was Ladhra; the first mortal that ever was upon the island,
according to those antiquaries, who say that Ireland was never
inhabited before the Flood but by Ceasar, and those who followed her fortune in that voyage. The mountain Sliabh Beatha
received its name from Beatha; Feart Fiontan, a place near
Lochdeirg, was so called from Fiontan; and from Ceasar a place
in Conacht was called Carn Ceasar. These new inhabitants,
when they had all landed, began to make discoveries in the island;
and they travelled together till they came to the fountain-head
of the rivers Steur, Feoir, and Berbha; here it was, that the
three men agreed to divide the fifty women between them. Fiontan, besides his wife Ceasar, had seventeen for his share; Bith
had his wife Barran, and seventeen more; and Ladhra had his
wife Balbha, and was satisfied with the sixteen that remained.
After this division Ladhra set out with his share of the women,
and came to Ardladhron, where he settled and died. His wife,
with the women that belonged to her, thought fit to remove and
return to Ceasar; these women were divided between Bith and
Fiontan; Bith took his number to Sliabh Beatha, where he
died. The women that he left applied themselves to Fiontan,
who, unable to comply with the expectations of his seraglio, resolved to leave them; and so ran away and came to Leinster.
His wife, Ceasar, upon the loss of her husband, removed to a
place called Ceasar's wood, in Conacht, where, out of grief for
her husband's absence, and the death of her father and brother,
she broke her heart. This happened but six days before the
Deluge; as the poet observes in the Psalter of Cashel.

> As iad Can iar nuair bheachta andaoigeadha animheachta,
> Ni raibh acht Seaehtmhain na ndhia uaithuibh gus an geathracha.

> And thus they died, as fate decreed they should,
> Six days before the rising of the Flood.

This is thought, by the Irish annals, to be an unaccountable relation, which it is impossible to give the least credit to; nor have I inserted it, in the beginning of this history, with any design that it should be believed, but only for the sake of order, and out of respect to some records of the kingdom, that make mention of it; but from whence intelligence could be had of what passed in this island before the Flood, it is out of my power to conceive; and I never read of any monuments or inscriptions upon pillars, to inform posterity of such transactions. To say that Fiontan preserved himself alive in the time of the Deluge, is incredible in itself, and contrary to the authority of Scripture, which mentions but eight persons that survived the Flood, and every one knows that Fiontan was not one of those persons. We have indeed some ancient manuscripts, that give a legendary account of four persons, Fors, Fearon, Andord, and this Fiontan, that, as they say, lived before and after the Deluge, and afterwards divided and possessed themselves of the four parts of the world; but our antiquaries, that are best acquainted with the history of Ireland, reject such fables with just indignation, supposing that those authors who thus endeavour to deceive mankind, have no other design but to bring the genuine antiquities of this kingdom into contempt. As for such of them, who say that Fiontan was drowned in the Flood, and afterwards came to life, and lived long to publish the antediluvian history of the island, what can they propose by such chimerical relations, but to amuse the ignorant with strange and romantic tales, to corrupt and perplex the original annals, and to raise a jealousy, that no manner of credit is to be given to the true and authentic chronicles of the kingdom?

Besides, supposing it were possible that this Fiontan could preserve himself in the Deluge, and live after it, how came it to pass that no authors of any character have transmitted an account of it to posterity; that no philosophers and men of universal learning of this nation, who were curious in discovering the antiquities of their own country, should omit taking notice of so memorable an event, and pass it over in silence and unregarded? The whole account, therefore, is no more than a spurious legend, and a poetical fiction, designed to surprise persons of low capacities, and to impose upon the superstitious vulgar, of too weak a judgment to apprehend to detect the falsehood of it.

I must own there is a very good reason for me to believe, that there was a very old man in the time of St. Patrick, who lived some hundred years before, and gave him a particular account of the history of the island ; not only relating to some of the most remarkable transactions of his own time, but he delivered down the traditions he had received from his ancestors, that concerned the antiquities of the kingdom : but the name of this person was Tuam, the son of Carril, if we believe some antiquaries ; or, if we give credit to others, Roanus, that is Caoilte Mac Ronain, who was above three hundred years old, and informed Saint Patrick of the observations he had made through the course of a long life, relating to the affairs of his own country. This Caoilte was certainly the man that was afterwards called Roanus or Ronanus ; for there is not an old record or manuscript of any authority in this kingdom which makes mention of Fiontan by those names ; and, therefore, Giraldus Cambrensis could have no foundation but his own fancy for calling Fiontan by the name of Roanus or Ronanus ; and, to show his ignorance the more, confounds the names, and understands the one for the other. This author deserves no manner of regard or credit to be given him, and his chronicle is the most partial representation of the Irish history that was ever imposed upon any nation in the world : he has endeavoured to make the venerable antiquities of the island a mere fable, and given occasion to the historians that came after him, to abuse the world with the same fictitious relations. This Caoilte, therefore, must be the person who went afterwards by the name of Ronanus ; for the ancient manuscripts of the kingdom always mention him by this name, and he is so called in a book that he wrote himself, (to be found among the works of Saint Patrick), under the title of Historia Hiberniæ; for in the title page, where the name of the author is particularly expressed, it is said to be written Authore Ronano.

There is another falsehood to be met with in Dr. Hanmer's Chornicle, which I am obliged to observe in this place ; not only to show the partiality of that writer, but to vindicate the Irish nation from those vile aspersions that such retailers of history have fixed upon them, who study to represent them as the most ignorant and superstitious people upon the face of the earth. This author, for reasons best known to himself, would have us believe, that the Gadelians, or the old Irish, had a great veneration for the memory of this Fiontan, whom he calls Roanus, for the account he gave of the antiquities of the kingdom. He lived, it seems, before the Flood, preserved himself in the Deluge, and continued alive about two thousand years after.

In his travels about the island he met with St. Patrick, and related to him the transactions of many past ages : this saint made
a convert of him to Christianity, and baptized him ; about a
year after he died. He was buried near Loch Ribh, in a place where
he says there is a church dedicated to him by his own name, which
is now to be found in the calendar of the Irish saints. But there
is not an antiquary, or a manuscript of any authority, that en-
courages these romantic tales ; and it is a common pratice of the
English writers to debase the antiquities, and to raise a character of their own nation, upon the ruins of the ancient Irish ; but
withal they sufficiently expose their own ignorance and incapacity for historical writings, by reason they give three several names
to the very same person. He is called Fiontan, (but Roanus by Giraldus Cambrensis,) and Caoilte Mac Ronain, who was baptized by
St. Patrick, and discovered to him the original accounts of the island;
and Ruan, who consecrated Lothra, in Ormond, near Loch Dierg,
not Loch Ribh, as Hanmer would impose upon us. But I have
no more time to throw away in refuting the falsehoods of this dis-
ingenuous author, or the writers he followed. As for the name
Roanus, I suppose Giraldus mistook and at first wrote it for
Ronanus, which led others who came after him into the same
error ; and so it has been taken upon trust, and delivered down ;
and Roanus is the current name with common historians to this
day.

AN ACCOUNT OF THE FIRST INHABITANTS OF IRELAND AFTER THE FLOOD.

The first person, who set foot upon the island after the Deluge,
was, according to some antiquaries, a messenger, whose name was
Adhna, the son of Beatha, sent by Niou, the son of Pelus, to discover the soil of the country. He landed upon the coast about
seven score years after the Flood, but made no stay ; he only
plucked up a handful of grass as a proof, and returned with it to
his master. This adventure is mentioned by an old poet, whose
verses are to be found in the Psalter of Cashel, and begin thus,
Fuairios, see Psalter of Cashel.

> Adhna, Beatha's son, we all agree,
> After the Flood, first tried the Irish sea.
> He prov'd the soil, and from the earth he tore
> A handful of rich grass, then left the shore,
> And so returned.

This, as our antiquaries observe, ought not, strictly speaking,
to be reckoned a peopling of the island ; because the messenger

made no stay, and left no inhabitants behind him ; but, for the sake of method, it was thought not improper to mention it, the better to introduce the history of the first colony, who settled in and took possession of the country.

The kingdom of Ireland lay wild and uninhabited for the space of three hundred years after the Deluge, till Partholanus, son of Seara, son of Sru, son of Easru, son of Framant, son of Fathocda, son of Magog, son of Japhet, son of Noah, arrived there with his people.   This the poet takes notice of after this manner.

> The western isle three hundred years lay waste,
> Since the wide waves the stubborn world defaced,
> Till Partholanus landed.

By this computation I am induced to believe, that it was about two and twenty years before Abraham was born, that Partholanus came into Ireland, and in the year of the world 1978; as the poet observes.

> A thousand and nine hundred years had past,
> And seventy-eight, since Adam first was formed,
> Till righteous Abraham was born.

I am not of the opinion of those authors, who imagine that Partholanus landed in the island about 1002 years after the Flood ; and at the same time allow that he was in Ireland in the time of Abraham.   We are satisfied by Scripture, that Abraham was no more than the eighth in a direct descent from Noah inclusive ; and it is not to be supposed that a thousand years should include no more than seven generations : so that we have more authority to believe that Partholanus reached the Irish coast about three hundred years after the Deluge.   He began his voyage from the country of Migdonia, in the middle of Greece, and steered towards Sicily ; leaving Spain upon the left, he came into the Irish sea, and landed upon the fourteenth of May, at a place called Inbher Sceine, in the west of Munster ; as the poet observes in these lines.

> The fourteenth day of May the Greeks came o'er
> And anchors cast, and landed on the shore
> Of Inbher Sceine.

The persons that attended Partholanus in this voyage, were his wife Dealgnait, and his three sons, Rughraidhe, Slainge, and Laighline, with their three wives and a thousand soldiers ; as we have the account from Ninus and the Psalter of Cashel.   The place where Partholanus fixed his residence was at Inis Samer, near Earne. and it received that name from a greyhound which Partholanus killed in that isle : the place, therefore, was so called from Inis which signifies an isle ; and Samer being the dog's name it was styled Inis Samer, or the Dog's isle. The death of this greyhound was occasioned by the passion and resentment of Par tholanus, who was informed of the loose behaviour of his wife with one of her footmen, whose name was Togha. This lady it seems was of a perverse disposition, and having disgraced herself with her menial, sought to palliate her misconduct by some highly indecorous observations.

When reproached by Partholanus, she replied to him in a strain quite at variance with all morality. She made light of her crime and, as it were to justify it, quoted some licentious verses from a profane poet, who was as ignorant as he was disregardless of a woman's dignity and duty. As yet, however, Ireland lay plunged in idolatry and superstition, and we are not to wonder if in the absence of Christianity, many of the inhabitants were given to the practices so inveterate and cherished amongst the heathens.

This incident is recorded by the poet :

*　　*　　*　　*　　*　　*　　*

*　　*　　*　　*　　*　　*

Partholanus, astonished at her audacious reply, in a fit of passion seized upon her favourite greyhound, and threw it with all his force upon the ground, and it died upon the spot. The name of the greyhound was Samer, as we observed before, and the place is called Inis Samer to this day. This is the first instance of jealousy and female falsehood in the Irish history. Seventeen years after Partholanus landed in Ireland, one of his followers died, whose name was Feadha, the son of Tartan ; he was the first person that died in the island, and from him Magh Feadha received its name.

The reason why Partholanus left his own country, and undertook this voyage, was, because he slew his father and mother in Greece, in order to obtain the crown, and hinder his elder brother of the succession ; but the vengeance of God overtook the inhuman parricide, and destroyed some time after nine thousand of the posterity of his colony by the pestilence : they were carried off within the space of a week, at Binneadair, now called the Hill of Hoath, near Dublin.

There is an account in some authors, though of no credit with the Irish antiquaries, of a sort of inhabitants in the island, before Partholanus brought over his colony. These people were under the government of Ciocall, the son of Nil, son of Garbh, son of Uadhmoir, (who gave a name to the mountain Sliabh,) whose mother was Loth Luaimhneach, and they lived two hundred years by fishing and fowling upon the coast. Upon the arrival of Partholanus and his people, there was a bloody battle fought between them at Muigh Jotha, where Ciocall and his whole army were destroyed. The place where Ciocall landed with his followers is said to be Inbher Domhnonn; he came over in six ships, and had fifty men and fifty women in every ship; as the poet observes in the following verses:

> The brave Ciocall, with three hundred men,
> Cast anchor in the bay of Inbher Domhnon;
> But, fighting to repel the bold invaders,
> Were all cut off.

In the time of Partholanus, seven lakes broke out in the island, which were these; Loch Measg, in Conacht, Loch Con, and twelve years after his arrival Loch Diechiodh began to flow; and a year after, Slainge, one of his sons, and the fourth great officer in the government, died, and was buried at Sliabh Slainge; Laighline, another son, died about a year after that, and as his grave was digging, the Loch Laighline sprang out of the hole, from whence it was called Loch Laighline: the next year Loch Eachtra broke out, between Sliabh Mudhoirn and Sliabh Fuaid, in Oigialladhn; then flowed Loch Rughraidhe, where Rughraidhe, another son of Partholanus was drowned; and in the same year Loch Luain began to flow. Partholanus found but nine rivers and three lakes in the whole island: the lakes were Loch Luimhnidh, in Desmond; Fion Loch Cearra, at Jerrous Domhnonn, in Conacht; and Loch Foirdreamhuin, at Sliabh Mis, near Tralee, in Munster. This is observed in a poem in Psalter na ran, which begins thus, Achaomh chlair chuin chaomhsheang, and the verses are these:

> Three pleasant lakes at first adorned the isle,
> Loch Foirdreamhuin, Loch Lumnigh. and Fionn Loch.

The nine rivers were, Buas, between Dalnaruidhe and Dalinda, this river is called Ruthatch; Liffea, which runs through part of Leinster to Dublin ; Lagi or Lee, that passes through part of Munster to Cork ; Sligo, Samer and Muaidh, in Conacht ; Mudhorn, that runs through Tireogain ; Buas, that passes, between Tireogain and Tirconuill, and the river Banna, whose streams flow between Lee and Eille ; as the poet mentions in a poem that begins in this manner, Adhamh athair sruith ar sluagh &c.

> The ancient streams, that made the country fruitful,
> Were Leoi, Buas, Banna, Bearbh,
> Saimer, Sligo, Mudhorn, Muadh, and Liffee.

Four years after the first flowing of Loch Murthola, Partholanus died, in the plains of Moynealta, where he was buried : the place was called Sean-mhagh-ealta Eadair, because the soil was barren, and not so much as a shrub would grow upon it ; for the word Sean-mhagh-ealta signifies a barren plain ; it was likewise called Maghnealta or Moynealta, from the number of fowl that used to flock thither to bask themselves in the sun, as was before observed. The death of Partholanus happened thirty years after his arrival upon the island, and, as some antiquaries say, in the year of the world 2628 ; though I am induced rather to follow the other computation, which makes it appear that it was in the year of the world 1986. Others imagine, that there were 520 years between the death of Partholanus and the destruction of his people by the plague ; but the learned antiquaries are of another opinion, who allow that the island lay waste and uninhabited but thirty years, after the posterity of Partholanus and his followers were thus destroyed, till Nemedius landed upon the coast as we are informed by the following verses :

> A dreadful plague laid all the island waste,
> Thro' ev'ry house and ev'ry town it pass'd:
> Not one remain'd alive. For thirty years
> The country desolate and wild appears,
> Till new inhabitants arrived.

We are informed by Charles Mac Cuillenan, in the Psalter of Cashel, that it was three hundred years from the time that Partholanus arrived in Ireland till the plague swept away the people, and for his opinion he refers to the authority of Eochaidh ó Flinn, a poet of some repute, who has left us these lines :

> Three hundred years this warlike progeny
> Possess'd the island till the plague destroy'd
> Th inhabitants, and left the country waste.

The most learned antiquaries have always allowed of this computation; and therefore they who reckon above 500 years between the death of Partholanus and the destruction of his people by the pestilence, must be mistaken in their account of time; for it seems incredible, that the country should be inhabited above 500 years, and that the number of souls should amount to no more than 9000 of both sexes; especially, when it is considered that Partholanus brought over with him 1000 when he first took possession of the island.

THE DIVISION OF IRELAND BETWEEN THE FOUR SONS OF PARTHOLANUS THAT WERE BORN IN IRELAND

The four sons of Partholanus were Er, Orbha, Fearon and Feargna; and we are to observe that Milesius had four grandsons of the same name. These four divided the kingdom into four parts, and shared it between them. Er possessed all the country from Oileach Neid, in the north, to Dublin, in Leinster. Orbha governed all from thence to the isle of Barrymore, in Munster; Fearon enjoyed all from thence to Galway, in Connaght, and Feargna ruled the whole tract back to Oileach Neid aforesaid. Eochaidh ó Flinn, an antiquary, and poet of great note amongst the Irish, gives a particular account of these divisions in this manner:

It was an honour to the aged monarch,
The dying Partholanus, that his sons,
Four valiant youths, deserv'd the kingdom after him.
These princes equally the island shared;
They lived in friendship and without ambition ·
Their love in early infancy appear'd,
And rose as childhood ripen'd into man.
Ireland was then a wilderness, untill'd,
O'errun with brambles, and perplex'd with thorns,
Till by the mutual pains and hard fatigue
Of these young heroes, it began to bear
And yield a harvest suited to their hopes.
Er was the eldest, noble, wise, and brave,
He governed northward from Oileach Neid
To Dublin; and from thence to Barrymore,
A pleasant isle, the bounds of his command,
Orbha possessed.
Fearon, from the grave of great Nemedius,
Enjoy'd the fruitful tract, with plenty stored,
To Galway; and from thence Feargna ruled
A spacious territory to Oileach Neid.
These youths were, by th' indulgent care of heaven,
Design'd as blessings on their native isle.

The persons of distinction that attended Partholanus into Ireland were Tochacht, Tarbha, Trenjomus, Eathachbeal, Cul, Doroha, and Damhliag. There were four learned men brought over in this expedition; their names were Lag, Leagmhadl, Jomaire, and Eithrighe. The first that promoted hospitali and good neighbourhood was Beoir, who made an entertainment, and introduced the custom of feasting into the island, which gave occasion to Samaliliath to invent the use of cups for the conveniency of drinking. Breagha recommended the pernicious practice of duelling and single combat. The three principal druids were Fios, Eolus, and Fochmair; and their most expert generals, who had distinguished themselves in battle, were Muca, Mearan, and Municneachan; the merchants who first began to establish a trade were Biobhal and Beabal.

Partholanus had ten daughters, whom he married to husbands of the first quality among his own countrymen; the posterity of Partholanus, and his followers, transported with him, continued in the island 300 years, from the time that this prince arrived in the country, till the whole number of the inhabitants, who were 9000 persons, were destroyed by the plague, at the Hill of Hoath, in that kingdom. It was 300 years after the Deluge that Partholanus landed upon the coast, which makes up 600 years from the Flood till this colony perished by that dreadful visitation.

AN ACCOUNT OF THE SECOND PEOPLING OF IRELAND, BY NEMEDIUS AND HIS SONS.

Ireland, we observed, continued without inhabitants for thirty years after the death of the Partholanians, till Nemedius, the son of Adnamhain, son of Paim, son of Tait, son of Seara, son of Sru, son of Easru, son of Fraimaint, son of Fathochta, son of Magog, son of Japhet, son of Noah, arrived upon the coast. All the original inhabitants of the island were the descendants of Magog: for the learned antiquaries are of opinion that the account of Ceasar that we have mentioned is fabulous, and deserves no credit. The relation between Partholanus and Nemedius is to be carried no higher than to Sru, the son of Easru; the Firbolgs, the Tuatha de Danans, and the Gadelians were the posterity of Seara, and are several branches of the same family. These tribes, notwithstanding they were dispersed into different countries, retained the same language, which was Scotbhearla, or the Irish, and it was spoken as the mother tongue by every tribe. This we have reason to believe from the testimony of authentic writers, who relate, that when Ithus, the son of Breogan, arrived in Ireland, from Spain, he conversed with the Tuatha de Danans in their own language ; as will more particularly appear in its proper place.

Others are of opinion that Nemedius descended from one of the sons of Partholanus, called Adhla, who was left behind in Greece, and did not attend his father in the Irish expedition. Nemedius began his voyage from the Euxine sea, which is the boundary between the north-west part of Asia and the north-east of Europe. He passed by the mountains of Sleibhte Rife, on the left hand, and came to a place called Aigen, in the north ; from thence arrived upon the coast of Ireland. His fleet consisted of four-and-thirty transports, and he manned every vessel with thirty persons. Nemedius had four sons, who followed his fortune ; their names were Stairn, Jarbhainiel Faidh, Ainnin, and Fergus Leathdhearg.

There broke out four lakes in the island in the time of Nemedius : Loch Breanuin, at a place called Magh na Sul Anuibh Niallain ; Loch Muinramhair, at Magh Sola, in Leinster ; and, ten years after his arrival, Loch Dairbhreach, and Loch Ainnin, at Magh Mor, in Meath, began to flow : the lake Ainnin sprang out of the grave that was digging for Ainnin, the son of Nemedius, and was called after his name. The poet gives this account of these lakes :

> Then the four lakes began to flow,
> And water'd all the plains below ;
> Loch Dairbhreach, and Loch Breannuin,
> Loch Muinramhair, and Loch Ainnin.

Macha, the wife of Nemedius, died before her son Ainnin, after she had been in Ireland about twelve years ; from her Armagh received its name, because she was buried in that place. Nemedius built two royal seats in the island, which were called Cinneich, at Joubhniallain, and Raith Ciombhaoith, in Seimhne. These places were erected by the four sons of Madain Muinreamhair, who were called Fomhoraicc ;* their names were Bog, Robhog, Rodin, and Ruibhne. These master builders, and their

* The apparent difference between our translator and General Vallancey, in the translation of this word, may be easily reconciled. Fomhoraicc, or Fo muireaig, with O'Connor, sea-robbers, is by General Vallancey rendered, marine sovereigns ; yet, in early ages, there was, perhaps, little difference between pirates and sovereigns of the sea.—See Gen. Vallencey's Irish Grammar, p. 16 new Dub. 1781.

countrymen, were distinguished by the name Fomhoraicc, because they were a sort of pirates or sea-robbers, that came originally from Africa, and settled from that time in the north of
Ireland. The next morning after these palaces were finished,
Nemedius commanded the four builders to be slain, out of jealousy, lest they should afterwards erect other structures that
should exceed his in state and magnificence. These brothers
were killed at a place called Doire Lighe, and there they were
buried.

Nemedius, designing to improve the soil of the country, cut
down twelve woods of a very large extent, and laid the land
open ; their names were, Magh Ceara, Magh Neara, Magh Culle
Tolla, Magh Luirg, in Conacht ; Magh Tochair, in Tireogaiu :
Leacmhadh, in Munster ; Magh Breasta, in Leinster ; Magh
Lughaidh, at Jobh Turtre ; Magh Seireadh, at Seabhtha ; Magh
Seimne, at Dalnaruidhe ; Magh Muirtheimhne, at Breagmhuigh,
and Magh Macha, at Oirgialladh.

Those African pirates, called Fomhoraicc, were the descendants of Shem ; they fitted out a fleet, and set sail from Africa,
and steering toward the western isles of Europe, landed upon
the Irish coast. The design of their voyage was to separate
themselves from the posterity of Ham, who was cursed by Noah,
his father, lest they should be involved in the same punishment,
which they thought they should avoid by flying and settling in
another country. But, some time after they arrived, Nemedius
engaged them in three bloody battles, and came off conqueror ;
the first battle was fought at Sliah Blaidhmia, the second at
Ross Fraochain, in Conacht, where Gan and Geanan were slain,
the two principal commanders of the Africans. They fought
the third battle at Murblrlg, in Dailraidah, where Stairn, the
son of Nemedius, was killed by Conuing, the son of Faobhar
But, in the fourth battle, which was the most bloody and desperate, and was fought at Cnamhruis, in Leinster, Nemedius was
defeated, and his forces, which were most of the men he had
in his kingdom, were cut to pieces. Among the slain was Arthur,
the son of Nemedius, born in Ireland, and Jobhchon, the son
of his brother Stairn. This misfortune broke the heart of Nemedius, who died soon afterwards, with two thousand of his
subjects, men and women, with him, at a place called Oilean
arda Nemhid, now called the isle of Barrymore, in the coun y
of Cork, in the province of Munster.

The Africans, upon the death of Nemedius, a prince of great
bravery and courage, and whose very name before had been a

terror to those pirates, pursued their victory, and made an entire conquest of the country. They resolved to revenge upon the Nemedians the loss they had sustained in so many bloody battles, and, taking advantage of the death of the Irish general, they immediately assembled their forces, and with small difficulty made themselves masters of the whole island. So that these vagabond Africans, who settled at Tor Inis, or (as some call it Tor Conuing) in the north of Ireland, entirely subdued the old inhabitants, and made them tributaries.

Marc, the son of Dela, and Conuing, the son of Faobhar, (which gave the name to Tor Conuing,) to support themselves in their new conquests, fitted out a fleet, and strengthened themselves with a standing army, and by these military methods harassed the unfortunate Nemedians, and obliged them to bring the tax and contributions they laid upon them, from the several parts of the island, to a place called Magh Gceidne, between Drobhaois and Eirne, and to deliver their tribute punctually upon the first day of November every year. These conquerors were very cruel and severe in their exactions upon the vanquished; for they demanded two parts of their children, of their cattle, of their milk, butter and wheat, which was collected in this manner. The Africans employed a woman to be the general receiver of their tribute, and she obliged every family in the island to pay three measures of wheaten meal, three measures of cream, and three measures of butter every year, and compelled them to bring their contributions to Magh Gceidne before mentioned. This place receives its name from the violence that was used upon the Nemedians in the collecting of their taxes; for the word Magh signifies a field or plain, Gceidne signifies compulsion or force; and the two words, when they are joined, make Maghceidne, which signifies the field wherein the Nemedians were forced to pay the tribute that their masters, the barbarous Africans, thought fit to exact; as the poet observes in these lines,

> Three measures of a larger size,
> Of cream and butter scarce suffice,
> The haughty victor's avarice.
> As many measures they demand
> Of wheaten meal, as tribute for their land.

The Nemedians, unable any longer to bear the oppression of these tyrants, resolved to shake off the yoke, and to make one vigorous effort to recover their liberty; the principal of them met and concerted measures for a general revolt; they agreed to summon all the force they were able, and to try the fortune of a pitched battle with the Africans ; accordingly they formed an army under the command of three expert generals, whose names were Beothach, the son of Jarbhanell, Fathach, the son of Nemedius, and his brother Fergus Leathdhearg ; and to give their men the greater courage, there were three brothers, who appeared in the field, and were officers of more than common bravery and conduct, Earglan, the son of Beoan, son of Stain, son of Nemedius, and his two brothers, Manntan and Jarthacht ; these were champions of the Nemedians, who offered to expose themselves in the hottest of the engagement, and to repel the fury of the enemy. Their army by land consisted of thirty thousand able men, and they had the same strength by sea ; as the poet observes in this manner :

> Now the Nemedians bravely make a stand,
> Eager of fight, and only wait command,
> With sixty thousand men by sea and land.

The Nemedians fell desperately upon the enemy, and a bloody battle ensued, wherein Conuing, the African general, with all his children, was slain ; and his garrison, which he had fortified, was taken and destroyed.

During this attempt of the Nemedians to free themselves from slavery, Morc, the son of Dela, was absent with his fleet in Africa ; but he returned soon after the battle, and landed at Tor Inis with sixty sail, and a numerous army on board ; and as they attempted to come on shore, the Nemedians opposed them, and a most desperate fight followed. The two armies fought with equal courage, upon the strand, without any sign of victory on either side, and the greatest part of their men were slain. The action was so hot, that they did not observe how the tide flowed in upon them, till they were quite surrounded, and when they offered to retire upon the land, they were hindered by the depth of the waters, so that those who had escaped the sword were drowned. Morc, the son of Dela, had the good fortune to make his way to his shipping, and having the advantage of his fleet, with the remains of his forces took possession of the whole island. Of the Nemedians, no more than thirty brave officers and three principal commanders escaped, in a sloop, out of the whole army. The names of the three generals were. Simon Breac, the son of Stairn, the son of Nemedius ; Joblath, son of Beothach, son of Jarbhannell Fathach, son of

Nemedius ; and a grandson of Nemedius, called Briotan 'Maol, the son of Fergus Leathdearg.

The chief of the Nemedians, upon this unfortunate defeat, after they had consulted among themselves, resolved unanimously to quit the island, rather than submit again under the yoke of the Africans ; but they were seven years before they had an opportunity to put this design in execution. Then these three generals divided the shipping, which Nemedius first brought into the island, between them, and receiving as many of their people as would venture to follow them, they weighed anchor, and stood out to sea. The Nemedians that remained in the country, were miserably oppressed by the tyranny of the conquerors, and lived in this state of servitude, under the government of ten principal commanders, till the Firbolgs landed in the island.

Simon Breac, the son of Stairn, the son of Nemedius, who was one of the three generals that left the country, arrived at Greece with the people he had on board, and instead of finding that liberty which he expected, he and his followers only exchanged one slavery for another ; from this Simon Breac, the Firbolgs derive their origin, as will be observed in its proper place. The second general was Jobhath, another grandson of Nemedius, who sailed, with his men, to the northern parts of Europe ; and some antiquaries are of opinion, that the Tuatha de Danans descended from him. The third general was Briotan Maol, the son of Feargus Leathdhearg, son of Nemedius, who landed in the northern parts of Scotland, and there settled, and his posterity were long possessed of that country. The number of ships the Nemedians procured, upon this occasion, consisted of eleven hundred and thirty sail of sloops, barks, and boats, some of which were covered with leather, and called, in the Irish language, Naomhogs. The posterity of Briotan Maol, and his followers, continued in the north of Scotland, till the Picts sailed from Ireland, to inhabit that part of Scotland, in the time of Heremon, the son of king Milesius, as will appear hereafter, when we come to the reign of that prince.

We are informed by Charles Mac Cuillenan, in his Psalter of Cashel, that the Welsh, in Britain, descended originally from this Briotan Maol, and the most ancient manuscripts of Ireland give the same account ; as the poet observed in his poem, which begins thus, Adamh athair sruith ar sluagh, Adam was our father, &c., the verses follow.

————— The brave Nemedian train,
Under Briotan launch into the main ;
A prince, whom all the ancient annals trace,
As the great founder of the British race.

Another poet and antiquary makes the same remark in this manner.

The warlike Welsh the great Briotan claim,
To be the founder of the British name.

And we have more reason to suppose that the word Britannia was derived originally from this Briotan, than from Brutus the Trojan, which is a fable that some historians are very fond of ; for if it were so, it would rather be called Brutannia. Besides we are informed by Geoffry of Monmouth, that the ancient name of the country was changed by the three sons of Brutus ; his son Laegrus called his part of the kingdom Laegria ; Camber, the second son, distinguished his share by the name of Cambria ; and Albanactus, the third son, would have his part known by the name of Albania. So that this account, from the authentic records of the Irish nation, gives a great light to the name of Britain, and deserves our belief, rather than the fabulous relations of partial and romantic writers, who have been the bane and destruction of true history.

The Nemedians, who remained in Ireland, were sorely oppressed by the tyranny of their African masters, till the posterity of Simon Breac, the son of Stairn, the son of Nemedius, who had settled in Greece, came into the island. These people were called Firbolgs, and landed in the country 217 years after Nemedius first arrived upon the coast. This is the observation of an old poet, who has these lines,

Seventeen above two hundred years had past
Since first Nemedius landed on the coast,
Till the bold Firbolgs left the Grecian shore,
For liberty, and would be slaves no more.

THE INVASION OF IRELAND BY THE FIRBOLGS.

Simon Breac, the son of Stairn, the son of Nemedius, with his followers landed in Greece, where the posterity of these adventurers settled, and in process of time increased to be a numerous people. The Grecians, out of fear they should attempt against the government, and occasion disorders in the state, resolved to use them like slaves more than subjects ; they oppressed them with hard labour and the severest drudgery ; they

F

forced them to sink pits, and dig clay in the valleys, and carry
it in leathern bags to the top of the highest mountains, and the
most craggy rocks, in order to form a soil upon those barren
places, and make them fruitful, and bear corn.   The Nemedians,
groaning under the weight of this servitude, came to a resolution to shake off the yoke, and to quit the country; this design
was kept so secret, that the chief of the Nemedians seized upon
some of the Grecian shipping, as the White book, called Cion
Droma Sneachta, gives the account, and with five thousand that
followed them they set to sea, and sailed till they arrived upon
the coast of Ireland.   This tribe, whose ancestors came to
Greece with Simon Breac, the son of Stairn, landed in the
island about 216 years after the death of Nemedius.   They had
five principal leaders in this voyage, Slainge, Rughraidhe, Gann,
Geanann, and Seangann.   These commanders were the sons of
Loich, son of Triobhuaith, son of Othoirbh, son of Goisdean,
son of Oirtheachta, son of Simon, son of Arglamb, son of
Beoan, son of Stairn, son of Nemedius, son of Adnamuin, son
of Pamp, son of Tait, son of Seara, son of Sru, son of Easru,
son of Framaint, son of Fathochta, son of Magog, son of Japhet,
son of Noah.   They had their five wives with them, Fuaid, Eadair,
Anuist, Cnucha, and Labhra; as the poet records in these lines,

> These brave commanders, Slainge, Gann, and Seangann,
> With Geanann and Rughraidhe, heroes all,
> And their five wives, the beautiful Fuaid,
> The fair Eadair, Aduist the chaste,
> The virtuous Cnucha, Labhra born for love,
> Cheerfully followed by five thousand men,
> Who scorn'd the Grecian servitude, set sail,
> And safely landed on the Irish shore.

These five princes, the chief leaders of the Firbolgs, divided
the island between them into five almost equal parts: as the
poet observes in this manner,

> Five warlike chiefs, Geanann, Rughraidhe,
> Gann, Slainge, and Seangann, shared the island.

Slaigne, from whom Inbher Slainge, by Wexford, received its
name, had to his share the province of Leinster, from Inbher
Colpa, near Drocheda, to the meeting of the three streams, and
a thousand persons were allotted to him.   Gann possessed all
from thence to Bealach Conglais, and he took his thousand
with him.   Seangann ruled the country from thence to Lime-

rick, and had a thousand for his share. Geanann governed the province of Conacht, from Limerick to Drabhaois, near Drocheda, he had likewise his thousand; and Rughraidhe, with his thousand followers, enjoyed the province of Ulster, from Drobhnois to Drocheda. From these five sons of Dela, and the people that followed them, descended the Firbolgs, the Firdhomhnoins, and the Firgailiains, who were so called for these reasons. The Firbolgs were those Nemedians whose business it was, in Greece to carry those leathern bags of earth before-mentioned, and from nence they received their name; for the word Bolg signifies a bag, and Fir signifies men, which, compounded, make Firbolgs. The second tribe were called Firdhomhnoins; their office was to sink deep pits in the earth, and dig out the clay for their fellows to carry; they were called Firdhomhnoin, because Fir signifies men, and Domhnoin signifies deep, which relates to the deep holes they were obliged to dig, and the words when they are joined, sound Firdhomhnoin. The third tribe were always under arms to protect the other tribes in their work, and to guard them from their enemies, who otherwise might come upon them fatigued and unarmed; they were called Firgailiains, for Fir signifies men, and Gailiain signifies a spear, which they used in their defence, which words, put together, make Firgailiain.

These five sons of Dela arrived in Ireland in the compass of a week; Slainge landed upon a Saturday at Inbher Slainge, which for that reason was so called, for Inbher signifies a river, and Slainge sailing up that river, and landing in that place, the stream was afterwards called Inbher Slainge; this river runs through part of Leinster to Wexford. Gann and Seangann, the Tuesday following came on shore, at Jorrus Domhnoin, in Conacht; and Geanann and Rughraidhe arrived the Friday after, at a place called Tracht Rughraidhe. The Nemedians, that followed Slainge, were called Firbolgs, and the two thousand that belonged to Geanann and Rughraidhe went by the name of the Firdhomhnoins. Some antiquaries are of opinion, that these two princes, with their number of men, landed in the north-west of Conacht, at a place called Inbher Domhnoin, which afterwards for that reason, was distinguished by that name; yet, generally speaking, all the people who followed the five sons of Dela in this expedition, were known by the name of Firbolgs, and before these five generals arrived in the island, we have no account of any that could properly be called kings of Ireland; as the poet informs us in these lines:

Fifty-six years the Firbolgs royal line
Were kings, and then the sceptre they resign
To the Tuatha de Danans

AN ACCOUNT OF THE FIRST KINGS OF IRELAND, AS RECORDED IN THE BOOK OF INVASIONS.

1. Slainge, the son of Dela, son of Loich, the chief commander of the Firbolgs, was the first monarch of Ireland ; he reigned one year, and died at a place called Dumha Slainge.

2. Rughraidhe, son of Dela, son of Loich, succeeded ; he enjoyed the crown but two years, and was drowned in the Boyne.

3. Geanann and Seangann, sons of Dela, ruled the kingdom together ; their reign lasted but four years, and they died at a place called Freamhain.

4. Gann, the son of Dela, son of Loich, succeeded his brothers he governed five years, and was slain by Fiacha Cinnfionnan.

5. He was succeeded by Fiacha Cinnfionnan, the son of Stairn, son of Rughraidhe, son of Dela, son of Loich ; he reigned five years, and was slain by Riondal, son of Geannan, son of Dela, son of Loich. This monarch was called Fiacha Cinnfhionnan, because most of the Irish, in his time, were remarkable for their white or fair hair ; for the word Cinnfhion signifies white heads, which was the occasion of that part of his name.

6. His successor was Riondal, the son of Geanann, son of Dela, son of Loich ; he enjoyed the crown six years, and was killed in an engagement by Fiodhbhghean, at a place called Craoibhe.

7. Fiodhbhghean, the son of Seangann, son of Dela, son of Loich, succeeded him ; he reigned four years, and fell in battle, as he fought against Eochaidh, son of Eirc, at a place called Muigh Muirtheimhne.

8. Eochaidh, son of Eirc, son of Riondal, son of Geanann, son of Dela, son of Loich, succeeded and enjoyed the crown longer than any of his predecessors, for he reigned ten years. This was a very fortunate prince ; for in his time the weather was temperate and healthy, the produce of the earth was not damaged by any immoderate rains, and plenty and prosperity prevailed through the whole island. He was the first monarch who restrained the outrages of his people by laws, and kept them in obedience and civility by wholesome punishments. He at last fell in battle, engaging with the three sons of Neimhidh, son of Badhraoi, at a place called Muighe Tuirridh. The names of these brothers were Ceasarb, Luacro and Luaim. In the reign of this prince who was the last monarch of Ireland of the Fir

bolgs race, the Tuatha de Danans invaded the island. He married Tailte, the daughter of Maghmore, king of Spain ; when she
died she was buried in a place, which from her was called Tailtean, and it is known by the same name to this day.

The king of the Tuatha de Danans, when they invaded Ireland,
was Nuadha Airgiodlamh, that is silver-handed. This prince
engaged Eochaidh, and a most desperate battle was fought at
Mugh Tuirriodh, between the two kings, in which Eochaidh, the
son of Eirc, was routed, and ten thousand, or according to others
an hundred thousand of the Firbolgs were slain. In this action
Nuadha Airgiodlamh lost his hand, and the wound was seven
years under cure, and he was forced to have a silver hand fixed
to his arm, from whence he was called Nuadha Airgiodlamh, that
is, Nuadha the silver-handed. The Firbolgs, who escaped this
defeat retired to the isle of Arran, Eilie, Rachruin, Inis Gall,
and other places for safety, where they could best secure themselves from the Tuatha de Danans, and there they remained till
the provential times, when every one of the provinces of Ireland
was governed by its own king. About that time the Picts expelled them out of these places, and forced them to apply to
Carbry Niafer, king of Leinster, who received them, and gave
them lands to cultivate as tenants under him ; but he exacted
such rents of them, and was so oppressive in the revenues he
demanded, that they were obliged to give up their farms, and
move to Conacht. They desired the protection of Meidheibh
Curachna, the queen of that province, who prevailed upon her
husband Oliolla, to bestow some lands upon them for their support. Anogus, the son of Nuadmor, was the prince of the Firbolgs at that time ; and the possessions they enjoyed in Conacht
are known to this day by some of the names of that people ; such
are Cime, Ceithirchinn, Roinn, Jamhain, Loch Cathro, Rinn,
Meadhra, Molinn, Dun Aonguis, in Arran, Carn Conuil, Magh
Naduir, Magh Nasuil, Magh Maoin, Loch Uair, and many others.
The Firbolgs were dispersed into several islands, and other parts
of the country, till Congcuilion and Conuil, Cearnach and Ulster,
quite drove them out of the kingdom. We have no account, in
our annals, that the Firbolgs, during their continuance in the
island, erected any royal seats or edifices of note, or made any
great improvements, by clearing the lands of woods, or that any
lake or river began to flow since their arrival at first till the time
they were finally expelled the country.

There are three families in Ireland, as our antiquaries inform
us, that are lineal descendants of the Firbolgs, and not of the

Gadelian race, which are Gabhraidhe, in Succa, in Conacht ; Ui
Tairsigh, in Crioch ó Failge, and Gailiuin, in Leinster.   And this
is all the account of the Firbolgs that can be extracted from the
ancient records of Ireland ; and we have no small assistance, in
writing the history of the people, from the famous antiquary Tanuidhe, ó Maol Conaire, who begins his poem in this manner ,

> Under five chiefs the Firbolgs once possess'd
> The island, till at last, by force oppress'd,
> They fled.

THE INVASION OF IRELAND BY THE TUATHA DE DANANS.

The Tuatha de Danans were the posterity of those who followed
the third son of Nemedius out of Ireland, when the Africans had
usurped the kingdom, and enslaved the inhabitants.   This people, rather than bear the heavy oppressions of those pirates,
left the island, under the command of Jarbhainel Faidh, a son
of Nemedius, and arrived, if we believe some antiquaries, in
Bœotia ; others say that they came to Athens, and settled near
the city of Thebes ; yet the truest account is, that they landed
in Achaia, a country of Greece, that borders upon Bœotia, and
near it stands the city of Thebes, according to the account of
Pomponius Mela.   Here it was that the Tuatha de Danans learned
the art of necromancy and enchantment ; and they became so
expert in magical knowledge, that they had a power of working
wonderful feats, so far as seemingly to raise the dead : for when
the country of Achaia, and the city of Athens was invaded by
the Assyrians, and several battles fought between them, these
sorcerers would use their diabolical charms, and revive the bodies
of the dead Athenians, and the next day bring them into the
field, which so dispirited the Assyrians that they began to despair of victory, and thought to give over the enterprise, and to
return into their own country ; for to what purpose was it to
fight, and come off conquerors one day, when they were to encounter the same enemies the next ? and these enchanters were
so dexterous in their art, as, by the assistance of evil spirits, to
infuse fresh life and vigour into the bodies of the slain, so that
the Athenians were sure never to be overcome.   But the Assyrians resolved to take the advice of a druid of great learning
among them, and, if possible, to discover in what manner they
could defeat the skill of those necromancers, and break the power
of their charms.   The druid told them, that after a battle was
over, they should thrust a club or a stake of quick-beam wood
through every one of the dead bodies, which would have this

effect, that if it was the power of the devil by which they were brought to life, this counter-charm would defeat the skill of the enchanters, and the bodies could never more be revived, but it it was the hand of heaven that brought to pass this wonderful event, it was impossible to withstand an Almighty power, and their securest way was, to desist from the undertaking. The Assyrians, relying upon the advice of the druid, immediately challenged the Athenians to a pitched battle, when they fought with great courage, and obtained a complete victory; and after the fight, they drove stakes through the bodies of the dead Athenians, and so the evil spirits had no more power to take possession of them, and the sorcerers were disappointed. The Tuatha de Danans, perceiving their art to be ineffectual, came to a resolution of quitting the country, for fear of falling into the hands of the Assyrians; accordingly they set out, and wandered from place to place, till they came to Norway and Denmark, where they were received with great hospitality by the inhabitants, who admired them for their learning and skill in magic, and the wonderful effects of their enchantments.

The person, who was the principal commander of these people in their travels, was Nuadhah Airgiodlamh, that is, the silver-handed, who descended from Nemedius. The Danes, being a very barbarous and illiterate nation, entertained such a regard for these strangers, that they gave them four cities to inhabit, where they should erect schools to instruct the youth of the country in their diabolical learning. The names of these cities were Falias, Gorias, Finnias, and Murias. In each city the Tuatha de Danans appointed tutors as presidents of these schools; they were persons of the greatest skill among them; Moirfhias was to teach in the city Failias, Arias in the city Finnias, Erus in the city Gorias, and Semias in the city Murias.

When the Tuatha de Danans had continued for some time in this country, they thought fit to move, and look out for a new settlement; and they arrived in the north of Scotland, where they continued seven years, near Dobhar and Jardobhar. From the four cities which they possessed in Denmark and Norway, they brought away four curiosities or monuments of great antiquity. The first was a stone, which was called Lia fail, and was brought from the city of Falias; from which stone that city received its name. This stone was possessed of a very wonderful virtue, for it would make a strange noise, and be surprisingly disturbed, whenever a monarch of Ireland was crowned upon it; which emotion it continued to show till the birth of Christ, who contracted the power

of the devil, and in a great measure put an end to his delusions.
It was called the Fatal stone, and gave a name to Inis fail, as the
poet observes in these verses :

> From this strange stone did Inisfail obtain
> Its name, a tract surrounded by the main.

This stone called Lia fail, had likewise the name of the Fatal
stone ; or the Stone of destiny ; because a very ancient prophecy belonged to it, which foretold, that in whatever country
this stone should be preserved, a prince of the Scythian race,
that is, of the family of Milesius, king of Spain, should undoubtedly govern ; as Hector Boetius gives the account, in his history
of Scotland.

> Ni fallat fatum, Scoti quocunque locatum
> Invenient lapidem, regnare tenentur ibidem.

In the Irish language it runs thus :

> Cineadh Suit saor an fine munab breag an f haisdine,
> Mar abhfuigid an Lia fail dlighid flaithios do ghabhail.

In English :

> Unless the fix'd decrees of fate give way,
> The Scots shall govern, and the scepter sway,
> Where'er this stone they find, and its dread sound obey.

When the Scythians were informed of the solemn virtue of
this stone, Fergus the great, the son of Earca, having subdued
the kingdom of Scotland, resolved to be crowned upon it.   For
this purpose, he sent messengers to his brother Mortough, the
son of Earca, a descendant from Heremon, who was king of Ireland at that time, to desire that he would send him that stone,
to make his coronation the more solemn, and to perpetuate the
succession in his family.   His brother willingly complied with
his request ; the stone was sent, and Fergus received the crown
of Scotland upon it.   This prince was the first monarch of
Scotland of the Scythian or Gadelian race ; and, though some of
the Picts had the title of kings of Scotland, yet they were no
more than tributary princes to the kings of Ireland, from the
reign of Heremond, who expelled them the kingdom of Ireland
and forced them into Scotland, where they settled.   Fergus,
therefore, was the first absolute monarch of Scotland, who acknowledged no foreign yoke, nor paid any homage to any foreign
prince   This stone of destiny was preserved with great venera-

tion and esteem, in the abbey of Scone, till Edward I. of England carried it away by violence, and placed it under the coronation chair in Westminster-abbey, by which means the prophecy that attended it seems to be accomplished; for the royal family of the Stuarts succeeded to the throne of England soon after the removal of this stone; a family that descended lineally from the Scythian race, from Maine Leamhna, son of Corc, king of Munster, son of Luighdheach, son of Oilioll Flanbeg, son of Fiacha Muilleathan, king of Munster, son of Eogan Mor, son of Oilioll Ollum, king of Munster, who descended lineally from Heberus Fionn, son of Milesius, king of Spain, every prince of which illustrious family successively received the crown upon this stone.

The second valuable monument of antiquity, that the Tuatha de Danans brought away from the Danes, and carried with them into Ireland, was the sword which Luighaidh Lamhfhada, that is, the Long-handed, used in battle, which they conveyed from the city Gorias. The third curiosity was a spear, which the same prince used to fight with; it was lodged in the city Finias, but removed by these necromancers into Ireland. The fourth was a cauldron, called Coirean Daghdha, that was carried off from the city Murias. These transactions are recorded in a poem, to be found in the Book of Invasions: the verses are these:

——————— The Tuatha de Danans,
By force of potent spells and wicked magic,
And conjurations horrible to hear,
Could set the ministers of hell at work,
And raise a slaughter'd army from the earth,
And make them live, and breathe, and fight again.
Few could their arts withstand or charms unbind.
These sorcerers long time in Greece had felt
The smart of slavery, till sore oppress'd,
And brought in bondage, the bold Jarbhanel,
Son of Nemedius, son of Adnomhoin,
Resolv'd no longer to endure the yoke
Of servitude, a fleet prepar'd, and wandering
Long time from sea to sea, at length arriv'd,
With all his followers, on the coasts of Norway.
The kind Norwegians receiv'd the strangers,
And hospitably lodg'd them from the cold.
But, when they saw their necromantic art,
How they had fiends and spectres at command,
And from the tombs could call the stalking ghosts,
And mutter words, and summon hideous forms
From hell, and from the bottom of the deep.
They thought them gods, and not of mortal race,

And gave them cities, and ador'd their learning,
And begg'd them to communicate their art,
And teach the Danish youth their mysteries.
The towns wherein they taught their magic skill
Were Falias, Finias, Murias, Gorias.
Four men, well read in hellish wickedness,
Moirfhias the chief, a wizard of renown,
And subtle Erus, Arias skilled in charms,
And Semias fam'd for spells—these fonr presided
In the four towns, to educate the youth.
At length these strolling necromancers sail'd
From Norway, and landed on the northern shore
Of Scotland; but perfidiously convey'd
Four monuments of choice antiquity,
From the four cities given them by the Danes:
From Falias, the stone of destiny;
From Gorias they brought the well-try'd swerd
Of Luighaidh; from Finias, a spear,
From Murias, a cauldron.

The Tuatha de Danans continued seven years in the north of Scotland, and then they removed to Ireland. They arrived there upon the first Monday in the month of May, and immediately set fire to their shipping; as the poet observes in this manner,

They land upon the shore, and then they burn
Their ships, resolving never to return.

When they came upon the coast, they had recourse to their enchantments to screen them from the observation of the inhabitants; and accordingly, by their magic skill, they formed a mist about them for three days and three nights, and in this undiscerned manner they marched through the country, without being discovered by the Firbolgs, till they came to a place called Sliabh an Jaruin, from whence they dispatched ambassadors to Eochaidh, son of Eirc, and to the nobility of the Firbolgs, to demand the kingdom, or challenge them to a decisive battle. This audacious summons surprised the king, who immediately raised an army, and, with all the forces of his country, he advanced to give them battle. This prince, and his soldiery, engaged with great bravery against the Tuatha de Danans, and the fight was bloody and desperate on both sides; but the Firbolgs, unable to withstand the enchantments of their enemies, were at last defeated, with the loss of ten thousand, or, as other histories, with more probability, inform us, of an hundred thousand, upon the spot. It was the distance of thirty years between he battle of south Muighe Tuirreadh, and the battle of north Muighe Tuirreadh ; as the poet computes in these verses :

> Since the sharp fight at south Muighe Tuirreadh
> To the battle fought at north Muighe Tuirreadh,
> Where Ballar, the great general, was slain.
> Was thirty years.

Some of the antiquaries of Ireland are of opinion, that the Tuatha de Danans were so called, because they were the descendants of the three sons of Danan, the daughter of Dealbaoith, son of Ealathan, son of Neid. The names of these brothers were Bryan, Juchor, and Juchorba; their grandfather was Dealbaoith, son of Ealathan, son of Neid, son of Jondaoi, son of Allaoi, son of Tait, son of Tabhairn, son of Eana, son of Baath, son of Ibath, son of Jarbhainel Faidh, son of Nemedius. This colony of people were called Tuatha de Danans, as they were the posterity of the three sons of Danan, who were so expert in the black art, and the mystery of charms and enchantments, that the inhabitants of the country where they lived, distinguished them by the name of gods ; as appears from an old poem that begins thus, Eisdig a Eolacha gan on, &c., wherein these three brothers are styled deities ; the lines are these :

> The Tuatha de Danans had their name
> From the three brothers, Bryan, Juchorba,
> And Juchor, slain by Logha, son of Eithlean.

From Danan, the mother of these brothers, the two hills at Luachair Dheagha, in Desmond, were called da Chidh Danan.

There is another opinion among learned antiquaries, that the Tuatha de Danans were so called, because they were divided into three tribes. The first was known by the name of Tuatha, and consisted of the nobility and the principal leaders of the colony; for Tuatha signifies a lord or commander ; and from hence it was, that the two beautiful women Beachoil and Danan, were called Bantuathachs, that is, ladies ; as the poet remarks in this manner :

> Beachoil and Danan, whose charms divine
> In every air and every feature shine,
> Were ladies, deeply versed in magic skill,
> But by decree of fate untimely fell.

The second tribe of the Tuatha de Danans was called Dee, that is, gods ; these were druids or priests. The third tribe

was styled Dee Danans, that is, Gods of Danan; they chiefly
applied to the study of poetry, and the art of composing verses;
for Dan signifies art, and likewise a poem or song. The three
sons of Danan, Bryan, Juchor, and Juchorba, were called gods,
from their surprising performances in the black art; and they
had the name also of Tuatha de Danans, because they were the
chief lords and commanders of the whole colony.

THE GENEALOGY OF SOME OF THE PRINCIPAL NOBILITY OF THE TUATHA DANANS.

The family of Eochaidh Ollamh was descended from Daghdha,
Ogma, Alloid, Breas and Dealbhaoith, the five sons of Ealthan,
son of Neid, son of Jondaoi, son of Allaoi, son of Tait, son of
Tabhairn, son of Eana, son of Bathath, son of Jobhath, son of
Beothaidh, son of Jarbhainel Faidh, son of Nemedius, son of
Adnamain and Mananan, son of Alloid, son of Dealbhaoith.
The six sons of Dealbhaoith were Ogmha, Fiacha, Ollamh,
Jondaoi, Bryan, Juchor, and Juchorba. Aongus, Hugh, Cearmad
and Midhir, were the four sons of Daghdha. Lughaidh, the
son of Cein, son of Dianceacht, son of Easaraig, son of Neid,
sons of Jondaoi Gabhneoin; also Ceidne, Dianceacht, and Luch-
tain Carbry, the famous poet, son of Taro, son of Turril
Bithro, son of Carbrie, Caitchean, son of Tabhairn, Fiacha, son
of Dealbhaoith, and his son Ollamh, son of Fiacha Caicer Neachtain, son of Mamaith, son of Echoaidh Garbh, son of Duach
Doill Siodhmall, son of Cairbre Crom, son of Ealomhuir, son
of Dealbhaoith. Eire Fodhla, and Banba, were the three
daughters of Fiacha, son of Dealbhaoith, son of Ogma; and
Einin, the daughter of Eadarlamh, was the mother of these three
sisters. Their female deities were Badhbha, Macha, and Morio-
gan. Their ladies of beauty and quality were Danan and Beo-
chuill; Bridhid was a poetess of note. They had two eminent
princes, Fec and Mean, who gave the name to Magh Feidh-
mhuin, in Munster: they possessed Triathre Torc, from whence
Trithtirne, in Munster, was so called. They defeated the
African pirates in the battle of north Muighe Tuirreadh; and
routed the Firbolgs in south Muighe Tuirreadh. In the first of
these engagements Nuagatt had his hand cut off, in the latter
he lost his head.

AN ACCOUNT OF THE KINGS OF THE TUATHA DE DANANS, AND THE TIME
OF THEIR REIGN.

Nuadha Airgiodlamh, or the silver-handed, the son of Eachtach, son of Eadarlamh, son of Ordan, son of Allai, son of Tait,
son of Tabhran, son of Eana, son of Baath, son of Jobhath, son
of Beothach, son of Jarbhainel Faidh, son of Nemedius, son of
Adnamain, reigned king of Ireland thirty years, and was slain
by Ealadh, son of Dealbhaoith, and by Ballar na Neid, in the
battle of north Muighe Tuirreadh.

Breas, son of Ealathan, son of Neid, son of Jondaoi, son of
Allai, son of Tabharn, son of Eana, son of Baath, son of Ibhath,
son of Beothach, son of Jarbhainel Faidh, son of Nemedius,
succeeded and reigned seven years.

Luighaidh Lamfnadha, or the long-handed, was his successor;
he was the son of Cein, son of Dianceatch, son of Eachtairg-
breac, son of Neid, son of Jondaoi, son of Allai, and his reign
continued forty years. This prince first ordained the assembly
of Tailtean, in honour to the memory of Tailte, the daughter of
Magh Mor, king of Spain. She was wife to Eochaidh, son of
Eirc, the late king of the Firbolgs, and was afterwards married
to Duach Doil, a great general of that colony; she took care of
the education of this Luighaidh, in his minority, and had him
instructed in the maxims of government: in gratitude for the
favours he had received, from the care and tuition of this lady,
he instituted the assembly of Tailtean, and appointed tilts and
tournaments as a tribute to her memory. These warlike exercises resembled the old Olympic games, and were observed upon
the first of August every year; a day which is still distinguished by the name of Lughnansa, from this Lughaidh, king of
Ireland.

Daghdah the Great succeeded; he was the son of Ealathan,
son of Dealbhaoith, son of Neid, son of Jondaoi, son of Allai,
son of Tait, son of Tabhairn, son of Eana, son of Baath, son of
Iobhath, son of Beothach, son of Jarbhainel Faidh, son of Nemedius; his reign was seventy years.

Dealbhaoith, the son of Oghmhagrian Eigis, son of Ealathan,
son of Dealbhaoith, son of Neid, son of Jondaoi, son of Allai,
son of Tait, son of Tabhairn, son of Eana, son of Baath, son of
Iobhath, son of Beothach, son of Jarbhainel Faidh, son of Nemedius, reigned next; he was king of Ireland ten years.

Fiachadh succeeded: he was the son of Dealbhaoith, son of
Ealathan, son of Dealbhaoith, son of Neid, son of Jondaoi, son

of Allai, son of Tait, son of Tabhairn, son of Eara, son of Baath, son of Jobhaith, son of Beothach, son of Jarbhainel, son of Nemedius ; he sat upon the throne ten years, and was slain by one Eogan, at a place called Ard Breac.

Macuill, Maceacht and Mac Greine, the three sons of Cearmada Mirbheool, the son of Daghdha, succeeded. These princes reigned thirty years, and some of the Irish antiquaries imagine that the island was divided between the three brothers, into three equal parts : they depended upon the authority of an old poet, who says,

> Three brothers, Macuill, Maceacht, and Mac Greine,
> Divided equally the isle between them.

But this appears to be a mistake, for the kingdom of Ireland was never thus divided. These three princes, I confess, ruled alternately, one every year, which seems to give occasion for this opinion. The reason why they were called Macuill, Maceacht, and Mac Greine, was, because the idols they severally worshipped were distinguished by these names. Macuill adored for his deity, Cuill, that is, a log of wood ; Maceacht worshipped Ceacht, in English, a plough-share ; and Mac Greine chose Grian for his god, which signifies the sun. But the proper names of these princes were, Eathoir, Teathoir, and Ceathoir. Eathoir, or Maceacht, had Banba for his wife ; Teathoir, or Macuill, was married to Fodhla ; and Ceathoir, who was called Mac Greine, was the husband of Eire. The right name, likewise, of Oirbhsion, was Mananan ; from him Loch Oirbhsion was so called, because, when his grave was digging, the lake broke out ; as the poet thus observes,

> ———————————— Eathoir,
> A fierce, a cruel, but a warlike prince,
> Paid homage to a log ; his wife was Banba.
> Brave Teathoir the charming Fodhla chose,
> A hero, wise and valiant, but ador'd
> A rusty plough-share for his god ; his brother
> Was Ceathoir, generous and bold, his queen
> Was the fair Eire, and his god, the sun.
> Oirbhsion properly was Mananan called ;
> From him Loch Oirbhsion received a name.

The Psalter of Cashel computes the whole time that the Tuatha de Danans continued in Ireland, to be a hundred and ninety-seven years ; as the poet expresses it thus,

> A hundred and ninety-seven years complete,
> The Tuatha de Danans, a famous colony,
> The Irish scepter sway'd.

ORIGINAL OF THE MILESIANS,

WITH A SUCCINCT ACCOUNT OF THEIR TRAVELS, GENEALOGIES, AND ADVENTURES, FROM FENIUSA FARSA, KING OF SCYTHIA, TILL THE TIME OF THEIR FIRST INVASION OF IRELAND

In order to observe a method and regularity in describing the original of the Scythians, I am to take notice, that they were the posterity of Japhet, the son of Noah ; Moses, in settling the genealogy of the patriarchs, in the tenth chapter of the book of Genesis makes mention of two sons of Japhet, Gomer and Magog. Gomer, he says, had three sons, Ashkenaz, Riphath, and Togarmah, but the sacred penman gives no account of the sons of Magog, who was the great ancestor of the Scythian nation. It is the business of this history, therefore, to be as particular as may be, in tracing the lineal descendants of this son of Japhet, which I find recorded in the Book of Invasions, upon whose authority we may depend ; for the whole account is faithfully collected and transcribed, from the most valuable and authentic chronicles of the Irish affairs, particularly from that choice volume, called Leabhar dhroma sneachta, or the White book, that was written before St. Patrick first arrived in Ireland to propagate Christianity in the country.

We are informed by this ancient manuscript, that Magog had three sons, their names were Baath, Jobhath, and Fathochta ; from Baath, descended Feniusa Farsa, king of Scythia, who was the founder of the Gadelians. The posterity of Jobhath were, the Amazons, the Bactrians, and the Parthians. Fathochta was the ancestor of Partholanus, who first settled a colony in Ireland after the Flood. Nemedius, the Firbolgs and Tuatha de Danans, the Longorbardians, the Hunns, Goths, and many other nations, descended from Magog, and came originally out of Scythia. Atyla, who called himself the scourge of God, and the terror of the world, was likewise of the posterity of Magog. This warlike Scythian conquered Panonia, and troubled the Roman empire for many years ; he overran Italy, and fought with great bravery against the Germans. Peliorbes, the king of the Hunns, was a Scythian, who made war upon Justinian, the Roman emperor ; the inhabitants of Daunia, a part of the country of Apulia, owe their original to the Scythians, as do the greatest number of the people in the Turkish empire.

Epiphanius is of opinion, that the Scythian monarchy began soon after the Flood, and continued to the captivity of Babylon; he says, farther, that the laws, customs, and manners of the Scythians were received by the other nations as the standards of policy, civility, and polite learning, and that they were the first after the Flood, who attempted to reform mankind into notions of courtesy, into the art of government, and the practice of good manners. Johannes Boemus, in the ninth chapter of his second volume, where he treats of the laws and customs of all nations, remarks, that the Scythians were never corrupted by the rude and savage behaviour of any foreign nation; and Josephus observes, that the Grecians call the Scythians by the name of Magogi, because they were the descendants of Magog.

It is the observation of Johannes Nauclerus, that the Scythians were always famous for worthy and heroic acts, and that historians, when they speak of them, give them the character of a brave and generous people. Herodotus, in his fourth book, tells us, that Darius the powerful, king of Persia, was expelled by the Scythians out of their country, with infamy and disgrace : and this is confirmed by Justin, the abbreviator of Trogus, who, enlarging upon the military exploits of the Scythian nation, gives this glorious account of them :* " The Scythians were either always free from the attempts of any other nation, or came off conquerors when they were attacked ; they drove Darius, the Persian king, out of Scythia, who was glad to save himself by a cowardly and ignominious flight ; they killed Cyrus and his whole army ; they fought with the same success against Zopyron, one of Alexander's generals, and destroyed him and all his forces ; they had heard indeed of the arms of the Romans, but never felt them." A character that no other people of the world so eminently deserved, and which we have no reason to suspect of partiality, as it came from an author who was a Roman, who seldom bestows too large encomiums upon the military exploits of any foreign or barbarous nation.

The author of the Polichronicon, in the thirty-seventh chapter of his first book, informs us, that the posterity of Gadelas were called Scythi or Scythians. The word Scythi, he says,

* Scythæ ipsi perpetuo ab alieno imperio aut intacti aut invicti manserunt; Darium, regem Persarum, turpi ab Scythia summoverunt fuga; Cyrum, cum omni exercitu, trucidarunt; Alexandri, magni ducem Zopyrona, pari ratione cum copiis universis deleverunt; Romanorum audivere sed non sensere arma.

is derived from Scuit. It is certain, that the Milesians may with equal propriety, be called Scythians, from the word Scuit as the old English in Ireland are styled Goill, from Gallia, which is the country from whence they were originally descended ; so that the Gadelians may, with the same right, be called Scythians, from Scythia, as the old English are called Goill, from the coun try of Gaul, from whence they came.

These observations, which I have collected from the learned manuscripts and annals of our own nation, and from the authority of foreign historians, make it evident, I presume, that the Gadelians, and by consequence the Milesians, are properly distinguished by the name of Scythians ; as they owe their original to those illustrious people, and are descendants from a nation so famous for civility, for good laws, and good government ; and, their posterity, the Gadelians, always approved themselves worthy of so brave ancestors, for they retained the same love for politeness, for learning and learned men, they fought valiantly in the field, were faithful allies, peaceable to their neighbours but severe revengers of broken leagues and abused faith. Their monarchy continued in Ireland under eighty-one absolute kings, of their own blood, and of the Gadelian family, not to mention a great number of their provincial princes, and other illustrious nobility, by which they may justly claim a relation to the warlike, the civilized, and learned Scythians, who make such a figure in history, and are justly esteemed the standards of probity, bravery, and honour, throughout the world.

Nor are we to forget in this place, that the posterity of Niul, the son of Feniusa Farsa, were generally called Scythians. This Niul was the second son of Feniusa Farsa, and had no share of the government allowed him by his father, or his elder brother, who succeeded. He was sent abroad with a numerous attendance, to travel into foreign parts ; and when he came near the borders of Egypt, he ordered his people, whom he designed to settle as a colony in some convenient country, not to forget that they were the natives of Scythia, that they should distinguish themselves by the name of Scuit or Scots, that their posterity might be ever mindful of their original, and glory in being descendants of the Scythian nation. This young prince had no other portion given him by his father, but the privilege of travelling, the benefit of the public schools, and to improve himself in the seventy-two learned languages, for Feniusa Farsa left his monarchy entire to Neauul, his eldest son.

G

A PARTICULAR ACCOUNT OF THE ORIGINAL OF THE GADELIANS, AND OF
THEIR ADVENTUR S TILL THEY INVADED IRELAND.

There are some of the Latin authors, who imagine that Gadelas was the son of Argos or Secrops, who was king of the Argivi,
that is, the Grecians, called in the old Irish Gaoidheal : but
this must be a mistake, because St. Austin informs us, that the
family of Cecrops began about the time that Jacob was born,
which was about 432 years after the Deluge ; and the same
father allows the crown to continue in that line but 215 years ;
by which computation it follows, that about 667 years after the
Flood, the government was removed out of their family, and
their monarchy expired. It is impossible that Gadelas should
be the son of Argos or Cecrops, because Hector Boetius, in his
History of Scotland, says, that the Gadelians were in Egypt
when Moses was working wonders in that country for the delivery
of the Israelites ; and the book of the Irish Invasions agrees with
that computation.

The Book of Invasions gives an account that about this time
Gadelas was born ; he was the son of Niul, son of Feniusa
Farsa, king of Scythia, son of Baah, son of Magog ; his mother
was Scota, the daughter of Pharaoh Cingris, king of Egypt.
Moses began to govern the Israelites in Egypt, about 797 years
after the Deluge ; and, according to that computation, there
were about 355 years from the reign of Cecrops till Gadelas was
born ; so that it was impossible for Gadelas to be a son of
Cecrops.

Other authors are fond of insisting that the Gadelians came
from Greece into Scythia, and from thence travelled by land into
Egypt. These writers are of opinion, that the word Scythia is
as much as to say Jath Sgeach or Sceachach, which they suppose
signifies land ; but upon comparing the word Scythia, in the
pronunciation, with either of these, especially the last letters of
it, we shall find there is no manner of analogy in the sound, between th, dh, th or ch, and ia, which are the last letters of the
word Scythia. This mistake arises from a profound ignorance
of some authors in the Irish language, and the forwardness of
others to guess and deliver their sentiments about what it is
impossible they should understand. They will have it, that the
Gadelians must come originally out of Greece, because the solemnity of the Gadelian triumphs, their sports, tilts and tournaments, and many other of their customs, bear a very near resemblance to the practice of the Grecians : from whence they

unadvisedly conclude, that the Gadelians were originally natives of Greece : but this similitude of manners and customs will be soon accounted for, if we consider that the several invaders of Ireland, after the Deluge, except Nemedius and the Milesians, took Greece in their way to Ireland, and resided there for some .ime. Partholanus, we have observed, came out of Midonia, supposed to be Macedonia, in Greece ; the Firbolgs set out from Thracia, and the Tuatha de Danans from Achaia, near Bœotia, and the city of Thebes ; so that those invaders, who either came out of Greece, or travelled through part of it, in their way to Ireland, may be supposed to retain some of the manners and usages of that country ; and we may presume, the Gadelians, when they came to Ireland, learned of the inhabitants they found there, some of those customs which the followers of Partholanus, or the colony of the Firbolgs, had introduced into the island. But to assert positively, that the Gadelians were originally descended from the Greeks, is what has no foundation in history, nor the authority of any faithful writer to support it : it is a mere conjecture, built only upon a distant resemblance of certain sports and exercises between the Greeks and the Gadelians, which we have very easily accounted for. It seems strange that any person should attempt to write the history of any nation whose language he is unacquainted with, and who can come at no more knowledge of antiquity than he receives through the corrupted cnannel of tradition, or the relation of foreign authors. The Irish tongue is obscure, and difficult to be understood ; and the natives of Ireland, who speak it properly enough, can hardly at .ain the knowledge of its characters, especially to read and becon. perfectly acquainted with the ancient records ; which ought to discourage a foreigner from writing about the origin of the Irish nation, and likewise render a faithful translation of the Irish manuscripts the more valuable in the opinion of every one who bears any regard to the genuine antiquities of the kingdom

A FULL ACCOUNT OF THE MOST ILLUSTRIOUS FENIUSA FARSA, GRAND-FATHER OF GADELAS, TILL HIS RETURN FROM MAGH SEANAIR ; WITH THE PARTICULARS OF HIS DEATH.

The great Feniusa Farsa, king of the Scythian nation, was a prince who applied himself to the study of letters, and made it his business to understand the several languages of the world, which began from the general confusion of tongues at the tower of Babel. From the time o. Adam till the building of that tower, there was but one universal language, which the ancient chronicles of Ireland call Gartigarran, which signifies the human tongue ; but when Nimrod and his profane confederates attempted to erect that structure, Providence thought fit to interpose and put a stop to the undertaking, by perplexing the workmen with a diversity of speech, and confounding them with strange languages, which effectually hindered their design, and prevented the finishing of the building : but the wisdom of God thought fit to preserve the genuine and original language, which was the Hebrew, in the family of Heber, from whom it was called the Hebrew tongue.　This good man, being informed of the wicked attempts of Nimrod and his accomplices, and that they proposed, by erecting a tower, to secure themselves from a second deluge, which they apprehended would again overflow the world, opposed their design, and refused to assist them in raising the structure.　He told them it was a vain and audacious enterprise, carried on in defiance of Heaven, whose decrees it was impossible to withstand or disappoint.　But this remonstrance made no impression upon the projectors, who thought to raise their tower to a height which the waters could never reach, and by that means secure themselves and their families from the danger of another flood ; but a confusion of language broke all their measures, and the faithful Heber, for his piety, was rewarded with a continuance of the original speech in his own family, who preserved it uncorrupt, and in its native purity delivered it to posterity.

Feniusa Farsa, the Scythian monarch, desirous to attain the knowledge of the Hebrew tongue, and to have it taught in the public schools which he designed to erect, resolved to go in person to Magh Seanair, which was near the place where the Hebrew was the common language of the inhabitants.　After the confusion at Babel, it is supposed, there arose seventy-two different tongues, which this Scythian prince designed if possible to be master of.　For this end he dispatched seventy-two persons of learning, with a number in case of mortality to supply their places, to the several parts of the known world ; and commanded them to stay abroad for seven years, that each of them might be perfectly acquainted with the language of the country where he chanced to reside ; then they were to return to Scythia, and instruct the youth in the several languages.　Upon the return of these learned linguists into Scythia, Feniusa Farsa began his journey to Magh Seanair, and left the government of the kingdom in his absence to Nenuall, his eldest son ; as the poet informs us in his poem that begins thus, Canoimh Bunadhus na ngaoidhiol, &c.

One was at first the language of mankind,
Till haughty Nimrod, with presumption blind,
Proud Babel built; then with confusion struck,
Seventy-two diff'rent tongues the workmen spoke.
These languages the Scythian monarch strove
To learn, and in his schools his youth improve.

It was sixty years from the building of the tower of Babel till Feniusa Farsa set out from the north, from his country of Scythia, and arrived at Magh Seanair, and there began his schools for the universal languages. This computation we receive from chronicles of great antiquity; and the poet agrees with it in the following verses:

From the confusion at the tower of Babel,
Till Feniusa Farsa from the north
Arriv'd, was sixty years.

This learned prince laid the foundation of an university at Magh Seanair, near the city called Athens, whither he invited the youth of the adjacent countries to frequent his schools, in order to attain the knowledge of the universal languages; as the poet observes in these lines:

In Magh Seanair, after the lofty tower
Of Babel was erected, the first school
At Athens was erected, where the languages
Were taught with care, and the industrious youth
Instructed.

The persons who had the care of these schools, were Feniusa Farsa, king of Scythia, Gadel, the son of Eathoir, of the posterity of Gomer, who was a Grecian; and Caoh Saion Shreathach, who came from Gudea, and was likewise called Gar Mac Neamha, as the poet writes in this manner:

The tutors who presided in the schools,
Were Gadel, son of Eathoir, and Gar,
The learned son of Neamha, the Hebrew
And Fenius, the principal of all.

Another poet is of the same opinion, which he expresses thus:

The learned monarch Feniusa Farsa,
And Gadel, perfect in the foreign tongues,
And Caoth, turned to truth, first took the charge
Of teaching youth the languages.

These three eminent linguists first invented the alphabet. in three principal languages, in Hebrew, Greek and Latin, which they inscribed upon tables of wood ; as the learned Cionfhaola, who writ in the time of St. Columbanus, or Colum Cill, justly observed.   The same author says, that Nion, the son of Pelus, the son of Nimrod, was then the sole sovereign and monarch of the universe ; and remarks farther, that Niul, the second son of Feniusa Farsa, was born at Magh Seanair about that time, for whose sake Feniusa continued twenty years,-as the president of the schools he had erected, that he might have his son under his immediate care, and make him perfect in the universal languages.   It was in the forty-second year of the reign of Nion, the son of Pelus, (as the Chronicles inform us,) that the king of Scythia first began to build and establish his schools at Magh Seanair ; so that we may suppose he continued at Magh Seanair ten years after the death of Nion, the son of Pelus ; for all the writers agree that he presided, as a tutor over those schools, for twenty years.   It likewise appears, from the computation of Bellarmine, in his Chronicle, that the schools at Magh Seanair were first begun by Feniusa Farsa, 242 years after the Flood.   The same author, in his Chronicle, computes, that it was in the year of the world 1850, when Nion, the son of Pelus, began his monarchy, and governed the nation of the Hebrews, which, according to the Hebrew computation allowed by Bellarmine, proves that Nion began to reign 200 years after the Flood : for from the Creation to the Deluge, by the account of Scripture, was 1656 years, to which we are to add forty two years of Nion's reign, that were spent before Feniusa Farsa, king of Scythia, began his universal schools : so that by this calculation it appears, that the foundation of the schools was laid 242 years after the Flood ; and they were kept open twenty years, ten years in the reign of Nion, and ten years afterwards.

When Feniusa Farsa, the Scythian king, had presided twenty years over the universal schools he had erected, he returned to Scythia, and began to build seminaries of learning in his own country ; Gadel, the son of Eathoir, he ordained president, and commanded him to digest the Irish language into form and regulation, and to divide it into five several dialects.   The firs: was the Finian dialect, which was spoken by the militia and the soldiery of the island ; the second was the poetical, the third the historical, the fourth was the dialect of the physicians, the fifth was the common idiom, or the vulgar Irish, used in general by the people of the country : this dialect received its name from Gadel, the master of the schools, and was called Gaoidhealg, that is, Irish, and not from Gadelas, as others imagine. This Gadel, the son of Eathoir, was so highly esteemed by Fe niusa Farsa, that, in respect to him he called the young prince, which he had by Scota, the daughter of Pharaoh Cingcris, by the name of Gaodhal, or Gadelas, as the learned Ceanfhoelta mentions in his history.

It is a question among authors, from whence the word Gaod Lal, or Gadelas, is derived : Becanus is of opinion, that it comes from Gaodin, or Gaothin, which signifies gentle, and by adding the syllable all, it sounds Gaodhal, which signifies all gentle. Others imagine that it proceeds from the Hebrew word Gadal which signifies great ; because Gadel, the son of Eathcir, (who was first called Goadhal, that is Gadel,) was a great proficient in learning, and in the universal languages. Our historians inform us, that he was called Gaodhal, or Gadel, from the Irish word Gaoith dil, which signifies a lover of learning ; for learning in English, in the Irish language is Gaoith, and love is the English for the word Dil. The Grecian philosophers explain the word in the same manner, and by Gaoith dil they mean a lover of learning.

It is not observed by the Irish chronicles, that Feniusa Farsa had any more children than two sons, Nenuall, who was the eldest, and Niul, the younger brother ; as the old poet remarks:

> The aged monarch happy in his sons ;
> The learned Niul, born near the tower of Babel,
> And valiant Nenuall, by birth a Scythian.

When Feniusa Farsa had reigned two and twenty years over the Scythian monarchy, and had returned home from Magh Seanair, he fell sick ; and, when he was near the point of death, he demised the kingdom of Scythia to Nenuall, his eldest son, and left nothing to Niul, the younger brother, but the advantage arising from the public schools he had erected, and the benefit of instructing the youth of the country in the learned languages.

AN ACCOUNT OF THE TRAVELS OF NIUL, FROM SCYTHIA INTO EGYPT, AND OF HIS ADVENTURES TILL HIS DEATH.

This young prince had employed himself for some time with great applause, in educating the Scythian youth, insomuch, that the fame of his learning and accomplishments was carried into distant countries, till at length it reached the ears of Pharaoh Cingcris, king of Egypt. This monarch was so charmed with

the report that he had heard. that he immediately dispatched
messengers into Scythia, to invite Niul into Egypt, to instruct
the youth of that country ; as the poet mentions in these lines :

> Th' Egyptian monarch heard of Niul's fame,
> From distant Scythia, and admir'd his learning.

Niul accepted of the invitation, and when he had been in Egypt
a small time, the king, delighted with his learning and the modesty of his behaviour, bestowed upon him his daughter Scota,
a princess of great beauty, and gave him the lands of Capacirunt,
that lie upon the coasts of the Red Sea.   This is universally allowed by our chronicles, and observed by the poet Giolla Caom-
nan, in his poem, which begins thus, Gaodhal glas odtaid Gaoid-
hil.

> The Scythian soon complied with the request,
> But, when he came, soft love his heart possess'd,
> And, for reward, he was with charming Scota bless'd.

After his marriage with the princess, he erected schools and
seminaries of learning in Capacirunt, and taught the sciences and
the universal languages to the youth of Egypt.   At this time
his wife Scota was delivered of a son, who, by the command of
Niul, was called Gaodhal, that is Gadelas.

It may seem strange perhaps, that Niul, (who was the fifth
descendant from Japhet,) should be contemporary with Moses,
especially considering that it was the space of 997 years from the
Deluge, till Moses took upon him the command of the Israelites.
This difficulty will be answered, if we observe, that it was not
impossible for Niul to live some hundred years ; for in those ages
of the world, the lives of mankind were very long, as may be
proved by the testimony of Scripture.   Heber, the son of Saile,
the fourth descendant from Shem, lived 464 years, and Shem
himself lived 500 years after his son Arphaxed was born.   This
account we find in the eleventh chapter of the book of Genesis ;
so that we are not so much to admire that Niul should live from
the forty-second year of the reign of Nion, the son of Pelus, to
the time that Moses came into Egypt ; and the wonder abates still,
if we may give credit to Marianus Scotus, who says, that it was
331 years after the Flood, when the confusion of languages happened at the tower of Babel ; and we have the evidence of the
most authentic records, to prove that Niul was born a considerable
time after that confusion ; so that the age of this prince is not
at all incredible, nor is the testimony of the Scottish author invalid, who places Niul as contemporary with Moses.

During the time that Niul resided at Capacirunt, near the Red Sea, with his wife Scota, and Gadelas his son, the children of Israel, under the conduct of Moses and Aaron, attempted to free themselves from the slavery of Egypt, and encamped near Capacirunt. Niul, somewhat surprised at the number of those itinerants, who had fixed themselves in his neighbourhood, went himself in person, to make discoveries, and to know their business, and to what nation they belonged. When he came to the outside of the camp, he met Aaron, of whom he inquired the reason of their encampment, and the country they were of. Aaron very courteously gave him satisfaction, and beginning the history of the Hebrew nation, related the adventures of that people he informed him of the bondage they had endured, for many years, under the taskmasters of the Egyptian king; and how the God they worshipped had worked wonders and miracles for their deliverance, and had punished, with the most dreadful judgments, the cruelty of that barbarous prince. Niul, affected with this relation, immediately offered his friendship and service to Aaron, and asked whether he had sufficient provision for so numerous a people; and, if they were in any distress, he promised to furnish him with corn, and all other necessaries which his country produced. This generous act could not but be well received by Aaron, who returned him thanks for his civility, and took his leave. When he returned to the camp, he gave an account to Moses of the adventure he had met with, and the kind offers that were made him by a neighbouring prince. Niul likewise, when he came home, related the history of the Israelites to some of the principal of his people, and repeated the conversation he had with one of their commanders.

It happened, that upon the same night, the young prince Gadelas, the son of Niul, had the misfortune to be bit in the neck by a serpent; some say as he was swimming in a river, though others assert that the serpent came out of the adjacent wilderness, and bit him in his bed. The venom instantly spread itself through his veins, and poisoned the whole mass of blood, so that the prince languished, and was reduced to the very brink of death. This dreadful accident alarmed Niul and his people, who, upon consultation, resolved to carry the expiring prince to the camp of the Hebrews, and entreat the humanity of Moses, that he would pray for his recovery to that Almighty God, who had displayed his power, in so wonderful a manner, among the Egyptians. Moses complied with their request, and addressed himself fervently to God, for the safety of the young prince; and laying his rod, that was in his hand, upon the wound, the youth immediately recovered, and was perfectly healed, but there remained a green spot upon the place where the bite was. From this green spot the prince was afterwards called Gaodhal glas, but by modern authors Gadelas ; Glas signifies green, and Gaodhal (as the moderns corruptly pronounce it, though Gadel was the proper name) being joined with it, is the reason that he is generally called Gadelas ; and from this Gaodhal, or Gadelas, the Irish are called Clana Gaodhal, which is as much as to say, the posterity of Gaodhal, or Gadelas.

When Moses had so miraculously cured this bite of the serpent, he prophesied, that wherever that young prince or his posterity should inhabit, the country should never be infested with any venomous creature. This prediction is fulfilled in the island of Crete, now called Candia, where some of the descendants of this prince remain to this day : and it is well known that no poisonous creature will live in that island, but die immediately upon their arrival there, as they do in Ireland. Some, I confess, are of opinion, that there were serpents in Ireland, till St. Patrick arrived to propagate Christianity in that country ; but this assertion depends upon the figurative manner of expression, which is to be understood of devils or infernal spirits, that may properly be called serpents, and were expelled the island by the piety and preaching of this saint. But we have no account in our ancient annals of any serpents in Ireland since the invasion of the country by the Gadelians ; and, by the universal silence of our historians, we may with great reason collect, that there were no such creatures ; and, as a farther testimony, we are to observe, that the infernal fiends, or the devils, are generally called serpents, in the life of St. Patrick.

We have an account, from some antiquaries, that Moses locked a chain he had in his hand about the neck of Gaodhal, or Gadelas ; and from thence he was called Gaodhal glas, that is Gadelas ; for the word Glas, by another termination, in the Irish language, signifies in the English, a lock, and by joining together the words Gaodhal Glas, we come at the name Gaodhalglas or Gadelas. In those times every principal and chief commander wore a rich chain about his arm, as a badge of his office, and a distinction of his authority. But as an evidence that this young prince had the syllable Glas added to his name, from the impression of the serpent's teeth, (which occasioned a green spot upon the wound, in Irish called Glas,) and not from a chain locked about his neck, I have inserted the following verses, extracted from the Royal Records of Tara.

> The hissing serpent, eager of his prey,
> Ascends the couch where sleeping Gadel lay
> In winding mazes then himself he roll'd,
> And leap'd upon him in a dreadful fold,
> And shook his forked tongue, and then around
> His neck he twists, and gives a deadly wound;
> From his black gums he press'd the killing foam,
> And from his mouth the blasting vapours come.
> The subtle poison spreads through every vein,
> No art, no juice of herbs, can ease the pain,
> Till Moses, with his never-failing wand,
> Touched the raw wound which heal'd at his command,
> But a green spot the tender skin distain'd.
> From hence the princely youth receiv'd his name,
> And was called Gaodhal glas.

Other antiquaries are of opinion, that he was called Gaodhal glas, or Gadelas, from the brightness of his armour, and the shining of the weapons he used in the wars; as the poet observes in this manner,

> ———— This prince, the virtuous Scota bore,
> From the bright lustre of the arms he wore,
> Called Gaodhal glas.

From this Gaodhal glas, or Gadelas, the Gadelians derive their name; and the Irish, from him, are called Clana Gaodhal Upon this account an ancient poet has these lines:

> From Gadelas the Irish had their name,
> The Scots from Scota, Feine from Fenius.

Some of the Irish chronicles assert, that the reason why Scota, the mother of Gadelas, was so called, was, because the father of Gadelas was descended from the Scythian race, among whom it was a custom to call the women after their husband's names.

It is to be observed, that this princess was a different person from that Scota, who was the wife of Golamh, afterwards called Milesius, king of Spain, by whom he had six sons; for the father of Scota, the mother of Gadelas, was Pharaoh Cingcria, king of Egypt, who pursued the children of Israel, as they fled from slavery, and perished in the Red Sea with all his army; but the father of that Scota, who was the wife of Milesius, king of Spain, was the fifteenth king of Egypt in succession from the Pharaoh above-mentioned, and distinguished by the name of Pharaoh Nectonebus.

When Niul had received the prince, his son, in perfect health, by the prayers of Moses, and in return had supplied the Israelites with provisions, and what was necessary for their journey. he began to be apprehensive that his father-in-law would he displeased at the civility he showed a people, whom he esteemed as a company of slaves, in a state of rebellion against his authority. He communicated his fears to Moses, who persuaded him to remove himself and his people, and accompany him into the promised land, where he should have a part of the country assigned him for his own support, and the maintenance of his followers ; or if he refused this proposal, he would deliver up the shipping which belonged to the crown of Egypt, into his hands, where he might dispose of himself and his subjects with safety, till he found how the great God would deal with Pharaoh, who resolved to pursue the Hebrews, and force them back to slavery. This motion Niul complied with, and accordingly Moses dispatched 1000 men, well armed, who made themselves masters of the ships, and delivered them into the possession of Niul, who, with all possible speed, went on board with all his people, and stood out to sea, in expectation of the event. Upon the next day the waters of the Red Sea were divided, and a wonderful passage made for the Israelites to go through ; and Pharaoh, with the choicest forces of his kingdom, attempting to follow them, were all drowned. Upon this memorable transaction, an old poet has these lines :

> The haughty monarch, with a heart elate,
> Resolv'd to follow, and to tempt his fate.
> He rush'd into the deep, the waters close,
> And with impetuous rage his pride oppose:
> They cover all his host, and, in their course,
> Sweep away 60,000 foot, and 50,000 horse.

This overthrow of the Egyptians was brought to pass about 797 years after the Deluge.

Niul, observing from his ships that Pharaoh and the Egyptian army were destroyed, resolved to return, and fix himself and his people in their former settlement : he brought his ships to land, and went on shore with all his followers. After this enterprise he had many children, and lived till his sons were able to bear arms, and then died, leaving behind him the character of one of the most learned and valiant princes of his age. Gadelas, after the decease of his father, took upon him the command, and admitted his mother Scota into a share of the government, and they reigned together with great wisdom and unanimity.

It was observed before that Moses had prophesied, that the countries wherever Gadelas or any of his posterity should inhabit should not be infested with any poisonous creature; and he likewise added this prediction, that the posterity of this prince should encourage the sciences, and be the constant patrons of poets, philosophers, historians, and men of learning in all professions. This account we receive from an ancient poet, in the following verses, to be found in the Psalter na rann :

The holy prophet was inspir'd to see
Into events of dark futurity ;
And said, for thee, young prince, has heav'n in store
Blessings that mortals scarce enjoy'd before ;
For wheresoe'er thy royal line shall come,
Fruitful shall be their land, and safe their home
No poisonous snake or serpent shall deface
The beauty of the field, or taint the grass ;
No noisome reptile with envenom'd teeth,
Nor deadly insect with infectious breath,
Shall ever bloat that land, or be the cause of death.
But innocence and arts shall flourish there,
And learning in its lovely shapes appear.
The poets there shall in their songs proclaim
Thy glorious acts and never-dying name.

Gadelas had a son born him in Egypt, whom he named Easru ; he was the father of Sru, who possessed and ruled over the territory of his ancestors. The successor of Pharaoh Cingoris, who perished in the Red Sea with his whole army, was Pharaoh an Tuir; he was a prince of a military disposition, and recruited the forces of his kingdom after that wonderful overthrow in his predecessor's reign. The kings of Egypt were successively called Pharaohs, till the time of Pharaoh Nectonebus, who was the fifteenth in succession from Pharaoh Cingoris, that possessed the throne of the Egyptian monarchy.

AN ACCOUNT OF THE EXPULSION OF THE POSTERITY OF NIUL AND HIS PEOPLE OUT OF EGYPT, BY PHARAOH AN TUIR.

Pharaoh an Tuir, upon his succession to the crown of Egypt immediately set himself to repair the loss sustained in the last reign ; and raised a numerous army, with a design of revenge upon the posterity of Niul and the Gadelians, for seizing the shipping, and assisting the Israelites with provisions when they encamped upon the borders of the Red Sea : and when he had completed his forces, he marched towards the country of Capacirunt, and entered it with fire and sword. Walsingham, in his

book called Hypodigma, gives the same account, where he says :*
"'The Egyptians being overwhelmed by the Red Sea, those that
remained drove out a Scythian prince, who resided among them,
lest he should take advantage of the weakness of the government, and make an attempt upon the crown.   When he was
expelled the country, with all his followers, he came to Spain,
where he and his people lived many years, and became numerous, and from thence they came into Ireland."

We are to observe, that this Scythian prince was Sru, the son
of Easru, son of Gadelas, and not Gadelas himself, as Hectoi
Boetius, and some ignorant English writers that followed him take
the freedom to assert.   But such pretenders to history will be of no
authority, when compared with the testimony of the Irish chronicles, which affirm positively, that Gadelas was the son of Scota,
the daughter of Pharaoh Cingcris, ring of Egypt ; that he remained there his life-time, and there died.   We are informed by
the same records, that this prince never came out of Greece, as
others imagine ; but his father, who was Niul, the son of Feniusa
Farsa, came directly from Scythia.   Nor is the account of Walsingham to be wholly credited ; for this Sru, upon his expulsion
from Egypt, did not direct his course towards Spain, but arrived
in Scythia, and it was Dagha, the son of Bratha, the fifteenth
descendant from Sru, that came first into Spain, as the antiquities of Ireland inform us.   However, it is certain, that Sru
was the commander and prince of the Gadelians, in their voyage
from Egypt, when they were driven out by Pharaoh an Tuir.
This is confirmed by the authority of Giolla Caomhan, a celebrated poet, who wrote a poem upon the subject while he was at
sea, and has these verses :

> Sru, son of Easru, son of Gadelas,
> The founder of the great Gadelian race,
> Left the Egyptian shore, expell'd by force,
> And sail'd with four ships.   He had in every transport
> Twenty-five nobles of the chiefest rank,
> Attended by their virtuous ladies.

The Irish records of the best authority agree, that Gadelas
and his son Easru, lived and died in Egypt, and that Sru, the
son of Easru, son of Gadelas, was the commander of the Gade-

* Egyptiis in mari Rubro submersis, illi qui superfuerunt expulerunt a se
quendam nobilem Scythicum qui degebat apud eos, ne dominium super eos in-
vaaeret.   Expulsus ille cum familia, pervenit ad Hispaniam, ubi et habitavit
annis multis et progenies ipsius, familiæ multæ multiplicata est nimia, et inde
venerunt in Hiberniam.

ians in this expedition. He landed with his followers in the island of Crete, where he died ; and was succeeded in the government by Eibher, or Heber Scot, his son, who was the head of that people, and sailed with them from Crete, and brought them to Scythia.

There is an author of some note, who is of opinion, that the Irish and Scots, were generally called Scots from this Heber Scot, who sailed with the Gadelians from Crete to Scythia, because the word Scot signifies a soldier, or a man of valour ; and it is certain, that this prince was a person of great bravery, and an expert bowman, from whom, this writer supposes, that his posterity were called Scots, and made use of bows and arrows in their wars and huntings, after the example of their ancestors, till late years, when they thought proper to use other weapons. But I am not to believe this author, when he contradicts the evidence of the most ancient of the Irish chronicles, which assert that he Gadelians in general were called Scots, because they originally came out of Scythia.

Gadelas, we are to observe, was contemporary with Moses, and was eighty years old when Pharaoh and his army were destroyed in the Red Sea. The fourth descendant from him, in a direct line, was this Heber Scot, son of Sru, son of Easru, son of Gadelas who was born in Egypt before the Gadelians were expelled thence. Some antiquaries imagine, that it was 440 years from the destruction of Pharaoh till the sons of king Milesius arrived in Ireland ; and this account is confirmed by an old poet, in these lines :

> From the destruction of Pharaoh Cingeris,
> Till the descendants of Milesius sailed
> From Spain, and landed on the Irish shore,
> Was forty and four hundred years.

The Book of Conquests, or Invasions, computes but 283 years from the time that Moses governed the Israelites in Egypt till the sons of Milesius arrived in Ireland ; and the Irish chronicles agree, that the posterity of Milesius first invaded the country 1080 years after the Flood. The book above-mentioned reckons, that it was 300 years after the Deluge when Partholanus came into Ireland ; that his posterity continued there 300 years, and that the country was uninhabited and waste 30 years after the extinction of the Partholanians, till the Clana Neimhidh, or the posterity of Nemedius landed upon the coast. The Nemedians governed the island 217 years ; the Firbolgs succeeded them, and reigned 36 years ; they were subdued by the Tuatha de Danans, who were governors of the country 197 years; and by adding the whole numbers together, they amount to 1080 years, which is the distance of time agreed to be from the Deluge till the posterity of Milesius first came into Ireland. If this computation be compared with the 797 years that were between the Flood and the government of Moses over the Israelites, it will appear evidently, that, from that time till the arrival of the Milesians in Ireland, there passed no more than 283 years; so that the above supposition is false, and without authority, which asserts, that the posterity of Milesius landed in Ireland 440 years after the passage of the Israelites through the Red sea.

Some antiquaries are of opinion, that when Sru and his followers set sail from Egypt, he steered west and by north into the Ægean sea, and left Trepofane, by some called Tarobain, and Asia Minor upon his right hand, and so he sailed round the coast of Asia northwards upon the left, and from thence westwards to mount Riffe, on the west and by north side of Asia; he steered then into the narrow sea that divides Europe from Asia, and from thence into Scythia. But it is certain, that this was not the course by which Sru attempted to steer from Egypt into Scythia; for he began his voyage from the mouth of the river Nile, and so sailed to the island of Crete, now called Candia, where he continued till he died; and as an evidence that some of this posterity remain there to this day, no serpent or venomous creature will live in the place, which is as free from those creatures as the country of Ireland. From Crete the Gadelians sailed through the Ægean sea into Pontus Euxinus, and up the river Tanais as far as navigable, and then marched his men under the conduct of Heber Scot before mentioned, who was their commander in all their voyages and adventures. If it should be thought impossible to come by sea from Egypt into Scythia, which was a kingdom of great extent in those times, it is to be observed, that the historians in their accounts of Scythia agree, that the river Tanais runs into Pontus Euxinus, which hath communication with the Ægean, and the Ægean with the Mediterranean, which sea extends to the coasts of Egypt, and to the mouth of the Nile, and Tanais was always accounted to be a river of Scythia. Herodotus, in his fourth book, gives this description of the river Tanais :* "The river Tanais, which divides Asia from Europe, is reckoned to be one of the rivers of Scythia."

* Tanais fluvius, dividens Asiam ab Europa, enumerature inter flumina quæ apud Scythas sunt.

When the Gadelians arrived in Scythia, from whence they originally descended, they were harassed with continual wars by their kindred, the posterity of Nenuall, the son of Feniusa Farsa, king of Scythia, who were afraid they would put in some claim to the government of the country; and in one of the engagements between them, Agnon, the son of Tait, the son of Heber Scot, fought hand to hand with his own cousin Reffleior, the son of Riffil, the son of Nenuall, and king of Scythia, and slew him. Their dissensions continued seven years; as the old poet, Giolla Caomhan, observes in the verses following, extracted from the poem which begins thus: Gaodhal glas otaid Gaoid-hill.

> For seven long years the Scythian wars continued,
> Till Reffleior (engaged with the valiant Agnon)
> Was slain.

THE EXPULSION OF THE GADELIANS OUT OF SCYTHIA.

When Reffleior, king of Scythia, was slain, he had two sons, Nenual and Riffil, who resolved to revenge their father's death, and, with a great army they had raised, to drive the Gadelians out of the country. The Gadelians, unable to engage with the Scythian forces, consulted together, and came to a resolution to leave the country before they were pressed to a battle; and accordingly they retired with all possible speed into the territories of the Amazons, where they continued for the space of a year, under the conduct of Adnoin and Heber, the two sons of Tait, son of Agnamon, son of Beogamon, son of Heber Scot, son of Sru, son of Easru, son of Gadelas.

Adnoin had three sons, whose names were Ealloid, Lamhfionn and Lamfhglas: Heber had two sons, Caicer and Cing; Adnoin died. After they had continued for the space of a year in that country, the Gadelians set to sea in three ships, threescore persons in each ship, and every third person had a wife. In this voyage they had six commanders; and they sailed westwards till they came into the narrow sea that flows from the Northern Ocean, where they were surprised with a violent storm, that drove them upon an island called Caronia, in the Pontic sea. In this island they staid a year and a quarter; and here Heber, the son of Tait, and Lamfhglas, one of the sons of Adnoin, died, and were interred with great pomp and solemnity, if we consider the rudeness and simplicity of those times. The principal commanders in this voyage were Ealloid, Lamhfionn, Cing and Caicer. They were persons tolerably experienced in adventures,

H

and directed their voyage with great skill; but they encountered great difficulties, partly owing to the inclemency of the weather, and in some measure to the rocks that lay concealed under water, and made sailing extremely dangerous. Uncertain which way to steer their course, they applied themselves to Caicer for advice. This person was a principal druid among them, and by his prophetic knowledge informed them, that there was no country ordained for them to inhabit till they arrived upon the coast of a certain western isle, which was Ireland; but that it was decreed they should never set foot in that country, yet it should be enjoyed by their posterity. It must be understood, that a druid signifies a priest, and a person of singular learning and wisdom; and the Gadelians were always happy in the attendance of some of these extraordinary sages, in all their travels and adventures, till they came to Ireland, and afterwards to the birth of Christ, which put an end to their idolatry and pagan priesthood.

The Gadelians, overawed by this prediction, proceeded in their voyage, and landed in Gothland, where Lamhfionn had a son of uncommon wisdom and courage, who was called Heber Glunfionn. In this country these people continued thirty years, and some of their posterity are inhabitants there to this day; as the learned Giolla Caomhan relates in a poem of his in this manner:

> The warlike sons of the Gadelian race
> Remain'd among the Goths for thirty years,
> And there shall some of their posterity
> Remain till the world's end.

But we have Irish records of great authority which contradict this account, and assert that the Gadelians continued in Gothland an hundred and fifty years, and this appears to be the truest computation; for it is certain that eight generations of that people died in that country. The eight successive descendants from Heber Glunfionn to Bratha are these: Bratha, the son of Deaghatha, son of Earchada, son of Alloid, son of Nuagatt, son of Nenuaill, son of Eibric, son of Heber Glunfionn, who was born in Gothland, the son of Lamhfionn, the principal commander that conducted the Gadelians into that country; and since it is impossible to think that the space of thirty years could consume eight generations, the last computation we must depend upon as the best authority.

Other chronicles assert that the Gadelians continued in Gothland three hundred years; yet this account is far from being

true, because the histories of the several invasions of the island
agree that there were not complete three hundred years, from
the destruction of Pharaoh and his army in the Red sea, till
the son of king Milesius landed upon the Irish coast. This
computation therefore must be false, because within that space
of time it was that the Gadelians finished all their voyages and
travels, from Egypt to Crete, from Crete to Scythia, from
Scythia to Gothland, from Gothland to Spain, from Spain back
to Scythia, from Scythia to Egypt, from Egypt to Thrace, from
Thrace to Gothland, from Gothland to Spain, and from thence
to Ireland.

THE VOYAGE OF THE MILESIANS FROM GOTHLAND TO SPAIN.

Bratha, the son of Deaghatha, the eighth descendant from
Heber Glunfionn, was the principal commander in the voyage,
and conducted the Gadelians from Gothland into Spain. He
had but four transports, and disposed twenty-four men, and as
many women, and four mariners, in every ship. The officers
who commanded under Bratha in his expedition, were Oige,
Vige, (the two sons of Ealloid, the son of Nianuall,) Mantan,
and Caicer. He sailed from Gothland, with Crete upon his left
hand, and steered south-west of Europe, and so landed in Spain.
The posterity of Tubal, the son of Japhet, were the inhabitants
of the country at that time; and with them the Gadelians,
upon their arrival, fought many desperate engagements, and
came off victorious over the natives in many battles. About
that time the family of Ealloid were all swept away by a dreadful pestilence, except ten persons, who increased and multiplied,
and in a few years in great measure supplied the loss.

Bratha had a son born to him in Spain, whom he called
Breogan, who proved to be a prince of great bravery and military conduct, and with his bold Gadelians, engaged the Spaniards
in many bloody battles, and always fought with success. It was
he that built Brigantia, near Cruine; and from him the city
had the name of Bragansa, as the learned Giolla Cuomhan observes in these lines :

> The brave Breogan chas'd the Spanish troops,
> Follow'd by victory where'er he fought,
> And rais'd the city of Brigantia.

This warlike prince had ten sons : their names were Cuailgne,
Cuala, Blath, Aibhle, Nar, Breagha, Fuad, Muirtheimhne, Ith,
and Bille. as the same author mentions in this manner

Ten were the sons of Breogan, their names
Breagha, Fuad, Muirtheimhne, Sula,
Cuailgne, Blath, Aibhle, Nar, Ith, and Bille.

The famous Gallamh, who was called Milesius of Spain, was the son of Bille, son of Breoghan, who, though he be the last named of all the brothers, yet the most authentic records of the kingdom allow him to be the eldest son. The family of Breogan obtained such a character among the Spaniards, that, by the assistance of their hardy Gadelians, they almost made a conquest of the whole country, and obtained some of the principal offices in the government. The young prince Gallamh was the son of Bille, and after he had fought with great bravery in many engagements against the natives, he resolved to undertake a voyage to Scythia, to visit his royal relations in that country. Accordingly he fitted out thirty ships, and when he had furnished his fleet with sufficient necessaries and provisions, he manned it with the stoutest of the Gadelian troops, and weighed anchor. He steered his course through the western sea till he came into the Mediterranean, and passing by Scythia and Crete he sailed northwards, through the Ægean into the Euxine sea, and so entering the river Tanais he landed in Scythia. He immediately despatched a courier to the Scythian court, to give notice. to Reffleior, the king, of his arrival. This prince was related to Reffleior, the son of Riffil above mentioned. The king of Scythia received this visit with great civility, and by his messengers invited him and his retinue to court, where the Spaniard behaved himself with so much gallantry, that he soon found a way into the affections of the king, who made him his prime minister, and generalissimo of all his forces, and bestowed his daughter upon him, whose name was Seang, by whom he had two sons, Donn and Aireach Feabhruadh. Milesius, having the sole command of the army, suppressed the growing power of the neighbouring princes, enlarged the bounds of that monarchy, and in many battles subdued all the enemies of the Scythian nation. By the continued course of his victories, he became the darling of the populace, which raised a jealousy in the king, who resolved to crush and put an end to his greatness, lest his ambition, supported by the love of the people, should animate him to make attempts upon the government, and to fix himself on the throne ; and therefore he determined, when a proper opportunity offered, to dispatch him. Milesius, informed of his bad design, assembled the principal officers of his Gadelians, and they came to a resolution of forcing their way into the palace and killing the king, which they immediately put in execution: then they retired to their shipping, and left Scythia. They went on board in the river Tanais, and sailed through the Euxine and the Ægean seas, till they came to the Mediterranean ; and so they steered towards the river Nile, and landed on the coast of Egypt. When Milesius and his attendants came on shore, he sent messengers to Pharaoh Nectonebus, the Egyptian king, to notify his arrival, who returned him his compliments, and invited him with great civility to the Egyptian court. He assigned a tract of land for the support of the Gadelian forces, and entertained Milesius as became the dignity of his character. This transaction is confirmed by the testimony of the learned Giolla Caomhan, in this manner :

> Milesius slew the monarch in his palace,
> Assisted by his brave Gadelian troops,
> Then sail'd away, and left th' ungrateful shore,
> And landed on the Egyptian coast.

In this voyage Milesius was followed by his two sons, Donn and Aireach Feabhruadh, whom he had by the princess Seang, the daughter of Reffleoir, but she died before he left Scythia. The Gadelians, when they arrived in Egypt, found that country engaged in a desperate war with the Ethiopians. Pharaoh Nectonebus, observing the valour of Milesius, and finding him to be an expert soldier, made him the general of the Egyptian forces, and depended upon his conduct in the whole management of the war. He first reduced his troops to a strict military discipline, and marched his army against the Ethiopians, and engaging in many bloody encounters, victory was always on his side ; and he made that use of success, that at last he quite broke the spirits of his enemy's soldiery, and made them tributaries to the crown of Egypt. The war being thus fortunately ended by the bravery and conduct of Milesius, his fame spread into all the adjacent countries, and he was so well esteemed in the Egyptian court, that Pharaoh Nectonebus gave him in marriage the princess Scota, his daughter, a lady of great virtue, and of excellent beauty. This princess was called Scota, for the same reason that Scota, the daughter of Pharaoh Cingcris, who perished in the Red Sea in pursuit of the Israelites, obtained that name, who was the wife of the famous Niul, the great ancestor of the Gadelians. Milesius, by this princess, in Egypt, had two sons, Heberus Fionn and Aimhergin. Upon his arrival in that country he appointed twelve of the most ingenious youths that came over with him, to be instructed in the curious arts and sciences of Egypt, with a design, when they were perfect masters in their several professions, to teach his own countrymen the trades and mysteries of the Egyptians.

When he had continued seven years in Egypt he remembered the remarkable prediction of Caicer, the principal druid, who foretold that the posterity of Gadelas should obtain the possession of a western island, which was Ireland, and there inhabit. Confiding in the truth of this prophecy, he fitted out sixty ships, and furnished them with provisions necessary for a voyage, then taking leave of the Egyptian court, he went on board with his followers, and sailed from the mouth of the river Nile into the Mediterranean till he came near Thrace, where he landed : in this place the princess Scota was delivered of a son, whom he named Ir. Soon after Milesius and his people left Thrace, and crossed many countries till he came to another island called Gothiana, which lies in the narrow sea (now called the British sea) that divides the Baltic from the ocean northwards. Here he continued for some time, and in this isle his wife Scota was delivered of another son, whom he named Solpa : he was the sixth son of Milesius, and was afterwards called the Swordsman. From hence he sailed with his Gadelians, till he arrived at the kingdom of the Picts, formerly called Albania, now Scotland. Here he landed, and plundered all the country that lay upon the coasts, and conveying his booty on shipboard, he sailed away, leaving Britain on his right hand, and having France west by south upon the left, he arrived upon the coast of Biscay, or Biscany, in Spain, where he unladed his ships, and set all his people on shore.

The certainty of his arrival was soon spread over all Biscany, and was carried with all possible speed over the whole kingdom. He found the Spaniards in the most deplorable circumstances, overrun by the Goths and other plundering foreigners, who took the opportunity of his absence and ransacked the whole country. Milesius, resolving to prevent the farther incursions of these barbarians, and deliver his subjects from the tyranny of these invaders, summoned the whole force of the Gadelians that continued in Spain, and forming them into regular troops, he joined them with those that followed him in his voyages, and offered battle to the Goths and their auxiliary foreigners, and put them to a general rout. He pursued his blow, and with the same good fortune defeated them in fifty-four several battles, and quite drove them out of the kingdom. By this means Milesius and his relations who were the family of Breogan, the son of Bra became masters of almost the whole kingdom of Spain.

The sons of Milesius were, in the whole, thirty-two, and twenty-four of them were illegitimate : he had eight sons by his two wives, Seang, a daughter of the king of Scythia, and the princess Scota, the daughter of Pharaoh Nectonebus, king of Egypt ; but no more than eight, which he had by his wives, arrived in Ireland as the poet testifies in this manner,

> Milesius, the warlike Spanish king,
> Had two-and-thirty sons and heroes all.
> But only eight born from the marriage bed,
> Arrived in Ireland.

Twenty-four of the sons of Milesius, we observed, were born to him by his concubines, before he began his voyage from Spain to Scythia ; the other eight legitimate princes he had by his two wives ; Seang, the daughter of Reffleoir, king of Scythia, bore him two sons in that country, Donn and Aireach Feabhruadh ; and Scota, the daughter of Pharaoh Nectonebus, king of Egypt, was the mother of the remaining six ; their names were Heber Fionn and Aimhergin, who were born in Egypt ; Ir, born in the island Irene, situated in the Thracian sea ; Colpa, called the swordsman, born in Gothiana ; and Aranann and Heremon, born in Galicia. This is observed by a poet of great antiquity, in the following lines :

> The valiant Gallamh, who was called Milesius,
> And fought a thousand battles with success,
> Had eight young princes of his royal blood ;
> Aireach Feabhruadh, and the noble Donn,
> Both born in Scythia ; near the river Nile,
> In Egypt, Heber Fionn and Aimhergin
> Drew their first breath ; the most courageous Ir
> A hero, who in fight surpass'd them all,
> Born in Irene, near the Thracian shore ;
> Culpa, a prince that well could wield a sword,
> The princes Arannan and Heremon,
> Born in the tower of Brigantia.

The children of Breogan, the son of Bratha, increased in Spain to be a numerous progeny, and had that confidence in the courage of their soldiers, that they resolved to attempt a conquest of some other country, and make it a place for their abode. They came into this design, because there had been a great scarcity of corn and other provisions in Spain, occasioned by the burning heats and dryness of the seasons ; and they were so continually alarmed with the inroads of the Goths and other foreigners, that they were obliged to be perpetually in the field in arms, for fear of being surprised. The principal persons of that family met in council, to debate upon this important subject, to come to a resolution which way they should steer their course, and who was the most proper to employ in the discovery of a country that was capable of supporting themselves and their people. After frequent consultations upon this affair, they agreed unanimously to dispatch Ith, the son of Breogan, a prince of great valour and penetration, and possessed of many other excellent qualities, to make a discovery of the western island, which by an old prediction was foretold should be inhabitated by that family. When this prophecy of the learned druid Caicer was mentioned in the council, the Gadelians were transported with joy, and depended upon success in the undertaking; and Ith with great satisfaction accepted of the chief command in that intended expedition. The place where this assembly met to consult was Bragunsa or Brigantia, in Galicia, in the kingdom of Spain.

This was certainly the occasion of the voyage of Ith, the son of Breogan, to Ireland; and what some imagine is more than a fiction, that he discovered the island in a starry winter night, with a telescope, from the top of the tower of Brigantia; for we have the greatest authority from the ancient chronicles of Ireland, to believe that there was a strict friendship and correspondence by navigation and traffic, between the Spaniards and the Irish, from the time that Eochaidh, the son of Eirc, the last king of the Firbolgs in Ireland, was married to Tailte, the daughter of Maghmore, king of Spain; so that the people of the two nations were well acquainted with one another long before Ith, the son of Breogan, was born. And this account is sufficient to destroy the credit of that idle fancy, that Ith, and the family of Breogan, first discovered the country of Ireland with an optical instrument, from the top of the tower of Brigantia; and puts it beyond dispute, that there was long before a constant familiarity and acquaintance between the Irish and the Spaniards.

Ith, who, as we observed before, was a prince of great learning and prudence, was of an enterprising genius, and furnished with many other princely accomplishments, fitted out a ship with provisions and necessaries, and manned her with 150 of the most resolute and hardy soldiers of the Gadelians. He took with him on board his son Lughaidh or Laugadius, weighed anchor, and set sail for Ireland. He arrived upon the northern coast of the island, and when he had landed his men, he sacrificed with great devotion to Neptune, the god of the seas, but the omens were not propitious. A number of the inhabitants soon came to the shore, and called to him, in Irish, to know his business, and the country he was of; he answered them distinctly in the same language, and told them, that he was of the same tribe, descended from the great Magog as well as themselves; and that the original Irish was the language in use, and inviolably preserved in his family.

From this transaction in the Book of Conquests, the most ancient of the Irish antiquaries conclude, that the Irish tongue was the genuine language of Nemedius and his people, and consequently, of the Firbolgs and the Tuatha de Danans. And this seems to be more than probable from what was observed before, that Gaoidhal, the son of Eathoir, by the direction and command of Feniusa Farsa, king of Scythia, reduced the Irish language into method and regularity; and from this Gaoidhal the grammarian, the Irish tongue, in the same language, is called Gaoidhalg, though by a strange corruption, it is called by the English the Irish tongue. This Gaoidhal, we have said, instructed the Scythian youth in the public schools, before Nemedius began his voyage from Scythia to Ireland; and the Irish tongue was the common language in Scythia, when Nemedius came from thence. The Irish chronicles agree, that the Irish was the genuine language of Nemedius and his followers, when they arrived in Ireland, and was made use of afterwards by the posterity of that people; not to say that the Irish was the natural language of the posterity of Milesius, and the Gadelians in general, from the time that Niul first departed from Scythia. The learned Richard Creagh, primate of Ireland, confirms this opinion by this remark :* " The Irish language is in common use in Ireland, from the coming of Nemedius, 630 years after the Flood, even to this day." And therefore it is no way incredible, that Ith, the son of Breogan, and the Tuatha de Danans, should converse intelligibly together in the same language.

Ith, upon his landing, inquired of the inhabitants the name of the island, and what was the name of the prince that governed it at that time. They answered him, the name of the island was Inis alga, and that it was under the dominion of three princes, the three sons of Cearmada Miorbheoil, the son of Daghdha, as was before mentioned. They told him likewise

---

* Gallica locutio est in usu in Hibernia, ab adventu Nemedi, anno 630 Diluvio, in hunc usque diem

that these three kings were all together at a place called Oil-each Neid, on the confines of the province, of Ulster, and were quarrelling about a number of jewels that were left them by their ancestors ; and the dispute ran so high, that the contest, in all likelihood, would be decided by the sword.

Upon this information Ith made choice of 100 of his trusty Gadelians, leaving the remaining 50 to guard the ship, and be-gan his march with all expedition to Oileach Neid. When he arrived, he found there the three princes of the island, the sons of Cearmada, who received him with great civility, and all out-ward marks of respect, and related to him the occasion of the controversy that was between them. Ith returned their com-pliments, and told them, that it was by chance that he came into the island, and was driven upon the coasts by stress of weather ; that he had no design to continue long, but to return with all convenient speed into his own country. The three kings, observing the prudence of his answers, and that he was a person of great abilities, resolved, by general consent, to choose him umpire of the differences between them, and obliged them-selves to be determined by his arbitration. Upon a fair stating of the dispute, Ith was of opinion that the jewels ought to be equally divided between them.

When the debate was at an end, Ith took upon him to recom-mend friendship and unanimity to the brothers ; and told them he thought they had no occasion to quarrel among themselves, since Providence had made them princes of so fruitful an island, that abounded with honey, acorns, milk, fish, and plenty of corn ; that the air was neither hot nor cold, but exceeding temperate and wholesome for human bodies ; and that the coun-try was of so large an extent, that if it was divided equally be-tween them, there would be sufficient to satisfy the wants, or even the ambition of every one of them. When he had ended his advice, and gratefully acknowledged their civilities, he took his leave, and departed with his retinue, in order to go on board.

The three brothers, the sons of Cearmada, observing what encomiums this foreigner bestowed upon the island, and how feelingly he expressed himself upon the air and the fertility of the country, were jealous he would give so great a character of the kingdom of Ireland, upon his return, that the Gadelians would soon pay them a visit, in order to make a conquest of it ; and therefore Mac Cuill, one of the brothers, was immediately dispatched, with 150 select resolute soldiers, in pursuit of Ith.

1. ey overtook him, and immediately fell upon his rear; Ith perceiving the attack, came to the relief of his men, and by his conduct and uncommon bravery made good his retreat, till he came to a place called Muigh Ith, called so from this Ith, the commander of the Gadelians. Here the Gadelians faced about, and both companies advancing in order, a most desperate and bloody battle was fought for many hours; and Ith, notwithstanding he was supported by the bravest handful of troops that ever the world bred, was mortally wounded in the action. His followers, perceiving their general in this distress, and despairing of victory, carried him off, and retired safely with him on shipboard, where he died of his wounds, before they were able to reach the Spanish coasts. I am sensible some of the Irish historians assert, that Ith was killed at Dromligon, and there was buried; yet I choose to follow this account, because I find it related by the undoubted testimony of the best Irish authors.

Before the soldiers of Ith arrived in Spain, that incomparable prince, Mclesius, died, after he had reigned in that country for thirty-six years. He was, as the chronicles of Ireland give his character, a prince of the greatest honour and generosity; and for courage, conduct, and military bravery, the world never saw his equal since the Creation. When Lughaidh, the son of Ith, had landed his father's body, he showed it to the sons of Milesius, and related the treacherous circumstances of his death, which so enraged the Gadelians, that they solemnly vowed revenge upon the three sons of Cearmada, and engaged to sacrifice their blood to the manes of their grand-uncle, and to drive them out of the kingdom.

But before I begin to give an account of this adventure of the Milesians, in order to the invasion of Ireland, it may not be im proper to answer the peevish objections of some ignorant authors, who have the front to assert, that it was impossible the Gadelians, who knew nothing of navigation, and understood neither sea-card or compass, should attempt a voyage from Spain to Ireland; and that there were no ships or shipwrights in the world, when the Milesians are said to invade the island. But a small acquaintance with history will inform us, that, soon after the Deluge, the posterity of Noah began to build ships in imitation of the Ark, and, by continued practice, became great proficients in that art; insomuch, that not long after the Flood, they had invented several sorts of transports, to convey colonies of people from the continent of Armenia, where Noah lived, into remote islands and distant countries. Can any one think it possible. that the posterity of Noah, who, by the direction of

Providence, were to inhabit almost all parts of the earth, and
were spread all over the face of it, could possibly arrive over
rivers, and seas, and oceans, into countries they were to possess,
without the use of shipping and navigation? And it is to be
denied, that several islands and distant parts of the world, which
could never be come at by land, were peopled by the posterity
of Noah, long before the sea-card or compass was discovered?
This is so obvious to common understanding, that it is needless
to insist farther upon it. And it is evident beyond dispute,
that the islands in the Mediterranean, the Adriatic, Pontic, and
Western seas, and many others, were inhabited long before the
modern methods of navigation were known in the world ; as
appears from the histories of the first discoveries of those islands,
that give the earliest accounts of the inhabitants, and the first
peopling of them.

We meet frequently, in the Irish histories, with many voyages
made by a sort of Africans, who often landed upon the island ;
and there we have an account of certain stars, and the names
of them, that were worshipped by the mariners, and were supposed to derive a power from the god of the sea, either to misguide
the ship, or to conduct her safe into the port. Infinite is the
number of authors that mention the siege and destruction of
Troy by the resolute Grecians, which happened, as Scaliger
computes, 1240 years before the birth of Christ, though Euse-
bius places it earlier by 21 years ; but be it more or less, we
are certain the Greeks fitted out a numerous fleet, consisting al
most of an incredible number of ships of all rates. The Africans, the Grecians, and all other nations of the world, are allowed by all authors, ancient and modern, to have had fleets at
sea, and to make long voyages, before the use of a sea-card or
compass was ever known. But I am not surprised at the partiality of these petty historians, who exclude the Gadelians, a people ever esteemed the most ingenious and enterprising of any
in the world, from the use of shipping and navigation, when
they prostitute their pens upon all occasions, to obscure the
glory, and to deface the venerable antiquities of the Irish nation.

Let me for once recommend to them the twenty-seventh and
twenty-eighth chapters of the Acts of the Apostles, where the
holy writer gives a relation of St. Paul's voyage from Jerusalem
to Rome, with these memorable circumstances, that the ship
was of a large size, and able to contain 276 persons ; that she
had sails and anchors, and that the mariners steered by the

stars, long before the chart or compass was discovered : so that this objection is of no manner of force, but designed only to destroy the authority of the Irish records, which give an account of the voyage of the Gadelians from Spain into Ireland ; and to impose upon the world with a fiction, that the Gadelians came from some other country, and were accidentally driven upon the Irish coasts ; and for no other reason but because they could not steer by the compass, which at that time was undis- covered. But the ancient chronicles of Ireland shall ever be a guide to me ; and unless we depend upon their authority, it is impossible to arrive at any certainty of the antiquities, and the religious or political state of that kingdom.

AN ACCOUNT OF THE VOYAGE OF THE MILESIANS FROM SPAIN INTO IRELAND
THEIR ADVENTURES, AND THEIR CONQUEST OF THE ISLAND

Hector Boetius, in his history of Scotland, is of opinion that Heber and Heremon were the sons of Gadelas ; but this asser- tion is opposed, for very good reasons, by the learned Cormac Mac Cuillenan, who affirms, that Gadelas was cotemporary with Moses ; and observes likewise, from the Book of Conquests, or Invasions, that the Milesians invaded Ireland 283 years after Pharaoh Cingcris, king of Egypt, perished in the Red sea, and therefore it is impossible that Gadelas should be the father of Heber and Hemeron : which appears yet more evident, from the computation of Cormac Mac Cuillenau of the several ances- tors of Gallamh, otherwise called Milesius, king of Spain, who was the father of Heber and Hemeron. I shall represent the distinct genealogy of Milesius, to show that Gadelas was not the father of these two young princes, but lived nineteen gene- rations before them. This pedigree is extracted from that most valuable record, the Psalter of Cashel.

Gallamh, or Milesius, son of Bille, son of Breogan, son of Bratha, son of Deaghatha, son of Earchada, son of Alloid, son of Nuagatt, son of Nenuaill, son of Foibhrioglas, son of Heber Glunfionn, son of Lamhfionn, son of Adhnoin, son of Tait, son of Ogamhan, son of Heber Scot, son of Sru, son of Easru, son of Gadelas, son of Niul, son of Feniusa Farsa, son of Baath, son of Magog, son of Japhet, son of Noah, son of Lameoh.

Whoever reads the Scottish history of Hector Boetius would be apt to imagine, that he intended another Gadelas, from whom the Gadelians in Scotland were derived, different from that Gadelas who was the great ancestor of the Irish ; but I depend upon the testimony of a learned author, who asserts that the

Gadelians in Ireland and Scotland originally descended from the same founder. Johannes Major affirms, in proof of this,[*] " My opinion is, that from whomsoever the Irish were derived, the Scots owe their original to the same founder." And venerable Bede, in the first chapter of his Ecclesiastical history, agrees with the judgment of this author ; where he says,[†] " In process of time, the country of Britain, after it had been inhabited by the Britons and Picts, was possessed on the side of the Picts, by a nation of the Scots, who came out of Ireland. under the conduct of Reuda, and made themselves masters of those lands, either by friendship or by the sword, which they enjoy to this day." From whence it appears, that the Scottish race came originally out of Ireland into Scotland, under Reuda their general, and that the present Scots are the descendants of that colony. Humfredus, a Welsh author, thus delivers his opinion upon the same subject.[‡] " The Scots themselves, and others, well know that the Scots are the offspring of the Irish, and that our countrymen, the Welsh, called them both by the same name. Guidhil, that is, Gadelians." Giraldus Cambrensis, in the 16th chapter of the third distinction of the book he wrote upon the history of Ireland, says, that Niall, of the nine hostages, was the monarch of Ireland ; that the six sons of Murieadhach, or Mortaugh, king of Ulster, made a voyage to Scotland, where they grew powerful, and by their courage made themselves masters of the country, and obtained the principal command of it ; and that at that time they gave it the name of Scotia, or Scotland. His words are,[§] " The Scottish nation descended from them is particularly so called to this day." So that what Hector Boetius attempts to prove upon this subject, in his history of Scotland, is a downright falsehood ; and he is to be esteemed fabulous, when he asserts that Gadelas was the father of Heber and Heremon, the sons of Milesius, and would impose another Gadelas upon the world, as the ancestor of the Scottish nation, different from that Gadelas who was the founder of the Milesians and made a conquest of the kingdom of Ireland.

Buchanan, a Scottish writer in his history of Scotland, would

---

[*] Dico ergo, a quibuscunque Hiberni originem duxerunt, ab eisdem Scoti exordium capiunt.

[†] Procedente autem tempore Britannia, post Britones et Pictos, Scotorum nationem in Pictorum parte recepit, qui duce Reuda de Hibernia egressi, vel amicitia, vel ferro, sibimet inter eos sedes, quas hactenus habent, vindicarunt.

[‡] Scotos Hibernorum prolem, et ipsi et omnes optime norunt, eodemque nomine a nostratibus scilicet Guidhil appellantur.

[§] Gens ab his propagata specificato vocabulo Scotica vocatur in hodiernum.

have it believed, that the progeny of Milesius came directly from France into Ireland ; and in confirmation he gives three reasons which he thinks sufficiently prove it.

The first, the kingdom of France was grown so populous, that from that part of it only, called Gallia Lugdunensis, there went out a colony of 300,000 able men, with a design to make a conquest of other countries ; and some of these, he says, were the posterity of Gadelas, and came into Ireland. But this author seems to be grossly ignorant of the time when the Milesians got possession of the island, and could therefore have no knowledge whether the country of France was over-stocked with inhabitants or not. But supposing that France could spare great colonies of its people, at the time when the Milesians invaded Ireland, is there not the same reason to believe, that the kingdom of Spain, not far distant, abounded with inhabitants, and was equally populous, and sent out colonies ? so that this argument is no way convincing, to prove that the Gadelians came out of France; for, by the same reason, they might as well set out from Spain. or from any other country whose people were too numerous, and therefore obliged to send colonies abroad.

His second reason carries just as much evidence with it as the first ; the Milesians, he says, must unavoidably come out of France, because there is a great resemblance between the French and the Irish languages, particularly in the words Dris and Dun, with some others which have the same signification in both. In answer we are to observe, that there are many words, borrowed from all languages, to be met with in the fourth degree of the Irish tongue, that have been admitted from the reign of Feniusa Farsa to the present time ; and as we find many French words intermixed, so there are a great many Spanish, Italian, Greek and Hebrew words, and others of the other principal languages of the world, to be discovered in the modern Irish, which, by reason of the intercourse of other nations, is strangely different from the purity of the original language. But this is no proof that the Milesians came out of France ; for notwithstanding there may be words of the same signification in both languages, yet the reason of it was, as Julius Cæsar observes, in the sixth book of his Commentaries, because the druids, who were a sort of priests and soothsayers, went from the British isles into France, and were received with such veneration in the country, that they were advanced to be their judges, and were invested with large patrimonies, privileges, and immunities, by the nobility and gentry of that nation. et perhaps these and other words were introduced into France by Manann, that was subject to the Gadelians, and whose natural language was the Irish tongue.

Artelius observes that the pure Irish was the genuine language of Manann, from whence it appears that the British druids or augurs went out of the island of Ireland into France; for in those ages Ireland was the fountain of knowledge and learning and by the druids, who travelled abroad, the youth of the neighbouring countries were instructed in the liberal arts and sciences; and since the natural language of these druids must be the Irish, it is easy to suppose that the French youths collected many Irish words, and introduced them into their own tongue, and they are so continued to be used to this day.

The learned Camden, in his Britannia, informs us, that the druids or soothsayers more commonly taught the youth in their schools by word of mouth, than by writing and books; and as a farther reason how some Irish words came to be intermixed in the French tongue, it must be known, as the Book of Conquests observed, that the French and Irish had a correspondence with one another by navigation and traffic; and that the daughter of the king of France was married to Ugainemore, one of the monarchs of Ireland, who made war with the French; and likewise, that Cricmhthan, the son of Fiodhadh, another king of the island, attempted to conquer the country. The Irish often transported their forces into France. Niall, of the nine hostages, long after Ugaine, at the head of a numerous army, designed to over-run the country, and make it tributary to the Irish, and, humanly speaking would have succeeded in his invasion, had he not been treacherously shot with an arrow by Eochaidh, the son of Eana Dinnsealach, king of Leinster, by the river Loire, in France; as shall be more particularly related in the course of this history Dathi, the son of Fiachradh, another Irish monarch, raised a great army, and landed in France; he marched through the country, and spoiled the inhabitants as far as the Alps, and designed entirely to subdue the kingdom; but he was destroyed by Providence before he had accomplished his purpose, and slain by a thunderbolt at the foot of the Alps. We have the testimony likewise of Cornelius Tacitus, that there was a great correspondence, by means of trade, between Ireland and France: and therefore the wonder seems to be at an end, how it came to pass, that the Irish and French borrowed some words one of another, and admitted them into their own language; for the reasons that we have produced evidently show that it was impossible it should be otherwise, and sufficiently overthrow the argument of Buchanan, by which he offers to prove that the Gadelians sailed from France into Ireland.

His third supposition is of no more credit than the two we have already confuted. He fancies that there is a great resemblance between the manners and customs of the French and Irish, and therefore the Gadelians must necessarily come out of France : but Johannes Belinus, in his book wherein he describes the customs and manners of all nations in the world, makes no such remark ; and therefore the observation of Buchanan in this case is singular, and like other fictions to be met with in his history deserves no credit.

Having answered the reasons of this Scottish writer, I am now to reply to the opinion of some English authors, who pretend to treat of Ireland, and assert that the Gadelians, or the posterity of Milesius, came originally from Britain, and got possession of the island. Their arguments are much the same with those already answered : and first they say, that many words in the British and Irish language have the same signification ; but this can be no evidence that the Gadelians were the inhabitants of Britain, and so removed into Ireland, because the country of Britain received its name from Briotan Maol, a Scythian by descent, whose language was the pure Irish. Camden says,* "Britain was so called from a prince whose name was Briotan." The learned Cormac Mac Cuillenan, in his Psalter of Cashel, and the Book of Conquests, and the Invasions of Ireland, gives the same account ; and observes, that Britain received its name from Briotan Maol, the son of Fergus Leathdearg, son of Nemedius, whose language was the original Irish. This Briotan Maol (descended from that noble Scythian, Nemedius) lived in Britain, and his posterity after him, till Heremon, the son of king Milesius, sent the Picts to make a settlement in the country of Scotland. They were afterwards invaded by Brutus, the son of Silvius, as some chronicles relate and afterwards they were attacked by the Romans, the Saxons, the Danes, and then by William the Conqueror, and the French ; so that after so many confusions and invasions of enemies, it is not to be wondered, that the Irish tongue, the genuine language of Briotan Maol and his posterity, from whom descended the warlike Britains, should be strangely corrupted, and almost utterly destroyed. But notwithstanding the alterations that language has received, yet some part of it remains pure

* Britannia dicta est a quodam qui vocabatur Britanus.

I

and unmixed, and is the same with the ancient Irish, that was spoken by Briotan Maol and his posterity.

Another reason to account for the near resemblance between the British and the Irish languages, is this observation, that the island of Ireland was the common refuge of the Britains in their wars, when they were pressed hard, and driven out of their own country by the Romans, the Saxons, and other enemies who invaded them; so that many families, for fear of slaughter and captivity, fled into Ireland, and were not only protected and secured by the arms of the generous and warlike Irish, but had lands assigned them for their support, exempt from all taxes and public contributions, as long as they thought fit to stay in the country. During their residence among these hospitable people, no doubt but the children of the Britains became acquainted with the Irish language; and from them many of the villages they inhabited retain their name to this day; such as Graig na Mbreathnach, Sliabh na Mbreathnach, Bally na Mbreathnach, and many others. When these Britains thought they might return with safety into their own country, they left the island, and constantly used many Irish words and expressions, and so did their posterity. This is a just account of the reason of the analogy there is between the British and the Irish language: and how far this will be admitted as an evidence, that the Gadelians came originally from Britain, every impartial person is at liberty to judge.

I confess there is a very remarkable resemblance between the Irish and the Britains in their manners and customs. They are both a warlike, a generous, and a brave people, distinguished for their justice and integrity; free and hospitable in their houses; lovers of learning and learned men; curious in chronology, and exact in the genealogies of their families; admirers of poets and music, and particularly delighted with the harp; and in other commendable instances, there is a very near likeness in the disposition, the genius, and practice of both nations. But this is so far from being a testimony, that the Gadelians came out of Britain into Ireland, that it rather confirms what was observed before, that the Britains borrowed their language, their manners, and customs from the Irish; and farther it is certain, that some of the principal officers, who followed the Milesians into Ireland, did afterwards leave the island and settled themselves in the country of Britain.

The sons of Breogan, who came with the Gadelians into Ireland, were Breogha, Fuaid, Muirtheimhne Cuailgne, Cuala,

Eibhle. Blaidh, and Nar; and from the posterity of Breogan, no doubt, descended the people called Brigantes, as the ancient chronicles of Ireland inform us: and what confirms this opinion is, the remark of Thomasius, in his Latin Expository Dictionary, who says, that the Brigantes, or the children of Breogan, were descended from a family in Ireland, notwithstanding they inhabited the counties of York, Lancaster, Durham, Westmoreland and Cumberland in Great Britain. So that the difficulty is cleared, and we are now sufficiently informed of the reason that many words of the same signification are to be found in the respective languages as british and Irish; and that the Britains copied after the Irish, not only in their language, but in many of the polite customs and manners of that illustrious people.

The learned Camden (an author fond of the honour of his own country) asserts that the original inhabitants of Ireland came out of Britain. But this writer, though ever so well versed in the antiquities of the English nation, must yet be a stranger to the early histories of Ireland, because he was unacquainted with the language they were wrote in; and therefore I choose to be directed by the ancient records of the kingdom, rather than by the ill-grounded supposition of any modern whatsoever.

Giraldus Cambrensis, in his legend concerning the Irish affairs, relates, that the Milesians came originally from Biscany into Ireland, by the command or permission of a king of Britian; and that by the persuasion of the same king they possessed themselves of the Orcades, and from thence transported a colony of many families into Ireland. His design it seems, by inviting these foreigners, was to bring the island into his own power, and to reduce it into the form of a tributary province to his own kingdom. The name of this prince, if we believe this writer, was Gorgundus, the son of Peilin. But this is an apparent fiction and falsehood, as will appear evidently, if we consult the chronicle of Stow, which proves to demonstration that Gorgundus was king of Britain not much above 300 years before Julius Cæsar made a conquest of the kingdom, in the eighth year of the reign of Cassibelan, who was king at that time: and the same author observes, that there were not many above 52 years from Julius Cæsar to the birth of Christ: so that by the computation of Stow, there were not full 400 years from the reign of Gorgundus till Christ was born. Now we are assured by the faithful Cormac Mac Cuillenan, in his Psalter of Cashel, and in the book of the Conquests of Ireland, that the Milesians landed in the island about 1300 years before the birth of Christ. The author of the Polychronicon agrees with this account, where he says,* "From the coming of the Milesians into Ireland to the death of St. Patrick, are 1800 years :" This is as much as to say, that the Milesians landed in the island about 1300 years before Christ was born ; for by subtracting the 492 years that passed between the coming of Christ and the death of St: Patrick, the remaining years will be about 1300, which is about the number between the coming of the Milesians into Ireland, and the birth of Christ. So that we have the testimony of Cormac Mac Cuil-.enan, the book of Invasions, and the Polychronicon, to balance against the fabulous account of Cambrensis. And by these authorities it appears, that the Milesians were in Ireland above 900 years before Gorgundus was king of Great Britain ; which overthrows the fiction of this idle writer, who would have it believed, that Gorgundus invited the Milesians from Biscany, that they landed in the Orcades, and sent a colony of families into Ireland to inhabit the country ; when that king was not born, by many hundred years, as the ancient records of the kingdom inform us ; to whose authority I shall pay the utmost deference, as it is impossible without them to open a light into these distant transactions, and to confute the errors and falsehoods of modern historians, who attempt, without the assistance of the Irish Chronicles, to write about the antiquities of that kingdom. These difficulties being cleared up, I now proceed directly to the course of the history.

It has been observed before that when Luighaidh, the son of Ith, had brought the body of his father on shore, he exposed it openly, and related the perfidious manner of his death before an assembly of the descendants of Milesius, and the sons of Breogan. The tragical sight, and the treachery of the Irish princes, had that effect upon the spectators, that they came into a resolution unanimously to invade the island, to destroy the inhabitants, and the cruel tyrants that governed them, and fix a new settlement in the country. Pursuant to this design, they fitted out a fleet, and raised a gallant army of the Gadelians, in order to wrest the kingdom from the power of the Tuatha de Danans. Some chronicles assert, that the Milesians began their voyage from a place called Mandoca, near the river Verundo, in Biscany ; and the ground of this opinion is, because they say Milesius was king of Biscany only in the latter part of his life ; for he was

---

* Ab adventu Hiberniensum, usque ad obitum Sancti Patricî sunt anni mille octi centi.

driven out of Spain by the incursions of foreigners, who, with their united force, had the better of him in several engagements, and confined him and his people within the narrow territories of that country, and there he continued till his death ; for the country was fortified by nature, very difficult of access, and impossible to be subdued, by reason of the vast woods and mountains that inclosed it. But this is opposed by the testimony of the most valuable and authentic records, which affirm, that the Milesians set sail for Ireland from Tor Breogan in Galicia. And this seems to be the truest account, for the book of Conquests or Invasions says, that Tor Breogan was the place they held a council, and determined to send Ith into Ireland ; and thither Luighaidh returned from Ireland with the dead body of his father, when he exposed his wounds to the family of Milesius, and the sons of Breogan ; and therefore it seems reasonable to believe, that they steered from that place to invade the island.

Milesius being dead before Luighaidh returned, Scota, his wife, resolved to leave the country, and to follow the fortune of the sons she had by Milesius in this expedition : for the kingdom of Spain was rent in pieces by intestine wars, and the continual inroads of foreign enemies. The Milesians, therefore, having put their provisions and their men on board, weighed anchor, and were impatient till they landed upon the Irish coast, to revenge the death of the valiant Ith, who was inhumanly slain, in defiance of the established laws of nature and of nations. This invasion they undertook under the command of forty brave commanders. The learned Eochaidh ô Flinn has transmitted to us their names in a poem of his, which begins thus, Taoisig na luing sin tar lear.

> The valiant chiefs of the Milesian race,
> Who led the bold Gadelians into Ireland,
> Were Eibhle, Fuaid, Breagha, Bladhbhin,
> Luighaidh, Muirtheimhne, Amergin, Buas,
> Breas, Buaighne, Donn, Ir, Heber, Heremon,
> Colpa, the swordsman, Eibher, Aireach,
> Arranan, Cuala, Cualgne, Narumne,
> Muimhne, Luighne and Laighne,
> Fulman, Mantan, Bile, Er, Orba, Fearon,
> Feargin, En, Un, Eadan, Goisden, Seagda,
> Sobhairce, Suirge, Palap, son of Heremon,
> The learned Caicer, son of Maman, warriors all,
> Full of revenge, sailed towards the Irish coast.

The number of their ships was thirty, and they disposed hirty of the most courageous of their troops in every ship :

they had their wives likewise on board, and many others followed them, out of a prospect of obtaining possessions in this new plantation.

From these principal officers, who commanded in this expedition, many places in Ireland obtained their names. Breagha, son of Breogan, gave the name to Moighe Breagha in Meath : Cuala, son of Breogan, gave the name to Sliabh Cuala : Cualgne, son of Breogan, gave the name to Sliabh Cualgne : Bladh, son of Breogan, gave the name to Sliabh Bladhma : Fuaid, son of Breogan, gave the name to Sliabh Fuaid : Muirtheimhne, son of Breoghan, gave the name to Sliabh Muirtheimhne, other· wise called the plain of Muirtheimhne : Luighaidh, son of Ith, who came to Ireland to revenge his father's death, gave the name to Sorca-Luighe, in Munster : Eibhle, the son of Breogan, gave the name to Sliabh Eibhle, in Munster : the generals Buas, Breas and Buaighne, the three sons of Tigeharnbard, the son of Brighe Nare, gave the name to Ross Nare, at Sliabh Bladhma : Seagda, Fulmane, and Mantane, Caioer and his son Sobhairce, Er, Orba, Fearon and Feargna ; the four sons of Heber, En, Un, Eadan and Goisdean ; Sobhairce, whose father is unknown ; Bille, the son of Frighet, son of Breogan ; the eight sons of Milesius, Donn, Aireach, Fabhruadhe, Heber Fionn, Amergin, Ir, Colpa the swordsman, and Arranhan the youngest ; the four sons of Heremon, Muimhne, Luighne, Laighne, and Palpa ; Heber or Eibher, the only son of Ir, the son of Milesius: these were the forty commanding officers who conducted the Gadelians into Ireland. Iriel the prophet, the son of Heremon, was born after they arrived in the island.

The Milesian fleet first attempted to land upon the northern coast of Leinster, at a place then called Inbher Slainge, but now known by the name of the harbour of Wexford. The Tuatha de Danans, alarmed at the number of the ships, immediately flocked towards the shore, and by the power of their enchantments and diabolical arts they cast such a cloud over the whole island, that the Milesians were confounded, and thought they saw nothing but the resemblance of a Hog ; and for this reason the island was called Muicinis. The inhabitants, by these delusions, hindered the Milesians from landing their forces, so that they were obliged to sail about the island, till at last, with great difficulty, they came on shore at Inbher Sceine, in the west of Munster. From thence they marched in good order to a mountain called Sliabh Mis ; here they were met by Banba, attended by a beautiful train of ladies, and followed by her druids and scothsayers. Amergin, the Milesian, addressed himself to her, and desired the honour to know her name; she answered, her name was Banba, and from her the island was called Inis Banba. From thence they proceeded on their march, and arrived at Sliabh Eibhline, where the princess Fodhla met them, with a retinue of ladies and druids about her; they desired to know her name, and she replied, her name was Fodhla, which also was the name of the island. They went on, and came to Visneach, where they were met by Eire and her attendants; she was likewise desired to discover her name, and she told them her name was Eire, and from her the country was called Eire. This transaction is confirmed by the testimony of an ancient poet, who, in a poem that begins thus, Sanna bunadhus na ngaoidhiol, has these lines:

> Banba they met, with all her princely train,
> On Sliabh Mis; and on the fruitful plain
> Of Sliabh Eibhline, Fodhla next they spied.
> With priests and learned druids for her guide,
> And all her charming court of ladies by her side;
> Then virtuous Eire appeared in pomp and state,
> In Visneach's pleasant fields, majestically great.

These ladies were married to the three sons of Cearmada, whc divided the island between them, though some of the Irish chronicles assert, that each of them ruled alternatively over the whole kingdom, and the country was for the time called by the name of the reigning prince. This appears from the following verses:

> These Irish kings alternatively reigned.
> And for their consorts chose three princesses,
> Fodhla, Banba and Eire.

The Milesians, after this adventure, continued their march till they came to the palace of Teamair, where the sons of Cearmada kept their court, and appeared in great grandeur and magnificence, encompassed with their enchanted guards. Amergin immediately addressed himself to the three kings, and resolutely demanded of them to resign their government, or be decided by the hazard of a pitched battle; and this he insisted upon in revenge for the death of the valiant Ith, whom they had treacherously slain. The prince of the Tuatha de Danans, surprised at this bold summons, made answer that they were not prepared to decide the dispute in a military way, because they had no standing forces, and could not instantly bring an army into the field; but they were willing the whole affair should be determined by the arbitration of Amergin, who they perceived was a person of great judgment and abilities, but threatened him withal, that if he imposed any unjust conditions, they would certainly destroy him by their enchantments. Amergin imme diately ordered the Gadelians to retire to Inbher Sceine, and with all possible expedition to hasten on shipboard, with the rest of the Gadelians, and to sail out of the mouth of the harbour, or as others say, nine waves from the shore ; then he made this proposal to the Tuatha de Danans, that if they could hinder his men from landing in the island, he, with his whole fleet, would return into Spain, and never make any other attempt upon the country ; but if he and his resolute Gadelians could, in defiance of them, land upon their coast, the Tuatha de Danans should resign the government and become their tributaries. This offer was well accepted by the inhabitants, who, depending upon the influence of their art, thought they should soon get rid of these insolent invaders ; for they had that command over the elements by their enchantments, that they made no question of preventing them from ever setting foot upon the shore again.

In obedience to the command of Amergin, the Milesians returned to their shipping, and he went on board with them ; they weighed anchor, and moved no more than the distance of nine waves from the shore. The Tuatha de Danans perceiving the ships were afloat, confiding in their art, had immediate recourse to their enchantments, which succeeded so far as to raise a most violent and tempestuous wind, which soon disordered the Milesian fleet, and drove them foul one upon another. Amergin and Donn, the sons of Milesius, knew the storm proceeded from no natural cause, and Arrauan, the youngest son of the brave Milesius, went up to the topsail to make discoveries, but was unfortunately blown off by a gust of wind, and falling upon the hatch he instantly died. The Gadelians began to be in great confusion, for the ships were dreadfully tossed, and the whole fleet was in danger of being lost : the vessel which Donn commanded, was, by the violence of the storm, separated from the rest of the fleet, and was broken to pieces, and himself and all the crew were drowned. By the wreck of this ship there perished four-and-twenty common soldiers, four galley slaves, twelve women, fifty brave Gadelians, who went volunteers, and five captains, whose names were Bille, the son of Brighe, Air-cach Feabhruadh, Buan, Breas, and Cualgne. The valiant Ir the son of Milesius, with his ship, met with the same fate ; for he was divided from the fleet, and was driven upon the western coast of Desmond, in the kingdom of Ireland, where he split upon the rocks, and every man perished. The body of this unfortunate prince was cast upon the shore, and was buried in a small island called Sceilg Mithill.

This place, by reason of its peculiar qualities, deserves a particular description. It is a kind of rock, situated a few leagues in the sea, and since St. Patrick's time, much frequented by way of piety and devotion ; the top of it is flat and plain, and though the depth of the earth be but shallow, it is observed to be of a very fattening nature, and feeds abundance of wild fowl that are forced to be confined upon it ; I say they are forced, because the surface of the ground, it is supposed, has that attractive virtue, as to draw down all the birds that attempt to fly over it, and oblige them to alight upon the rock. The people who live nigh, resort hither in small boats, when the sea is calm, to catch these birds, whose flesh being very sweet, they use for provision, and their feathers for other occasions ; and it is observed, that these fowl, though almost innumerable, are exceeding fat, notwithstanding the circumference of the top of the rock is but small, and does not exceed three acres of land. This isle is surrounded with high and almost inaccessible precipices, that hang dreadfully over the sea, which is generally rough, and roars hideously beneath. There is but one track, and that very narrow, that leads up to the top, and the ascent is so difficult and frightful, that few are so hardy as to attempt it.

This Ir, who was so unhappily lost, was a prince of great bravery, and military experience, always in the front of an engagement, at the head of his stout Gadelians, attended with success whenever he fought, the guardian and protector of his followers in battle, by his very name a terror to his enemies. The posterity of this warlike general were the noble Clana Rughruaidhe, who kept a splendid and magnificent court, for the space of 900 years, at Famhain Macha, in the province of Ulster, and for 700 years of the time, were the heroes of the age they lived in, and were reputed the celebrated champions of the western parts of Europe, as shall be particularly observed in the progress of this Irish history.

The learned Eochaidh ó Flinn has taken notice of these misfortunes that befel the Milesians at sea, in a poem of his, which begins thus, Taoisig na luing tar lear, the lines are these :

> The ruffling winds the foaming billows rise.
> The face of heaven is ravished from their eyes
> Art fails, and courage fails, no succour near,
> As many waves as many deaths appear.
> The giddy ships run round, and then are tost,
> Then bulge at once, and in the deep are lost.
> The brave Milesians, to the bottom borne,
> Attempt to rise, but never must return.
> Don, Bille, Buan, with his virtuous bride,
> Dill, Aireach, Buas, Breas, Cualgne.
> All plunged into the deep, are buried by the tide

It was observed before, that the ship wherein Ir was, separated from the rest of the fleet, and was lost in the storm, and his body driven on shore, and buried ; this shipwreck, and the loss of this prince and his two brothers, is lamented by an old poet, in these verses :

> Amergin, learned and valiant, fell in battle,
> At Billeteinn ; Ir was cast away
> Near the rocky cliffs of Sceilg , and Arranan
> Was shipwrock'd on the Irish coast.

Heremon, with part of the Milesian fleet, was driven to the left, towards the island, and with great difficulty arrived safely at Inbher Colpa, now called Drocheda. The place was called Inbher Colpa, because Colpa, who went by the name of the swordsman, another son of Milesius, was unfortunately drowned as he attempted to come on shore. It appears that this enterprise of the Gadelians was fatal to the five sons of Milesius, who were lost before the country was conquered, and the Tuatha de Danans were dispossessed of the government. The death of these five princes is recorded and confirmed by an old poet in this manner :

> The sorcerers, by force of wicked magic,
> Summon'd the winds, and in the storm destroy'd
> Five princes of the famed Milesian race.

The names of these brothers who perished before the conquest of the island, were Donn, Ir, Aireach, Feabhruadh, Arranan, and Colpa the swordsman, who were all lost by the enchantment of the inhabitants, and no more than three sons of Milesius survived this dreadful tempest, to possess the country ; their names were Heber, Heremon, and Amergin, and they landed at Inbher Sceine.

Three days after Heber and his followers were got on shore, they were attacked by Eire, the wife of Mac Breine one of the princes of the country, at Sliabh Mis, or the mountain of Mis ; this lady was attended by a strong body of men, and a desperate battle followed, where many were destroyed on both sides. In this action Fais, the wife of Un mac Vighe, was slain in a valley at the foot of a mountain, which, from her, obtained the name of Blean Fais, which signifies the valley of Fais. The death of this lady is thus observed by an old poet

> The valley where the lovely Fais fell,
> From her, as ancient Irish records tell,
> Obtained the name of Blean Fais.

Scota, the relict of king Milesius, was likewise slain in this engagement, and was buried in another valley on the north side of the mountain Sliabh Mis, adjoining to the sea. This valley, which was the place of her interment, was called Glean Scoithin, or the valley of Scota, as an old poet testifies in these verses :

> Beneath a vale its bosom does display,
> With meadows green, with flowers profusely gay ;
> Where Scota lies, unfortunately slain,
> And with her royal tomb gives honor to the plain
> Mix'd with the first, the fair virago fought,
> Sustain'd the toils of arms, and danger sought ;
> From her the fruitful valley had the name
> Of Glean Scoith, and we may trust to fame.

This was the first battle that was fought between the Milesians and the Tuatha de Danans for the empire of the island, as we are informed by the same author in this manner :

> The stout Gadelians first their courage try
> At Sliabh Mis, and rout the enemy ;
> Where heroes, pierced with many a deadly wound,
> Choak'd in their blood, lay gasping on the ground ;
> Heroes, whose brave exploits may justly claim
> Triumphant laurels, and immortal fame.

The persons of note that fell on the side of the Milesians, in this action, were the princess Scota, and the lady Fais ; they likewise lost two of their principal druids, whose names were Uar and Eithir : but there were no more than 300 of the Gadelian soldiers missing after the fight, notwithstanding they defeated the Tuatha de Danans, and slew 1000 of them. Eire, the wife of Mac Greine, one of the princes of the country, with as many of her flying troops as she could keep together, retired to Tailton and there related the misfortunes she had met with, and how she was routed by the enemy, and the choicest of her men were slain. The Milesians continued upon the field of battle, burying their dead, and celebrating the funeral rites of the two druids with great solemnity. An old poet makes honourable mention of this battle, and confirms some of the particulars in these verses.

On Sliabh Mis our warlike squadrons stood,
Eager of fight, and prodigal of blood ;
Victorious arms our stout Gadelians bore,
Ruin behind, and terror march'd before :
A thousand of the enchanted host are slain,
They try their charms and magic arts in vain,
For with their mangled limbs they cover all the plain.
Three hundred only of our troops are kill'd,
Who bravely turned the fortune of the field.
The learned Uar rush'd among the rest,
But, with repeated blows and wounds oppress'd,
He fell, and by his side expiring lay
Either, a priest, and gasp'd his soul away.
The victors then the funeral rites prepare,
Due to their dead companions of the war.

It was observed before, that eight of the commanding officers of the Milesians were unfortunately destroyed at sea, by the enchantments of the Tuatha de Danans : Ir was lost at Sceilg Mihchil ; Arranan was dashed to pieces by a fall from the topsail ; Donn, with five of the principal Gadelians, was drowned at a place called Teach Duinn, in the west of Ireland. Eight ladies likewise of the first quality perished at sea ; two lost their lives when Donn was shipwrecked ; their names were Buan, the wife of Bille, and Dil, the daughter of Milesius, the wife and sister of Donn. Sceine, the wife of Amergin, was unfortunately cast away at Inbher Sceine. From the misfortune of this lady the river was called Inbher Sceine, or the river of Sceine, for Inbher signifies a river ; and it is known by the same name in the county of Kerry, to this day.

Fial, the wife of Lughaidh, was a lady of strict virtue and uncommon modesty ; for she was so confounded with shame, because her husband had seen her naked as she was swimming in the river Feil, that she languished, and died with grief. The stream received the name of Inbher Feile from this fair Milesian, and is so called to this time. Scota and Fias, two other ladies of the Gadelians were slain in the battle of Sliabh Mis before mentioned.

The wife of Ir, and the wife of Muirtheimhne, the son of Breogan, likewise died before the battle of Tailton was fought ; these made up the eight ladies of the Milesians who were dead before that engagement. The names of seven of them are recorded in the book of the Conquests of Ireland, and are Scota, Tea, Fial, Fias, Liobhra, Oghbha, and Sceine. The same number of principal officers of the Gadelians perished before that action with the Tuatha de Danans, whose names are expressed before. An old antiquary, in one of his poems, has given us the names of even of these female adventurers, who came into Ireland.

> Seven ladies of the chiefest quality
> Followed the fortunes of the stout Gadelians,
> When they resolved to conquer or to die.
> Tea, the virtuous queen of Heremon;
> Fial, the consort of the brave Lughaidh;
> Fias, a princess of distinguished beauty was,
> And the beloved wife of Un; and Sceine
> Was wedded to Amergin's princely bed;
> Liobhradh was the royal pride of Fuaid;
> Scota, the relict of the great Milesius:
> And Oghbha strictly chaste in widowhood.

The Gadelians, who were under the command of Heber, and came off with victory at the battle of Sliabh Mis, when they had buried their dead, and recovered themselves from the fatigue of the fight, they marched to Inbher Colpa, now cal'ed Drocheda, in the province of Leinster, where they joined a strong body of Milesians, with Heremon at the head of them: with this reinforcement they sent a summons to the three princes of the island, the sons of Cearmada, to come to a pitched battle at a place appointed, in order to decide the government of the country. The Tuatha de Danans accepted of the challenge, and advanced with their choicest troops, led on by their three princes, and began the fight; the Milesians received the charge with great bravery, and, greedy of revenge for the death of Ith, fell desperately upon the enemy, when a most bloody action followed. Both sides maintained their ground, and victory was in suspense for some time; but at length the Gadelians broke the ranks of the Tuatha de Danans, and occasioned such confusion among their forces, that they were put to the rout with great slaughter, and driven out of the field. The three princes of the country were slain in the engagement; Mac Greine fell in an encounter with Amergin; Mac Ceacht was killed by Heremon, and Mac Cuill was slain by Heber Fionn. This memorable transaction comes to the notice of posterity from the following verses of an old poet:

> The princes of the island kept their court
> At Tailton; but the bold Gadelians

> Punished their treachery to the valiant Ith :
> Mac Greine, though fierce in fight, Amergin slew,
> Mac Cuill fell beneath the dreadful sword
> Of Heber ; and Heremon, hand to hand,
> O'erbore Mac Ceacht, and pierced him to the ground.

In this action were slain likewise the consorts of these three princes, who were Eire, Fodhla, and Banba. The same poet gives this account of their death :

> This fatal day the virtuous Eire was slain
> By Siurge ; Fodhla by the sword of Headan
> Fell dead ; and Banba sunk beneath
> The avenging arm of Saicer.

The Tuatha de Danans, perceiving the death of their three commanders, despaired of victory, and fled in great disorder. The Milesians followed their success with great slaughter of the enemy, but in the pursuit they lost two of their leading officers, Cualgne, the son of Breogan, at Sliabh Cualgne, and Fuaid his brother at Sliabh Fuaid : but the Gadelians, no way discouraged, pressed hard upon the vanquished, destroyed numbers of them in their flight, and put them to a general rout. The inhabitants were never able to recruit their forces, but were obliged to submit to the victors, and deliver up the government of the island.

Some of the Irish antiquaries are of opinion, that after the Milesians had obtained this victory, Heber Fionn and Heremon divided the country into two parts between them ; the northern part, from the river Boyne and Sruibh, fell to the share of Heremon, and from thence to the main ocean southwards, came to the possession of Heber Fionn. A poet of great antiquity makes mention of this division in this manner :

> The two commanders shared the isle between them ;
> The north division Heremon enjoyed
> From the rich vale, where, in delightful streams,
> The Boyne, the darling of the ocean, flows ;
> Southwards from thence the royal Heber reigned,
> And his dominion to the sea extended.

Five of the Milesian officers attended upon Heremon to his part of the country, and had lands assigned them for their support, where each of them erected a castle upon their own estate, and there they resided with their families. The names of those five commanders were Amergin, the son of Milesius

Goisdean, Seaghda, Sobhairce and Siurge. Heremon also built a magnificent palace, where he kept his court, at Airgiodross, upon the bank of the river Feoir, in Ossery, and called it Rath Beothach ; Amergin raised the castle of Turlagh Inbher More, now called Arcloe; Sobhairce built the fort of Dunn Sobhairce ; Seaghda erected Dunn Deilguisis in the territory of Cualann ; Goisdean built Cahair Nare, and Siurge called his seat by the name of Dunn Eadair.

Some of the principal of the Milesians likewise followed Heber Fionn into his division of the country, who generously allowed them an honourable subsistence, and gave them lands for the support of their families ; their names were Caicer. Mantann, Eadan, Vige, and Fulman. Each of these Gadelian. nobles raised very stately structures upon their own estates ; Heber Fionn built a royal palace for himself in Leinster, and called it Rath Loamhuin ; Caicer erected the Castle of Dunn Inn, in the west of Ireland ; Mantann was the founder of Cumh dach Cairge Bladhruidhe ; Unn the son of Vige built Rath Arda Suird, and Fulman built the fort of Cairge Feadha.

But this division of the island is opposed by some of our antiquaries of great authority, who assert, that Heber possessed himself of the two provinces of Munster ; the province of Leinster and Conacht fell to the share of Heremon ; the province of Ulster they divided between Eimhir or Heber, the son of Ir the son of Milesius, their brother's son, and some others of the principal Gadelians ; and the canthred of Corckaluighe, in the county of Cork, in Munster, they assigned to Lughaida, the son of Ith, who was treacherously slain by the princes of the country, in revenge of whose death the Milesians first engaged in this expedition.

This latter division of the island seems to deserve the greatest credit ; because it is certain, that the royal palace of Heremon, called Rath Beothaic, was built at Airgiodross, upon the bank of the river Feoir, in Leinster ; and it appears likewise, that the posterity of Heber Fionn resided for many years in the province of Munster. The descendants of Heremon inhabited in Conacht and Leinster ; and the family of Eimhir or Heber, the son of Milesius, commonly called Clana Rughraidhe, remained for many generations in the province of Ulster, and are the original and the most ancient inhabitants of Ulster of all the posterity of the Milesians. They were a tribe who kept their royal seat at Eamhain, for the space of 900 years, and for their valour, their generosity and military exploits, they were the glory of the Irish nation ; as the most authentic records, particularly the Psalter of Cashel and the royal Psalter of Tara, inform us. They flourished in great honour, and were the renowned heroes of the western parts of Europe for many ages, till, sinking under the weight of their own greatness, they were destroyed by intestine quarrels and irreconcileable breaches in their families, as will be related hereafter ; by which means the royal seat of Eamhaim fell to ruin, and the tribe separated and fixed themselves in other provinces of the island. The descendants of the brave hero Connall Cearnach removed to Laoighis, (in English, Lex) in the province of Leinster, and the posterity of Bergus Mac Roigh obtained settlements in Conmacne, Conacht, Careamruadh, and Kerry, in Munster : these families were originally derived from the same ancestors, and were called, in general, by the name of Clana Rughraidhe. The same changes and divisions happened likewise in other tribes of the Milesians, who, by reason of animosities among themselves, separated from the possessions that were first assigned them ; particularly in the family of the O Dwyers, or as some write them, O Divir, in Irish called O Duibhidhir, descended from Cairtre, the son of Conchorb, who lived four generations before Cathoir More, monarch of Ireland, of the line of Heremon. The same alterations appear likewise in the tribe of the O Ryans, who were of the same family, and removed from the province of Leinster to Munster, where their posterity remain to this day ; but the revolutions that arose in these families, and their removal from the lands where they first settled, happened many years after Heber and Heremon divided the island as before mentioned.

It is evident, that the three Collas, with all their relations and dependants, went into Ulster about the year of our Redemption 130 ; where, by their valour, they dispossessed the former inhabitants, and fixed themselves. The lands which they obtained in this province, were called Modhoirn ui Macuais, and Ui Chriomhuin, where some of their posterity remain to this time. It was in the reign of Muireadhach Tireach that they got into the enjoyment of these new estates. The noble earl of Antrim, Mac Daniel by surname, is descended from Collauais ; and the most illustrious family of the Mac Mahons, in the province of Ulster, the Maguires, in Irish, Maguidhir, and the O Hanlauns, with several other branches derived from the same stem, were the lineal descendants of Colla da Chrioch, as will be confirmed particularly in the progress of this history

In the reign of Cormack Mac Airt, a descendant from the posterity of Heremon, called Deisig, (in English, Desie,) the O Faolains, the kings of Desie, came into Munster, and got possession of a great part of the country. And in the reign of Oilioll Ollum, king of Munster, the learned Cairbre Musc, a gentleman of the line of Heremon, presented a most ingenious poem, in Irish, to Oil.oll Ollum, wherein he celebrated the valour, the generosity, the magnificence and grandeur of his royal patron; who so graciously accepted the performance, that as a reward, he bestowed upon him the two Urmhumhain, in English, the two Ormonds, but known then by the name of Muscruidhe, so called from Cairbre Musc before mentioned. These counties contained all the canthred from Bealach mor, in Ossery, to Carrignasuire, now styled Carrig. These were the lands conferred upon that excellent poet, and not the Muscruidhe, in the county of Cork; but they continued only a short time in the possession of his issue, for his family was soon extinct.

It was not long after this, that some of the posterity of Heber Fionn, descended from Cormac Gaileangadh, removed out of Munster, and settled themselves, and their families, in very large estates in Conacht and Leinster. The lands which they obtained were called Gaileangadh and Luigne; and from the descendants of this Cormac Gaileangadh, the noble families of O Hara, (in Irish O Headhra,) and of O Gara (in Irish O Gara) are derived. So that it appears by what means these several families got possession of large tracts of land in the island; and that they did not receive their estates from the donation of Heber and Heremon, when they laid out the division of the country. And this account is reason sufficient for us to believe, that Heber and Heremon did not, after their conquest of Ireland, attempt to share the country between them in the manner we have observed before; because we find that Heremon built his palace within the territories of Heber Fionn, (called Rath Beothach, and situated at Airgiodross, in the province of Leinster,) which it is impossible to suppose: but the last division has the best authority to support it, which asserts, that Heremon was possessed of the province of Leinster, where he erected his royal seat and kept his court.

The Milesians brought over with them, in the Irish expedition, a very skilful musician and an eminent poet; the name of the poet was Cir mac Cis, and the musician was called O Naoi. These two persons being very excellent in their profession, there was some contest between Heber and Heremon

K

about them ; for they were both delighted with their company, and resolved, if possible, to detain them ; but they agreed, at length, to decide the dispute by lots, and determine to whom they should belong ; by this means the musician fell to Heber, and the poet was to attend upon Heremon.   From this contro-versy, as the chronicles inform us, arose that laudable custom among the Irish, to show great honour and munificence to their poets, historians, philosophers, and men of learning ; and the musician being to attend upon Heber in the southern part of the country, that division of the island is observed to be more particularly delighted with music ; as an old poet remarks in this manner :

> The learned princes, Heber and Heremon,
> Contended which should, with the poet's art,
> And the musician's skill, be entertained.
> They cast the lots; the northern prince enjoyed
> The pleasing charms of poetry ; and Heber
> With music first his southern subjects bless'd.
> From hence the generous Irish, with rewards,
> Did bountifully crown the poet's skill,
> And music flourished in the southern coasts.

In the Milesian invasion of Ireland there came over twenty mechanical persons of several occupations, and a number of labouring men, fit only for servile work, whose business was to clear the country by cutting down the woods, and to render it proper for tillage or pasture ; accordingly these four-and-twenty labourers, soon after their arrival in the island, laid open twenty-four large tracts of land, which by cultivating became fruitful. The names of these tradesmen were Aidhne, Ai, Asal, Meidhe, Morba, Meide, Cuibh, Cliu, Ceara, Reir, Slan, Leighe, Liffe, Line, Leighean, Trea, Dula, Adhar, Aire, Deisi, Deala, Fea, Femhean, and Seara ; and the plains that were cleared at that time are literally known by these names to this day.

The princess Tea, the daughter of Lughaidh, the son of Ith, and the wife of Heremon, the son of Milesius, gave orders for erecting a royal palace for herself in Lyatrim, which seat is now called Teamhair, from this lady, who was the foundress of it ; for Mur signifies a seat or a palace, and Tea being the proper name of that princess, by joining the words they sound Tea-mhuir, and by another termination in Irish they are pronounced Teamhair ; but in construction they are the same, for they both signify the royal seat or palace at Tara.

The two principal Gadelians, Heber and Heremon, adminis-

tered the government together, with great affection and unanimity, for the space of a year, and then an unfortunate difference
arose, attended with very fatal consequences. The occasion of
the dispute was the possession of three of the most fruitful valleys in the whole island ; their names were Druim Clasach, in
the territory of Maine, Druim Beathach, in Maonmuighe, and
Druim Finginn, in Munster. Two of these valleys lay in the
division of Heber Fionn, and he received the profits of them ;
t. his wife, being a woman of great pride and ambition, envied the wife of Heremon the enjoyment of one of these delightful valleys, and therefore she persuaded her husband to demand
the valley of Heremon, and upon a refusal, to get possession of
it by the sword ; for she passionately vowed she would never
be satisfied till she was called the queen of the three most fruitful valleys in the island. The wife of Heremon, a lady of masculine spirit, prevailed upon her husband to insist upon his
title, and to defend his right : and this resolution occasioned a
war between the two princes, who, by consent, led their whole
forces to the plains of Geisiol, in Leinster, where a desperate
battle was fought, in which the eldest brother, Heber Fionn,
and three of his chief commanding officers, Siurge, Sobhairce, and
Goisdean were slain. The death of these brave Gadelians, we
perceive, was wholly owing to the pride of this woman, who, to
quicken her husband in this unjust undertaking, swore she
would not sleep a night more in the island till she had accomplished her purpose. This transaction stands thus upon record
in the verses of an old poet :

> The royal princes, Heber and Heremon,
> With mutual consent, and kind affection,
> The isle divided ; and they reigned in peace,
> Till the ambition of a woman's heart,
> The wife of Heber, urged them on to war
> By pride o'ercome, she thirsted to enjoy,
> And to be called queen of the Three Vales,
> The most delightful lands in all the isle.
> She vowed, and, raging passionately, swore,
> That she would never sleep on Irish ground
> Till she was mistress of those fruitful plains.
> A battle followed on Geisiol's fatal field,
> Where Heber Fionn fell a sacrifice
> To the ambition of a haughty wife.

This relation is confirmed by the concurring testimony of the
learned Tanuidhe ó Conaire, who has these lines

> Three of the fruitful valleys of the isle,
> Druim Finginn, Druim Clasach, and Druim Beathach,
> Occasioned the fierce battle of Geisiol,
> Where valiant Heber fell.

Heremon, after this victory over his brother, the unfortunate
Heber, succeeded in the whole government, and reigned sole
monarch of the kingdom of Ireland for the space of fourteen
years. There is some difference in the ancient records, concerning the death of Prince Heber ; for some of our antiquaries
assert, that he was slain at the battle of Airgiod Ross, as these
verses intimate :

> Heremon was monarch of the isle
> Full fourteen years after the bloody fight
> Of Airgiod Ross, where Heber lost his life.

But this opinion is contradicted by some authors of great
fidelity, who with good authority deny that Heber was slain at
the battle of Airgiod Ross, and justly place his death at the
fight of Geisiol before mentioned. In the reign of King Heremon the desperate battle of Cuil Caicer was fought, where Caicer,
one of the principal officers of Heber Fionn, was slain by
Amergin, the son of Milesius. This action happened about a
year after the death of Heber ; and in the year following the
fight of Caicer, Amergin, the son of Milesius, was killed by his
brother Heremon, in the battle of Bile Teiuiodh, at Cuil Breagh.
In the same year the nine rivers of Eile broke out, and the
three streams of Va Niolliolo, in Ireland, began to flow. In
the third year following, Mantan and Fulman, two of the principal officers of Heber Fionn, were slain by Heremon, in the
battle of Breaghuin, in Freamhain.
During the monarchy of Heremon over the whole island, the
nine following lakes discovered themselves ; Loch Cime, on
Magh Sreing, Loch Buadhaice, Loch Bagha, Loch Rein, Loch
Fionnmhaighe, Loch Greine, Loch Riach, which spreads its
waters over all the plain of Magh Maoin, Loch da Choidh, in
Leinster, and Loch Laoigh, in Ulster. Four years afterwards the
Gadelian commanders, En, Un, and Eadan, were slain by Heremon, in the fight of Comhraire, in Meath, where they were
likewise buried. In the same year three rivers broke out in
Conacht, which were all known by the name of Succa.
Some of the Irish historians assert, that after Heremon had
obtained the victory over Heber Fionn, he divided the island into
five provinces, among some of his commanding officers. The

province of Leinster he gave to Criomhthan Sciathbheil of the Domhnonchuibh, a gentleman of great worth, and descended from the ancient Firbolgs. He bestowed the two provinces of Munster upon Er, Orbha, Fearon, and Feargna, who were the sons of Heber Fionn, his brother. The province of Conacht he conferred upon Un, the son of Vige, and Eadane, two noted generals, who came along with him out of Spain ; and the province of Ulster he settled upon his other brother's son, whose name was Heber or Eimher, the son of Ir, the son of Milesius, king of Spain.

In the beginning of the reign of this Irish monarch, the Picts, who resided in Thrace, left their own country, and landed with a numerous army upon the coasts of Ireland. The reason why they quitted their country is thus related by Cormac Mac Cuillenan, in his Psalter of Cashel. Policornus was king of Thrace at that time, and, being an effeminate prince, he resolved to seize by violence upon a beautiful young lady, the daughter of Gud, generalissimo over the Picts, and to keep her as a concubine. This design was seasonably discovered to Gud, who, by the assistance of his faithful Picts, who were then in pay under the crown of Thrace, found means to destroy Policornus, whom they slew, and then fled the country. They marched through the dominions of several princes, till they came into France, where they were kindly received, and admitted into pay by the French king, who assigned them a tract of land for their support, where they built a city, and properly gave it the name of Pictaviam, now called Poictiers. When Gud, the commander of the Picts, had related to the king of France the occasion of his leaving Thrace, and that his design was to secure the honour of nis daughter, that prince also resolved to debauch her himself, and made some attempts to force her out of her father's hands ; who, so soon as he perceived his intention, summoned his people together, and by stratagem seized upon the French shipping, weighed anchor and stood out to sea ; they came upon the coasts of Ireland, and landed at Inbher Slaigne, but the young lady unfortunately sickened and died in the voyage.

The venerable Bede, in the first chapter of his Ecclesiastical history of England, agrees with this account, with this difference only, that he says that these wandering Picts landed in the northern part of the island. His words are these : * " It happened,

---

* Contigit gentem Pictorum de Scythia, ut perhibent, longis navibus non multis oceanum ingressam, circumagente flatu ventorum fines omnes Britanniæ Hiberniam pervenisse, ejusque septentrionales oras intrasse, atque inventa ibi gente Scotorum, sibi quoque in partibus illis petiisse locum, nec impetrasse potuisse.

as fame goes, that a nation of the Picts from Scythia, setting to sea in a few long ships, after they had by the varying of the wind sailed round the coast of Britain, came at last into Ireland, and landed in the northern part of 'the island : there they found the nation of the Scots, among whom they desired a settlement, but their request was denied." But one circumstance of this relation is a mistake, for they did not land in the north of Ireland, but they came on shore in the harbour of Wexford, as it is now called.

At that time Criomhthan Sciathbheil was governor of Leinster by commission from Heremon, who, as soon as these people arrived, received them hospitably, and entered into a strict alliance with Gud, and Cathluan, his son, who were the commanders of the Picts; because he wanted their assistance against some mischievous Britons (called Tuatha Fiodhga) who spoiled and made great depredations on both sides the river Slainge ; and to terrify the Milesian soldiery, they violated the law of nations, by poisoning the heads of their arrows and their other weapons, which had that effect as to make the least wound mortal or incurable. Criomhthan relating this savage practice of the Britons to his new associates, they told him there was a very eminent druid, who came over with them, that, by his skill in physic, knew how to prepare an antidote against the poison, and hinder its operation. The name of this druid was Trosdane, who, when he was applied to by the Milesian general, confessed that he understood a method which would destroy the barbarous designs of the Britons, and expel the venomous quality of their weapons ; accordingly he advised him to procure 150 white-faced cows, and when he had digged a pit near the place where he usually fought with the Britons, to empty their milk into the hole, and when any of his soldiers were wounded by the enemy, they should immediately go into the pit, and bathe themselves in the milk, which would prove a sovereign antidote against the poison and hinder its effect. Criomhthan followed the advice of the druid, and when he had made the pit near the field of battle, and filled it with milk, according to his directions, he drew up his forces against the Britons, and a most desperate fight followed, (called the battle of Cath Arda Leamhnachta,) and the Milesians obtained a complete victory : for when any of the Gadelian soldiery perceived themselves wounded, they immediately removed to this bath of milk, where they washed, and became perfectly cured. This defeat of the

Britons, who were called Tuatha Fiodhga, is transmitted to posterity, by a very ancient poet of good authority, in these lines:

> The wandering Picts, after a tedious voyage
> Around the British coasts, at length arrive
> Upon the Irish shore; where the Gadelians
> Were fighting with the Britons fierce and cruel.
> Who, with envenom'd arrows, certain death
> Dispensed; and many a brave Milesian
> Languished with wounds incurable, till relieved
> By a prevailing antidote, prescribed
> By the wise Trosdane, of the Pictish race.
> This learned druid, exquisitely skill'd
> In poison, did expel the subtle venom
> By a warm bath of milk, which from the dugs
> Of an hundred and fifty bald-faced cows distilled
> The soldiers here soften'd their rankling wounds,
> And washed, and to the fight returned unhurt.
> nus were the Britons routed in the field,
> And all their barbarous art defeated

After this victory over the Britons, Gud, and his son Catn iuan, who were the leaders of the Picts, formed a conspiracy, and resolved to possess themselves of the government of Lein ster, and there to settle with their followers. This design was timely discovered to Heremon, the king of Ireland, who immediately raised an army to suppress these foreigners, and drive them out of the country. But before they came to engage, the Picts, unable to resist the Milesian troops, with great humility and submission surrendered themselves up to the mercy of the king, who with great generosity pardoned them, and withdrew his forces, but gave them notice withal, that there was a country lying east and by north of Ireland, where they might transport themselves and obtain a settlement. The Picts immediately came to a resolution to leave the island; but first desired some of the Milesian women to go along with them, upon whose issue, they solemnly swore that the government of the country, if ever it came into their hands, should devolve, and continue for ever in their family. Upon these assurances Heremon complied, and delivered to them three women of quality, who were widows; they were the relicts of Breas, Buas, and Buaigne, one of whom Cathluan, the chief commander of the Picts, took to himself. They immediately set sail, and arrived at Cruithantuath, now called Scotland, where Cathluan, the Pictish general, obtained the sovereignty of the country, and was the first monarch of the Pictish line; and of this family, after the demise of this prince, there were 70 successive kings in Scotland; as is observed in the following verses, extracted from the Psalter of Cashel, out of·a poem that begins thus, Eolach Alban vile :

> The Picts, unable to withstand the pow'r
> Of the Milesian troops, a truce implore;
> And, willing to be gone, their anchors weigh'd
> And boldly the Albanian coasts invade,
> Where seventy monarchs of the Pictish race
> With great exploits the Scottish annals grace.
> 'Twas Cathluan began the royal line
> Which ended in the hero Constantine.

The learned Trosdane, who by his art assisted·the Gadelians in subduing the Britains, and five more of principal note among the Picts, did not follow the fortune of Cathluau in the Scottish expedition; their names were Oilean, Ulpra, Neachtain, Nar, and Eneas, and these six that remained in Ireland had estates assigned them for their support, in Breagmhuigh, in Meath.

Heremon, the king of Ireland, after a reign of fourteen years died at Airgiod Ross, in Rath Beothaice, near Feior, and there he was buried; and in the same year the river called Eithne broke out, and began to flow, between Dial na Ruidhe and Dial riada.

The chronicles of Ireland give an account, that Heremon sent away a great number of the posterity of Breogan, that is, the Brigantes, and of the Tuatha de Danans, along with the Picts, in their invasion of Scotland; and from these descendants of Breogan were the Brigantes derived, who afterwards possessed themselves of very large settlements in England. Such of this family (called in Irish Clana Breogan) as survived the battle of Tailtean, separated, and some of them followed Heber Fionn into Munster. others attended upon Heremon into Conacht and Leinster, and part of them went into Ulster with Heber, the son of Ir. These Brigantes, some time afterwards, understanding that the Picts, and their relations that followed them, had been successful in the Scottish invasion, and had wrested the government out of the hands of the former inhabitants, a number of them, animated with this success, resolved to transport themselves thither, and obtain a settlement in the country; thither therefore they came, and had lands and estates bestowed upon them for their maintenance. But in process of time, they with the Picts were driven out of the country, by the prevailing power of the Dalriada, and afterwards by Fergus the Great; as will be particularly mentioned in the further progress of this history.

Some of the Irish chronicles assert, that the posterity of Breogan, afterwards called the Brigantes, came into Ireland, Albion, and Britain, as they fled out of Spain, to avoid the cruel tyranny of the Goths, and the incursions of other hostile nations, who miserably ravaged that country after the sons of Milesius had left it; so that we have reason to conjecture, that the Brigantes of England removed thither from Ireland, Albion, and Spain, when they fixed themselves in some of the counties of that kingdom.

A.M. 2752.
Upon the decease of Heremon, king of Ireland, the crown devolved upon his three sons, Muimhne, Luighne, and Laighne; these princes reigned jointly and peaceably for the space of three years, at which time Muimhne died at Magh Cruachain, and the remaining brothers, Luighne and Laighne, were slain by the sons of Heber Fionn, at the battle of Ard Ladhran.

2755.
The succession then came into the hands of Er, Orbha, Fearon, and Feargna, the four sons of Heber Fionn, who governed the kingdom together for one year, and were slain in an engagement by Irial, the son of Heremon.

2756.
They were succeeded by Irial, the son of Heremon, who was a learned prince, and could foretell things to come: the reason of his entering into war with the sons of Heber Fionn was, because they had basely taken away the lives of two of his elder brothers, who died without issue, so that the crown came by succession to him, and he governed the kingdom ten years. During the reign of this monarch, a great part of this country was laid open, and freed from woods; particularly the following places were cleared, and made fit for tillage and pasture: their names were Magh Reidchiodh, now called Lex Magh Neilm, in Leinster; Magh Comair, Magh Feile, in Jobh Neill; Magh Sanuis, in Conacht; Magh Ninis, in Ulster; Magh Midhe, Magh Luigne, in Conacht; Magh Teachta, in Jobh mac Uais; Magh Fearnmuighne, at Oirgialladh; Magh Cobha, at Jobh Beathach; Magh Cumaoi, at Jobh Neil; Magh Cuille Feadha, Magh Riada, Magh Nairbhrioch, at Fotharthuathaibh Airbhrioch, in Leinster. This prince adorned his country with seven royal palaces, where he kept his court: they were called Rath Ciombaoith, at Nemhuin, Rath Coincheada, at Seimhne; Rath Mothuig, at Deag Carbad; Rath Buirioch, at Sleachtaibh; Rath Luachat, at Glas Carn; Rath Croicne, at Maghnis; and Rath Boachoill, at Latharna.

The year after these seats were erected, the three rivers, called the three Finns, in Ulster, broke out and began to flow. The following year this prince won four remarkable victories over

his enemies: the first was at the battle of Ard Inmath, at
Teabtha, where Stirne, the son of Duibh, son of Fomhoir, was
slain; the second was at the battle of Teanmhuighe, which he
fought against a sort of pirates, called Fomhoraioc, and slew
Eichtghe, the leader of them; the third was at the battle of
Loch Muighe, where Lugrot, the son of Moghfeibhis, was slain;
and the fourth was at the battle of Cuill Martho, where he
overcame the four sons of Heber. The second year after this
victory Irial died, at a place called Magh Muagh, where he was
buried. These battles are recorded by an old poet in these
verses :

> Irial, the youngest of the royal line,
> Was king of Sliabh Mis, and king of Macha :
> Success attended him whene'er he fought,
> And in four battles he was crowned with victory.

A.M. 2766.
Eithrial, the son of Irial, son of Heremon succeeded
in the government, and reigned twenty years as monarch
of the whole kingdom. This prince was distinguished
for his excellent learning, for he wrote with his own hand the
history and travels of the Gadelians; nor was he less remarkable for his valour and military accomplishments. In his reign
seven plains or woods, that covered a great tract of land, were
cut down: they were called Tean mhagh, in Conacht; Magh
Liogat, Magh Bealaig, at Jobh Turatire; Magh Geisile, at Jobh
Failge; Magh Ochtair, in Leinster; Loch mhagh, in Conacht;
and Magh Rath, at Jobh Eachach. After this long reign of
twenty years this prince was killed by Conmaol, the son of
Heber Fionn, at the battle of Soirrean, in Leinster.

2786.
Conmaol, the son of Heber Fionn, by this victory
obtained the crown, and governed the kingdom of Ireland thirty years, and was the first absolute monarch of the
Heberian line. He was continually engaged in wars with the
family of Heremon, and fought twenty-five pitched battles
against them, and came off with victory in all. The names of
nine of them were as follow: the battle of Ucha, the battle of
Conucha, the battle of Sliabh Beatha, the battle of Geisille,
where Palpa, the son of Heremon, was slain; the battle of Mud-
huirn, where Samhro, the son of Jonbhotha, was killed; the
battle of Lochlein, where Magrot was slain; the battle of Beirre,
the battle of Aonach Macha, where Conmaol, a valiant prince,
lost his life, by the hands of Heber, the son of Tighermhas, of
the line of Heremon. After the battle he was buried upon the

south side of Aonach Macha, in a place called Feart Chonmaoil, which signifies the grave of Conmaol; for the Irish word Feart in the English signifies a grave.

A.M. 2816.
Tighermhas, the son of Follain, son of Eithriall, son of the learned Irial the prophet, the son of Heremon, succeeded and reigned fifty years. He was continually alarmed with the pretensions of the family of Heber Fionn, but engaged them in twenty-seven battles, and had always the victory. The names of these several actions stand thus upon record : the battle of Eille, where Rochorb, the son of Gullain, was slain ; the battle of Comair, the battle of Maighe Teacht, the battle of Loch Moighe, where Deighiarno, son of Goill, son of Gullain, was killed ; the battle of Cuillard, at Moighinis; the battle of Cuill Fraochain, the battle of Atguirt, in Seimhne the battle of Ard Niadh, in Conacht ; the battle of Carn Fearradhoig, where Fearradhoch, son of Rochuirb, son of Gullaii was slain ; the battle of Cluain Cuis, in Teabtha ; the battle or Comhnuidhe, at Tuath Eibhe ; the battle of Cluain Muireag, in the north of Breifne ; the battle of Cuill Faibhair, at Earbus ; the seven battles of Luglocht, by Loch Lughach ; the two battles of Cuill, at Airgiod Ross ; and the battle of Reibh, where most of the posterity of Heber Fionn were destroyed by the forces of Tighermhas.

The following year nine streams broke out of the earth, and began to flow : their names were Loch Cea, which covered the plain of Magh Falchuir ; Loch Nualline, in Conacht ; Loch Niarun, Loch Nuair, Loch Saiglean, Loch Gabhair, in Meatl and Breagmhaigh; Loch Feabhuil, at Tir Eogain, which drowned the whole tract of land called Feabhuil Mac Loduin and Magh Fuinsighe, by which names the country it overflowed was called ; Dubh Loch at Ard Cianachta ; and Loch Dabhuil, in Oirgialladh. About this time the three black rivers in Ireland discovered themselves, Fubno, Torruin, and Calluin.

The first golden mine in this country was found out in the reign of this prince. It was discovered near the Liffee, by a person called Juchadhan, who had the management of the ore, and was very curious in the working of metals. In his time, likewise, the colours of blue and green were invented, and the people began to be more polite in their habits, and set off their dress with various ornaments. This prince established a law through his whole dominions, that the quality of every person should be known by his garb ; and for a distinction he enacted, that the clothes of a slave should be of one colour ; the habit of a soldier he allowed to be of two colours ; he permitted three colours to be the dress of a commanding officer ; the apparel of gentlemen, who kept hospitable tables for the entertainment of strangers, was to consist of four colours ; five colours were allowed to **the** nobility of the country ; the king and queen and the royal family were confined to six colours, and the chronologers and persons of eminent learning were indulged the same number.

This prince died at Magh Sleachta, and three parts of his subjects, by the judgment of heaven, perished with him the same night ; it was upon the eve of the festival of All Saints, and he was struck as he was worshipping his idol Crom cruadh, the same God that Zoroaster adored in Greece. The Irish antiquaries agree, that Tighermhas was the first that introduced idolatry, and erected Pagan alters in the island, and began to establish his religion about 100 years after the Milesians arrived in the country. From the adoration paid to this idol, and the kneeling posture of those who worshipped it, the field in Breifne, now in the country of Lahain, was called Magh Sleachta. After the decease of this prince, some of our authors are of opinion that there was an interregnum, and the country was without a king for the space of seven years, and then they placed upon the throne of Ireland, Eochaidh Faobharglas, the son of Conmaol ; but this is a mistake, and is contradicted by the regal table of the Irish monarchs, which particularly mentions that the successor of Tighermhas was Eochaidh Eadgothach, a descendant of Lughaidh, the son of Ith ; and this account has authority sufficient for us to follow.

A.M. 2866. Eochaidh Eadgothach, son of Datre, son of Conghal, son of Eadambuin, son of Mail, son of Lughaidh, son of Ith, son of Breogan, succeeded Tighermhas in the throne of Ireland. His reign continued four years, and then he was slain by Cearmna, of the line of Ir, son of Milesius.

2870. Cearmna and Sobhairce, two brothers of the sons of Eibhric, son of Eibher, son of Heber, son of Ir, son of Milesius, succeeded, and reigned joint monarchs of Ireland forty years. These were the first Irish princes that came out of Ulster, and were of the line of Ir. They agreed to divide the kingdom between them ; and the boundary between each division extended from Inbher Colpa, now called Drocheda, to Limerick, in Munster. The north part of the country was possessed by Sobhairce, who erected a magnificent palace in his own share, and called it Dunn Sobhairce. His brother, Cearmna.

was prince of the southern division, in which Le likewise built a royal seat, where he kept his court, and gave it the name of Dunn Cearmna; it is now called Dunn Patrick, and is situated in Courcie's country. Sobhairce was killed by Eochaidh Mean, and Cearmna was slain in the battle of Dunn Cearmna, by Eochaidh Faobharglas, a prince of the family of Heber Fionn.

A.M. 2910. Eochaidh Faobharglas, son of Conmaol, son of Heber Fionn, son of Milesius, obtained the crown, and sat upon the Irish throne 20 years. He was distinguished by the name of Eochaidh Faobharglas, because the two javelins he used in the wars were green and sharp-edged, and he wore a sword of the same colour; for the word Glas signifies green, and Faobhar signifies sharp-edged, and these two epithets being joined sound Faobharglas. This prince was the first of the Milesian kings that, by his arms, reduced a part of Albain, or Scotland, to become tributary to the crown of Ireland; for the Picts, who settled themselves in that country, notwithstanding they bound themselves with solemn oaths to pay homage to the king of Ireland, broke out into frequent rebellions, since the time of Heremon, and gave great disturbance to the Irish government. This prince was annoyed by the posterity of Heremon, against whom he fought the following battles, and came off with success: the battle of Luachair Deaghadh, in Desmond the battle of Fosuighe da Ghort, the battle at the meeting o. the three streams, the battle of Tuam Dreogan, at Breifne, and the battle of Drom Liathain. He laid open the country by cutting down seven great woods, which were known by the names of Magh Smearthuin, in I've Failge; Magh Laoighin, Magh Luirg, in Conacht: Magh Leamhna, Magh Manair, Magh Fubna, and Magh da Ghabhol, at Oirgialladh. Eochaidh was at length killed by Fiachadh Labhruine, who was descended from Heremon, at the battle of Corman.

2930. Fiachadh Labhruine, son of Smiorgioill, son of Eanbothadh, son of Tighernahas son of Follain, son of Eithrial, son of Irialfaidh, son of Heremon, succeeded and reigned monarch of Ireland twenty-four years; though some of our antiquaries assert that he reigned twenty-seven years. The reason why he was distinguished by the name of Fiachadh Labhruine was, because in the time of this prince the stream of Inbher Labhruine began to flow. There likewise broke out, during his government, the rivers Inbher Fleisge and Inbher Maige; as did the lake called Loch Eirne, which overflowed a

great tract of land that was known by the name of Magh
Geanuinn.

This Irish monarch had a son, called Aongus Ollbhuagach,
who was a prince of great courage and singular conduct, and
engaged the Scottish Picts, and the old Britons that inhabited
that country, and defeated them in every action.   The effect
of his victories was an entire conquest of the country, and a
reduction of that warlike people, the Scots, as well as the Picts
to pay homage to the crown of Ireland.   For though the Picts
had, from the time of Heremon, been tributaries to the Irish
for the space of 230 years after the Milesians first possessed
themselves of the island, yet the Scots never owned themselves
under subjection till they were conquered by Aongus Ollbhuagach, who compelled the whole kingdom of Scotland to obedience, and forced the inhabitants to pay a yearly tribute.

Fiachadh Labhruine, king of Ireland, engaged the family of
Heber Fionn in four battles : they were called the battle of
Fairge, the battle of Galluig, the battle of Claire, and the
battle of Bealgadain, in which action he fell by the hands of
Eochaidh Mumho, the son of Mofeibhis.

Eochaidh Mumho, the son of Mofeibhis, son of Eochaidh
Faobharglas, son of Conmaol, son of Heber Fionn, son of
Milesius, sat next upon the Irish throne.   His reign continued twenty-two years, and he was slain by Aongus Ollmuchach,
at the battle of Cliach.

A.M. 2054.

2975.

Aongus Ollmuchach succeeded.   This king was the
son of Fiachadh Labhruine, son of Smiorgoill, son of Irial
faidh, son of Heremon, son of Milesius.   He reigned eighteen
years, though some antiquaries assert that he governed twenty-
one years.   The reason why he was called Ollmuchach was, because he was famous for having a breed of swine of a much
larger size than any in Ireland ; for the Irish words Oll and Muca
signify great swine, which gave occasion to his name of Ollmuchach.   He was a valiant and warlike prince, and fought the
following battles ; the battle of Cleire, the battle of Sliabh Cao-
lite, where Baiscion was slain ; the battle of Moigein Cgiath, in
Conacht, the battle of Glaise Fraochain, where Fraochan Faidh
was killed ; and he fought thirty battles against the Picts, the
Firbolgs, and the inhabitants of the Orcades.

In the reign of this prince three lakes began to flow ; Loch
Einbheithe Anoirghiallaibh, Loch Failcheadain, and Loch Gasain,
at Muigh Luirg ; and by his industry the following plains were
laid open, and cleared of wood, Magh Glinne Dearcon, in Cineal

Conuill ; Magh Niouagiach, in Leinster ; Magh Cuille Caol, in
Boguine ; Aolmagh, at Callroigbe ; Magh Mucraine, in Conacht ;
Magh Luachradh Deaghadh, and Magh Arohuill, in Kerry Cuach-
radt. Aongus was at length slain by Eana, son of Neachton,
a person of authority in Munster ; though I am rather induced
to believe he was killed by Eana Firtheach, in the battle of Car-
man, because not only the histories which treat of the kings of
Ireland assert the same, but the poems, which are of great authority, and begin with these words, Aongus Ollmuchach adbath,
are likewise an undeniable evidence of this opinion.

A.M.
2993.
Eadna Airgtheach, the son of Eochaidh Mumho, son
of Modh Feibhis, son of Eochaidh Faobharglas, son of
Conmaol, son of Heber Fionn, son of Milesius, succeeded,
and reigned monarch of Ireland twenty-seven years. This prince
took care to reward the courage of his soldiery ; and to incite
their bravery he ordered a number of silver shields and targets
to be made, which he bestowed among the most valiant and deserving of the Irish militia, without partiality or affection, and
regarded nothing in the distribution but merit and military experience. He was unfortunately killed by Rotheachta, son of
Maoin, son of Aongus Ollmuchach, in the battle of Raighne.

3020.
Rotheachta after him enjoyed the crown. He was the
son of Maoin, son of Aongus Ollmuchach, son of Fiachadh
Labhruine, son of Smiorgoill, son of Eanbotha, son of Tighermhas, son of Follain, son of Eithriall, son of Irialfaidh, son
of Heremon ; he governed the kingdom twenty-five years, and
was slain by Seadhna, son of Artri, at Rath Cuachain.

3045.
Seadhna, was the next monarch of Ireland : this prince
was the son of Artri, son of Eibhric, son of Eibher or
Heber, son of Ir, son of Milesius, king of Spain ; he unhappily
fell by the hands of his own son, when the Dubloingois, that is,
the pirates, came to Cruachan, after a reign of five years.

3050.
Fiachadh Fionnsgothach, the son of Seadhna, son of
Artri, son of Eibhric, son of Heber, son of Ir, son of Milesius, succeeded, and governed the kingdom twenty years. The
reason why he was called Fiachadh Fionnsgothach was, because
in his reign it was observed that there grew abundance of white
flowers, which the inhabitants squeezed into cups, and used the
juice for drink, which was likewise very medicinal in many dis-
tempers ; for the word Sgoth signifies a flower, and Fionn signifies white, which being joined, is pronounced Fionnsgothach.
This prince was killed by Muinheamhoin, the son of Cas Clothach.

A.M.
3070.
Muinheamhoin obtained the government: he was the son of Cas Clothach, son of Firarda, son of Rotheachta, son of Rosa, son of Glas, son of Nuaghatt, son of Eochaidh Faobharglas, son of Conmaol, son of Heber Fionn, son of Milesius king of Spain, and reigned five years. This prince ordained, that the gentlemen of Ireland should wear a chain about their necks, as a badge of their quality, and to distinguish them from the populace: he also commanded several helmets to be made, with the neck and forepieces all of gold; these he designed as a reward for his soldiers, and bestowed them upon the most deserving of his army. He died of the plague at Magh Aidne.

3075.
Aildergoidh, the son of Muinheamhoin, son of Cas Clothach, son of Firarda, son of Rotheachta, son of Rosa, son of Glas, son of Nuaghatt, son of Eochaidh Faobharglas, son of Conmaol, son of Heber Fionn, son of Milesius, king of Spain, succeeded, and reigned seven years; he was the first prince that introduced the wearing of gold rings in Ireland, which he bestowed upon persons of merit, that excelled in the knowledge of the arts and sciences, or were any other way particularly accomplished. He was at length killed by Ollamh Fodhla, in the battle of Ceamhair, or Tara.

3082.
Ollamh Fodhla was his successor in the throne: he was the son of Fiachadh Fionnsgothach, son of Seadhna, son of Artri, son of Eibhric, son of Heber, son of Ir, son of Milesius, king of Spain, and his reign continued thirty years. This prince was possessed of many excellent qualities, which gave occasion to his name: for Ollamh signifies a person that excels in wisdom and learning, and Fodhla was the name of the island, and the character by which this monarch is distinguished in the Irish chronicles, justly merited that denomination; for he was certainly a prince of the most comprehensive knowledge, and of the strictest virtue, that ever sat upon the Irish throne. He instituted the most useful laws for the government and the advantage of his people, and was so indefatigable in his studies, that he undertook to transmit to posterity, in a very correct history, the several travels, voyages, adventures, wars, and other memorable transactions of all his royal ancestors, from Feniusa Farsa, the king of Scythia, to his own times; and in order to purge and digest the records of this kingdom, he summoned his principal nobility, his druids, the poets, and historiographers, to meet him in a full assembly at Tara, once in every three years, to revise the body of the established laws, and to change or correct them as the exigence of affairs required. In testimony of this, I shall

produce the following verses of great antiquity, and to be found
in writings of good authority :

The learned Ollamh Fodhla first ordained
The great assembly, where the nobles met,
And priests, and poets, and philosophers,
To make new laws, and to correct the old,
And to advance the honour of his country.

This illustrious assembly was called by the name of Feis
Feamhrach, which signifies a general meeting of the nobility,
gentry, priests, historians, and men of learning, and distinguished
by their abilities in all arts and professions : they met by a
royal summons, in a parliamentary manner, once every three
years, at the palace of Tara, to debate upon the most important concerns of state ; where they enacted new laws, and re-
pealed such as were useless and burthensome to the subject, and
consulted nothing but the public benefit in all their resolutions.
In this assembly the ancient records and chronicles of the island
were perused and examined, and if any falsehoods were detected they were instantly erased, that posterity might not be
imposed upon by false history ; and the author, who had the
insolence to abuse the world by his relation, either by per-
verting matters of fact, and representing them in improper
colours, or by fancies and inventions of his own, was solemnly
degraded from the honour of sitting in that assembly, and was
dismissed with a mark of infamy upon him : his works likewise were destroyed, as unworthy of credit, and were not to be
admitted into the archives, or received among the records of
the kingdom. Nor was this expulsion the whole of his punishment, for he was liable to a fine, or imprisonment, or whatever sentence the justice of the parliament thought proper to
inflict. By these methods, either out of scandal or disgrace,
or of losing their estates, their pensions and endowments, and
of suffering some corporal correction, the historians of those
ages were induced to be very exact in their relations, and to
transmit nothing to after-times, but what had passed this
solemn test and examination, and was recommended by the
sanction and authority of this learned assembly.

In this parliament of Tara, that wise prince Ollamh Fodhla
ordained, that a distinction should be observed between the
nobility, the gentry, and other members of the assembly : and
that every person should take his place according to his quality, his office, and his merit. He made very strict and whole

L

some laws for the government of his subjects, and particularly expressed his severity against the ravishment of women, which, it seems, was a piece of gallantry and a common vice in those days, for the offender was to suffer death without mercy ; and the king thought fit to give up so much of his prerogative, as to put it out of his power either to extend his pardon, or even to reprieve the criminal. It was a law, likewise, that whoever presumed to strike or assault a member of the parliament during the time of the sessions, or give him any disturbance in the execution of his office, either by attempting to rob him, or by any other violence, he was condemned to die, without any possibility, by bribes, by partiality, or affection, to save his life, or escape the sentence.

The members of this triennial convention usually met together, though not in a parliamentary way, six days before the beginning of the session ; that is, three days before the festival of All Saints, and three days after, which time they employed in mutual returns of friendship and civility, and paying their compliments one to another. A poet of great authority, and very ancient, has given the following account of this assembly

> Once in three years, the convention sat,
> And for the public happiness debate ;
> The king was seated on a royal throne,
> And in his face majestic greatness shone.
> A monarch for heroic deeds designed :
> For noble acts become a noble mind :
> About him summon'd, by his strict command,
> The peers, the priests, and commons of the land,
> In princely state and solemn order stand ;
> The poets likewise are indulg'd a place,
> And men of learning the assembly grace.
> Here ev'ry member dares the truth assert,
> He scorns the false, and double-dealing part :
> For a true patriot's soul disdains the trimmer's art.
> Here love and union, ev'ry look confess'd,
> And joy and friendship beat in every breast.
> Justice by nothing biass'd or inclin'd,
> Is deaf to pity, to temptation blind :
> For here with stern and steady rule she sways,
> And flagrant crimes with certain vengeance pays
> The monarch ever jealous of his state,
> Inflexibly decrees th' offender's fate,
> Tho' just, yet so indulgently severe,
> Like Heav'n, he pities those he cannot spare.

The place appointed for the meeting of this assembly was a convenient room in the palace of Tara ; the apartment was very long, but narrow, with a table fixed in the middle, and seats on both sides. At the end of this table, and between the seats and the wall, there was a proper distance allowed, for the servants and attendants that belonged to the members, to go between and wait upon their masters.

In this great hall this triennial parliament assembled ; but before they entered upon public business, they were entertained with a magnificent feast, and the order wherein every member took his place was in this manner. When the dinner was upon the table, and the room perfectly cleared of all persons, except the grand marshal, the principal herald, and a trumpeter, whose offices required they sholud be within, the trumpeter sounded thrice, observing a proper distance between every blast, which was the solemn summons for the members to enter. At the first sound all the shield-bearers, that belonged to the princes and the chief of the nobility, came to the door, and there delivered their shields to the grand marshal, who, by the direction of the king at arms, hung them up in their due places upon the wall on the right side of the long table, where the princes and nobility of the greatest quality had their seats. When he blew the second blast, the target-bearers, that attended upon the generals and commanding officers of the army and of the militia of the kingdom, advanced to the door, and delivered their targets in the same manner, which were hung in their proper order upon the other side of the table. Upon the third summons the princes, the nobility, the generals, the officers and principal gentry of the kingdom entered the hall, and took their places, each under his own shield or target, which were easily distinguished by the coat of arms that was curiously blazoned upon the outside of them ; and thus the whole assembly were seated regularly without any dispute about precedency or the least disorder No person was admitted beside the attendants that waited, who stood on the outside of the table. One end of the table was appointed for the antiquaries and the historians, who understood and were perfectly skilled in the records and ancient monuments of the kingdom ; the other end was filled by the chief officers of the court : and care was particularly taken, that their debates should be kept secret, for which reason no woman was ever to be admitted.

When dinner was ended, and every thing removed, they ordered the antiquities of the kingdom to be brought before them, and read them over, and examined them strictly, lest any falsehoods or interpolations should have crept in ; and if they found any mistakes or false representations of facts, occasioned either by the prejudice or the ignorance of the historians, they were scratched out, after they had been censured by a select committee of the greatest learning, appointed to inspect into those old records. The histories and relations that were surveyed and found true and perfect, were ordered to be transcribed, after they had passed the approbation of the assembly, and inserted in the authentic chronicles that were always preserved in the king's palace, and the book wherein they were written was called the Psalter of Tara. This ancient record is an invaluable treasure, and a most faithful collection of the Irish antiquities; and whatever account is delivered in any other writings repugnant to this, is to be esteemed of no authority, and a direct imposition upon posterity.

In this solemn manner did the Milesians, a learned and generous people, preserve from the most early times the monuments of every memorable transaction that deserved to be transmitted to the world; and in the interval between every session of this triennial parliament, not only the professed antiquaries, but the gentry, and persons of abilities in all professions and capacities, did with all diligence and fidelity collect what was worthy to be observed in their several districts and provinces, and laid their remarks before the next assembly, to be examined; and, if they were approved, to be transcribed in the royal records for the benefit and information of their descendants. If the same care had been taken by other nations, we should not see so many fabulous histories abroad that are founded upon no authority, but supported only by the effrontery of the relaters; but this method it seems was peculiar to the ancient Irish, whose policy and civil government have been the wonder, and ought to have been the example and standard of after ages. And this form of assembling, and bringing their antiquities to a public scrutiny. was followed till the time of St. Patrick, and continued with some alterations, but rather with more care and exactness than to any disadvantage, as will be observed in the course of this history in its proper place.

I am obliged to mention it as the singular glory of the Irish nation, that their Milesian ancestors had so great a veneration, and valued themselves so much upon the nobility of their extract, that they preserved their pedigrees and genealogies with the strictest care; and it is evident, that in former times there were above 200 principal annalists and historians in the kingdom, who had a handsome revenue. and a large estate in land

assigned them, to support themselves in the study of heraldry
and chronology, and to gain a perfect knowledge in those useful
professions. Every nobleman of any quality retained a number of these learned men, on purpose to record the actions of
himself and his family, and to transmit them to posterity, besides such as were in constant pay and attendance for the service of the public. But these private antiquaries had no liberty
of themselves to enter any thing upon record, unless it had been
first approved by the great triennial assembly, whose confirmation gave authority to all the private as well as the public
records of the kingdom. The same generosity and encouragement was likewise extended to men of learning in other professions; the physicians, the poets, and harp-players, had estates
settled upon them, that they might not be disturbed by cares
and worldly troubles in the prosecution of their studies: and
they lived without dependance, and were obliged to no service,
but to employ themselves for the use of their noble patrons that
retained them. In the time of war, or any other public calamities, they were bound to no military attendance or contributions; their persons were inviolable, and it was the greatest of
crimes to kill them, and esteemed sacrilege, whatever distress
the public were in, to seize upon their estates, so that they were
never molested in improving themselves in their several professions; every one followed his proper study under these noble
encouragements, which were never wanting when merit and industry were to be rewarded. And when an eminent antiquary,
a physician, a poet, or harp-player died, his eldest son was not to
succeed him, either in his estate or his salary, unless he was the
most accomplished of the family in that profession; for his successor in his office and the fortune he enjoyed, was to be the
most learned and expert of that tribe he belonged to; which was
the occasion that every person in the family studied to perfect
himself in the knowledge of that art or science to which he proposed to succeed in, in order to obtain the revenue and honour
that belonged to it. And this emulation, supported by such encouragements, advanced all the branches of learning to such a character in the kingdom, that it became the centre of knowledge, and
polite and generous education, and was so esteemed by all the
neighbouring nations, especially in the western part of the world,
as appears evidently by the general testimony of foreign as well as
domestic writers, who have undertaken to treat of the affairs of
this kingdom.

The military discipline in use among the Milesians, is differently related by the Irish authors ; but they all agree in this, that in the forming of their armies, and giving battle to their enemies, they observed an exact regularity, and knew well how to improve all advantages. The common soldiers were always perfect in their exercise, and advanced to fight with great bravery, and in close order. Every company was four or eight deep, according to the number of men they had, and the conveniency and disposition of the ground they were to engage upon. It was death without mercy, by the military law, for a soldier to retreat a foot of ground, but he was still to advance boldly forward, if not countermanded by the commanding officer. They had always a general appointed over the whole army, whose orders were absolute, and to be obeyed by all inferior officers without dispute or appeal. Every lower officer had his coat or arms blazoned curiously upon his banner, that he might be distinguished, and either rewarded for his courage, or punished for his cowardice, in the time of battle. They were always attended in their marches, and when they were engaged, by their antiquaries and annalists, who were employed to take notice of the behaviour of every officer ; and when they found a commander who had signally distinguished himself against the enemy, his name and his exploit was immediately entered into the records of the family he belonged to, and transmitted down from father to son, in order to inspire the several branches of that tribe with emulation and courage, and spur them forward into an imitation of that great example ; and this transaction was not only recorded in the private history of the family, but an exact copy of it was to be laid before the next triennial assembly, and upon approbation to be inserted in the royal records of the kingdom. This monarch likewise, for the encouragement of learning, made a law, that the dignity of an antiquary, a physician, a poet, and a harp-player, should not be conferred but upon persons descended from the most illustrious families in the whole country.

Having observed that the princes, the nobility, and the gentry of the Milesians made use of coats of arms, as badges and distinctions of their quality, it will be useful, I am persuaded, as well as entertaining, to take notice from writers of the best authority, of the original of this practice, and by what means it was first introduced among them.

It must be understood, therefore, that the Israelites, being oppressed by the tyranny and persecution of the Egyptians, resolved, under the conduct of Moses, to free themselves from that cruel bondage; and accordingly the twelve tribes assembled together, under the command of that great officer, who designed to deliver them from slavery, and lead them out of that barbarous country. In this expedition every tribe had a banner, and a certain device or a coat of arms distinctly blazoned upon it. In their march they came to Capacirunt, where Niul, the father of Gadelas, resided with his people, near the borders of the Red Sea, through which, by an Almighty power, a way was wonderfully opened, and the whole nation of the Hebrews passed through, as we have before related.

In process of time it happened, that Sru, a great-grandson of Niul, was banished out of Egypt by the prince who then reigned, with his whole family and descendants; and as he conducted his people out of the country, he followed the example of the Israelites, and, in imitation, had a banner, with a dead serpent and the rod of Moses painted upon it for a coat of arms; and he made a choice of this device, for this reason particularly, because Gadelas, who was his grandfather, was bit by a serpent, and the wound was cured by Moses, who laid his wonder-working rod upon it, and saved his life. From this example the posterity of Sru always made use of banners and coats of arms, as an honourable distinction of their families; and this account is confirmed by the annals of Leath Cuin, which is supported by the additional testimony of the book called Leabhar Leatha Cuin, in this manner. The author, treating upon this subject, gives this account of the coats of arms of the twelve tribes: the tribe of Reuben had a mandrake painted upon their banners; Simeon, a spear; Levi, the ark; Judah, a lion; Issachar, an ass; Zebulun, a ship; Naphthali, a deer; Gad, a lioness; Joseph, a bull; Benjamin, a wolf; Dan, a serpent; and Asher, a branch of a vine.

Our Irish annals are very particular in accounting for the arms and devices borne by several eminent persons, and the most flourishing nations. They inform us, that Hector, the Trojan hero, bore sable two lions combatant, Or; that Osiris bore a sceptre royal ensigned on the top with an eye; Hercules bore a lion rampant, holding a battle-axe; the arms of the kingdom of Macedon were a wolf; Anubis bore a dog; the Scythians, who remained in the country and made no conquests abroad as the Gadelians did, bore a thunder-bolt; the Egyptians bore an ox; the Phrygians, a swine; the Thracians painted the god Mars upon their banners; the Romans, an eagle; and the Persians, bows and arrows; the old poet, Homer

relates, that several curious devices were raised upon the shield
of Achilles, such as the motions of the sun and moon, the stars
and planets, a sphere with the celestial bodies, the situation of
the earth, the ebbing and flowing of the sea, with other uncommon decorations and ornaments that rendered it beautiful and
surprising.   Alexander the Great bore a lion rampant, and ordered his soldiers to display the same arms upon their shields,
as a distinguishing mark of their valour and military achievements ; Ulysses bore a dolphin and the giant Typhon belching
out flames of fire ; the arms of Perseus was a Medusa's head ;
Antiochus chose a lion and a white wand for his ; Theseus bore
an ox, and Seleucus, a bull ; Augustus Cæsar bore the image of
the great Alexander ; sometimes he laid that aside, and used
the sign Capricorn : at other times he blazoned a globe, or the
helm of a ship, supported commonly by an anchor and dolphin.
Simon, the high priest of the Jews, dressed himself in his ponti-
fical robes, which were very splendid, and set off with various
ornaments and representations, when he went out of Jerusalem
to meet the victorious Alexander, who resolved to level the city
with the ground ; and, by the curiosity and solemnity of his
habit, he overawed that invincible conqueror, and suppressed
his designs.   In the same manner almost, Pope Leo adorned
himself, and mollified the anger of Attila, that warlike Scythian,
who threatened to sack the city of Rome ; and Pope Benedict
used the same method to prevail upon Totilas, a valiant Goth,
to withdraw his forces out of Italy.

   There was a custom likewise in use among warriors of old, to
adorn their helmets with a crest, that represented some savage
beast, or fierce bird of prey ; by these figures to distinguish
themselves in the field of battle, to impress a dread and terror
upon their enemies, and to encourage, and with a nobler air to
lead their own troops, and engage them to fight.   Nor were
these representations and devices confined only to set off the
shields and helmets of the ancient heroes, but they were at
length used to adorn the prows of ships and smaller vessels ;
such figures were from very ancient times introduced to beau-
tify and grace their fore-decks, and besides the ornament they
gave, they served to distinguish one ship from another ; and this
we have authority to believe, from the testimony of the holy
penman, who, in the twenty-eighth chapter of the Acts of the
Apostles, particularly mentions, that the ship wherein St. Paul
was to be conveyed to Rome, was distinguished by the sign of
Castor and Pollux.

Now to show the insufferable partiality of the English writers. I am obliged to take notice, that these under-workmen in history never take upon them to deny the use of banners with coats of arms, among the Hebrews, the Greeks, the Romans, and other nations; but the Gadelians and the oid Irish, it seems, have no claim to this honorary privilege. Every account that is given of this ancient and worthy people, they esteem fabulous; and they would, if their arguments and integrity were equal to their malice, erase the very name of a Gadelian out of all records, and destroy the memory of them among men. But notwithstanding the feeble efforts of these little authors, we have the testimony of the best historians, to prove that the Gadelians were a family as illustrious, and made as early a figure in the chronicles of the world, as any tribe in the universe; and as an unquestionable evidence upon this subject, they preserved their own monuments and records with the strictest care, and faithfully delivered them to posterity; and therefore prejudice and ignorance are the only inducements that could prevail upon the English writers who pretend to treat of Irish affairs, to deduce their accounts of Ireland from no higher a period than the reign of William the Conqueror; and because the histories of their own country cannot be traced with any tolerable authority farther than the time of that prince, therefore it must needs follow, that the Irish annals are of the same modern date, and every chronicle beyond that point of time must be a fable and romance. How conclusive this argument is, any unprejudiced person will easily determine. However this is certain, that the old chronicles of England were destroyed by the victorious Romans, Goths, Saxons, Germans, Normans and other foreigners, who made a conquest of the kingdom; but the Irish records were kept sacred, and were never in the hands of any invading enemy, nor was the island ever absolutely subdued, so as to be under a foreign yoke, from the first arrival of the Milesians unto this day.

It is therefore certain, that the Milesians, from the time they first conquered the island, down to the reign of Ollamh Fodhla, made use of no other arms of distinction, in their banners, than a dead serpent and the rod of Moses, after the example of their Gadelian ancestors. But in this great triennial assembly at Tara, it was ordained by a law, that every nobleman and great officer should, by the learned heralds, have a particular coat of arms assigned him according to his merit and his quality, whereby he should be distinguished from others of the same rank, and be known to any antiquary or person of learning wherever he appeared, whether at sea or land, in the prince's court, at the place of his own residence, or in the field of battle. Upon the death of this great monarch, the crown devolved by an hereditary right upon his son.

A.M. Fionnachta succeeded in the government of Ireland.
3113. He was the son of Ollamh Fodhla, son of Fiachadh Fionns- gothach, son of Seadhna, son of Artri, son of Eibhric, son Heber, son of Ir, son of Milesius, king of Spain. His reign conti- nued 15 years, though some authors assert that he filled the throne 20 years. The reason why he was distinguished by this name was, because abundance of snow fell upon the island in his reign, and for a long time covered the whole country. There is an account, but of no manner of authority, that when this snow came to thaw and dissolve it turned into natural and perfect wine. This is certainly a fiction, for though the word Fion in the Irish signi- fies wine, yet by adding another N to it, and spelling it thus, Fionn, which is the first syllable of this prince's name, it signi- fies white ; the following word Acta, or Sneacta, is the genuine Irish for snow, and these words, when they are joined, are pro- nounced Fionnachta, not Fionachta ; so that by observing the proper spelling of this name, the writers of the best credit are induced to believe that this monarch obtained his name from the great quantity of snow that fell in his time ; and reject, as idle and fictitious, the other opinion, which asserts that he was so called, because the snow when it dissolved became true wine. This prince died at Magh Inis, and there was buried.

3128. Slanoll was his successor. He was another son of Ol- lamh Fodhla, son of Fiachadh Fionnsgothach, son of Seadhna, son of Artri, son of Eibhric, son of Heber, son of Ir, son of Milesius, and he wore the crown of Ireland fifteen years. The reason why he was distinguished by the name of Slanoll was, because the people of the country enjoyed so perfect a state of health, that very few or none of them fell sick, or died of any malignant distemper, during his whole reign ; for the syllable Oll in the Irish is the same as great in the English, and Slan signifies health, which, by being transposed and joined with the other word, is pronounced Slanoll. This prince died at Tara, in the house of Modhchuarda, but the distemper that occasioned his death was never known.

3143. Geide Ollgothach succeeded him. He was the third son of Ollamh Fodhla, son of Fiachadh Fionnsgothach, son of Seadhna, son of Artri, son of Eibhric, son of Heber, son of Ir, son of Milesius, and he sat upon the throne seventeen years. He received the name of Geide Ollgothach, because the people of Ireland, in his time, had a custom of being very loud and noisy when they spoke ; for the syllable Oll, as was before observed, signifies great, and the word Gothach signifies talking or speaking, which, when they are joined together, sound Ollgothach, that is, great or loud talking. This prince was at length killed by Fiachadh, the son of Fionnachta.

A.M.
3160 Fiachadh, the son of Fionnachta, son of Ollamh Fodhla, son of Fiachadh Fionnsgothach, son of Seadhna, son of Artri, son of Eibhric, son of Heber, son of Ir, son of Milesius, obtained the crown and reigned 20 years, as some of the chronicles assert ; though upon a strict inspection 1 am induced to believe, that he governed four years more, for the regal table admits of no interregnum, and the book of the reigns of the Irish kings speaks very dubiously concerning the reign of this prince. It seems to intimate, that there were other competitors with him, who raised pretences to the government, and particularly observes, that Bearngall, the succeeding monarch, made war upon him for some years before he lost the sovereignty : the four years therefore that passed, while the crown was in dispute, may be placed to the reign of either of these princes, for the reasons above mentioned. This king was at length dethroned and slain by Bearngall, the son of Geide Ollgothach.

3184. Bearngall was his successor. He was the son of Geide Ollgothach, son of Ollamh Fodla, son of Fiochadh Fionnsgothach, son of Seadhna, son of Artri, son of Eibhric, son of Heber, son of Ir, son of Milesius. His reign continued twelve years, and he was killed by Oilioll, the son of Slanoll.

3196. Oilioll, the son of Slanoll, son of Ollamh Fodhla, son of Fiachadh Fionnsgothach, son of Seadhna, son of Artri, son of Eibhric, son of Heber, son of Ir, son of Milesius, king of Spain, sat next upon the throne. He reigned sixteen years, and lost his life by the hands of Siorna Saoghalach, son of Dein.

3212. Siorna Saoghalach succeeded. He was the son of Dein, son of Rotheachta, son of Maoin, son of Aongus Ollmuchach, son of Fiachadh Labhruine, son of Smiorgoill, son of Eanbotha, son of Tighermas, son of Follain, son of Eithriall, son of Irialfaidh, son of Heremon, son of Milesius, king of Spain ; and his reign lasted twenty-one years. He was called Siorna Saoghalach, because he lived to an exceeding great age, beyond any of his time. as his name plainly imports. He was slain by Rotheachta, the son of Roan, at Aillin ; as the old poet gvies us to understand in the following lines, taken out of a poem which begins thus, Eir ard Inis na Roig.

> Siorna reigned one-and-twenty years,
> And prosperously wore the Irish crown ;
> But, though long lived, he died a fatal death,
> Unfortunately slain by Rotheachta,
> At Aillin.

A.M. 3233.   Rotheachta succeeded him ; he was the son of Roan, son of Failbhe, son of Cas Cead Chaingniodh, son of Aildergoid, son of Muineamhoin, son of Cas Clothach, son of Firarda, son of Rotheachta, son of Rosa, son of Glas, son of Nuaghatt Deaglamh, son of Eochaidh Faobharglas, son of Conmaol, son of Heber Fionn, son of Milesius. His reign was not long, for he governed but seven years, and died at last terribly, for he perished by fire at Dunn Sobhairce.

3240.   Eilm was his successor. He was the son of Rotheachta, son of Roan son of Failbhe, son of Cas Cead Chaingniodh, son of Aildergoid, son of Muineamhoin, son of Cas Clothach, son of Firarda, son of Rotheachta, son of Rosa, son of Glas, son of Nuaghatt Deaglamh, son of Eochaidh Faobharglas, son of Conmaol, son of Heber Fionn, son of Milesius. He was slain, after a reign of one year, by Giallacha, son of Oliolla Olchaoin.

3241.   Giallacha obtained the crown. He was the son of Oliolla Olchaoin, son of Siorna Saoghalach, son of Dein, son of Rotheachta, son of Aongus Ollmuchach, son of Fiachadh Lahruine, son of Smiorgoill, son of Eanbotha, son of Tighermas, of the posterity of the line of Heremon. His reign continued nine years, and he was killed by Art Imleach, at Moighe Muadh

3250.   Art Imleach succeeded. He was the son of Eilm, son of Rotheachta, son of Roan, son of Failbhe, son of Cas Cead Chaingniodh, son of Aildergoid, a descendant from Heber Fionn. He sat upon the throne twenty-two years, and was killed by Nuadha Fionn Fail.

3272.   Nuadha Fionn Fail was his successor. He was the son of Giallacha, son of Oliolla Olchaoin, son of Siorna Saoghalach, of the line of Heremon. His reign lasted twenty years, and he was slain by his successor Breasrigh, the son of Art Imleach.

3292.   Breasrigh, the son of Art Imleach, son of Eilm, son of Rotheachta, son of Roan, a prince of the posterity of

Heber Fionn, succeeded. He governed the kingdon nine years, and fought many successful battles against the pirates that infested the coasts. He was killed by Eochaidh Apthach, at Carn Chluain.

A.M. 3301. Eochaidh Apthach obtained the crown. He was the son of Fin, son of Oliolla, son of Floinruadh, son of Roithlain, son of Martineadh, son of Sitchin, son of Riaglan, on of Eochaidh Breac, son of Luigheach, son of Ith, son of Breogan. His reign was but short, for he sat upon the throne but one year. He was distinguished by the name of Eochaidh Apthach, because during the short time of his reign there was a great mortality among his subjects, that swept away most of the inhabitants; for once in every month the whole island was infected with a malignant distemper that was incurable. The Irish word Apthach signifies a plague or infection. He was killed by Fionn, son of Bratha.

3302. Fionn, the son of Bratha, son of Labhra, son of Cairbre, son of Ollamh Fodhla, a descendant in succession from Ir, the son of Milesius, obtained the crown. He governed twenty years, and was slain by Seadhna Jonaraicc.

3322. Seadhna Jonaraicc was his successor. He was the son of Breasrigh, son of Art Imleach, of the line of Heber Fionn, and reigned twenty years. He was called Seadhna Jonaraicc, because he was the first monarch of Ireland that settled a constant pay upon the officers and soldiers of his army, and maintained them, by a fixed salary, according to the quality of their posts and commissions. He likewise ordained military laws, and instituted a form of discipline that was a standard to the Milesians for many ages. This unfortunate prince was inhumanly murdered by his successor, and had his limbs violently drawn asunder, which put him to inexpressible torture.

3342. Simon Breac by this barbarous act obtained the crown. He was the son of Nuadh Fionn Fail, of the line of Heremon. His reign continued six years; but the Divine vengeance pursued him in an exemplary manner, for he was seized by Duach Fionn, the son of his predecessor, who justly punished him with the same ignominious death he had inflicted upon his father, and ordered his body to be torn to pieces.

3348. Duach Fionn, son of Seadhna Jonaraicc, son of Breasrigh, a descendant from Heber Fionn, succeeded, and reigned five years. He was slain by Muireadhach Balgrach.

3353. Muireadhach Balgrach was his successor. He was the son of the cruel Simon Breac, of the posterity of Heremon. He governed the kingdom four years, and then was killed by Eadhna Dearg, the son of Duach Fionn.

A.M. 3357. Eadhna Dearg, the son of Duach Fionn, son of Seadhna Jonaraice, of the line of Heber Fionn, succeeded, and reigned twelve years. The reason why he was distinguished by the name of Eadhna Dearg was, because he was remarkable for a fresh and sanguine complexion. It was in the reign of this prince that a mint was erected, and money coined, at Airgiodross. He did not die by the sword, as did most of his predecessors, but was destroyed by the plague, which depopulated most part of the island, and was buried at Sliabh Mis.

3369. Lughaidh Jardhoinn obtained the government. He was the son of Eadhna Dearg, son of Duach Fionn, of the posterity of Heber Fionn, and was monarch of the island nine years. He was called Lughaidh Jardhoinn from the colour of his hair, which was a very dark brown; for the word Jardhoinn, or Dubhdhonn, in Irish, is the same as dark brown in English, which gave occasion to his name. This prince was killed by Siorlamh, the son of Fionn, at Roth Clochair.

3378. Siorlamh, the son of Fionn, son of Bratha, son of Labhra, son of Cairbre, son of Ollamh Fodhla, a descendant from Ir, the son of Milesius, king of Spain, succeeded in the throne, and governed the island sixteen years. He was known by the name of Siorlamh, from the extraordinary length of his hands; for the word Sior, in the Irish language, has the signification of long in English, and Lamh is the same with hands. And indeed this monarch was called so with great propriety, for nature had furnished him with hands so long, that when he stood upright his fingers would touch the ground. His successor, Eochaidh Uairceas, slew him, and put an end to his reign.

3394. Eochaidh Uairceas seized upon the crown. He was the son of Lughaidh Jardhoinn, son of Eadhna Dearg, a descendant from Heber Fionn, and ruled the kingom twelve years. He was called by the name of Eochaidh Uairceas, from a sort of skiffs or small boats, of which he was the inventor. This prince was banished, or driven out of the kingdom of Ireland, two years before he came to the government; and, when he was obliged to quit the island, he summoned and took with him a select number of his followers and friends, and in thirty ships well manned with choice troops and expert mariners, he set to sea, (this was his security all the time of his banishment,) but he would often come upon the coasts, and spoil the inhabitants; and for the convenient landing of his men he invented a

rt of cock-boats, that were easy to manage, and covered them
ith the skins of beasts. By this device he would frequently
et a body of his men on shore, and make great depredations
pon the coasts, and plundered all the maritime parts of the
ountry. This invention gave occasion to his name ; for the
ord Uairceas, or (as others pronounce it) Fuarceas, signifies a cold
kiff, or a cock-boat, in English ; because these small vessels were
sed in the cold and severest weather for the conveniency of
ndiug. These skiffs are called in the Irish language by the
ame of Curachs or Curachain, and are made use of in some parts
f the island to this day. This Irish monarch was slain by Eo-
haidh Fiadhmhuine.

**A.M.
046.** Eochaidh Fiadhmhuine, and his brother, Conuing Beg
Aglach, obtained the sovereignty. They were the sons
of Duach Teamhrach, son of Muireadhach Balgrach, son
f Simon Breac, of the royal line of Heremon. They reigned
int monarchs of the island for five years. The eldest of these
rinces was distinguished by the name of Eochaidh Fiadhmhuine,
ecause he took great pleasure in the chasing of deer and other
ild beasts, which he frequently hunted in the woody and wild
arts of the country ; for the word Fiadh in Irish signifies a deer,
nd Muine is the same as a wood or desolate wilderness in English,
hich words, when they are joined, make Fiadhmhuine. These
rothers lost the kingdom, and Eochaidh Fiadhmhuine was slain
y Luighaidh Lamhdhearg, the son of Eochaidh Vairceas.

111. Luighaidh Lamhdhearg, the son of Eochaidh Vairceas,
a prince of the posterity of Heber Fionn, succeeded, and
igned seven years. He was known by the name of Luighaidh
amhdhearg, because he had a remarkable red spot upon one
his hands. He was killed by Conuing Beg Aglach, who made
ar upon him, and by that means revenged his brother's
eath.

118. Conuing Beg Aglach obtained the crown. He was the
son of Duach Teamharach, son of Muireadhach Balgrach,
n of Simon Breac, of the line of Heremon. When he had
vercome his competitor, he resumed the government, and
igned ten years. He received the name of Conuing Beg
glach, because he was a prince of an undaunted spirit, exposed
s life with the greatest bravery, and was always seen in the
eat of action ; for the words Beg Aglach signify resolute and
arless. This monarch was of a strong constitution of body,
nd was inspired with a soul capable of designing and executing
e greatest actions. The glory of the Irish nation was raised

to a considerable height, during the reign of this king, who not only fought successfully against the enemies of his country, but governed his subjects at home with justice and moderation, and ruled absolutely in the hearts and affections of his people. But these excellent qualities could not protect him from the attempts of Art, who succeeded him, and slew him; as a poet of great antiquity observes in this manner.

> Conuing the brave, with love of glory fired,
> Oppress'd by force, triumphantly expired;
> He raised his courage for the last debate,
> And with a princely soul undaunted met his fate,
> Slain by the sword of Art.

A.M. 3428. Art succeeded to the crown. He was the son of Luighaidh Lamhdearg, of the line of Heber Fionn, and governed the kingdom six years; he lost his life by the hands of Duach Laghrach, who, with the assistance of his father, slew him.

3434. Fiachadh Tolgrach, the son of Muireadhach Balgrach, son of Simon Breac, son of Aodhain Glas, a prince of the posterity of Heremon, was his successor, and was monarch of the island for seven years. His life and reign were ended by the sword of Oilioll Fionn, who slew him.

3441. Oilioll Fionn possessed the throne. He was the son of Art, the son of Luighdheach Lamdhearg, of the line of Heber Fionn, and he wore the crown nine years, but was killed by Airgeadmhar, with the assistance of Fiacha and his two sons.

3450. Eochaidh, the son of Oilioll Fionn, son of Art, son of Luighdheach Lamdhearg, of the posterity of Heber Fionn, succeeded, and he governed the island seven years. He would not admit of a partner in the throne, and refused to allow Airgeadmhar a share in the government. He made a peace with Duach, which continued but a short time, for he was afterwards slain by him, after a reign of seven years.

3457. Airgeadmhar was his successor. He was the son of Siorlamh, son of Finn, son of Bratha, a prince of the posterity of Ir, the son of Milesius, king of Spain. He filled the throne for twenty-three years, and was at last killed by Duach Laghrach, and by Lughaidh Laighde.

3480. Duach Laghrach seized upon the crown. He was the son of Fiachadh Tolgrach, son of Muireadhach Bolgrach, son of Simon Breac, descended from the family of Heremon, and

governed the island ten years. The reason why he was distinguished by the name of Duach Laghrach, was because he was
so strict and hasty in the execution of justice, that he was impatient and would not admit of a moment's delay, till the criminal was seized and tried for the offence : for the word Ladh-
rach in the Irish language signifies speedy and sudden, which
gave occasion to his name. He was killed by Lughaidh Laighe.

A.M. Lughaidh Laighe was his successor. He was the son
3490. of Eochaidh, son of Oiliolla Fionn, of the posterity of
Heber Fionn, and he was monarch of the island seven years.
An old book, called the Etymology of Names, asserts, that this
Lughaidh was one of the five sons of Daire Domhtheach, and
that all the brothers went by the same name. The same author
relates, that a certain druid, who had the skill of prophecy,
foretold to Daire, the father, that he should have a son, whose
name should be Lughaidh, who should one day sit upon the
throne of Ireland. Daire, it seems, afterwards had five sons,
and the more effectually to bring about this prediction, he gave
the same name to every one. When the five brothers were
come to a maturity of years, Daire took an opportunity to call
upon the druid, and inquired of him which of his sons should
have the honour of being monarch of the island ? The druid,
instead of giving him a direct answer, ordered him to take his
five sons with him on the morrow to Tailtean, where there was
to be a general convention of all the principal nobility and
gentry of the kingdom, and that while the assembly sat he
should see a fawn or young deer running through the field,
which should be pursued by all the company ; his five sons
likewise would run among the rest, and whosoever of them
overtook and killed the fawn, the crown should be his, and he
should be sole monarch of the island. The father followed the
direction of the druid with great exactness, and accordingly the
next day set out with his five sons, and came to Tailtean, where
he found the assembly sitting, and looking about him, he spied
the fawn running over the fields, and the whole assembly left
their debates and pursued her; the five brothers ran
among the rest, and followed her close till they came to
Binneadair, now called the hill of Hoath ; here a mist,
that was raised by enchantment, separated the five sons of
Daire from the other pursuers, and they continued the chase,
and hunted her as far as Dail Maschorb, in Leinster, where
Lughaidh Laighe, as the druid foretold, overtook the fawn, and
killed her. From this transaction this prince was called Lugh-

M

aidh Laighe, for the word Laighe in the Irish signifies a fawn.
There goes an old story of no great credit concerning this
monarch, which, though it be a fiction, I shall mention, out of
respect to its antiquity; for it is a fable of many hundred years'
standing. This prince, it seems, as he was hunting in one of
the forests of Ireland, and was divided from his retinue that
followed him, was met by an old withered hag, who, after some
discourse with him, prevailed to be admitted into his embraces,
and accordingly they retired to a private place of the wood,
where, when the king attempted to caress her, he was surprised
with the appearance of a most beautiful young lady, and instead
of a deformed old woman, he found a lovely maid in his arms.
This vision represented, as the legend observes, the genius of
the kingdom of Ireland, which this monarch obtained with great
difficulty and danger; but though he underwent very grievous
hardships before he had the crown fixed upon his head, yet he
was amply rewarded for his sufferings, with the possession of the
sovereignty and the riches of one of the most fruitful islands in
the whole world. So far is the relation of this ancient writer;
but I much question his fidelity, and every one is left to judge
for himself. But notwithstanding the account given of this
prince in the fore-mentioned book of Etymology, that he was
the son of Daire Doimhthach, yet I am apt to believe that the
king I am speaking of was a person different from his son, and
that the prediction of the druid belonged to another man of
the same name. Lughaidh Laighe, after a reign of seven years,
was slain by Aodh Ruadh, son of Badhurn.

3497.   Aodh Ruadh succeeded in the government. He was
the son of Badhurn, son of Airgeadmhar, son of Siorlamh,
son of Finn, son of Bratha, son of Labhradh, son of Carbre,
son of Ollamh Fodhla, of the family of Ir, the son of Milesius,
king of Spain. He was monarch of the island twenty-one years,
and was unfortunately drowned at Easruadh.

A.M.   Diothorba, the son of Diomain, son of Airgeadmhar,
3518.   son of Siorlamh, of the posterity of Ir, the son of Milesius, succeeded him. He likewise governed the kingdom twenty-one years, and died of a malignant distemper at
Eamhain Macha.

3539.   Ciombaoith, son of Fionntan, son of Airgeadmhar,
son of Siorlamh, son of Finn, a descendant from Ir, the
son of Milesius, succeeded, and reigned over the island twenty
years; he was at last destroyed by the plague at Eamhain
Macha.

Macha Mongruadh obtained the crown. She was the A.M. daughter of Aodh Ruadh, son of Badhurn, son of Sior-3559. lamh, a descendant from Ir, the son of Milesius ; and she reigned seven years. It was in the government of this princess that the royal palace of Eamdaih was erected : and the reason why that magnificent structure was called Eamhain Macha is thus related in the Irish records. There were three princes in the province of Ulster, who for a long time waged continual wars for the government of the island : their names were Aodh Ruadh, the son of Badhurn, from whom Easruad obtained its name ; Diathorba, the son of Demain, from Visneach Meatn ; and Ciombaoith, the son of Fionntan, from Fionnabhair. Tnese three kings, after they had worn one another out with struggling for the crown, came at last to an agreement, and consented that every one should reign monarch successively, for the space of twenty or twenty-one years ; and by the force of these articles they had all their turns, and sat upon the throne according to the treaty. Aodh Ruadh was the first of these three princes that wore the crown, and died ; but left only a daughter behind him, whose name was Macha Mongruadh, or the red-haired princess. Diathorba, according to the agreement, obtained the government, and reigned the whole time that was allotted him : then he resigned, and by the articles Ciombaoith, who was the third prince in succession, reigned his time ; for Aodh Ruadh died, as we observed before, and left no son behind him. But the princess Macha Mongruadh claimed the throne, as she was the daughter of Aodh Ruadh, and insisted upon her right of inheritance, because her father, if he had lived, should have succeeded next. Diathorba, meeting with this unexpected opposition, sent for his five sons, who were persons of great courage and ambition, and, when he had informed them of the design of this young lady, they all came to a resolution to stand by the former treaty, and vindicate their pretensions by the sword ; for they could not bear that a woman should fill the throne of Ireland, and attempt to govern so brave and warlike a people.

The princess Macha was a lady of an invincible spirit, of a strong robust constitution. able to endure hardships, of a bold enterprising genius, and is always mentioned with great honour and respect by the Irish historians. As soon as she heard of the preparations of Diathorba and his sons, she resolved not to be surprised, and therefore she sent a summons to the principal nobility who took her part, and commissions to raise a strong body of troops, and with all possible expedition to attack the enemy. Diathorba and his sons were supported by a numerous army, well disciplined. In a short time the two competitors met, and their whole forces engaged, and a most desperate battle was fought, when the princess Macha obtained a complete victory. This success fixed the crown firmer upon her head, and gave peace to the kingdom for some time ; for Diathorba did not long survive the misfortune, but died with grief, and left five sons, whose names were Baoth, Buadhach, Bras, Uallach, and Borbchas, to insist upon their claim, and when opportunity offered, to defend their rights.

It was not long before these five brothers, by the interest of their friends, raised a considerable body of men, and resolved once more to appear in the field, and decide their pretensions to the crown. But before they offered battle they dispatched a herald to the princess, to demand the government and the possession of their right, to which they had a just claim, not only by the treaty, but upon the account of their family, as they were descended from the royal line of the Irish monarchs. The princess, instead of complying with the summons, sent the messenger away with indignation, and told him she would soon chastise his masters for their insolence, at the head of her victorious army ; and she was as good as her word, for soon after both armies engaged, and fought with great bravery, and victory was a long time in suspense, for no less than the kingdom of Ireland depended upon the event, and was to be the prize of the conqueror : but after a bloody and sharp action, the confederate army of the brothers was broken, and a general rout followed, and by this success the princess got absolute possession of the throne.

After this defeat the brothers were close pursued, and forced to conceal themselves in the woods and marshes of the country ; but they were discovered to the queen, who resolved upon a stratagem to apprehend them, very dangerous and difficult in the execution. It seems that after this battle she was pleased to marry Ciombaoith, the son of Fionntan, and to him she left the government of the kingdom, and the command of the army, while she took upon herself to go in quest of the five pretenders, and if possible to secure them from any farther attempts upon the crown. To bring this to pass she laid by her robes of state, and disguised herself in an ordinary habit, suitable to her design, and changed the colour of her hair, which was remarkable for its redness, by powdering it with the flower of rye.

In this obscure dress she set forward, without any attendants, towards the woods of Buirrinn, where the brothers were concealed; and after some search she found them together, boiling part of a wild boar which they had hunted and killed. When she advanced near them, she was observed by the young men, who were surprised at the sight of a woman in so solitary a place; but when they recovered themselves they civilly asked her to sit down, and partake of what entertainment she found, for their misfortunes had obliged them to that way of life, and their desperate circumstances could supply them with no other provision. She courteously accepted of the invitation; and after she had eaten, one of the brothers, with an air of gallantry, said, that the lady, though she was none of the handsomest in the face, yet she had fair lovely eyes, and therefore declared he could not withstand the temptation, and resolved to have a nearer acquaintance with her. Accordingly he took her by the hand, and leads her to a close thicket at some distance, and attempted to debauch her; but she, observing her opportunity, laid hold upon his arms, and, after some struggle, by main force overcame him; and having brought cords with her for the purpose, she bound him fast, and returned to the four brothers.

They were somewhat surprised to see the lady without her gallant, and asked what was become of her lover; she told them she supposed he was ashamed to appear and show his face, after he had condescended so much below his quality as to converse with so mean a person; and this reply she delivered in so modest a manner, that they resolved in turns to withdraw with her, and use her as they pleased, which they attempted one after another, but she played the same part with them all, and so secured them. By this dangerous stratagem she brought them away prisoners with her, and returned to court, where her husband, and the principal nobility and commons of the kingdom, were impatiently expecting the event. When she had related the particulars of the adventure, she was applauded and congratulated by the whole company, and with a noble carriage she delivered up her captives.

The five competitors for the crown being thus apprehended, the council of the kingdom sat to determine what sentence should be passed upon them; and they unanimously agreed, that the peace of the government would never be settled unless they were all put to death. But the queen who was of a merciful disposition, interposed, and as she had hazarded her own royal person to secure them, she desired their lives might be saved, for it would be contrary to the established laws and customs of the land to proceed to execution; and insisted, that, instead of death, their punishment might be, to erect a stately palace in that province, where the prince should always keep his court. They agreed to the justice of her request, and upon that condition the five brothers saved their lives.

The queen undertook to draw the plan of this structure, which she did with her bodkin that she wore on her neck, and served to bind her hair. The name of this royal fabric is Eamhuin Macha, and it was so called from the pin or bodkin that the queen used in laying out the area of it; for Eo in the Irish language signifies a needle or bodkin, and Muin is the same as neck in English, which words together sound Eomuin, and sometimes it is read Eamhuin, because it signifies the pin of the neck, which gave occasion to the name. This word, with the name of the queen joined to it, was the reason that this building was called Eamhuin Macha.

There is another account, mentioned in some Irish chronicles, different from what we have now related, and asserts, that the palace of Eamhuin Macha received its name from a woman so called, who was wife to Cruin, the son of Adnamhuin. This woman, it seems, was obliged (for what reason is uncertain) to run a race with the horses of Connor, king of Ulster, and (as the story goes on) she out-ran them, and came first to the goal: she was with child at the time, and near her delivery, and when she fell in labour was delivered of twins, a son and a daughter. The barbarity of this action, and the pains she suffered in travail, so incensed the unfortunate woman, that she left a curse upon the men of Ulster; and heaven heard her, for the men of that province were constantly afflicted with the pains of child-bearing for many years, from the time of Connor, who then reigned in Ulster, to the succession of Mal, the son of Rochruide. This Irish heroine governed the kingdom for many years, in a magnificent manner. She was the delight of her subjects, and the terror of her enemies, but was at last slain by Reachta Righdhearg, who succeeded her.

Reachta Righdhearg was the next monarch. He was A.M. 3566. the son of Lughaidh Laighe, son of Eochaidh, son of Oilioll Finn, son of Lughaidh Lamdhearg, son of Eochaidh Uaircens, a prince of the posterity of Heber Fionn, and governed the kingdom twenty years. He was distinguished by the name of Reachta Righdhearg, because one of his arms was exceeding red, for the word Rig in the Irish language signifies

an arm : he was killed by Ugaine More, in revenge for his foster-
mother.

Ugaine More, who was surnamed the Great, obtained
the crown. He was son of Eochaidh Buaidhaig, son of
Duach Laidhrach, a descendant from the royal line of Heremon, and was monarch of the island thirty years, or, as some writers assert, governed it forty years. He was known by the name of
Ugaine More, because his dominions were enlarged beyond the
bounds of his predecessors ; for he was the sovereign prince of
all the western European isles. This prince had a very numerous issue ; for he had twenty-five children, twenty-two sons and
three daughters.

A. M. 3586.

When his sons were grown up, each of them took upon himself to raise a company of soldiers, and in a military manner
they would march through the kingdom, and raise contributions
upon the country for their support ; and no sooner had one
troop left a place, but another came and consumed all the provisions that were left. This oppression was insupportable, and
the subjects were forced to represent their grievances to the king,
and complain to him of the distressed state of the country.
Upon this remonstrance Ugaine convened his council, and consulted how he should suppress these violent measures of his
sons, that were of the most destructive consequence to his people.
It was their advice, that the kingdom of Ireland should be
divided into five-and-twenty parts, and shared equally between
his children, under this restriction, that the young princes should
content themselves with the portion assigned them, and confine
themselves within the bounds of their own territories, without
presuming to encroach upon the dominions of their neighbours.
In confirmation of this division, we meet with the following lines
in a very old poet :

> Ugaine. the monarch of the western isle.
> Concerned at the oppression of his people,
> Divided into equal parts his kingdom
> Between his five-and-twenty children.

And by the rules of this division, the public taxes and revenues of the island were collected by the king of Ireland, for the
space of three hundred years after, from the time of this monarch down to the provincial ages.

I confess the kingdom of Ireland was also divided in a manner different from this ; but that division was not made by
Ugaine the Great, but by Eochaidh Feidhliach, who, by his

royal donation, conferred the country upon his prime ministers. The province of Ulster he settled upon Feargus, the son of Leighe ; the province of Leinster he bestowed upon Rossa, the son of Feargus Fairge ; the two provinces of Munster he gave to Tighernach Teadhbheamach and Deaghadh. He divided the province of Conacht between three of his favourites, whose names were Fiodhach, son of Feig, Eochaidh Allat and Tinne, sons of Conrach. But a particular account will be given of these transactions when the course of this history brings us to treat of the reign of Eochaidh Feidhliach, a succeeding monarch in the government of the country.

Ugaine left behind him two sons, Laoghaire Lorck, and Cobhthach Caolmbreag, by whom the royal line of Heremon was continued ; and to these princes all the future branches of that family owe their descent. After a long reign this great monarch was slain by Badhbhchadh, the son of Eochaidh Buaidhaig, but he did not succeed him.

A.M. 3586. Laoghaire Lorck, the son of Ugaine More, laid claim to the government, and fixed himself in the throne. He was the grandson of Eochaidh Buaidhaig, son of Duach Laidhrach, a descendant from Heremon ; and he wore the crown two years. His mother was a French princess, her name was Ceasair Cruthach, a daughter of the king of France, she was the wife of Ugaine More, and had issue, this monarch and his brother Cobhthach Caolmbreag. This king was distinguished by the name of Laoghaire Lorck, because he seized upon the murderer of his father, who was Badhbhchadh, the son of Eochaidh Buaidhaig, and slew him ; for the word Lorck, in the Irish language, signifies murder or slaughter. But he was afterwards most perfidiously slain himself, by his brother Cobhthach Caolmbreag, at Didhion Riogh, near the bank of the river Bearbha. The circumstances of this inhuman act are thus related in the records of Ireland. The king Laoghaire Lorck was very kind and indulgent to his brother, and settled a princely revenue upon him ; but his bounty and affection met with very ungrateful returns, for Cobhthach envied his brother the enjoyment of the crown, and nothing less than the whole kingdom would satisfy his ambition ; and because he could not obtain his ends he perfectly languished, through grief and madness, for his constitution was broken, and his body daily wasted, which brought him into so bad a state of health that his life was despaired of. As soon as the king heard of his sickness, and the melancholy circumstances he was in, he resolved to pay him a visit, and set out with his body guards and his household troops about him for that purpose. When he came to his bed-side, the sick prince, observing that his brother was attended by men in arms, asked the reason of such a military retinue, and seemed to resent it, as if he suspected his fidelity, and dared not trust himself with a sick man without such a warlike attendance. The king courteously answered, that he never entertained the least suspicion of his loyalty or affection, but came in that manner only for state, and to keep up the dignity of his royal character; but that rather than make him uneasy he promised the next visit he made him he would be without a guard; and so, with the most tender and compassionate expressions, he took his leave.

The perfidious Cobhthach, reflecting that his brother would soon come to visit him alone and unattended, resolved upon his death; but not relying upon his own capacity, he communicated his design to a wicked druid, and advised with him in what manner he should accomplish his purpose. The infamous soothsayer, instead of detecting the treason, encouraged the conspirator; and upon consultation it was agreed, that Cobhthach should feign himself to be dead, and when his brother came to lament over his body, he was to stab him with a poniard that was to be concealed by him. And this barbarous stratagem had its desired success; for when the news of his brother's death came to Laoghaire, he immediately came to the body, and as he was lying upon it, expressing his sorrow, his brother secretly thrust his poniard into his belly, and killed him.

But he thought he was not sufficiently secure in his usurpation by the murder of the king, unless he destroyed all the princes of the blood, that might claim a right or give him any disturbance on the throne; he therefore murdered Oilioll Aine, the son of Laoghaire; and likewise designed to take away the life of a young prince, who was the grandson of his brother; but he was saved almost by a miracle, for when the cruel tyrant sent for the child, he forced him to eat part of the hearts of his father and grandfather; and to torture him the more, he caused him to swallow a living mouse, and by such inhuman methods resolved to destroy him: but by a strange providence the child was so affrighted by these barbarities, that he seemed distracted, and by the convulsions and agonies he was in perfectly lost the use of his speech; which when the usurper perceived he dismissed him with his life, for he thought he would never recover his senses, and therefore could not be able to assert his right, or give him disturbance in the government.

This young prince was called Maion, and was conveyed away by his friends to Corcaduibhne, in the west of Munster, where he was entertained for some time by Scoriat, who was the king of that country ; from thence he removed into France, with nine of his friends, (though some antiquaries are of opinion that he went into the country of Armenia,) who, soon after his arrival, discovered to the French king the circumstances of his royal birth, and the tragical history of his misfortunes. The king was so affected with this relation, that he received him into his service, and soon after advanced him to be his general in chief, and fixed him in the command of his whole army. He had by this time his voice restored, and in this post he behaved with so much bravery and conduct, that his character and reputation increased daily, and was carried abroad into all the neighbouring countries, and at length came to the knowledge of the loyal party in Ireland, many of whom resorted to him to avoid the tyranny of the usurper The monarch, Laoghaire Lorck, being murdered, after a short reign of two years, his brother seized upon the crown.

A.M. 3618. Cobhthach Caolmbreag set the crown upon his own head. He was the son of Ugaine More, the son of Eochaidh Buaidhaig, of the royal line of Heremon. Notwithstanding his usurpation, and the disaffection of his subjects he reigned thirty years, and, if we believe some chronicles, he governed the kingdom fifty years. His mother, as was observed before, was the daughter of the king of France. He was known by the name of Cobhthach Caolmbreag, because his body was so macerated and worn away, by envy and ambition, that ne seemed to be a walking shadow : he had no flesh upon his bones, nor scarce any blood in his veins, and the consumption had reduced him to a skeleton ; for the Irish word Caol signifies small and lean, and the place where he resided in his sickness was called Maghbreag, for which reason he had the name of Caolmbreag, After this long reign vengeance overtook him, and he was set upon and slain by Maoin, who was called Labhradh Loingseach, as a just sacrifice to the ghosts of his father and grandfather.

3648. Labhradh Loingseach was his successor. He was a son of Oilioll Aine, son of Laoghaire Lorck, son of Ugaine More ; and wore the crown eighteen years, but fell at last by the sword of Meilge, the son of Cobhthach Caolmbreag. This mon-

rch was a learned and valiant prince, and acquired such repu-
ation when he commanded the army of France, that Moriat,
ie daughter of Scoriat, the king of Fearmorck, in the west of
Lunster, charmed with the relation of his exploits, conceived a
onderful affection for him, and fell desperately in love with
im ; and to discover her passion, and recommend herself to his
iteem, she employed an eminent musician that was then in Ire-
nd, whose name was Craftine, to carry over a letter to France,
ith a noble present of jewels, and to deliver them in a proper
ianner to the general, as a testimony of her love and the value
ie had for him. The musician faithfully executed his message,
id, arriving in France, he found a way to have access to Labh-
idh.   When he was introduced to him, he delivered his cre-
:ntials, and then took out his harp, and played a most ravish-
ig tune, which was the better received because he sung with it
poem that was composed by the young lady in praise of the
:roic actions of the general.   From this happy adventure Labh-
idh resolved to vindicate and prosecute his right to the crown
: Ireland; and when he had communicated his design to some
: the prime ministers of the French court, that were his friends,
id concerned for his interest, they took an opportunity to re-
ind the king of the pretensions of Labhradh to the Irish throne,
id desired he would be pleased to assist him in the recovery of
is right.   The king, convinced of the justice of the cause, com-
lied with their request, and gave immediate orders for a body
: 2200 choice troops to be ready, and a number of ships to trans-
ort them.   With these forces Labhradh set to sea, and landed in
ie harbour of Wexford.   Upon his arrival he had intelligence
iat Cobhthach Caolmbreag, who had usurped the crown, re-
ded at that time at Didhion Riogh, where he kept his court,
:tended by his ministers and nobility who had submitted to his
rranny.   Labhradh resolved if possible to surprise him, and
ierefore marched with all expedition, and came upon him un-
repared, and put the old usurper and all his retinue to the
vord.   He immediately insisted upon his hereditary right, and
as proclaimed king of Ireland.
  After he had killed the tyrant in his own court, surrounded
y his nobles, and cut off all his favourites and attendants, the
ironicles relate, that a certain druid, surprised at the bravery
: this action, asked some of his retinue who was that gallant
ero, who had the policy to design, and the courage to execute
ich an exploit ; he was answered, that the name of the general
as Loingseach.   Can Loingseach speak ? says the soothsayer,

It was replied, he can.; for which reason that monarch was
called by the name of Labhradh Loingseach, for Labhradh in
the Irish language signifies to speak; and by this additional
title was Maoin always distinguished in the history of Ireland,
wherever he is mentioned.

This prince was the inventor of a sort of green-headed par-
tisans, in the Irish called Laighne, and gave orders that they
should be used by his whole army. From these military weapons it was that the inhabitants of the province of Gailean,
now called Leinster, were known by the name of Laighne; as
the poet makes the observation in this manner:

> Two thousand and two hundred of the Gauls,
> With broad green partisans of polish'd steel,
> Landed at Wexford, on the Irish coasts;
> From whence the province, called of old Gailean,
> Obtained the name of Leinster.

When Labhradh had destroyed the tyrant, and fixed himself
in quiet possession of the government, he resolved to make his
addresses to the young princess who so generously offered him
her love, and first inspired him with resolution to vindicate his
right to the crown of Ireland. He therefore waited upon her
with a noble retinue, and took his favourite, Craftine, the musician, with him, and had the happiness to be well received by the
father of the lady, and they were soon married with great
solemnity.

If it should be demanded why this monarch, when he was forced
to fly out of Ireland, chose rather to apply for refuge to the
French court than to retire to any other country, we are to consider, that he was nearly related by blood to the French king;
for it was observed before, that Ceasair Chruthach was a daughter
of a king of France, and was married to Ugaine More, by whom
she had two sons, Laoghaire Lorck and Cobhthach Caolmbreag;
and this prince, whose life we are writing, was the grandson of
Laoghaire Lorck. Another inducement, which prevailed upon
him to fly to France for protection, was, because there was
a very strict league and familiar intercourse between the province
of Leinster and the kingdom of France; and it is observed
that every province of Ireland maintained a correspondence with
the country beyond the seas that was nearest to it. The
O'Neills were in friendship and alliance with Scotland; the
province of Munster with England; the province of Ulster with
Spain; the province of Conacht with Wales; and the province

f Leinster, as before mentioned, with the kingdom of France. 'his friendly intercourse is taken notice of by the famous Torna) Mac Cionaire, who, in his time, was one of the principal poets nd antiquaries of the island. The lines are these :

> Each of the Irish provinces observ'd
> A strict alliance with the neighbouring nations
> O'Neills corresponded with the Scots,
> The men of Munster with the English,
> The inhabitants of Ulster lov'd the Spaniards,
> Of Conacht, lived in friendship with the Britons,
> Of Leinster traded safely with the French.

We are to remark, in this place, that all the princes that go-
erned the province of Leinster, were the lineal descendants of
his Irish monarch Labhradh Loingseach, except O'Nuallain,
rho was of the posterity of Cobhthach Caolmbreag.

From this mutual correspondence and intercourse, kept up
etween the provinces of Ireland and the neighbouring countries,
rose that resemblance to be observed in the carriage and de-
ortment of the Irish with the manners of those adjacent fo-
eigners.

The names of the principal families, that were to be found in
Leinster, are these following: O'Connor Falie, with all the
ranches derived from him, who was descended from Rasa Failge,
he eldest son of Cathaoir More ; the families of the Cavanaghs,
he Murphys, the Tooles, in Irish O'Tuathaill, the O'Branains,
he O'Macgiolla Patricks, in English Fitz Patricks, the O'Dunns,
)'Dempseys, O'Dwyres, O'Ryans, and the several descendants
hat came from them. The greatest part of the inhabitants of
Leinster proceeded from Cathaoir More, but Macgiolla Patrick
id not descend from him ; for the branches parted in Breasal
Breac, the son of Fiachadh Fobharaicc, fourteen generations be-
ore Cathaoir More, including Cathaoir and Breasal. This Brea
al Breac, we are to observe, had two sons, and their names were
Lughaidh Lothfin and Conla. The province of Ulster was di
ided between these brothers : Lughaidh and his posterity pos-
essed the country from the river Bearbha eastwards ; and from
hence westwards to Slighdhala was the portion of Conla and
is descendants. And this division is taken notice of in a
ery ancient poem, which begins in this manner, Naoimsheau-
hus Inis Fail.

> Lughaidh and Conla, princes of renown
> Descended from the valiant Breasal Breac;

> The men of Ossery were derived from Conla;
> And Lughaidh, eldest of the two, began
> The noble family of the O'Dwyres

This ancient tribe of the O'Dwyres was divided in the fifth degree before Cathaoir More, in this manner ; Cathaoir More was the son of Feidhlim Fiorurglas, son of Cormac Gealtagaotn, son of Niachorb, son of Cormac Gealtagaoth, son of Conchorb, who had a son called Cairbre Cluthiochair, who was the great ancestor of this illustrious family. The tribe of the O'Ryans descended from Nathy, son of Criomthun, son of Eana Cinn-sealach, the seventh generation from Cathaoir More. From the second son of Ugaine More, whose name was Cobhthach Caolmbreag, was derived the posterity in general of Sioll Cuin.; and likewise the tribes of Fiachadh Sreabhthine, and Eochaidh Dubhlein, and all other branches of those families that descended from Capa ; as will be more particularly observed when the genealogy of the Milesians comes to be considered.

There is a fable to be met with in the ancient manuscripts of Ireland, that relates to this prince Labhradh Loingseach. No doubt it refers to some very remarkable transactions in his reign, but at this distance of time it is impossible to trace out the moral of it ; every person, therefore, is at liberty to draw what consequences from it he pleases : I shall transcribe it faithfully, observing only that some of the incidents of it are very curious, and because of its antiquity it may not be unworthy of a place in this history.

As the story goes, therefore, this monarch, Labhradh Loingseach, had ears of a very immoderate length, which resembled the ears of a horse ; and, to conceal this deformity from the notice of his subjects, when he had his hair cut, the person that served him in that office was sure to lose his life ; for he was immediately killed, lest he should discover this blemish in the king, and expose him to the contempt and ridicule of his people. It was, therefore, a custom among the hair-cutters of the kingdom, to determine by lots who should succeed in this desperate employment, which always became vacant once every year ; for once within that time the king was constantly used to have his hair cut from below his ears, and by that means exposed the length of them to his barber. It happened that the lot to officiate in this post fell upon a young man, the son of a poor widow, and he was her only child ; the sorrowful mother apprehending the loss of her son, was overwhelmed with grief, and applied herself to the king, lamenting her misfortune, and entreating his roya mercy to spare her child. This moving scene had the effect to obtain the life of the young man ; but it was on this condition, that he would never divulge a secret that should be committed to him, nor reveal what he should observe, under the penalty of forfeiting his life. The young man joyfully complied with these terms, which he thought very favourable and easy to observe, and cut the king's hair ; but, when he discovered his ears, he was somewhat surprised, but outwardly took no notice, yet when he came home he fell desperately sick, (for secrecy it seems was ever a burden,) and was so oppressed with the weight of the discovery he made, that he would admit of no remedy, and was reduced to the very brink of death. His mother, sorely afflicted with this misfortune, applied herself for advice to an eminent druid, who was a physician, in the neighbourhood, who came to the youth, and soon perceived that his distemper was not the effect of a natural cause ; and examining his patient, he told him his art was ineffectual in his cause, for his recovery was impossible, unless he was disburdened of an important secret, which lay heavy upon him. But even the remedy was as bad as the disease, for if he divulged it he was sure to lose his life ; and this miserable difficulty, and the apprehension of death either way, was the true occasion of his sickness. The druid represented the circumstances of the young man to his mother, and by way of remedy, contrived a method between the two extremes, that would answer the purpose and have the desired effect ; he observed to her, that though her son was under strict obligations not to discover the secret to any person living, yet this did not hinder but he might divulge and repeat it in the open air ; and therefore he advised him to go to a neighbouring wood, and, when he came to a meeting of four highways, to turn upon the right hand, and the first tree that he came to, to apply his lips close to it and whisper the secret. The young man exactly followed the prescription of the druid, and a willow tree being the first he came to, he delivered himself of the secret, and found immediate ease, for he soon recovered of the distemper, which began to leave him in his return home.

Soon after this it happened that the harp of Craftine, the king's principal musician, was broke, and he came to this wood to cut down a tree, that was proper to make him a new instrument, and by chance he made choice of the willow that the young hair-cutter had whispered the royal secret to. The musician carried the tree home, and made a harp out of it ; and when it was strung and put in order, it would sound but one tune,

the words of which in Irish are these : Da chluais chapuil ar
Labhradh Loingseach, which is in English, Labhradh Loingseach has the ears of a horse.   This surprised the musician, and
the fame of this wonderful instrument was carried all over the
kingdom ; others of the same profession attempted to touch it,
but it was always in the same tune, which so amazed the king,
that he thought the hand of heaven was concerned in this miracle,
which he believed was sent by the gods, who were offended at
his cruelty, for putting to death so many of the young men of
his kingdom, only to conceal his deformity from his subjects.
And this reflection had that impression upon his mind, that he
repented of the barbarity he had used, and openly exposed his
long ears all his life afterwards.   This relation, though according to the letter of it, it must be false, yet I am apt to believe,
could we come at the genuine moral of it, the circumstances of
the fable would appear very beautiful.

A.M.
3666.
Meilge Malbthach got possession of the throne of Ireland.   He was the son of Cobhthach, son of Cobhthach
Caolmbreagh, of the royal line of Heremon.   His reign
continued seven years, till he was killed by Modhchorb, the
son of Cobhthach Caomh.

3673.
Modhchorb was his successor.   He was the son of
Cobhthach Caomh, son of Reachta Righdearg, son of
Lughaidh Laighe, a prince of the posterity of Heber Fionn,
He governed the kingdom seven years, and was slain by Aongus
Ollamh.

3680.
Aongus Ollamh, son of Oiliolla, son of Labhradh
Loingseach, a descendant from Heremon, succeeded.   He
reigned eighteen years, and fell by the sword of Jeran Gleofathach, son of Meilge.

3698.
Jaran Gleofathach was the succeeding monarch.   He
was the son of Meilge, son of Cobhthach Caolmbreagh,
son of Ugaine More, lineally descended from Heremon.   His
reign continued seven years, and he was slain by Fearchorb, son
of Modhchorb.   The reason why he was distinguished by the
name of Gleofathach was, because he was a person of great
wisdom and judgment, and fine natural parts, which he improved by study, and became a very accomplished prince.

3705.
Fearchorb obtained the crown.   He was the son of
Modhchorb, son of Cobhthach Caomh, of the royal pos-
terity of Heber Fionn, and governed the island eleven years.
He lost his crown and his life by the sword of Conla, the son of
Jaran Gleofath

A.M.
3716.
Conla Cruaidh Cealgach, son of Jaran Gleofathach, son of Meilge, son of Cobhthach Caolmbreag, son ot Ugaine More, a descendant from Heremon, was his successor. He wore the crown four years, but the manner of his death is not recorded in the history of the Irish monarchs. It may be supposed he died naturally, because he was succeeded by his son.

3720.
Oiliolla Caisfhiaclach, son of Conla Cruaidh Cealgach, son of Jaran Gleofathach, of the royal line of Heremon, was the succeeding prince. He reigned over the kingdom twenty-five years, and was slain by Adamhar Foltchaoin, at Tara.

3745.
Adamhar Foltchaoin sat next upon the throne. He was the son of Fearchorb, son of Modhchorb, a lineal descendant from Heber Fionn, and reigned five years

3750
Eochaidh Foltleathan succeeded. He was the son of Oiliolla Caisfhiaclach, son of Conla Cruaidh Cealgach, a prince of the posterity of Heremon, and was monarch of the island eleven years. He was slain by Feargus Fortamhuill.

3761.
Feargus Fortamhuill was his successor. He was the son of Breasal Breac, son of Aongus Gailine, son of Oiliolla Brachain, son of Labhradh Loingseach, descended from the line of Heremon, and reigned twelve years. He was known by the name of Feargus Fortamhuill, because he was a prince of exceeding great strength of body, and brave beyond any of his time, but fell at last by the victorious sword of Aongus Tuirmheach.

3773.
Aongus Tuirmheach got possession of the throne. He was the son of Eochaidh Foltleathan, son of Oiliolla Caisfhiaclach, of the posterity of Heremon. He governed the kingdom thirty years, and according to the computation of other writers, he was monarch sixty years. He was distinguished by the name of Aongus Tuirmheach, on account of the invincible shame he conceived for violating the chastity of his daughter, and getting her with child. He could never bear to be seen publicly, he was so much concerned at that abominable act, though it was committed when he was overcome with wine. The effect of this incestuous crime was a son, whose name was Fiachadh Fearmara. We are to observe, that the word Tuirmheach, in the Irish language, signifies a sense of bashfulness or shame, which gave occasion to the name of that prince. The son the young lady bore him was called Fiachadh Fearmara, because he was conveyed away privately, and exposed in a small boat, without any attendants, to the mercy of the sea, but care was taken to furnish him with very rich mantles, and

N

other conveniencies ; and, to defray the expense of his maintenance and education, there was a number of very valuable jewels
laid by him, which was a testimony of his extraction, and that
he was a child of no ordinary quality.   In this manner the infant was exposed, and must have perished, if the boat had not
soon been discovered, floating on the sea, by a company of fishermen, who instantly made up to it, and took out the distressed
babe, and provided a nurse for him with all the care that the
meanness of their condition was capable of.   This Aongus
Tuirmheach had a son that was legitimate, whose name was Eanda
Aighnach, from whom the tribe of Sioll Cuin in general descended.
This Irish monarch was slain at Tara.

A.M. 3803.   Conall Callamhrach succeeded in the throne. He was
the son of Eidirsgeoil, son of Eochaidh Foltleathan, son
of Oiliolla Caisfhiaclach, descended from the line of Heremon, and governed the kingdom five years.   He was killed
by Niadh Seadhamhuin, a prince of the posterity of Heber Fionn.

3808.   Niadh Seadhamhuin was his successor. He was the
son of Adamhar Foltchaoin, son of Firchorb, descended
from Heber Fionn, and reigned over the island seven years.   In
his reign the wild hinds would come of their own accord from
the woods and mountains, and suffer themselves to be milked as
quietly as cows and the tamest cattle.   They, it seems, were
under the enchantment of a woman, who was the mother of this
monarch, and a sorceress of distinction in those times, whose
name was Fleidhis : but her art could not preserve the life of her
son, for he was slain by Eanda Aighnach.

3815.   Eanda Aighnach obtained the crown.   He was the son
of Aongus Tuirmheach Teamharach, son of Eochaidh
Foltleathan, descended from the royal stem of Heremon, and was
possessed of the government twenty-eight years.   This prince
was called by the additional name of Eanda Aighnach, because
he was of a very bountiful disposition, and exceedingly munificent
in his donations ; for the word Aighnach in the Irish language
signifies liberal, free, and hospitable.   This monarch lost his life
by the hands of Criomhthan Crosgrach.

3843.   Criomhthan Crosgrach filled the throne of Ireland.
He was the son of Feidhlim Fortruin, son of Feargus
Fortamhuill, son of Breasal Breac, of the line of Heremon,
and governed the kingdom seven years.   He was distinguished by the title of Criomhthan Crosgrach, because he behaved
with such bravery at the head of his army, that he was victorious in every battle he fought ; for the Irish word Crosgrach

signifies slaughter and bloodshed. He was slain by Rogerus, the son of Sithry.

A.M. 3850. Rughraidhe, surnamed the Great, was his successor. He was the son of Sithrighe, son of Dubh, son of Fomhar, son of Airgeadmhar, son of Siorlamh, son of Fionn, descended from the illustrious line of Ir, the son of Milesius, king of Spain. He was monarch of the island thirty years; but, if we give credit to another computation, he sat on the throne seventy years, and died a natural death at Airgiodross.

3880. Jonadhmhar, the son of Niaseaghamhuin, son of Adamhar, derived from the princely stock of Heber Fionn, succeeded. He reigned three years, and lost his life by the sword of Breasal Bodhiabha.

3883. Breasal Bodhiabha fixed himself in the government. He was the son of Rughraidhe, son of Sithrighe, son of Dubh, son of Fomhar, son of Airgeadmhar, son of Siorlamh, descended lineally from Ir, the son of Milesius, king of Spain. He was known by the name of Breasal Bodhiabha, because, during his reign, a most pestilential murrain happened, which raged with such fury among the cows and black cattle, that most of them through the whole kingdom died; for the word Bodhiabha, in the Irish language, signifies the mortality of kine or black cattle. This prince, after a reign of eleven years, was killed by Lughaidh Luaghne.

3894. Lughaidh Luaghne seized upon the crown. He was the son of Jonadhmhar, son of Niaseaghamhuin, of the royal posterity of Heber Fionn, and governed the kingdom five years. He was slain by Congall Claringneach,

3899. Congall Claringneach, the son of Rughraidhe, son of Sithrighe, son of Dubh, descended from the line of Ir, the son of Milesius, king of Spain, succeeded. His reign continued thirteen years, and he fell by the sword of Duach Dalta Deaghadh.

3912. Duach Dalta Deaghadh was his successor. He was the son of Carbre Loisgleathan, son of Lughaidh Luaghne, son of Jonadhmhar, of the royal stock of Heber Fionn. He ruled the kingdom of Ireland ten years. This prince was distinguished by the title of Duach Dalta Deaghadh, because his father, Cairbre Loisgleathan, had two sons, the monarch we are speaking of, whose name was Duach, and another that was called Deaghadh. These two brothers were princes of great valour and military conduct and equally worthy of the Irish throne; but the right of succession was invested in Duach,

who was the elder brother, who therefore seized upon the sovereignty, and fixed himself in possession. The younger brother,
Deaghadh, resolved to dispute with him in the field ; and to support his pretensions, raised an army ; but before he had put
himself at the head of his forces, his brother, who was the reigning prince, was advertised of the treason, and sent for him to
court, but in a friendly manner, as if he understood nothing of
his purpose. He accordingly came, and no sooner arrived, but
he was taken into custody, and his eyes put out, to make him
incapable to pursue his ambitious designs ; but still he allowed
him a handsome revenue, and maintained him like a prince all
his lifetime. From this transaction Duach received the additional names of Dalta Deaghadh ; for the word Dalta, in the
Irish language, signifies a foster-father, which this prince was to
his brother Deaghadh, by the care he took of him as long as he
lived. But this method to secure himself in the throne could
not defend him from the attempts of Fachtna Fathach, who
slew him, and reigned after him. This event, concerning the
blindness of Deaghadh, is observed by an ancient poet in these
lines :

> Deaghadh, invited to his brother's court,
> Inhospitably had his eyes scoop'd out ;
> His crimes did scarce deserve a milder fate,
> For treason must be punished without mercy.

**A.M.
3922.** Fachtna Fathach was the succeeding monarch. He
was the son of Rughraidhe, son of Sitrighe, son of Dubh,
son of Fomhar, son of Airgeadmhar, a descendant from
the line of Ir, the son of Milesius, king of Spain, and governed the
kingdom eighteen years. He was known by the name of Fachtna
Fathach, because he was a prince of great learning and wisdom,
and possessed many excellent accomplishments. He established
most wholesome . laws for the government of his people, whom
he ruled with signal prudence and moderation : for the Irish
word Fathach, signifies wisdom or discretion. This monarch,
notwithstanding his princely qualities, was slain by Eochaidh
Feidhlioch.

3940. Eochaidh Feidhlioch filled the throne. He was the
son of Finn, son of Finlogha, son of Roighnein Ruadh,
son of Easamhuin Eamhna, son of Blathachta, son of Labhra
Luirc, son of Eana Aighnach, son of Aongus Tuirmheach, descended from the line of Heremon, and he governed the kingdom
twelve years. The mother of this prince was Benie. the daugh-

ter of Criomthan ; and the reason for which he was known by the name of Eochaidh Feidhlioch was, because he laboured under so melancholy a dejection of spirits, that he was quite oppressed with vapours, and would draw out his sighs to a very immoderate length ; for the word Feil, in the Irish language signifies as much as a great length in English, and Uch or Och is the Irish term for a sigh, which gave occasion to his name. He contracted this sadness of mind upon the loss of three of his sons, who were princes of very promising hopes, but were unfortunately slain in the battle of Dromchriadh, and the habit of sighing that was upon him followed him to his grave. These ...ree brothers were called the three Fineamhnas because they were all born at a birth ; for the word Amaoin, in the Irish tongue, signifies to deny, for none of them ever denied the extraordinary manner of their birth, but took pleasure upon all occasions to relate the circumstances of it. The names of these young princes were Breas, Nar, and Lothar, and their mother was Clothfionn, a very virtuous lady, and the daughter of Eochaidh Uchtleathan.

This monarch, Eochaidh Feidhlioch, was the first that laid out the division of the Irish provinces. The province of Conacht he divided into three parts, between three of his favourites ; their names were Fiodhach, son of Feig, Eochaidh Allat, and Tinne, the sons of Conrach ; he conferred upon Fiodhach all the country from a place called Fiodhach, to Limerick ; upon Eochaidh Allat he bestowed the territory from Jorrus Domhnan and Galway to Daibh and Drobhaois ; to Tinne, the son of Conrach Magh Sambh, he gave the tract of land that extends from Fiodhach to Teamhair Broghaniadh ; he likewise gave him possession of all the ancient territories of Taodin. Feargus, the son of Leighe, was settled by his authority in the province of Ulster : he invested Rossa, the son of Feargus Fairge, in the province of Leinster ; the two provinces of Munster he bestowed upon Tighernach Teadhbheamach and Deagbadah ; and this division and investiture of the country continued during his whole reign.

Eochaidh, after he had thus divided the kingdom, went into Conacht, for he determined to erect a royal palace in that province, and there to keep his court. Upon his arrival he summoned the three petty princes of the province to attend him, and, informing them of his design, required that they should agree upon a proper place for the building of this fabric, where he resolved to fix his residence. Two of these princes, Eochaidh Allat, and Fiodhaidh, absolutely refused to comply with his demand, and told him to his face, that the revenue which belonged to their share of the country, and what taxes and contributions fell to them, they would pay as usual into the royal exchequer at Tara; but the third prince, who was Tinne, the son of Conrach, being a courtier, made an offer of any part of his country for the king to build upon; which compliance of his so pleased the king, that he bestowed upon him his daughter, a very beautiful lady, whose name was Meidhbh, whom he soon married, with the consent of the princess; and in a short time he had, by the nobleness of his carriage, and his other princely accomplishments, so recommended himself to the favour and esteem of the king, that he conceived a very great affection for him, and admitted him in all his councils of state, made an inviolable league and friendship with him, and advanced him to be prime minister of the kingdom.

It being agreed that a royal palace should be erected in the province of Conacht, the king consulted with his druids and soothsayers what parts of the country would be most propitious for the undertaking. They immediately had recourse to their art, and found that Druin na ndruagh now called Cruachan, was the most proper and fortunate place for this royal building. The plan was drawn by the most eminent architects, and they set about the work with such application, that the ditch, which was very large and to surround the whole pile, was finished within the compass of one day. This fabric went under the name of Rath Eochaidh, and was likewise called Rath Cruachan.

Upon the marriage of Tinne with this Irish princess, the king bestowed upon him the sovereignty over all the province of Conacht, and made him the king of it: and a difference arising between him and one of the petty princes, Eochaidh Allat, he slew him in an engagement, and gave away his share of the province to Oilioll Fionn. Meidhbh who was called queen of Conacht, made a present of the palace of Rath Eochaidh to her mother, whose name was Cruachan Crodhearg; from whom that royal structure changed its name, and is called Rath Cruachan to this day. This transaction is delivered down to posterity, by a very ancient poet, in this manner: .

> The royal palace of Rath Eochaidh,
> Was called Druim Druagh and Tuluig Aidhne;
> But afterwards obtained a nobler name,
> Of Rath Cruachan, from the virtuous lady
> Cruachan Crodhearg.

Tinne, the son of Conrach, reigned with his queen Meidhbh for many years over the province of Conacht, but he was at last slain at Tara, by Monuidhir, otherwise called Maceacht. After his decease Meidhbh administered the government for ten years; then she married Oilioll More, the son of Rossa Ruadh, who came out of Leinster; but it is supposed he was born in Conacht, for his mother, whose name was Matha Muireasg, was originally a lady of that province; she bore seven sons to Oilioll More, who were distinguished by the name of the seven Maine; her husband was at length run through with a lance by Conall Cearnach, notwithstanding he was of a great age. The place where this act was committed was Cruachan; but the inhabitants, and the neighbouring people were so alarmed at this murder, that the whole country of Conacht were up in arms, and made so close a pursuit after Conall Cearnach, that they overtook and killed him, in revenge for the death of Oilioll More, who was very much esteemed in that province.

After the death of Oilioll More the government returned a second time into the hands of Meidhbh; and, whilst she was a widow, and the queen of Conacht, there arose a most unhappy difference between her subjects and the inhabitants of Ulster, over which province Connor was then king, This contest broke out into open hostilities, and occasioned a long war. But to give a particular relation of these occurrences, I am obliged to trace the account of them to the very beginning, and to particularly take notice of the death of the three sons of Visneach, which was the true cause that gave birth to these fatal commotions.

Connor, who at that time was possessed of the government of Ulster, being invited to a splendid entertainment at the house of one Feidhlim, the son of Doill, principal secretary of state to the king, it happened that the wife of Feidhlim fell in labour and was delivered of a daughter. An eminent druid, that always attended the king's person, being present at the feast, by his prophetic skill foretold, that the child just born should occasion great disturbances in the province of Conacht, and turn the government into confusion. This prediction surprised the nobility and the great officers that waited upon the king, who unanimously advised, that the public welfare required that the child should be immediately destroyed. But Connor opposed this resolution, and persuaded them to spare the life of the infant; for that he would take care to disappoint the accomplishment of the prophecy, by breeding up the child under his own

inspection, and, perhaps, when she arrived at maturity of years
he might think it proper to make her his wife; by which means
he diverted the nobles from their purpose, and preserved the
child; and, as he undertook the education of the girl, immediately removed her from her father's house, and carried her to
his own court. The druid insisted upon the truth and authority
of his prediction, and called the child by the name of Deirdre.

To secure the infant, and to prevent the consequences of the
druid's prophecy, the king conveyed her to one of the strongest
garrisons in his province, and placed her in a well fortified tower,
almost inaccessible; and gave strict orders, that none should be
admitted within the child's apartment but her necessary attendants, and a woman, who was the favourite of the king's, whose
name was Leabharcham. This woman, who was a great poetess
and could deliver verses extempore on any subject, was much
respected by the nobility of the country.

Within the walls of this castle was the young Deirdre confined till she became marriageable; and as she grew up she appeared to be a lady of singular beauty, and those who had the
care of her education had been so faithful to their trust, that
she was the most genteel and accomplished person in the whole
kingdom.

It happened that, as Deirdre and her governess were looking
out of the window, upon a snowy day, they saw a slaughter-man
of the garrison killing a calf, for the use of her table, and some
of the blood fell upon the snow, when a raven came and fed upon
it. This sight occasioned a strange passion in the young lady,
for notwithstanding her confinement she was of a very amorous
disposition, and, turning to Leabharcham, "Oh," says she, "that
I could but be so happy as to be in the arms of a man, who
was of the three colours I now see; I mean, who had a skin as
white as the driven snow, hair as shining black as the feathers
of a raven, and a blooming red in his cheeks as deep as the calf's
blood." Her governess was at first surprised at this uncommon
wish; but, out of tenderness to the young lady, for whom she
had an unalterable affection, she told her, that there was a young
gentleman, belonging to the court, exactly agreeing with that
description, whose name was Naois, the son of Visneach, Deirdre began immediately to be in love with him, and begged of Leabharcham that she would contrive a method to bring him privately into the castle, and introduce him into her apartment,
for she was passionately charmed with his features and complexion, and was in torment till she saw him. The indulgent

governess promised she would ease her of her pain upon the first opportunity; and in a short time found means to inform Naois, the young gentleman, of the love of the lady; and assured him, that if he had gallantry enough to venture his person, she would find means to convey him into the tower, and give him possession of one of the finest women in the world. It was impossible for the young Naois to withstand so generous an offer; and soon after, by the policy of Leabharcham, he got within the garrison, and was conveyed into the lady's chamber, where after many endearments, and solemn protestations of love, she entreated that he would deliver her from confinement, and remove her out of the castle.

The lover promised he would release her, or die in the attempt; but the enterprise was of the utmost danger, for the tower was well fortified, and strictly guarded. He therefore communicated his design to his brothers Ainle and Ardan, who generously resolved to support him, and, with the assistance of 150 resolute soldiers, they surprised the garrison, and carried off the damsel. They immediately left the country, and fled to the sea coasts, and upon the first opportunity they went on board, and arrived safely in Scotland.

Upon their arrival the king of Scotland received them hospitably; and when he understood the quality of his new guests, he settled a revenue upon Naois and his followers; but he was soon informed of the beauty of the young lady, which left such an impression upon him that he resolved to force her from the arms of her husband, and, if he met with opposition, to run the utmost hazard to obtain her. Naois was made acquainted with his design, and put himself into a posture of defence. There were many skirmishes and engagements between the king's troops and the Irish, but at last Naois was forced to fly, and with his wife and followers got possession of an adjacent island, expecting to be instantly attacked. In this distress he sent to some of his friends, among the nobility of Ulster, for a supply of forces; and his request was so favourably received, that the principal nobility of the province interceded with king Connor that they should be relieved, and have liberty to return to their own country; for they said it would be barbarous to suffer the three sons of Visneach to be destroyed upon the account of a lewd woman. Connor seemingly consented, and complied with this representation of his nobles, and, as a testimony that he had no treacherous design upon the three brothers when they returned, condescended to deliver two of his favou   into the hands of some of the friends of Naois, and his followers, as hostages for their security.   The names of these two princes were Feargus, the son of Roigh, and Cormac Conloingios.   Depending upon the honour and sincerity of the king, Feargus, the son of Roigh, sent his own son, with a sufficient number of forces, to relieve Naois, which was soon accomplished ; and he brought Naois, his wife, his brothers and followers with him, safely into Ireland.

The king, when he had notice of their landing, despatched Eogan, the son of Durtheacht, who was the principal commander of Fearmoighe, to conduct the three brothers to Eamhain ; but gave him secret orders to fall upon them in the way, and kill every man of them.   Eogan met with the sons of Visneach in the plains of Eamhain ; and, when he fixed his eyes upon Naois, who was in the front, he advanced towards him, as if he designed to salute and congratulate him upon his return to Ulster, but he suddenly thrust him through with a spear, and he fell dead upon the spot.   This action was so treacherous in itself, and was so resented by Fiachadh, the son of Feargus, who was sent to assist those distressed Irish, and bring them into their own country, that he attacked Eogan with all his might, but with ill fortune to himself, for he was thrust through the body, and died instantly.   Animated with this success, Eogan, who was, it must be confessed, a person of singular bravery, fell upon the two brothers, the remaining sons of Visneach, and slew them likewise, and routed all the forces they had, then seizing upon the unfortunate Deirdre, he carried her to the court of Connor, the king of Ulster.

One of the two hostages for the king's honour, whose name was Feargus, the son of Roigh, was so incensed at this breach of faith, that he resolved to revenge it upon the king, especially because his son Fiachadh, who was sent to conduct those distressed Irish, was treacherously slain.   He communicated his design to Dubthaig, who accepted of the proposal ; accordingly they raised a large body of resolute troops, and advanced towards Eamhain, where the king was.   Connor was not to be surprised, therefore opposed them with all his forces, and a most bloody fight followed, wherein Maine, one of the king's sons, was killed, with 300 of his choicest men, and the flower of all his army.   This defeat gave the victors an opportunity to seize upon the palace of Eamhain, which they plundered, and put all they met to the sword, not sparing the ladies of the seraglio, whom the king kept for his own pleasure

Cormac Conloingios, we have observed, was the other hostage. He likewise raised a body of stout men among his friends, to the number of 3000, and marched with them into the province of Conacht, then under the government of Queen Meidhbh. From this queen they met with kind reception, and continued under her protection for some time; but in the night they would send strong detachments into the province of Ulster, to burn and ravage the country, which they harassed with such dreadful hostilities, that the inhabitants, and the fruits and provisions of the whole province, were in a manner all destroyed by fire and sword. The country of Crioch Cuailgne particularly suffered in these calamities, which was the cause of those contests and heart-burnings kept up between the two provinces for seven years afterwards.

During the time of those provincial wars it was, that Feargus, the son of Roigh, found means to insinuate himself into the affections of Meidhbh, the queen of Conacht, who proved with child by him, and was delivered of three boys at a birth. The names of these three princes were Ciar, Corc, and Conmac; as the poet has long since related in this manner.

The valiant prince, Feargus, son of Roigh
Was master of the charms of Meidhbh Cruachna,
Who bore him three sons, whose names in history
Are Ciar, Corc, and Conmac.

From these three brothers it is certain, that some families of principal distinction in Ireland derive their extraction. Ciar, the eldest brother, gave name to Ciaruidh, that is, Kerry, in the province of Munster: and the excellent O'Connor, of Kerry, is a descendant of some of his posterity. Corcamruidh was so called from Corc, and from him is derived the illustrious O'Connor, of Corcamruidhe; and from Conmac sprang all the worthy families of the Comaicnies, in Conacht. And to illustrate this with more authority, I refer to a very ancient poem, composed by Lughair, an eminent poet and antiquary, the first verse begins thus, Clann Feargusa clann os Caoh; where it appears evidently, that the three sons of Meidhbh obtained possessions and authority, as well in the province of Conacht, as in Munster, which may be farther proved by observing, that the countries in those two provinces are known by the names of these princes to this day.

The unfortunate Deirdre, who, as the prediction foretold, was the unhappy occasion of all these calamities was confined by

Connor, the king of Ulster, one whole year, after the death of her husband and the tribe of Visneach ; in which time she was so afflicted with the loss of her beloved Naois, that she was perfectly inconsolable ; she never raised up her head, nor was seen to smile, but was almost distracted with grief, and would admit of no comfort. The king was moved with a sense of her misfortunes. for she was beautiful in her tears, and, after he had tried in vain to mitigate her sorrow, he sent for the perfidious Eogan, son of Durcheacht, the chief commander of Fearmoighe, who was the executioner of her husband, and to torment her the more, made a present of her to him, to be used at his pleasure. She was immediately put into the chariot along with him, who resolved to carry her to one of his seats in the country, there to be confined a close prisoner. The cruel Connor vouchsafed to ride a few miles with his favourite general, in order to secure his prey, which so enraged the distracted Deirdre, that she took an opportunity to discover her anger, by looking upon them both with such sternness and indignation, that the king took notice of her, and told her, that the cast of her eyes between them two was like the look of a sheep between two rams. This remark so incensed the poor lady, that she started out of the chariot, and fell with such violence upon her head that she beat out her brains, and instantly died. And this is the account given by the records of Ireland, concerning the banishment of Feargus, the son of Roigh, of Cormac Conloingios and Dubthaig Daoluladh, and the miserable death of the unfortunate Deirdre.

We have observed before, that Connor was king of Ulster at the time when Meidhbh was possessed of the government of Conacht ; which province was under the power of that princess for many years, for she reigned after the death of Tinne, son of Conrach, who was her first husband, ten years ; she was the wife of Oilioll More eight years, and, after his decease, continued eight years a widow, but at last was slain by Ferbhuidhe, the son of Connor. This princess's reign was ennobled by many memorable transactions, and produced many eminent personages, whose brave exploits deserve a place in this history. I shall, therefore, for the sake of posterity, give an account of some of their heroic exploits and military achievements ; and to observe an order in this relation, I am obliged to take notice of the death of Connor, king of Ulster. which was brought about in this manner.

AN ACCOUNT OF THE DEATH OF CONNOR, KING OF ULSTER.

It was one of the commendable customs of the ancient Irish to encourage the youth of the kingdom, and train them up in a military life, that they might defend their country in time of distress, and make conquests, and become formidable abroad. To incite their valour, and to inspire them with generous and warlike sentiments, it was established, that whoever was the victor in single combat, should be distinguished with the spoils of the vanquished as a trophy and testimony of his bravery. This honour and encouragement was the occasion of violent contests and disputes, and stirred up an emulation in the minds of the youth, which seldom ended without duelling and bloodshed. The principal heroes in these times, were Connall Cearnach, Congcuillin, and Laoghre Buadhach, in Eamhain. The first of these champions insisted upon a pre-eminence above the other two ; and to convince them that he was of superior courage, he commanded the brains of a great soldier, called Meisgeadhra, to be brought as an evidence of his merits : this Meisgeadhra had the character of one of the bravest persons in the island, and had distinguished himself upon all occasions, but was killed in a trial of skill, by Connall Cearnach. Congcuillin and Laoghre Buadhach being satisfied of the truth of this victory, submitted, and gave up their pretensions to the laurel ; for they thought it in vain to contend with so illustrious a champion, who had slain the best swordsman of the age.

The reason why this great hero called for the brains of his adversary, in proof of his courage, was, in compliance with a remarkable custom in those times, that whenever a champion overcame his adversary in single combat, he took out his brains, and, by mixing them with lime, made a round ball, which by drying in the sun became exceeding solid and hard, and was always roduced in public meetings and conventions, as an honourable istinction, and a trophy of experienced valour and certain vicory.

At this time it happened that there were two natural fools belonging to the court of Connor, king of Ulster ; and this prince, having in his possession one of these noble badges, made of the brains of Meisgeadhra, took great care to preserve it, which the fools taking notice of, supposed it to be of great value, and therefore resolved to steal it out of the palace. This trophy was then lodged in one of the royal seats of Ulster called Craobh Dhearg Besides this there were three stately fabrics in that province ;

the principal was the palace of Eamhain, where the kings of Ulster generally resided and kept their court. Adjoining to this stately fabric was the lodge of Teagh na Craoibhe Ruadhe, which, in English, signifies the house of the red branch, where the most renowned champions lodged their arms, and hung up their honourable trophies, and the spoils they had taken in the wars, when they came off victorious over foreign enemies. The third building of note was the royal hospital of Broinbhearg, which signifies the house of sorrow and affliction; for here the sick and wounded were provided for and supported till they were perfectly cured. The champions, whose trophies and arms were placed in the palace of Teagh na Craoibhe Ruadhe, were distinguished by the title of Champions of the red branch, and were known by that name in foreign countries; for they were a military order of brave soldiers, whose courage had obtained them an honourable character over all the western part of the world.

This palace being the place appointed to preserve the most valuable jewels and monumental trophies of the kingdom, this ball of brains was there laid up for security; but the two fools above-mentioned, observing where it was, found means to convey it away undiscovered. When they had it in their possession, they immediately went to the green of Eamhain, and began to play and divert themselves, by tossing it in the air from one to another. As they were sporting upon the green, a very eminent hero of those times, whose name was Ceat, the son of Magach, happened to come by. This champion belonged to the province of Conacht, and was an implacable enemy to the government of Ulster; he rode up to the fools, and, finding they were diverting themselves with one of these military trophies, he prevailed upon them to give him the ball, which he carried with him into his own province.

The contests and disputes among the men of Ulster and the inhabitants of Conacht, broke out some time before into open hostilities, and there were many battles fought between the two provinces; and this Ceat, by way of insult to his enemies, when he came into the field, would threaten them with this ball of brains, which he always tied to his belt, and which, according to an old prediction, was some time or other to be of fatal consequence to the province of Ulster. The prophecy it seems foretold that Meisgeadhra, of whose brains this ball was composed, should, after his death, be fully revenged upon the men of Ulster, for the indignities he had suffered from them; and Ceat, obtaining this trophy by stratagem, always wore it about him, being persuaded that the prediction would be accomplished by him; for he resolved upon the first opportunity to enter the lists with the boldest champion of Ulster, and this ball of brains was the weapon he chiefly designed to use in the combat.

The war was still carried on with vigour between the two princes, and Ceat, at the head of a powerful army, made incursions, entering the province of Ulster with fire and sword, plundered the country, and drove away all their cattle. These hostilities enraged Connor, who drew together all his forces, and, supported by a well-disciplined army, marched with all possible expedition towards the enemy, and resolved to give them battle. By this time Ceat had received a choice body of recruits from the province of Conacht, and with these reinforcements he drew up, and both armies were prepared to engage.

But Ceat was unwilling to come to a decisive battle with Connor, and therefore contrived a statagem to surprise and destroy him without fighting. It seems that most of the principal ladies of Conacht were standing upon the top of a hill, viewing the two armies, expecting the event of the battle. It was resolved that these women should send a messenger to Connor, as if they had something of importance to communicate, and desired he would be pleased to come to them ; for no danger could be apprehended from a company of women, and therefore his person was secure. Connor being a prince of great gallan-try, fell into the snare, and accepted the invitation ; confiding in the honour of the ladies, with great indiscretion, he went to the top of the hill, without his guards, and unattended. He immediately paid his compliments to the ladies, but the treacherous Ceat had found a way to conceal himself in the company, and, observing his opportunity, placed his ball of brains in a sling, with a design to discharge it at the king of Ulster, and so by killing him put an end to the war ; but Connor perceiving the villany, immediately retired towards his forces. Ceat pursued him close, and, overtaking him at Doire da Bha-oith, he let fly, and was so sure of his mark, that he hit Connor full on his head, and broke his skull. His army, perceiving him in this distress, hastened to relieve him, which forced Ceat to make his way towards his troops, and so by flight preserved his life.

The ball of brains made a contusion in the head of Connor, and when one of the principal surgeons was sent for, whose name was Fighnin Faithaig, he found that the wound was of dangerous consequence, though, if the nobles would give their consent he promised to use the utmost of his skill in the operation, and, if possible, to preserve his life. The nobility and principal officers that were attending, readily agreed to this proposal; for they said that the happiness of the whole province depended upon the king's life, and they were sensible that, though the sacred person of the king must be hazarded in the attempt, yet a desperate case would admit of no cure but what was desperate The wound, however, was in a short time cured, by the care and skill of this surgeon: but it had such effect upon the brain, that, upon the least passion or heat of the spirits, it was in danger of breaking out again, and a relapse might be attended with very fatal consequences. Fighnin, therefore, thought it his duty to represent the truth of the case to Connor, and advised him, in a submissive manner, to avoid all immoderate exercise, that might disorder or put his blood into a ferment, particularly not to ride hard, or be incontinent any way, but to keep his spirits cool and in a proper motion.

The king strictly observed the directions of the surgeon; for the violence of heat or passion would force the wound open and by that means bring his life into the utmost danger; and in this state Connor continued for seven years, to the great joy of his subjects, till (as some of the Irish chronicles, though of no great authority, assert) the Friday on which our Saviour was crucified; and then the king, being surprised at the dreadful and supernatural eclipse, and shocked at the horrid darkness and convulsion of nature, that followed the death of the Son of God, consulted with one Bacrach, an eminent druid of Leinster, to know the occasion and design of that wonderful event. The pagan prophet replied, that the cause of those strange and violent alterations arose from a barbarous murder that day committed by the wicked Jews, upon a most innocent and divine person, Jesus Christ, the Son of the everlasting God. The king resented that inhuman act with such passion, that he cried out, if he were a spectator of the villany, he would be revenged upon those barbarous Jews, who had the insolence to destroy his Lord, the Son of the great God of the whole earth. He immediately drew his sword, and went to an adjacent grove, and, distracted almost to madness at the thoughts of that abominable act, he hacked and cut the trees, protesting, if he were in the country of the Jews where this holy person was executed, he would be revenged upon his murderers, and chop them to pieces as he did those trees; and by the violence of his anger, his blood and spirits were disordered and fermented, which had that effect, that the wound burst open, and some of his brains followed, so that he died upon the spot. The grove of trees where this accident happened was called Coill Lamhruadhe, from the hand of this Connor, king of Ulster.

After the death of this prince there was some dispute about the succession, which was at last accommodated by this resolution, that whoever would undertake to carry the body of Connor from the place where it lay to the palace of Eamhain, without resting by the way, should succeed to the throne of Ulster. This proposal worked upon the ambition of a footman that belonged to the deceased king, whose name was Ceann Bearruidhe, who, encouraged with the prospect of wearing a crown, resolved to try his fortune, though he died in the attempt; and therefore he took the body, that was of a great weight, upon his shoulders, but when he came to the top of Sliabh Fuaid, he sunk under the burden, for his heart was broke, and he died instantly. And from this transaction there arose a proverbial saying in the country, when a person undertakes a trust or charge upon himself that he is unable to manage, he miscarried like the government of Ceann Bearruidhe, whose ambition put him upon this desperate attempt, which cost him his life.

But the authors, who deliver this account of Connor, king of Ulster, are not to be respected, when they contradict the more solemn testimony of the Irish records, which assert directly that Connor was dead long before the birth of Christ. It must be confessed that some circumstances of the above-mentioned relation are supported by good authority; for it is certain that Bacrach, a famous druid of Leinster, did prophecy to the people of that province, and foretel that a most holy and divine person should be born in a wonderful manner, and be barbarously murdered by the great council of his own nation, notwithstanding his design of coming into the world was for the happiness and salvation of the whole earth, and to redeem them from the delusions and tyranny of infernal demons, whose office was to torture them with insupportable pains in a future state. And these cruel and ungrateful indignities, that were to be offered to this innocent and god-like man, made such an impression upon Connor, that he was overcome with indignation and resentment, and, drawing his sword, he hacked and chopped the wood like a person distracted, which so inflamed his spirits that the ball of brains dropped off, and he fell down dead. But the death of this king happened long before Christ was born, and therefore that circumstance of the history must be false

o

If it should be thought incredible that a pagan prophet should be so inspired as to foretel the birth and the crucifixion of Christ, I desire that it might be considered that Almighty God, to accomplish the ends of His all-wise designs, might, if He pleased, vouchsafe such a measure of inspiration to a pagan as to be able to deliver such a prediction ; and, as an evidence upon this occasion, the oracles of those heathen prophetesses called sybils will prove that the circumstances of Christ's birth and passion have been foretold by those who knew nothing of the true God, but lived in the dark ages of ignorance and idolatry.

AN ACCOUNT OF THE DEATH OF CEAT, THE SON OF MAGACH.

This Ceat was the general over the army of Conacht, and was one of the most celebrated champions of those times : he seldom failed of victory when he engaged, and was so inveterate an enemy to the men of Ulster, that by his frequent inroads and cruelties he had almost ruined the whole province. He plundered and spoiled the country wherever he came, and so harassed the inhabitants, that his name was a terror to them ; for he had often routed them in the field, and under his oppression they became a miserable and dispirited people. It happened that this hero of Conacht made incursions into Ulster in the time of winter, when the country was covered with deep snow ; he had met with some opposition, but after many skirmishes and engagements he obtained his purposes, and by his conduct and bravery was returning home loaden with spoils. In this expedition he had fought three of the stoutest champions of Ulster, and killed them in single combat, and designed to carry their heads with him into Conacht, but in his march he was pursued by Connall Cearnach, who overtook him at Athceitt, and offering him battle, a most bloody action followed, in which Ceat was slain by the general of Ulster ; but he sold his life dearly, for in the engagement Connall himself was so desperately wounded, and lost so much blood, that he fell down in a swoon, upon the very spot where the combat was fought. In this fainting state he was found by another renowned swordsman of Conacht, whose name was Bealchu Breifne, who, perceiving the wounds of one of the combatants, and that the other was killed outright, was pleased with the sight, and said that he never received more satisfaction in his lifetime than he enjoyed at present; for two implacable competitors, whose ambition had involved the whole kingdom of Ireland in confusion, and had occasioned so much bloodshed, were destroyed by one another, and met with a fate suitable to their deserts. Connall was so incensed by being insulted in this manner, that he desired Bealchu to despatch him at once out of his misery, for his reflections were insupportable; and he chose rather to die by his hand, because it would vindicate and raise his character, for then it could not be said, with justice, that he fell by the sword of one man, but two champions of Conacht overcame him. But Bealchu generously spared his life, and with great honour assured him that he would not only give him his life, which he thought could not continue long, but he would endeavour to recover him of his wounds, and, when he was perfectly cured, he would fight him in single combat, and give him satisfaction; and accordingly he saved him from the fury of the soldiers, and took him with him in his chariot. The most eminent surgeons of the kingdom were ordered to attend him, and to take care of his wounds, which by proper skill and application were soon healed, and Connall obtained his perfect health.

But Bealchu observing that Connall so suddenly recovered, and enjoyed his full strength and former activity, was afraid to fight him fairly, but resolved to dispatch him another way; and accordingly he fixed upon his own sons for the executioners, who by agreement were to surprise him in the dead of the night, and murder him in his bed. But Connall was acquainted with this treacherous design soon enough to prevent it; and therefore upon the night when this barbarous act was to be committed, he boldly addressed himself to Bealchu, and desired him to change beds with him, or he would instantly take away his life. Bealchu was unwilling to gratify his request; but, when he considered the case, he complied, and accordingly went to the bed where Connall lay, and Connall removed into his bed. In the night the ruffians entered the room, and fell upon their own father through mistake, and killed him. Connall, observing his opportunity, rushed upon them by surprise, and slew the three brothers. He took their heads and that of their father along with him, and soon after arrived at the palace of Eamhain, where he related the particulars of the adventure, and exposed the heads of his enemies, as infallible proofs of his courage and success. This transaction is transmitted to posterity, by a very old poet, in this manner:

Connall Cearnach was renowned in arms,
And, with a courage not to be subdued,
He fell upon the ruffians in the chamber,
Three brothers, sons of Bealchu Breifne,
And slew them all.

In this manner died Bealchu Breifne, who was a person of
great bravery, and his three sons, who were to be the executioners
of the illustrious Connall ; and the account which I have given,
contains likewise the particulars of Ceat's death, the son of Magach.   I could set off this history with many great actions in
chivalry, performed by this valiant knight Connall, what combats
he fought, and victories he won, were it consistent with my present design ; but I observe, in short, that the Irish records make
very honourable mention of this champion, and speak of him
with the greatest applause, as the best swordsman, and the invincible hero of the western world.

AN ACCOUNT OF THE DEATH OF FEARGUS, THE SON OF ROIGH.

It has been observed before, that Feargus underwent a volun-
tary exile in the province of Conacht, and retired to Oilioll and
Meidhbh at the royal castle of Mayeo.   During his banishment
it happened that the king and queen and their guest were walk·
ing, in the summer season, upon the bank of a lake that was
near the palace ; Oilioll desired Feargus to strip himself, and divert him by swimming the lake, Feargus complied, and when he
was undressed he plunged into the water.   The sight of so comely
a person naked had that effect upon the queen, that she longed
to be near him, and desired leave from her husband to bathe
herself, for the weather was exceeding hot, and promised to bathe
in a secret and distant part of the lake.   He thought himself
secure of the honour of his wife, and therefore, to please her
humour, he gave his consent.   She immediately retired to a private place, and, after having undressed, jumped in ; but, being
very expert in swimming, she could not though in the sight of
her husband, forbear approaching the gallant Feargus, which so
enraged the jealous Oilioll, that he commanded a kinsman of his,
who was one of the retinne, to throw a partisan, that he had
in his hand with all his violence at Feargus ; which he did
with such dexterity, that he wounded him sorely in the body, but
did not disable him from making to shore, though the wound
was exceeding painful, and proved mortal.   When he came

to land he twisted the spear out of his body, and flung it with all his might at Oilioll, but missed his mark, and pierced a greyhound to the ground, that stood near the chariot of the king so that it died upon the spot. Feargus, after he had thrown the javelin, fainted with the loss of blood, and, falling to the ground, immediately expired, and was buried upon the bank of the lake. This unfortunate prince was a person of consummate courage, and had exerted himself often with applause in single combat and the field of battle. He it was that killed Fachtna, the son of Connor; and those formidable champions, Geirgin, the son of Nialladha, and Owen, the son of Durtheachta, the brave commander of Fearmoighe, felt the metal of his sword. He likewise foiled many resolute swordsmen, whose names, and the accounts of their combats, it would be tedious to mention: but we are not to forget what rich spoils he brought away from Ulster, and how he ravaged and sacked the country, and over-run the province with fire and sword, insomuch, that the calamities he brought upon the people of Ulster were not repaired in many years; for the strangers, who followed the fortune of this prince, were for seven, or as others assert, ten years plundering the country, which reduced the inhabitants to the extremest misery. These incursions were occasioned by the treacherous death of the sons of Visneach, who were barbarously slain; which cruelty the men of Conacht undertook to revenge, but they met with great opposition in their hostilities, for the forces of Ulster would often penetrate into the province of Conacht, and captivate the people, and carry off very considerable booty. This enmity and heart-burning produced perpetual wars between the two provinces, which were waged with different success, but brought such insupportable calamities upon the people, that whole volumes have been written upon the miseries that attended these commotions; but the nature of this history will not admit of a particular account, but requires other matters to be considered of more importance to the present design.

AN ACCOUNT OF THE DEATH OF LAOGHAIRE BUADHAIG.

That famous prince, Connor, king of Ulster, retained a poet in his court, whose name was Hugh, the son of Ainin, who was suspected to be very intimate with the queen, and to hold a criminal correspondence with her. This intrigue was discovered at length to the king, who, enraged at the baseness of the action, gave immediate orders that the poet should be drowned in a pond that was adjacent to the house of Laoghaire Buadhaig. The command was instantly obeyed, and the poet was seized and designed for execution, but the principal shepherd of Laoghaire was resolved to prevent the sentence, and boldly asked the guards that attended, whether they could find no place more proper to drown the poet than before the door of his master, and declared he would prevent it as far as his life went, because it would occasion a fright, and give great offence to the family. Laoghaire, hearing the debates, and observing there was more than a common disturbance, started up in haste, and, in running out, struck his head against the upper part of the door, which with the violence of the blow, fractured his skull; but the wound was not immediately mortal, for he lived to call his servants about him, who fell bravely upon the king's guards, and those who attended the execution, and, putting them to flight, he obtained his purpose, and saved the life of the poet; but he did not survive this action, for after the encounter he died upon the spot. This was the unfortunate end of Laoghaire Buadhaig, as Irish chronicles expressly assert.

AN ACCOUNT OF THE DEATH OF MEIDHBH CRUACHNA.

Oilioll More, the husband of Meidhbh, being killed by the hand of Connall Cearnach, Meidhbh removed her place of residence to Inis Chroithoin, situated upon the bank of the lake Ribh; and, having the conveniency of a sweet water, she used in the summer mornings to retire into the pond, and divert and refresh herself by swimming. Forbuidhe, the son of Connor king of Ulster, being a prince of very severe resentment. hearing of this custom of the queen, found means privately to come to the lake, and with a line he had for that purpose, he measured the exact distance between the one side and the other, where Inis Cloithroin formerly stood, and returned back to Ulster undiscovered. As soon as he arrived, he drove two stakes of wood into the ground, at the same distance with the length of the line which measured the breadth of the lake; and when he had placed an apple at the top of the stakes, he stood at the other, and for some time made it his practice to cast a stone at the apple with a sling. He used this exercise so long till he could fling to the greatest nicety, and became so dexterous, that he never missed his mark. At that time there was an appointed meeting between the principal inhabitants of Ulster and Conacht, upon one side of the river Shannon, at Inis Cloithroin. It was to compose some differences between the two provinces; and Forbuidhe, the son of Connor, came with his father's deputies, and was the principal person in the management of the treaty. This he thought was a proper time to execute his design against the queen of Conacht; and an immediate opportunity offered to accomplish his purpose, for the queen, according to custom, came in the morning to divert herself in the lake, and when she was in the water, Forbuidhe flung a stone at her with his sling, and was so expert in the art, that he smote her full in the forehead when, sinking to the bottom, she died instantly. In this manner fell this heroic queen, after she had enjoyed the government of Conacht ninety-eight years, as before mentioned. It was thought proper to give an account of the death of some of the most illustrious princes of the island, and of the memorable exploits and achievements of those brave persons that were called the champions of the western isle; and this was thought the most proper place to introduce these transactions, because they happened in the reign of Meidhbh, queen of Conacht. But lest it should be thought a digression, if we stay too long upon this subject, we shall return and take notice of the children of Eochaidh Feidhlioch, who makes so great a figure in the Irish history.

This prince, Eochaidh Feidhlioch, had three sons and three daughters; the names of his three sons were Breas, Nar, and Lughair, and the three daughters were known by the names of Eithne Vathach, Clothra, and Meidhbh Cruachna. A very ancient poet gives the same account, which authority is sufficient for us to follow.

> The valiant Eochaidh Feidhlioch
> Left three fair daughters of his royal line,
> Each would adorn a monarch's nuptial bed,
> Their names were Eithne Vathach, Meidhbh, and Clothra.

A FARTHER ACCOUNT OF THE EXPLOITS OF CONNOR, KING OF ULSTER.

This prince is so honourably mentioned by the historians of Ireland, that it would be injustice to his memory, as well as to posterity, to rob the world of any of those memorable actions, which so eminently distinguish this prince in the ancient records of the kingdom. It must be observed, therefore, that Neasa, the daughter of Eochaidh Salbuidhe, was mother of this excellent monarch; and wherever we find his genealogy, he is always said to be Connor, the son of Neasa, &c. His father was Fachtna Fathach, the son of Caia, son of Rughraidh, a descendant from the royal line of Ir, the son of Milesius, king of Spain. One of the daughters of Connor was married to Carbre Niadfar, king of Leinster, who, to obtain her, made over part of his own dominions to her father; and when the provincialists insisted upon laying out the distinct bounds of each province, it appeared that a great part of Leinster was claimed by Connor, king of Ulster, as settled by the marriage of his daughter; and he added to his own territories all the country from Loch an Choigeadh and Teamhair, that is, Tara, to the main ocean. This tract of the island is known to include three complete territories; as a poet of great antiquity observes in the following lines:

> Connor enlarged the bounds of his command;
> And, as a dowry for his daughter's beauty,
> Obtain'd three fruitful tracts of land from Leinster,
> And join'd them to his own dominions

The name of the lady who procured these three territories for Connor, the king of Ulster, was Feidhlin Nuadhcrothach; but she had more regard for the grandeur of her own family than for the honour of her husband or her own character, for she found means to make her escape, and fled from Leinster, with a young gallant called Connall Cearnach.

Connor, notwithstanding his own accomplishments, by one action obscured the glory of his reign; for upon a time, when he had drank to excess, he attempted familiarity, and had the misfortune to be allowed to commit incest with his own mother, Neasa; which abominable crime produced a son, whose name was Cormac Conloingios. But the vengeance of Heaven severely punished the mother, who was most concerned in the guilt of this wickedness, with the loss of all her other children, except these three sons, who died without issue; the names of the surviving three were Beanna, from whom Beantry obtained its name; Lamha, who gave the name to Lamhruidhe; and Glaisne, from whom Glasruidhe is derived: and to perpetuate the infamy of that unnatural act, Providence, as our Irish annals inform us, has taken care that at this day there is not one descendant, even from these three, living upon the face of the earth.

AN ACCOUNT OF THE DEATH OF CONLAOCH, SON OF CONGCULIONN.

The Irish records deliver these particulars concerning the death of Conlaoch. Congculionn, it seems, discovered a martial disposition, and delighed in arms from his youth ; and, to perfect himself in the discipline of war, he went into Scotland, where there was a lady of masculine bravery and great experi ence, whose name was Sgathach, and to her he applied to be instructed in the exercise of his weapons, under whose care and inspection he soon improved, and became one of the most accomplished warriors of his time. But the soft passion of love notwithstanding, found a way into the heart of the young sol- lier ; for there was a most beautiful young lady in Scotland, whose name was Aoife, the daughter of Ardgeine, who was so charmed with the comeliness of his person, and the generous manner of his deportment, that she conceived the most violent passion for him, which she soon found means to acquaint him with. The cavalier with great gallantry accepted of her love ; and upon the first sight of her was moved with the most tender sentiments, and though he had not any opportunity of marry- ing her, yet he attempted the lady's virtue, who yielded upon the first summons, and she proved with child by him. He now began to think of returning into Ireland, and, taking leave of the distressed Aoife, he gave her a chain of gold, and charged her to keep it safely, till the child, if it proved a son, came to the estate of a man ; and then he ordered her to send him to Ireland with that token, by which he should discover him to be his son, and promised that as such he would entertain him but withal he gave her this injunction particularly, that she should lay the strictest command upon him to observe her direc tions in three things : the first, that he should never give the way to any person living, but rather die than be obliged to turn oack : the second, not to refuse a challenge from the boldest champion alive, but to fight him at all hazards, if he was sure to lose his life : the third, not to confess his name upon any account, though threatened with death for concealing it. These obligations she was to lay upon him with a parent's authority, which she promised to execute faithfully, and with these assur- ances Congculionn returned to Ireland.

The unfortunate Aoife was soon after delivered of a son, who was named Conlaoch. whom she carefully educated, and, when he came of age, she placed him under the tuition of Sgathach, the virago of Scotland, to be instructed in the use of arms, and in the art of war and military discipline. He discovered the same genius with his father, and when he had finished his exercises with applause, his mother, as she was ordered, sent him into Ireland to Congculionn.

As soon as he arrived upon the coasts, he resolved to go directly to the court of Connor, king of Ulster, which was then kept at a seat called Thracht Eise, because that was the most convenient place for the reception of his principal nobility and commons, who were then assembled to debate upon some important affairs that related to the government of the province. When the young cavalier appeared at court, Connor sent one of his commanding officers to inquire who he was, and upon what business he came; but the stranger resolved to observe the commands of his mother, and refused absolutely to give him satisfaction upon that head, and declared that his name was not of much importance, but he would not discover it to the stoutest man living. The messenger, whose name was Cuinnire, surprised at this insolent answer, returned to the king, and related what had happened. Congculionn was at that time at court, and, willing to be fully satisfied who this stranger was, desired leave to go to him, saying he did not doubt of giving the king a good account of him. He was accordingly sent, with a full commission to use him as he pleased, and to force him, if he continued obstinate, into compliance and good manners. When he came he demanded, with an air of authority, what his name was; but the stranger would by no means give him satisfaction, which so enraged his father, whose passion had overcome his reason, that he struck at him with his lance, and a most desperate combat followed between the two champions, the father and the son, equally brave and expert in the management of their arms. They fought a considerable time with doubtful success; at last Congculionn, unable to sustain the force of his son's youthful heart, who charged him briskly, was obliged to give way, and, notwithstanding he had fought so many duels killed many renowned swordsmen, and understood his weapons as well as any man living, and had courage to use them, yet he engaged with a young hero of superior strength, who pressed him very hard, and forced him to take the refuge of a ford to defend his life. He was perfectly distracted with this repulse, and, forgetting the reason of his quarrel, which should have engaged him to receive the stranger with the greatest tenderness and honour, he called to an officer that belonged to him, and was a spectator of the combat, to give him the spear called in the Irish language Gai Builg, with which he was sure to destroy his adversary, and put an end to the dispute. His friend, whose name was Laoigh, the son of Righe Gabhra, finding him in distress, and close pursued, gave him the weapon, which Congculionn instantly threw with all his might, and pierced the unfortunate Conlaoch through the body; which decided the fortune of the combat, for the young hero fell dead upon the spot by the hands of his own father.

It were easy to enlarge and set off this history with numerous relations of adventures of this nature, between the most renowned champions of those warlike ages. I could, if my bounds would allow me, give an account of the death of Congculionn, who was slain by the children of Cailetin; in what manner the brave Feardia, the son of Domhnoin, was killed by Congculionn, and how the seven brothers, who were called the Maines, and were the sons of Oilioll More, and the famous Meidhbh, queen of Connacht, lost their lives. These, and many more transactions, that relate to Congculionn, and other champions of those times, might be particularly mentioned; but volumes would not contain all the military exploits of the Irish heroes, and therefore they are not to be expected within the compass of this history; but whoever desires to be acquainted with those illustrious events may, if he understands the ancient language of the country, have recourse to manuscripts, that are now preserved in the kingdom of Ireland, and whose authority was never yet questioned. They are of easy access to the curious, and the antiquaries are glad of the opportunity of communicating them. The books, which treat of the actions of these heroes, are these, Brislioch Muigh Muirtheimhne, Oideadh na gcurruidhe, Tain bo Cuailgne, Tain bo seaghamhain deargruathar Chonuill Chearnuig, Feis Eamhnr tain bo Fleidhis, and many others upon the same subject.

But notwithstanding the bounds set to this history, it will be of some use to take notice of the death of a most distinguished champion, whose fame is alive to this day among the Irish, his name was Conrigh, the son of Daire; and what makes it proper to introduce this transaction at this time is, because this valiant hero was cotemporary with Connor, king of Ulster, and was one of the most eminent warriors of the age. The mother of this illustrious person was Morann Manannach, the daughter of Ir, the son of Virsighe, and sister to Eochaidh Eichbheoil; and this account we receive from a poet of great antiquity, in the following manner;

The virtuous lady, Morann Mananrach,
Daughter of valiant Ir, son of Virsigbe,
Sister to Eochaidh Eichbheoil.
Was mother of the most courageous Conrigh
The son of Daire.

It must be observed, that there were three principal tribes, or orders of knights, or renowned champions in Ireland, at that time, that were the bravest persons of the age they lived in, and were so confessed by all nations abroad ; for their valour, their tallness, and the proportion of their bodies, were made the wonder of all foreign countries, and their exploits are not to be paralleled in history ; nor was the famed Fionn of Leinster able to engage any of them. The first tribe of these warriors was called, the Champions of the Red Branch, in the Irish language Curruidhe na Croibhe Ruadhe ; and these were under the command of Connor, king of Ulster. The second order was those who had the government of Jorrus Domhnoinn, in Conacht ; and the master of these knights was Oilioll Fionn. The third consisted of a select family of hereditary courage, called The shildren of Deaghdha, who were under the authority of Conrigh, the son of Daire, and they had their residence in the west of Munster. These tribes were the most celebrated heroes of those times ; and they were never to be overcome by all the shampions of the world, nor could they be conquered, unless they quarrelled among themselves, and by that means fell by each other's arms.

A PARTICULAR ACCOUNT OF THE DEATH OF CONRIGH, THE SON OF DAIRE.

Notwithstanding the bravery of this great warrior, his death was brought about in this manner ; as the genuine records of Ireland particularly mention. It happened that the champions of Craobh Ruadh, or the Red Branch, had intelligence of a rich island near the coast of Scotland, that abounded with gold, silver, jewels, and other valuable commodities, which they resolved to attack and plunder, and return home laden with spoils ; and, as an inducement to sharpen their courage, they had heard that there was a most beautiful maiden lady in the island, who exceeded all the women of her time, the daughter of the governor of the country, and her name was Blanaid. Conrigh, understanding that the knights of the Red Branch were going upon this design, and had made themselves ready for the expedition, had recourse to his necromantic art, in which he was very expert, and which was a polite study in those times ; and by the assistance of his skill he transformed himself into a disguised shape, so that nobody knew him ; and under this cover he conveyed himself on shipboard, and landed with them upon the island.

When they arrived, they found the inhabitants in a consternation, and for security, and to prevent surprise, the governor had removed his daughter, and her jewels, and the most valuable treasure of the country, into a strong castle, well fortified, and almost impossible to be stormed ; and what added to the difficulty, the defenders of it were almost as skilful in magic as the besiegers, and summoned all their art to defend the castle. There were several attempts made by the Irish without, but with no success ; and, after some fruitless assaults, they began to despair of accomplishing their design, and had some thoughts of quitting the island. But Conrigh, in the habit of a mean person, in a gray habit, whose heart was fixed upon the young lady, conveyed himself among the commanding officers, who were debating the matter in a council of war ; and when he found they resolved to break up the siege, boldly, and with a good grace, opposed their return to Ireland before they had taken the castle ; and engaged, under the penalty of losing his life, that, if he would give him the liberty of choosing one of the jewels within the garrison, he would soon make them masters of it, and they might plunder it at their pleasure. Congcullionn, who was the Irish general, joyfully accepted the proposal, and promised him upon his honour he should have his choice of the plunder, and the liberty to take which jewel he pleased. Upon this security Conrigh put himself at the head of the troops, for he was to command in the assault, and, advancing to the walls of the castle, he thought it rashness to depend wholly upon the bravery of his forces, and therefore made use of his necromantic art, which had that effect as to stop the motion of an enchanted wheel that was placed at the castle gate to prevent the entrance of the besiegers. When he had removed this difficulty, he forced the gate, and made way for the whole army, who entered, and put all the enclosed islanders to the sword, except the beautiful Blanaid. They plundered the fort of all the riches and jewels they could find, and, with great treasure and valuable spoils, they returned to their shipping, and went on board and landed in Ireland.

They directed their way towards Eamhain, and when they came there they resolved to divide the prey they had taken.

Conrigh, in his gray habit, applied himself to the general for his choice of what jewel he pleased, which he obliged himself upon honour to allow him. Congculionn made no objection; and Conrigh immediately took the young lady by the hand, and said, this is the jewel I choose as a reward for all my services. The general, who had depended upon her for himself, resolved to sacrifice his honour to his love; and, forcing the lady from him, told him he had deceived him by the manner of his expression, and that he would stand by the contract only in the sense he understood it, which was, that he might choose which of the precious stones he would, and that he might do if he pleased; but he would not deliver up the lady, neither did the laws of honour oblige him to it. This answer surprised Conrigh, who upbraided the general with the breach of his word, and resolved upon the first opportunity to seize her, and to convey her out of his reach; and he found means to effect this in a short time, for though he was not able to accomplish it by force, yet his magical art never failed him, and by enchantment he stole away the damsel unperceived, and carried her off. Congculionn soon perceived his fair plunder was gone; and the man in the gray habit being missing at the same time, he began to suspect that Conrigh, the son of Daire, made use of that disguise to steal her away, and instantly ordered messengers every way to pursue them; and he himself, by good fortune, set out towards Munster, and overtook Conrigh at Solochoid. He commanded him to give up the lady; but Conrigh had more gallantry than to comply, and told him that they would decide their pretensions in single combat, and the victor should claim the lady as his prize. Congculionn accepted of the challenge; and the rivals fought desperately, and the victory was a long time doubtful, but Conrigh proved the happy man, and overcame the general, whom he used in an ignominious, and, were it not the custom of the country, in an ungenerous manner; for he tied him neck and heels, and, what was the greatest testimony of disgrace, he cut off his hair with his sword, and left him in a very deplorable condition. When he had secured his rival, and exposed him to all imaginable shame, he pursued his journey and came with his fair jewel into the west of Munster.

He had no sooner left the place of combat, but Laoigh, the son of Riogh an Gabhra, a servant to Congculionn, came up to his master, and, when he had unbound him, took care of his wounds, and they retired with all possible expedition into the wilderness of Ulster, near a place called Beanaibh Boirche; and

In this solitude the disgraced general, attended with his man, continued for the space of a year ; in which time they never appeared in public, but lived privately, and concealed them-selves from the knowledge of the inhabitants. And the reason of this resolution was, because it was a sign of cowardice, and the most infamous scandal to a champion or a professed soldier to be without his hair. When the year was expired, Congculionn, as he wandered about, came to the top of Binn Boirche, and, looking about him, he observed a great flight of large black birds, flying from the north sea, and landing upon the shore. He immediately advanced towards them, and with an engine called Taithbheim, he pursued them incessantly day and night, and killed a bird of them in every county of the kingdom, till he came to Srabh Broinn, in the west of Munster.

In his return he was surprised with the sight of the beautiful Blanaid, near the bank of Fionnglaise, a river in the county of Kerry, where Conrigh had a noble seat, and lived in great state and magnificence. Congculionn addressed himself to her, and she immediately knew him ; and, after they had conversed for a short time, the lady could not forbear confessing she loved him above all men living, and entreated him to believe it was against her consent she was divorced from him ; and therefore desired that, about the next Allhallow-tide, he would come with an armed force, and deliver her from the tyranny of a man whom she hated, and she would take care that Conrigh should have no guards about him to oppose the design, which she was confident, if he had but the courage to attempt, she could assure him of success. Conculionn gallantly promised that he should be prepared for the adventure by that time, and depended upon her management for the happy issue of it, and with the most endearing expres-sions on both sides they took their leave. He directly went to the court of Connor, king of Ulster, to whom he communicated the engagements he was under to the lady, and entreated that he would supply him with a sufficient number of troops for the pur-pose. The king approved of his design, and promised him all suitable assistance and protection.

In the meantime Blanaid, the better to carry on the intrigue, and make it safe for her lover, advised Conrigh, over whom she had great influence, to erect a stately palace for his residence, that should exceed all the buildings in the kingdom ; and to make it more noble, and the better to provide materials, she thought it not improper, since he was in peace with his neighbours, to employ his soldiery, who were distinguished by the name of Clana

Deagha, to gather all the stones of a larger size, that stood up-right, for the foundation of the building, with design that all the experienced warriors that belonged to Conrigh, should be dis-persed over the kingdom, at the time that Congculionn pro-mised to relieve her and carry her off. The unfortunate husband deceived by this stratagem, complied, and gave immediate orders that all his forces should scatter themselves over the country, to collect stones for the fabric ; and his commands were obeyed, for he did not reserve so much as a troop to guard his person, or to imploy upon any emergencies of the government.

The news that Conrigh had sent away his army, was soon conveyed to Congculionn, who thought this time the most proper to execute his purpose, especially since the forces made up of the Clana Deagha were likewise removed ; for these made up a formida-ble band, and were some of the bravest soldiers in the world. He accordingly put himself at the head of a resolute body of troops, that were given him by Connor, king of Ulster, and began his march. He soon arrived near the seat of Conrigh, and privately lodged his men in a thick wood near the palace. His first busi-ness was, to dispatch a messenger to Blanaid, to notify his arri-val with a sufficient force to carry her off, which he would attempt in whatever manner she proposed. The lady was transported with the news, and sent him word, that she would take care Con-righ should be unable to make opposition for she would steal his sword ; and that he should know what time was the most proper to attack the palace by this sign : there was a brook, which ran from the seat where Conrigh lived, through the wood where Cong-culionn had encamped ; into this rivulet she proposed to pour a large quantity of milk, sufficient to discolour the stream, and Congculionn was to observe when the water ran white, and im-mediately to draw out his men and break into the castle. The messenger returned, and the general, strictly observing the di-rections, discovered the brook to be white with milk, when, sallying out, he forced his way into the palace without opposition, and slew Conrigh, who had not so much as a sword for his defence, otherwise he would have sold his life dearly. Blanaid threw her-self into the arms of the conqueror, who carried her away with him into Ulster. The rivulet obtained its name from this me-morable transaction ; and from the whiteness of the water, oc-casioned by the milk, was called Fionnglaise ; for the word Fionn, in the Irish language, signifies white, and Glaise is the same with the word brook, and by joining both words they form Fionn-glaise.

But the perfidious Blanaid did not long survive her treachery; for the unhappy Conrigh retained a poet in his court, whose name was Feircheirtne, who pursued the conqueror and his mistress into Ulster, resolving to sacrifice the base woman to the ghost of his murdered master. When he arrived he found Congculionn and Blanaird, with many of the principal nobility, attending upon Connor, the king of that province, who diverted himself by walking upon the top of a very steep rock, called in the Irish language Rinchin Beara. The poet, watching his opportunity, observed Blanaid standing upon the very edge of the cliff, and addressing himself, as if he made his compliment to her, he seized upon her violently, with all his force, and, clasping her in his arms, he threw himself headlong with her down the precipice, and they were both dashed to pieces.

I shall no longer interrupt the connexion of this history, by relating the heroic exploits and achievements of the ancient worthies of Ireland; but so much was thought proper to be observed, as a specimen of the bravery of those ancient champions, and to convince posterity, that the ancestors of the genuine Irish were a warlike and generous people, and deserve to have their names and their actions recorded for their own honour, and for the example and improvement of future ages. I shall now proceed regularly to the successive reigns of the Irish monarchs.

A.M. 3952. Eochaidh, who had the surname of Aireamh, succeeded in the throne. This prince was the son of Fin, son of Finloga, son of Roighnein Ruadh, son of Easamuin Lamhna, son of Blathachta, son of Labhra Lorc, a descendant from the royal line of Heremon, and governed the island twelve years. He was distinguished by the name of Eochaidh Aireamh, because it was he that first introduced the custom of burying the dead in graves dug within the earth, for the Irish word Aireamh signifies a grave. The Milesians, and their posterity, before the reign of this monarch, were used to cover their dead by raising great heaps of stones over their bodies, which practice this prince abolished, as not so decent and secure. He lost his life by Siodhmali, at Freamhain Teabhtha.

3964. Eidersgeoil was his successor. He was the son of Eogan, son of Oilioll, son of Jar, son of Deagha, son of Suin, son of Roisin, son of Trein, son of Rothrein, son of Airindil, son of Maide, son of Forgu, son of Fearadhach, son of Oiliolla Euron, son of Fiacha Fearmara, son of Aongus Tuirmheach, son of Eochaidh Foitleathan, of the posterity of Heremon, and wore the crown six years, but was killed by Nuaghadh Neacht, at Aillin.

Nuaghadh Neacht was the succeeding monarch. He was A.M. 3970. the son of Seadna Siothbach, son of Lughaidh Loitfin, son of Breasal Breac, son of Fiacuadh Fiorbric, son of Oiliolla Glas, son of Fearaidhach Foglas, son of Nuaghat Follamhain, son of Alloid, son of Art, son of Criomthan Cosgrach, son of Fearaidhach Fionn, son of Breasal Breagamhuin, son of Aongus Gailine, descended from the line of Heremon, and reigned but half a year. He was known by the name of Nuaghadh Neacht, from the Latin word Nix, which signifies snow; for his skin was so exceeding white as to be compared to the driven snow. This prince fell by the sword of Conaire, the son of Eidersgeoil.

3970. Conaire, who was surnamed the Great, seized upon the government. He was the son of Eidersgeoil, son of Eogan, son of Oiliolla, descended from the line of Heremon, and filled the throne thirty years, or, if we believe another computation, he reigned seventy years. It is to be observed, that from this monarch the noble families of the Earnighs, in Munster, and of the Dailriadhs, in Scotland, descended. The Earnighs first went into Munster, in the time of Duach Dalta Deaghadh ; and the occasion of their settling there, as the ancient poet Cormac Mac Cuillenan records, in his Psalter of Cashel, was the superior force of the Clana Rughraidhe, of the posterity of Ir, the son of Milesius. who expelled them out of their former possessions, and routed them in eight several engagements, which forced them to fly for refuge into Munster, where they became powerful, and got large estates ; and they flourished in this province, from the time of Duach Dalta Deaghadh to the reign of Mogha Nuagat, insomuch that they were obliged to extend their settlements ; and in process of time they spread themselves westwards of Iverahagh, and from thence to the western islands in Munster, as the history of that province particularly mentions. This tribe arrived to so great authority, as to take upon themselves the command of the whole country, which they governed till the reign of Mogha Nuagat, by whom they were expelled, and forced to seek new habitations. Conaire, the monarch of Ireland, was deprived of his crown and his life, by Aingeal Caol, son of the king of Wales.

4000. Lughaidh Riabhdearg filled the throne. He was the son of Fineamhnas, son of Eochaidh Feidhlioch, son of Fian, son of Finlogha, descended from the royal line of Heremon, and reigned over the kingdom twenty years. This monarch entered into alliance with the king of Denmark, whose daughter, Dcarborguill, hc obtained for his wife. He received the title of Lughaidh Riabhdearg on the account of two red circles, one of which encompassed his neck, the other surrounded his body. Upon some discontent he put an end to his own life, by falling upon his sword. There is an account to be met with in some of the Irish chronicles, that this prince was begot by three brothers, by committing incest with their own sister, when they were intoxicated with wine ; the brothers and sister, as the same authority asserts, were the children of Eochaidh Feidhliooh, one of the kings of Ireland.

A.M. 4020. Connor Abhradhruadh succeeded in the government. He was the son of Feargus Fairge, son of Nuaghadh Neacht, son of Seadna Siothbhaic, a prince of the posterity of Heremon, and wore the crown but one year. The reason why he was distinguished by the name of Abhradhruadh was, because the hair of his eye-brows was red ; for the Irish word Abhradhruadh signifies red eye-brows.

4020. Criomhthan Niadhnar was his successor He was the son of Lughaidh Riabhdearg, descended from the line of Heremon, and reigned monarch of the island sixteen years. He was known by the name of Criomthan Niadhnar, because he was one of the bravest and most victorious champions of the age he lived in ; for in the Irish language the word Niadh signifies a bold hero. It was in the twelfth year of the reign of this prince that Jesus Christ, the Saviour of the world, was born. His death was occasioned by an unfortunate fall from his horse.

A.D. 4. Fearaidhach Fionfachtnach obtained the government. He was the son of Criomthan Niadhnar, son of Lughaidh Riabhdearg, of the posterity of the line of Heremon, and he reigned twenty years. His mother was Nar Tath Chaoch, daughter of Laoch, son of Daire, who lived in the land of the Picts, or Scotland. He was distinguished by the honourable title of Fearaidhach Fionfachtnach, because he was a prince of strict justice, and governed his subjects with equity and moderation all his reign ; for the Irish word Fachtnach signifies just and equitable ; and he had the most lawful claim to that title, for a monarch of more integrity and virtue never sat upon the throne of Ireland. In the reign of this prince it was, that Moran, the son of Maoin, lived, and was the chief justice of the kingdom. He was called, by way of eminence, the just judge ; and he was the first that wore the wonderful collar, called in the Irish language Jadh Morain. This collar was attended with a most surprising virtue · for if it was tied about the neck of a wicked judge, who intended to pronounce false judgment, it would immediately shrink, and contract itself close, and almost stop the breath ; but if the person that wore it changed his resolution, and resolved sincerely to be just in his sentence, it would instantly enlarge itself, and hang loose about the neck. This miraculous collar was also used to prove the integrity of the witnesses who were to give evidence in the court of judicature ; and if it were tied about the neck of a person who designed to give a false testimony, it would wonderfully shrink close, and extort the truth, or continue contracting itself till it had throttled him. And from this practice arose the custom, in the judicatories of the kingdom, for the judge, when he suspected the veracity of a witness, and proposed to terrify him to give true evidence, to charge him solemnly to speak the truth, for his life was in danger if he falsified, because the fatal collar, the Jadh Morain, was about his neck, and would inexorably proceed to execution. This Fearaidhach Fionfachtnach died a natural death at Liatrym.

A.D. 24. Fiachadh Fion, from whom descended lineally the Dial Fiathach, was the succeeding monarch. He was the son of Daire, son of Dluthig, son of Deitsin, son of Eochaidh, son of Suin, son of Rosin, derived from the princely stock of Heremon. He sat upon the throne three years, and fell by the sword of Fiachadh Fionoluidh.

27. Fiachadh Fionoluidh was his successor. He was the son of Fearaidhach Fionfachtnach, descended from the posterity of Heremon, and governed the kingdom twenty-seven years. He was called the prince of the white cows ; and the reason of this distinction was, because all the time of his reign the greatest number of the cows were white over all the kingdom : this gave him the name of Fionoluidh ; for the word Fionoluidh, in the Irish language signifies white cows, Fionn is the same as white, and Oluidh is in the English a cow. It must be observed in this place, that the Chronicle of Stow asserts, that the Scots had possessed themselves of the kingdom of Scotland in the year of our redemption 73, which was before Carbre Riada was born. This Fiachadh was murdered by the plebeians of Ireland, called Aitheach Tuatha.

54. Cairbre Cinncait filled the throne. He was the son of Dubthaig son of Rughraidhe, son of Diochuin, son of Tait, son of Luighre, son of Oiris, son of Earnduilbh, son of Rionoil, son of the king of Denmark, who came into Ireland with Labhra Loingseach, to the fort of Tuama Teanbhoith ; and he

sat upon the throne five years. He was, as some of the chronicles assert, descended from the posterity of the Firbolgs, and was known by the name of Cairbre Cinncait, because his ears were of an uncommon shape, and resembled the ears of a cat. This prince fixed himself in the government by one of the most barbarous acts of treason that is to be met with in history. The manner was thus.

There was a conspiracy formed by the common people of the kingdom, the ordinary mechanics and meanest of the plebeians, to dethrone the reigning monarch, to murder the nobility and gentry, and by that means to seize upon the government. To accomplish their design, which was carried on with the utmost secrecy, they resolved to provide a most magnificent entertainment, and to invite the king, the petty princes, and the nobility and gentry of the kingdom, to a feast that was to be celebrated at a place called Magh Cru, in the province of Conacht. This feast was three years in making ready, for they could not furnish suitable provision for so numerous an assembly in less time; and within that space the conspirators reserved and laid up the third part of their corn, and other necessaries, to furnish the entertainment. When everything was thus prepared, with great state and plenty, the king and princes, the nobility and gentry of the island were invited, and fatally accepted the invitation, to their own ruin. The principal guest was Fiachaidh Fionoluidh, the monarch of Ireland, who brought his queen along with him, her name was Eithne, daughter to the king of Scotland; the second in quality was Feidh, son of Fidheigh Chaoich, king of Munster, who had his wife with him, whose name was Beartha, daughter to the king of Wales; the third was Breasal, the son of Firb, king of Ulster, his wife likewise was present at the entertainment, and her name was Aine, daughter of the king of England. These princes were attended with a numerous and splendid retinue, which consisted of the prime nobility and gentry of the kingdom.

There were three persons particularly, who were the ringleaders and principally directed this conspiracy: their names were Monarch, Buan, and Cairbre Cinncait, that usurped the government of Ireland, who was the chief traitor, and by his wicked policy contrived the entertainment. The feast continued for the space of nine days in great splendour, and when that time was expired, the plebeians, and the vilest scum of the people, led on by their generals, fell suddenly upon the royal guests, the nobility, and all the company, and put them to the sword, without distinction,

except the three queens, who by good providence were all big
with child, and moved the compassion of the traitors : but they
resolved not to trust long to their mercy, for upon the first opportunity they made their escape, and landed safely in Scotland.
Here they fell in travail, and each of them was delivered of a son,
whose names were Tuathal Teachtmar, Tiobruide Tirioch, and
Corbulan.

These confusions so distressed the people, that they were reduced to the utmost extremities, and to a state of despondency :
they had no encouragement to follow their business and occupations ; the fields lay unmanured; and a most desperate famine
followed.   These were the effects of the usurpation, which at
last opened the eyes of the inhabitants, who began to inquire
after the young princes, and resolved to restore them to their
just rights.   When they had intelligence that they were in Scotland, they invited them in the most submissive manner to return to their country, and deliver their subjects out of the
hands of those tyrants, who had oppressed them for many years ;
and they promised to vindicate their titles, and put them in
possession of their crowns.   The princes, unwilling to rely wholly
upon the loyal tenders of the unsteady populace, would not accept of the invitation, unless they would bind themselves by an
oath of allegiance. to continue in their obedience, which they
willingly submitted to ; and accordingly the exiled kings returned into Ireland, where they were received by the general
acclamations of the people, the tyrants were destroyed, the country was restored to its former state of plenty and happiness, and
a final end put to usurpation.

Since we are relating the lives of the ancient monarchs, it may
not be improper to obviate an objection that might be offered,
concerning the genealogy of these princes ; for if it should be
thought surprising, that the Irish writers of late ages deduce
the descent of the kings, either from the sons of Milesius, or
from Lughaidh, the son of Ith ; and likewise if it should seem
unaccountable, that the principal families of Ireland to this day
derive their original from some of the branches of the Milesian
line, without owning themselves to be the descendants of any
officer or other soldier, who came over in this expedition, and.
it may be presumed, left a posterity behind them.   In answer
to these difficulties, it must be observed, that the ancient records of the kingdom, particularly the books that treat of the
reigns and conquests of the kings, take express notice of the
ruin and extirpation of the posterity of the Milesian soldiery ;

for in process of time they degenerated into a barbarous and rebellious race of men, and used their princes in the most seditious and inhuman manner; for which turbulent and disloyal practices the monarchs by degrees weeded them out of the kingdom; and those few that remained, were so vile and infamous, that the antiquaries never preserved their genealogies but passed them over in oblivion, as a reproach and scandal to the Irish nation. But to return to our history.

A.D. 59.

Elim obtained the government of the island. He was the son of Conragh, son of Rughruidhe, son of Sithrighe, son of Dubh, son of Fomhoir, of the royal line of Ir, the son of Milesius, king of Spain, and reigned twenty years, but was at length slain by Tuathal Teachtmar, at the battle of Aichle.

79.

Tuathal Teachtmhar was his successor. He was the son of Fiachadh Fionoluidh, son of Fearaidhach Fionfachtnach, son of Criomthan Niadhnar, of the posterity of Heremon, and filled the throne thirty years. He received the name of Tuathal Teachtmhar from the state of plenty and public prosperity which he settled over the whole kingdom, by succeeding in the government; for the word Teachtmhar, in the Irish language, signifies fruitfulness and prosperity. This Tuathal Teachtmhar was the only child of Fiachadh Fionoluidh, and his mother was big with child of him when she was forced to fly into Scotland, some time after the bloody massacre of Magh Cru, in Conacht, when the plebeians rebelled, and, by murdering the reigning princes, the nobility and gentry of the kingdom, seized upon the government. The mother of this monarch took great care of his education, and brought him up suitable to his quality till he was twenty-five years of age. It has been observed before, that the kingdom of Ireland suffered great calamities under the tyranny of the usurpers, and was particularly distressed by a sore and long famine: these miseries at length roused up the spirits of the people, who applied themselves to their learned druids and soothsayers to know the cause of their misfortunes, and what remedy would be effectual to redress them. The priests had recourse to their art, and upon consultation they found that the cause of all their afflictions was the barbarous murder of the kings, the nobility and gentry, and the expulsion of the lawful heirs; and therefore they told the plebeians, that nothing could atone to heaven for their disloyalty and barbarities and remove the famine out of the land, but a resolution to return to their allegiance, to recall their exiled monarch, and to establish him upon the throne of his ancestors, which was the only method to recover the state out of confusion, and settle the tranquillity of the nation. The plebeians, reduced to the last extremity by want, were pleased with this answer, and finding upon inquiry that Fiachadh Fionoluidh had a son in Scotland, whose name was Tuathal, they consulted together to send messengers to Scotland, with a tender of their loyalty, and an offer to fix the injured king upon the throne of his progenitors.

And to favour the restoration of this young prince, there were some of the nobility and gentry remaining in the country, who had the fortune not to be present at the entertainment when the massacre was committed. These were upon all occasions promoting the interest of Tuathal Teachtmhar, and disposing the people to insist upon his return : the chief of them was Clanduin Deasuig, out of Leinster.

But there were two gentlemen, Fiachadh Caisin, and Fionmal his cousin, who signally distinguished themselves, in these dangerous times, against the party of the usurpers ; for they raised five hundred resolute men, and when they were well armed and disciplined, they ranged about the country spoiling and killing the plebeian rebels in all parts of the kingdom, which was a great support to the royal cause, and by degrees so dispirited the malcontents that they began to long for a change of government, and passionately desired a revolution.

The messengers of the people arriving in Scotland, delivered their credentials to Tuathal Teachtmhar, who being informed of the deplorable state of his oppressed country, resolved to attempt a recovery of his right, and abolish the tyranny of the usurpers. Accordingly he went on board with all possible, expedition, and, taking his mother with him, who was Eithne, the daughter of the king of Scotland, and a strong body of old experienced soldiers, landed safely at Jorris Domhrionn. Here he met with the loyal party of forces, headed by the brave Fiachadh Caisin, who were plundering and destroying the country of the rebels with fire and sword, and, joining with their troops, directed his march to Tara, where he found the principal men of the kingdom assembled in his favour, who received him with joyful acclamations, and in a solemn and magnificent manner proclaimed Tuathal king of Ireland.

Elim, the son of Conragh, had then possessed himself of the government of Ireland, being an elective king chosen by the suffrage of the plebeians, after the death of Cairbre Cinncait The usurper, alarmed at these proceedings, prepared for defence, and having raised what power the exigency of the time would permit, marched with what forces he had against Tuathall, and gave him battle at Aichle, where his new raised army was soon broken and defeated, and he himself slain This success so animated the royal party, that they pursued their victory, and fell upon the plebeians, and routed them in all parts of the kingdom. But this was not accomplished without great difficulty, for the rebels had made themselves strong by a possession of twenty-five years, and tried their fortune in several engagements before they were absolutely quelled, but at length by the superior bravery of Tuathal's troops, they were reduced ; for they were defeated in twenty-five battles in Leinster, in twenty-five battles in Conacht, and in twenty-five battles in Munster.

Tuathal, by these repeated victories, put an end to the usurpation, redeemed the nobility and gentry from the oppression of the commons, and restored happiness and tranquillity to the kingdom. When he had fixed himself in the government, he convened the general assembly of Tara, after the example of his royal predecessors in the throne of Ireland, who always summoned a parliament in the beginning of their reigns, to debate upon the affairs of the state, and to consult the welfare and peace of the public. The nobility and gentry of the island joyfully met him, and in this convention recognised his title to the crown, confessed him to be their lawful and rightful monarch, and promised to support his government against all foreign and domestic enemies ; and, as a farther testimony of their loyalty, engaged to continue the succession in his family for ever ; in the very same manner as they promised to Ugaine More, one of his predecessors.

In this assembly it was that Tuathal separated a tract of land from each of the four provinces, which met together at a certain place ; and of that part which he took he made the country of Meath, as it appears at this day. For though the territory of land that is adjacent to Visneach, was known by the name of Meath, from the time of the sons of Nemedius till the reign of this monarch, Tuathall, yet the proportion that was thus separated and divided from the rest was not so called till the death of this prince, who established it as a distinct part of the country from every one of the provinces, as before mentioned.

In each portion taken out of the provinces, Tuathal erected a magnificent palace. In the tract he divided from Munster, and added to Meath, he built the royal seat of Tlachtga, where the fire Tlachtga was ordained to be kindled. The use of this sacred fire was to summon the priests, augurs, and druids of Ireland, to repair thither, and assemble upon the eve of All Saints, in order to consume the sacrifices that were offered to their pagan gods ; and it was established, under the penalty of a great fine, that no other fire should be kindled upon that night throughout the kingdom, so that the fire that was to be used in the country was to be derived from this holy fire ; for which privilege the people were to pay a Scraball, which amounts to three pence, every year, as an acknowledgment to the king of Munster ; because the palace Tlachtga, where this fire burned, was the proportion taken from the province of Munster, and added to the country of Meath.

The second royal palace that was erected, was in the proportion taken from the province of Conacht, and here a general convocation was assembled, of all the inhabitants of the kingdom that were able to appear, which was called The Convocation of Visneach, and was kept upon the first day of May, where they offered sacrifices to the principal deity of the island, whom they adored under the name Beul. Upon this occasion they were used to kindle two fires in every territory of the kingdom, in honour of this pagan god. It was a solemn ceremony at this time, to drive a number of cattle of every kind, between these fires, this was conceived to be an antidote and a preservation against the murrain, or any other pestilential distemper among cattle, for the year following. And from those fires, that were made in worship of the god Beul, the day, upon which the Christian festival of St. Philip and St. James is observed, is called, in the Irish language, La Beultinne. The derivation of the word is thus , La in Irish signifies a day, Beul is the name of the pagan deity, and Teinne is the same with fire in the English, which words when they are pronounced together, sound La Beultinne. The inhabitants at this time, for want of the conveniency of coined money, would change and barter their horses, their arms, or what other valuable things they had, for different necessaries which they had occasion for, which was the way of buying and selling in those ages. The king of Conacht, as a tribute and acknowledgment, had a horse and arms for every lord of a manor, or chieftain of lands, that came to this assembly ; and the reason of this claim was, because the tract of Visneach was a proportion separated from the province of Conacht. in order to enlarge the borders of Meath.

The third royal seat erected by Tuathal, was the palace of Tailtean, which was a territory added to Meath, and originally belonged to the province of Ulster. At this place was the celebrated fair of Tailtean held, which was the more remarkable, as the inhabitants of the island brought their children thither, that were of a suitable age, and contracted with one another about the marriage of them. The strictest and most becoming order was observed in this meeting ; for the men were placed by themselves, the women likewise had a peculiar place at a convenient distance assigned them, where they treated about the disposal of their children, and when the articles were agreed upon they proceeded to the ceremony.

It must be observed here, that Lughaidh Lamhfhada was the first monarch who established the fair of Tailtean, in honour to the memory of Tailte, the daughter of Maghmor, king of Spain, and wife to Eochaidh, the son of Eirc, the last king of the Firbolgs, as before mentioned. In this field that renowned queen was buried, by Lughaidh Lamhfhada, who, in commemoration of her, instituted the fair of Tailtean ; because she had taken care of his education in his minority, and accomplished him in polite learning, and the discipline of arms, till he was grown a man. This fair was then kept upon the day known in the Irish language by the name of La Lughnasa, in the month of August, which is as much as to say, the day ordained by Lughaidh, and is called in the English Lammas-day, observed upon the first day of the month of August. But notwithstanding the fair of Tailtean was ordained before the reign of Tuathal Teachtmhar, yet there was no palace erected in that place till the time of this monarch ; and because the seat of Tailtean, in the country of Meath, was separated from the province of Ulster, the king of that province laid claim to a tribute of acknowledgment, arising from that fair, which consisted in an ounce of silver from every couple that were contracted and married at that time.

The fourth royal seat, erected by Tuathal Teachtmhar, was the palace of Teamhair, that is, Tara, which was added to Meath, and originally belonged to the province of Leinster. In this stately fabric the general meeting of the several estates of the kingdom was held, which convention was called the royal assembly of Tara. This parliament was summoned once in three years, and was also distinguished by the name of Feas Teamhrach. The business of this assembly was to enact wholesome laws for the government of the kingdom, to examine into the ancient chronicles and records, to purge them of all false and spurious relations, and to settle the genealogies of the renowned Gadelians. The pedigrees and noble exploits of the several families in the island, were brought before this assembly, who appointed a select committee of the most learned antiquaries, to search into the truth and authority of them ; and if they were approved and passed the scrutiny, they were admitted by the parliament, and transcribed into the royal records, called the Psalter of Tara ; so that whatever laws, customs or genealogies were offered to be introduced, if they were not upon inquiry to be found in this venerable and authentic journal, were not admitted as genuine. but were rejected as an imposition upon posterity.

The bounds of this history will not allow of a particular account of the several laws and institutions established by this convention. which I am certain will take up a vo ume of themselves, and may hereafter. upon proper encouragement, be communicated to the public ; yet it may be convenient to repeat, in some measure. what was observed before, and speak of the regularity and decent order observed in the magnificent entertainments, provided for the several members of this triennial parliament during the time of their session.

This assembly did not only consist of the principal nobility and gentry of the kingdom, but the military officers, and the principal commanders of the army, were admitted to a place in these debates ; and the name of every officer, that was in full pay, and employed in the defence of the country, with the date of his commission, was enrolled by the learned antiquaries in the royal records. The nobility and gentry likewise had their names inserted in the list, by public authority, according to their several qualities ; and by the superiority of their degrees, every member had a right to a place at these entertainments.

When the dinner was prepared, and the apartment ready, every guest had a servant to attend upon him, and to carry his target, which he delivered to the antiquaries, who hung them up, according to their enrolments. The dining-room was a long and narrow building, with tables placed against each side of the room, only allowing a space for a waiter to stand behind. Above the table were hooks fixed in the wall, at convenient distances, upon which the targets of the nobility, the gentry. and commanding officers, were hung up, by the learned antiquaries or heralds, whose office it was, by which means every member knew the place appointed for him to sit, for they were to take their places under their own targets, which were easily dis. tinguished by the coats of arms blazoned upon the outside of them, so that there was no dispute about precedence and preeminency, for by these methods it was impossible to mistake.

The table on the right hand was appointed for the nobility, who were possessed of the greatest estates ; that on the left hand was for the principal officers who had the highest posts in the army, and for the rest of the members. The end of the apartment was allotted to the antiquaries, the historians, the judges, the poets, and men of learning in all professions, who were allowed to sit in this convention. A space was left between the table and the wall for the attendants. Before the dinner every person was to go out of the room, and the members were to be called in by three loud blasts of a trumpet ; and several other ceremonies were observed, to raise the state and solemnity of this convention, which are particularly described in the reign of Ollamh Fodhla, a preceding monarch.

It was this prince, Tuathal Teachtmhar, that first laid the tribute, or chief rent, called Boiroimhe, upon the province of Leinster, which he exacted as satisfaction for the death of two young princesses, his daughters, who lost their lives on the account of the king of Leinster ; their names were Fithir and Dairine. The king of this province, called Eochaidh Ainchean, was married to Dairine, the eldest sister, and brought her away with him to his royal palace in Leinster. About a year after the marriage, this lascivious prince, not contented with the embraces of his lady, craftily went to Tara, the court of Tuathal Teachtmhar, and told him, that his daughter Dairine was dead, which loss could no way be repaired to him, unless he would condescend to bestow her sister upon him ; for he valued the honour of his friendship, which would be more sacred and lasting by this alliance, and in some measure contribute towards the public peace of the kingdom. This request was complied with by the king of Ireland, and the princess Fithir was delivered to Eochaidh Ainchean, who married her, and took her with him to his own province. When she arrived she found her sister Dairine, and was so surprised and overcome with shame at the sight of her, that she fainted away, and could not be recovered, for she instantly died. The unfortunate Dairine, not suspecting the virtue of her sister, was so affected with the loss of her that she threw herself upon the dead body, and her grief was so violent, that she fell into convulsions, which immediately put an end to her life. This melancholy accident is taken notice of by a very ancient poet, in this manner :

> Two princesses, the daughters of Tuathal
> The fair Dairine, and the lovely Fithir.
> Fell by the lust of Eochaidh Ainchean,

The virtuous Fithir died with guiltless shame,
And Dairine overcome with grief,
Would not survive her sister's fate.

The Irish monarch, informed of the tragical end of his two daughters, resolved to revenge their death upon the king of Leinster, whose treachery and falsehood had destroyed two of the most beautiful ladies in the whole kingdom. He therefore immediately dispatched messengers throughout the island, to complain of the indignity offered him ; and demanded assistance of the principal nobility and gentry, to vindicate his abused honour, and to chastise the baseness of the unfaithful Eochaidh. They received his letters, and, resenting the affront in a proper manner as became good subjects, they raised an army with all expedition, and when they were well fitted out they were sent to Tuathal, to support the justice of his cause, and to invade the territories of the king of Leinster.

Supported with a numerous and resolute body of troops, Tuathal marched into the province of Leinster with fire and sword, making most dreadful depredations, and miserably distressing the inhabitants. Eochaidh, informed of the miseries of his people, designed at first to raise an army, and give battle to the enemy ; but when he understood the strength of the Irish forces, he found he was unable to make head against them in the field, and therefore, in the most submissive manner, desired a cessation of arms, and by treaty to compound the dispute. The king of Ireland had it in his power to destroy and overrun the whole province, but being of a merciful disposition, he consented to withdraw his troops, and restrain them from plundering the country, if the king and people of Leinster would bind themselves by solemn engagements, to pay a certain tribute, every second year, to him and his successors in the throne of Ireland, which contract should oblige the king and the inhabitants of the province for ever. These terms were accepted by Eochaidh and his subjects, with great satisfaction ; and the tribute and acknowledgment, that was demanded by Tuathal for the death of his daughters, was, threescore hundred cows, threescore hundred hogs, threescore hundred wethers, threescore hundred copper cauldrons, threescore hundred ounces of silver, and threescore hundred mantles. This tribute was ordered to be disposed of in this manner ; a third part of it was to be paid to the people of Oirgiallach, a third part to the inhabitants of Conacht, and the remaining part to Jobh Neill. A poet of great antiquity has transmitted an account of this transaction in the following lines, which exactly agrees with the old history called Boiroimhe Laighean, or the fine of Leinster.

> As tribute for the death of the two princesses,
> And in revenge for the base act of Eochaidh,
> The men of Leinster were obliged to pay
> To Tuathal, and all the monarchs after him,
> Threescore hundred of the fairest cows,
> And threescore hundred ounces of pure silver,
> And threescore hundred mantles richly woven,
> And threescore hundred of the fattest hogs,
> And threescore hundred of the largest sheep,
> And threescore hundred cauldrons strong and polish'd.
> This tribute was appointed to be sent,
> A third part to the inhabitants of Conacht,
> Another third to Oirgiall, and the rest
> To Jobh Neill.

This tax was known in Ireland by the name of Boiroimhe Laighean, or the tribute of Leinster, and was duly paid every second year during the reign of forty monarchs in Ireland, after Tuathal, who first received it ; as the poet has given us to understand in this manner :

> To forty royal monarchs of the isle,
> This heavy tribute was exactly paid,
> From the renowned Tuathal's restoration,
> To Fianachta's happy reign.

The province of Leinster was delivered from the payment of this tax by the intercession of St. Moling, who obtained from Fianachta a forbearance till Monday, as he expressed it. The saint, it seems, had an equivocal evasion, for he meant the Monday after Doomsday, by which artifice he overreached the king, who remitted the tribute.

It has been observed that this fine of Leinster was paid for many ages ; but sometimes, when the kingdom of Ireland was invaded or disturbed by civil commotions, the king of the province would refuse to send his tax, which occasioned many wars and fatal disputes ; for the Irish monarchs would insist upon their right and defend it by arms, and by these contests and quarrels many of the nobility and gentry were slain on both sides, but the greatest calamities generally fell upon the province.

During the reign of Tuathal Teachtmhar, as the Irish records of Tara expressly mention, there were two general assemblies convened within the kingdom of Ireland: the first was summoned to the palace of Eamhain, in Ulster ; the other met at

Cruachan, in the province of Conacht. The most remarkable
ordinances and laws, that were debated and established in these
great councils of the nation, were those that follow. It was
enacted, that all the annals, histories, and other public chronicles of the kingdom should be examined and revised, and the
same method should be used in fixing their authority, as was
ordained by the committee of the triennial parliament, in the
reign of that illustrious monarch Ollamh Fodhla; for great
corruptions had been introduced from the murder of Fiachadh
Fionoluidh, under the usurpation of the plebeians, and those
conventions had been discontinued till the restoration of Tuathal.

It was likewise established in that august assembly, by the
king and his nobles, that the artificers, the tradesmen and handi-
craftsmen of the kingdom, should be brought under regulation ;
for which end the mechanics of all occupations, smiths, carpenters, musicians, and all other ingenious professions, were summoned to attend upon these triennial parliaments : when they
came, a select committee was appointed to examine into the
skill and abilities of every mechanic, and to make choice of sixty
of the most eminent in their several professions, who had authority by commission to govern and be supervisors over the rest.
Every one of these had the proper extent of his jurisdiction settled ; and their office was to reform all abuses in their several
professions, and suspend such as were unskilful, or by misman-
agement brought their art into disrepute, from the exercise of
their trades ; so that no person was allowed publicly to practise
his art, or profess any mechanical employments, without a license from these commissioners, after he had been strictly examined, and accepted, by reason of his abilities, in the trade and
business he designed to follow. These supervisors, invested with
this authority, were known in the Irish language by the name of
Jollanuidh, which signifies skilful and able mechanics. Before
this time, it must be observed, that very few of the posterity of
the Milesians professed any trade or occupation, but were generally persons of some estate, or employed in the army, or in
other public posts of the government. The mechanics of the
country, in those days were the remnant of the Tuatha de
Danans, who were permitted to stay in the kingdom, the Brigantes, and some of the principal plebeians : the lower branches
of the Milesian race were the militia of the island, the historians,
antiquaries, harpers, physicians, and Brehon or judges, and other
public officers of the state. who would not submit to any manual

honour, lest they should degrade and bring a stain upon the honour of their families. This monarch, Tuathal Teachtmhar, was slain by his successor, Mal, the son of Rughruidh.

A.D. 109. Mal, the son of Rughruidh, seized upon the government. His grandfather was Cathbhadha, son of Giallchadha Finn, son of Fionchadha, son of Muireadhuagh, son of Fiachadh Fionnamhaig, son of Iriel Glunmar, son of Connall Cearnach, son of Amergin Jargiunaig, son of Cas Trillsigh, son of Fachtna, son of Cana, son of Gionga, son of Rughruidh More, (from whom Clana Rughruidhe obtained its name,) a descendant from the posterity of Ir, the son of Milesius, king of Spain. He filled the throne of Ireland four years, and fell by the sword of Feidhlin Reachtmar, son of Tuathal Teachtmhar Feidhlin.

113. Feidhlimhidh Reachtmar was his successor. He was the son of Tuathal Teachtmar, son of Fiachadh Fionoluidh, derived from the royal line of Heremon, and wore the crown nine years. The mother of this Irish monarch was Baine, the daughter of Sgaile Balbh, the king of England. This prince was distinguished by the name of Feidhlimhidh Reachtmhar, because he governed his subjects, and administered justice among them, by the most equitable law of retaliation. Every sentence and decree that he passed upon an offender was strictly conformable to this ancient law, which he enjoined with the same exactness in all the public judicatories of the kingdom. If a criminal had defrauded another of his cattle, his sheep, or any part of his property, or had destroyed the use of a leg, an arm, or an eye, or of whatever nature the offence was, he was obliged to make satisfaction by this law. And by the dread of this severe though just decree, the inferior subjects of Ireland were terrified into humanity, integrity, and good manners, and became an honest and worthy people. From this method of punishment and retribution was this prince distinguished by the name of Feidhlimhidh Reachtmar: and Providence rewarded him for the justice of his administration, for he did not fall by the sword, as did most of his predecessors, but died a natural death.

122. Cathaoir More, who was surnamed the Great, was the succeeding monarch. He was the son of Feidhlimhidh Fionirglais, son of Cormac Gealta Gaoth, son of Niadh Corb, son of Concorb, son of Modha Corb, son of Conchabhar Abhraruadhe, son of Feargus Fairge, a prince descended from the posterity of Heremon, and governed the kingdom three

Q

years. This king had thirty sons, as an old poet gives us to understand in this manner :

> Descended from the loins of Cathaoir More
> Were thirty princes, most renown'd in arms.
> Most comely personages, and heroes all.

Yet we are assured that twenty of those princes died, and left no issue behind them ; the remaining ten married, and had many children. The names of those brothers who survived were Rosa Failge, Daire Barrach Breasal, Eineach Glass, Feargus, Oilioll, Criomthan Dearg Maisneach, Eochaidh Teimhin, Aongus, Fiachadh Baiceada, who was the youngest prince of the family. This last branch obtained the government of the province of Leinster, and were kings of that country for many ages.

From Rosa, the eldest son of this monarch, Cathaoir More, who was surnamed Failge, which signifies the hero of the rings, descended the most princely and illustrious family of O'Connor Faly. The word Faly, it must be observed, is an evident corruption of Failge, which in the Irish language signifies rings. For this prince Failge, who was the eldest son of the posterity of Cathaoir More, was distinguished by the honourable name of O'Connor Faly, or Failge ; as appears evidently from all the authentic records of Ireland in general, and particularly by the genealogy, preserved through so many ages, of the illustrious family of O'Connor Faly, which testifies, that the hereditary princes of Leinster successively retained the ancient title of Failge, in proof of their royal extraction from Rosa Failge, whom they justly claim as the greatest ancestor of the family. And they have exerted themselves as a posterity worthy of such progenitors ; for they have shown themselves a valiant and generous tribe, free and hospitable, and true patriots, when the cause of their country required their arms ; they were so free of their blood in its defence, that the family, in process of time, was reduced to a small number, for the bravery of this illustrious house of Leinster exposed them to the greatest dangers and difficulties, and they would never fly or retreat, though oppressed by superior strength, but rather chose to sell their lives dearly upon the spot. From this prince, Rosa Failge, descended other noble families, as the O'Dempseys, lords of Clanmalier, and O'Dunne, with several others of principal note, as will be particularly observed when we come to adjust the pedigrees of the Milesians.

It is certain, that Fiachadh Baiceada, though a younger brother to Mosa Failge, is placed in many books of genealogies before any of the nine sons of Cathaoir More, who left issue behind them; and for this reason, because the province of Leinster was governed by more kings of his posterity than of any of the other brothers. From him descended the princely families of Mac Morough Cavanagh, in the Irish language Mac Murchadha Caomhanach, king of Leinster; of O'Tool, in Irish O'Tuathail, who were some time the monarchs of that province; of Byrn, in Irish O'Broin, who were not only kings of Leinster, but lords of Wicklow, for many generations. From this Fiachadh were derived likewise the noble families of the Murphys, in the Irish O'Murchudha; of Dowling, in Irish O'Dunluing; of Ryan, in Irish O Riain, and in some chronicles of Ireland it is called O'Maoilrian; of Cinsealagh, of O'Mulduin, of O'Cormac, or O'Duffy, and many others.

From Cairbre, the son of Concorb, who lived four generations before Cathaoir More, were descended the families of O'Dwyre, in the Irish O'Duibhidir, who were kings of Carbry, Coillnamanach, &c.

From Conla, the son of Breasal Breac, who preceded Cathaoir More by fourteen generations, was derived the princely family of Fitz Patrick, in the Irish language Macgiollaphadruigh, who were the kings of Ireland for many ages · and from the same noble stem proceeded the heroic tribe of O'Braonain, of Vibhduach, who were distinguished by their military achievements, and were some of the most renowned champions of the times they lived in.

A.D. 125. Conn Ceadchathach, who for his valour obtained the title of the Hero of the hundred battles, obtained the government. He was the son of Tuathal Teachtmhar, descended from the royal line of Heremon, and wore the crown twenty years; but was at length slain by Tiobraidhe Tireach, son of Mail, son o. Rochruidhe, king of Ulster. He was barbarously murdered in the territory of Tara, when he chanced to be alone and unattended by his guards; the executioners were fifty ruffians, disguised for that purpose in the habit of women, and employed by Tiobraidhe Tireach to fall upon him when opportunity favoured, and put an end to his life. The mother of Conn Ceadchathach was Ughna, the daughter of the king of Denmark This prince was attacked, and so overpowered by Modha Nuagat, king of Munster, that he lost half his dominions, after he had been defeated in ten battles, and was forced to deliver them into the possession of the conqueror.

The mother of the victorious Modha Nuagat was Sigoda, the daughter of Floin, son of Fiachrad, of the Earnaidhe ; and the reason of his quarrel with the king of Ireland was, upon the account of the Earnaidhs, who were descended from the posterity of Fiachadh Fearmara, and derived from the princely stock of Heremon. This family by continual victories had the better of the descendants of Heber Fionn, in Munster ; so that there were three, who at the same time raised pretensions to the crown of that province Lughaidh Allathach, Daire Dornmore, and Aongus. When Modha Nuagat perceived that the royal house of Heremon had possession of the government of Munster, he did not think it safe to stay in that province, but removed into Leinster, where he had his education and support with Daire Barrach, the son of Cathaoir More. There grew an intimate friendship between these two young princes ; so that Modha Nuagat requested of his royal companion, that he would favour his right, and supply him with sufficient forces to recover the crown of Munster. His friend complied, and immediately put him at the head of a stout body of troops. Modha, with his assistance, marches into the province in a hostile manner, and halted at Vibh Liathain · here Aongus made head against him, with a numerous army and a fierce and bloody battle commenced ; but after a sharp dispute, with doubtful success, Modha Nuagat was victorious, who routed the enemy, and pursued them so close, that he drove them out of the province. This battle was fought upon a spot of ground fortunate for the conqueror ; for in the same place he fought the battle of Ard Neimhidh.

Aongus after this defeat, fled directly to Conn Ceadchathach, the monarch of Ireland, and entreated his assistance ; the king supplied him with a reinforcement of fifteen thousand men ; with this army he enters the province of Munster, and, prompted by indignation and revenge, resolved to recover the crown he had lost, or die upon the spot. He halted at Crioch Liathain, where Modha Nuagat was ready to receive him, and offered him battle. The two armies engaged with great bravery, but the forces of Modha. accustomed to victory, broke through the adverse troops, and destroyed the greatest part of them, with a terrible slaughter, and put the rest to a general rout.

Animated with this success, Modha Nuagat banished the Earnaidhs out of the province of Munster, but with this restriction, that as many as submitted peaceaoly to his government might continue in the country. It was the assistance that Conn Ceadchathach gave to Aongus, that was the cause of those dreadful wars between that king and Modha Nuagat; but the Irish monarch was unfortunate in most engagements, for he lost the day in ten several battles. He was defeated in the battle of Broisne, the battle of Sampaite, the battle of Greine, the battle of Athlone, the battle of Moigh Criooh, in which actiou Fiachadh Rioghfhada, the son of Feidhlimhidh Reachtmar, was slain; the battle of Asail, the battle of Sliabh Mosaigh, the battle of Suamaigh, the battle of Gabhran, and the battle of Visnigh. And these contests and dissensions continued between the two princes, till Modha Nuagat, by a constant course of success, had got possession of one half of the kingdom; so that his territories extended from Galway and Dublin, and Eiskir Reada was the bounds of his government. From this conquest the southern part of the kingdom is known to this day by the name of Leath Modha, or Modha's half, who was the victorious prince we are now speaking of, and was likewise distinguished by the name of Eogan More. The northern part of the island is called to this time by the distinction of Leath Cuinn, or Conn's half, from this Conn Ceadchathach, king of Ireland.

Modha Nuagat had another opportunity of enlarging his conquests, that could not fail of success, and prevailing upon the affections of the people; for it happened that seven years before, an eminent druid, whom he retained in his family, discovered by his art that there should be a most dreadful famine throughout the island, and so great a scarcity of provision, and the fruits of the earth, that the inhabitants would be compelled to feed upon one another's flesh, to preserve their lives; and, therefore, to obviate these calamities, he advised him to support himself and his retinue, by feeding on fish and fowl, of which at that time there was great plenty in all parts of the kingdom; by this means he had the advantage of saving all the corn, and other fruits for subsistence, when that desolation and misery should fall upon the land; and, as a farther provision against the approaching famine, he persuaded him to build storehouses, and to buy in all the corn of the country, and to lay out all the revenue of his province, that could be spared from other uses in the purchase. Modha Nuagat was so convinced of the integrity of the druid, that he gave belief to the prediction, and for the space of seven years he and his subjects lived upon fish and fowl, and secured the corn, and other necessaries of life, in granaries and proper places, and sent factors all over the kingdom, to buy all the provision that was exposed for sale, as far as the whole income of his province would extend. At the time foretold, there was a miserable scarcity throughout the whole island, and the people were reduced to the most desperate extremities; but when they were informed of the provident care of the prince of Munster, who had laid in great quantities of corn and other necessaries, they applied to him in great numbers, and relying upon his mercy and humanity, entreated him to support them with bread, and save the lives of the whole kingdom. Modha made use of this advantage, and though he resolved to relieve the miseries of the people, yet insisted upon an acknowledgment as an equivalent, and promised to assist them with corn in this distress, upon condition that they would submit to a constant tribute, and pay a tax to the crown of Munster. These terms were joyfully accepted by the starved petitioners; and so the granaries and store-houses were opened, and necessaries were distributed, but with a sparing hand, among the people. The circumstances of this transaction are confirmed by the concurring testimony of an authentic poem, that begins thus, Eogan More ia mor a raith; the lines are these:

> And now, alas! came on the deadly year,
> And dreadful blasts infected all the air,
> The fields no chearful hopes of harvest bring,
> Nor tender buds foretel a coming spring,
> Nor bladed grass, nor bearded corn succeed,
> But scales of scurf and putrefaction breed;
> And men, and beasts, and fowls, with hunger pined,
> And trees and plants in one destruction joined.
> The scattered vulgar search around the fields,
> And pluck what'er the withered herbage yields.
> Famished with want, the wilds and deserts tread,
> And fainting wander for their needful bread;
> But, tired at length, unable to sustain
> Afflictive want, and hunger's pinching pain,
> They pray to Modha as a guardian god,
> And bless, with hands upheld, the place of his abode.
> " Let fall," they cry, " some pity on our grief,
> " If what we beg be just, and we deserve relief."
> The prince, with pity moved extended wide
> His granaries, and all their wants supplied;
> But, as a most deserved reward, commands
> A tax, and lays a tribute on their lands.

This prince, Modha Nuagat, it must be observed, was known by four different names: he was called Eogan Fidhfheathach,

Eogan More, Eogan Taithlioch; and Modha Nuagat; as an ancient poet has given us to understand in this manner:

> The prince of Munster is known in history
> By four most noble titles, Eogan More,
> Eogan Fidhfhecthach, Eogan Taithlioch,
> And Modha Nuagat.

To understand the true occasion why this prince was distinguished by these several appellations, the curious may consult that ancient treatise, called the Etymology of Names, which will give him satisfaction concerning the derivation of them. Eogan More was the son of Modha Neid, and was married to Beara, the daughter of Heber More, son of Miodhna, king of Castile, in the kingdom of Spain. By this Spanish princess he had one son and two daughters; the name of his son was Oilioll Olum, the eldest daughter was called Sgoithneamh, and the youngest Coinioll. This is confirmed by a poet of great antiquity in these verses:

> The Spanish princess, beautiful Beara,
> Daughter of Heber, the Castilian king,
> Was mother of the valiant Oilioll Olum,
> And of the virtuous ladies Sgoithneamh
> And Coinioll.

Modha Nuagat, the king of Munster, was at length treacherously slain by Conn Ceadchathach, the monarch of Ireland, who, as some chronicles assert, killed him in his bed, in the morning of the day when they intended to fight the battle of Maigh Leane. The reason why this king Conn was surnamed the hero of a hundred battles, was, because he subdued the provincialists, and triumphed over them in so many engagements; to confirm this, we have the testimony of the following lines:

> The warlike Conn came off with victory
> In Munster, and an hundred battles won;
> So many times with laurels was he crowned,
> And triumphed over Ulster, and in Leinster
> He fought in sixty battles with success.

But the good fortune of this prince at last forsook him, and he was slain by Tiobraide Tireach, as before mentioned.

Conaire was the succeeding monarch. He was the son of Modha Lamhadh, son of Luigheach Allathach, son of Cairbre Cromcinn, son of Daire Durnmore, son of Cair-

A.D.
145.

bre Fionnmor, son of Conair More, son of Eidersgeoil, descended
from the royal line of Heremon, and governed the kingdom
seven years.   He was killed by Neimhidh, the son of Sruibh-
chin.   The mother of this prince was Eithne, the daughter of
Lughaidh, son of Daire.   From this Conaire, king of Ireland,
descended the Dailraids, in Scotland, as did the Baisgnigh from
Leim Congculionn, as the old poet observes in this manner :

> The noble tribe of the Dailriads
> Descended from the illustrious Conaire;
> Musgraidh proceeded from the royal stock
> Of the same monarch ; and the famed Baisgnigh
> From great Congculion's loins their lineage drew.

**A D.
152.**   Art Aonfhir, the Melancholy, sat next on the throne of
Ireland.   He was the son of Conn Ceadchathach, son of
Feidhlimbhidh Reachtmhar, a prince of the posterity of
Heremon, and reigned thirty years.   His queen was Meidhbh
Leathdearg, the daughter of Conann Cualann, and from this princess Rath Meidhbhe, near Tara, obtained its name. The cause of
this monarch's being distinguished by the title of Art Aonfhir
was, because he was the sole survivor of his two brothers, who
were unfortunately killed by the brothers of Conn, the hero of
the hundred battles.   The names of these princes were Conla
and Crionna ; and the brothers of Conn, who slew them, were
called Eochaidh Fionn, and Fiachadh Suidhe.   This transaction
is confirmed by the testimony of an ancient poet, whose authority was never yet questioned, in these lines :

> Eochaidh Fionn, and Fiachadh Suidhe,
> Brothers of Conn, the hero of the island,
> Destroyed the princes Conla and Crionna,
> Brothers of Art ; at whose unhappy fate
> He grieved, and with continued sorrow pined,
> And so was called The melancholy Art.

Conn, the monarch of Ireland, had six children ; the two sons,
who were killed, as before mentioned, and Art, who succeeded
him in the government ; and three daughters, whose names
were Maoin, Sadubh, and Sarah, as an old poet gives us to understand in these verses ,

> Six children from the royal loins of Conn
> Descended; three brothers, worthy of a crown,
> Conla, Crionna, and melancholy Art ;
> Three daughters, beautiful and virtuous,
> Maoin, Sadubh and Sarah.

The princes Coula and Crionna were slain by their uncles, their father's brothers; the princess Sarah was married to Conaire, the son of Modha Lamhadh, by whom she had three sons, called the three Cairbres; their names were Cairbre Rioghfada, Cairbre Baschaoin, and Cairbre Muisg. The posterity of Cairbre Rioghfhada, the eldest of the brothers, remo ed into Scotland, and are distinguished in that country by the name of Dailriadas. One of the descendants of this prince, w ao was called Eochaidh Munramhar, had two sons, whose names were Earcha and Tolchu; from the eldest of these brothers were derived the Dailriadas of Scotland; from the youngest sprang, in a lineal descent, the Dailriadas that settled in the province of Ulster, and were called Ruthach. The princess Sadhbh, another daughter of Conn, was married to Macniadh, the son of Lughdheach, derived from the posterity of Ith, the son of Breogan, by whom she had a son, whose name was Lughaidh, and sometimes he was distinguished by the title of Mac Conn. Her husband Macniadh died, but she was soon married to Oilioll Olum, by whom she had nine sons; seven of these young princes were unfortunately killed in the battle of Magh Muchruime, as Oilioll Olum has confirned in a poem composed by himself.

> The tender father for his sons laments;
> Seven princes, the only hopes of my old age,
> Fell in one day: Eogan, Dubmerchon, Modchorb,
> Lughaidh, Eochaidh, and Diothorba.

The two brothers that escaped the battle of Magh Muchruime, were called Cormac Cas and Cian. And though Oilioll Olum had nineteen sons in the. whole, nine by the daughter of Conn, and ten by other women, yet but three of them left any posterity; as we have sufficient reason to believe, from the testimony of an ancient poet in this manner,

> Nineteen young heroes were the valiant sons
> Of Oilioll Olum, a renowned prince;
> But, by untimely fate destroyed, sixteen
> Childless; three alone were blessed with issue,
> And to posterity delivered down
> The princely line of the Heberian race.

The sons of Oilioll Olum, that had children, he had by his queen Sadhbh, the daughter of Conn, the monarch of Ireland. The eldest of the three brothers was called Eogan More, and he fell in the battle of Magh Muchruime, by the victorious sword of a Welsh hero, Beine Briot, who was son to the king of Wales. This prince, Eogan More, left a son behind him, called Fiachadh Muilleathan, from whom descended all the illustrious families of the Clancarthy Mores, the Mac Carthys, O'Sullivans, and the O'Bryens, with all the spreading branches of those noble tribes, who have appeared very glorious in the Irish nation. The mother of this Fiachadh Muilleathan was Muncha, the daughter of Dil da Chreaga, and he was born at Ath Uisioll, that lies upon the river Suir. He was distinguished by the title of Fiachadh Fear da Liach, by reason of the sorrowful news which was brought; for the word Fiach in the Irish language signifies news. The melancholy account that was brought, was the death of his father, Eogan More, at the battle of Magh Muchruime, soon after he was conceived, and before he was born, and the painful death of his mother, who died in travail with him. When he came to the years of understanding, he was made acquainted with the unhappy fate of both his parents, which gave occasion to his name; and he was afterwards called Fiachadh Fear da Liach, upon account of the sorrow and grief he conceived at the loss of them. Oilioll Olum composed a poem upon the celebrated battle of Magh Muchruime, where this transaction is recorded in an elegant and pathetic manner; the verses are these:

> The prince, with more than common grief oppress'd,
> Heard the strange death, and sorrow swelled his breast;
> His father, brave in arms, untimely slain;
> His mother, torn asunder, died with pain
> In childbirth. Thus o'ercome with sad surprise,
> A stream of fruitless tears ran trickling from his eyes.

This young prince was also called Fiachadh Muilleathan. What gave occasion to this name was this: his mother's father, it seems, was endued with a prophetic skill; and, among others of his predictions, he foretold to his daughter, that, if she could forbear the delivery (for she was then in travail) for the space of twenty-four hours, the child that should be born should be advanced to great honour, and one day fill the throne of Ireland; but if he came into the world immediately, he should never be promoted to a crown, but should prove an eminent druid, and be of principal note for his divinations. The mother, though in the utmost pain, resolved, if possible, to prevent the birth; for it was her ambition she designed to gratify, though it cost her her life, and she told her father she would take care the child should not be born within the time, unless it forced a way through the sides of her belly; and accordingly, as an expedient, she instantly ran into a ford of the river Suir, which ran near her father's house, and, wading into a proper depth, she sat, for the space of twenty-four hours, in the cold water, upon a stone, which effectually prevented her delivery. Upon her return home the child was born, but, as the just reward of her pride, she fainted and expired. This transaction gave a name to the infant, who was called Fiachadh Muilleathan; for the crown of his head was, by his mother's sitting upon the stone, pressed in and made flat, and in allusion he was known by the title of Muillcathan, which word, in the Irish language, signifies flat-headed.

The second son of Oilioll Olum was Cormac Cas, from whom, in a lineal descent, are derived the renowned tribe of the Dailgeais, or the O'Bryens, MacMahons, the Macnamaras, otherwise called Sioll Aodh, with many other branches of noble and heroic blood, as shall be particularly observed in its proper place. To this son, Cormac Cas, Oilioll Olum demised the perpetual government of the province of Munster, after his decease; but when he had intelligence that Fiachadh Muilleathan was born, he thought proper to alter his will, and in this manner settled the succession : that his son, Cormac Cas, after his death, should wear the crown of Munster during his natural life, any then it should devolve to Fiachadh Muilleathan, the son of Eogan More ; the sovereignty then was to return into the family of Cormac Cas, and so the province was to be governed alternately by the heirs of these two illustrious tribes, without quarrels or disputes ; and the will of Oilioll Olum was held in that veneration by his posterity, that there were no contests between the two families for the crown of Munster for many ages.

The third son of Oilioll, that left issue behind him, was Cian, from which prince descended the most noble family of O'Carrol, who were kings of Ely for many generations ; from him likewise derived O'Meachair, O'Hara, O'Gara, and O'Connor Ciannachta.

It must be observed that Oilioll Olum was the first king that reigned in Munster, of the royal line of Heber Fionn, and he begins the list of those princes in the royal tables, and the public records of the kingdom : of those, I mean, who presided over the two divisions of that province, for Oilioll Olum was in possession of the government before he had expelled Mac Con, (Mac Con, who descended from the posterity of Dairine, of the

noble line of Lughaidh, the son of Ith, son of Breogan,) and
was a branch of the family of Deirgthene, whose great ancestor
was Heber Fionn. When the tribe of Dairine had the command
in the province of Munster, the descendants of Deirgthene were
admitted into the principal offices of the state, and were the
established judges of the country ; and when the posterity of
Deirgthene obtained the government, the family of Dairine were
invested with a great share of authority, they presided in the
public courts, and administered justice to the subjects ; and this
succession in the posts of honour and trust continued till
Mac Con was detected of corruption in pronouncing judgment,
for which he was degraded by Oilioll Olum, who as a just
punishment banished him the island.

In this state of exile Mac Con continued for some time, but
being a person of a factious and turbulent disposition, he began
to think himself injured, and resolved upon revenge, and by
violence to return into his country, against the express sentence
of the king. To accomplish his design he projected an open
invasion ; but having no forces to support him, he applied himself to Beine Briot, son to the king of Wales, who promised to
assist him with a competent number of troops, and fix him in
the possession of his authority ; and the more easily to engage
this young prince, the crafty conspirator assured him he had a
considerable party in the island, who resented the injustice of
his sentence, and were ready to declare in his favour as soon as
he arrived upon the coast.

Confiding in the integrity of Mac Con, the prince of Wales
raised a numerous army, and enlisted into his service men of all
nations, that offered to follow him in the expedition ; and when
he had provided a sufficient number of transports he weighed
anchor, and landed upon the Irish shore. When they arrived
they held a council of war, where it was resolved to dispatch a
herald to the melancholy Art, who was then monarch of the
island, and require him to resign the government, or to give
them battle, and decide the contest with the sword. The challenge was a surprise to the king, but he accepted the summons,
and sent orders to the general of his militia to attend upon him
with his trained bands ; for he had raised an army to oppose
the insolent invaders, which if it should give way, and offer to
fly, he was ordered to assist with his fresh body, and by that
means, recover the fortune of the day. But the perfidious Fionn
had been bought off from the service of the king, and had sold
his loyalty to Mac Con for a sufficient bribe which engaged him

to get out of the way, and carry himself as a neuter in the dispute.

The king of Ireland soon perceived the treachery of his general, who not only refused to attend upon him in his own person, but seduced the principal officers of the militia, and engaged them to be absent, and not appear in the fight; but these discouragements did not prevent the king from making head against the enemy; and accordingly, after he had laid a solemn curse upon the traitor, he marched with the forces he had against Mac Con, who had drawn out his army, and was ready to receive him. The Irish troops were supported by the assistance of nineteen sons of Oilioll Olum, who brought with them a considerable body; and the army of the invaders consisted chiefly of foreigners, of all nations, but were well disciplined by the care and vigilance of Beine Briot, the prince of Wales, who was an accomplished general, of a robust constitution of body, and for his courage and conduct in arms was one of the most renowned heroes of the age. The fight began with great fury on both sides, and victory was in suspense for some hours, but the king of Ireland, for want of his militia, who were resolute and hardy soldiers, was forced to give way to the superior force of the foreign troops, who followed their blow, and put the Irish to a general rout. In this action, called the battle of Magh Muchruime, was Art, monarch of Ireland, and the son of Conn, the hero of the hundred battles, unfortunately slain, by Lughhaidh Laga, the brother of Oilioll Olum, who took part with the invaders, and turned the fortune of the day. The death of the king so dispirited his troops, that they fled instantly, and were pursued with great slaughter by the conquerors, who in that engagement destroyed the bravest soldiers of the kingdom, for they gave no quarter, but put all to the sword. Among the slain were seven of the sons of Oilioll Olum, that he had by Sadhbh, the sister of Art, the king of Ireland, and daughter of Conn, the renowned hero of the hundred battles.

It must be observed in this place, that Oilioll Olum was properly called Aongus; but his name was changed upon this occasion. It happened that Oilioll Olum, being an amorous prince, offered violence to a young lady, whose name was Aine, the daugher of Ogamuill: the lady, resenting this injury, resolved to revenge herself upon the ravisher, and finding an opportunity, when she was in bed with him, observing he was asleep, bit off part of his ear. By this action she thought she had fixed a badge of infamy upon Oilioll for the abuse he had offered her, and in some measure revenged the death of her father, whom he slew. This transaction, as some chronicles assert, was the cause of changing his name.

But there are records of some authority, that give another account of this matter, and relate, that he received the title of Oilioll Olum, from the words Oil Oll, which, in the Irish language, signify shame or reproach. This prince, it seems, was distinguished by three remarkable blemishes, which were esteemed a great disgrace to him, and attended upon him to his grave. He was deformed, as was observed before, by the loss of the greatest part of his ear; his teeth were exceeding black, and his breath very offensive, and had a nauseous smell. These imperfections befel him upon the account of the rape he committed upon the young lady, who had no sooner bit his ear than he seized a spear or partizan, that was placed near him, and, thrusting it through her body, he fixed her to the ground. The head of the spear struck against a stone, and, by the force of the blow, the point of it was bent; Oilioll having drawn the weapon out of her body, put the point of the spear into his mouth, intending to straighten it with his teeth, but the metal, being envenomed with a strong poison, changed the colour of his teeth into black, and had that effect upon his breath, that it afterwards had a nauseous smell not to be endured. These were the three blemishes, which gave the name of Oilioll Olum to this prince, who was the less to be excused, because he had warning long before, by a prediction, concerning this spear, which foretold that he should be afflicted with three great misfortunes, if he suffered the point of that spear to touch a stone, or if he applied it to his teeth, or attempted with it to kill a woman; but the prophecy found no credit with Oilioll Olum, for which reason he deservedly fell under those calamities, which occasioned the change of his name, and which he carried with him to his grave.

A.D. 182.

Luighaidh, who had the name of Mac Con, by his victory got possession of the government. He was the son of Macniadh, son of Luighdheach, son of Daire, son of Firuillne, son of Eudbuilg, son of Daire, son of Siothbuilg, son of Firuillne, son of Deagamhrach, son of Deagha Dearg, son of Deirgtheine, son of Nuagatt Airgtheach, son of Luchtaire, son of Logha Feidhlioch, son of Ereamhoin, son of Eadamhuin, son of Gosamhuin, son of Sin, son of Maithin, son of Logha, son of Eadamhuin, son of Mail, son of Luighaidh, son of Ith, son of Breogan, and filled the throne of Ireland thirty years. The mother of this prince was Sadhbh, the daughter of Conn, as before mentioned. He obtained the name of Mac Con from a greyhound that was called Ealoir Dearg, that belonged to Oilioll Olum. This king, in his infancy, was educated in the court of Oilioll Olum, and being a child of a very weak and tender constitution, he was very fretful and difficult to be pleased; but when he could not be pacified by other methods, those who had the care of him procured a young greyhound for him to play with, which, by its fondness and diverting postures, so amused the child, that he conceived a wonderful kindness for the dog, and was never easy or contented without him; and from this playing with the greyhound, he was known by the name of Mac Con, but he was properly called Lughaidh. The victory he obtained in the battle of Magh Muchruime put him in possession of the kingdom; for within the compass of a week, by pursuing his success, he fixed himself in the sovereignty of the whole island, and governed it securely thirty years; as is particularly mentioned in the following verses, transcribed from a very ancient poem, which begins in this manner, Cnocha cnoc os cion liffe.

> Within seven days the fortunate Lughaidh
> Obtained the scepter of the western isle;
> And reign'd in honour and prosperity,
> For thirty years, as ancient records tell,
> But he was at last slain by treachery,
> Sitting 'n state in the assembly.

It must be observed, that this Mac Con, the Irish monarch we are speaking of, was not a descendant from the posterity of Heber Fionn, as he is expressly mentioned to be, in the poem that begins with these words, Coniare caomh chaomhuin chuin, but was derived from the family of Lughaidh, the son of Ith, son of Breogan; Ith, and Milesius, the king of Spain, who was otherwise called Gollamh, were brothers' children; and notwithstanding that Lughaidh, the son of Ith, and his posterity, were descended from Gadelas in a lineal succession, yet they are not to be reckoned of the line of Milesius, but were cousin-germains to that family: and this account is confirmed by the testimony of a poet of great credit and antiquity, who, speaking of the three renowned tribes that were derived from the posterity of Lughaidh, the son of Ith, has these verses:

> Three princes, famous in the Irish annals,
> O Cobhthaig, generous and hospitable;

O Floin Arda, invincible and brave;
And the most valiant Heidersgeoil,
Were not descended from the royal line
Of great Milesius.

From Lughaidh, the son of Ith, the following surnames deduced their original; O'Laoghaire, in the English language called O'Laoery, or Leary; O'Baire of Aronn, in Carbry; Magh Flanchy, of Darthruidhe; Magh Amalgadh, of Callruidhe; O'Curnyn, and Mac Aillin, in the kingdom of Scotland.

This Mac Con, it must be understood, was the third monarch of Ireland, who was of the royal line of Ith. The first monarch of that family was Eochaidh Eadgothach, the son of Daire, who possessed the government of the island four years, and fell by the sword of Chermana, the son of Eibhric, the son of Ir. The second of that line was Eochaidh Apthach, who sat upon the throne one year, and was slain by Fionn, the son of Bratha. The third, descended from this illustrious house, was this Mac Con; as appears evidently by the authority of an ancient poet, who has transmitted to us the following verses:

From the most noble race of Ith descended
Three princes, who the Irish scepter sway'd;
Eochaidh Eadgothach, Eochaidh Apthach,
And the renowned Lughaidh, who reveng'd
The cruel death of their great ancestor.

Comain Eigis, the son of Fearcio, formed a conspiracy by the persuasion of Cormac, the son of Art, the Melancholy, against Mac Con, and slew him with a remarkable spear, known in the Irish language by the name of Righde. This treacherous act was committed at Feimhin, in Leinster, as the king was returning from Munster. The unfortunate journey of the king into that province, was occasioned by the prediction of his druid, who foretold that he should not wear the crown of Ireland for half a year, if he removed the place of his residence from the royal house of Tara. Influenced by this prophecy, he came to Munster, to solicit the friendship and assistance of his relations in that province, who descended from Oilioll Olum; but this family, instead of favouring his request, resolved to destroy him; for they could not forget the revenge they owed him for the death of Eogan More and his brothers, whom he slew in the battle of Magh Muchruime. Mac Con, upon this repulse, returned back to Leinster, where he was treacherously killed, in the manner before-mentioned. He lost his life in the field called, in the Irish language, Gort an oir, which signifies the Golden field, at Magh Feimhin, near Dearg Rath, that lies on the north side of Ath na garbat, or the Chariot's ford. The place is known to this day by the name of Gort an oir, or the Golden field; which title it received, because Mac Con, when he was slain, was distributing his liberality, and rewarding the poets and principal artists of the kingdom with large sums of gold, when the murderer came behind him undiscovered, as he was standing near a large rock, and most barbarously thrust him through with a spear.

A.D. 212. Feargus, who was distinguished by the name of Black Teeth, was the succeeding monarch. He was the son of Fionnchada, son of Eogamhuin, son of Fiathach, son of Finn, son of Daire, son of Dluthach, son of Deisin, son of Eochaidh, son of Sin, son of Rosin, son of Trein, son of Rothrein, son of Airiondil, son of Maine, son of Forga, son of Fearadhach, son of Oilioilaran, son of Fiach Fearmara, son of Aongus Tuirmheach, descended from the royal line of Heremon, and sat upon the throne one year. It was in the reign of this prince, that the inhabitants of Ulster expelled Cormac by force out of that province into Conacht, notwithstanding he made an entertainment at Magh Breag, and feasted them plentifully. It was at this feast the king of Ulster commanded one of his servants to set fire to Cormac's beard with a lighted candle, which was accordingly done, and then he was banished the province. The three principal persons, concerned in the disgrace and exile of this noble man, were the three Feargus's, the sons of Fionchada, son of Eogamhuin; their names were, Feargus, who was surnamed Dubhdheadach, or Black Teeth; the second brother was called Feargus, surnamed Caisfhiachlach, which signifies Crooked Teeth; and the youngest was Feargus, surnamed Foltleabhair, or Longhaired.

Cormac, inflamed with resentment at this ungenerous usage applied for protection to Thady, the son of Cein, son of Olioll Olum, who was a person of authority and great interest in the country of Ely. When he arrived he represented his misfortunes, and the indignities he had received, with so moving an address, that the generous Thady promised to support him against his oppressors, and restore him to his just rights, if he would engage to settle a tract of land upon him, after he had triumphed over his enemies. Cormac joyfully complied with the conditions, and gave him security, that he should be put into possession of as much land as he could surround with his

R

chariot upon the day of battle, when the fight was over, and he had obtained a complete victory over the three brothers   Thady relying upon his honour and integrity, resolved to espouse his cause with all imaginable vigour ; and, to intimidate his enemies, he told Cormac that he knew where the invincible hero, Lughaidh Laga, lay concealed; and assured him, that if he could prevail upon that bold champion to appear at the head of his troops, and present himself in the front of the battle, the day would be his own ; and, as an undisputed sign of success, the heads of the three Feargus's, he made no question, would be cut off by this intrepid warrior, and laid at his feet He further informed him, that this stout soldier had retired, and lived an obscure life at Atharla, near Sliabh Crett, where he would be sure to find him.

Encouraged by these assurances, Cormac went instantly to Atharla, and upon a strict search he found the brave Lughaidh in a poor despicable cottage, lying along upon the ground, with his face upwards.   When he perceived him in that posture, he pricked him gently with the end of his lance ; upon which the old soldier demanded, with a stern countenance, who it was that presumed to disturb him in so insolent a manner.   Cormac replied mildly, and told him his name ; and Lughaidh answered, that if he had been pleased, he might justly have taken away his life, in revenge for the death of his father Art, the Melancholy, who fell by his hand.   Cormac told him, he thought he was obliged to make him a suitable recompense for that action ; that I promise you, says Lughaidh, for I will make you a present of a king's head in the time of battle.   By this time Cormac had made known his business ; and after he had received his word that he would assist him to the utmost of his life, and give him revenge over his enemies, they set forward together towards Ely, where Thady, the son of Cein, kept his residence.

By this time Thady had raised a numerous army, with a design to destroy the province of Ulster with fire and sword ; and was the more easily induced to engage in this expedition, because Feargus Dubhdheadach, or the Black Teeth Prince, who was the elder brother, had some time before slain the father of Thady in the battle of Samhna.   This resolute army marched to Brugh mac anoig, and Criona chin comar, where the brothers were ready to receive them with the forces they had raised, and resolved to engage at all events.   In this place was the memorable battle of Criona fought, between Cormac and the three Feargus's ; but Thady would not permit Cormac to enter in o the fight, but persuaded him to be spectator of the action upon the top of a hill, near the field where the battle was fought, and expect the event.

The sign was given, and both armies engaged with signal courage, and the victory was undetermined for some hours; but the valiant Lughaidh resolved to turn the fortune of the day, and, rushing into the hottest of the action, made his way through heaps of slain, till he came to Feargus Foltleabhair, or the Long-haired, whom he fell upon with desperate fury, and cut off his head; he retired with the spoil of his enemy in his hand, and coming to the place where Cormac was supposed to be, he advanced up to him, and threw the head of this Feargus at his feet.

It seems that Cormac, apprehensive of some danger from the fury and outrageous passion of Lughaidh, who, in the heat of the battle, when his blood was in ferment, would divert himself with the slaughter of his friends and enemies without distinction, had before the engagement changed his habit with one of his servants, whose name was Deilion Druth. Lughaidh therefore brought the head of his enemy, and throwing it at the feet of Cormac, as he imagined, demanded whether that was the head of Feargus, king of Ireland. The servant, assuming an air of state to himself, answered him, that it was not. The champion immediately forced his way into the hottest of the battle, and dealing his blows terribly about him, he met Feargus Chais-fhiaclach, or the Crooked Teeth, and rushed upon him so violently, that he slew him without much resistance, and likewise cut off his head. With this trophy he returned to the supposed Cormac, and, showing him the face, asked him, was not that the head of the king of Ulster? The disguised servant replied it was not his, but the head of his brother. Enraged with these disappointments, he resolved to accomplish his purpose, and with dreadful slaughter of the enemy, he made his way to the king, whom he engaged with such fury, that he slew him before he could be relieved, and brought his head away with him in triumph. He came joyfully to the supposed Cormac, and demanded whether that was not the head of Feargus Dubhdheadach, king of Ulster? The servant, when he had examined the face, answered, it was. The victor, proud of his conquest, threw the head with his whole force at the servant, who appeared in the habit of his master, and the blow was so violent that he fell dead at his feet. This happy stratagem preserved the life of Cormac; for this Lughaidh was so untractable and fierce, that in his fury he delighted in bloodshed, and were it not for the disguise, Cormac must certainly have fallen a sacrifice to the passion of this ungovernable and savage warrior. But Lughaidh, notwithstanding his reputation and conduct in arms, was wounded desperately, and lost so much blood that he fainted away. The fight was bloody on both sides, and the victory was won with great loss, for the army of Ulster, though obliged to give way, rallied seven times with bravery; but the victorious Thady, the son of Cein, with his hardy troops, pierced into the main body of the enemy, and, after a sharp contest, put them to the rout, and drove them out of the field; he pursued them with great slaughter from Criona to Glaise an Eara, near Drom Ionasgluinn; as the learned Flanagan, whose authority is indisputable, observes in his poem in this manner:

> Feig Mac Cein, from Rath Cro, subdued
> The army of Ulster tho' seven times they rallied,
> And fought; but, with superior force o'erborne,
> They fled, and were pursued from Rath Criona
> To Ard Cein.

After the action was over, the valiant Thady, the son of Cein, was obliged by the sore pain of the wounds he received, to be carried out of the field in his chariot; for he was miserably galled by three spears, in three several places of his body. His design was to surround as large a tract of land as he was able; for this, as was before observed, was to be his reward, if he came off with victory. Accordingly, he commanded the driver of his chariot to make all possible expedition; for in the circuit of the day he proposed to encompass the royal palace of Tara, and to drive on as far as Dublin. But the anguish of his wounds, and a large effusion of blood, had reduced him to so weak a state, that he perfectly languished; yet, intent upon the enlarging his territories, he called to the driver, and asked him, whether he had yet surrounded the royal seat of Tara? the servant told him he had not; upon which Thady was so enraged, that he summoned all his strength, and flung his spear so violently, that he transfixed his body, and he instantly dropped the reins and died.

At this time Cormac came to the place, and perceiving Thady in that miserable condition, by the pain of his wounds, called to a surgeon that was in his company, and with the most barbarous design commanded him, under a pretence of dressing one of his wounds, to convey an ear of barley into it;

into the second wound he ordered him to inclose a small black worm; and in the third he was to conceal the point of a rusty spear; and then he was to take care, in the administering of his medicines, that the wounds should seemingly be cured, and the surface of the skin closed, but they were not to be searched to the bottom, in order to give him the more pain, and by degrees to affect his life. This I think is the most ungrateful instance of cruelty to be met with in the Irish history; but Thady was a person of great courage, and had a brave army at his command, which gave Cormac a suspicion that he would seize upon the government himself, and therefore he resolved by this inhuman method to destroy him.

In this deplorable state the unfortunate Thady continued for the space of a year, and suffered most exquisite tortures, and his life was in the utmost danger. The condition of this young prince was lamented by his whole army, but particularly by Lughaidh Laga, who, not suspecting the treachery of Cormac, went to Munster, and brought away with him an eminent surgeon, who had performed wonderful cures in that province, and through the whole kingdom. When he came to examine into the wounds of his patient, he ordered his three pupils, who attended him, to lance the skin, and with proper instruments to probe the wounds. Thady could not bear the pain occasioned by this operation, but gave a most pitiful sigh, and almost fainted under the hand of the operator. The surgeon asked the eldest of his pupils, who was the most expert in his profession, what was the reason the young prince sighed so lamentably, and in what state the wound was? He answered, that he was not surprised to hear the patient cry out and lament, for there was an ear of barley inclosed within the wound. Thady was in the utmost pain when the second wound was searched; and unable to conceal the torment he suffered, sighed again, which made the surgeon examine into the reason; and the second pupil told him that he discovered a living black worm that gnawed upon the flesh and occasioned the most acute torture. The third wound was now to be examined; and notwithstanding the compassionate care of the young operator, Thady could not forbear crying out when the probe was within the skin; and upon inquiry into the reason, the third pupil told his master, that notwithstanding the surface of the skin was healed, yet the flesh was putrified and corrupted within, for the rusty point of an old spear lay concealed at the bottom. The surgeon, surprised at so uncommon a case, gave orders that a ploughshare should be heated in the fire till it was red hot ; which being brought to him he took it in his hand, and with a cruel stern countenance, he ran violently at his patient, as if he would have forced the iron through his body : Thady, surprised at this attempt, started out of his bed to avoid the push, and by the violence of his motion occasioned by his fear, his wounds were forced open, and he fortunately discharged the car of barley, the black worm and the rusty iron ; which had that happy effect that the surgeon, by applying proper medicines, soon accomplished his cure, and he was perfectly recovered. Thady, after this act of treachery, employed his forces in making conquests in the country, and his arms were attended with that success, that he subdued large territories in Leath Cuinn ; so called because it was part of the dominions of Conn, who lost half the island, and was forced to be content with the remaining part which was known by this name, Leath Cuinn.

The victorious Thady was the son of Cein, son of Oilioll Olum ; from Jomhchaidhe, the son of Conla, descended the noble families of the O'Carrolls ; from Fionachta, the son of Conla, the tribe of O'Meaghair was derived ; from Cormac Gaileangach proceeded the families of O'Hara, O'Gara, O'Cahaise, and O'Connor Cianachta. They extended their conquests over the country in this manner : Gaileanga was victorious eastward and westward, Cianachta southward and northward. The posterity of Heber Fionn got possession of other countries in Leath Cuinn, or the half of Ireland, under the sovereignty of Conn. This part of the island was conquered by the posterity of Conhlan, son of Lorcan, son of Dathin, son of Teachuire, son of Sidhe, son of Ambhile, son of Big, son of Aodhan, son of Dealbhaoth, son of Cas, son of Conall Eochluath, son of Luighdherah Mean, who made swords-land of all the countries from Limerick to the mountain of Eachtuighe, son of Aongus Tireach, son of Firchairb, son of Modha Chorb, son of Cormac Cas, son of Oilioll Olum. The territories that fell into the hands of the conquerors were these ; the seven Dealbhnas, that is, Dealbhna more, Dealbhna beg, Dealbhna eathra, Dealbnna jathar, Midhe dealbhna sithe neanta, Dealbhha cuill fabhair, and Dealbhna lire da looh, in Conacht. This Feargus, the Irish monarch we are treating of, was slain as before mentioned by Lughaidh Laga, at the instigation of Cormac, the son of Art.

A.D. 213. Cormac Ulfada, after his victory, seized upon the government, He was the son of Art, son of Conn, the renowned hero of the hundred battles, and he killed the

throne forty years. The reason why he was distinguished by the name of Cormac Ulfada, was, upon the account of his beard and the hair of his head, which was exceeding long ; or he might receive this title from the word Ulfada, or Ulafad, which signifies. in English, far or remote from Ulster ; for we have observed, that the inhabitants of Ulster expelled him out of that province, and he continued in banishment sixteen years, or, according to other computations, he was in exile ten years, before he returned and became the monarch of the island. The mother of this prince was Eachtach, the daughter of Ulcheataigh, who was by his profession a blacksmith. His father, who was Art, the Melancholy, the son of Conn, was charmed with the beauty of this fair plebeian, who bore him this king Cormac, not long before the battle of Magh Muchruime. This young woman he used as a concubine ; for it was a custom in those times, that a king's son might lay his commands upon any poor mechanic to deliver up his daughter, and it was thought honourable to the family to have a child admitted within the embraces of a prince; but the father might refuse to give up his daughter, unless the prince engaged to endow her with a handsome portion. By this means the mother of Cormac became the concubine of Art ; for she was not his lawful queen, his wife being Meidhbh Leathdearg, the daughter of Conan Cualan, from whom Rath Meidhbh, adjoining to the palace of Tara, received its name. This concubine, Eachtach, the mother of Cormac, had a dream one night as she was in bed with Art, the young prince, that her head was chopped off, and that a tree grew out of her neck, whose branches overspread the whole kingdom of Ireland ; but the sea rose to a prodigious height, and destroyed that tree, and then retired ; from the root of this tree sprang out another, but this was blasted by a westerly wind, and so it died. When she awaked in the morning, she was surprised at the strange circumstances of her dream, and with great concern related the particulars of it to Art. The prince being well accomplished in soothsaying and divination, interpreted the dream in this manner : You are to observe, says he, that the head of every woman, by the law of nature, is the husband, and me you will certainly lose in the battle of Magh Muchruime, where I shall be slain. The tree that you supposed grew out of your neck, is a son you will bear to me, who, I foretel, shall one day sit upon the throne of Ireland. The overflowing of the sea, by which he was destroyed, implies that this prince shall die by the sticking of a bone of a sea-fish in his throat ; the tree you perceived to spring out of the root of the former, will be the son of that king, who like-wise shall obtain the sovereignty of the kingdom ; and the blast of the west wind, by which it withered and decayed, signifies, that a desperate battle will be fought between himself and the Irish militia, who will rise in arms against him, when he shall be slain. But the Fiana Eirionn, or the militia of Ireland, shall have no occasion to boast of their victory obtained by treason and rebellion, for they shall never flourish or prosper after that action, but their courage shall fail them, and they shall become a prey to their enemies. And in process of time the interpreta-tion of this dream was exactly accomplished in the persons of Art, his son Cormac, and Cairbre his grandson. Art was slain in the battle of Magh Muchruime, Cormac was choked by the bone of a sea-fish, and Cairbre Liffeachair lost his life in the battle of Gabhra, by the Fiana Eirionn, or the standing militia of the kingdom.

The wife of Cormac, king of Ireland, was, if we give credit to some chronicles, Eithne Taobhfada, the daughter of Cathaoir More; but that must be a mistake, and to assert that Eithne Cathach was the mother of Cairbre Liffeachair is equally false, and impossible to be proved ; for there was the distance of four-score and eight years between the death of Cathaoir More, and the time that Cormac took upon him the command of Ireland, which may be computed in this manner. Conn reigned twenty years ; Conaire More held the government seven years ; Art was monarch of the kingdom thirty years ; Mac Con reigned as many, and Feargus Dubhdheadach wore the crown one year before he was dethroned by Cormac, who fixed himself in the succession. And we have undoubted authority to believe that Eithne Ollamhdha, daughter of Dunluing, son of Eana Niadh, was the mother of Cairbre Liffeachair ; and the same testimony informs us, that this lady was fostered and educated by Bui-ciodh Brughach, an eminent and wealthy herdsman, who lived in the province of Leinster.

This Buiciodh Brughach was a very hospitable person, and made it his practice to have a large cauldron always boiling upon the fire, full of flesh and provision for the entertainment of all passengers who came that way, who he relieved generously upon free cost, without asking any questions, or demanding of his guests who they were, or to what part of the island they be-longed. This herdsman abounded in cattle of all kinds : he had in his possession at one time seven herds of cows, each herd con-sisted of seven score ; he was furnished with a noble stud of

fine horses, and had flocks of sheep not to be numbered. The
gentry of Leinster, with their whole families and retinue, would
often visit the house of this herdsman, and quarter themselves
upon him for a long time ; and when they left him, they would
bring away with them a drove of his cows, or take his horses
and mares, or whatever else they pleased, without asking his consent, and never make him any return.   This ungrateful practice of the guests soon impoverished their benefactor, who was
at last by this method stript of all his cattle except seven cows
and a bull.   With this small remaining part of his fortune he
removed privately in the night from Dun Buiciodh, taking
along with him his wife and his foster-child Eithne.   He travelled with his little family till he came to a great wood, adjoining to Ceanannanus, in the country of Meath, which Cormac
generally made his place of residence.   In this solitude Buiciodh
resolved to spend the rest of his days ; and, as a defence against
the weather, he built a small tent, with turf and boughs, where
he lodged his wife and his fair charge Eithne, who, in her rus-
tic dress, discovered a singular beauty, and attended upon her
foster-parents in the quality of a servant.

It happened that Cormac rode out and diverted himself in
this wood ; and his fortune directing him towards this little
hermitage, he spied the beautiful Eithne very cheerfully milk-
ing the cows ; she had two vessels, which she made use of, to
separate the thin milk from the richer and more substantial, for
when she began to milk a cow she disposed of the first part of
the milk into one vessel, and the latter part of the strippings
she poured into the other, which method she observed till she
had gone over the whole number : when she had finished, she
took up the vessels and carried them home.   Cormac followed
her at a distance, admiring her sagacity and the niceness of
her care, perfectly charmed with the modesty of her looks
and the fine shape and beauty of her person.   The young
milkmaid did not stay long in the cottage, but came out again,
with two other vessels and a bowl in her hand, and went to
a spring of water not far from the hut ; she stooped to the
brink of the spring, and laded with the bowl, with the water
that was near the surface she filled one vessel, and into the other
she poured the water that was laded from the middle of the
spring, which was cooler and clearer than the rest.   When her
vessels were full she returned home ; Cormac still having his
eye upon her, and surprised at her innocent behaviour and exact
judgment : she soon came out again, for she was obliged to do

all the menial offices of the family, with a reaping-hook in her
hand, and she had not gone far before she found a place that
abounded with rushes ; there she began to work, and when she
had cut a handful of rushes, she separated those that were long
and green from such as were short and withered, and laid them
in different heaps ; which distinction she used till she had as
many as she designed to carry.   The amorous Cormac observed
her at a distance, and, unable to stifle his passion, rode up to
her.   She was somewhat surprised, at first, to see so genteel a
person in so solitary a place ; but the young prince, by the
courtesy of his address, soon removed her fears, and assured her
that she was in no danger, notwithstanding she was alone ; for
it would be the greatest barbarity to offer violence to a maid of
so innocent a carriage, and whose beauty deserved to be removed
from woods and wildernesses into the courts of princes.   After
some of these polite compliments had passed, and the fair
Eithne was recovered from her surprise, Cormac asked her the
reason of the distinction she had used in separating the milk,
the water, and the rushes, and desired to know who was that
happy person whom she was so careful to oblige, as to preserve
the best of every thing by itself, and to distinguish by particular
marks of her favour and esteem.   The maid, with a blush rising
in her face, answered, that the person upon whom I bestow the
choicest of what I can provide, is one, to whom I owe all the
services of my life, and to please whom is my duty and the
utmost of all my care.   The prince inquired who this fortunate
person was, she told him it was the unhappy Buiciodh Brughach ; what, says Cormac, the generous herdsman, so remarkable
for his hospitality in the province of Leinster !   The very same,
sir, replies the maid ; why then, says he, your name must be
Eithne, and you are the daughter of Dunluing, and foster-child
to this herdsman, who has taken care of you from your infancy,
and bred you up.   Yes, sir, she answered, I perceive you know
my family and the circumstances of my fortune : I do, fair
maid, says he, and I am so charmed with your modesty, and
the beauty of your person, that I scorn to make any unbecoming attempts upon your honour, but resolve by the ties of marriage to make you a partner in my bed.   Sir, she replied, though
a poor maid may justly be ambitious to be thus advanced upon
any terms, yet I retain that duty to my foster-father, that I
would not presume to dispose of myself, without his consent, to
the greatest monarch of the universe.   Cormac applauded her
resolution, and desired to be conducted to the cottage where

Buiciodh was ; and when he came, he informed him of his design, and the sincerity of his passion ; and engaged, upon the honour of a prince, to remove him out of that solitary retirement, and bestow wealth and lands upon him, suitable to the generosity of his soul, if he would consent that the beautiful Eithne should be his wife. Buiciodh rejoiced at this good fortune, especially because his fair charge, whom he affectionately loved, was to be the wife of a prince, and soon complied with his request. Cormac fulfilled his promise to Buiciodh, and gave him the tract of land called Tuath Odhrain, that is situated near the palace of Tara, and furnished him with a great stock of cattle and other necessaries, by which means he was made happy during his life : and then the marriage was consummated with the beautiful Eithne, by whom he had a son, who made a great figure in the Irish history, called Cairbre Liffeachair.

This Cormac, the monarch of Ireland, it must be observed, was a prince of the most consummate wisdom, who perfectly understood the maxims of government, and the most accomplished statesman of the age ; and, as a testimony of his learning and political knowledge, he wrote a tract, for the use of his son, Cairbre Liffeachair, intituled, Advice to Kings, which is worthy to be inscribed in golden characters, for the information of princes, and as a most complete standard of policy to all ages. He was very solicitous in revising and purging the ancient laws of the people, and established new acts and ordinances for the regulation of his subjects, exactly calculated to the genius and temper of his people. He was likewise a prince of great munificence and hospitality, and supported the royal dignity of a king in the utmost state and grandeur. We may form a judgment of the splendid and magnificent court of this monarch, by the description of the palace where he kept his residence, called in the Irish language, the royal seat of Miodchuarta. The account of this noble fabric we received from the relation of Amergin, the son of Amalgadha, son of Maolruadhna, an eminent poet, retained in the family of Diarmod Mac Carrol, and to be found in the book that treats of the Description of Places and Buildings, written by this learned author. This palace of Miodchuarta was built, it must be confessed, a long time before Cormac came to the crown ; for in this house it was, that Slanoll, one of the monarchs of Ireland, died, many years before Cormac was born : but it was repaired and enlarged by this prince, and made a banqueting-house, for the reception and entertainment of his own nobility, and the ambassadors of foreign princes. The length of this structure was 300 cubits; it was 30 cubits in height, and 50 cubits in breadth ; a lanthorn of curious workmanship and of a large size, hung up in the middle of the state room ; fourteen doors belonged to the house, and the lodging apartments were furnished with 150 beds, beside the royal bed of state, where the king himself usually lay. Never was there a monarch in the throne of Ireland, that was attended with a more noble retinue ; for he had in constant pay 150 of the most distinguished champions of the kingdom, as the yeomen of his guard, to wait upon his person, especially to serve him at his table when he dined in public ; at which time he was served in an hundred and fifty cups of massy gold and silver. The household guards, that were in constant attendance, consisted of a thousand and fifty of the bravest men in his whole army ; and other ensigns and distinctions of royalty he had about him, which would have been no reproach to the dignity of the greatest princes. A poet of great antiquity has transmitted to us the character of this munificent king, the lines are these :

> The melancholy Art, who fill'd the throne
> Of Ireland, had but one son, the brave Cormac ;
> A prince most generous, liberal, and free,
> Who raised the grandeur of the Irish nation,
> And made it famed throughout the world

Cormac had a numerous issue ; his children were three sons and ten daughters, as an eminent poet has given us to understand in this manner :

> Ten princesses of most accomplished beauty
> Were daughters of Cormac, the Irish king ;
> Three sons he had of a superior courage,
> Their names were Daire, Cairbre and Ceallach.

The first-named of the three young princes was slain at Dubhrois, near the banks of the river Boyne, at Breag ; Ceallach, another of the brothers, fell by the hand of Aongus Gaothbhuailteach ; as the following verses, composed by a poet of great veracity, inform us :

> The valiant Aongus Gaothbhuailteach
> Slew Ceallach, a prince, the son of Cormac ;
> His brother Daire unfortunately fell
> With the renowned Thady, son of Cein,
> At Dubhrois, near the river Boyne.

It may not be improper, in this place, the better to illustrate this part of the history, to mention particularly the genealogies of some of the principal persons concerned in the government, and in the public administration of the Irish affairs. It must be observed, therefore, for this purpose, that Feidhlimhidh Reachtmhar had three sons, whose names were, Conn Cead-chathach, who was known by the title of The hero of the hundred battles, Eochaidh Fionn, and Fiachadh Suidh, as before mentioned. The posterity of Conn were kings, and governed in Tara ; the second brother, whose name was Eochaidh Fionn, went into Leinster, at the time that Cuchorb, the son of Modh-achorb, was king of that province. Laoighseach Cean More, the son of Connall Cearnach, had his education with the prince Eochaidh Fionn, and at this time the inhabitants of Munster made incursions into Leinster, and conquered a large proportion of that province ; and by the success of their arms were in possession of Ossery and Laoigheis, as far as the top of Maistean. Cuchorb then reigned in Leinster, and, perceiving that the forces of Munster had got footing in his province, and were not easily to be expelled by his own strength, he entreated the assistance of Eochaidh Fionn to drive them back into their own territories ; Eochaidh complied with his request, and sent commissions to his friends and allies, to attend upon him with a complete number of troops, to engage in this expedition. His orders were faithfully obeyed, and he advanced his companion, Laoighseach Cean More, who was bred up with him, to be the general of his forces ; Cuchorb put himself at the head of what men he could engage to follow him, and joined his ally, who thought it proper that his friend Laoighseach should be commander in chief of the whole army.

Thus united, they marched towards the Momonians, or the men of Munster, who, apprehending that they should be attacked, were prepared to receive them. The two armies soon engaged, and a bloody action followed, in which both sides fought with great valour and bravery, and it was difficult for some time to judge which way the victory would incline, but fortune, after a sharp dispute, declared in favour of the confederate army, who broke the ranks of the enemy, with terrible slaughter, and routed them from the top of Maistean to the river Bearbha. The battle was fought at Athtrodain, now known by the name of Athy, situated upon the river Bearbha, now called Barrow. And the Momonians, in this engagement, were defeated, and the flower of their troops lay dead upon the spot.

The Lagonians, or the men of Leinster, animated with this success, continued the pursuit; and, perceiving that a strong body of the enemy had rallied, and were drawn up in order at Cainthine, on Magh Riada, now called Laoighis, that is, Laise or Leise Riada, the victors fell upon them with desperate fury and put them to flight : they then pursued them to Slighe Dhala, now called Bealach More Ossery, where the forces of Leinster made so dreadful a slaughter of the Momonians, that they were forced to desist for want of enemies to kill; which victory resettled the state of that province, and so discouraged the men of Munster, that they never attempted to enlarge their bounds, but were glad to confine themselves within their own territories.

Cuhorb, being reinstated in his dominions by the assistance of Eochaidh Fionn, out of gratitude thought himself obliged to recompense his services, and therefore generously bestowed upon him the seven Fothortuaths; and confirmed this donation, by perpetuating the right to his posterity for ever. Laoighseach, the general of the confederate army, who had his education with Eochaidh Fionn, he rewarded with the seven Laoighises, to be enjoyed by him and his heirs; for he confessed, that the success of the expedition was owing to the valour and conduct of the general, whose military experience gave him advantages over the incapacity of the commanding officer in the enemy's army, which he made such use of as to obtain a complete victory.

From this instance of gratitude to Laoighseach, the posterity of this general took upon themselves the title of kings of Leix or Leise; and the king of Leinster, being sensible that he owed his crown to the bravery of this commander, obliged himself, and his successors in that province, to make a perpetual acknowledgment to the kings of Leix, in memory of the service he received from Laoighseach, who restored him to his throne. He established it by law, that the kings of Leix should have a just claim for ever, to a sirloin of every beeve that was killed in the royal slaughter-house, for the use of the kings of Leinster; and that one of the king of Leinster's galloglachs, or receivers, should attend constantly in the king of Leinster's court, and should have a salary allowed him for that purpose, whose sole business it should be to supervise and collect this tribute for the use of the king of Leix.

It was ordained, likewise, that the king of Leix for the time being, should be allowed a place at the council-board of the king

f Leinster, and was to take his place in the fourth degree at
ll public assemblies and entertainments, and but three were
lmitted to sit above him nearer the king. He was to enjoy
1e principal office in the treasury, and to distribute the king's
ounty and munificence to the gentry, the antiquaries, the
oets, the musicians, and the learned in all arts and professions,
hose abilities entitled them to a reward; and whatever pre-
:nts or acknowledgments were sent to the king, were trans-
itted to him, and passed through his hands. It was enjoined
irther, that seven of the royal family of Laoighis, or Leix, should
onstantly attend the person of the king of Leinster, as a fixed
uard, for which service they were to be honourably maintained,
; the charge of the crown of Leinster. But the king of Leix,
1 return for these privileges, was obliged to maintain, at his
wn expense, one hundred and fifty stout soldiers, to serve in
1e army of the king of Leinster, who were bound to execute
1e most difficult and dangerous commands; to force the lines
f the enemy, though with the utmost hazard; to beat them
ut of their quarters, and to distinguish themselves in the hot-
:st part of the battle.

It was observed before, that Laoighseach Ceanmor, the first
ing of Laoighis or Leix, was brought up, and had his educa-
ion with Eochaidh Fionn, son of Feidhlimhidh Reachtmhar,
1e first king of Fothortuath; for which reason it was, that the
ings of Leix were obliged to be ready upon all occasions, with
competent number of troops, to assist the king of Fothortuath
pon the first summons; and this custom was faithfully observed
y the kings of Leix to the time of Henry II. king of England.

The third brother of Conn, the hero of the hundred battles,
ras called Fiachadh Suidhe. This prince was very powerful,
nd in possession of a large tract of land near the palace of
'ara, that was known by the name of Deisie Teamhrach, but he
ras never fixed in the sovereignty of the kingdom. He had
hree sons, whose names were Rosa, Aongus, who was distin-
uished by the title of Gaothbhuailteach, and Eogan; the
econd brother, Aongus, was the most accomplished soldier of
he three, for he had signalized himself in several engagements,
ras very expert in military discipline, and victory scarce ever
ailed him.

At this time it happened, that there was a person of principal
1ote in the kingdom, who, by his misbehaviour, had fallen under
:he displeasure of Cormac, who could not be induced, by the
ipplication of his greatest favourites, to receive him into his

esteem, till Aongus undertook to be his advocate, and humbly intereeded for his pardon. The king was at first inflexible, but when Aongus offered himself to be bound for his fidelity and good conduct for the time to come, Cormac was prevailed upon to forbear his resentments, and admit the discarded favourite into his court. This reconciliation, procured by the intercession of Aongus, was so disagreeable to the young prince, Ceallach, the son of Cormac, that he seized violently, and without commission, upon the forgiven offender, and when he had him in custody he never asked the consent of his father, but in revenge put out both his eyes. Aongus, being informed of this barbarity, resented it in an outrageous manner, and, being incensed at the treachery of the action, raised a numerous army, and, appearing himself at the head of them, marched towards Tara, to chastise the insolence of the young prince, and to do justice to his injured friend. Cormac, alarmed at this formidable rebellion, prepared to defend himself and his son; but Aongus made a vigorous attack, and slew Ceallach with his lance, as he stood by his father's side, and likewise at another throw he struck out one of the king's eyes with his spear.

But Cormac, nothing discouraged at these misfortunes, resolved to crush the rebellion; and, having a gallant army about him, he offered battle to the haughty traitor, and, with a terrible slaughter of his best troops, drove him out of the field. After this defeat Aongus and his brother retired for protection to the province of Leinster, where they continued for one year; from thence they removed to Ossery, but this place was no safe refuge for them, which obliged them to fly to the court of Oilioll Ollum, who they supposed would be inclined to succour them, because he had married the princess Sadhbh, the daughter of Conn, to whom they had a near relation.

Oilioll Ollum was moved with compassion at the miserable distress of the three brothers, and bestowed upon them, for their present support, the territories of Deasie, in the province of Munster; and the reason he conferred this tract of land upon them was, because they were in possession of the Deasie, near the palace of Tara, before this misfortune happened, and by their defeat were obliged to seek for new settlements, or fall a sacrifice to the arms of the conqueror.

The brothers gratefully accepted of the lands assigned them, and, without quarrel or dispute, they divided the country between them, in three equal parts. Some of the old records assert, that these young princes were the lineal descendants of

Oilioll Aram, and were called Earnaighe ; but this appears to
be a mistake, for they were improperly distinguished by that
name, because the Earnaighe were the posterity of Conaire, the
son of Mogha Lamha, justly speaking, who are particularly mentioned in the preceding part of this history. The reason why
these brothers, the sons of Fiachadh Suidhe, applied to the court
of Munster for protection was, the persuasion of Corc Duibhne,
the son of Cairbre Muisc ; and the posterity of these princes
were known by the name of Deasies. This tribe was conducted
into this province by Eochaidh Fionn, the son of Reachtmar,
and the three brothers, Rosa, Eogan, and Aongus Gaothbhuailteach.

At the time when these young princes arrived in Munster,
Cairbre Muisc had a considerable interest in that province ;
but his wickedness was a scourge to the whole country, for during his residence there the fruits of the earth were all destroyed,
and the corn was blasted, which occasioned a very dreadful famine. The particular act of impiety, that was supposed to pro-
voke the vengeance of heaven was, his committing incest with
his own sister, whose name was Duibhin, who proved with child.
When the time of her delivery came, she had two sons, whom she
named Cormac and Corc. The father and mother of this incestuous issue were the children of Modha Lamha, and of Sarah his
wife, who was the daughter of the renowned Conn, the hero of
the hundred battles.

The inhabitants of Munster, particularly the principal gentry
of the country, were so alarmed at the miserable scarcity of
provision, that they applied to Cairbre, and inquired if he could
inform them of the occasion of the dreadful famine that raged
through all the province. Cairbre, being conscious that his guilt
deserved so severe a judgment, told them he was of opinion
that his own impiety was the cause of that visitation, particularly an act of incest he committed with his own sister, who
bore him two sons, whom he called Corc and Cormac. The
gentry were moved with horror and indignation at so base a
crime, and demanded, by way of atonement, that the children
should be delivered into their hands, whom they proposed to
put to death, to burn their bodies to ashes, and to cast the dust
into a stream that was near the place.

When this transaction happened, there was a druid in the
company, whose name was Dionach ; this soothsayer had recourse to his art, and found it expedient that one of the brothers, called Cormac, should be given up to the people ; but

S

Core, the younger son, he desired to be delivered into his hands, and he promised to convey him out of Ireland. This motion was agreed to by the whole assemby, and accordingly the prophet took up the child assigned to him, and travelled to the sea shore, where he procured a vessel, and weighed anchor, and landed with the infant at a small island called Inis Baoi. It had this name from an old woman styled Baoi, who lived there, and to her the druid delivered the child, who took care of him for the space of a year, and then the druid, who never left him, rewarded the nurse for her trouble, and returned with him back into Ireland. When he arrived, he brought him to his grandmother by his father and mother, whose name was Sarah, delivering withal a strict charge, that she should give him handsome education with all imaginable privacy, and secure him from the knowledge and resentment of the people of Munster.

The Deasies, affected with these calamities of the province, consulted the most eminent druids, whether the country should be destroyed, or enjoy a state of happiness for the time to come? For if they learned there would be any wars or commotion among the inhabitants, they were resolved not to abide the issue, but to remove and seek for new settlements. The soothsayers gave them to understand, that it was proper they should continue in the country; and informed them withal, that the wife of Eana Cinnsealach, whose name was Cuingion, was far gone with child, and would be delivered of a daughter; and that, as soon as she was born, they were to apply to the father, to desire the nursing and the education of her; if he refused their request, they were to make a suitable present to the father, and that would prevail with him to resign her to their disposal: the reason of these instructions was, because it was foreseen that this child should consult the interest, and bestow great advantages upon that family. The Deasies gave belief to the prediction, and, following the advice of their druids, obtained the child of the father. But the prophecy being not to be accomplished till the child was marriageable, they were impatient till she was of a suitable age; and to forward her growth they slew many young children, and fed her with their flesh. This method of dieting her promoted her inclinations, and she was capable of marriage some years sooner than the usual age. The name of this lady was Eithne Vathach, whose husband, it was predicted, should be a fast friend to the tribe of the Deasies; and therefore they made inquiry for a husband for her, and when the articles of marriage were settled, they bestowed her upon

Aongus, the son of Nadhfraioch, king of Munster. But this prince could not obtain her without a gratuity to the family that brought her up; and therefore Aongus delivered as a dowry, into the possession of the Deasies, the lands of Magh Feimhin, consisting of the third part of Cluain Mell, and the middle third; but he was first obliged to drive the people of Ossery out of those estates, who at that time were the possessors of tnem. A considerable time after this, Aongus and his lady Eithne were slain by the people of Leinster, in the battle of Ceallosnadh, four miles eastward of Laithglin.

The posterity of Fiachadh Suidhe, who were distinguished by the name of Deasies, had not, when they first came into Munster, any lands in that province, except that part of the country called Deasie Deisgceart, or the South Deasie, which extends itself from the river Suir to the south sea, and from Liosmore to Ceann Criadain, till the marriage of this lady Eithne with the prince Aongus, son of Nadhfraioch, king of Munster ; for then it was, in accomplishment of the prediction, that he conferred upon the tribe of Deasie the country called Tuasgirt, or North Deasie, which contains the tract of lands from the river Suir aforesaid, to Corea Athrach, known now by the name of Machaire Chaisil, or the plains of Cashel.

There was a prince called C'Fao'an, who descended lineally from the family that was king of North Deasie, and he erected a stately palace, and kept his court, westward of Dunleamhnachta, which structure continues the name of Don Faolan to this day. He had a relation of the same family, who fixed himself in the possession of Deasie Deisgceirt, or the South Deasie, and from him O'Bric received its name. His royal seat was situated near the coast of the south sea, called Oilean O'Bric, or the island of Bric ; and between these two families was the government of the two divisions of the Deasie continued, till the death of O'Bric, who left no issue behind him, and then the government of both parts fell into the hands of Faolan, whose descendants possessed the sovereignty for many years and successions, till they were driven out of the North Deasie by the prevailing power of the posterity of Heber Fionn, the son of Milesius, who conquered that part of the country, and left no more to that tribe than the South Deasie : and in this posture were both Deasies found by the English, who were brought into Ireland by Diarmuid Mac Morough, king of Leinster.

It must be observed in this place, that Aongus Ossery, and his followers, had the command of Magh Feimhin, called the

North Deasie, and that Aongus was forced to abandon his possessions of Magh Feimhin, and was expelled the country by the posterity of Fiachadh Suidhe, with all his relations and dependants; so that from this general defeat of Aongus Ossery it is, that Baille Urluidhe, and Mulloch Aindeonach, are known by the same name to this day; for the word Urluidh, in the Irish language, signifies the blows or irresistible strokes of valiant men, and Aindeonach is as much as to say a violent expulsion.

Cormac, the son of Art, king of Ireland, had at that time a numerous family to maintain, and his revenue was so small, that he was not able to find provisions, especially a sufficient quantity of flesh to support them suitable to his quality. He therefore advised with his treasurer, who had the principal management of his affairs, and knew the exigency of his fortune, on what method he should take to keep up the dignity of his table, and to subsist his attendants, till his subsidies and tributes would become due, and enable him to defray the expense. His treasurer, being sensible of the wants of his master, gave his opinion, that there was no other redress left, but to raise a number of resolute and well-disciplined troops, and enter the province of Munster in a hostile manner, and demand of the king of Munster the revenue that lay in arrear: for, sir, says he, there are two provinces in Munster, and you receive contributions but from one of them; your business, therefore, is to insist upon your right, to demand what you have been defrauded of, and, if he should deny your claim, to plunder the country, and to force a just acknowledgment from the inhabitants.

This advice was well received by Cormac, who immediately put it in execution. He therefore dispatched a proper messenger to Fiachadh Muilleathan, the king of Munster, and made a demand of the revenue arising from one of the provinces, which had been unjustly detained from him. The message was received with contempt, and Fiachadh returned this answer, that the demand was unprecedented, none of his predecessors, the kings of Ireland, ever received an additional tribute from the province, neither would he distress his subjects by raising new contributions, which they had no right to pay. Cormac, upon the return of the messenger, was incensed with this denial, and raised an army with all expedition, and directed his march towards Munster. He entered the province as an enemy, and came as far as Druim Da Maire, (which place is now called Crup

Luinge,) where he halted and encamped with his forces. Fiachadh Muilleathan, the king of Munster, perceiving he should be
attacked, was ready to receive him, and encamping with his army
in the very face of Cormac, resolved to try the issue of the
battle.

But Cormac, not confiding wholly in the courage of his forces,
had recourse to policy, and, having a great number of Scottish
druids and enchanters in his army, desired the assistance of their
skill to annoy and dispirit the enemy. These necromancers
made use of their art, and, by charms and incantations, occasioned the greatest trouble and inconveniences to the army of
Munster ; particularly their magical skill had that success, as
to dry up the water that was in the enemy's camp, so that the
soldiers and the cattle were in the utmost distress, and were
ready to expire for thirst.

The king of Munster lamented this sad calamity among his
forces, and, hearing of an eminent druid that lived in Ciarruidhe
Luachra, whose name was Modharuith, he sent to him, and requested him to deliver his armies out of these difficulties ; but
the crafty druid, taking advantage of the misfortune of the
king, denied his assistance, unless he had confirmed to him, as
a reward, the two territories, now called Roche's country and
the country of Condon, and settled upon his posterity for ever ;
upon that condition he engaged to deliver the army of Munster
from the power of the Scottish enchanters, and to procure plenty
of water in the camp.

The necessity of the king's affairs obliged him to comply with
this unconscionable demand, and the druid had immediate recourse to his art. The counter-charm, which he used upon this
occasion, was an enchanted dart he had in his hand, which he
flung into the air with all his force, declaring, that from the
spot of ground upon which the arrow fell, there should spring a
fountain of the purest water sufficient to supply the wants of
the whole army ; and so it came to pass. By this means the
soldiers were relieved and inspired with fresh courage ; and, enraged with the miseries they had endured, they desired the king
to lead them against the enemy, and promised him full revenge,
and assured him of victory. He accordingly drew out his forces,
and offered battle to the king of Ireland, who, distrusting the
courage of his soldiers, fled for his security without striking a
blow, and was pursued so closely by the king of Munster, that
he was overtaken at Ossery, and obliged to capitulate. The
conditions insisted on were, that he was to deliver up hostages,

which were to be the principal of his nobility, and send them from Tara to Raith Naoi, now called Cnoc Rathfann, as a solemn assurance that he would repair all the losses the people of Munster had sustained by the plundering and depredations of his army, from the time that he first entered the province. These terms were accepted, for they were offered sword in hand : and the testimony of an old poet, who wrote of these affairs, confirms this account in these lines :

> The valiant Fiachadh Muilleathan,
> The warlike monarch of the southern coasts,
> Received the hostages, who came from Tara
> To Rathfuin and Rath Naoi.

This prince, the victorious Fiachadh Muilleathan, had two sons, whose names were Oilioll Flan More and Oilioll Flan Beag. Oilioll Flan More, who was the eldest, died without issue ; and all the posterity, descended from Fiachadh Muilleathan, were the offspring of Oilioll Flan Beag, whose descendants were very numerous, and of great authority, in the province of Munster. This is taken notice of in the verses of an old poet, in this manner :

> Two worthy princes of the royal blood
> Of Fiachadh Muilleathan,
> Were Oilioll Flan More, and Oilioll Flan Beag.
> The eldest with a child was never blest :
> The youngest with a numerous progeny
> O'erspread the province.

The prince, Oilioll Flan More, having no child of his own, by public authority adopted his brother, Oilioll Flan Beag, for his son, and demised to him all his fortune and estate, upon this condition, that his name should be inserted in the lineal genealogies, between the name of his father, Fiachadh Muilleathan, and that of his brother, in order to make posterity believe that he was the father of Oilioll Flan Beag ; and the pedigrees belonging to all the spreading branches of that line, have the name of Oilioll Flan More disposed according to the contract agreed to by the two brothers, and are delivered down in the same form through many ages. The Psalter of Cashel, likewise, and others of the most ancient and authentic chronicles of Ireland, take notice of these genealogies, with the name of this prince placed next to his father's ; though the writers of those times were sensible, that Oilioll Flan More was not the father.

of Oilioll Flan Beag: notwithstanding, the public records of the kingdom always mention the name of Oilioll Flan More in the genealogy of Fiachadh Muilleathan, but with no design to impose upon posterity, only in observance of the agreement between the two brothers, upon the consideration before mentioned.

We are now come to the death of this renowned prince Fiachadh Muilleathan, who was treacherously slain by Conla, the son of Thady, son of Cian, son of Oiliolla Olum, at the ford talled Aith Uisiol, upon the river Suir. This barbarous act was accomplished in this manner: Conla, it must be observed, had his education with Cormac, monarch of Ireland, where he was instructed in military discipline, and the polite parts of 'learning, and was bred up suitably to his descent and quality. When he was young, it happened that he had a sharp humour in his blood, which occasioned a scabby and leprous scurf all over his body; the most eminent physicians were applied to, and they administered medicines, but without success: the young prince became a most frightful object, for his whole body was broken out, and covered as it were, with scales. This misfortune was lamented by the whole court, but by none more than by Cormac himself, who had conceived a sincere affection for him, as he was his companion from a child. In those times it was esteemed the highest accomplishment to understand divination and soothsaying, and Cormac was become so great a proficient in those studies, that, for the service of his friend, he tried the utmost of his skill; and upon consultation was able to foretel, that he should never be delivered from that distemper, but would without remedy continue afflicted with the leprosy, unless he could find means to wash his body all over with the blood of a king. Soon after this prediction, Conla, despairing of a cure, took leave of Cormac and his court, and came into the province of Munster, over which Fiachadh Muilleathan was then king, and kept his residence at Rath Rathfuinn, now called Cnoc Rathfuinn. In the court of this prince he was received with great favour and civility, and, notwithstanding the appearance of his distemper, he was admitted near the person of the king. Some time after it happened that Fiachadh, attended by his nobles and his retinue of state, had resolved to divert himself by swimming in the river Suir, and Conla, who was his near relation, was so well esteemed as to have the honour of carrying his lance. When they arrived upon the bank of the river, his servants undressed him, and he plunged into Aith

Uisiol, to bathe and refresh himself. He had not been long in the water, till Conla observed him swimming towards him, and making his way towards the shore. The prediction of Cormac instantly came into his mind, and, thinking this a proper opportunity to accomplish it, he basely violated the laws of gratitude and hospitality, and ran the king through the body with ais own spear. The wound was mortal, and the attendants, advancing to take full revenge upon the traitor, the expiring prince laid his dying commands upon them, to save his life, and pardon the murderer. His orders were faithfully obeyed; Conla had his life spared, and the king was carried on shore and instantly died.

It was observed before, in a preceding part of this history, that Cormac, king of Ireland, had ten daughters; yet the ancient records being silent, and mentioning nothing memorable of eight of these princesses, what they have related of the other two will be properly introduced in this place. The name of one of these ladies was Graine, who was married to Fionn, the son of Cumhall; but being of an amorous disposition she left him, and stole away with her gallant Diarmuid O'Duibhne; the other was called Ailbhe, who was married to her sister's husband, Fionn, the son of Cumhall.

From this Fionn the established militia of the kingdom were called Fiana Eirionn; and if it should be asserted either through ignorance or prejudice, that there was no such standing body of troops in the island as these trained bands, to evince the contrary, let it be considered that this part of history is supported by evidence not to be opposed. The constant tradition of the ancient Irish, concerning the militia, which has delivered down from father to son a continued account of many great and memorable exploits, performed by the bravery of these troops for many ages, is a testimony of sufficient force, with an impartial judgment, to prove that the brave Fiana, or Trained Bands, were fixed upon the Irish establishment, and were the standing army of the kingdom. As a further argument upon this occasion, let it be observed, that to deny the authority of this tradition is not only to suppose that the ancient Irish, for many centuries, conspired to abuse posterity with a fiction, but by this means the reputation of the most authentic records is disputed, which particularly relate the actions of the Irish militia. Besides, there remain to this day several unquestionable monuments of these old soldiers, to deny which, is to disbelieve matter of fact, and to oppose the common reason of mankind.

Some of the remaining footsteps of these old warriors are known by their first names at this time ; as, for instance, Suidhe Fionn, or the palace of Fionn, situated at Sliabh na Mban, or the Woman's Mountain, which seat was so called from Fionn O'Baoisgne. Gleann Garruidh, in Vibh Fathach, received its name from Garruidh Mac Morna ; Leaba Dhirmuda, and Graine, which signifies Diarmuid and Graine's Bed, and stood at a place called Poll tighe Liabain, in Vibh Fiachrach, in O'Shaghnusie's country. Many instances to the same purpose might be produced, to prove that many places in the kingdom retain, to this day, the names of some of the old Irish militia , but these are sufficient ; and to mention more would occasion too wide a breach in the progress of this history.

If it should be objected, that it is not to be supposed some particular transactions, relating to O'Fionn, and his Fiana Eirionn, or the Irish militia, can obtain belief, because some of the circumstances are impossible in fact, and therefore must be absolutely false, I confess, indeed, that the history of Ireland, in some degree, labours under the same misfortune with most of the old chronicles that were written in the times of idolatry and paganism ; and there is scarce a country upon earth, I suppose, whose primitive records are not disguised with fable and some incredible relations ; and even since Christianity appeared in the world, and the clouds of superstition and ignorance were in some measure dispelled, many strange and romantic accounts have been delivered with an air of truth, and obtained credit among weak judgments, notwithstanding the monstrous inconsistencies they abound with. But it is an unjustifiable consequence to conclude from thence, that the old records and chronicles of all nations are fables and rhapsodies ; as if antiquity was a sure and infallible mark of falsehood, and that the ancient writers were a gang of cheats and impostors, who conspired together to transmit lies and to impose upon posterity.

It cannot be denied, however, that many poetical fictions, and suspected relations, are foisted into the chronicles that treat of Fionn and his Irish militia ; such as, the battle of Fionn Tragha, Bruighean Chaorthuin, Achtra, and Ghiolla Dheacair, which are accounts, not so much designed to gain credit, as to relieve the reader, and to embellish and set off the history ; and therefore to weaken the authority of the whole, upon the account of some poetical fables interspersed, is too severe and unjustifiable a piece of criticism, and contrary to the common candour allowed to such ancient writings.

In some of the records, which treat of the old militia of Ireland, it is asserted that they were a body of men, so strong, and so tall of stature, as is really incredible; for it is certain, though there were a brave and undaunted number of troops, yet the size of the persons did not exceed the common proportion of those times. They were no more than a standing well-disciplined army, under the monarchs of Ireland, in whose hands the militia ever was, that were kept in regular and constant pay. Their business was to defend the country against foreign or domestic enemies, to support the right and succession of their kings, and to be ready at the shortest notice, upon any surprise or emergencies of the state. They were to guard the sea coasts, and to have a strict eye upon the creeks and havens of the island, lest any pirates should be lurking there, to plunder the country, and infest the inhabitants; and they were established for the same purpose as a standing body of forces are kept up in any nation, to defend it from invasions, to support the rights and prerogatives of the crown, and to secure the liberty and property of the people.

The way of subsisting these troops was by billeting them upon the country, from Allhallow-tide to the month of May, which was the winter season; during the other part of the year they were obliged to fish and to hunt, and find provision for themselves. But they were confined to perform their military exercise, and to be under discipline. The officers were enjoined not to oppress, but to defend the inhabitants from the attempts of thieves and robbers, and to promote the peace and happiness of the people: it was their duty to quell all riots and insurrections, to raise fines, and secure forfeited estates for the use of the king; to inquire into, and suppress all seditious and traitorous practices in the beginning, and to appear in arms when any occasion of the state required.

For these services they were allowed a regular pay, as the princes of Europe at this day maintain their armies; for though this militia had no pay from the kings of Ireland, but when they were in winter quarters, from Allhallow-tide to the month of May, yet, as was observed before, they had the privilege, for the other part of the year, to fish and fowl for their support, which was equivalent to their settled pay, for the flesh of what they killed they eat, and the skins they had liberty to sell, which afforded a good price.

The method of dressing their meat was very particular; for when they had success in hunting, it was their custom in the

forenoon to send their huntsman, with what they had killed, to
a proper place, where there was plenty of wood and water; there
they kindled great fires, into which their way was to throw a
number of large stones, where they were to continue till they
were red hot; then they applied themselves to dig two great
pits in the earth, into one of which, upon the bottom, they used
to lay some of those hot stones as a pavement, upon them they
would place the raw flesh, bound up hard in green sedge or bull-
rushes; over these bundles was fixed another layer of hot stones,
then a quantity of flesh, and this method was observed till the
pit was full. In this manner their flesh was sodden or stewed
till it was fit to eat, and then they uncovered it; and, when the
hole was emptied, they began their meal. This Irish militia, it
must be observed, never eat but once in twenty-four hours, and
their meal time was always in the evening. When they had a
mind to alter their diet, instead of stewing their meat, as we
have before mentioned, they would roast it before these fires
and make it palatable and wholesome.

And, as an undisputed evidence of these fires, the marks of
them continue deep in the earth, in many places of the island,
to this day; for they were very large, and burned exceeding
fierce, and the impression they left is now to be met with many
feet deep in the ground. When any husbandman in Ireland
turns up with his plough any black burnt earth, he immediately
knows the occasion of it; and the soil of that colour is known,
with great propriety, by the name of Fulaeht Fian to this time.

When the Irish militia came to these fires to dress their meat,
before they went to eat they would strip themselves to their
shirts, which they modestly tied about their middles, and go
into the other pit dug in the ground, which was very large, and
filled with water. Here they would wash their heads and necks,
and other parts of their bodies, till they had cleansed themselves
from the sweat and dust occasioned by their hunting; and this
custom was very wholesome and refreshing, for they would rub
their limbs and their joints till they had forgot all their fatigue,
and became as sprightly and active as when they began their
sport in the morning: when they were perfectly clean, they
would put on their clothes, and begin their meal.

After they had eaten they would apply themselves to build
huts and tents, where they made their beds, and designed to repose themselves for the following night. These beds were composed and laid out with great exactness They cut down branches
of trees, which they placed next the ground; upon these was

laid a quantity of dry moss, and upon the top of all was strewed a bundle of green rushes, which made a very commodious lodging. These beds, in the ancient manuscripts, are called Tri cuilceadha na feine ; which in English signifies the three beds of the Irish militia.

Campian, an author of little veracity, would impose upon the world, by asserting that Fionn, the son of Cumhall, was known by the name of Roanus ; but this is either an ignorant mistake or a signal instance of the prejudice of this writer, for the father of Cumhall was Trein More, the fourth lineal descendant of Nuagadh Neacht, king of Leinster, and the mother of Fionn was Muirn Munchaomh, the daughter of Thady, the son of Nuagatt, an eminent druid, retained in the family of Cathaoir More. Almhuin, in the province of Leinster, was the native country and inheritance of Thady, the son of Nuagatt, upon which account Fionn obtained possession of Almhuin, in right of his mother ; yet Fionn was invested with the country of Formaoilna Bhfian, in Cinseallach, where Limerick, in Leinster, now stands, by the donation of the king of Leinster.

Hector Boetius, another fabulous writer, in his history of Scotland, imposes upon the world, by asserting that Fionn was of a gigantic size, and that he was fifteen cubits high ; but by the ancient records of the kingdom, whose authority will be for ever sacred with me, it appears that Fionn did not exceed the common proportion of the men of his time : and there were many soldiers in the militia of Ireland, that had a more robust constitution of body, and were of a more extraordinary stature , and the reason why Fionn was the general and first commanding officer over the Irish militia was, because his father and grandfather enjoyed the same dignity before him, and had the honour to be at the head of those invincible troops ; but upon this account more especially he had the principal command of the standing army, as he was a person of superior courage, of great learning and militar[y] experience, which accomplishments advanced him in the esteem of the soldiery, who thought him worthy to lead them. His uncommon stature, therefore, and gigantic strength, are mere fictions, designed to abuse the world, and to destroy the credit of these historians who treat upon the affairs of the old Irish government.

The constant number of those standing forces, that were quartered upon the kingdom of Ireland, was three battalions, each battalion consisting of 3,000 able men. But this was the establishment only in time of peace, when there were no dis turbances at home, or fear of any invasions from abroad. But if there were any public discontents, or any apprehensions of a rebellion or a conspiracy; if there arose any contests between the king and his nobility, or the king found himself under a necessity to transport a body of troops into Scotland, to assist the Dailriads, or upon any surprise or difficulties of the state, Fionn increased his forces to the number of seven battalions, which was strength sufficient to assist his friends, the Dailriads, in Scotland, and to defend the kingdom of Ireland from the attacks of domestic or foreign enemies.

It has been observed, that Fionn was the commander-in-chief of the Irish militia, but he had several inferior officers, who, in their degrees, exercised an authority under him, by his commission. Every battalion or legion was commanded by a colonel; every hundred men were under the conduct of a captain; an officer, in the nature of a lieutenant, had fifty under him; and a sergeant, resembling the Decurio of the Romans, was set over five-and-twenty: but when an hundred of these militia were drawn out, by ten in a rank, there was an officer appointed over every ten of them commonly called the commander of ten; and, therefore, when the chronicles of Ireland make mention of Fear Comhlan Cead, or Fear Comhlan Caoguid, which signifies a man able to engage with a hundred, and another to fight with fifty, it is not to be understood as if the first was able to encounter an hundred himself, and conquer them with his own hand, or the other had the courage to engage with fifty, and come off with victory; the meaning is, that such an officer had the command of an hundred men, with whom he would fight hand to hand with the same number of enemies; and that an officer who had fifty under him, would engage with any fifty that opposed him, with their commander at the head of them.

Every soldier that was received into the militia of Ireland by Fionn, was obliged, before he was enrolled, to subscribe to the following articles : the first, that, when he was disposed to marry, he would not follow the mercenary custom of insisting upon a portion with a wife, but, without regard to her fortune, he should choose a woman for her virtue, her courtesy, and good manners. The second, that he would never offer violence to a woman, or attempt to ravish her. The third, that he would be charitable and relieve the poor, who desired meat or drink, as far as his abilities would permit. The fourth, that he would not turn his back, or refuse to fight with nine men of any other nation that set upon him, and offered to fight with him.

It must not be supposed, that every person who was willing to be enlisted in the militia of Ireland, would be accepted ; for Fionn was very strict in his inquiry, and observed these rules in filling up the number of his troops, which were exactly followed by his successors in command, when they had occasion to recruit their forces.

He ordained, therefore, that no person should be enlisted or received into the service, in the congregation or assembly of Visneach, or in the celebrated fair of Tailtean, or at Feas Teamhrach, unless his father and mother, and all the relatives of his family, would stipulate and give proper security, that not one of them should attempt to revenge his death upon the person that slew him, but to leave the affair of his death wholly in the hands of his fellow-soldiers, who would take care to do him justice as the case required ; and it was ordained, likewise, that the relations of a soldier of this militia should not receive any damage or reproach for any misbehaviour committed by him.

The second qualification for admittance into these standing forces was, that no one should be received unless he had a poetical genius, and could compose verses, and was well acquainted with the twelve books of poetry.

The third condition was, that he should be a perfect master of his weapons, and able to defend himself against all attacks ; and to prove his dexterity in the management of his arms, he was placed in a plain field, encompassed with green sêdge, that reached above his knee ; he was to have a target by him, and a hazle stake in his hand of the length of a man's arm. Then nine experienced soldiers of the militia were drawn out, and appointed to stand at the distance of nine ridges of land from him, and to throw all their javelins at him at once ; if he had the skill, with his target and his stake, to defend himself, and come off unhurt, he was admitted into the service ; but if he had the misfortune to be wounded by one of those javelins, he was rejected as unqualified, and turned off with reproach.

A fourth qualification was, that he should run well, and in his flight defend himself from his enemy ; and to make a trial of his activity he had his hair plaited, and was obliged to run through a wood, with all the militia pursuing him, and was allowed but the breadth of a tree before the rest at his setting out ; if he was overtaken in the chase, or received a wound before he had ran through the wood, he was refused, as too sluggish and unskilful to fight with honour among those valiant troops.

It was required, in the fifth place, that whoever was a candidate for admission into the militia, should have a strong arm, and hold his weapons steady ; and if it was observed that his hands shook, he was rejected.

The sixth requisite was, that when he ran through a wood his hair should continue tied up, during the chase ; if it fell loose, he could not be received.

The seventh qualification was, to be so swift and light of foot as not to break a rotten stick by standing upon it.

The eighth condition was, that none should have the honour of being enrolled among the Irish militia, that was not so active as to leap over a tree as high as his forehead ; or could not, by the agility of his body, stoop easily under a tree that was lower than his knees.

The ninth condition required was, that he could, without stopping or lessening his speed, draw a thorn out of his foot.

The tenth and last qualification was, to take an oath of allegiance to be true and faithful to the commanding officer of the army. These were the terms required for admission among these brave troops ; which, so long as they were exactly insisted upon, the militia of Ireland were an invincible defence to their country, and a terror to rebels at home and enemies abroad.

It happened, that, when Cormac was monarch of Ireland, some of the principal gentry of the province of Ulster transported themselves into Scotland, and committed great hostilities upon the coasts : and, in some of their incursions, they had the fortune to surprise the beautiful Ciarnuit, daughter to the king of the Picts. With this fair prize, and other valuable booty, they returned into Ireland. The beauty of this captived lady could not be long concealed, and came at length to the ears of Cormac, who, before he saw her, was so transported with the relation of her charms, that he demanded her of the gentry who brought her out of her own country , accordingly she was presented to the king, who fitted up an apartment for her in his palace, and valued her beyond all the ladies of his court.

But her beauty, and the place she had in the king's favour, occasioned her many enemies ; and the queen resolved upon revenge, for robbing her of her husband's love, and soon found means to put her designs in execution. The queen of Cormac at this time was Eithne Ollamhada, the daughter of Dunluing, and, being a lady of great spirit, she resented the indignity she had received in so violent a manner, that she boldly told the king, that, unless he would deliver into her hands this mistress

of his, she would leave the court, and separate herself from him
for ever. Cormac, unwilling to incense his injured queen, and
to drive her to extremities, resigned the fair Ciarnuit into her
hands, whom she used with great severity, and, as a punishment,
obliged her every day to grind with a quern or hand-mill nine
quarters of corn. But notwithstanding the close confinement
she was under, the king could not give up his passion, but found
means to be admitted privately where she lay, and got her with
child. Her slavery was continued by the queen, who insisted
on the quantity of meal ; but when she grew big she became
weak and faint, and unable to perform the task enjoined her.
In this distress, upon the first opportunity, she applied herself
to the king, and complained so tenderly of her misfortunes, that
he dispatched a messenger to Scotland, who brought over with
him one of the most expert carpenters of the kingdom. This
skilful mechanic in a short time erected a mill, by means of
which the unfortunate Ciarnuit was delivered from the daily
servitude enjoined her by the queen, as a just revenge for de-
frauding her of the esteem and affections of the king. This
transaction continues upon record, in the verses of an ancient
poet, in this manner :

> The lovely Ciarnuit, forced away
> And taken captive by her enemies,
> Was made a present to the Irish monarch,
> The royal Cormac, who, by beauty's charms
> Subdued, esteem'd her mistress of his heart.
> The jealous queen, with keen resentment fir'd,
> Demanded, in revenge, the Scottish lady,
> To be delivered to her mercy. The king
> Unwillingly consented ; for the fair
> Unfortunate Ciarnute was obliged
> To turn a mill, and, with her tender hands,
> To grind of corn nine quarters every day.
> In this distress, and in her poor apartment,
> The king would privately be introduced
> Till she grew big with child, and then, unable
> To undergo the slavery of the mill,
> She cried, and humbly begg'd her royal lover
> To send to Scotland for a skilful workman,
> Who, by his art, could make a proper engine
> To grind without her hand. The king complied ;
> The workman came, and, by his cunning skill,
> He made a mill, and eas'd her of her pains.

In the reign of Cormac, king of Ireland, it was, that the famous Fiothall flourished, who was the chief justice of the king-

dom. This learned judge had a son, whose name was Flaithrighe : when he was upon his death-bed he sent for his son, who
was a person of great learning and every way accomplished :
and, when he had given him his blessing in the most affection-
ate manner, he obliged him, by the bonds of his duty, to observe
four particulars, that would be of great service in the future
management of his life :—The first, that he should not undertake
the charge of educating and maintaining a king's son : the second, that he should not impart any secrets of importance to
his wife : the third, that he should not advance, nor be concerned
in promoting a clown, or a person of low birth and ill manners :
the fourth, was not to admit his sister into the government of
his affairs, nor trust her with the keeping of his house, or of
his money. These were the injunctions the expiring father laid
upon his son, who, after his decease, resolved to make trial whether it was of any consequence to observe them, and whether
any signal misfortune would attend the breach of them.

Accordingly he took upon himself the education of the son
of Cormac, king of Ireland, and engaged to breed him up.
When the child was able to go of itself, and to speak intelligibly, Flaithrighe carried him into a wood, and committed him
to the care of one of his herdsmen, an honest man, and whose
fidelity he could confide in ; he strictly commanded him to conceal the child in the most retired place of the wood, and admit
no body to the sight of him, unless he sent him a certain token, which was the sign that he might safely trust the person
to see him. When he had thus provided for the security of the
child, he returned home, and pretended to be exceedingly sorrowful and dejected, as if some misfortune of consequence had
befallen him : his wife observing him seemingly oppressed with
grief, inquired into the reason of his sorrow, which would be
eased by being discovered to her, who would willingly endure
a part with him in his sufferings. He gave her no answer at
first, which increased her curiosity, and she repeated her importunity, and more passionately entreated him to communicate to
her the cause of his affliction ; at last he complied, but upon
this condition, that she would never discover what he told her
to any creature living : she immediately bound herself to secrecy by a solemn oath, and he, upon this security, informed
her, that the reason of his melancholy was, that he had unfortunately killed the young prince committed to his care. The
woman, forgetting the obligation of her oath, and unmindful of the
duty she owed to her husband, immediately cried out, and basely

T

breaking her trust, she called the servants of the family to seize upon their master, who was a murderer and a traitor, for he had destroyed the king's son. The servants, surprised at the cruelty of the action, and urged by the instigation of their mistress, seized upon Flaithrighe, and when they had bound him they delivered him into the hands of justice.

In this manner were the two first injunctions of the father violated by the son, in order to make trial of the force and importance of them. The third he proved, by advancing the son of one of his shepherds, who was an illiterate person, and of no education, and promoting him to a good estate and an honourable employment. The fourth he made an experiment of, by committing, after his father's decease, the greatest part of his fortune to his sister, and trusting her with the principal management of all his affairs.

Flaithrighe was brought to trial for the murder of the king's son, and being convicted by the evidence of his wife, to whom he had confessed the fact, he was cast for his life, and by express sentence from the judge he was condemned to die ; and the most violent enemy in his misfortunes was the ungrateful son of the shepherd, whom he raised from poverty into plenty and granduer ; for he thought that, when Flaithrighe was executed, he should have an opportunity of purchasing his forfeited estate of the king, which he was able to do, by the great riches conferred upon him by his benefactor, whose life he resolved if possible to destroy. The unfortunate Flaithrighe thought that a sum of money, if well applied among the courtiers, might procure him a reprieve, and therefore he sent a messenger to his sister, to desire she would send him the bags he had intrusted her with, for his life was in the utmost danger, and if she denied him he was sure to be executed in a few days. The sister most inhumanly refused, adding this falsehood to her cruelty, that she never received any money from him, and wondered at the insolence of his demand. Flaithrighe, astonished at this reply, and the time of his execution approaching, desired, before his death, to be admitted into the king's presence, for he had a matter of great importance to communicate. His request being granted, he humbly asked pardon for reporting that the prince was dead, and assured him that his information was false, for he was alive and in perfect health ; and, says he, if your majesty distrust the truth of this, I will immediately send for him, and he shall appear safe before you. The king was surprised at this discovery, and commanded him to dispatch a messenger for the youth, and bring him instantly to court ; threatening him withal, that in this account of his proved false, he should be loaded with irons, and suffer the most ignomious and cruel death. The prisoner, as he was ordered, sent to his herdsman, and gave the messenger the sign agreed upon, whereby he was sure that the prince would be delivered. The child was soon brought to court and into the presence of the king, where his foster-father was, and when the youth beheld him fettered as a malefactor, he cried out, and humbly entreated the king, that the irons should be taken off. Flaithrighe was immediately released, and received into the king's favour, as a testimony of his innocence.

Cormac, being fully satisfied when he saw his son alive, demanded of Flaithrighe, what was the reason of this behaviour of his, and for what ends he brought himself under those difficulties, as to suffer imprisonment and fetters, and to put his life into the utmost hazard ? He answered that his design was only to prove the importance of four notable injunctions that his father laid upon him before his decease. The first, says he, was that I should not take upon me the care of educating and breeding up the son of a king, because if the youth comes to mischance or dies, the life of the foster-father is in the king's hand, and he lies wholly at his mercy. The second was, not to commit a secret to a woman, because the whole sex are talkative and unguarded, and oftentimes bring the life and honour of their husbands into danger, by discovering what they are bound by the most solemn obligations to conceal. The third command was, that I should not be concerned in advancing the son of a clown, of mean extract and low education ; because he soon forgets his benefactor, that raised him from poverty and rags into plenty and honour ; his principle is ingratitude, and he often contrives the destruction of his friend, in order to conceal the lowness of his descent and the baseness of his original. The last injunction was, that I should not commit the keeping of my wealth, or any valuable part of my fortune, into the hand of my sister ; and for an infallible reason, because it is the practice of women to make a prey of what they get into their hands, and what they receive only in trust, they understand as a gift, they rifle their nearest relations, and, if opportunity offers, will plunder them of all they have.

It was an established law, in the reign of Cormac, king of Ireland, that every monarch of the kingdom should be attended by these ten officers, which he was obliged to have always in his retinue; a lord, a judge, au augur or druid, a physician, a poet.

an antiquary, a musician, and three stewards of his household.
The duty of the lord was, to be a companion for the king, and to
entertain him with suitable discourse and conversation.   The
office of the judge was, to administer justice to the subjects, to
publish the laws and customs of the country, and to preside in
courts of judicature under the king, who was generally present
in those assemblies. The function of the druid was, to regulate
the concerns of religion, and the worship of the gods, to offer
sacrifices, to divine and foretel, for the use and advantage of
the king and country. The physician was to preserve the health
of the king, the queen, and the royal family, and to administer
medicines upon proper occasions.   The poet was to transmit to
posterity the heroic and memorable actions of famous men, of
whatsoever quality they were ; to compose satires upon de-
bauchery and vice ; and to lash the immorality of courtiers
and inferior persons, without partiality or affection.   The office
of the antiquary was, to preserve the genealogies of the kings
of Ireland, to correct the regal tables of succession, and to deliver down the pedigrees of every collateral branch of the royal
family.   He had likewise authority to supervise the genealogies
of the gentry and other private persons, and enter them into
the public records of the kingdom.   The musician was to divert
the king with his instruments, to sing before him, when he was
pleased to throw off public cares, and to ease his mind from the
business of the state.   The three principal stewards of the
household were to provide for his table, to wait upon the king
when he dined or eat in public, and to govern the inferior
officers and servants of the kitchen, and when they offended to
inflict proper punishments upon them.

These regulations and orders were observed strictly, for many
ages, by the successive monarchs of the kingdom, from the
reign of Cormac, to the death of Bryen, the son of Kennedy,
without any alteration.   But when the kings of Ireland were
received into the Christian faith, they dismissed the druid, who
was a pagan, and admitted into his place a Christian priest, as
a confessor, whose business it was to instruct the king in the
principles of his holy faith, and to assist him in his devotions.
These ancient customs of the Irish kings are confirmed by the
testimony of an eminent poet of great antiquity, who upon
this occasion has left these lines :

Ten royal officers, for use and state,
Attend the court, and on the monarch wait :

A nobleman, whose virtuous actions grace
His blood, and add new glories to his race.
A judge, to fix the meaning of the laws,
To save the poor, and right the injur'd cause.
A grave physician, by his artful care
To ease the sick, and weaken'd health repair.
A poet, to applaud and boldly blame,
And justly to give infamy or fame;
For without him the freshest laurels fade,
And vice to dark oblivion is betray'd.
The next attendant was a faithful priest.
Prophetic fury roll'd within his breast ·
Full of his god, he tells the distant doom
Of kings unborn, and nations yet to come;
Daily he worships at the holy shrine,
And pacifies his gods with rites divine,
With constant care the sacrifice renews,
And anxiously the panting entrails views.
To touch the harp, the sweet musician bends,
And both his hands upon the strings extends;
The sweetest sound flows from each warbling string,
Soft as the breezes of the breathing spring.
Music has pow'r the passions to control,
And tunes the harsh disorders of the soul.
  The antiquary, by his skill, reveals
The race of kings, and all their offspring tells.
The spreading branches of the royal line,
Traced out by him, in lasting records shine.
  Three officers in lower order stand,
And, when he dines in state, attend the king's command.

Cormac, the monarch of Ireland, it must be observed, was a prince of great virtue and strict morality, and very exact in the worship of the Deity, as far as the light of nature informed him; and his piety and devotion found acceptance and a reward from above, for the merciful God was pleased to deliver him from the obscurity of pagan darkness, and enlightened him with the true faith of the gospel. He was converted seven years before his death, during which time he refused to adore his false deities, and instead of bowing to his idols, he did homage as a devout Christian to the true God; so that this prince was the third person who believed in the faith of Christ, before the arrival of St. Patrick in Ireland. The names of these converts were Connor, the son of Neasa, who was informed of the sufferings of Christ, and the redemption of mankind, by Bacrach, a pagan druid; Moran, son of Maoin, the second, and Cormac, king of Ireland.

This prince kept his court, as did most of his predecessors in the throne of Ireland, at the royal palace of Tara, till he had

the misfortune to lose his eye by Aongus Gaothbhuailteach, as
before mentioned ; and from that time till he died, he lived in
a very mean house, covered with thatch, at Anachuill, in Ceananus. The reason of retiring from his court was, because the
principal nobility and gentry of the kingdom supposed it to be
a bad omen for the happiness of the public, if a king, who had
any blemish upon him, should reside in the royal palace of
Tara ; and therefore Cormac resigned the government to his
son, whose name was Cairbre Liffeachair, and contented himself
with that ordinary house at Anachuill, which was not far from
the court. In this contented privacy he spent the remainder
of his life ; and, being a prince of great learning, and an accomplished statesman, here it was that he drew up that admirable
treatise, called Advice to kings, for the use of his son, as was
observed before ; and during his retreat from public business,
he banished all rites of superstition and idolatry, and improved
himself in the worship and knowledge of the true God.

In those pagan times, one of the idols of the ancient Irish
was a golden calf, and it happened, that when Cormac was em-
ploying himself in devotion in his thatched house, some of the
druids that belonged to the court, brought this image into his
presence, and, as their custom was, fell down before it, and
adored it with divine worship ; but the king continued his addresses to the true God, and would not comply with their idolatry. Maoilogeann, who was the principal of these pagan
priests, perceiving that the king acted in contempt of their
holy rites, demanded of him the reason why he did not comply
with the religion of his ancestors, and pray to the golden calf,
and conform to the established worship ? The king answered,
that it was beneath the dignity of a rational being to adore a
brute, which he determined never to do, much less a log of wood
fashioned by the workman's hand, who was no more able to
make a God than to create himself, and therefore he would direct
his addresses to that supreme Being, who formed the carpenter
and the tree, superstitiously converted into a god. The druid
then conveyed away, the image, and soon after brought it to the
king, and presented it before him, dressed in the most magnificent attire, decked with jewels, and confidently demanded,
whether he would not address himself to a deity so splendidly
arrayed, and of so majestic appearance ? Cormac replied, that
it was in vain to tempt him to idolatry, for he was resolved to
pay no divine homage but to the one supreme God, the Creator
of the heavens and of the earth, and of a place of punishment

for the wicked. who corrupt his worship, and disobey his laws. This resolution of the king, it is supposed, cost him his life ; for the very same day, in the evening, a salmon was provided for his supper, which the sorcery and magical art of this pagan priest had' so enchanted, that a bone of the fish stuck in the king's throat, and choked him. Other authorities assert, that as the king was at supper eating the fish, a number of infernal fiends were raised by the charms of the druid Maoilogeann, who set upon the king, and strangled him : but before he expired, he gave orders to his servants not to bury him in the royal sepulture of the Irish monarchs ; for he would not have his dust mixed with that of his pagan predecessors.

His commands were obeyed, and another place was appointed for his interment ; but as his body was carrying upon a bier, after the custom of the country, the river Boyne was so enlarged, and overflowed its banks in so wonderful a manner, by the wicked arts of these infernal spirits, that the bearers could not attempt to pass over the channel ; for these furies of hell would not admit his body to be buried in a temple devoted to their service, because he refused to conform to their abominable rites, and introduced a way of worship in opposition to the established religion. This stratagem these cursed spirits made use of three several times, in order to prevent the interment of the body ; but the servants, intrusted with the care of the funeral, did not desist from their duty, for, notwithstanding these dreadful discouragements, they made a fourth attempt to carry the royal corpse over the river, but the body was whirled out of their hands by a hurricane, and dropped into the stream, which was so rapid, that it rolled it along to Rosnaroigh, where it was washed off from the carriage. Upon this account that part of the river Boyne is distinguished by the name of Athfuaid to this day : for Ath in the Irish language signifies a ford, and the word Fuaid, a bier, which, being joined, are pronounced Athfuaid. The body, when it was found, was taken up, and buried solemnly at Rosnaroigh.

A long time after this action, as the chronicles of Ireland inform us, the head of this monarch was found by St. Collum Cill, or, as modern authors call him, St. Columba, who buried it ; and in the same place he continued till he had celebrated thirty masses for his departed soul, which gave occasion to the erecting of a church over the grave, which remains to this day.

In those times there were two remarkable temples, or burying-places, where most of the Irish monarchs were interred. The names of these royal repositories were, Brugh na Boine, and Roilic na Riogh, near Cruachan, in the province of Conacht. The latter of these was of principal note, and contained the bodies of most of the ancient kings ; as the learned Torne Eigis, an eminent poet, gives us to understand, in the following verses :

> This sepulture preserves the royal dust
> Of the renowned monarchs of the isle.
> Here Dathy lies (whose acts were sung by fame)
> Near Cruachan's pensive walls : close by whose side,
> For great exploits in war and equal arms
> Dreaded, Dungalach sleeps ; who from his foe,
> Wrested by greater might, to his own sway,
> Numbers of captiv'd hosts in fetters bound,
> Witnessing thraldom.   Near the mournful shade
> These weeping marbles cast, are also laid
> The great remains of Conn, who sway'd with fame
> Hibernia's royal sceptre ; nor deny
> To hold the kindred dust, in love once join'd,
> Of Tuathal and Tumultach, who their sire,
> While mortal, Eochaidh Feidhlioch own ;
> He too, great parent of three sons as brave,
> Mingles his dust with those he once inspir'd
> With happy life ; nor does the grave refuse
> To keep the breathless dust, by death disjoin'd,
> Of Eochaidh Airiamh, who his fate
> Ow'd to Mormaol's sword, with blood distain'd.
> Nor could thy beauty, lovely once, secure
> Thee Clothro, or from death's subduing arm
> Guard thy all-conquering eyes, whose lance destroy'd
> (With thee in blood alike and charms allied
> Thy sisters Meidhbh and Murasg ; here entomb'd
> They rest in silence, near thre royal queens,
> (Forgetful now in death they ever reign d ,
> Eire, Fodhla, Banba, from the scepter'd line
> Sprung of the Tuatha de Danans, far renown'd
> For dire enchanting arts and magic power.
> In this repository sleep in peace
> Cearmada's royal sons ; three warlike names,
> While life and vigour could their arm inspire,
> Now lifeless each, nor more intent on fame.
> Here valiant Midher rests, to death a prey,
> While the still monument seems proud to hold
> The relicts of great Caol and Ugaine,
> Mixt with the brother dust, which lies entomb'd,
> Of Cobhthach and Badhbhcha, who, in happier times
> Were born, now sleep near Oilioll's princely urn.

Eochaidh Gunait succeeded in the throne of Ireland. A.D. 253. He was the son of Feig, son of Jomachaidh, son of Breasal, son of Fionchadha, son of Fiachadh Fionn (from whom Duilbfiath obtained its name). son of Dluthaig, son of

Deithsin, son of Sin, son of Rosin, son of Airndill, son of Maine, son of Forga, son of Feargus, son of Oilioll, son of Fiachadh Fearmara, son of Aongus Tuirmheach, of Tara, a prince descended from the royal line of Heremon. He was monarch of the island one year, and was slain by Lughaidh Feirtre.

A.D. 254.
Cairbre Liffeachair, the son of Cormac, son of Art, son of Conn, the hero of the hundred battles, succeeded, and governed the kingdom twenty-seven years. He was distinguished by the name of Cairbre Liffeachair, because he was nursed near the banks of the river Liffee, in Leinster. The mother of this prince was Eithne Ollamhda, the daughter of Dunluing, the son of Eana Madh; and he was slain by Simeon, the son of Ceirb, who came from the confines of Cource, or the borders of Leinster, in the battle of Gabhra, that was fought between this monarch and the militia of the kingdom, who took up arms against him. The reason of this rebellion, and the engagement that followed it, is recorded in this manner.

There was a lady, the daughter of Fionn, the general of the Irish militia, whose name was Samuir; her father bestowed her upon Cormas Cas, son of Oilioll Olum, by whom she had two sons, who were called Tinne and Conla. Upon account of this relation it was that Modha Corb, the son of Cormac Cas, kept, as his confident, his uncle Oisin, the son of Fionn and Clana Baoisgine, expressly contrary to the consent and order of Cairbre Liffeachair and Aodh Caomh, son of Gai idh Glandubh, of Clana Morna. At this time, it must be observed, that Clana Morna had authority to quarter and billet the militia of the kingdom, who were in a state of mutiny and rebellion against Fionn and Clana Baoisgine, and had been so for seven years before. For this reason Clana Morna attempted to persuade Cairbre Liffeachair, and the provincialists of Ireland, to re-establish Modha Corb in the throne of Munster, from a prospect that Clana Baoisgine would be expelled the province; which was the true occasion of the battle wherein this monarch lost his life.

281.
Fathach Airgtheach and Fathacl Cairptheach, the two sons of Mac Con, son of Macniadh, son of Luigheach, descended from the posterity of Ith, the son of Breogan, possessed themselves of the government; but their reign was short, for they did not govern a whole year before they were slain. Fathach Cairptheach fell by the sword of his brother Fathach Airgtheach; but he did not long survive this fratri-

cide, for he was soon dethroned by the militia of the kingdom,
who killed him in the battle of Ollarbha.

Fiachadh Sreabhthuine was the succeeding monarch.

A.D. 282. He was the son of Cairbre Liffeachair, son of Cormac
Ufada, derived from the royal line of Heremon, and sat
upon the throne thirty years, but fell at last by the sword of the
three Collas, in the bloody battle of Dubhchomar. This prince
obtained in marriage Aoife, the daughter of the king of Gall
Gaodhal, by whom he had a son called Muireadhach Tireach.
He was known by the name of Fiachadh Sreabhthuine, because
he was bred up, and had his education in Dun Sreabthuine, in
the province of Conacht.

To enlighten this part of the history, as far as the ruins of
time will give leave, it is proper to take notice of the reason
that gave occasion to this battle of Dubhchomar, which stands
recorded in that valuable record, the Psalter of Cashel ; and
likewise some account should be given of the genealogies that
belong to the relations of the Collas, which Fiachadh Sreabhthuine, son of Cairbre Liffeachair, divided ; Clana Gcolla, and
the Oirgiallaidh, from Clana Neill, and the posterity of the
same family, in the province of Conacht. This prince, Fiachadh
Sreabhthuine we have observed, was the son of Cairbre Liffeachair, and was the grandfather of Eochaidh Muighmeodhain,
son of Muireadhach Tireach, son of Fiachadh Sreabhthuine ;
from this prince Muireadhach descended Clana Neill, and those
of the same tribe in the province of Conacht. Eochaidh Dubhlein, the son of Cairbre Liffeachair, was likewise brother to Fia-
chuadh Sreabthuine ; this Eochaidh, we find, had three sons, who
were distinguished by the title of the three Collas, from whom
descended Ui Mac Vais, Ui Criomthan, and Mogh Drona. The
proper names of these three brothers, called the Collas, were
Cairioll, Muireadhach, and Aodh ; and this we understand by
the testimony of an ancient poet, who has transmitted the
account to us in these lines .

Three princes, once the glory of the isle,
Known by the name of the three warlike Collas.
Were sons of Eochaidh ; and in battle slew
The Irish monarch, for heroic deeds
Renown'd, and seiz'd upon the Irish sceptre;
These brothers are in ancient records call'd
Aodh, Muireadhach, and Cairioll,
Or for distinction otherwise express'd,
Cairioll Colla Uais, Aodha Colla Mean,
And Muireadhach Colla da Chrioch.

The wife of Eochaidh Dubhlein was Oilean, the daughter of the king of Scotland, whose glory it was to be the mother of these three martial princes, the three Collas; who, entering into a conspiracy against their native prince, Fiachadh Sreahhthuine, by the success of their treason, in a decisive battle, wrested the sovereignty out of his hands, and put an end to his life. The true occasion of this rebellion is recorded in this manner.

Fiachadh Sreabhthuine, the Irish monarch, had a son, whose name was Muireadhach Tireach. This young prince soon discovered a military genius, and obtained such experience in the art of war, that his father, convinced of his bravery and abilities, made him generalissimo of all his forces, and delivered into his hands the absolute command of his armies; for at that time the king never exposed himself at the head of his forces, his royal life being of that importance as not to be hazarded upon the uncertain issues of a battle. Upon some provocations from the king of Munster, it was thought necessary to send a strong body of troops into that province, under the command of Muireadhach, the young prince; and fortune, whose darling he was, followed him in all his undertakings, for he succeeded in this expedition beyond his hopes, and brought away with him a great number of captives, and an immense booty. His father, Fiachadh Sreabhthuine, king of Ireland, was encamped at that time at Dubhchomar, near Tailtean, with a numerous army; for the three Collas, his brother's sons, had raised a considerable body of troops, and joined the forces of the king, who by these forces became formidable, and resolved to do himself justice upon his enemies.

Now the success of the young prince, in the province of Munster, was known in the king's camp, which gave great satisfaction to his father, but was not so well received by the three Collas, who envied him the glory of his conquests, and therefore conspired to destroy the king, and seize upon the government; for they apprehended that when the young prince came to the throne, he would resent some indignities he had received from them, and at least banish them the court, if not take away their lives. They began, therefore, to concert measures, in order to execute their designs; and, prevailing upon some officers of the king's troops, they thought themselves able, with the forces they had brought along with them, and this additional strength, to engage with the Irish army, and give them battle; and if they came off with victory, they would be in a capacity to defeat the succession of the young prince, and to seize upon the crown.

It happened that at this time the king had a very eminent druid in his retinue, with whom he consulted upon this occasion; for he was made sensible of the treachery of the three brothers, who had separated their forces from the Irish army, and withdrawn to some distance, with a design to fall upon the king. The druid, whose name was Dubhchomair, made use of his art, and informed his master, that he found it would be of the last importance to himself and his family, to save the life of the three Collas, notwithstanding their rebellion; for if he destroyed them, the crown of Ireland should not be worn by any of his posterity, but descend into another line. The king was somewhat surprised at this reply, but upon recollection made this gallant answer, that he would joyfully resign his life, so that he might secure the succession to his descendants, rather than, by destroying those three traitors, be instrumental in fixing the crown upon the heads of their posterity; and armed with this resolution, which added to his natural bravery, he drew out his forces, and fell upon the enemy; but his destiny, and the prediction of the druid followed him, for he was slain in the action.

A.D. 315.   Colla Uais, obtaining a complete victory, was proclaimed monarch of the kingdom. He was the son of Cairbre Liffeachair, a descendant from the posterity of Heremon, and supported his title to the goverment four years. But the lawful heir, Muireadhach Tireach, the son of the deceased king, kept his pretensions on foot, and with a brave body of loyal troops engaged the usurper, and his success was equal to the justice of his cause, for he dethroned him, and drove him out of the kingdom. He fled for refuge with his two brothers to the court of the king of Scotland, where they were hospitably received, and allowed protection. The reason that prevailed upon them to fly into that country was, because they bore a very near relation to the king; for the princess Oilean was a daughter to the king of Scotland, the wife of Eochaidh Dubhlein, and the mother of these three ambitious brothers. This ursurper was distinguished by the name of Colla Uais, as he was of a more noble and martial disposition than his brothers, and as he found means to fix the crown of Ireland upon his head for some time, which the other two were so far from accomplishing, that they were obliged to leave their country, and remove into a foreign land to save their lives.

A.D.
319.
Muireadhach Tireach succeeded the usurper. He was the son of Fiachadh Sreabhthuine, son of Cairbre Liffeachair, descended from the royal line of Heremon, and governed the kingdom thirty years; but was at length killed by Caolbhach, the son of Cruin Badhraoi. The consort of this prince was Muirion, the daughter of Fiachadh, king of Cinneal Eoguin, and the mother of Eochaidh Muighmeodhoin.

The three Collas, being expelled the kingdom of Ireland, were forced to fly for refuge to the king of Scotland, who supported them suitable to their quality, and entered 300 soldiers, that followed them, into the regular pay of his own army; for they were a handful of brave hardy men, and wonderfully esteemed by the king, for the comeliness of their persons, and undaunted resolution and courage. The three brothers continued in Scotland for the space of three years; till tired at length of residing in a strange land, they called to mind the prediction of the druid before-mentioned, which foretold, that if they fell by the hand of the king of Ireland, the crown should devolve upon their posterity; they resolved, therefore, to accomplish this prophecy, at all hazards, and settle the succession upon some of their descendants. Arriving in Ireland, with no more than nine persons to attend upon each of them, they directed their march towards the court, with a design to offer their lives into the king's hands, who, incensed with indignation and revenge, they expected would sacrifice them to the manes of his murdered father. When they came to Tara with so small a guard, they were admitted into the presence of the king, who, instead of committing them to prison, or punishing them with immediate death, as traitors and rebels, received them courteously, and congratulated them on their return to their own country. He asked them what news there was from Scotland, and whether they were not dejected at the melancholy state of their affairs? They replied, that they were surprised at this unexpected reception, especially since they were the executioners of his royal father, which action sat very uneasy upon their minds, and gave them the utmost anguish in reflecting upon it. The king answered, that clemency was one of the brightest jewels in the crowns of princes, and therefore he was contented to forgive their past crimes, and leave them to the justice of the immortal gods, and the sharp remorse of their own minds, which was the most severe torment that could be inflicted on the guilty; and as a testimony that they might depend upon the promise of a king, he conferred upon them

very signal marks of his favour, he settled a princely revenue
upon them, and made them principal officers in the command
of his army.

In these posts of trust and honour they continued for some
time, till the king, either jealous of their fidelity, or from a
principle of friendship and affection, told them, that the places
they enjoyed, and the salary attending them, would expire with
their lives, and not descend to their families ; and therefore he
recommended to them to consider of some provision for their
children, who would be left destitute, unless they took care to
secure an estate for them in their life-time.   He assured them
they might rely upon the continuance of his favour ; and, as an
evidence of his esteem, he generously offered them a number of
troops, sufficient to support them in their attempts, and to make
a conquest of lands and estates, that would be a dependance for
their posterity.   The brothers gratefully accepted of the king's
proposal, and desired to know what country was most proper
for them to invade : the king replied, that the province of
Ulster formerly offered such an indignity to one of their family,
that it demanded full revenge ; his advice therefore was, that
they should enter the country with fire and sword, and have
satisfaction of the inhabitants for banishing Cormac, son of Art,
after they had infamously branded him, by burning his beard
with a candle, at Magh Breag.   This injured prince was forced
to fly for security into Conacht, after he had been inhospitably
treated by the king of Ulster, at whose command a servant held
the lighted torch to his face ; and therefore they had a right,
he thought, not only to do themselves justice upon the people,
but to attempt the crown, and seize upon the government.

Accordingly the three brothers, supported by a numerous and
well-disciplined army, entered the province of Ulster ; and, instead of opposition from the inhabitants, they were joined upon
their arrival with a body of 7000 troops, and some of the principal nobility of the country at the head of them, who promised
to assist them in their pretensions, and stand by them with
their lives and fortunes.   This reinforcement put a good face
upon the enterprise, and raised the courage of the brothers, who
directed their march towards the provincial army, and came to
Carn Eochaidh Leathdhearg, in Fearmuighe.   Here the king of
Ulster was ready to receive the invaders, and both armies engaged ; a most desperate and bloody action it was, and after a
sharp dispute, the three brothers won the field.   The king
rallied his broken forces, and again offered battle to the victors,

but without success ; for his army was routed in seven several
engagements, one day after another, within the compass of a
week. The last dispute ended with a most terrible slaughter of
the king's troops ; and Feargus Fodha, king of Eamhain, was
slain : his army instantly fled, and were pursued with incredible
fury and bloodshed by the victors, who covered the earth with
their dead bodies, from Carn Eochaidh to Gleanrighe. By this
time the swords of the conquerors were so drenched and fatigued with the execution they made, that they were forced to
aesist, or not a man of the provincial army could possibly have
escaped.

The three Collas, animated with this victory, returned with
their forces to the palace of Eamhain, where the king of Ulster
kept his court. This royal seat they plundered, and set it on
fire ; by which means, though the fabric was not wholly consumed, yet it became so ruined and unfit for service, that it
could never recover its former magnificence, nor be used as a
palace by the kings of that province.

The brothers resolved to make the most of their success, and
made an absolute conquest of the countries of Modernuigh, Ui
Criomhthain, and Ui Mac Uais. Colla Mean, after he had dispossessed the inhabitants, fixed himself in the possession of
Modernuigh ; Colla da Chrioch obtained the territory of Criomhthain ; and Colla Uais settled himself in Mac Uais. With these
transactions we shall conclude the reign of Muireadhach Tireach, king of Ireland, who was slain by Caolbhach, the son of
Cruin Badhraoi.

A.D.
352.

Caolbhach was the succeeding monarch. He was the
son of Cruin Badhraoi, son of Eachadh Ghobhna, son of
Luighdheach, son of Jomchoda, son of Feidhlim, son of
Cas, son of Fiachadh Aruidhe, son of Aongus Gaibion, son of
Feargus Foglas, son of Tiobhruidhe Tireach, son of Breasal, son
of Firb, son of Mail, son of Rochruidhe, a descendant from the
posterity of Ir, the son of Milesius, king of Spain. He possessed the sovereignty one year, and fell by the sword of Eochaidh Moighmeodhin. The mother of this prince was Inniaoht,
the daughter of Luighdheach.

353.

Eochaidh Moighmeodhin was the succeeding monarch.
He was the son of Muireadhach Tireach, son of Fiachadh
Sreabhthuine, a descendant from the royal line of Heremon, and governed the island seven years. This prince obtained in marriage, for his first wife, Mung Fionn, the daughter
of Fiodhuigh, by whom he had four sons, Brian, Fiachradh,

Feargus, and Oilioll. After the decease of this lady, his second consort was a Welsh princess, whose name was Carthan Cas Dubh, daughter of the king of Wales, by whom he had a son, who for his valour and military exploits was known by the name of Niall of the nine hostages. This king was distinguished by the title of Eochaidh Moighmeodhin, because his head, and the features of his complexion, resembled his father, but the size and shape of his body was like a common labourer, whose name was Miongadhach. This prince was at war with the king of Leinster; and the celebrated battle of Cruachan Claonta was fought between him and Eana Cinsalach, who had the government of that province. In this engagement a most eminent druid, whose name was Ceadmuithach, who was an attendant upon the king of Ireland, was taken prisoner by the army of Leinster. When he was brought before Eana Cinsalach, he asked his officers how they came to spare the life of the priest, and did not put him to the sword without giving him quarter? The druid, incensed with this question, boldly told the king, that whatever came of his life, he might be assured that he should never fight with success out of that field where he then stood. The king was enraged at this reply, and, with a scornful smile, instantly thrust his spear through the captive's body. The priest, perceiving himself ready to expire, had only time to assure the king, that the insulting smile, which attended the thrust that gave him his death's wound, should be a reproach to his posterity as long as one of them remained alive, for it should give them a name that would not be forgotten. This prediction was literally accomplished, for the family of this prince was afterwards known by the name of Vibh Cinsalach: the word Salach, in the Irish language, signifies foul or reproachful, a character that this royal line of Leinster could never wipe off. This king, Eana Cinsalach, was a fortunate and martial prince, and the most powerful and formidable of any of the petty princes of the island; as a poet of credit and antiquity has confirmed in the following lines:

The great Eana, that with honour fill'd
The throne of Leinster, and by victory
Followed where'er he fought, advanced the glory
Of the province: as an annual tribute, raised
An ounce of gold on every village; he forced
From every house in Leath Cuin, a tax
Of three pence yearly, as a just confession
Of his imperial sway; for to withstand
His power and his commands were certain death.

Though rage and cruelty did ever stain
His royal breast, adorn'd with numerous triumphs
He comes transmitted to posterity.

The Psalter of Cashel, whose credit and authority will admit of no dispute, has it upon record, that the aforesaid Eana fought fifteen battles in Leath Cuin, and came off with victory in every engagement.

A.D. 360.
Criomthan sat next upon the throne of Ireland. He was the son of Fiodhuig, son of Daire Cearb, son of Oilioll Flanbeg, son of Feachadh Muilleathan, son of Eogan More, son of Oilioll Olum, descended from the posterity of Heber Fionn, and wore the crown seventeen years. The royal consort of this prince was Fidheang, the daughter of the king of Conacht. This monarch carried his arms into foreign nations, and overcame the Scots, the Britons, and the French, in several engagements, and made them tributaries. A poet, whose authority is unquestionable, has given this account in the following manner:

The fam'd Criomthan sway'd the Irish sceptre:
And, dreaded for the fury of his arms,
His sovereignty extended cross the seas,
Unmindful of the dangers of the waves.
He with insuperable force subdued
The Scots, the Britons, and the warlike Gauls,
Who paid him homage, and confess'd his sway.

This renowned monarch bestowed the kingdom of Munster upon Conall Eachluath, who had his education with him from his youth. The donation of this province to a stranger, was thought unjust by the posterity of Fiachadh Muilleathan, who judged it proper to represent to Conall, that he was put into possession of what he had no right to enjoy; for though he was their kinsman, yet he could have no pretension to the crown of Munster, so long as the lawful heir was alive; that the government of the province ought to descend lineally to Core, the son of Luighdheach, who descended from the line of Fiachadh: and worthy he was to fill the throne of his ancestors, being a prince of consummate wisdom and undaunted bravery. This remonstrance had such an influence upon Conall, that he was willing to refer the case of the succession to proper arbitrators, that were learned in the law, and promised to abide by their determination The matter was debated on both sides before the umpires, who came to this resolution, that Core, the son of Luighdheach,

U

should first take possession of the government of Munster, as
he was of the eldest branch, but the crown should not descend
to his heirs; for the succession was limited and settled upon
the posterity of Cormac Cas.

The family of Fiachadh Muilleathan agreed to this award,
and engaged themselved by sureties, and the most solemn secu-
rities, that after the decease of Corc the crown should devolve
upon Conall Eachluath, if living, or his immediate heir, without contest or disturbance. This act of succession was conformable to what Oilioll Olum had before established upon the
same account; for he ordained that the two families should
have an alternate right to the crown of Munster successively,
and the throne be filled with the lineal posterity of Fiachadh
Muilleathan, and the lawful descendants of Cormac Cas.

Upon this arbitration the just and generous Conall resigned
the government of Munster into the hands of Corc, who, after
a short reign, died; and then he re-assumed the crown, as his
right, according to the establishment. By this uncommon act
of equity Conall was had in such esteem by Criomthan, king of
Ireland, that he delivered into his custody all the prisoners and
hostages that he brought over with him in triumph from the
kingdoms of Britain, Scotland, and France; for he thought he
could rely upon the integrity of a prince who delivered up the
possession of a crown that he was able to defend, for no other
reason but because he had no right to it, and who therefore
thought it would not sit easy upon his temples. This transaction is confirmed by a poem, to be found in the Psalter of
Cashel, composed by that son of the Muses, Cormac Mac Cuillenan.

> The kings of distant lands were forced to own
> The victor's power, and to the great Criomthan
> Tribute and homage paid; a worthier prince
> Ne'er fill'd a throne, nor sail'd to foreign shores,
> Unnumber'd captives he in triumph led,
> And hostages, the bonds of true submission.
> These pledges, and the prisoners of his wars,
> He trusted in the hands of the brave Conall;
> Than whom, a prince of more integrity,
> And stricter justice, never wore a crown.
> This prince, for arms and martial skill renown'd,
> Enlarg'd the bounds of his command, and rul'd
> With equity the countries he had won;
> He govern'd Fearta Conuill, in Feimhin,
> And Druin Cormaic Aine, and Dungar;
> His was the celebrated seat of Cashel,
> And Maig and Duncearmna.

The king Criomthan, notwithstanding his princely accomplishments, could not be secure from the villanous attempts of his own sister, whose name was Mung Fionn, for she resolved to destroy him, and prepared a dose of poison for that purpose, out of a prospect to obtain the crown for her son Brian, whom she had by Eochaidh Moighmeodhin. She found means to administer the draught, which had the desired effect, for the king died at Sliabh Vidhe an Riogh, that lies northward of Limerick. But vengeance close pursued the wicked executioner, who, the more securely to recommend the dose to the king, tasted of it herself, which despatched her at Inis Dornglass.

A.D. 375. Niall, distinguished by the name of the nine hostages, succeeded. He was the son of Eochaidh Moighmeodhin, son of Muireadhach Tireach, descended from the royal line of Heremon, and governed the kingdom twenty-seven years. The mother of this prince was Carthan Casdubh, daughter to the king of Britain. His first queen was Inne, the daughter of Luighdheach, who was the relict of Fiachadh ; his second consort was Roigneach, by whom he had seven sons, who are known in history by these names, Laoghaire, Eane, Maine, Eogan, two had the name of Conall and Cairbry.

This prince, at the request of the Dailriads, in Scotland, who were harassed and oppressed by the savage Picts, transported a numerous army into that kingdom to assist them. When he arrived he changed the old name of the country, and called it Scotia, at the request of the Dailriads and the Scots themselves, but it was upon condition that Scotland was to receive the honour of that appellation ; for it was agreed that it should be called only Scotia Minor, but Scotia Major was to be the name of Ireland. The occasion of this name was in honour and memory of the lady Scota, the daughter of Pharaoh Nectonebus, king of Egypt, who was queen to the famous Gollamh, otherwise called Milesius, king of Spain : from this monarch the Dailriads descended, and therefore they made choice that the island should be called by the name of Scotia Major, rather than Hibernia, or any other appellation. The authority of the learned Camden might be insisted upon in confirmation of this account, for he asserts, in his chronicle of Britain, that Scotland was called Scotia Minor, and Ireland Scotia Major; and declares that there is no certain evidence upon record, to prove that the inhabitants of Scotland were known by the name of Scots, before the time that Constantine the Great was emperor of Rome.

This judicious antiquary very justly calls the Irish Scotorum

Atavi, "the ancestors of the Scots," as an argument that the people of Scotland were originally derived from the ancient Irish; and the same author proceeds upon the same subject, and has this expression,* "The Scots came from Spain, and arrived in Ireland in the fourth age." To confirm the testimony of this writer, Nemius, a Welsh author of great credit, agrees with this opinion, which is so consistent with the Irish history, that it cannot be denied.

It is evident, from the ancient records of the island, that the country of Scotland was known by the name o. Albain, till the reign of Niall, distinguished by the title of the nine hostages; and as the tribe of the Dailriada prevailed that the country should be called for the future by the name of Scotia, so they and their posterity continued there, and enjoyed large territories for many ages. The kingdom of Scotland was styled Albania, from Albanactus, the third son of Brutus, to whom the country was assigned by lot, when the father was making provision for his children. This prince, Brutus, as Jeoffry of Monmouth relates, had three sons, and their names were Leagrus, Camber, and Albanactus, to whom he gave proper settlements: England he bestowed upon Leagrus, which after his name was called Lagria; the territory of Wales he conferred upon his son Camber, called after him Cambria; the country of Scotland fell to the share of Albanactus, from whom it obtained the name of Albania, and continues to be so called to this day.

Nial, the Irish monarch, upon some provocation, carried with him a great army from Scotland into Lagria. or England; and from thence transported it in a numerous fleet into Armorica, now called Bretagne, in the kingdom of France. These troops made great devastations in the country, for they met with little opposition; and, after plundering the inhabitants, returned with rich spoils and valuable booty. But the most considerable part of their prey consisted of 200 children, descended from the most noble blood in the province, whom they brought home with them, and among the rest was St. Patrick, a youth of about sixteen years of age; his two sisters, whose names were Lupida and Dareroa, were likewise carried into captivity, and the rest of the number were of the first rank.

Many are the authorities that might be urged to prove that the kingdom of Ireland was called Scotia, and that the inhabitants were known by the name of Cineadh Scuit. Among others,

---

* Scoti ex Hispania in Hiberniam quarta

Jonas the abbot, speaking of St. Collum Cill, in his second chap ter has this expression;* "Columbanus, who is also called Columba, was born in Ireland, a country inhabited by the nation of the Scots." The venerable Bede, in the first chapter of the history of England, asserts, that the Scots were the inhabitants of Ireland:† "Ireland is the original country of the Scots." And the same learned author, giving an account of the saints, speaks thus:‡ Saint Kilianus, and his two companions, came from Ireland, an island of the Scots." From the testimony of this faithful writer it appears, that the Irish were called Scots or Cineadh Scuit, in the time of Bede, who flourished about 700 years after the birth of Christ.

Orosius, who lived much earlier, in the fourth century, agrees with the evidences before produced ; and, in the second chapter of the first book, expresses himself thus:§ "Ireland is inhabited by the nation of the Scots." It is most certain, that the island was called by the name of Scotia by most authors. Serapius informs us, that "the blessed St. Kilian descended from the Scots;" his words are, beatus Kilianus Scotorum genere : and near the same place he says,|| "Scotland, which is also called Ireland ;" so that this island was known by both names. But as the clearest testimony in this matter, the expression of Capgravius must not be omitted. This author, writing of St. Collum Cill, has these words:¶ "The kingdom of Ireland was anciently called Scotland ; from whence came the people of the Scots that inhabit Albany, which joins to a part of the greatest Britain, and is now called Scotland." This evidence is supported by Marianus, a Scottish author, in this manner ; he is writing of St. Kilian, and speaks thus:** "At this time that part of Britain, which borders upon the north of England, is properly called Scotland ; but venerable Bede does not only

* Columbanus, qui Columba vocatur, in Hibernia ortus est, eam Scotorum gens incolit.
† Hibernia propria Scotorum patri est.
‡ Sanctus Kilianus et duo socii ejus ab Hibernia Scotorum insula veneruct.
§ Hibernia Scotorum gentibus colitor.
|| Scotia quæ et Hibernia dicitur.
¶ Hibernia enim antiquitus Scotia dicta est, de qua gens Scotorum Albania Britanniæ majori proxima, quæ ab eventu modo Scotia dicitur, originem duxit et progressum habuit.
** Etiamsi hodie Scotia proprie vocatur ea Britanniæ pars, quæ ipsi Angliæ continens ad septemtrionalem vergit, olim tamen eo nomine Hiberniam non tantum fuisse ostendit venerabilis Beda, cum ex Scotia Pictorum gentem in Hiberniam venisse ait, ibique Scotorum gentem invenisse.

prove that Ireland was formerly known by that name, when he says, that the nation of the Picts came from Scotland into Ireland, and there they found a nation of the Scots."

This opinion, that Ireland was formerly distinguished by the name of Scotia, is yet confirmed by the authority of Cæsarius, who lived about 500 years after Christ ; the words of this writer follow :* "Whoever doubts whether there be any such place as purgatory, let him go to Scotia, let him enter into the Purgatory of St. Patrick, and he will no longer disbelieve the pains of purgatory." This expression may justly be depended upon to prove that Scotia was then the proper name of the island ; for there is no place to be found, in Scotland, that goes by the name of St. Patrick's Purgatory, and it is certain that there is such a place in Ireland, to be met with at this day.

Cæsarius, speaking of St. Boniface, delivers his sentiments in this manner ;† "Ireland was properly known by the name of Scotia, out of which island a colony of Scots removed, and settled themselves in the part of Britain that was possessed by the Picts. They were called Dailreudins originally, from Rheuda, their general, as the venerable Bede observes ; and they expelled the Picts out of that country, and possessed themselves of all the northern coast, which they distinguished by the ancient name of their own nation. So that though the nation of the Scots was one, yet there were two countries known by the name of Scotia, the one the old Scotia, which is properly the kingdom of Ireland, the other the new, which is in north Britain." From the expression of this author, it is proper to observe, that he was persuaded that the Irish were the genuine Scots ; that the tribe of the Dailriads were the first called Scots, in Scotland ; and that the ancient name of Ireland was Scotia Major as Scotland was distinguished by the title of Scotia Minor which name was imposed upon that country by Cineadh Scuit.

Buchanan, a Scottish author of some note, has a passage in the second book of his history of Scotland, agreeable to the

---

* Qui de purgatorio dubitat, Scotiam pergat, Purgatorium Sancti Patricii intret, et de purgatorii pœnis amplius non dubitabit.

† Hibernia Scotia sibi nomen etiam vindicabit, qua tamen ex Hibernia ista Scotorum pars quædam egressa est, in eaque Britanniæ ora quam Picti jam habebant consederunt ; ii qui principio a duce suo Rheuda Dailreudini dicti fuerunt, ut ait venerabilis Beda ; postea tamen Pictos inde ipsos exegerunt ; et boreale totum illud latus obtinuerunt, eique vetus gentes suæ nomen indiderunt ; ita ut Scotorum gens una fuerit, sed Scotia duplex facta sit, una vetus et propria in Hibernia, recentior altera in septemtrionali Britannia

opinion of the writer above mentioned. His words are :* "All the inhabitants of Ireland were originally called Scots, as Orosius testifies; and our annals give an account, that the Scots of Ireland removed more than once into Scotland." From whence it is to be collected, that not only the Dailriads transported themselves from Ireland into Scotland, but that more of the inhabitants left the island, and obtained settlements in Scotland. And this is agreeable to the ancient records of the kingdom, which particularly mention several colonies, that from time to time invaded the country, and by their valour and other methods made themselves masters of new possessions, which continued in their families for many ages.

The Irish chronicles assert, that Aongus Ollmuchach, the son of Fiachadh Labhruine, was sent into Scotland, by the king his master, to settle and collect the tribute that was imposed upon the Picts, as an acknowledgment of homage and submission to the crown of Ireland; and this happened about 250 years after the Milesians were in possession of the island. At a considerable distance of time Reachta Righdhearg, king of Ireland, went into Scotland upon the same design, and imposed a tax upon the inhabitants. Cairbre Riada likewise transported a number of forces, and attempted to make a conquest of the eastern part of Scotland, from whom the Scottish Dailreudini, as the learned Bede observes, were lineally descended. Mac Con also had great authority in the government of Scotland and Wales, and from thence he came into Ireland, to the battle of Magh Muchruime. where Art, the son of Conn, the hero of the hundred battles was slain; by which success Mac Con obtained the sovereignty and was the succeeding monarch of the island. Some time afterward Fatha Canain, the son of Mac Con, with a resolute body of troops, invaded the coasts of Scotland, and got possession of large territories in the country. The posterity of this prince were the Mac Allens and their descendants. Colla Uais, and his followers, transported themselves into Scotland, and by their bravery and success obtained a settlement for their families; from this commander derived the noble and illustrious tribe of the Clan Donalls, in Scotland and Ireland. Criomhthan, the son of Fiachadh, the king of Ireland, made an invasion upon the Scottish dominions, as did Earc, the son of Eochaidh Munramhar, son of Aongus Firt, a prince descended from

---

* Scoti omnes Hiberniæ habitatores initio vocabantur, ut indicat Orosius, nec semel Scotorum ex Hibernia transitum in Albaniam factum nostri annales referunt.

Cairbre Riada, whose posterity are distinguished by the names
of Clan Eirc, and Cineal Gabhrain, in Scotland, and Cineal
Lodhairn, Cineal Comhghaill, Cineal Naongusa, and Cineal
Conchriche, in Nilii, with all the spreading branches of those
ancient families.   Maine Leamhna, the son of Corc, son of
Luighdheach, invaded the kingdom of Scotland, and succeeded
so far in his design, that he made a conquest of a large territory,
which from him was called Mormor Leamhna, now the duke-
dom of Lenox; and to this prince the noble family of the house
of Lenox owe their original.   Eoganach Moigh Geirgin descended from a brother of this Maine Leamhna, whose name
was Cairbre Cruithniach.   These two brothers, some time after
the reign of Niall of the nine hostages, went into Scotland, and
there settled themselves.   After them the six son of Muireadhach, the son of Eogan, son of Neill, encouraged by the success
of their countrymen, made an attempt, and got possessions in
the country; they were known by the names of the two Lo-
dains, two Aongus's, and two Feargus's : from whence it appears that the principal of the Scottish families were originally
d scended from the ancient Irish, to whom they owe the nobility
of their blood, and the glory of their families.

But it must be confessed, that the Scottish tribes that inhabit
near the borders of England, have no pretence to a descent
from the Irish ; because their ancestors were banished out of
England by William the Conqueror; which may be easily collected by the resemblance of manners and customs to be observed at this day between the borderers of both nations.

Many other families likewise, that have possessions in Scotland, have no right to boast of an Irish extraction, being the
posterity of the old English.   In testimony of this, we have
the authority of the laborious Stowe, who in his Annals gives
this account : Henry II. king of England, was engaged in a war
with the Scots, and took William, king of Scotland, prisoner,
whom he ordered into custody, and to be close confined at
Roan, in Normandy, where he continued a captive till he was
dismissed by paying a ransom of 400 pounds, after which both
kings made peace, and became friends.   The king of Scotland,
after his release, prepared to return into his own country ; and
determined, from a principle of gratitude, to take with him a
number of English gentlemen, who had obliged him by many
civilities in his restraint, and bestowed settlements upon them
among his subjects.   This he generously did, upon his return,
and appointed a large territory for the support of his English

attendants, and their heirs for ever, which estates are enjoyed by some of their posterity to this day. The names of the principal English, who followed the king into Scotland, are transmitted to us ; as, Balioll, Bruce, Rawly, Moubry, Sinclair, Hangiford, Ramsey, Barkley, Landell, Bisey, Wallegene, Royse, Montgomery, Walley, Colly, Milly, Fricer, Greme, Garley, and many others.

Buchanan, the Scottish author, agrees with this relation, in the second book of his history of Scotland, where he has this expression :* "Since the natives of Ireland, and the colonies sent from thence into Scotland, were originally called Scots ; in order to distinguish between the Irish and these Scots, they began to call those transplanted Irish by the name of Albanian Scots." From the testimony of this historian we are to observe, that the Scots, who inhabited Scotland, were originally natives of Ireland, and removed from thence to obtain new settlements ; and likewise, that the ancient Irish were originally known by the name of Scots. To confirm the opinion of this author, we have the concurring sentiments of the English annalist, the celebrated Stowe, which may be properly introduced in this place, before we treat particularly of the reign of Niall of the nine hostages ; because what we have to observe concerning that prince will receive an additional credit, by the authority of this great antiquary, who has been ever esteemed a writer of singular integrity and reputation.

The learned Stowe gives an account, that in the year of Christ 73, one Marius was king of England, and that Rogerus, king of the Picts, invaded the British territories with a numerous army out of Scotia, a strong body of hardy Scots, who entered the country with fire and sword, and by continued hostilities and incursions mightily distressed the inhabitants. The king of England, with a number of choice forces, made head against the invaders, and gave them battle, wherein Rogerus and most of his army were slain. The victor used his success with moderation ; for such of the enemy as surrendered to his mercy, he spared, and assigned them a competency of lands in the east part of Scotland, for their support. Here they settled, but having no women among them to perpetuate their families, they sent into Wales for a supply ; but they were denied, which

* Principio cum utrique id est Hiberniæ incolæ et coloni eorum in Albium missi Scoti appellarentur, ut discrimine aliquo alteri ab alteris distinguerentur initio conpare alteri Scoti Albani vocant.

made them to address the Irish, who complied with their request. So far we have followed the testimony of Stowe, as a collateral evidence upon this occasion. It was observed before, that the general of the Pictish army transported women out of Ireland with him, in the time of Heremon, which was about 300 years before Marius was king of England; and this transaction happened, as the same author asserts, in the year of Christ wherein Vespasian was elected emperor of Rome, which was ten years before the abbey of Glastonbury was built, and 272 years after the beginning of the Christian era, when Aurelian presided over the empire, and first attempted to adorn his head with an imperial crown.

A.D. 395.

Pelagius, a native of Wales, began first to broach his heresy, at which time it was, that the emperor Aurelian selected a number of the Roman clergy, and sent them into Great Britain, to instruct the inhabitants, and settle the Catholic religion among them. When they arrived they found the Scots and the Picts plundering and harassing the country without opposition. The Britons, in this extremity, sent their deputies to Honorius, the emperor, and implored his assistance; but the emperor at that time could not spare any troops to defend their conquests at so great a distance, and therefore the Britons received no other answer, than that they must provide for themselves in the best manner they could, for they were not to expect any succours from Rome. By this means the invaders brought the Britons under servitude, and cruelly fleeced the inhabitants, who were unable longer to bear the yoke, or to answer the exorbitant demands of the conquerors. Reduced to this distress, they again depute messengers, and send them to Rome, who succeeded so well in their negociations, that a legion was sent over with them; but this assistance was too weak to repel the victorious Picts, who had considerably enlarged their conquests, and almost overrun the whole kingdom. The Roman legion, upon their arrival, made several attempts upon the enemy, but with small success, for they could not boast of any advantage over the invaders, who fatigued them with continual skirmishes, and made them resolve to give over the attempt, and return to Rome; but, before they left the country, they persuaded the Britons to raise a strong fortification upon the borders of England, between them and their enemies, which would be a means to prevent the incursions of the Scots and Picts, and be a great security to the inhabitants.

The Roman auxiliaries departed, and when they were gone,

the Britons, perceiving themselves destitute of foreign succours, thought proper to put in execution the advice of fortifying their borders, and opposing the inroads of their neighbours; accordingly they made a deep trench, and raised a high bank of sods, from sea to sea; but this defence proved ineffectual to restrain the attempts of their enemies, for when the Scots and Picts had intelligence that the Romans had left the island, they immediately set upon the abandoned Britons, broke down the partition of turf, and, by plundering and other cruelties, brought great distress upon the inhabitants. These calamities were insupportable, and therefore the Britons, unable to bear or to redress these misfortunes, were obliged to send their deputies to Rome a third time, and by representing the deplorable state of the country, to humbly supplicate for relief. The Romans thought themselves obliged to defend their allies, and therefore sent a force over to their assistance. When they arrived, the Britons drew together their scattered forces, which, with the auxiliary legion, made a considerable army. With these troops they marched against the enemy, who, unable to bear the shock of the Roman courage, were obliged to fly with great loss, and were so dispirited with continual skirmishes and bad success, that they despaired of maintaining what they had acquired, and retired toward their own borders. Hither they were pursued by the victors, with great slaughter, and forced to retreat beyond the fortification erected by the Britons, and fly far into their own country to save their lives.

The Romans, having thus delivered the Britons from the cruel tyranny of the Scots and Picts, resolved to return; for they found it of small importance to undertake such long marches, and hazard their lives, when no rewards followed their victories, and their allies were in so low a condition, by the miseries of a long war, that they were unable to make them suitable satisfaction. Under these discouragements they left the island, and the distressed Britons, to the mercy of an enraged enemy, who soon had notice of their departure, and prepared themselves for another invasion. The Britons, apprehensive of their design, used their utmost diligence to repair the wall upon the borders, which they proposed to fortify with stronger materials than turf and dirt, and began to raise it with stone-work eight feet broad, and twelve feet high; as the learned Bede particularly relates in the fifth chapter of his English history.

By this time the Scots and Picts were ready for their attempt, and encouraged by the absence of the Romans, were certain of success ; for the enemies they were to engage with were broken-hearted, and accustomed to fly at the first attack. Accordingly they marched their forces, that were very numerous, towards the borders, and, making a wide breach in the partition-wall, they entered the country with dreadful hostilities, committing the most unheard-of outrages, and so dispirited the Britons, who dreaded their cruelty, that, without attempting to hinder their incursions, they were obliged, with their wives and families, to leave their habitations, and fly to the woods and wildernesses to preserve their lives. The invaders pursued them closely, resolving to extirpate the whole race of them, and besieged them within those inaccessible places, wherein they sheltered themselves, insomuch that the Britons were constrained to feed upon wild beasts and the natural produce of the earth ; for if they attempted to peep out of their fastnesses, they were in danger of being taken by the Picts and Scots, who used them barbarously, and put them to the most tormenting death.

In these miserable extremities they continued for some time, till at last their indefatigable and sharp-sighted enemies had driven them into a corner of the country, with the sea behind them, and the victorious invaders in front. This distressed condition obliged them to solicit mercy of the Romans once more ; and accordingly they found means to dispatch a messenger, with a most supplicating letter, to Boetius, one of the consuls. This epistle most pitifully represented the circumstances of their hard fate, how they were confined within a narrow compass, between the sea and the enemy; so that, if they attempted to fly, they were sure of being drowned ; and if they stirred out of their camp, they fell into the hands of the besiegers, the most inhuman and relentless enemy of the two, concluding in the most submissive manner, and imploring the assistance of the Romans against the Scots and Picts, who would unavoidably, in a short time, destroy the old Britons, and make themselves masters of the whole island. This transaction is particularly mentioned by the venerable Bede, in the thirteenth chapter of his history of England, where he has preserved the very expression made use of in that epistle to the consul ; the words are these :* " The barbarians drive us back to the sea, the sea beats us again upon the barbarians ; so that between these two enemies we have two sorts of death before us, we are either butchered or drowned."

* Repellunt barbari ad mare, repellit mare ad barbaros, inter hæc oriuntur duo genera funerum, aut jugulamur aut mergimur.

By the success of the Scots, in their invasions of the English, it appears that the Irish Scots, (as they all originally were,) had the Britons in subjection, and made them tributaries. Nonnius, an ancient British author, as Speed in his chronicle observes, asserts that the Scots and Picts were victorious over the Britons, who were a conquered people for the space of four hundred years; and the learned Camden confirms this opinion, where he says ;* "Five hundred years after Cæsar first entered the island, the kingdom of Britain was left abandoned to the Picts and Scots;" which farther deserves our belief, because the judicious Bede, in the fourteenth chapter of the first book of the before-mentioned history, has this expression :† "The audacious Irish plunderers are returned home, designing after a short time to invade us again." From whence it is obvious to collect, that the Irish were professed enemies to the Britons, and made frequent invasions into their country; for when the Romans would not interpose in their quarrels, but withdrew their succours, they were sorely harassed by the Scots and Picts, who reduced them to the lowest misery, and exercised an insupportable tyranny over them.

But the continual inroads and barbarities of their enemies was not the only calamity that oppressed the Britons; for about that time the Pelagian heresy gave them great uneasiness, which was propagated with great industry, and found kind reception among the populace. To stop the infection of these wicked principles, the Britons, unable to exercise any church discipline, by reason of their servitude, summoned a convention, and agreed in council to apply to the church of France, and desire they would send over some of their eminent prelates and divines to recover the people out of this filthy heresy, and establish them in the orthodox faith. The Gallican church held a meeting upon this message; and after some debates they resolved to dispatch two celebrated bishops, Germanus and Lupus, into Britain, to oppose the progress of the Pelagian doctrines. The prelates, when they arrived, applied themselves vigorously to the business they came about, and by the irresistible force of their arguments, and the piety of their lives, they so prevailed upon the affections of the people, that they renounced the impious tenets of Pelagius, and were confirmed in the principles of the true religion.

* Anno 500 a Cæsaris ingressu Britannia, Pictorum immanitati relinquuntur.
† Revertuntur impudentes grassatores Hiberni domum, post non longum tempus reversuri

The Scots and Picts, we have observed, were continual thorns in the sides of the Britons, and wars were waged between the two nations, until the reign of Vortigern, king of Britain, which was in the year of our Redemption 447. The inhabitants of Britain, at this time, were a very wicked people ; and heaven, for their impieties, delivered them under the power of the Scots and Picts, who were sore scourges in the hand of Providence, and ruled them with a rod of iron; insomuch, that the Britons were forced to send messengers to two Saxon princes, Hengist and Horsa, and desire their assistance. These foreigners landed in the island, attended with a numerous army, and in several engagements repelled the insolence of the Scots and Picts, and obliged them to give over their attempts, and to cease their hostilities. By the assistance of these German forces the Britons were freed from the incursions of their neighbours, who kept within their own borders, and the kingdom was settled in peace, to the universal joy and satisfaction of the inhabitants.

The indefatigable Stowe, in his British Chronicle, printed at London in the year 1614, at the fifty-second page, gives an account, that these Germans or Saxons were so pleased with the air and the fertility of the island, that they barbarously murdered, at one massacre, 480 of the nobility and gentry of Britain ; and that Aurelius Ambrosius, then king of Britain, caused the stones, that were brought by Merlin, from mount Clare, in the province of Munster, to be erected in the same place where the barbarous execution was committed, as an eternal monument of the German cruelty upon the natives of Britain. Some time afterwards Aurelius himself was buried in the same place ; and the same author observes, that these stones, when they were fixed, were called Chorea Gigantum, but now are known by the name of Stone Henge, upon Salisbury plain. That historian asserts farther, that the Irish brought these stones with them from Africa, and what Geoffry of Monmouth observes is very remarkable, that not two of those stones, came originally out of the same part of that country.

From the testimony of this English historian it is easy to believe, that the Irish fleets were accustomed to sail to Africa, that they made voyages abroad with honour and success, and obtained considerable authority in other countries beside their own ; and whoever disputes the grandeur and great character of the ancient Irish, betrays his ignorance of antiquity, and confesses that he never conversed with old records, which are the

ountain from whence an historian is to draw out his observa-
ions. Some persons would willingly be acquainted with the
elebrated transactions of past ages, without the trouble of read-
ng and study; for which reason they are mere pedants, and take
ıp with superficial relations, without searching into the original
ıf kingdoms, or turning over the old chronicles, that preserve
he memory of those renowned times. It is the observation of
Macrobius, in the sixth book of his Saturnalia;* "We are ignorant
ıf many things with which we might be acquainted, would we
nake the reading of the ancient annals familiar to us." And
his remark is in no instance more exactly verified than with
elation to the Irish history.

For when we assert that the kingdom of Britain was formerly
ributary to the Scots and Picts; if the integrity of our rela-
ion be suspected, we can immediately refer to the testimony oı
he learned Camden, who, in his chronicle, has this expression:+
'In the year 476 the Britons became tributary to the Scots
,nd Picts." And when we say that the Picts were afterwards
overpowered and suppressed by the Scots, we have liberty to
all in the evidence oı the same writer, who informs us, that
,bout the year 850, or, as others suppose, 839, when Cionaoth,
he son of Alpin, was king of Scotland, the Picts were brought
n subjection to the Scots. If the credit of this history should
xe questioned, because we insist that no other foreign powers
ıossessed the sovereignty of the kingdom of Ireland, but those
ırinces we have taken notice of, and whose succession we have
ıccounted for, such as Partholanus, Clana Neimidh, Firbólg, the
Tuatha de Danans, and the Milesians, we have authority to
ustify our relation, by citing the testimony of a reputable au-
hor, Gulielmus Nubirgensis, who says expressly in the twenty-
ıixth chapter of his second book,‡ "The kingdom of Ireland
ıever submitted to a foreign power." And lastly, if we trans-
nit to posterity some remarkable exploits of Niall, the hero of
he nine hostages, that were scarce ever heard of before, espe-
ially in the latter ages, we declare that we abhor to impose
ıpon the world with fictions of romantic adventures; but our
ıuthorities are the most valuable ancient records of the king-
lom, which we peruse with great caution and industry, and
from thence extract our materials, and are directed in our method
ınd the management of the subject before us.

* Multa ignoramus quæ non laterent, si veterum lectio nobis esset familiaris.
† Britanni facti sunt tributarii Scotis et Pictis, anno 476.
‡ Hibernia nunquam externæ subjecit ditioni.

There is an old manuscript in vellum, exceeding curious, entitled the life of St. Patrick, which treats likewise of the lives of Muchuda Albain and other saints, from whence I shall transcribe a citation that relates to St. Patrick, and particularly mentions that he was of Welsh extraction ;* "Patrick was a Briton born, and descended from religious parents." And in the same place he has the following remark :† "The Irish Scots, under Niall their king, wasted and destroyed many provinces of Britain, in opposition to the power of the Romans. They attempted to possess themselves of the northern part of Britain ; and, at length, having driven out the old inhabitants, those Irish seized upon the country, and settled in it." The same author, upon this occasion, remarks, that from thenceforth Great Britain was divided into three kingdoms, that were distinguished by the names of Scotia, Anglia, and Britia.

This ancient writer likewise asserts, that when Niall, the hero of the nine hostages, undertook the expedition of settling the tribe of the Dailriada in Scotland, the Irish fleet sailed to the place where St. Patrick resided :‡ "At this time the fleet out of Ireland plundered the country in which St. Patrick then lived, and, according to the custom of the Irish, many captives were carried away from thence, among whom was St. Patrick, in the sixteenth year of his age, and his two sisters, Lupida and Darerca ; and St. Patrick was led captive into Ireland in the ninth year of the reign of Niall, king of Ireland, who was the mighty monarch of the kingdom for twenty-seven years, and brought away spoils out of England, Britain and France." By this expression it is to be supposed that Niall of the nine hostages waged war against Britain, or Wales, and perhaps made a conquest of the country ; and it is more than probable that when this Irish prince had finished his design upon the kingdom of Wales, he carried his arms into France, and invaded the country, at that time called Armorica, but now Little Britanny, and from thence he led St. Patrick and his two sisters into captivity.

* Patricius Brito natus, ex parentibus religiosis ortus.

† Scoti de Hibernia sub rege suo Niall, diversas provincias Britanniæ contra Romanum imperium multum devastabunt, contendere incipientes aquilonalem Britanniæ plagam, tandem, ejectis veteribus colonis, ipsi Hibernienses eam occupaverunt et habitaverunt.

‡ Hoc tempore quædam classis Hibernica deprædavit patriam, in qua morabatur Divus Patricius, et consueto Hibernorum more, multi inde captivi ducti sunt, inter quos erant Divus Patricius, ætatis suæ anno decimo sexto, et duæ ejus sorores, Lupida et Darerca, et ductus est Divus Patricius in Hiberniam captivus, anno nono Niall, regis Hiberniæ, qui potenter 27 annis regnavit, ac Britanniam, et Angliam, et Galliam devastavit.

And this I am rather induced to believe, because the mother of St. Patrick was the sister of Martin, the bishop of Turin, in France ; and I have read in an ancient Irish manuscript, whose authority I cannot dispute, that St. Patrick and his two sisters were brought captive into Ireland, from Armorica, or Britanny, in the kingdom of France. It is evident likewise, that when Niall, the king of Ireland, had subdued the Britons, he dispatched a formidable fleet to plunder the coasts of France, and had so great success, that he carried away numbers of the natives with him into captivity, one of which, it is reasonable to suppose, was the young Patrick, who was afterwards distinguished by the name of the Irish saint.

Niall, encouraged by the number of his captives, and the success of his arms in France, resolved upon another expedition ; and accordingly raised a gallant army of his Irish subjects for that purpose, and sent a commission to the general of the Dailriada in Scotland, to follow him with his choicest troops, and assist him in the invasion. Niall, having prepared a sufficient number of transports, and a competency of provision, weighed anchor with his victorious Irish, and, steering his course directly to France, had the advantage of a prosperous gale, and in a few days landed upon the coasts : he immediately began to spoil and ravage the country near the river Loire ; here it was that the general of the Dailriada found him, and both armies being joined, they committed dreadful hostilities, which obliged the inhabitants to fly, and leave the country to the mercy of the invaders.

The commanding officer of the Dailriada, in this expedition, was Gabhran, the son of Domhanguirt, who brought over with him Eochaidh, the son of Eana Cinsalach, king of Leinster. This young prince had been formerly banished into Scotland by Niall, but resolving to be revenged, when opportunity offered, he desired to be admitted as a volunteer in the service, and by that means was transported into France. The king of Ireland being informed of his arrival, would on no account permit a visit from him, nor suffer him in his presence, but Eochaidh soon found an opportunity to execute his design, for one day perceiving the king sitting upon the bank of the Loire, he conveyed himself secretly into an opposite grove, on the other side, and shot Niall through the body with an arrow ; the wound was mortal, and he instantly expired.

The difference between the king of Ireland, and Eochaidh, the prince of Leinster, arose upon this occasion : the ambition of

Eochaidh incited him to keep his residence at Tara, as monarch
of the island, in express opposition to the command of the king,
and accordingly, by way of taking possession, he abode there
nine days and nights.   This attempt of his was censured by a
druid of principal note, who informed him, that by this practice
he had violated the ancient and solemn customs of Tara, which
enjoined, that no person should presume to keep his court in
that royal palace, before he was admitted into the order of
knighthood.   This intelligence had that effect, that Eochaidh
withdrew from Tara, and relinquished his pretensions to the
crown of Ireland.   When he was gone, Niall removed thither,
and kept his court as the king of Ireland ; and, lest Eochaidh
should again renew his claim to the crown, after many skirmishes and sharp disputes, he was banished into Scotland.

The king of Ireland received another provocation from Eochaidh, which incensed his resentment, and in some measure occasioned his banishment ; for when Eochaidh had abandoned
the royal seat of Tara, and was upon his way towards his own
province, he came to the house of Laidhgin, the son of Bair-
ceadha, a principal druid, who was in great favour with the
king of Ireland.   While he continued there the son of this
druid had the imprudence to throw out some contemptuous expressions against Eochaidh, which he so resented, that he fell
upon him, and killed him on the spot.   This action so enraged
the father, that he instantly applied himself to Niall for satisfaction, and, representing the fact in the most aggravating circumstances, prevailed upon the king, who promised to revenge
the death of his son upon the prince and people of Leinster.

Niall, with all expedition, prepared an army to invade the
province, which he entered with fire and sword, and miserably
distressed the inhabitants.   The druid followed the army into
Leinster, and perceiving the miseries the innocent people suffered by this dreadful invasion, he took pity on their misfortunes, and told them, that the king's forces should commit no
further disorders, if they would deliver Eochaidh, who was the
only criminal, into his hands.   The inhabitants, reduced to the
last extremities, accepted of this expedient ; and, though with
great reluctance, seized upon the prince, and surrendered him
into the power of his enraged enemy.

The druid, full of revenge, designed to execute his prisoner by
a lingering death, and therefore caused his body to be chained
to a great stone, that stood upright, and is now to be seen on
the west side of Slainy, between Cill Brighde and Tullach

O'Feidhlin. The unfortunate prince was obliged to stand with his back towards the stone ; and when he had remained there for some time, loaded and galled with the weight of the chain, the druid resolved to dispatch him, and put an end to his life ; he therefore commanded nine soldiers to set upon him, for Eochaidh was a person of great strength and invincible bravery, and he supposed would not fall without resistance. The prince perceiving the executioners advanced towards him, summoned all his courage, and forcing the chain with more than mortal strength, unrivetted the pin which fastened the ends of the chain, and obtained his liberty. Unarmed as he was, he fell upon the soldiers, and twisting their weapons out of their hands, he killed some of them, and, making good his retreat with safety, found means to escape into Scotland. When he arrived, he requested the protection of Gabhran, the son of Domhanguirt, the general of the Dailriada, with whom he came into France, and slew Niall, who was the occasion of all his misfortunes.

When this prince Eochaidh was in exile in Scotland, it happened that his wife, whose name was Feidhlin, the daughter of Cobhthain, son of Dathi, was with child ; and at the same time the wife of Gabhran, the son of Domhanguirt, whose name was Ingeanach, was likewise with child ; and both ladies, it seems, were equally near their travail, for they were both seized with pains, and delivered on the same night. For convenience, and by reason of the friendship that was between them, the two princesses lodged in the same apartment ; there were no persons admitted in the room but the midwife, all the other attendants being commanded to stay without the door till they were called. The Irish princess was delivered of two sons, and the Scottish lady, who had borne many children, but all females, and who passionately desired a son, the more to please and engage the affections of her husband, was delivered of a daughter. Therefore when she understood, that the other lady was delivered of two sons, she desired that she would part with one of them to her ; the Irish princess consented, and her friend received the infant into her bed with the greatest transport and satisfaction.

The artifice was concealed from the attendants, who, upon their admission into the room, perceiving that the Scottish lady had a son, instantly carried the joyful news to the father, who caressed the infant with the fondest endearments, and called him by the name of Eogan, not suspecting the fraud, but supposing it to be his own. He likewise complimented the Irish lady upon the birth of her young prince, who was known by the name of Raudubh, son of Eochaidh.

After the death of Niall, the hero of the nine hostages, Eochaidh returned into Ireland, and sent for his lady and his son from Scotland. He took possession of the government of Leinster, and was king of that province for many years. His friend Gabhran, the general of the Dailriadas, obtained the sovereignty of Scotland, and settled the succession upon his supposed son.

Eogan, the young prince, after the death of Gabhran, laid claim to the kingdom of Scotland by hereditary right, and was crowned without opposition ; and when he had settled the state of his affairs, he prepared a number of shipping, and a gallant army, to invade Ireland ; for he justified his pretensions to the kingdom, as he was a lineal descendant from Cairbre Riada. His forces consisted of English, Welsh, and Scots. When he landed upon the Irish coast, he began hostilities upon the province of Leinster. Randubh being unable, with the strength of his provincial troops, to oppose the invaders, was forced to see his subjects pillaged, and consult his own safety. His mother lived with him at that time, who, lamenting the distressed circumstances of her son, advised him not to sink under his misfortunes; for she would go in person to the king of Scotland, and by stratagem was confident she could put a stop to his spoiling of the country, and persuade him to retire out of the province. This motion came very seasonably, for the king of Scotland had then sent to the king of Leinster, to demand a heavy tribute from him, and, if refused, he threatened him with military execution, and the utmost miseries of fire and sword.

The good old lady, as she promised, set out for the Scottish camp, and when she arrived demanded audience of the king ; Eogan was surprised at the adventure, and supposing she was distracted, he admitted her into his presence. She then boldly expostulated with him upon the subject of his invasion, and, representing the cruel depredations he had committed upon the province of Leinster, she demanded with intrepid bravery, what provoked him to so barbarous and unwarrantable an undertaking. The king, enraged at this question, replied, that he was not obliged to answer the impudence of every old hag that should ask him questions, and commanded her to make the best of her way out of the camp. The lady, not discouraged at this reply, told him, that his mother was as much a hag as she, and if he pleased to give her liberty of speaking with him in private, she engaged to convince him, and inform him of a secret that was of the last importance to his interest. The king complied, and taking her aside from his attendants, was impatient to hear this weighty discovery. Sir, said she, I told you that your own mother was such a hag as myself, which is literally true; for I am your own mother, and Randubh, the king of Leinster, whom you seem resolved to drive out of his country is your own brother; and to evince my honour and veracity upon this occasion, I beseech you to send instantly to your supposed mother, the queen dowager of Scotland, who, I am confident, will assert the truth, and confess that you are my son; only let me entreat you to cease hostilities and outrages upon the province until the messenger returns. The king was astonished at this relation, and thought it of such importance, that he instantly dispatched a messenger into Scotland to his mother, and desired she would come to him into Ireland with all possible haste; for her presence was of absolute necessity, and concerned him in the most tender circumstances of his whole life. She complied with the request of her son, and, landing in Ireland, was conducted to the camp. The king of Scotland acquainted her with his message, and the surprising account he had heard from the queen of Leinster, and desired that she would satisfy him in the truth of the discovery, and declare upon her honour whether he was her son or not. The old lady openly confessed the whole intrigue between her and the queen of Leinster, and convinced the king in the point of his birth, who desired they would keep the matter secret, lest his right to the crown should be disputed, and an attempt made to prevent the succession of his family in the throne of Scotland. For if the tribe of the Dailriadas should be informed that he was not the son of the deceased king, they would dispute his title, and disturb his government. The ladies bound themselves to secrecy, a peace was immediately made, and a strict friendship established with Randubh, the prince of Leinster, and Eogan withdrew his forces from the island, and returned to Scotland.

Niall, the king of Ireland, had eight sons, who left a numerous posterity behind them, from which some noble families in the country claim an extraction at this day; but it will be improper, in this place, to speak particularly of their offspring and descendants, because they will be mentioned with more method, when we treat of the genealogies and spreading branches of the Milesians, or the Clana Mileadh. The reason why this prince was distinguished by the title of hero of the nine hostages, and is called in the Irish language Niall Naoighiallach, was because he had nine hostages in his custody, five from the provinces

of Ireland, and four from the kingdom of Scotland, in order to
secure the fidelity of his enemies in both countries, who he suspected would offer to raise commotions, and disturb the peace
of his reign; for the word Niall in the Irish, signifies in English, a prisoner or hostage.   This transaction is upon record, in
the verses of an ancient poet, who mentions it in this manner:

> Niall, the martial hero of the Irish,
> The son of the renowned Eochaidh,
> By force of arms, and military skill,
> Subdued the rebels who opposed his right;
> And, as a plege of their allegiance,
> Detain'd five hostages of noble blood;
> And, to secure the homage of the Scots,
> He kept confin'd four hostages of note:
> From whence this prince, the ancient records call,
> The Hero of the Nine Hostages.

A.D.
308.

Dathy was the succeeding monarch.   He was the son
of Fiachradh, son of Eochaidh Moighmeodhin, son of
Muireadhach Tireach, descended from the royal line of
Heremon, and he governed the kingdom twenty-three years.
His first consort was Fial, the daughter of Eachach, from whom
Feile Cruachan obtained its name.   His second queen was
Eithne, the daughter of Orach, by whom he had a son called
Oilioll Molt: his third wife was Ruadh, the daughter of Artigh
Uchelathan, the son of Fir Conga, and this lady was mother of
Fiachadh Ealgaigh, but unfortunately died in travail.   From
Dathy, king of Ireland, descended the noble families of the
O'Sheagnasy, king of Vibhfhiachrach, O'Dowd, in the Irish
O'Dubhda, O'Heyn, kings of Aidne, Kilkelly, in the Irish
Giollachealaigh, O'Cearaigh, O'Comain, O'Clierigh, O'Fahy, and
many illustrious tribes that will be particularly inserted in the
course of this history.   This monarch was distinguished by the
name of Dathy, because of his wonderful sprightliness and activity of body; for he was so accomplished, that he handled
his weapons dexterously, and put on his armour before he was
at the estate of a man; for the word Dathy signifies nimbleness
and agility.   This prince received his death by a thunderbolt,
as he was pursuing his conquests in the dominions of France,
where he had carried his arms with great success.   He died
near the foot of the Alps, from whence his army carried his
body with them into Ireland, and interred it with great solemnity at Roilicna Riogh, in Cruachan, after he had governed
the island twenty-three years.

THE SECOND BOOK.

Giving an account of the most memorable transactions of the ancient Irish, form their reception of Christianity to the invitation of the English in the reign of Henry II., king of England.

HAVING deduced the General History of Ireland from the first inhabitants of the kingdom to the death of Niall, the hero of the nine hostages, in whose reign St Patrick was brought into the island, we are now to prosecute the account of this nation, till the English were introduced by King Henry II., who went into the island in person, and, upon the submission of the nobility and principal gentry, confirmed the inhabitants in their estates and ancient liberties.

There is an author, one Sanders, whose legendary writings have ever been rejected by the lovers of truth, that has the confidence to assert, in his first book of the English wars, that as soon as the Irish had received the Christian faith, they submitted themselves, their consciences, and estates, to the management and direction of the Pope of Rome, and that they acknowledged no other sovereign prince in that kingdom but the Roman Pontiff, from the first establishment of Christianity in the island, till it fell into the hands of the English, under King Henry II. His expression is this .* "The inhabitants of Ireland, immediately upon embracing the Christian faith, surrendered themselves, their estates and fortunes, under the dominion of the Pope of Rome, nor did they own any other supreme prince, in that kingdom, besides the Roman Pontiff, down to that time." But the falsehood of this assertion is evident from the testimony of that ancient record, the Psalter of Cashel, which, speak-

---

* Hibernia initio statim post religionem acceptam, se suaque omnia in Pontifices Romani ditionem dederunt, nec quemque alium supremum principem Hiberniæ ad illud usque tempus preter unum Pontificem agnoverunt.

ing of the prophet Irial, a renowned monarch of Ireland, and a
son to Heremon, relates that many of that illustrious line filled
the throne, both before and for many ages after Christianity was
received in that kingdom. His words upon this occasion are
these : * "Irial the prophet reigned ten years, and before the
faith of Christ was propagated in Ireland by St. Patrick, there
were fifty-seven kings of his race, who governed that kingdom,
and after the time of St. Patrick, there were fifty kings in succession of the same family." And his account is consistent with the
ancient records of the kingdom, which take no notice of subjection to the see of Rome, but mention in the regal tables a
succession of princes of the royal Irish blood, and that the island
was governed independently by its own kings.

The author of the Polichronicon agrees with the preceding
account ; the words are,† "From the arrival of Saint Patrick
to the time of Feidhlim, there were thirty-three kings, who governed the kingdom for 400 years : in the reign of this prince,
the Norwegians made a conquest of the country, under Turgesius, their general."   Feidhlim was king of Munster in whose
time the king of Norway transported a body of hardy troops,
and brought the island into great troubles ; and from this citation it appears, that the Pope had not the sovereignty of the
kingdom, but that it was governed successively by many monarchs of the Milesian race, after the time of St. Patrick, till
the invasion of the Norwegians, who are otherwise called Fionn-
lochlannuig.   The same author has this expression in the same
place :‡ "From the time of Turgesius to the reign of Roderick,
the last monarch in Conacht, there were seventeen kings on the
throne of Ireland." From these testimonies it is evident, that
the Roman Pontiff had not the supreme authority in the island,
from the time of St. Patrick till the English arrived, under
Henry II., and settled in the country.

This account is farther confirmed by the testimony of Anselm.
archbishop of Canterbury, who inscribes his thirty-sixth epistle,§

---

* Irial propheta per decem annos regnavit, et antequam regula Christi per
Patricium seminata esset in Hibernia, de semine ejusdem regis quinquaginta septem reges regnaverunt super Hiberniam. et post Patricium de prole ipsius quinquaginta reges.

† Ab adventu Sancti Patricii usque ad Feidhlimidii regis tempora, triginta
tres reges per quadringentos annos in Hibernia regnaverunt: tempore autem
Feidhlimidii Norvecienses duce Turgesio terram hanc occuparunt.

‡ A tempore Turgesii usque ad ultimum monarchum, Rodoricum, Conaciæ
regem, decem et septem reges in Hibernia regnaverunt.

§ Moriardacho glorioso, gratia Dei, regi Hiberniæ.

"To the illustrious Moriartach, or Mortough O'Bryen, by the grace of God, king of Ireland." This epistle is to be found in the works of archbishop Usher, that learned prelate, who has, with indefatigable pains, collected the epistles that were sent between England and Ireland, and other great persons of both nations, and preserved them to posterity. The same archbishop Anselm wrote another letter to the same prince, and calls him expressly the renowned king of Ireland; and archbishop Lanfranc, one of his successors in the see of Canterbury, wrote a letter to Terlagh O'Bryen, king of Ireland, in the year 1074, and introduces it in this form :* "Lanfranc, a sinner, and the unworthy archbishop of the holy church of Canterbury, to the most magnificent Terlagh, king of Ireland, our benediction with our service and prayers." The learned Usher, in the same book, has preserved an epistle of great importance upon this subject, wherein Henry I., king of England, wrote to Rodolphus, archbishop of Canterbury, recommending to him, for holy orders, one Gregory, that upon admission into the priesthood he might be consecrated, at the request of the king of Ireland, to the bishopric of Dublin. This epistle was written in the year 1123, wherein is this expression :† "The king of Ireland has given me to understand, that by his writ, and by the consent of the burghers of Dublin, this Gregory is chosen to be a bishop, and they send him to you to be consecrated; my will therefore is, that you satisfy their desire by consecrating him without delay."

From what has been before said upon this subject, and from the concurring testimony of so many authorities, it appears that the kingdom of Ireland was governed by monarchs of the Milesian line, till the English invaded and settled in the country; and it is likewise evident, that the Roman Pontiff had no right of sovereignty, nor exercised any jurisdiction in the island, from the time of St. Patrick, than what he administered and laid claim to in other nations, not only in France and Spain, but in most of the countries of Christendom, which were go-

* Lanfrancus peccator, et indignus sanctæ Dorovernensis, ecclesiæ archiepiscopus, magnifico regi Hiberniæ Terdeluaco benedictionem cum servitio et orationibus.

† Mandavit mihi rex Hiberniæ per breve suum et burgenses Dubliniæ, quod elegerunt hunc Gregorium in episcopum, et eum mittunt tibi consecrandum: unde tibi mando ut petitionem eorum satisfaciens ejus consecrationem sine dilatione impleas.

verned by their own kings, and paid no homage to the see of Rome as to a temporal prince.

It must be confessed, notwithstanding, that about seventy-seven years before the English invitation, Donough, the son of Bryen Boiroimhe, undertook a journey to Rome, and had a commission from the principal nobility and gentry of the island, to offer themselves as subjects to the see of Rome, and implore the protection of the Roman Pontiff: and the reason of this act of submission was, because the petty princes of the island were continually quarrelling about the bounds of their territories; and these contests had so harassed and impoverished the island, that the inhabitants chose rather to submit themselves to a foreign power, than to be subject to the tyranny and oppression of their own kings. And what seemed to induce the people to offer their submission to the see of Rome was, that the Pontiff was not only a spiritual, but a temporal prince, of great interest and authority throughout Christendom, and able, by his assistance or mediation in the courts of foreign princes, to establish the peace, and secure the liberties and privileges of the country. But this surrender of the island into the hands of the Pope, is no evidence to confirm what is asserted by some authors, who relate that the emperor Constantine, upon his receiving the Christian faith, conferred the western isle of Europe, which is Ireland, upon Pope Sylvester; which is impossible to be true, for this reason, because this island was never conquered by the Romans, nor in the possession of Constantine, or any other emperor of Rome; and therefore it would be ridiculous in that emperor, or any other, to make a grant of an island to a prince, which he had no right to himself, and was never under his authority. Nor can it be supposed with reason, that an island so fruitful, so populous, so wealthy, and of so considerable an extent as the country of Ireland, should be without a king to command it for so many ages, but be governed by the Pope, and by his deputies, from the time of St. Patrick till the invasion by the English, who subdued it, and made it a tributary province; but we have been too long in refuting the falsehood of Sanders, an author of no credit, though it was proper to remove this objection before we proceeded farther in the course of this history.

Laogaire was the succeeding monarch. He was the A.D. 427. son of Niall, the hero of the nine hostages, and wore the crown thirty years; the mother of this Irish king was Roigheach. In the fourth year of this prince's reign, Pope Celestine commissioned St. Patrick with proper powers, and sent him into Ireland to propagate the Christian faith, and to establish the inhabitants in the belief of the Gospel. It was observed before, that St. Patrick was brought a captive from France into Ireland by Niall, in the ninth year of his reign, and that this saint was then a youth of sixteen years of age. Niall, after his victories in France, and his return home with his captives, enjoyed the crown eighteen years : Dathy, as we said before, was his successor, and he reigned twenty-three years. Now by adding the eighteen years of Niall, after St. Patrick arrived in Ireland, to the whole reign of Dathy, we come to the number of forty-one years ; with which, if we reckon sixteen years, that was the age of the saint when he was carried into captivity, and join to them four years of the reign of Laogaire, it is evident, that St. Patrick was sixty-one years of age when Pope Celestine sent him into Ireland to convert the country, and introduce Christianity among the inhabitants.

And to confirm this computation, we have, as evidence, the concurring testimony of a book, entitled, "Martyrologium," which asserts, that St. Patrick was 122 years of age when he died ; which proves that his age was sixty-one years when he arrived in Ireland to execute his commission, and preach the Gospel ; for it is beyond dispute, that he continued in the country sixty-one years, in converting the inhabitants, before his death. But St. Patrick was not the first person deputed by Pope Celestine to recommend the Christian faith to the Irish, for Palladius, a bishop, was sent before him, in the year 430, as the venerable Bede, in his English annals, particularly mentions ; his expression is,* "Palladius was the first bishop that was sent by Pope Celestine to the Christian Scots." The arrival of this prelate in the island, was in the third year of the reign of Laogaire, which was in the year preceding the landing of St. Patrick, as his successor, on the same important negociation.

Palladius, in this expedition, was attended by twelve clergymen ; with them he arrived in Ireland, and landed in the north part of the province of Leinster, at a place called Inbher Deaghadh. Here he erected three churches, which he consecrated, and dedicated them to three eminent saints ; the first was called Cillfinne, where he deposited his books, and some valuable relics of the apostles St. Peter and St. Paul ; the second was Teach na Romhanach ; and the third had the name of

---

* Anno quadringentesimo tricesimo Palladius ad Scotos in Christum credentes a Celestino Papa orimus mittitur episcopus.

Domhnach Arda. When he had finished the solemnity of consecration, and before he had an opportunity of making any
number of proselytes among the inhabitants, he was seized by
Nathi, the son of Garchon, a violent bigot for the old pagan
religion, who had the principal command in that part of the
country, and obliged Palladius and his followers to abandon
their design, and quit the island to preserve their lives.

One year after the expulsion of Palladius, St. Patrick, not
discouraged by the ill fortune of his predecessor, came into Ireland, and, resolving to prosecute his designs with vigour and
Christian zeal, he brought over with him twenty-four of the
Roman clergy to assist him in his undertaking. This account
is in some measure opposed by Henricus Antisiodorensis, who,
in the life of St. Germanus, in the 128th chapter, asserts, that
St. Patrick brought with him thirty holy men of the episcopal
order, and dispersed them over the country. These are the
words of that author,* "The blessed St. Patrick, having finished
his journey from a very distant country, not only comforted his
followers by his presence, but he appointed thirty bishops, whom
he had gathered together from the parts beyond the sea, after he
had consecrated them, into the Lord's harvest, because it was
great and the labourers were few" From hence it appears, that
St. Patrick proposed to himself the conversion of the whole
island, which it was impossible for him to accomplish in his own
person, and therefore he brought over with him a number of
pious and learned associates to carry on the work, and the more
effectually to propagate the faith ; and when he arrived in the
country, he inquired after those Scots who had embraced the
Gospel from the preaching of Palladius, whom he received into
communion, and ordained laws and canons for regulating his
converts, and forming them into discipline ; which injunctions
were religiously observed by the Irish Christians throughout the
kingdom, for 400 years after the death of St. Patrick, until the
island was invaded by the Danes. About the time that this
Irish apostle entered upon the execution of his office, there was
a mint erected at Ardmach and Cashel, and money coined for
the service of the state.

Henricus Antisiodorensis above mentioned, in his 174th chapter, asserts that St. Patrick laid out the whole kingdom into cer-

---

* Benedictus Patricius itinere longo de regione longinqua peracto, et prae-
sentia sua suos exhilarabat, et triginta episcopos ex transmarinis partibus con-
gregatos, et a se consecratos in Domini messem, eo quod esset multa et operarii
pauci, destinabat.

tain divisions, and disposed the inhabitants, their cattle, their goods, and all their effects into such a method, that he knew the produce of all the land, and understood the private fortune, and the abilities of all the people. The tenth, not only of the fruits of the earth, but of the inhabitants, their cattle, and their substance, he separated for the support of the clergy : the men he ordained into some religious order of the Roman Catholic church; the women he settled in convents and nunneries by themselves; for he had erected monasteries and other structures for their reception, and appointed a sufficient revenue for their constant support. This author is express to this purpose, where he delivers himself in this manner :* "He built a great number of monasteries, for the convenience of the men, whom he made monks, and of the women, whom he separated as nuns, and assigned the tenth part of the lands and of the cattle for their maintenance." The same writer observes farther upon this subject, that by the order and prudent management of St. Patrick, there was not the least part of the whole kingdom that did not abound with religious persons of exemplary piety, whose devotion and holy lives were admired and had in reverence among the neighbouring nations, who usually distinguished the country of Ireland by the name of the island of saints.

Nonnius, a Welsh author, in the history of Wales, bestows great encomiums upon St. Patrick, and, among other excellencies of his character, relates* that "he founded 355 churches, and consecrated the same number of bishops; but for presbyters he ordained 3000 of them." The testimony of this writer is confirmed by the authority of an old poet, who delivers the same account in the following lines :

> The bless'd St Patrick, with his priestly hands,
> The rite of consecration did confer
> Upon the most religious of his clergy,
> Three hundred and fifty-five in number.
> He likewise, for the service of the church,
> As many sacred structures did erect,
> And presbyters ordained three thousand.

If it should seem improbable, and not easy to be credited, that so great a number of bishops should be consecrated and

---

* Omnes ergo mares monachos fœminas sanctas moniales efficiens, numerosa monasteria edificavit; decimamque portionem terrarum ac pecudum corum sustentationi assignavit.

† Ecclesias 355 fundavit, episcopos ordinavit eodum numero; presbyteros autem usque ad tria millia ordinavit

disposed in the island at one time by St. Patrick, let the testimony of St. Bernard be admitted, to take off this difficulty, who, treating in the life of St. Malachias concerning the ecclesiastical customs and discipline originally established in the Irish church, makes use of this expression,* "The bishops are changed and multiplied at the will and discretion of the metropolitan ; so that one bishopric was not content with one bishop, but every particular church was governed by its own particular bishop. From the testimony of this writer it appears that the bishops of Ireland were very numerous when Christianity began to be established in the time of St. Patrick ; and indeed the necessity of the church, that was then in her infancy, required the joint endeavours of many faithful pastors to compose and qualify the minds of new converts, and to guard against the attempts of the great enemy of mankind, whose kingdom was shaken by the zeal and devotion of these prelates, and in apparent danger of being overthrown. And, as a farther evidence upon this subject, let it be considered that the ancient records of the kingdom inform us, that every deanery in the island had a bishop to preside over it : and the old chronicles relate that St. Patrick consecrated two archbishops in the country ; the archbishop of Ardmach, who was primate of all Ireland, and the archbishop of Cashel. The first of these prelates exercised a plenitude of power over the whole kingdom, especially his jurisdiction extended over Leath Cuinn ; the other had authority over Leath Modha, but in obedience and subordinate to the primate and metropolitan.

The reason of this distribution of ecclesiastical power seem to be because the sovereignty of the kingdom was in possession of the royal line of Heremon, of whose posterity was the monarch then reigning, Laogaire, the son of Niall, the renowned hero of the nine hostages. There were many personages of rank and quality descended from the royal branches of this family who became early converts to the Christian faith, and received the initiation of baptism from the hands of St. Patrick upon his first publication of the Gospel. The most eminent of these most noble proselytes were Eogan and Conall, who, with the principal relations of their family, insisted that the metropolitical church, that was to preside over the kingdom, should be erected

* Mutantur et multiplicantu episcopi pro libitu metropolitani ; ita ut unus episcopatus uno non esset contentus, sed singulæ penæ ecclesiæ singulos haberent episcopos.

and established at Leath Cuinn, and should have the precedency, and exercise a jurisdiction in spirituals over all the bishops in the island ; and this privilege they were the more importunate to obtain, because they had the supreme command over the kingdom at that time, and they were willing that the new archiepiscopal see should be honoured with the same rights and dignities, and be equally extensive with their temporal power. For the same reason it was that the descendants from the line of Heber Fionn desired and obtained from St. Patrick that the see in the second degree of jurisdiction and authority should be appointed in the division of the country which they enjoyed, and wherein they had the supreme command ; and accordingly the archiepiscopal diocese of Cashel, in Leath Modha, was established, because there lay the estate of that illustrious family, who were invested with great immunities and privileges in these parts, which they were in possession of from the reign of Conn, and exercised under the successive monarchs of the kingdom : and this receives an additional evidence from the testimony of the most authentic records of the island, which not only mention the archbishop of Cashel under the title of the archbishop of Munster, but likewise he is particularly called the archbishop of Leath Modha in the ancient records.

Some have imagined that Imliooh Jobhair was the seat of an archbishop in the time of St. Patrick, but the reason of this conjecture evidently arose from hence, that the archbishop and his clergy of Cashel, were violently banished from Cashel by the victorious Danes, who had almost subdued the whole kingdom, and supported themselves in their conquests by the most barbarous outrages and military executions. Maolseachlin, the son of Molrony, had fixed himself in possession of Meath, in the reign of Niall Caille over Ireland, and Olchabhair had seized upon the government of Munster, and seated himself in that province; and Turgesius, the Danish general, had spread a terror over the whole kingdom, and by his arms was in command of exceeding large territories. The country labouring under the heavy yoke of these foreigners, and the inhabitants flying from their settlements to preserve their lives, it may be supposed with great reason, that Foranan, who then was primate of Ardmach, retired from Cashel with his clergy, for their security, and absconded to Imlioch Jobhair, to conceal themselves from the cruelty of the Danes, who in their plunderings observed no distinction of sacred persons and things, but most dreadfully ravaged the country, and forced the inhabitants into slavery. In this solitude, that was defended by thick woods and dangerous bogs, did this primate and his college of clergy take up their residence, during the tyranny of the merciless Danes, which continued a long time, and reduced these most pious and excellent divines to great miseries and distress.

Nor does it appear from the ancient annals of the kingdom, that there were originally constituted any more archbishops in Ireland than the primate of Ardmach and the archbishop of Cashel. But the number afterwards increased; for in the year of our Lord 1152, the Roman cardinal, Johannes Papiron, made a voyage into Ireland, attended by Giallo Chriost O'Connaire, bishop of Lismore, who was commissioned with a legatine authority from the Pope. When they arrived they summoned a general convocation of the clergy, and assembled at Ceananus, in Meath; and in this convention an archbishop was consecrated for the city of Dublin, and another consecrated and appointed for the diocese of Tuam. These prelates, in this ecclesiastical assembly, obtained a Pallium, as will be particularly expressed hereafter, from the authority of the Irish annals, that were original'y written at Cluain Aiduach.

In the reign of Laogaire, king of Ireland, it was, as was before observed, that St. Patrick entered upon the execution of his ministerial office, and began to introduce the Gospel in the kingdom; at which time Aongus, the son of Nadfraoch, was king of Munster. This prince, being informed that St. Patrick was propagating the faith in some part of that province, resolved to apply himself to him in person, and went with his retinue as far as Magh Feimhin, where he found him preaching; he invited him to his royal seat at Cashel, where Aongus was instructed in the Christian principles, and was admitted by baptism into the communion of the church. This transaction is expressly upon record, in the life of St. Patrick above mentioned, where are these words :* " When St. Patrick went about the province of Munster, Aongus, the son of Nadfraoch, the king of Munster, went to meet him at Magh Feimhin, in the lands of the Deisies, and joyfully conveyed him to the royal city of Cashel, which is in the country of Eoganacht, where the king believed and was baptized." The same writer gives an account of a misfortune that happened at the time when the

* Dum vero Momoniam proficisceretur venit obviam ei rex Momoniæ Aongus, filius Nadfraoch, in campo Feimhin, in terra Deisi, eumque duxit in civitatem regalem, nomine Caisil, quæ est in regione Eoganacht. ibique credidit rex Aongus et baptizatus est.

king was standing at the font, and relates that St. Patrick, striking the end of his episcopal staff, that was defended with a spike of iron, with some vehemence, designing to fix it in the ground, he struck it through the foot of the king, which put him into great disorder; but notwithstanding the acute pain he suffered, and the abundance of blood which flowed from the wound, he had that regard for the religion into which he was baptized, that he would not stir from the place till the solemnity of the office was finished. This transaction is transmitted by the same authority in the following words,* "While St. Patrick was pronouncing the benediction over the king, who was standing to receive it, the point of the staff was fixed in the king's foot." From the testimony of this writer it appears that it was Aongus, the son of Nadfraoch, who had his foot transfixed with the episcopal staff; notwithstanding, it is the opinion of some, that the person who received this wound was Eogan, the son of Niall, king of Ulster; and as an indisputable evidence upon this occasion, the history of Leath Cuinn, very ancient, and of great authority, gives the same account, in the following verses, that were composed by the celebrated poet Torna O'Mulconaire.

His royal foot transfix'd, the gushing blood
Enrich'd the pavement with a noble flood.

Aongus, the king of Munster, had a numerous issue; for his children were twenty-four sons and as many daughters; and he showed that regard to the piety and institutions of St. Patrick, that he devoted twelve of each sex to the service of God, and confined them to a religious and monastic life. This prince settled a fixed revenue upon St. Patrick and the clergy of Ireland, to secure them from poverty and the contempt of the people. He ordained that every person that was admitted to baptism within the province of Munster should pay three pence for the service of the church; but the king, considering that it would be inconvenient for the clergy to collect their fees themselves, and divert them from the conscientious discharge of their office, ordered by law that this tax should be paid into the king's exchequer, who, in consideration of it, obliged himself and his successors to deliver to the convents and religious houses founded by St. Patrick, 500 cows, 500 bars of iron, 500 shirts, 500 mantles, and 500 sheep, which were to be duly provided every

* Cumque Sanctus Patricius regem stando benedixisset, cuspis baculi sancti fixa est in pede regis.

Y

year for the support and maintenance of the clergy ; and this triennial tribute was constantly paid into the treasury of the province till the time of Cormac Mac Cuillenan.

There is an account to be found in the Red Book of Mac Eognine, that Aongus, the son of Nadfraoch, king of Munster, was a pious prince ; that he retained two bishops, ten priests, and seventy-two persons of other religious orders, to attend upon him in his court, to say mass in his royal chapel and to offer up prayers to heaven for the happiness of himself and the whole kingdom ; and this he did by the direction of St. Patrick, who was the spiritual guide of this prince, and kept up the spirit of devotion in the court of Munster during the reign of Laogaire, the son of Niall, king of Ireland.

Bryen, the son of Eochaidh Moidhmeodhin, had twenty-four sons in the reign of Laogaire, the Irish monarch, at the time that St. Patrick was executing his commission in the kingdom. The principal of these brothers was Eichin, who had a large territory, and was of greatest authority in the province of Conacht. To him St. Patrick applied himself, with a design to recommend the Christian faith, and convert him from the pagan religion. But this prince was a violent bigot for the idolatry of his ancestors, and, instead of receiving the holy missionary with reverence suitable to his character, he was so transported with passion. that he fell upon him, and beat him without mercy ; and not contented with this barbarity, he commanded his brothers that were with him to correct him with blows, and show him no favour. The brothers obeyed the orders, and inhumanly cudgelled the saint, and bruised him all over his body : but the youngest, whose name was Duach Galach, was moved with compassion, and not only refused to strike him, but comforted him under his misfortune, and took care of his wounds, and entertained him honourably at his own house. This civility was so gratefully received by St. Patrick, that, as soon as he was able to go abroad, he went to the barbarous Eichin, and boldly expostulated with him concerning the severity of his usage ; and, as an exemplary vengeance from heaven, for treating the ambassador of Christ with stripes and contempt, he predicted to his face that neither he, nor any of his cruel brothers, or of the posterity descended from them, should ever arrive at the princely dignity, or have the honour to wear a crown ; but the youngest brother, the compassionate Duach Galach, who treated him with veneration and humanity, for the sake of the Great God, whose commissioner he was, should sit upon a throne, and his descendanis inherit the same blessing and honour for many ages. When the young prince heard of this prophecy, that was so im-. portant to himself and his family, he solemnly engaged to St. Patrick, that he would obey his commands in whatever he enjoined him ; which submission was so acceptable to the prophet that he gave him his benediction, and assured him of the truth of what he had foretold, that he himself should sit upon a throne, and the crown lineally descend to his posterity.

It was 430 years after the birth of Christ that St. Patrick opened his commission in Ireland, which was in the fourth year of the reign of Laogaire, as before-mentioned. He continued in Ireland sixty-one years, propagating the Christian doctrines with resolution and success, which number of years being added to the 430 above, make 491 from the beginning of the Christian era to the death of that Irish apostle ; who, as we are informed in the account of his life, was sixty-one years preaching the gospel in the island, and working miracles for the confirmation of the religion he recommended. This computation is supported by the concurring testimony of an ancient poet of good authority, who has transmitted the account in these verses subjoined :

> The holy saint, with zeal and Christian courage,
> Did propagate the Gospel of his Master,
> For one-and-sixty years, and miracles
> Performed, strong evidence of truth.

If it should be questioned whether there are any such verses upon record in the life of St. Patrick that is handed down to the present times, let it be considered, that we are informed by a manuscript chronicle of antiquity, that sixty-four persons have severally written the life of this reverend missionary ; and no doubt there is some difference to be observed in their relations ; and therefore it is not to be wondered that some particular transactions and miracles of that saint are expressed in some of these lives that are omitted in others ; but the authority of the whole is not to be overthrown for this reason, which would be a severe execution, and was never put in practice in judging of the truth of other histories.

In the reign of Laogaire, king of Ireland, Dubhthach, the son of Lughair, a poet, Fithall Feargus, and Rosa, the son of Tirchin, recommended to St. Patrick the examination of the chronicles and genealogies of the kingdom, and submitted them to his correction ; but the saint modestly refused to act in a matter of this importance, upon his own judgment, because he

was not thoroughly acquainted with the antiquities of the island
and the pedigrees of the families ; and therefore he addressed
himself to Laogaire, and desired him to issue out his royal
mandate, for a convocation of the principal clergy, historians,.
and antiquaries of the kingdom, and in the writs to express the
time and place of their meeting. The king was well pleased
with the method, and accordingly ordered out his summons, and
the most eminent of the three professions met and assembled
in convocation. The several genealogies, and the old record;,
were produced before the convention, who examined into their
authority with great care and exactness ; but considering the
number of the members that composed the assembly, and the
difficulty and the time that would be employed, if every particular person was to read over the whole and give his opinion ,
it was agreed by consent, that a select committee of nine should
be appointed, to whom the purgation and amendment of the
chronicles should be committed, and their corrections should
receive a sanction from the whole assembly. The nine deputed
upon this occasion were three learned kings, three eminent prelates, and three of the most accomplished antiquaries : the three
kings were, Laogaire, the son of Niall, the hero of the nine hostages ; Daire, king of Ulster, and Core, king of Munster. The
Christian bishops were St. Patrick, the pious Binen, and the
judicious Cairneach ; the antiquaries were Dubhthach, Feargus,
and Rosa. By this learned committee were the genealogies of
the principal families, and the ancient records of the kingdom,
carefully examined, and purged of all spurious relations, and
then disposed into the archives of the island, as a venerable and
authentic collection, whose veracity was to be relied upon, and
never was questioned by future ages, who called this body of
records the Great Antiquity. This convocation, and the select
committee, who had the particular inspection of these affairs,
are transmitted by an ancient poet in these lines that follow :

> The learned authors of those choice records,
> Which for their truth are called the Great Antiquity,
> Were nine, selected by the convocation,
> For wisdom and integrity renowned ;
> Three kings, three prelates, and three antiquaries :
> The prelates were, the most devout St. Patrick,
> The pious Binen, and the wise Cairneach ;
> The kings were Laogaire, the Irish monarch,
> A prince in heraldry exactly skill'd ;
> Join'd with him was the judicious Daire,
> The warlike king of Ulster ; the third,
> A prince for letters and for martial acts

Was famous, his name was Corc, the potent king
Of Munster: three antiquaries next survey'd
These old records, and purg'd them by their skill;
The faithful Dubhthach, and the sage Feargus,
And Rosa, nicely vers'd in foreign tongues.
These nine perus'd the annals of their ancestors,
Eras'd the errors, the effects of fraud
Or ignorance; and by the test of truth
Examin'd, they establish'd the records,
And every pedigree of noble blood;
And thus corrected they descend to us,
Unworthy issue of our brave progenitors.

The annals and records being thus perused and reformed, by the care and learning of this select committee, the king, by the consent of the nobility, ordained, that they should be committed to the trust of the reverend prelates of the kingdom, who had them transcribed in legible characters, and laid up in their principal churches for the benefit of posterity. There are many of these venerable manuscripts preserved to the present times, and many copies of them found in the custody of the curious at this day; such are the book of Ardmach, the Psalter of Cashel, the book of Glean da loch, the book called in the Irish language Leabhar na Huaidhchongabhala, the treatise of Cluain mac naois, the book of Fionta cluana haighneach, the Yellow book of Moling, the Black book of Molaiga, and several other ancient tracts, that relate to the antiquities of the kingdom, which have afforded great assistance in the collection of this history.

And farther, that the annals, the genealogies, and chronicles of the kingdom, might be preserved incorrupt, without falsehood or interpolations, it was established by law, that the substance, and the most important transactions, should be transcribed once in every three years into the royal Psalter of Tara, after they had been examined, and received a sanction from the approbation of the great assembly of the kingdom. But the particular account of these triennial conventions, and the nature of their debates, have been mentioned, when we spoke of the reign of Cormac, the Irish monarch, and therefore will be prosecuted no farther in this place.

The principal authors, who treated of the affairs of Ireland in the pagan times, were these following: Amergin Glungeal, Sean Macaighe, Brigh Banaghdar, from whom the word Brighe in the Irish language is become proverbial; Conla Caoin Bhreathach, the famous antiquary of the province of Conacht; Seanchan Mac Cuil Chiaoin, and the learned Fachtna his son; Seanchan, the son of Oilioila; Moran, the son of Maoin;

Feargus Fianaidhe, in Kerry ; Luachra, Feircheairtine, a celebrated poet ; Neidhe, the son of Aidhna ; Aitherne, the son of Amhnas ; Feargus, a poet of note, the son of Aithirne ; Neara, the son of Fionchuil, from Siodubh, Seadamus, the son of Moruinn ; Fearadach Fionnfathach, the principal author of the Wisdom of the king of Ireland ; Fithall Feargus, a good poet ; Rosa, the son of Tirchin ; and Dubhthach O'Lugair ; these three last mentioned delivered the annals and public records of the kingdom to St. Patrick, to be revised by him, which he refused to correct by his own judgment, without the assistance of the most learned professors in the kingdom.

In the times of paganism, it was ordained by law, that if any public antiquary had deviated from the truth in any state record, or in the private genealogy of a family, he was immediately degraded and not allowed for the future to act in his profession : if a judge, through ignorance or corruption, pronounced unjust judgment, he was never afterwards permitted to sit in the courts of justice. And there seems to be good authority to believe, that there were several concomitant marks and symptoms that attended the sentence of the judge, either in his own person or in some other remarkable way, whereby it was publicly known whether the decree pronounced was consistent with justice or not ; particularly we are informed by good evidence, that when an Irish judge, called Sean Macaighe, delivered an unjust sentence, there broke out visibly many large blisters upon his right cheek ; but when he was upright in his judgment, the skin remained smooth, and no pustules appeared.

The celebrated Conla Caoin Breathach administered justice with the strictest equity, was proof against the corruption of bribes, and delivered his sentence without affection or prejudice. Seancha Macuill was a person of consummate wisdom and integrity ; and when he presided in courts of justice, and was to pronounce his decree, he always fasted the night before. When his son Fachtna, who was a judge in those times, was unjust in his decision of causes, if it was in the time of harvest, a very remarkable event ensued, upon the night following all the acorns would fall from the trees in that part of the country, which was a great misfortune to the inhabitants ; but if his decree was consistent with justice, no calamity ensued, but the oaks retained their fruit. It was observed, that if a judge was corrupt in his administration in the spring, when the trees were in blossom, the cows forgot their natural instinct, and would not bear their calves to remain near them : and the famous Moran, the son of Maoin, who was one of the principal judges of the kingdom, when he sat upon the bench to administer justice, put the miraculous chain, called in the Irish language Jodha Morain about his neck, which was attended with that wonderful virtue, that if the judge pronounced an unjust decree, the chain would instantly contract itself, and encompass the neck so close, that it would be almost impossible to breathe ; but if he delivered a just sentence, it would open itself, and hang loose upon the shoulders.

A certain distinguished evidence of truth or falsehood was likewise observed to attend upon the historians and public notaries of the kingdom, which restrained them from corrupting the genuine chronicles, or altering the genealogies of private families ; but the particular signs that followed cannot be discovered at this distance of time, because many records of moment are lost, from whence we might expect information upon this subject. However, we have the same evidence to prove the authority of the Irish annals and public manuscripts, as is esteemed sufficient to confirm the histories of other nations ; and perhaps it would be no more than truth to affirm, that no people, except the Jews, whose writers were divinely inspired, have more genuine or earlier accounts of the concerns of their ancestors, than the chronicles and records that give being to the present history ; and for this reason, among many others, because no nation in the world could possibly be more exact in preserving their records, and transmitting them uncorrupt to posterity, than the ancient Irish ; especially considering they were corrected and confirmed by the most pious and learned prelates of the Christian church in that kingdom.

Laogaire, the son of Niall, king of Ireland, summoned a great convention to assemble at Tara, after the custom of his ancestors ; and when the principal nobility, gentry, and the most learned antiquaries met, at the time and place appointed, the ancient laws and records were read over ; and when they were purged and corrected, and the new statutes were transcribed and added, they were deposited in the most sacred archives, as a body of laws to be consulted upon occasions for the administration of justice and for the government and public happiness of the kingdom.

When this parliament assembled, the king of Ireland kept his court in a royal palace, which was appointed only for his own use and the reception of his attendants ; and this was called the house of Moidhchuarta. The king of every province in the

island had likewise a house assigned, for the convenience of himself and his retinue.   The king of Munster lived in the house
called in the Irish language Lung Muimhneach ; for Lung signifies a house, which being joined to Muinhneach, implies the
Munster house : the king of Leinster had for his house Lung
Laighneach, or the Leinster house : the house where the king
of Conacht resided, was known by the name of Coisirchon-
nachtach : and the palace of the king of Ulster was called
Euchruis Uladh.

There were three other houses at Tara, that were built for the
use of the public : the first was called Caircair ne Ngiall, which
was a strong building, where the state prisoners were kept and
secured ; the second was called Realta Nabhfileadh, where the
judges, the antiquaries, and the poets of the kingdom assembled
to decide suits at law, to impose fines and punishments upon
delinquents, and to regulate and adjust the customs of the country ; the third was a noble edifice, called Grianan na Ninghean,
where the provincial queens, and the ladies their attendants, resided during the assembly, and kept a very splendid court.   But
notwithstanding this structure was only one house. yet every
princess had a separate apartment magnificently fitted up, which
contributed in a great measure to the splendour and gallantry
of that triennial convention.

The provincial kings, it has been observed, had their separate
houses during the sitting of the parliament at Tara ; but when
they assembled upon the business of the kingdom, and to enact
or repeal laws for the benefit of the public, they met in the great
house of Miodhchuart, where there was a most noble room of
state, where every member of the assembly sat, according to his
profession and his quality, without disputes of precedency or
disturbance.

In the middle of the room there was a throne erected, and
under a canopy was placed a royal chair, where the king of Ireland always sat with his back to the east.   The situation of the
house, it must be observed, was directly east and west.   Upon
the left hand of the monarch sat the king of Munster ; the king
of Leinster sat before the king, with his face towards the throne;
the king of Conacht sat behind his back, and the king of Ulster
sat upon the king's right hand, towards the north ; the principal nobility and gentry of each province had their places near
the kings they belonged to ; so that the whole assembly made a
most solemn and splendid appearance. The manner of the sitting

of this parliament is upon record in the writings of a learned antiquary, in the following verses :

> The Irish monarch on a royal throne
> Conspicuous sat, in the middle of the house;
> The prince of Leinster in a chair of state
> Was plac'd, but with his back to the assembly,
> His face towards the king : behind the throne
> The prince of Conacht sat ; towards the south,
> Upon the king's left hand, the prince of Munster
> Grac'd the assembly ; and upon the right
> Sat in his splendid robes the prince of Ulster.

Laogaire, the king of Ireland, was disturbed in his government by Criomthan, the son of Eana Cinsalach, who, with the assistance of the provincial troops of Leinster, fought with the Irish army the memorable battle of Ath Dara, where the king's forces were defeated with terrible slaughter, and himself taken prisoner. Criomthán, having the king in his power, would not give him his liberty, unless he would promise and engage, with the most solemn oaths and imprecations, that he would never attempt to get possession of Boiroimhe, or challenge any right to it. The king being in his enemy's power, thought proper to submit to the conditions, and bound himself under the obligation of the strictest oaths ; but when he was released he broke through his engagements, which he insisted were the effects of necessity, and extorted from him by military violence. But the vengeance of heaven ever attending upon the guilt of perjury, would not be eluded by such sophistical evasions ; and therefore by a thunderbolt put an end to the life of the unfaithful king, at Greallach Dabhuill, near the Liffee, as we are informed by an old poet in this manner :

> Laogaire, the son of the renowned Niall,
> Was struck from heaven, in the delightful plains
> Near Liffee's fruitful streams, to death devoted
> For violating the bonds of solemn oaths.

This was the end of that unfortunate prince, designed by heaven as a perpetual example to succeeding kings, who trifle with treaties and oaths, and imagine they have a dispensing power to cancel the obligations of them at their own pleasure, or when that wicked engine, called reasons of state, seems to require it.

The consort of Laogaire was Aongus, daughter to the general who commanded the army of King O'Liathan, by which lady he

had a son, whose name was Lughaidh. There is a relation inserted in some old manuscripts concerning this princess and her
son, which, without doubt, is owing to the bigotry and superstition of those early times, which had that veneration for St.
Patrick, that almost every action of his life was esteemed a miracle ; this transaction that follows, it must be observed, is not
designed to gain belief, nor is it proposed, by relating it in this
history, to put it upon the same foot of certainty and credit with
other particulars, though nothing is impossible to God Almighty:
but as it was the foundation of an ancient custom practised to this
day by the genuine Irish, and not otherwise to be accounted for,
it must not be omitted absolutely. The story therefore is this:

St. Patrick, attended by the principal of the Irish clergy, made
a visit to the consort of Laogaire, who received them with great
courtesy and goodness, and when she had assured them of her
esteem and the continuance of her favour, she invited them to
an entertainment, that was provided on purpose, as a testimony
of her respect ; for the queen it must be considered, was bap
tized by St. Patrick, upon her marriage, and from that time had
the saint in great veneration. The young prince was placed
near his mother at the table, who, being hungry, and eating
hastily, he unfortunately attempted to swallow a large morsel,
but after all his endeavours, it stuck fast in his throat and stopped his breath. The whole company was astonished at this
misfortune, the court was in confusion, and the queen particularly was overwhelmed with grief, and was utterly inconsolable.
All methods were used to open the passage, but without success ;
so that the prince was given over for lost beyond recovery. The
queen, finding all human means ineffectual, addressed herself to
St. Patrick, and implored his assistance in this distress, whose
prayers to heaven she thought would restore her son, notwithstanding he seemed expiring. and in the very agonies of death.
The saint immediately ordered the youth to be removed into
another apartment, where no person was to be admitted but
himself By this time the prince, to all appearance, was quite
dead ; which was so far from discouraging the endeavours of St.
Patrick, that he applied himself by fervent prayer to heaven,
for the space of three days and three nights, and continued in
that supplicating posture without intermission, or refreshing
himself by eating or drinking ; for he justly thought, that the
duty of fasting was a necessary attendant upon the act of prayer,
and added an irresistible force to devotion. Upon the third
day, (as some legendary writer has corrupted the story, which

hitherto is far from being incredible,) St. Michael the Archangel, conveyed himself into the apartment, where St. Patrick was prosecuting his request with great perseverance and importunity, and stood before him in the shape of a pigeon. The dove immediately accosted the saint, and after he had informed him that he was the Archangel Michael under that humble appearance, he told him, that the Almighty God had heard his prayers for the recovery of the prince, who lay stretched at length upon his back with his mouth wide open, a posture very convenient for the operation that was to follow; for the dove, it seems, without any difficulty, thrust his bill down the throat where the stoppage was, and dexterously drew out the morsel that stopped the breath, and the prince immediately revived. The pigeon having executed his business, conveyed himself away without any ceremony, and vanished out of sight.

St. Patrick, leading the young prince by the hand into the presence of the queen, presented him alive ; and she was so transported with joy, that she received him upon her knees, and in that submissive posture returned her thanks to the saint, for his unwearied application to heaven, and congratulated him upon the success of his prayers. But he, with great modesty, refused to take upon himself the merit of the action, and relating to her the particular circumstances of his recovery, told her, that she ought to express her gratitude to Michael the Archangel, who was the great physician that restored the prince. The queen was so affected with the account, that she obliged herself, by a most solemn vow, never to forget the favour, and as an acknowledgment to St. Michael, she promised to bestow annually one sheep out of every flock she had, and a part of all the provision that came to her table, upon the poor, during her life : and to perpetuate the memory of this miraculous recovery of the young prince, and in honour to the archangel who effected this cure, it was ordained by law, that all the Christian converts throughout the kingdom of Ireland should conform to the practice of the queen, and constantly offer the same oblations. And in obedience to this injunction, arose the custom of killing St. Michael's sheep, called in the Irish language Cuid Mhichill, observed to this day; for it is most certain, that every family, upon the 29th of September, which is the anniversary festival in honour of St. Michael, at least of the ordinary sort of people, kill a sheep, and bestow the greatest part of it upon relieving the poor. This is the relation, which is impossible to be true in every circumstance, yet so much of it may deserve credit, that the young prince, the son of Laogaire, was by some accident in apparent hazard of his life, and was recovered by the care and advice of St. Patrick, upon Michaelmas Day ; in memory of which deliverance, the queen, from a principle of piety, did bestow such yearly charities upon the poor, whose example was followed by the whole kingdom, and is religiously observed by many families to this day.

Oilioll Molt succeeded Laogaire in the throne of Ireland. He was the son of Dathy, son of Fiachadh, son of Eochaidh Moidhmeodhin, descended from the royal line of Heremon, and governed the island twenty years. The consort of this prince was Uchtdealbh, the daughter of Aongus, son of Nadfraoch : and the reason why he was distinguished by the name of Oilioll Molt was, because his mother, whose name was Eithne, when she was big with child of him, passionately longed for a piece of wether mutton ; she communicated her desire to a gentlewoman, called Fial, the daughter of Eochaidh Sadaigh, who came to visit her when she was near her delivery, and when the child was born the lady insisted that his name should be Oilioll Molt. It was in the reign of this prince, that Amalgaidh, the son of Fiachadh, son of Eochaidh Moidhmeodhin, was king of Conacht, who died after he had governed the province twenty years. In his time Muireadhach Mundearg was king of Ulster, who died after a reign of twelve years. This provincial prince was the son of Feargna, son of Dallain, son of Dubhthaig, son of Mianaign, son of Lughaidh, son of Aongus Fionn, son of Feargus Dubhdheadhach.

A.D. 453.

This Irish monarch, soon after he was proclaimed, thought it convenient to assemble the convention of the states, at the royal palace of Tara, after the example of precedent kings. And here it may be proper to observe, that in ancient times there were three general convocations held in the whole kingdom of Ireand ; they were distinguished by the names of the convocation of Tara, the convocation of Eamhain, and the convocation of Cruachan. The first of these has been particularly described in the foregoing part of this history, the two others deserve our notice in this place.

It must be observed therefore, that the conventions of Eamhain and Cruachan were appointed to examine and inspect into the tradesmen and mechanics, to determine of their abilities in their several crafts, and to regulate their occupations. This assembly consisted of the principal nobility and gentry, with the most learned antiquaries of the kingdom ; and when they met, they selected threescore, who were the most expert in their several professions, and commissioned them with a power to separate and disperse themselves throughout the island, and to take cognizance of the accomplishments, the industry, or imperfections of the several tradesmen within their respective jurisdictions; and without an express license from one of these commissioners, no mechanic could exercise his art, or work publicly at his trade, in any part of the country. These were the principal affairs concerted in these assemblies, which were of great use towards the improvement of ingenuity, industry, and trade, and promoted order and uniformity among the people.

There is a manuscript extant, of great antiquity, called Leabhar Oiris, that mentions this Irish monarch, Oilioll Molt, under the title of king of the Scots; and in the reign of this prince it was, that Benignus, a comharbha of St. Patrick, that is, a clergyman of a religious order ordained by that missionary, departed this life. This king was engaged in a war with the people of Leinster, and he fought the memorable battle of Tuama Aichir with the inhabitants of that province, in which action many gallant soldiers perished, and the fight concluded with incredible slaughter on both sides. In the reign of this king, Ambrosius, king of Wales, had many encounters with the Scots and Picts; and about this time Conall Creamhtuine died, as did likewise Jarlaithe, the third bishop of Ardmach, when Simplicius was Pope of Rome. This Oilioll Molt did not enjoy the crown by right of succession; for Lughaidh, the son of Laogaire, was the hereditary prince, who promoted his title by the sword, and was supported in his pretensions to the crown by Mortough, son of Earca, Feargus Cearbheoil, Conall Creamhtuine, and by Fiachadh Lonn, the son of Caolbhadh, king of Dailraidhe, who raised a numerous army, and when they had joined the young prince, they engaged the king's army, and fought the battle of Ocha, where Oilioll Molt was defeated and slain.

Twenty years after Lughaidh obtained this victory, the six sons of Eochaidh Munramhar went to Scotland; they were known by the names of the two Aongus's, the two Loarns, and the two Feargus's. It was the distance of 300 years from the reign of Connor, the son of Neasa, to the time of Cormac, the son of Art; and 204 years had passed from the reign of Cormac to the memorable battle of Ocha; twenty years after which engagement the sons of Eirc, the son of Eochaidh Munramhar, transported themselves into Scotland. At this time Duach Galach, the son of Bryen, the son of Eochaidh Moidhmeodhoin, governed the province of Munster; he reigned seven years, and fell by the sword of Eochaidh Tormcharna.

A.D.
473.

Lughaidh succeeded to the crown of Ireland. He was the son of Laogaire, the son of Niall, the hero of the nine hostages, descended from the royal line of Heremon, and his reign continued twenty years. At this time Fraoch, the son of Fionchad, was king over the province of Leinster; and now it was that the battle of Cill Osnach was fought at Moigh Fea, in the county of Cabarlo, four miles eastward of Leithlin: in this action Aongus, the son of Nadfraoch, who had been king of Munster thirty-six years, lost his life; his wife also, whose name was Eithne Uathach, the daughter of Criomhthan, son of Eana Cinsalach, was slain by Mortough, the son of Earca, and Oilioll, the son of Dunluing, as a poet of sufficient credit informs us in these lines:

> The martial prince Aongus, son of Nad'raoch,
> Fought in Cill Osnach's bloody field, and fell
> By the victorious sword of Oilioll,
> Son of Dunluing.

After this action, Fraoch, the son of Fionachuidhe, son to the king of Leinster, was slain in the battle of Graine, by Eochaid, the son of Cairbre. In the tenth year of the reign of this Irish monarch, Felix, the third of the name, was elected Pope of Rome: and near the same time was fought the battle of Eamhna, by Cairbre, son of Neill, who afterwards engaged in the battle of Cinnailbhe, in the province of Leinster. About this time Mochaon Naoindroma died; and by Cairbre above mentioned was fought the famous battle of Seaghsa, where Duach Teangamhadh, the king of Conacht, was slain by Mortough, son of Earca, as the following lines particularly testify:

> The martial prince Duach Teangamhadh
> Engag'd in the three memorable battles
> Of Dealga Muchroma, Tuama,
> And Seaghsa.

About this time it was that the inhabitants of the province of Leinster engaged with a gallant army against Jobh Neill, and fought the battle of Loch Moighe, where there was much blood spilt, and a desperate slaughter on both sides; and now it was that Feargus More, the son of Earca, followed by the Dailriadas, made an attempt upon the kingdom of Scotland, and arrived at great authority in that country. In the four-

eenth year of the reign of Lughaidh, the son of Laognire, king
f Ireland, St. Patrick died, after he had, by indefatigable zeal
nd industry, propagated the Christian faith, and extended his
onquests over the pagan idolatry through the greatest part of
he island; the age of this saint was 122 years. The king of
reland did not long survive him, but died soon after by a stroke
rith a thunderbolt, which was the instrument of vengeance used
y heaven to punish him for opposing the preaching of St.
'atrick, and suppressing to the utmost of his power, the doc-
ines of Christianity, and preventing their admission among his
eople. Gelasius was the Pope of Rome in the last year of the
eign of Lughaidh, king of Ireland.

A.D.
J3.

Mortough obtained possession of the government. He
was the son of Muireadhach, son of Eogan, son of
Niall, the hero of the nine hostages, descended from the
oyal line of Heremon, and filled the throne twenty-four years.
'he mother of this Irish monarch was Earca, the daughter of
oar, who came from Scotland. In the beginning of the reign
f this prince the pious Ciaran was born, whose father was a
arpenter, but of eminent extraction, of the posterity of Ir, the
on of Milesius, king of Spain. This Ciaran was a person de-
oted to a religious life, and his name is often mentioned with
onour in the book that treats of the lives of the Irish saints.
n the fourth year of the government of Mortough, Anastatius,
ie second of that name was elected Pope; and about this time
ie famous Comhgall Beannchoir was born, and in process of
ime became an abbot of such note and authority, that he had
0,000 religious monks under his jurisdiction and command; the
haracter of this religious person, and the extent of his power,
 particularly expressed in the book called Leabhar Ruadh Mac
againe; the authority of which relation comes recommended
y the concurring testimony of St. Bernard, a writer of reputa-
on, who, in the life of St. Malachias, gives an account that an
minent disciple, whose name was Roanus, who had been edu-
ited under this Comhgall, was sent abroad by the holy abbot
ho, he says, had erected a hundred religious houses; and men-
on the particulars of his descent, that he was of the posterity
f Iriall, the son of Conall Cearnach, son of Amergin, of the
lustrious tribe of Clanna Ruighruidhe, descended from Ir, the
on of Milesius, king of Spain. This relation is farther sup-
orted by an ancient poem, extracted from the chronicle of
ints, wherein are these verses.

The most religious Comhgall Beannchoir,
Son of Seadhna, with undaunted courage
Met the approach of death; with Christian bravery
His soul surrender'd, and approv'd himself
Descended from the royal line of Ir.

Near this time died Anastius, the Roman emperor; and the pious St. Caineach Achadh Bo left the world; this devotionist was descended from Feargus, the son of Raogh, derived from the royal stem of Ir, the son of Milesius, king of Spain. In the reign of Mortough, king of Ireland, was born that great example of piety, Collum Cill, the son of Feidhlin, son of Feargus, son of Conull Gulban, son of Niall, the hero of the nine hostages. About this time died the most religious St. Bridget; this excellent person was the daughter of Dubhthaig, the son of Dreimne, son of Breasal, son of Deic, son of Counla, son of Art, son of Cairbre Niadh, son of Cormac, son of Aongus More, son of Eathach Fion Fuathnairt, son of Feidhlimidh Reachtmar, son of Tuathal Teachtmar, of royal extraction, and descend;d from the line of Heremon. She died after she had lived eighty-seven, or according to another computation, seventy years.

In the tenth year of the reign of Mortough, king of Ireland, Symmachus was elected Pope, and presided in the primacy fifteen years and eight months. In the twenty-first year of his reign Hormisda succeeded in the pontificate, and lived four years after his election. About this time the dead body of the blessed Antonius, a most religious monk, was miraculously found, and conveyed to Alexandria, and solemnly interred in the church dedicated to St. John the Baptist in that city. Mortough met with great disturbances and opposition in his government, and in one year was obliged to engage in the following memorable battles; the battle of Cinneich, the battle of Almaine, the battle of Cliach, the battle of Eibhline, and the battle of Moighe Hailbhe; not long after this last action, Mortough died at the house of Cheitthigh; and near the same time the devout St. Ailbhe Imiligh was translated to a better life.

Tuathal Maolgarbh succeeded in the throne. He was A.D. 515. the son of Cormac Caoch, son of Cairbre, son of Niall, the hero of the nine hostages, descended from the renowned posterity of Heremon, and governed the island thirteen years. The mother of this monarch was Comaoin, the daughter of Dall Bronuigh, and he was particularly distinguished by the name of Tuathal Maolgarbh, because his mother, as soon as she was delivered of him, struck his head against a stone, as a sort

of charm upon which his future fortune was to depend ; the
blow made an impression, and occasioned a flatness in his skull
which was the reason that gave him the title of Tuathal Maol
garbh. In the reign of this Irish monarch, Mootius, a person
of exemplary piety, and one of the disciples of St. Patrick,
died, after he had lived, as the chronicles assert, 300 years.
Under the government of this prince, Baoithin, a scholar of
Collum Cill was born ; and, it must be observed, that Collum
Cill and Baoithin were nearly related, for they were brothers'
children. About this time Comhgall, the king of Scotland,
departed the present life, and the devout Mobi, a very excellent
person, died near the same time ; he was otherwise called by the
name of Bearchain, a celebrated prophet, extracted from the
posterity of Fiachadh Baiceada, the son of Cathaoir More. The
noted battle of Tortan was fought by the people of the province
of Leinster, in the reign of Tuathal Maolgarbh ; in which engagement, Earca, the son of Oilioll Molt, from whom came Fir-
ceara, lost his life. The battle of Sligo was fought not long
afterwards, by the two young princes, Feargus and Daniel, the
two sons of Mortough, son of Earca, in which bloody action
Eogan Beal, who had governed the province of Conacht thirty-
five years, was unfortunately slain. About this time died the
excellent Oghran, the saint of Leathruidh, who lineally descended from the posterity of Conaire, the son of Modha Lamha ;
and the most religious Ciaran, the carpenter's son, was cut off
in the blossom of his age, having lived no more than thirty-one
years.

In the reign of this Irish monarch it was, that Bachach, which
in the Irish language signifies a sturdy cripple, had his head
struck off from his shoulders, by the vengeance of heaven, as a
punishment for swearing falsely, by the hand of Ciaran ; and
this execution, by the appointment of Providence, happened at
the great fair of Tailtean, in the sight of innumerable spectators.

Tuathal Maolgarbh was soon after slain by Maolmor, the son
of Niathire, at the request and instigation of Diarmuid, the son
of Feargus Ceirbheoil, at a place called Grealladh Eily. In the
reign of this monarch, Guaire, the son of Colman, took upon
him the command of the province of Conacht, and fixed himself in the throne, after the death of Eogan Beal, notwithstanding the deceased prince had a son, whose name was Ceallach
who had entered himself into a religious order, under the tuition of Ciaran, with a design to devote himself to a pious and
monastic life ; but by the persuasion and importunity of his

z

friends in the province, who resolved to assert and support his right, this young devotionist was prevailed upon to leave his cell, and appear at the head of a good body of forces, who determined to proclaim and establish him in the throne of Connacht. Ciaran soon missed him out of his monastery, and cursed him with a most dreadful imprecation, and implored heaven to blast his designs, by cutting him off by a sudden and untimely death. Ceallach had intelligence of the severe resentment of Ciaran, and dreading the influence of his prayers, he hastened to the convent, and prostrating himself with the most humble submission at the feet of the abbot, he promised to pay him implicit obedience for the future part of his life, and to engage in nothing without his approbation and consent. The compassionate Ciaran, imputing his conduct to the folly of youth and the importunity of his friends, immediately gave him his pardon and his benediction; but assured him withal, that his prayers were sealed in heaven by an irreversible decree, and that his death would be violent and unexpected. This answer surprised the young votary, who applied himself for the rest of his life to piety and charitable acts, and continued in the monastery under the care of Ciaran, till at length his merits advanced him into a bishopric in the country. But though he had relinquished his pretensions to the government of Conacht, and resolved to sequester himself from temporal affairs, yet he was willing that the crown of that province should descend to his family; and accordingly he used all possible endeavours to establish an interest, and place his younger brother in the government. But Guaire, by the industry of his spies, had notice of his preparations and designs, and imagining his reign would never be free from tumults and pretences, so long as Ceallach, who was a politic and indefatigable person, was on this side the grave, he, by sufficient rewards, prevailed upon three of the bishop's own servants to dispatch him, which they basely executed upon the first opportunity. Thus fell this noble prelate, and accomplished the prediction of Ciaran, who foretold his death, which heaven inflicted for renouncing his religious vow, and attempting a secular life after most solemn engagements to the contrary.

Diarmuid succeeded to the crown of Ireland. He was the son of Feargus Ceirbheoil, the son of Conall Creamhthaine, son of Niall, the hero of the nine hostages, descended from the royal stock of Heremon, and governed the kingdom twenty two years. The mother of this prince was Coru-

A.D. 528.

hach. the daughter of Maine, of the province of Leinster, and in his reign died the pious Tigearnach, the bishop of Cluain Eos, derived from the family of Daire Barach, son of Cathaoir More. About the same time expired Oilioll, the son of Mortough, that governed the province of Leinster nine years; in whose reign Cormac, the son of Oilioll, son of Muireadhach, son of Eochaidh son of Daire Cearb, son of Oilioll Flan Beag, was king of Munster.

The memorable battle of Cuill Conaire was fought at Ceara near this time, by the two princes, Feargus and Daniel, the sons of Mortough, son of Earca, where Oilioll Jonbhanda, the king of Conacht, and his brother Aodh Fortamhail, were unfortunately slain. In the reign of Diarmuid a most dreadful plague happened, that overspread the whole kingdom of Ireland, and made terrible devastations among the people, especially among the saints and the religious of the kingdom, particularly Mac Tuil, of Cil Cuilin, was carried off in this visitation, which, by way of distinction, was called Crom Chonuill. About this time was fought the bloody battle of Cuill, where great numbers of the inhabitants of the county of Cork perished; and it is said, that the bad success of this engagement was owing to the prayers of a most pious lady, called Suidhe Midhe, that was descended from the posterity of Fiachadh Suidhe, the son of Feidhlimidh Reachtmar, and occasioned the defeat, by soliciting heaven for revenge upon that people, who had injuriously treated her, and used her unbecoming her descent and character. The king of Ulster, who had governed that province twenty-two years, and was the first king of Dailnaruidhe, died about this time. The name of this prince was Eochaidh, and he was the son of Connla, son of Caolbhadh, son of Cruin Badhraoi, son of Eochaidh Cobha. Cormac, the son of Oilioll, king of Leinster, died under the government of Diarmuid, as did likewise that noted prophet Beg Mac De.

In the same reign was born the most devout St. Molua; he was the son of Sinil, son of Amergin, son of Duach, son of Eochaidh Moidhmeodhin, at which time happened the death of the bishop of Acha Cuingire, and St. Neasin the leper. In the government of this Irish monarch, the church of Cluain Feart, in the county of Kerry, was founded and completed by the charitable bounty of St. Breannuin, who claimed his extraction from the posterity of Ciar, the son of Feargus Gabhran, the king of Scotland, died in this year, and his enemy Gruige, the son of Maolchion, king of the Picts, fought successfully, and routed the

Scots in a pitched battle.   Another engagement about this time
was fought by Feargus and Daniel, the two sons of Mortough
the son of Earca, that was called the battle of Cuildreimne,
against Diarmuid, the son of Feargus, who was defeated with a
terrible slaughter of his troops, and obliged to fly for his life.
The unfortunate event of this action, wherein the greatest part
of his army was lost, was the effect of the prayers of St. Collum
Cill.   This excellent person had been reproachfully used by the
king, who had violently put to death Curnan, the son of Hugh,
the son of Tiormcharna, who was educated under the care and
protection of Collum Cill; and for this barbarous act the saint
applied to heaven for vengeance, which heard his prayers, and
punished the king with the loss of his choicest forces in the
battle before mentioned.   Diarmuid was attended with the same
ill fortune, when he fought the battle of Cuil Uinsion at Teabhtha, and was driven out of the field by Hugh, the son of Breanian,
king of Teabhtha, where the slaughter was incredible, and scarce
a man of the whole army remained alive.   Collum Cill, after
this defeat, removed into Scotland, to a place called Hoide Collum
Cill, and now he was about forty-three years of age.   Soon after
he arrived in that country, a most desperate battle was fought,
by Clanna Neill, in a part of the highlands, called the fight of
Monadoire, where seven petty kings of the Picts, with the flower
of their army, were left dead upon the field of battle.   About
this time died Colman More, the son of Cairbre, son of Dunluing,
who had governed the province of Leinster for thirty years.

There is an account in a very ancient chronicle, that in the
seventh year of the reign of Diarmuid, king of Ireland, a poor
woman, who was a nun, and had vowed a religious life, called
Sionach Cro, applied herself to the king, complaining of the
great injury she had received from Guaire, the son of Colman,
who had violently forced from her a cow, that was the only
means of her subsistence.   This injury was so resented by Diarmuid, that he selected a strong body of his troops, and directed
his march towards the River Shannon, and encamped upon the
banks of the stream.   Guaire had soon notice of his preparations
and his march, and, with a much less number of forces, resolved
to justify what he had done by the sword; and leading his
men towards the banks of the Shannon he faced the king's
troops on the other side.   In this posture of defiance the two
armies were drawn out; but Guaire, doubting of success, dispatched Cumin, one of his favourites, to Diarmuid, to desire he
would not attempt to cross the river with his forces within the

pace ot twenty four hours. The king promised that he would
ot, and told the messenger, that his request was but of small
importance, for he was assured of victory, depending not only
pon the justice of his cause, but the number and experienced
ravery of his forces. Diarmuid, as he had engaged, continued
1 his encampment till the next morning, upon the east side of
he river, and Guaire upon the west.

Cumin having intelligence of the number of the king's troops,
vas averse to an engagement, and, desiring to persuade Guaire
to make his peace by a timely submission, he expostulated with
im upon the uncertainty of the success, and wondered he would
ttempt to come to a battle under so great disadvantages ; but
Guaire, no ways discouraged, for his personal bravery was never
uestioned, replied, that victory was not always the consequence
f numbers, but depended upon the disposal of heaven, which
ften bestows success upon a few, and defeated a multitude ; and
hat he was satisfied in the courage of his soldiers, and therefore
he determined to face the enemy, and leave the event to Provi-
.ence. In this enterprise Guaire was attended by the principal
iobility and gentry of the provinces of Munster and Conacht,
who raised what forces they were able, and came to his assistance.
And now the two armies, drawn out in order of battle upon the
ianks of the Shannon, attempted to recover the opposite side,
iut the provincial troops were unable to oppose the undaunted
esolution of the king's army, which plunged into the stream,
.nd with incredible difficulty forced their way ; and notwith-
tanding Guaire, with all the conduct of an able and experienced
.eneral, attempted to hinder their landing, his forces were de-
eated with a dreadful slaughter, and the few that remained fled
or their lives.

The misfortune of this battle is attributed to the importunate
irayers of St. Caimin, who founded and consecrated the church
if Inis Cealtrach ; for that holy person, as the chronicles inform
is, had spent three days and three nights in devotion, and im-
iloring heaven to blast the designs of Guaire, and to confound
is army. This St. Caimin was a lineal descendant from the
iosterity of Fiachadh Baiceada, the son of Cathaoir More ; and
when Guaire was informed, before the engagement, that St. Cai-
nin was supplicating upon his knees against his success, and
irofessed himself an enemy to his cause, he applied himself to
he saint, and with great humility asking his pardon, and la-
nenting the misfortune of his displeasure, he entreated him to
ie reconciled, and to pray for his victory ; but the saint re-

mained inexorable, and told him, that his overthrow and the destruction of his army was determined, and the decree of heaven could not be revoked.

After the defeat of the provincial troops, Guaire had no security for his life but a secret and swift flight, and therefore he made his way through woods and solitary places, without any attendants, till he came to a small cell, where no person lived but a religious woman, who had retired thither for the benefit of devotion. When the woman saw him she inquired after his name, and the business that brought him into that unfrequented solitude ; he concealed his name, and told her that he was a friend to Guaire, who had been routed by the king's troops, and was obliged to fly to preserve his life. The woman replied that she was sorry for the defeat of Guaire, who was a prince of that goodness, bounty, and charity, as to deserve a better fortune ; and after she had enlarged upon the accomplishments and the calamities of the general, she welcomed him into her apartment, promised fidelity in concealing him, and supplied him with necessary accommodations, as far as her abilities and the circumstances of the place would permit. But this pious woman, concerned that the meanness of her provision was unsuitable to the quality of her guest, went to an adjacent brook, in order to procure some fish for the entertainment of the prince, and by good fortune espying a salmon, which of herself she was unable to catch, she returned to her cell, and joyfully relating her success, she desired him to go with her to the river, and assist her to catch the fish : he willingly followed her to the place, they drew the salmon out of the water, and Guaire, who was used to keep a splendid table, and generally consumed among his household ten oxen at a meal, made a supper of only the fish with great cheerfulness and satisfaction, and expressed his gratitude to Providence, and to the piety of his host, for his unexpected relief. The next morning the prince left the cell, and, wandering through the woods, met with a body of his troops who had survived the defeat ; they received him with great joy, and he put himself at the head of them : a council of war was immediately called, and the debate was, whether the prince should again try his fortune, and recruit his forces, or submit to the victor with his whole army ? After several arguments were offered on both sides, it was concluded, that a general submission best became the unfortunate posture of their affairs ; and Guaire, convinced of this advice, led his broken forces, and resolved to make his peace with the conquerors upon any terms.

Approaching the royal army, Guaire sent a messenger to offer his submission, which was accepted, and promising to lay down his arms, he was admitted into the presence of the king; he immediately fell upon his knees, and delivered up his sword into the king's hand, who obliged him to hold the point of it between his teeth, and in that humble posture he confessed disloyalty and the unwarrantableness of his designs, and bound himself by the most solemn obligations to atone for his miscarriages, by his future fidelity and obedience.

It was observed before, that Guaire was a person of the most exemplary goodness and extensive charity; and the king, suspecting the integrity of his outward virtues, resolved to make a trial while he had him at his mercy, who still continued upon his knees, lamenting his misfortune, and supplicating pardon. And for this purpose the king commanded an eminent druid, who always attended near his person, to ask some favour of Guaire, to try whether his charity and his great bounty proceeded from a principle of religion and goodness, or were the effect of a desire of popularity and ostentation. The druid obeyed his orders, and implored the charity of the unhappy prince, and begged he would bestow something upon him for the sake of his profession; but Guaire, suspecting his design, refused his request, being convinced that he was supported by the king, and could be under no necessity to desire his relief. Upon this repulse, a man, grievously afflicted with the leprosy, and a very miserable object, was sent to Guaire, who solicited his charity, and begged alms for God's sake. This, he supposed was an unhappy person worthy of his compassion, and accordingly, being incapable to relieve him any other way, he gave him the silver bodkin that stuck in his vest. The poor man retired with great gratitude, and applied to heaven for a blessing upon his benefactor; but the bodkin was taken from him by the king's order, and the leper returned to Guaire, to acquaint him of his misfortune, and again to entreat his charity. Upon his return, the good prince, affected with the relation and barbarity of the act, resolved to supply his wants to the utmost of his ability, and bestowed upon him a golden girdle of great value, that was tied about his waist. It was gratefully accepted by the beggar; but before he had gone far it was taken from him, by the king's command, which forced him to return again to the unhappy prince, who continued still upon his knees, with the point of the sword between his teeth, the king holding the hilt in his hand. When the leper had related the cruel circumstance of his usage, he implored his farther relief; upon which the compassionate Guaire, who had nothing more that he could bestow, was so concerned, that he burst out into a flood of tears. The king, observing him in this affliction, demanded the occasion of it, and asked him whether his sorrow and concern proceeded from the calamity of his affairs; because he had made his submission, and lay at his mercy, who had the power of the sword, and was able, if he pleased, instantly to dispatch him.

Guaire replied, that his melancholy fortune was the least subject of his grief, which arose wholly from reflecting on the distress of the miserable leper, and the incapacity of his condition to afford him relief. The king immediately commanded him to rise from the ground, and, being convinced of the humanity of his nature, and the sincerity of his virtue, generously received him into his friendship, and promised never to require any subjection from him, being sensible there was an Almighty Sovereign, to whom he himself owed homage, and whose vicegerent he was in the administration of his government.

The two kings being reconciled, entered into a strict league, and bound themselves in the most solemn manner not to violate their engagements. The king of Ireland invited Guaire to go with him to the great fair of Tailtean, which was the general mart of the whole kingdom; and to convince him of the sincerity of his affection, among other testimonies of his esteem, he promised to settle the succession upon him, and resolved to confirm the crown to him after his decease. The two princes, with a noble retinue, came to Tailtean, and Guaire carried with him a great quantity of money, to dispose of in acts of charity, and upon other occasions, as opportunity offered; but Diarmuid, understanding the generosity of his nature, and that his bounty admitted no limits, gave secret orders through the whole fair, that no person should presume, on any account, to apply to Guaire for his charity, or receive a gratuity from his hands. Three days after his arrival, Guaire, perceiving no miserable object to implore his relief, and being informed that the king had forbidden, by a strict injunction, that no person should beg alms of him, was so dejected, that he desired the king to allow him the attendance of a good bishop, to whom he might confess, and from whose hands he might receive absolution and the holy ointment. The king surprised, asked him, what he intended by this request? he answered, that his death, he was certain, was approaching; because he was unable to live without exercising his charity, which his royal mandate had absolutely put out of his power to do. The king immediately revoked his order, and by that means opened a way for the bounty of his royal companion, who, besides the large sums he expended in relieving the poor, with great generosity encouraged the men of learning in all professions, and by his benefactions procured the applause of the most eminent poets and antiquaries of the kingdom. There is an account in an ancient manuscript, the credit of which may perhaps be questioned, that the hand with which he extended his charity to the poor, was longer than that which bestowed his gifts upon men of learning. The king of Ireland proposed the succession of Guaire to the nobility and gentry of the kingdom, who confirmed his title with public demonstrations of joy; and this mutual affection and esteem continued inviolable between the two princes, till death dissolved their engagements, and put an end to their friendship.

The Irish annals give an account that Guaire had a brother, who devoted himself to a religious life, whose name was Mochua. This holy person observed all the fasts of the church with great obedience; and, designing to abstain from his common diet, and to eat no more than what was absolutely necessary to support nature, during the time of Lent, he retired for that purpose to a fountain of pure spring water, that lay southwards of Boirin, at the distance of five miles from Durlus Guaire; and he had no person to attend upon him but a clergyman of a lower order, whom he retained to say mass. In this retirement these votaries observed great abstinence and regularity in their eating and drinking, and their custom was, to refresh themselves with no more than one meal a day; which consisted of the meanest provisions, a small quantity of coarse barley bread with water-cresses, and spring water from the fountain. In this manner they spent the time of Lent till Easter-day, which festival the holy Mochua resolved to observe with the strictest devotion and reverence, and therefore he celebrated the mass himself, and performed other offices that belonged to the solemnity of the occasion; but his clerk, who attended upon him, was so tired with feeding upon herbs and such slender provisions, that he interrupted the saint before the prayers were over, and longed so impatiently to eat flesh, that he desired his master to give him leave to go to Durlus, to the court of Guaire, king of Conacht, and refresh and satisfy himself with flesh; for he was no longer able to support nature by that abstemious method he had used, and by a way of living that his constitution would not permit. Mochua did not oppose the reasonableness of his request, but persuading him to be patient and re-signed, he told him he would supply him with flesh without undertaking such a journey, for he would supplicate heaven in his behalf, and he was assured that his prayers would have the desired effect, and supply his wants ; accordingly he prostrated himself, and most importunately called upon God, imploring his bountiful hand to provide flesh for his servant, who had fasted the time of Lent with strict reverence, and was unable to pre-serve his health without immediate relief.

At that very instant it happened, (as some particular manu-scripts relate, but with small truth I am afraid,) that the ser-vants of Guaire, king of Conacht, were laying his dinner upon the table ; and to the great surprise of the attendants, the dishes were hurried away by an invisible power, and conveyed directly to the solitary cell, where Mochua was continuing his devotion, and his clerk expecting the event. The prince, with his whole court, was amazed at this wonderful accident ; and, enraged at the loss and disappointment of his dinner, he ordered a body of his horse guards to pursue the dishes travelling in the air, and he followed, with the principal of his nobility, resolving to re-cover them and bring them back to his court at Durlus.

It seems beneath the gravity as well as the dignity of an his-torian, to take notice of these legendary relations, which are certain rather to move the indignation and spleen than the be-lief of the reader ; but it must be considered, that the times we are writing of abounded with incredible relations, and the writers of those ages were always raising the characters of the saints, even to miracles, not foreseeing the disadvantage they bring to religion, which, instead of recommending it to the world, they ridicule and expose. And in the present case it can-not be supposed, that the transaction we are speaking of is put upon the least foot of credibility, but designed only to keep the thread of our history entire, and to give light to some material inci-dents, which otherwise would be obscure, and perhaps not easily to be accounted for. But to go on with our story :

When the dishes arrived at the cell, they presented themselves with great submission before the devout Mochua and his clerk, and after the saint had returned thanks to the bounty of hea-ven for so miraculous a supply, he desired his servant, that was so carnally inclined, to fall to and eat heartily. The clerk had scarce put bit in his mouth, but looking about him he spied a great company of horsemen advancing upon full speed, and making towards them. He was terribly affrighted at the sight, and, lamenting the voracity of his appetite, he told his master, that he wished the dishes had stayed at home ; for he was afraid they came with an evil design, and would certainly bring them into some misfortune. Mochua comforted his timorous clerk, and assured him, that it was his brother Guaire, the king of Conacht, with his retinue, that was pursuing the meat ; and to keep up his appetite, he engaged that they should not be able to move a step nearer, before he had filled himself, and eaten as much as he thought fit : and accordingly, the saint having offered up a short petition to heaven, the feet of the horses stuck fast in the ground, and the riders remained immoveable upon their backs, and had no power to stir a step before the hungry clerk had satisfied himself, and made a good meal of it. When he had dined, the saint addressed himself to God for the relief of the pursuers, and the horses immediately found themselves released, and the company, overcome with wonder and astonishment, advanced, and presented themselves before the saint.

Guaire and his retinue found the devout Mochua upon his knees : and he immediately quitted his horse, and in the most submissive manner entreated his compassion, and desired his benedicton. The saint gave him his blessing and his pardon, and desired him and his attendants to fall to and eat their dinner in that place ; they joyfully complied with the invitation, and without more ceremony they consumed most of the provision, and when they had reverently taken their leave of Mochua, Guaire, with his guards and his followers, returned to his palace at Durlus. Whatever share of credit or contempt this relation may meet with, it is most certain, that the road leading from Durlus to the fountain where St. Mochua and his clerk retired to fast, during the time of Lent, which is the length of five miles, is known to this day in the Irish language by the name of Bothur na Mias, which in the English signifies the Dishes road.

In this place, it must be observed, that some of the ancient chronicles assert, that Eogan More had another son besides Fiachadh Muilleathan, whose name was Diarmuid ; and the same authority informs us, that St. Beacan, who consecrated the church of Cill Beacan in Muskry Cuirc, was a descendant from the posterity of that Diarmuid, from whom likewise the antiquaries allow, were derived Oilioll Flan More, Oilioll Flan Beg, and Deachluath. Upon the extraction of these persons, an old poet composed the following verses ·

The holy Beachan from Diarmuid
Descended, and from the same progenitor
Sprung Oilioll Flanmore, a most renowned prince,
Oilioll Flan Beg, and Deachluath.

About this time it was that Breasal, the son of Diarmuid, king of Ireland, resolved to invite his father, and the principal nobility of his court, to a magnificent entertainment, which he designed to furnish in the most sumptuous manner at Ceananus in Meath; among other dishes for the feast he proposed to have a large piece of beef of exceeding fatness, and examining his own cattle for this purpose, he found them so lean, that they were not fit to be killed, especially upon so public an occasion. Under this disappointment he was informed that a religious woman had a cow that would suit his design; but when he applied to her to purchase the beast, she absolutely refused to sell her, and when she could not be prevailed upon to exchange her for seven cows and a bull that were offered, Breasal drove her away by violence, and killed her for the entertainment. This poor woman lived at Cill Ealchruidhe. The king of Ireland, with his courtiers and his royal retinue, came to the feast; and when they were in the height of their mirth, this injured woman forced herself into the room, and in the most affecting manner complained of Breasal to the king, and representing the circumstances of the wrong she had suffered, most passionately demanded justice. Diarmuid was so moved at the violence offered to her, and so highly resented the baseness of his son, that he was in a rage, and vowed he would revenge the injury, and put his son to death for the fact. Accordingly he commanded him to be seized, and taken into strict custody, and dragging him to the river Loch Ruidhe, he ordered him to be drowned, which unnatural sentence was immediately executed.

So far this story may deserve belief; but what follows, without doubt, was foisted in by the credulous writers of those dark ages, who were for heaping miracles upon the backs of their saints, which the present times are not expected to give credit to. But those obscure guides are the only authority we have to direct us, and therefore we are obliged to comply with the coarseness of our materials, and proceed regularly, lest our design should suffer more by omitting these legendary relations, than it possibly can by inserting them in the history.

The king having indulged his passion so far as to destroy his son, in his calmer moments began to lament his loss, and to condemn himself for the sudden violence of his resentment. He was perfectly overcome with melancholy, and when he reflected upon his death, the thoughts of it were insupportable. In this distracted condition he applied himself to Collum Cill, who advised him to go to St. Beacan, who lived in the province of Munster, and possibly from the prayers of that holy person he might find relief. The king followed this advice, and, attended by Collum Cill, came to the saint, who resided in a mean cell, upon the north side of mount Grott, which at this time is known in the Irish language by the name of Cill Beacan. When they arrived they found the saint with great labour digging a ditch to surround his churchyard, and working in his wet clothes, for it was a rainy day. When St. Beacan perceived that it was the king of Ireland, he cried out to him aloud, "O murderer, down to the ground upon your knees." The king instantly quitted his horse, and prostrated himself before the saint. Collum Cill, who attended upon the king, informed the holy Beacan of the business they came upon, and told him that the king was almost distracted with reflecting upon the barbarity of the act he had committed, and had no relief left him but his prayers to heaven, that God would be pleased to pardon him the offence, and restore him his son alive; and therefore he presumed that so religious a person would not refuse to intercede for him, since his life and happiness were so immediately concerned. The saint was moved with compassion, and addressed himself three times with great fervency to heaven, for the restoring of the young prince, and heaven heard his prayers, for, as the legend relates, the king's son was brought to life and presented to his father, who received him with inexpressible joy, and ever after held the saint in great veneration, whose devotion had power sufficient to work such wonders, and accomplish so miraculous an event.

The Irish chronicles go on and entertain us with transactions of no great importance, yet not so trifling as to be wholly omitted. They inform us that Guaire, the son of Colman, king of Conacht, Cuimin Fada, son of Fiachadh, and Camin of Inis Cealtrach, met at the great church of Inis, where it was agreed that three questions were to be proposed among them, and were to be severally answered. Camin was appointed to ask the first, and demanded of Guaire what he most passionately wished to be possessed of in this world? His answer was, an immense treasure of gold and silver. Then Guaire proposed to him what was the utmost of his wishes and desires? He replied, to their great surprise, a languishing and distempered body. The next question was offered by Guaire to Cuimin, who asked him what he would wish to obtain ? He replied, a number of pious and learned books, to make me capable of discovering the truth to the people, and instructing them in the doctrines of religion. It is said they all severally obtained their desires ; particularly we are informed that Camin ended his days miserably, his body being sorely afflicted with pains and diseases, being under the curse oi St. Mochua, who, as the Irish annals relate, implored heaven to punish him with the most dreadful visitations.

Guaire, the son of Colman, received provocations from the people of Munster, which he resolved to revenge by the sword ; and, after he had completed three battalions of choice troops, raised in Conacht, entered the province of Munster, with great terror and loss to the inhabitants. The king of Cashel at that time was Dioma, the son of Roanan, son of Aongus, who was followed by a gallant army, and resolved to oppose the hostilities of Guaire, and drive him into his own territories. The two armies met at a place called Magh Figinty, now known by the name of the heart or middle of the country of Limerick, where the two princes with great courage engaged at Carn Fearaidhaidh, and a terrible slaughter was made on both sides; but Guaire was at length compelled to fly, and most of his forces were slain upon the spot. In this action were lost seven of the principal gentlemen of the province of Conacht. The cause that induced Guaire to invade the province of Munster was, to support his pretensions to all the territories from mount Eachtuidhe to Limerick, which originally belonged to the old division of Conacht, but was separated from that province by Lughaidu Meoin, the son of Aongus Tireach, who defeated the forces of Conacht in seven successive battles ; in which terrible engagements, which were sharply disputed on both sides, seven kings were slain, who fought with great bravery, and unfortunately fell at the head of their troops. Lughaidh was at length so reduced, that the remaining part of his army consisted of raw undisciplined men, scarce of age, and of small experience ; so that he made swords-land of all the country from Beirn Tri Carbat, by Carn Fearaidhaidh, to Bealach Luchaidhe, and from Ath Boiroimhe, to Lein Congculoinn, as the ancient poet Cormac Mac Cuillenan observes, in the following manner :

> The martial prince Lughaidh Lamhdearg,
> Was crown'd with victory, and by his arms
> Contracted the old limits of the province,

And took from Conacht all the territories
From Carn Fearaidhaidh to Ath Luchat.

St. Mochua and St. Collum Cill lived in the same age, and, as a manuscript of some credit, though of small importance, relates, when Mochua, who was likewise known by the name of Mac Duach, was retired into the wilderness for the benefit of his devotion, he had no living creatures about him except a cock, a mouse, and a fly. The use of the cock was to give him notice of the time of night by his crowing, that he might know when to apply himself to his prayers : the mouse, it seems, had his proper office, which was, to prevent the saint from sleeping above five hours within the space of twenty-four ; for when the business of his devotion, which he exercised with great reverence and regularity upon his knees, had so fatigued his spirits, that they required a longer refreshment, and Mochua was willing to indulge himself, the mouse would come to his ears, and scratch him with its feet till he was perfectly awake : the fly always attended upon him when he was reading ; it had the sense, it seems, to walk along the lines of the book, and when the saint had tired his eyes and was willing to desist, the fly would stay upon the first letter of the next sentence, and by that means direct him where he was to begin. An excellent monitor ! but as fate would have it, these three sensible creatures unfortunately died, which was an affliction of that consequence to the saint, that he immediately dispatched a letter to Collum Cill, who was then in Scotland, lamenting the death of his companions, and entreated a proper message from him to support him in his sorrow. Collum Cill received the news with Christian magnanimity, and returned this comfortable answer, that he ought to mitigate his grief, for misfortunes attend upon all sublunary things ; that his three companions were mortal, and subject to the inexorable stroke of death, and therefore it became him not to be surprised, or in an immoderate manner to lament their departure. Not long after this it was, that Diarmuid, the son of Feargus, king of Ireland, fell by the sword of Hugh Dubh Mac Swyny, at a place called Rath Beag, in Muighline, and was buired at Cuinnirry.

A.D. 550. Feargus and his brother Daniel were the succeeding monarchs. They were the sons of Mortaugh, son of Earcha, son of Muireadhach, son of Eogan, son of Niall the renowned hero of the nine hostages, descended from the posterity of Heremon. These brothers governed the island without jealousy or dispute, for the space of one year. The mother of these princes was Duinseach, the daughter of Duach Teangabha, king of Conacht. These kings were obliged to engage with the inhabitants of Leinster, and they fought the memorable battle of Gabhrah Liffe with the subjects of that province, who in the action lost 400 of the principal nobility and gentry of the country, together with the greatest part of their whole army. About this time Dioman Mac Muireadhach, who governed the province of Ulster ten years, was unfortunately killed by Bachlachuibb. Feargus and Daniel died soon after ; but whether they fell by an untimely stroke, as did most of their predecessors, it is impossible at this distance to determine.

A.D. 550. Eochaidh, the son of Daniel, was the next successor in the throne of Ireland : he was the son of Mortough, son of Earca. This prince admitted with him into the government his uncle Baodan, son of Mortough, son of Earca, descended from the illustrious line of Heremon, and they governed the island three years. In the reign of these princes it was, that Cairbre Crom, the son of Criomthan Sreibh, son of Eochaidh, son of Nadfraoch, who was king over the province of Munster, departed the present life. This martial prince fought the battle of Feimhin, against Colman Beag, the son of Diarmuid, and defeated him, with a terrible slaughter of the greatest part of his forces : the victor was distinguished by the name of Cairbre Crom, because he was nursed and educated at a place called Cromgluisse. About this time died, as some of the ancient records of the kingdom inform us, Breannuin Biorra, who lived to the age of nine score years ; as a poet of great antiquity and good credit has transmitted to us in the following verses :

> Happy the man whom Providence preserves
> To the long life of Breannuin Biorra,
> Who lived in plenty and prosperity
> A hundred and eighty years, and then he died
> Lamented.

Some time after this, Fiachadh, the son of Baodhan, engaged in the bloody battle of Folla and Forthola, against the inhabitants of the counties of Ely and Ossory, and obtained a complete victory, by slaying incredible numbers of the enemy. In the reign of these kings died Conull, son of Comhguill, the commander of the Dailriada, in Scotland, after he had governed that illustrious tribe for the space of sixteen years. This Scottish general bestowed Aoii in that kingdom upon Collum Cill. These Irish princes, Eochaidh and Baodhan, were slain by Crouan, the son of Tiaghernaig, king of Conachta Glinne Geimhin.

A.D. 554.

Ainmereach was the succeeding monarch. He was the son of Seadhna, son of Feargus Ceanfada, son of Conull Gulban, son of Niall, the hero of the nine hostages, descended from the royal branch of Heremon, and administered the government three years. The wife of this prince was Bridget, the daughter of Cobhthach, the son of Oiliolla, descended from the noble family of the Leinsters of Ard Ladhran, by whom he had a prince whose name was Hugh. Ainmereach, after a short reign, was deprived of his crown and of his life by Feargus Mac Neil, at Carrig Leime an Eich.

557

Baodan sat next upon the throne of Ireland. He was the son of Nineadhadh, son of Feargus Ceannfada, son of Conull Gulban, son of Niall, the hero of the nine hostages, descended from the posterity of Heremon, and governed the island one year. The royal consort of this prince was Cacht, the daughter of the king of Fionngall : and in this king's reign it was, that St. Breanuin of Cluain Feart was translated to a better life. About this time was fought the bloody conflict of Bagha, in which engagement Aodh, the son of Eochaidh Tiormcharnadh, king of Conacht, was slain. The reign of this Irish monarch was memorable for the death of the renowned Cairbre Crom, king of Munster, and of Baodan, king of Ulster, and likewise of St. Ruadhan Lothra, derived from the family of Oiliolla Flan Beg, the son of Fiacha Muilleathan. Baodan, the king of Ireland, after one year's reign, was treacherously slain by the two Cuimins, that is, by Cuimin, son of Colman Beag, and Cuimin, the son of Libhrein, at a place called Carrig Leime an Eich. It is proper to observe in this place, that the venerable Bede, in the fourth chapter of the third book of his English history asserts, that St. Collum Cill removed into Scotland in the year of our redemption 565.

558.

Aodh, or Hugh, obtained the crown. He was the son of Ainmereach, son of Seadhna, son of Feargus Ceannfada, son of Conull Gulban, son of Niall, the hero of the nine hostages, of the royal line of Heremon. The mother of this prince, as was observed before, was Bridget, the daughter of Cobhthach. This Irish monarch had a long reign of twenty-seven years, and he fought the noted battle of Beallach Dathi, where he obtained a signal victory, and slew Colman Beag, the son of Diarmuid, and 5000 of the enemy were left dead upon the spot : by this means the prophecy of Collum Cill, who particularly predicted this defeat, was accomplished. In the reign of Hugh, the pious Seanagh, the bishop of Cluainoraird, departed

2 A

the present life; and during his government it was, that Fiachadh, the son of Baodan, son of Muireadhach, who governed
the province of Ulster twenty-five years, was killed by the sword
of Fiachadh, the son of Deamain, in the battle of Beathadh;
about which time died Feidhlim, the son of Tighernach, king of
Munster.

This Irish king summoned, by his royal mandate, the princes,
the nobility, and the clergy of the kingdom, to meet at the parliament of Dromceat: he had three reasons which induced him
to appoint this convention, but the principal occasion was, to
concert proper measures to expel and banish a numerous body
of men, who were called poets, out of the island: these professors were become very chargeable to the inhabitants, and being
of a covetous disposition, were a grievance insupportable to the
people; and upon account of the privileges and immunities
enjoyed by these versifiers, from the indulgence of former kings,
a third part of the whole kingdom passed under the notion of
poets, and professed themselves regular members of that society;
for it was a plausible cover to idleness and ease, it being ordained by law, that they should be supported by other men's
labours, and billeted upon the people throughout the island
from Allhallow-tide till May. This grievance being represented
to the king, he resolved to reduce their number by expelling
most of them the kingdom, and by that means to redress this
insufferable imposition, and satisfy the desires of his subjects.

But the great reason that incensed this monarch against the
poets, and provoked him to drive them out of the island wa-,
for their insolence in demanding the golden bodkin that fastened
the royal robes under the king's neck, and was esteemed so sa-
red and unalienable, that it was carefully delivered down from
one prince to another, as a royal jewel of singular worth and
virtue. This unprecedented demand enraged the king, but he
considered it might be of bad consequence to banish them the
kingdom, and therefore he resolved to confine them to Dailriada,
in the province of Ulster.

It must be observed that this was not the first time the poets
fell under the resentment of the Irish princes; for in the reign
of Connor Mac Neasa, king of Ulster, who reigned many years
before Hugh came to the throne, there was a design to prosecute
the poets with the utmost severity of law and justice; for they
had, by their behaviour, rendered themselves so obnoxious to
the state, and so burthensome to the people, that there was no
possibility of appeasing the inhabitants without expelling them

the island. But when this resolution of the government was known to the poets, the whole body of them, which amounted to one thousand, met to concert measures to preserve themselves from the impending storm: nor are we to wonder that they were increased to so great a number; for every principal poet, for a mark of distinction, retained thirty of inferior note as his attendants, and a poet of the second order was always followed by a retinue of fifteen. In this convention of poets, after many debates, it was resolved to leave the island before the sentence of their banishment was pronounced, and retire into Scotland. When the king of Ulster understood their design, he thought it would be inexpedient to transport themselves into that kingdom, and therefore he sent to them Congculion, one of his favourites, with a commission to treat with the malcontents, and allow them a continuance of seven years in the country, as a time of probation; and if they did not reform their conduct before the time expired, they were to be finally banished. An ancient poet has recorded this transaction in this manner:

> Connor, the most renowned king of Ulster,
> A friend to arts, a patron to the learned,
> Protected by his great authority
> The poets for seven years, who liv'd in peace
> Throughout the island.

Within the time allowed, the poets by degrees found means to disperse themselves over the whole nation, and gave no uneasiness to the people; so that they lived unmolested till the reign of Fiachadh, the son of Baodan, king of Ulster, and from the time of Fiachadh, to Maolchabha, son of Diomain, son of Carril, who governed the same province, and so they continued unpersecuted, till Hugh, the son of Ainmereach, became monarch of the island. Three several times this profession of men had rendered themselves offensive and insufferable to the people, who represented their oppression to the state, and petitioned for their expulsion; but they were still protected by the mediation of the kings of Ulster, who received them into that province, and were answerable for their behaviour. When the first attempt was made towards their banishment, Connor, king of Ulster, interposed, and professed himself their patron and advocate, and reprieved their punishment for seven years, notwithstanding they were above a thousand in number. The second persecution they brought themselves under, was taken off by the interest and authority of Fiachadh, the son of Baodan, who

governed the same province, and entertained them for the space
of one year; for by this time their number was reduced, the
whole body amounting to no more than seven hundred, with an
eminent poet at the head of them, called Eochaidh Riogh Eigeas,
as another poet has recorded in this manner :

> The learned Eochaidh Riogh Eigeas,
> The celebrated poet of the age,
> With all his followers of the same profession,
> Were kindly entertain'd by Fiachadh,
> And saved from punishment.

The third design to expel the poets was prevented by the seasonable intercession of Maolchabha, king of Ulster, who received them into his favour, and saved them from banishment ;
for at this time they made a considerable figure in the kingdom
by their numbers, which increased daily, and amounted completely to 1200.   The principal poets, who had a sort of a jurisdiction over the rest, were Dallan, Forguill, and Seanchan. This
deliverance of the poets is recorded in the following lines :

> The valiant Maolchabha, king of Ulster,
> From exile sav'd, by his authority,
> The poets of the island ; in his province
> He entertain'd them, abandon'd and forlorn,
> As the great patron of the Irish muse.

The second reason that prevailed upon the king to summon,
by his royal mandate, the great assembly of Dromceat, was, in
order to settle a constant tribute upon the tribe of the Dailriads in Scotland, who owed homage to the crown of Ireland,
and paid an acknowledgment, called Eiric, which signifies ransom
or kindred money, to the king.   This tax was first laid upon
them by Colmân, the son of Comhgealladh ; but they had of
late refused to contribute their proportion, which Hugh, the
reigning monarch was resolved to insist upon, and accordingly
the matter was fully debated in this convention.   Colman, who
first obliged them to be tributaries to the Irish, has taken notice
of their subjection in this manner :

> The Dailriads, I ordain, shall pay
> Eiric, as tribute to the Irish crown,
> And with their troops endeavour to support
> The king by sea and land.

The third occasion for which Hugh assembled this convention

of the nobility and gentry of the kingdom was, to deprive Scanlan More, the son of Cionfhaoladh, of the command of Ossery, who had refused to pay the revenue arising from that country into the public exchequer, and converted it to his own use. His post and authority the king designed to confer upon Jollan, the son of Scanlan, who was exceedingly well qualified to govern that people, and gave security to the king that he would be punctual in the payment of the taxes laid upon him. These were the reasons for which the king convened this parliament of Dromceat, as these ancient lines expressly testify :

> The Irish monarch summon'd by his writs
> The parliament of Dromceat ; the subjects in debate
> Were, the expulsion of the poets, the ancient tribute
> Of the Dailriads, and the just deposing
> Of Scanlan, prince of Ossery.

Having mentioned the convention of Dromceat, and the occasion of their meetings, it may not be improper to give a particular account of the members of that assembly, which consisted of the princes, and the principal nobility and gentry of the kingdom. There met, upon the summons from the king Criomhthan Cear, king of Leinster; Jollan, son of Scanlan, king of Ossery; Maolduin, son of Aodhna or Hugh Beannain, king of West Munster ; Guaire, son of Colman, king of Clan Fiachadh, north and south ; Firghin or Florence, son of Aodhna or Hugh Dubh, son of Criomhthan, king of the whole province of Munster ; Criomhthan Deilgeneach, king of West Ireland ; Ragallach, son of Uadhach, king of Tuatha Taighdean, and Breifne O'Rorke to Cliabhan Modhuirn ; Ceallach, son of Cearnach, son of Dubh Dothra, at Briefne ui Reyly, Congallach Ceanmhaguir Tirconconuill ; Fearguill, son of Maolduin on Oilioch ; Guaire, son of Conguill on Ulster ; the two kings of Oirgiall, their names were Daimin, son of Aongus, from Colchar Deasa to Fionn Carn at Sliabh Fuaid, and Hugh, son of Duach Gallach, from Fionn Carn at Sliabh Fuaid to the river Boyne. St. Collum Cill likewise attended this assembly at Dromceat ; for he had notice sent him into Scotland of the meeting, and the principal motives that occasioned it, and he immediately transported himself from Aoii, where he lived, and was accompanied by a great number of religious persons, who were allowed to sit in this assembly. This saint was followed into Ireland by a retinue of twenty bishops, forty priests, fifty deacons, and thirty students in divinity, who were not yet admitted into holy orders. This transaction is transmitted to posterity in the verses of an old poet called Amhra Colluin Cill, which may be translated thus :

> St. Collum Cill arrived at Dromceat,
> Followed by a retinue of his clergy ;
> By twenty prelates of superior order,
> By forty presbyters and fifty deacons,
> And thirty students in divinity
> Not yet ordained.

I confess it may seem surprising that Collum Cill, who was no more than an abbot, should be attended by prelates, who were of a more excellent order among the clergy ; but the seeming difficulty will cease, by observing what the venerable Bede asserts, in the fourth chapter of the fifth book of his English history, where he treats of the bishops of the island of Aoii, in Scotland, and declares that the Scottish bishops acknowledged the superior jurisdiction of the abbots of Aoii, and in the ancient times paid them spiritual obedience ; his expression is.* " The island of Aoii was used to have an abbot, who was a priest, for its governor, to whom not only the whole province, but also the bishops, by an unusual order, owed submission, after the example of the founder and the first teacher, who was not a bishop, but a priest and a monk."

From the testimony of this learned writer we are to understand, that St. Collum Cill was the first teacher that attempted to propagate the Christian faith among the Picts, in the north of Scotland ; for which reason, not only the priests and the monks submitted to the authority of Collum Cill, and his successors in the island of Aoii, but the prelates of the kingdom likewise were under their jurisdiction, and paid them obedience. And therefore the bishops, who were instructed in the doctrines of Christianity by Collum Cill, thought it their duty to attend upon him into Ireland, to the assembly of Dromceat. We have an account in the ancient manuscripts of a remarkable circumstance relating to this saint, who, it seems, had obliged himself never more to look upon Irish ground, and therefore to prevent his sight, he wore a sear-cloth over his eyes during the voyage, and all the time he continued in the island. There was a very holy person called St. Molaise, who had sent Collum Cill into

---

* Solet ipsa habere protectorem semper abbatem presbyterum, cujus viri et omnis provincia et ipsi etiam episcopi ordine inusitato debent esse subjecti, juxta exemplum primi doctoris illius qui non episcopus sed presbyter extitit et monachos.

Scotland, as a religious penance for some offence he had committed, and enjoined him, under solemn penalties, never more to behold Ireland with his eyes; and Collum Cill religiously observed his commands, and never was refreshed with a glimpse of light till the assembly broke up and he returned into Scotland. St. Molaise wrote a poem upon this occasion, wherein are these lines :

> The pious Collum Cill with his retinue
> Sail'd from the isle of Aoii, and arrived
> In Ireland; but by the discipline of the church
> Enjoin'd, he never with his eyes beheld
> The country.

The occasion of this severe penance inflicted by St. Molaise, was to correct the vindictive nature of St. Collum Cill, who had embroiled the kingdom in great confusion, and to gratify his revenge, was the promoter of the following bloody engagements; the battle of Cuill Dreimne, the battle of Cuill Rathain, and the battle of Cuill Feadha. The battle of Cuill Dreimne was fought, as St. Ciaran testifies, in an ancient manuscript called Jobhuir Chiaran, upon this occasion. During the time of the sessions of the royal parliament of Tara, that was summoned by Diarmuid, the son of Feargus Ceirbheoil, king of Ireland, it unfortunately happened, that Cuarnon, the son of Hugh, son of Eochaidh Fioncharna, killed a gentleman, against the established laws and privileges of that convention. The king, resolved to preserve the rights and the dignity of that assembly ordered Cuarnon to be executed; but he escaped the hands of justice at that time, and implored the protection of the two sons of Earca, Feargus and Daniel, who gave him refuge; and for the better security of his life, they committed him to the care of St. Collum Cill, as to a religious sanctuary, which no authority would presume to violate. But notwithstanding the piety and the character of his keeper, the crime of the offender was of that importance that justice found him out in his retirement and deprived him of his life. This sacrilegious violence, as it was judged to be, so enraged St. Collum Cill, that his passion urged him on to revenge; and incensing the northern Clanna Neill, with the injury he had received and the impiety of the fact, they took arms in defence of the saint; and in an outrageous manner demanded satisfaction of Diarmuid, for violating the holy asylum, and putting the offender to death; the king thought to chastise their sedition with the sword, and

marched against them with his forces ; a terrible engagement
followed, and after a bloody conflict the royal army, supported
by the provincial troops of Conacht, was defeated, and that martial clan obtained a complete victory, not a little owing (says
the manuscript) to the fervent prayers of Collum Cill.

There is another record, called the Black book of Molaga,
which gives a different account of the battle of Cuill Dreimne.
This chronicle relates, that there was a copy of the new testament transcribed from the book of Fiontan, which was claimed
by no proprietor, and therefore Fiontan insisted that the copy
was his, as it was written from the original which was in his
hands. Collum Cill was of another opinion, and strenuously
urged, that since it was unknown who wrote it, he might as well
lay claim to it as another, and resolved to prosecute the matter
to the utmost. This dispute was managed with great violence
and acrimony on both sides, and occasioned such disturbance,
that Diarmuid was obliged to interpose and decide the dispute.
The king heard the pretensions of both parties, and weighing
deliberately the arguments that were offered, he gave sentence
in favour of Fiontan, using this familiar proverb, that ' the cow
and the calf ought always to go together ;' and therefore the
proprietor of the original had an undoubted right in the copy,
till the transcriber, who was the true owner, thought fit to lay
in his claim. This repulse was resented by St. Collum Cill,
who found means to engage the king in a war, which occasioned
the memorable battle of Cuill Dreimne. The battle of Cuill
Rathain, fought between the Dailnaruidhe and the inhabitants
of Ulster, was occasioned by the resentment of St. Collum Cill,
who had received some affront from Comhgall, and resolved to revenge it with the sword. Comhgall raised the forces of that province to oppose him, and both sides came to an engagement. The
battle of Cuill Feadha was likewise fought by the procurement
of St. Collum Cill. In this action he encountered the forces of
Colman, the son of Diarmuid, who had raised a numerous army
in defence of his son Colman, who had unfortunately killed
Baodan, the son of Ninneadha, king of Ireland, at Leim an
Eich, which young prince was committed to the charge and
tuition of St. Collum Cill.

It has been observed before, that St. Collum Cill came out of
Scotland, attended by many prelates, presbyters, and deacons ;
and when he came near Dromceat, where the principal of the
kingdom were assembled, the wife of Hugh, king of Ireland,
was incensed at his arrival, and commanded her son Conall to

use these religious foreigners with contempt and disrespect, and not to regard their office, nor give them the least countenance or protection. This uncivil design was soon communicated to St. Collum Cill, who being of a quick resentment, refused to enter into the assembly, till he had obtained his revenge upon the queen and the prince for this treatment; and therefore he addressed himself to heaven, and importunately petitioned for an exemplary stroke of vengeance; which was, that the queen and her waiting lady, who attended near her person, might be punished with a disease, which, though not incurable, yet should afflict them with long and lingering pains. This infliction was sent by heaven, and obliged the queen and her attendant to confine themselves in their apartments, and not to come abroad. During the time that their distemper continued, the superstitious people of the country imagined that they were turned into cranes; for it happened that two cranes, that were never observed before, frequented an adjoining ford, which made the poor rustics fond of this opinion. A poet of that age severely lashes this superstitious conceit, and among other satirical lines has these following:

> The queen astonish'd at her feathers stood,
> And with her maid transform'd, frequents the flood:
> But when she sees a coming storm, she sails
> Above the clouds and leaves the lowly vales.

The reason of the saint's resentment against the servant was, because she was the messenger employed by the queen to the young prince, to prejudice him against the reception of St. Collum Cill and his attendants.

After St. Collum Cill had accomplished his revenge upon the queen and her servant, he entered the assembly, where he was received with singular respect, and had the honour to be placed next to Conall, the son of Hugh, son of Ainmereach, king of Ireland, and the nobility and gentry that belonged to him. But when the young prince observed that the clergy were admitted into the convention, and seated in so eminent a place, he was moved with indignation, and incensed twenty-seven of the most furious and passionate of his friends, who obeyed the commands of Conall, and in a most barbarous manner insulted the clergy, by pelting them with tufts and dirt, till they were covered with filth, and some of them very much bruised by this violent and uncivil treatment. St. Collum Cill was amazed at the indignity, and undertaking the cause and protection of his followers, he expostulated with the assailants, and boldly inquired at whose instigation it was, that the privileges belonging to that assembly were so outrageously violated, and the rights of the particular members so insolently invaded? and when he understood that Conall, the king's son, was the director and the principal cause of this barbarity, he warmly represented to the prince the heinousness of the fact; and, as the chronicle goes on, he caused twenty-seven bells to be rung, and by these bells he laid the most heavy curses and dreadful imprecations upon him; which had that effect, as to deprive Conall of his sense and understanding, and in the end occasioned the loss of his estate, and of the succession itself to the crown of Ireland. This cruel prince, from the curse laid upon him by ringing the bells, was afterwards distinguished by the name of Conall Clogach.

Hugh, the king of Ireland, had another son, whose name was Daniel, a prince of a more humane and courteous disposition than his brother, and who professed a reverend regard to the Christian religion, and the clergy that officiated in the administration of it. St. Collum Cill applied himself to this young prince, who received him suitable to his character and holy function; he instantly rose up, and kissed the cheek of the saint; and among other testimonies of respect, he resigned his seat, and placed St. Collum in his own chair. The saint was so affected with this uncommon courtesy and condescension, that he pronounced a benediction over the young prince, and prayed solemnly to heaven that his life might be crowned with prosperity and happiness, and after the decease of his father, he might succeed him in the throne of Ireland, and be a blessing to his people. The prayers of the saint had their desired success; for Conall, as his right and inheritance, his brother being incapable to govern, was possessed of the sovereignty of the island, and ruled the kingdom thirteen years.

After these civilites had passed between the saint and the young prince, St. Collum Cill addressed himself to the king, who was in a separate apartment from the rest of the assembly, and the young prince Daniel with him. The king was somewhat surprised at the appearance of the saint; for by the miracles which he had performed, and by the constant success of his prayers, he became terrible to the Irish court, and the king himself had a great awe upon him when he came into his presence; but, notwithstanding, he was received with great ceremony and outward respect, which proceeded perhaps more from fear than any sincere value for his person or his character. The saint was willing to prove the integrity of the reception, and to make trial of the king's favour, and therefore he told him that he had three requests to propose, which, if they were granted, he should be convinced that the civility and reverence showed him outwardly by the king was real and undisguised.. Hugh, afraid to disoblige the saint, replied, that whatever his petitions were, if it was in his power, they should certainly be granted. St. Collum made answer, that he was able to gratify his desires, which were, that he would retract his purpose of banishing the poets, and driving them out of the kingdom : that he would discharge Scanlan More, king of Ossery, from his confinement, whom he kept in his custody as a prisoner ; and that he would not transport his army into Scotland, to raise the chief rents and contributions of the Dailriada, or advance their tribute beyond what was paid to his predecessors. The king said in answer, that it would be of infinite prejudice to his government to give any protection to the poets, for they were a lazy, covetous, and insatiable body, and an insupportable grievance to the people ; that their numbers increased daily, every superior poet taking state upon himself, being followed by a retinue of thirty, and those of a lower order retaining a proportionable number of attendants suitable to their several degrees, so that a third part of the whole kingdom had entered themselves into the society of the poets, to the great decay of trade and industry, and the sensible impoverishment of the country ; and therefore he was obliged, for the ease of his subjects, and his own safety, to purge the island of them, and transplant them into new settlements. The saint patiently attended to the king's reasons, and convinced by the force of his arguments, he replied, that it was necessary that the college of poets should be reformed but not suppressed ; that he would consent to the reduction of their numbers, and the degrading of the greatest part of them ; yet it would be a support and emolument to the royal dignity, if his majesty, after the example of the preceding kings, retained a poet of honesty and distinction in his court, and would allow that every provincial prince in the island should enjoy the privilege of a learned poet in his retinue ; and that every lord of a cantred should likewise maintain a poet if he pleased, to preserve the exploits and record the genealogy of his family. This proposal was accepted by the king, the expulsion of the poets was prevented, and this regulation was the standard by which the society of poets were directed in future ages. This agreement between St. Collum Cill and the king of Ireland is thus

transmitted to us, in the lines of an old poet, called Maol-
ruthuin :

> The poets were secur'd from banishment
> By Collum Cill, who, by his sage advice.
> Soften'd the king's resentment, and prevail'd
> That every Irish monarch should retain
> A learn'd poet ; every provincial prince,
> And lord of a cantred, were by right allowed
> The same privilege and honour.

From this establishment by Hugh, the king of Ireland, and
St. Collum Cill, arose the continued custom for every Irish
monarch to maintain a most learned and accomplished poet in
his court, for his own use and service ; every provincial prince
and lord of a cantred had the same liberty allowed, and were
obliged to settle a fixed salary upon their poets, that was sufficient to afford them an honourable maintenance, and secure
them from the contempt of the people.   In those ages the persons of poets were esteemed sacred, and their patrimonies and
properties inviolable.   In public wars and commotions they
were exempted from plundering and contributions, they paid no
taxes or acknowledgments to the state, and their houses were
invested with the privilege of a sanctuary, and not to be forced
without sacrilege and impiety.   There were colleges erected,
and large revenues settled upon them in the nature of universities, where learning and arts were taught and encouraged.   Rath
Ceannaid was an academy in those times, and so were Masruidh
and Maigh Sleachta in Breifne : here free schools were opened,
and youth educated and instructed in antiquity, history, poetry,
and other branches of valuable and polite learning.
    In the reign of this Irish monarch, Eochaidh Eigeas was the
most excellent poet, and was president over the whole body
throughout the island ; he was known by another name, and by
some called Dallan Forgaill : this governor of the society had
authority to examine into the qualifications and abilities of
novices and candidates, and upon admission, he sent them into
the several provinces of the island ; particularly he recommended
Hugh Eigeas to Crioch Breag, and Meath Urmaol he ordained
the chief poet in the two provinces of Munster ; Seanchan, son
of Uairfeartaig, he appointed to the province of Conacht, and
Firb, the son of Muireadhach, he fixed in the province of Ulster,
and settled a poet of good learning and ingenuity in the family
of every lord of a cantred through the whole kingdom.   These

poetical professors had free lands and revenues assignad them for their support, by their several patrons ; they were exempted from tax and plunder, invested with valuable privileges, and, over and above their salaries, were paid for every poem they composed, by the person or family that employed them.

The second request that St. Collum Cill preferred to Hugh, the king of Ireland, was the release and enlargement of the king of Ossery ; but this petition was denied, which so displeased the saint, that he replied boldly, that Scanlan should be discharged, and that very night should untie the strings of his brogues at the time when he was offering up his midnight devotion.

The third favour, that St. Collnm Cill desired of the king of Ireland was, that he would not attempt to transport an army into Scotland, to raise the tribute and taxes that were usually paid by the tribe of the Dailriada ; for it would be an encroach-ment upon their ancient privileges, and contrary to the estab-lished laws of his predecessors, to commit hostilities upon that honourable clan, which was always ready to assist the Irish crown with their arms, and expose their lives with great bravery in its défence. But this remonstrance, how reasonable soever, had no effect upon the king, who resolved to invade Scotland with a powerful army, and compel that tribe to gratify his demand. The saint made answer, that Providence had taken that illustrious clan into its peculiar protection, which was able and resolved ta set bounds to the tyranny and exactions of the Irish crown, and would deliver the Dailriadas from so unjust and unprecedented oppressions ; and this was spoken with a prophetic spirit, and was afterwards literally accomplished. After this discourse be-tween the king and the saint, he with the retinue of the clergy took leave of the court, and prepared to return to Scotland. An ancient manuscript, called Leabhar Glin da Loch, observes, that Aodhan, the son of Gabhran, son of Domanguirt, was pre-sent at the assembly of Dromceat, and was allowed a place in the convention, and that he was among the attendants of Saint Collum Cill, when he had the last intercourse with the Irish monarch, and made his compliments at his departure. The same valuable record asserts, that the assembly of Dromceat sat con-stantly, without prorogation, for the space of a whole year and one month, where most excellent laws were established and ad-mitted, for the correcting of abuses in the state, and for the fu-ture government of the people.

. When St. Collum Cill had taken his final farewell of the king and the Irish court, he withdrew and came with his followers to

a place called Dubh Eeagluis, in luis Eogain, where Scanlan
the king of Ossery, was confined in close custody; and the night
after he arrived (as the old chronicle, tinctured, I am afraid,
with ignorance or superstition, particularly mentions) a most
miraculous event happened; for a large pillar, as it were or
fire, appeared in the air, which it enlightened, and directly hung
over the apartment where Scanlan was imprisoned, under a strong
guard, and loaded with chains.   The soldiers were astonished
at this fiery appearance, which was exceeding bright and terrible,
and under surprise fell flat upon their faces to the ground.   All
the castle was illuminated as at mid-day, and a beam of light
darted into the room where the king of Ossery lay, groaning
under the weight of his irons, and (as the tale goes on) he heard
a distinct voice, which called to him aloud, "Stand up, Scanlan,
give me your hand, fear nothing, leave your chains and fetters
behind you."   The king was in amaze at the vision and the
voice; but he took courage upon recollection, and rose up, and
gave his hand to an angel in human shape, who led him out of
the apartment, his feet being at liberty, and his chains falling
off of their own accord.   The guards were surprised as the angel
was conducting the king, and demanded who they were that
dared to force the prison against the king's command.   The
angel replied, that Scanlan, king of Ossery, was delivered from
his imprisonment; which answer confounded the soldiers, for
they thought it impossible that any human power would make
so desperate an attempt.   And by this means the king obtained
his liberty.

When they had passed the guards, the king was presented to
St. Collum Cill, with whom he was to continue that night; and
the saint being disposed to sleep, intended to take off his brogues,
but was prevented by the king, who untied them, as St. Collum
Cill had predicted.   The saint, in surprise, demanded who had
loosened his strings; the king answered he had done it, which
gave the saint great satisfaction, because he had frustrated the
design of Hugh, the king of Ireland, upon that prince, and procured his delivery from a cruel imprisonment.

The king of Ossery was severely used during his confinement;
his apartment was mean and unbecoming his quality, his diet
hard and exceeding coarse, his keepers allowed him nothing
but salt meat, which so violently inflamed his throat, and raised
his thirst, that when St. Collum Cill would have talked with
him about the circumstances of his usage, and the posture of his
affairs, his mouth was so dry, that he could not speak plain, or

give an answer, but made signs, and by a confused noise signified that he wanted drink. The saint immediately relieved his thirst, and commanded Baoithin, one of his followers, to give the king a large bowl top full, which the king joyfully accepted, and finished at three draughts. After his thirst was thus assuaged, and his throat cooled, he was able to discourse, and answered the saint particularly to every question, and made him acquainted with his nearest concerns. From the impediment that was in the speech of the king, occasioned by his thirst, the posterity of Scanlan, who succeeded him in the command o. Ossery, were observed to stammer, and to pronounce their words with a great deal of trouble and difficulty. The king being thus restored to liberty, was advised by St. Collum Cill to return to his government, and appear publicly in the administration of affairs. But Scanlan apprehended the resentment of Hugh, king of Ireland, who would be apt to seize upon him again, and commit him to prison, under a stronger guard, with worse usage. The saint told him not to fear, and to inspire him with courage, he bestowed upon him his episcopal staff, as a security and protection, with a command to leave it for him at his convent at Armuigh, in the county of Ossery. The king, under this sacred assurance of safety, returned to his court, and reigned over his people as long as he lived, without any disturbance or invasion from Hugh, king of Ireland.

Scanlan, from a principle of gratitude, acknowledged the favours he had received from St. Collum Cill, to whom he owed his life and delivery, and enacted a law, which should oblige his subjects, who were masters of families, to pay three pence a year towards the support of the convent, which St. Collum Cill had erected, at Armuigh, in the county of Ossery ; and this tax was to be levied from Bladhma to the sea-side. An old poet of good authority, who composed upon the Amhra or the Vision of St. Collum Cill, has recorded this transaction in the following lines.

> It is establish'd by my royal law,
> Which I require my subjects to obey,
> That every master of a family,
> Who lives within th' extent of my command,
> Should three pence offer, as a yearly tribute,
> To the religious convent of Armuigh.

After this revenue was settled upon the convent by a legal establishment, St. Collum Cill pronounced a solemn benediction upon the royal family ot Scanlan, and upon the whole country in general; but limited by this condition. that the king and the people should pay obedience to the governor of the convent, who was to exercise a sort of spiritual jurisdiction over all Ossery; and likewise, that they would be just and regular in the payment of the yearly revenue that was fixed by law upon themselves and their posterity. An account of this transaction is transmitted to us in the same poem, called the Vision of St. Collum Cill: the verses may be thus translated:

> The fruitful land of Ossery I bless,
> The king, his family, and all his subjects,
> Who from a conscience of religion
> Have bound themselves a yearly tax to pay,
> And fix'd the same on their posterity.

It is to be observed, that St. Collum Cill, whose memory is so valuable among the ancient Irish, was called originally at his baptism by the name of Criomthan; and, if we believe the book that gives an account of his Vision, (whose testimony may perhaps be questioned in some particulars,) his guardian angel, who always attended him, was known by the name of Axall; and his evil genius, who followed him as a plague to infect his mind and inspire him with impious thoughts and wicked designs, was called Demal. This we find recorded (though with what certainty it is hard to say) in the same treatise which relates the most memorable acts of this saint.

> The pious Christian hero, Collum Cill,
> When he was baptiz'd, received the name
> Of Criomthan O'Cuin; his guardian angel
> Was the most watchful Axall; but the demon
> Who, with infernal malice stung, attended
> Upon the saint to torture and torment him,
> Was called Demal.

This change of his name happened when he was under the tuition of Florence, or Finghin Moigh Bille, who was the tutor that instructed him in the doctrines of religion, and had the principal care and management of his education. This master allowed his pupil liberty, one day in the week, to divert himself, and go to the neighbouring town, to play with his companions, who were youths of the same age; and being a child of a very modest and agreeable disposition, his company was desired by all the children in the country, who, upon the day that he was to go abroad, would resort to the door of the monastery to receive him; and when they saw him coming to the gate they would from a transport of joy lift up their hands, and cry, " Here comes Collum na Cille," which in the Irish language signifies The pigeon of the church ; for he was a child distinguished for a meek behaviour, and the title was applied to him with great propriety. When the abbot Florence, who was his guardian, observed the name his companions had bestowed upon the youth, he began to think it was the will of heaven that he should be so called, and from that time he gave him the title of Collum Cill, and never used the name of Criomthan, which was given him at his baptism.

Nor is it surprising to find an alteration in the name of this saint ; for such changes happened frequently among the saints, who were often distinguished by new names. This we observe in a religious person called Muchoda, who was a disciple of St. Patrick, and was originally called Carthach ; the same we find in Caomhan, who at the font received the name of Mac Neile ; and St. Patrick himself was called Sicar at his baptism, but when he came to confirmation he had the name given him of Gemnus Magnus, and afterwards when Celestine, the Pope of Rome, sent him into Ireland to propagate the Christian faith, he again changed his name, and called him Patrick. Upon this occasion I might instance Fionnbhair of Cork, and many others of exemplary piety, who were distinguished upon occasions by different names, in the same manner as St. Collum Cill, who from his youth was known by that name, notwithstanding he received the name of Criomthan when he was baptised.

It must not be omitted in this place, that the father of St. Collum Cill was naturally an Irishman, his mother was likewise of the same country, and not of a Scottish descent, as some partial historians of that kingdom would willingly impose upon the world ; and to confirm this truth we have the authority of a book called the Chronicle of the Saints of Ireland, which expressly asserts, that Feidhlin, the son of Feargus Ceannfada, son of Conull Gulban, the son of Niall, the great hero of the nine hostages, was the father of St. Collum Cill ; and as a farther evidence it may not be improper to subjoin the following verses, translated from an old poet, whose testimony cannot be disputed :

The most religious Collum Cill
Descended from the royal race of Felix,
Son of Feargus, most renown'd in war,
Son of the invincible Conull Gulban.

2 B

This is the genealogy of St. Collum Cill by his father's line; and that he was likewise of Irish extraction by the family of his mother, appears from the testimony of the treatise before mentioned, called The vision of Collum Cill, which records, that Eithne, the daughter of Dioma, son of Naoi, who came from the posterity of Cairbre Niafer, king of Leinster, was the mother of this saint.   The following verses are translated from the same writer:

Eithne, a noble and virtuous princess,
Sprung from the illustrious line of Cairbre,
Was daughter of Dioma, son of Naoi,
And mother to St. Collum Cill.

. This Irish saint mortified his body by a continued course of abstinence and austerity, which by this severe usage became so macerated, that his bones had almost pierced through his skin; and when the wind blew hard through the wall of his cell, which was unplaistered, and forced aside his upper garment, his ribs became visible through his habit; for by his fasting and other acts of devotion he was no more than the image of a man, and was worn to a very ghastly spectacle.   An ancient poet has transmitted this description of St. Collum Cill in the following verses:

This pious saint, as a religious penance,
Lay on the cold ground, and through his garments
His bones look'd sharp and meagre; his poor cell
Was open to the inclemency of the winds,
Which blew through the unplaister'd walls.

The age of this saint, as the most authentic chronicles relate, was seventy-seven years.   This computation is justified by the account of Dallan Forguill, who wrote The vision of St. Collum Cill soon after his decease.   He was a poet, and upon this occasion has these verses:

St. Collum Cill, after a pious life
Of seventy-seven years, breath'd out his soul,
And was translated to the heavenly choir
Of angels and archangels, as a reward
Due to his virtues.

The first forty-three years of his life he spent in the kingdom of Ireland, which was his native country; then he removed into Scotland, where he continued thirty-four years.   The author of the vision of this saint has recorded these particulars of his life in the lines subjoined :

> Forty-three years this Christian hero liv'd
> Among his Irish countrymen, then inspir'd
> With zeal to propagate the Christion faith
> He visited the Scots, to whom he preach'd
> The gospel four-and-thirty years.

The three principal places where St. Collum Cill usually resided, are known by the names of Aoii, in Scotland ; Derry, in the province of Ulster, and Dunn da Leathghlass, where his body was solemnly interred. For these places of abode the saint ever retained a great affection, and mentions them with a particular fondness in these verses, which he composed himself :

> My soul delights to meditate and pray
> At Aoii, the happy paradise of Scotland ;
> Derry, the glory of my native isle,
> I celebrate thy praise, by nature bless'd ;
> To Dunn de Leathghlass I bequeath my bones,
> In life a sweet retreat.

St. Collum was naturally of a hale and robust constitution ; for the author of his life relates, that when he used to celebrate mass or to sing psalms, his voice might be distinctly heard a mile and a half from the place where he was performing his devotion ; and, as we find expressly related in his vision, no evil spirit could bear the divine and harmonious sound of his voice, but fled away far out of the reach of it. To confirm this, it is proper to introduce the evidence of an ancient poet, who, treating of the vision of St. Collum, particularly mentions it ; the lines may be thus translated :

> St. Collum by his sweet melodious voice
> Expell'd the evil spirits, who from the sound
> Precipitantly fled; for, by heaven inspir'd,
> He charm'd the good but was a scourge and terror
> To the profane.

There is an account of a wonderful event, to be met with in an old manuscript, which perhaps may be refused belief, but cannot wholly be omitted in this place. The chronicle relates, that when St. Collum Cill was in Ireland, there lived a pagan priest in the county of Tyrconnel, who erected a temple of great beauty and magnificence in these times, and among other curiosities of art and workmanship, he made an altar of fine glass,

which he superstitiously adorned with the representation of the
sun and moon. It happened that this priest was seized with a
sudden distemper, which took away his senses, and he was without motion, as if he had been in a swoon. The devil, who it
seems had a particular resentment against the man, took advantage of the opportunity, and seizing him with his talons, was
hurrying him away through the air; St. Collum looking up,
perceived the fiend upon the wing bearing his prey, and when
he was flying directly over him, the saint made the sign of the
cross in the air above his head, which so astonished the devil,
that he let go his hold and dropped the priest, who providen-
tially fell at St. Collum's feet. This deliverance was so gratefully received by the priest, that after a short discourse he became a convert to Christianity, and when he had dedicated his
temple to the Christian service, he bestowed it upon St. Collum,
and entered himself into a religious order, where he led a monastic life, and became an eminent confessor for the faith of
Christ. In the reign of Hugh, son of Ainmereach, king of Ireland, the celebrated St. Collum was removed to a better state.

It is to be cautioned in this place, that the saint we are
speaking of was Collum Cill, the son of Feidhlin, son of Feargus; for many excellent and pious persons in Ireland were
afterwards known by the same name. That valuable record,
called Leabhar Ruadh Mac Eogain, and the Chronicle of the
Irish saints, expressly assert, that many religious men, and exemplary women, and abbesses of that kingdom, had the same
name; they take notice that there were twenty-two saints in
Ireland called St. Collum, the first of which name was the saint
whose piety and virtuous acts have been described, and in honour of whose memory every one was desirous of that title, as a
sort of check and restraint upon immorality and vice, and a
signal example of temperance, charity, and every other Christian virtue.

We are told that there were fourteen religious persons in
Ireland, known by the name of Breannuin; the two principal
were Breannuin Biorra and Breannuin Ardfeart: and we find
that there were twenty-five saints in that kingdom called Ciaran,
particularly those holy men Ciaran Cluana Mac Naois, Ciaran
Saigre, Ciaran Tiabruide Naoi, and Ciaran Cille Fionmuidhe.
Thirty were distinguished by the name of Aodhan, and seven
called Bairrfionn, of whom Bairrfionn, who lived in Cork, was
of superior note; this person had another name, and was called
Fionnbhair of Cork, and was the son of Amergin, son of Dubh

Daibhin. son of Nineadha, son of Eochaidh, son of Cairbre Ard, son of Bryen, son of Eochaidh Moidhmeodhin, king of Ireland. In the convent of Cork, the governor of which religious house was this Fionnbhair, there were seventeen prelates constantly residing, and seven hundred of the clergy. There were fifteen holy women in Ireland, who were distinguished by the name of Bridget; the most eminent of them was Bridget, the daughter of Dubhthaig, who lived in the province of Leinster, and the character of this pious woman is highly valued and esteemed among the religious throughout Europe. It is certain that she descended lineally from the posterity of Eochaidh Fionn Fuath-nairt, who was a famous prince, and brother to the renowned Conn, the hero of the hundred battles; as we find it particularly mentioned in the chronicle of the Irish saints, where there is a poem that begins with these words, Naomh Sheanchus, Naomh Insi Fail, and has the genealogy of this lady expressed at large in this manner: Bridget, the daughter of Dubhthaig, son of Dreimne, son of Breasal, son of Dein, son of Conla, son of Art, son of Cairbre Niadh, son of Cormac, son of Aongus, son of Eochaidh Fionn Fuathnairt, son of Feidhlimidh Reacht-mar, son of Tuathal Teachtmar, king of Ireland. The religious women that were known by the name of Bridget in that king-dom were fourteen, and were those that follow: Bridget, the daughter of Dioma; Bridget, the daughter of Mianaig; Bridget, the daughter of Momhain; Bridget, the daughter of Eana; Bridget, the daughter of Colla; Bridget, the daughter of Eathtair Ard; Bridget, of Inis Bride; Bridget, the daughter of Diamair; Bridget, the daughter of Seannbotha; Bridget, the daughter of Fiadnait; Bridget, the daughter of Hugh; Bridget, the daughter of Luinge; Bridget. the daughter of Fiochmaine; Bridget, the daughter of Flainge.

It was in the reign of Hugh, the son of Ainmercach, king of Ireland, whose history is now under consideration, that Gaodhil gave over Manuinn Eogan Mac Gabhran, being very aged at that time. Under the government of this monarch St. Cain-catch Achadhbo, descended from the posterity of Feargus, son of Riogh, departed the present life. About this time it was, that Colman Rimidh engaged in the memorable battle of Sleamhna, where the royal army of Hugh, king of Ireland, with his son Conall at the head of it, was defeated; soon afterwards the battle of Cuill Caoll was fought by Fiachadh, the son of Baodan, in which action Fiachadh, the son of Diomain, was routed, and the greatest part of his army put to the sword.

After this defeat, Conall, the son of Suibhne, obtained, by his singular bravery, three complete victories in one day, when he conquered three generals of the name of Hugh, viz., Hugh Slaine, Hugh Buidhe, king of Omaine, and Hugh Roinn, king of O'Faile. These battles were fought at Bruighin da Choga, as the following lines expressly testify :

> The martial Conall with his valiant troops
> Three battles fought, and fortunately conquer'd
> The three renowned Hughs, Hugh Slaine,
> Hugh Roinn, and Hugh Buidhe who bravely fell
> With all their forces.

Fiachadh, the son of Baodan, and Fiachadh, the son of Diomain, who are mentioned before, were engaged in perpetual quarrels and disputes, which were fomented with great violence on both sides ; and they could not be persuaded to an interview and reconcilement, for St. Collum Cill interposed, and by the meditation of his prayers prevailed, that Fiachadh, son of Diomain, had always the advantage of his enemy, over whom he obtained several victories. The unfortunate Fiachadh, son of Baodan, having suffered many grievous defeats, applied himself to St. Collum Cill, and desired him to favour his interest ; for he was sensible he was not so much overcome by the arms of his enemies, as vanquished by the irresistible powers of his prayers. The saint expostulated the matter with him, and among other particulars, demanded whether it was his choice to lose his life in battle, and be happy afterwards in the kingdom of heaven, or to come off victorious over his enemies and be eternally miserable in another state. The ambitious and deluded prince replied, that he would trust his soul into the hands of Providence; but of all things he desired in this world, he would choose to subdue his enemies in battle ; for such exploits would make his name immortal and mentioned with honour to all posterity. This answer was very unwelcome to the saint, who lamented the folly of the young prince ; but proposing the same question to Fiachadh, son of Diomain, he made a more Christian choice, and preferred the happiness of a future life to all the titles of fame, and the glory of conquest, which attended the victorious in this world ; and the wisdom of this prince was so acceptable to the saint, that he received him under his immediate charge, entreated heaven for success in all his undertakings, and by his prayers obtained victory for him in every engagement.

Every principal family of the nobility and gentry throughout the kingdom of Ireland, expressed a singular veneration and reverence for some particular saint, whose name they invoked, and whose protection they implored upon all occasions ; and this will appear evidently from the instances that follow. The families of the Tuathallachs and Byrns applied themselves to St. Caoimhgin, of Glindaloch ; the Cinsalachs committed themselves to the care of Maoidog Fearna ; the Cavenaghs to Moling ; the Moores, in the Irish language O'Mordha, addressed to Fiontan of Cluain Aidnach ; Ossery called upon Caineach Achasdho ; the O'Bryens Apharlach directed their prayers to Seadhna ; Muskry Mac Diarmuid placed themselves under the care of Gobnuit ; Imocuille fixed upon St. Colman, with many other noble families that might be mentioned in this place. There was not a county or territory in all the kingdom but what had a particular saint, whose name they invoked in all emergencies, and who was made choice of as the guardian of themselves, their families, and fortunes. But the saints we have already mentioned were not the most distinguished ; for the most popular names throughout the island were such as Finghin or Florence, of Moigh Bille Ciaran Cluana, Comhgoill Beanchoir, Bridget of Kildare, Eilbe of Imligh, and St. Patrick. These saints are particularly recorded, with the provinces and families they had the charge of, by Aongus Ceilede, who composed the book called Psalter na Rann, from whence the following lines are extracted, that were written by the same author :

> The illustrious tribe of the O'Neills address'd
> Themselves, in their religious offices,
> To the devout St. Collum ; the men of Ulster
> Invok'd the help of Finghin Maigh Bille.
> The noble family of the Dalnaruidhe
> Implor'd the kind protection of Comhgoill.
> Bridget, a lady lineally deriv'd
> From a renowned race of kings, took charge
> Of Leinster ; and the most devout St. Ailbe
> Presided over Munster. These were saints
> Of an inferior order, when compar'd
> With the divine St. Patrick, who possess'd
> The first place in the Irish kalendar,
> And was the guardian angel of the isle.

In the reign of Hugh, son of Ainmereach, king of Ireland Brandubh, the son of Eochaidh, son of Muireadhach, son of Aongus, son of Feidhlim, son of Eana Cinsalach, was king of Leinster, and governed that province for one year. This provincial prince engaged in a war with Hugh, the Irish monarch,

and after several sharp disputes he defeated the royal army in
the celebrated battle of Beallach Dunbolg, where Hugh, the son
of Ainmereach, was unfortunately slain. After this victory,
the ancient records assert, that the inhabitants of Leinster rebelled against Brandubh, who raised a considerable force to suppress the traitors; but they were supported with superior numbers, and engaged the king in the battle of Camcluain, by Saran
Saoibhdearg of Seannboith, in which action the king, after a
terrible slaughter of his troops, lost his life. This memorable
event is related by an old poet of good authority, in the following lines:

> The most heroic Saran Saoibhdearg
> Of ancient Seannboith, with his sword
> Engag'd the valiant Brandubh, king of Leinster,
> And slew him hand to hand.

A.D.
587.
     Hugh Slaine seized upon the government. He was
the son of Diarmuid, son of Feargus Ceirbheol, son of
Conall Creamthuine, son of Niall, the hero of the nine
hostages, descended from the royal line of Heremon; and he
admitted as a partner in the sovereignty, Colman Rimidh, the
son of Mortough, son of Earca, derived from the same illustrious
family. These princes were the succeeding monarchs, and ruled
jointly with great friendship for the space of six years. The
mother of Hugh Slaine was Mungan, the daughter of Congear-
uinn, son of Duach, of the province of Conacht; and he contracted marriage with Eithne, the daughter of Breannuin Dall,
of the same part of the country: by this lady he had six sons,
and their names were Diarmuid, Donagh, Maolbreasail, Maolo-
dhar, Congall, and Oilioll. This king was particularly distinguished by the name of Aodha Slaine; and he was known by
that title, because his mother was delivered of him upon the
river Slaine. In the reign of these Irish princes, Gregory, the
Roman pontiff, deputed St. Augustine the monk, with a commission to propagate Christianity in Britain; into which country
ho came, attended with a great number of clergy, whose business was to obey his orders, and assist him in that religious undertaking. This transaction is contradicted by some writers,
who assert, that five missioners of the name of Augustine arrived in Britain at the same time, which account may be justly
suspected to be a mistake. Colman Rimidh fell by the sword
of Lochan Diolmhain, and Hugh Slaine was killed by Conull
Guthbin: such was the unfortunate end of these princes, who
sat jointly in the throne of Ireland

Aodh Uairiodhnach succeeded. He was the sou of A.D. 591. Daniel, son of Mortough, son of Muireadhach, son of Eogan, son of Niall, the famous hero of the nine hostages, descended from the posterity of Heremon; and was blessed with a long reign, for he enjoyed the sovereignty twenty-seven years. The mother of this prince was Bridget the daughter of Orca, son of Eiric, son of Eachach; and the occasion of his being called Aodh Uairiodhnach was, because he was troubled with acute pains, and frequently felt stitches in his side; for the word Jodnach in the Irish language, signifies in the English a cold stitch, and Uair is the Irish word for an hour, (because his distemper was regular in its attack, and seized him constantly at certain hours,) so that by joining these words together they sound Uairiodhnach. This tormenting disease was a great affliction to the king, and was very sharp and violent while it lasted, insomuch that the king would cry out as if upon the rack, and offer his kingdom to be eased of it for one hour. But notwithstanding he was subject to these pains in his body, he was a prince of a martial disposition, and could well endure the fatigues of war. His reign met with frequent disturbances from Aongus, the son of Colman, who was at length totally defeated in the memorable battle of Odhbha, in which bloody conflict Conall Laoghbreag, the son of Aodha Slaine, the preceding monarch, lost his life; soon after this action Aodh Uairiodhnach, king of Ireland, was killed in the battle of Da Fearta.

618. Maolchobha succeeded in the Irish throne. He was the son of Aodh or Hugh, the son of Ainmcreach, son of Seadhna, son of Feargus Ceannfada, son of Conull Gulban, son of Niall, the celebrated hero of the nine hostages, derived from the royal stock of Heremon, and administered the government four years. The consort of this monarch was Craoiseach, the daughter of Hugh Fionn, king of Ossery: and he fell by the victorious sword of Suibhne Meain, in the dreadful battle of Bealgadin.

622. Suibhne Meain seized upon the crown. He was the son of Fiachra, son of Fearadhaich, son of Mortough, son of Muireadhach, son of Eogan, son of Niall, the renowned hero of the nine hostages, a lineal descendant from the royal race of Heremon, and enjoyed the sovereignty thirteen years. It was in the reign of this Irish monarch that St. Caomhgin of Glindaloch was translated to a better state, after he had been blessed with a long life of 120 years. This religious person was the son of Caomhloga, son of Caomfheada, son of Curile, son

THE GENERAL HISTORY

of Feargus Laoibhdearg, son of Meisin Cuirb, who came from
the posterity of Labhra Loingseach. Under his government
likewise died Hugh, who was otherwise called Aodha Beanain,
king of Munster ; and about the same time was removed by
death out of the present world, the most pious St. Adamain,
son of Ronain, son of Tinne, son of Aodha, son of Coluim, son
of Seadha, son of Feargus, son of Conull Gulban, son of Niall, the
hero of the nine hostages. The wife of Suibhne Meain, king of
Ireland, was Rona, the daughter of king Ua Durtri. This prince
met with an untimely fate, as did most of his predecessors, and
was slain by Conall Claon, son of Sganlann Sgiath Leathan.

A.D.
635. Daniel possessed the sovereignty of Ireland. He was
the son of Hugh, son of Ainmereach, son of Seadhna,
son of Feargus Ceannfada, son of Conull Gulban, son of
Niall, the hero of the nine hostages, descended from the royal
posterity of Heremon, and sat upon the throne thirteen years.
It was this prince that fought the terrible battle of Dun Citherne,
where he engaged Conall Claon, whom, after a dreadful slaughter
of his best troops, he routed and drove out of the field. In the
reign of this Irish monarch, St. Fiontan, who was likewise known
by the name of Muna, exchanged this life for a better ; and
about the same time Carthach Mochuda was banished from
Rathan to Lismore. Under the government of this prince happened the death of Mochua and Molaise, the pious bishops of
Leithglin. Carthach Mochuda before mentioned, was a descendant from the noble family of Ciar, son of Feargus Mac Roigh,
and undertaking a pilgrimage from Kerry to Rathan, when he
arrived there he erected an abbey in that place, and settled some
monks in it, to the number, as an old record asserts, of 710.
These religious persons were distinguished by their piety and
holy lives, and their character was so valuable among the people,
that it was given out, that an angel usually conversed with every
third person in a familiar manner.

The great reputation of these monks of Rathan raised a jea
lousy among the religious who lived in the convent of Jobh
Neill, and lost ground considerably in the affections of the people. To recover their character they sent messengers to Mochuda, to desire him to leave Rathan, and repair to his own country, which was the province of Munster. The saint refused the
invitation, and replied resolutely, that he would never forsake
his pious monks of Rathan till he was compelled by violence,
either by a king or a bishop invested with proper authority.
This answer enraged the monks of Clanna Neill, who resolved to

force the saint from Rathan, incensed Blathmac and Diarmuid, who came attended by a body of the northern clergy, in a tumultuous manner, with a design to seize upon Mochuda, and drag him out of his convent. When the saint was informed of the violence projected against him, and that his enemies were approaching, he dispatched a Pictish nobleman of Scotland, who was a lay monk in the house, to treat with Blathmac, and desire the favour of continuing with his monks at Rathan for the space of a year longer without disturbance; the name of this religious Pict was Constantine. Blathmac was prevailed upon to allow a year's respite, and, without offering any violence, returned home with his followers. When the time was expired Blathmac came to Rathan, expecting Mochuda and his monks would quit the convent; and when he arrived he sent a clergyman into the house, to require the saint to fulfil the agreement, and leave the monastery without giving him the trouble of an ejectment; but Mochuda, unwilling to forsake the convent, which he had erected for a religious use, dispatched the pious Constantine to Blathmac, entreating him not to proceed in his design, and force him out by violence, and promising him withal, that if he would allow him to continue there with his monks for one year more, he would withdraw without giving him more trouble. This request with great difficulty was obtained, and the saint remained undisturbed till the time expired; but at the end of the year Blathmac with his clergy about him returned to Rathan, and when he found Mochuda and his monks continued in the convent, he raised a company of rude fellows in the neighbourhood, with a design to force the house and apprehend the saint. The leader in this enterprise was Diarmuid Ruaighnigh, who was followed by the principal of the tribe of Cluain Aongusa.

Supported with this assistance Diarmuid advanced towards the abbey gate, and not attempting to enter, he fixed himself behind the door on the outside, which stood wide open. Mochuda was soon informed of this attempt, and without any sign of fear or surprise he came to the gate where Diarmuid was, and when he had addressed him with great civility, he courteously invited him into the convent, but Diarmuid did not accept of the invitation, and could by no means be induced to go in. This denial astonished the saint, who expected to be used with violence, and demanded the reason of his refusal, and whether he did not come with such a number of followers on purpose to seize upon him and his monks, and by force to eject

them out of the monastery. Diarmuid acknowledged that the
design of his arrival, and those hostile preparations, were to apprehend him, and in case of resistance and opposition, to seize
him and turn him and his religious out by force; but, says
he, I find a compunction in my mind, and dare not prosecute this attempt, which I am concerned that I any way engaged in, for I have that veneration for your professed piety,
and the dignity of your sacred character, that I should incur
the guilt of sacrilege should I impiously lay hands upon you,
or presume to violate this structure, devoted to the purposes of
religion and the pure worship of God. May that God therefore, replied Mochuda, shower his divine blessings upon you and
your posterity; you are worthy to sit in the throne of Ireland,
which would be happy under the command of so pious a prince,
and I pray God that the crown may be fixed upon your royal
head, and by an uninterrupted succession descend to your family
for many ages. Nor, continued he, would I have you be concerned at the scoffs and indignities you will be apt to receive,
on your return to Blathmac and his profane companions; for
they will in derision bestow a title upon you, and call you by
the name of Diarmuid Ruaighnigh, yet that name shall be a
distinction of honour to yourself and your posterity.

With this encouragement from St. Mochuda, Diarmuid returned to Blathmac, who, expecting the saint and his monks,
passionately inquired why he had not entered the convent, and
forced away the members of the house if they refused to follow
him with consent. Diarmuid replied, that he never designed
to offer violence to so religious a person; to which answer
Blathmac returned scoffingly, "that, I confess, was Ruaighnigh,"
which was as much as to say, it was charitably done; for the
word Ruaighnigh in the Irish language signifies charitable in
the English. The whole company immediately derided him
with the same appellation, and by that means the prediction of
the saint was accomplished; upon the account of this circumstance the descendants of Diarmuid were called Sliocht Diarmuida Ruaighnigh for many generations.

Blathmac still persisted in his resolution of forcing the convent, and expelling the monks; and followed by a number of
rude profane people, he advanced towards the abbey. The gate
was found open, and he seized Mochuda, and using him in a
very rude and disrespectful manner, he thrust him and his
monks out of their apartment, and made fast the gates. This
barbarous treatment was so resented by the saint, that he cursed

him with dreadful imprecations, and implored heaven to revenge this cruel persecution upon his family.

Mochuda, after this expulsion, was uncertain whither to retire and conduct his followers, but at length he resolved to lead them towards the county of Deisies, in the province of Munster ; and while the saint was upon his journey, as the chronicle asserts, he performed many miracles, and worked wonders among the people. When he arrived in that country with his monks, he applied to the king of the Deisies, who gave him a courteous and honourable reception, and made provision for the saint and his followers ; and in a short time Mochuda was so sincerely respected by the king, that he committed himself and the affairs of his government to his care and administration, and took him with him to Dunsginne, which place has changed its name, and is the same with Lismore at this day. This is the account extracted faithfully from the Irish chronicles, concerning the expulsion of Mochuda and his monks from the abbey of Rathan, of their arrival in the county of Deisies, of the entertainment they received from the king, who made provision for them, and settled them in Lismore.

It is to be observed in this place, that the remarkable battle of Muighrath was fought by Daniel, the son of Hugh, son of Ainmereach, in which terrible conflict Conall Claon was unfortunately slain, after he had governed the province of Ulster ten years. In the reign of Daniel, the following saints, who were most eminent for their piety in those times, departed the present life, viz., St. Mochuo, who was descended from the posterity of Cathaoir More ; this religious person erected and consecrated Tigh Mochuo in Leix, otherwise called in the Irish language Laoeghis ; St. Mochuda, Molaise Leithgline, Comhdan mac da Chearda, and the devout Cronan, bishop of Caoindrom. This prince died soon afterwards, of a natural death ; which is the more remarkable, because most of his predecessors fell by the sword.

A.D. 648. Conall Claon obtained the sovereignty, and admitted his brother Ceallach as a partner in the government. These princes were the sons of Maolchabha, son of Hugh, son of Ainmereach, son of Seadhna, son of Feargus Ceannfada, son of Conull Gulban, son of Niall, the hero of the nine hostages, descended from the royal line of Heremon, and filled the throne with peace and unanimity thirteen years. In the reign of these brothers, Cuana, the son of Cailchine, derived from the illustrious posterity of Heber Fionn, and king of Fearney in south Munster, departed this life. This prince was called the renowned champion of Liathmuine, and was contemporary with the celebrated Guaire, son of Colman, king of Conacht, and resembled that noble person in his acts of munificence and charity ; for he was continually extending his relief to the poor and indigent, liberal to men of learning in all professions, and hospitable to strangers, which were accomplishments that Guaire was distinguished by, who is delivered down by the Irish writers as the standard of these princely and uncommon virtues to posterity.   Upon this occasion the following verses were composed by Conall and Comhdan, who had an excellent genius for poetry, and were the laureats of the age :

> The most illustrious Guaire, the son of Colman,
> A liberal and hospitable prince,
> Was equall'd in his virtues by Cuana,
> The brave and pious champion of Liathmuine.

In the reign of Conall Claon and his brother Ceallach, Ragallach, the son of Uadhach, who had governed the province of Conacht for 25 years, was killed by Maolbride, the son of Mothlachan, and met with an inglorious fate, from the hands of a base vile rabble of mechanics and labourers that were his immediate executioners.   This Ragallach had conceived a violent hatred and aversion for the son of his elder brother, whose right to the crown he had invaded, and was fearful lest he should be disturbed in his government by the pretensions of his nephew, who was the next heir in succession, and had a formidable interest in the affections of the people.   He resolved therefore to remove him out of the way, and had made several attempts upon his life, but without success ; but when he perceived his wicked designs defeated, and that it was impossible to murder him by open violence, by reason of his popularity, he had recourse to a stratagem which effected his purpose, and concluded in the death of the young prince.   Ragallach it seems was so concerned because he could not destroy the young prince, that he contracted a languishing disease, and fell into a consumption ; and to conceal his treachery the better, he sent a message to his nephew, to desire a visit from him before he died, for his disease, he judged to be incurable, and therefore he passionately expected to see him, for he designed to leave the government to him, and to settle upon him the crown of Conacht.   The prince and his friends soon discovered the meaning of this disguised friendship, and resolving to go to court upon the invitation, he raised a considerable force, to attend him as a guard, but he charged them to behave themselves without committing hostilities, only to have their swords drawn under their cloaks, and be in readiness if any violence should be offered by his uncle, whose treachery he suspected, and was apprehensive some attempt would be made upon his life. Under this strong guard the prince and his friends arrived at the court of Conacht, and being introduced into the king's presence, who lay languishing upon his bed, he courteously inquired after his health, and the nature of his distemper. The king was surprised when he saw the prince enter his chamber with so numerous a retinue, and with a seeming concern told him, that it was the greatest trouble of his whole life, to be suspected of insincerity by the person he fully designed should wear the crown after his decease ; for there could be no occasion for such a guard, and so many followers, unless he apprehended some danger, which was unreasonable to suppose from an expiring king, who so dearly valued him, and resolved to declare him his successor ; and therefore he desired to see him again the next morning, but without attendants, for he had something of importance to communicate, which was not proper to be divulged before company ; nor indeed, continued he, am I able to bear the suspicion of my dear nephew, who, by the number about him, must be jealous of my friendship, which confounds me upon a death-bed, when I am preparing to leave the world, and fix him in the succession to the crown of Conacht. The nephew, deceived by the hypocrisy of his perfidious uncle, went to visit him the next day, unattended and without his guards, and he had no sooner entered the chamber, but, upon a sign given, a body of soldiers, who were prepared for the execution, followed him, and falling upon him in a barbarous manner, left him dead upon the spot. Ragallach being thus delivered from his fears, by destroying the rightful heir, began to recover from his languishing state of health, his consumption daily abated, and his cure was perfected in a short time. He had now no apprehensions of a competitor to give him disturbance, and therefore he abandoned himself to ease and indolence, neglected the weighty affairs of his government, and consumed his time and his revenue in rioting, feasting, and sensuality.

This treacherous prince, Ragallach, had for his wife a compassionate and well-disposed lady, whose name was Marron, and she so lamented the miserable death of the young prince, that she was afraid that the gods, for she was a pagan, would revenge this cruelty upon her husband or herself in an exemplary man-per ; and therefore she had recourse to an eminent augur retained in the family, and inquired of him whether the vengeance of heaven was concerned to punish the murder, and who would suffer for that monstrous act, Ragallach, who contrived his execution, or herself, who was no way privy to it. The soothsayer replied by the rules of his art, that the death of her nephew would be revenged upon the king and herself, and that by the most unexpected means, and by the hands of her own child; for the child she had then in her womb would be the instrument appointed by Providence to punish this barbarous murder, which would be amply revenged upon Ragallach and herself. The queen, astonished with this answer, informed the king, who resolved to destroy the child as soon as it was born, and by that means defeat the prediction of the druid. The lady was soon after delivered of a daughter, and in obedience to the king's commands, the infant was thrown naked into a bag, and given to a swineherd to be destroyed ; but the man looking upon the child, was so moved with its cries and the sweet beauty of its face, that he relented with compassion, and resolving to preserve its life, he carried it privately to the door of a religious woman, who lived in a cell in the neighbourhood, and hung the bag upon a cross that stood in full view of the woman's house. In that condition the helpless babe lay exposed, and the swineherd, for fear of a discovery, returned by unfrequented ways to his own dwelling : but Providence ordered, that the woman came home within a short time, and hearing the mournful cries of a distressed infant, she soon perceived the bag hanging upon the cross, and taking it down, she found a most beautiful babe, which she assisted in the best manner she was able, and became so delighted with her fondling, that though her circumstances were mean, she resolved to breed her up at her own charge.

The child was nursed and educated with great care and tenderness, and when she began to grow up, she discovered so beautiful a complexion, and so complete a person, that the fame of her spread over all the country, and came at last to the ears of the king of Conacht. Ragallach, who was a very lascivious prince, was so charmed with the description of this rural maid, and the character of her uncommon beauty, that he sent a messenger to bring the girl to court ; and if the supposed mother refused to part with her, he was not to use violence upon the first summons, but return with all possible speed with an answer. The woman, who valued the maid with the most tender affections of a parent, refused to send her child, and the messenger returning with no-

tice of her refusal, the king was so abandoned to his passio..,
that he sent positive orders to force her away, and bring her to
the court of Conacht. His commands were faithfully executed
by the messenger; and when the maid was admitted into the
presence of Ragallach, he was so charmed with the modesty of
her carriage and the beauty of her person, that he resolved to
preserve her for his own use, and within a short time she was
received into his embraces. This contempt and indignity enraged the queen, who boldly represented to the king the injustice
and scandal of the action, but without success ; for he was resolved to gratify his pleasures at all hazards, and persisted in his
converse with this country beauty, whom he resolved to retain,
at the expense of his character, and of the indignation of a jealous queen, who resented this affront in the most outrageous
manner.

When the queen perceived that her persuasions and her me-
naces were ineffectual, she applied herself to the most eminent
clergy of the kingdom, to represent the wickedness of this
practice to the king, and prevail with him to dismiss his concubine ; and accordingly Feichin Fabhair attended with a great
number of eminent divines, and religious persons of several
orders, came to Conacht, to address the king upon this occasion,
and in the most submissive manner entreat him to desist from
that impious course of life, and banish his mistress the court.
They were soon admitted into the presence of Ragallach, and
used all possible arguments to prevail with him, but without
success ; for he was a prince of a libidinous disposition, and
refused absolutely to comply with their request ; which so enraged the clergy, that they left the court, and implored the jus-
t.ce of heaven to overtake the king by a most signal stroke : they
loaded him with the most dreadful imprecations, and prayed to
God that he might not live till the May following, that he might
receive his death by the most despicable weapons, that the meanest persons and the very scum of mankind might be the executioners of the divine vengeance, and that he might die in a place
unbecoming the majesty of a king, and end his days in a most
vile and ignominious manner. These imprecations of the clergy
were heard, and were accomplished in the most minute circum-
sance ; for, as the chronicle continues the relation, Ragallach
and his nobles were diverting themselves in an island by hunting a stag, the beast had received a wound, and coming near the
place where the king was expecting him, he threw a dart with
such force and judgment, that he pierced him through the body.

The stag in this extremity plunged into the lake, and the king with his followers pursued him through it. The beast reached the farther shore, and ran into a field where some labourers were cutting turf. The stag, by the pain of his wound, and the fatigue of swimming, was ready to drop, which when the rustics perceived they ran upon him, and killed him, and by consent divided the flesh equally between them. By this time Ragallach and his retinue came up, and finding the boors cutting up the beast, he was in a great passion, and commanded them to resign the stag, and deliver it to the huntsman to be carried to court; but the countrymen resolved not to part with their booty, and upon a short consultation they perceived the king had but few in his company, and found themselves able to defend their prey: accordingly they fell upon the king with their spades and other tools, and without much difficulty they dismounted Ragallach, and left him and most of his followers dead upon the spot. Thus did heaven confirm the prayers of the clergy, and punished a wicked and lascivious prince, who committed murder to secure himself upon the throne, and lost his life for the sake of a concubine. Marron, the queen of Conacht, did not long survive, for the neglect of her husband threw her into a melancholy distemper, which occasioned her death; nor did the daughter long enjoy the pleasures of a court, for she soon died unlamented, and vengeance justly punished such wicked and promiscuous mixtures.

In the reign of Conall Claon, king of Ireland, was fought the noted battle of Carn Conuill, by Diarmuid, the son of Aodha Slaine, in which engagement was killed Cuan, the son of Amholgadhg, who had governed the province of Munster ten years. In the same action fell Cuan Conuill, king of Figinte, and Talmonach, king of O'Liathain. This victory, we are told, was in a great measure owing to the incessant prayers of the religious belonging to the convent of Cluain Mac Naois, who fervently addressed themselves to heaven for the success of Diarmuid, who, after a bloody conflict and terrible slaughter, won the battle. The victor, when he returned, bestowed a valuable tract of land and great privileges upon the convent, and the estate he settled at that time, is known at this day by the name of Liathmantain; and he had that veneration for the abbey of Cluain Mac Naois, that he ordered by his will, that there his body should be interred, which was done accordingly. The most pious St. Fursa died about this time; she was of the royal line, descended from the posterity of Lughaidh Laga, brother to Oilioll Olum;

and St. Mocheallog, who erected and consecrated Cill Mocheallog, was soon afterwards translated to a better state : this religious person was derived from the family of Conaire, the son of
Eidersgeoil. The brothers, who sat jointly on the throne of Ireland concluded their reign in this manner : Ceallach was lost in
Brugh Os Boyne, and Conall was killed by Diarmuid, the son of
Aodh Slaine.

A.D.
661.
Blathmac and Diarmuid Ruaidhnaigh, the two sons
of Aodha Slaine, son of Diarmuid, seized upon the sovereignty. These princes descended from the royal line
cf Heremon, and reigned over the island seven years. In the
government of these brothers the memorable battle of Pancty
was fought, in which bloody engagement the king of England,
with thirty of his principal nobility, was slain. About this
time that religious person St. Oltan died, and Maoidog, descended
from the posterity of Colla Uais, monarch of Ireland, who built
and consecrated the church of Fearna, left the present world,
and was removed to a better ; he was followed by Cuimin Foda,
the son of Fiachradh the monk, and by St. Mannach, the son
of Finghin or Florence, King of Munster. These two brothers,
Blathmac and Diarmuid, died of the plague that for distinction
was called Buidhe Connuill.

668.
Seachnusach was the successor in the throne of Ireland. He was the son of Blathmac, son of Hugh, otherwise called Aodha Slaine, descended from the royal line of Heremon, and reigned monarch of the island six years. In the
government of this prince the battle of Feirt was fought between the inhabitants of the province of Ulster and the Picts,
where there was a terrible slaughter of both armies. In the
reign of this prince died the most pious Baoithin, abbot of Be-
anchuir. Seachnusach was afterwards killed by Dubh Duin of
Cineol Cairbre.

574.
Cionnfaola, the son of Blathmac, son of Aodha
Slaine, son of Diarmuid, possessed the sovereignty, and
reigned four years. Under the administration of this prince,
the convent of Beannchuir was consumed by fire to the ground,
and all the members of that religious house were dispossessed
and expelled by invading foreigners. This monastery was distinguished by the name of Beannchuir, upon the account of
Breasal Breac, king of Ireland. This prince transported a numerous army into Scotland, and was so successful in his expedition, that he returned with considerable booty, and among the
rest he brought over with him a great number of horned cattle.

When he arrived in Ireland he encamped with his forces in a place now called Beannchuir, where he was obliged for the support of his troops to kill many of these beasts, and their horns were scattered all over the plain, which from that time has been called by the name of Beannchuir, upon the account of these horns; for the word Beanna or Adharchadh, in the Irish tongue, signifies horns in the English. Many years after this encampment, the religious abbot Comhgall erected and endowed an abbey in the same place; and, regarding its original appellation, occasioned by scattering the horns, he retained the old name, and called it the abbey of Beannchuir. After this religious house was attacked and burned down by foreigners, Cion Faola, king of Ireland, was killed by Fionnachta Fleadhach, the son of Dunchada, in the memorable battle of Cealtrach.

A.D. 678.

Fionnachta Fleadhach obtained the government. He was the son of Dunchada, son of Aodha Slaine, derived from the illustrious line of Heremon, and he filled the throne of Ireland seven years. Under the administration of this prince, the people of Ireland were accustomed to make great feasts, and recreated themselves with noble and expensive entertainments; and from these sumptuous and magnificent banquets, the king was distinguished by the name of Fionnachta Fleadhach, for the word Fleadh in the Irish language signifies in the English a feast. In the reign of this prince died Colman, the pious bishop of Inis Bo Finne, and about the same time Fionnan, who pronounced his benediction over Ardfionan, left the world; this excellent person descended from the posterity of Fiachadh Muilleathan. The famous St. Aranan died not long afterwards. This Fionnachta, king of Ireland, fought the battle of Lochgabhair, against the inhabitants of the province of Leinster, in which engagement a great number of the provincial troops were cut off. The learned Cionnfaola died under the government of this monarch; and in the same year Dungall, the son of Scanlan, king of the Picts, and Cionnfaola, king of Cionnachta Glinne Geimin, were buried by Maolduin, son of Maolfithrigh, at Dunceithrin. In the same reign some of the principal commanders of the Welsh invaded Ireland, with a numerous and gallant army of their countrymen, and, as the venerable Bede relates in the sixth chapter of the fourth book of his history, committed dreadful hostilities, and made cruel devastations upon the Irish coasts. The same writer asserts, that in the year of our redemption 684, the forces of the king of England, under the conduct of an experienced general, whose name was Bertus, landed upon the island, and reduced the inhabitants to great extremities. His expression is,* " Bertus miserably ravaged that innocent nation, which was a most friendly ally to the English." In this invasion was fought the famous battle of Rathmore, at Muigh Glinne, in which action Cumasgach, king of the Picts, and a great number of the Irish were slain. These resolute and hardy Welsh transported themselves from thence to the isles of Orcades, which they subdued, and plundered the country without mercy. Some of these people landed upon the northern coast of Leinster, and spoiled the inhabitants with great cruelty, not sparing age or sex, or even the churches and the sacred vessels dedicated to divine service. After these ravages they returned, loaded with booty, into their own country. Fionnachta Fleadhach, king of Ireland, was killed by Hugh, the son of Dubhthaigh, and by Conning, at Greallach Dolling.

A.D. 685. Loingseach got possession of the crown. He was the son of Daniel, son of Hugh, son of Ainmereach, derived from the illustrious race of Heremon, and governed the kingdom of Ireland eight years. In the reign of this prince Adamhnan removed himself from Scotland, to propagate the Christian faith among the Irish, and about the same time Moling Lauchradh left the world. Under the government of Loingseach the Welsh invaded the island, by whom Magh Muirtheimhne was miserably plundered. Among other misfortunes of his reign, a most dreadful and consuming murrain raged among the cattle throughout England and Ireland, which occasioned a most terrible and afflicting famine among the inhabitants, so that the people were compelled to feed upon one another; and this visitation continued with great violence for the space of three years. Egbertus the saint undertook to preach the gospel in Scotland about this time, and Muireadhach Muilleathan, king of Conacht, died. The subjects of Ulster soon afterwards engaged the Welsh in the battle of Moigh Cuillinn, and obtained a victory over those foreigners, of whom a terrible slaughter was made, and almost their whole army slain. Adamhnan, the religious abbot of Aoii, in the kingdom of Scotland, died about the same time, after a life of seventy-seven years. It was within the reign of Loingseach, that the Saracens invaded the Grecian empire with an incredible number of forces, and attempted to make themselves masters of the capital city, Con-

* Bertus vastavit gentem innocentem misere et nationi Anglorum amicissimam.

stantinople ; but, after a siege of three years, they were repelled with considerable loss, and obliged to give over the undertaking. The pious Coibhdhean, bishop of Ardfert, was now removed to a better life ; and, soon after the decease of this prelate, the battle of Cormin was fought by Ceallagh, the son of Ragallach, who governed the province of Conacht seven years, in which bloody action Loingseach, the son of Aongus, king of Ireland, lost his life.

A.D.
693.
Congall Cionnmaghair succeeded in the throne. He was the son of Feargus Fanuid, son of Conull Gulban, son of Niall, the hero of the nine hostages, descended from the princely line of Heremon, and he was in possession of the sovereignty nine years. This Congall was a cruel persecutor of the Irish church,'and he burned the regular and secular clergy at Kildare without mercy or distinction. But the divine vengeance pursued him, and punished him with a sudden and unlamented death.

702.
Feargall obtained the government. He was the son of Maolduin, son of Maolfithrigh, son of Hugh, otherwise called Aodha Uairiodhnach, a lineal descendant from the line of Heremon, and sat upon the throne of Ireland seventeen years. The mother of this monarch was Cacht, the daughter of Maolchabha, king of Cineal Conuill. In the reign of this prince died Baodan, the bishop of Inis Bo Finne. About this time the Welsh, and the noble tribe of the Dailriadas, fought a most bloody and desperate battle, at a place called Clooh Mionuire ; the victory was in suspense, and the slaughter equal on both sides, for some part of the day, but the undaunted bravery of that ancient clan was not to be resisted, and the Welsh were routed with the loss of the greatest part of their army. In the same year Neachtan, the king of Scotland, expelled his dominions a convent of monks, who presumed to reprehend him for his conduct, and by that means promoted discontents among his subjects. The reign of this prince was remarkable for a very wonderful event that happened, and which gave a name to Niall Frasach, who was born about the same time ; for three showers fell from the heavens in the sight of a number of spectators, viz., a shower of honey at Foithin Beag, a shower of money at Foithin More, and a shower of blood at Magh Laighion.

But the most remarkable transaction in the reign of Feargall was the battle of Almhuinne, that was fought between Morough Mac Broin, king of Leinster, who had governed that province fifteen years, and this Feargall, the son of Maolduin, king of

Ireland. The royal army, raised by the king, consisted of 21,000 choice troops; and the provincial forces, that followed the king of Leinster, amounted in the whole but to 9000, supported by eighty-nine valiant and distinguished champions of hardy seasoned courage, and his household troops, that were inconsiderable in number, but of undaunted bravery. Both armies entered the field, and a most bloody and desperate engagement followed; but the provincial troops made so dreadful an impression in the beginning of the action, that they pierced into the king's army, and put them into confusion with incredible slaughter, and notwithstanding a great superiority of numbers, Feargall was forced to give way, victory declared for the king of Leinster, and 3300 of the enemy were left dead upon the field of battle. At the first onset an unaccountable terror seized upon the royal army, occasioned, as some authors assert, by a dreadful apparition that hung over them in the air, which put them into such dread and consternation that they were easily overthrown; which terrible sight, the chronicle relates, left such an impression upon the minds of some of the soldiery, that though they escaped with their lives in the action, yet after the defeat they ran distracted. Some accounts magnify the loss sustained by the king of Ireland, and express that 7000 of his men were killed upon the spot. The misfortune of the royal army, we are informed, was owing to a sacrilegious act committed by Feargall, as he was advancing to fight the king of Leinster; for it is said that in his march some of his forces broke into a church called Cillin, and carried away all the holy vessels, and violently drove away a cow that belonged to a hermit of that place. This injustice was so resented by the pious old man, that he laid dreadful imprecations upon the king, and applied to heaven for exemplary vengeance upon his army; and the prayers of that holy person prevailed, and occasioned the loss of the battle, wherein Feargall, king of Ireland, and his sacrilegious forces lost their lives.

A.D. 719. Fogarthach was the successor to this unfortunate prince. He was the son of Neill, son of Cearmuigh Sotuill, son of Diarmuid, son of Hugh, otherwise called Aodha Slaine, of the royal line of Heremon, and reigned monarch of the island one year. He lost his life by Cionaoith, the son of Jargallach, in the battle of Beilge.

720. Cionaoith fixed himself in the sovereignty. He was the son of Jargallach, son of Conuing Charraig, son of Congaille, son of Aodha Slaine, derived from the princely stock

of Heremon, and administered the government four years. In the reign of this prince the relics of the pious Adnomhan were removed from Scotland into Ireland. The bloody engagement of Drom Curran was fought soon afterwards, by Flaithbheartach, the son of Loinseach, with Cionaoth, king of Ireland ; in which action the royal army received a general defeat, and the king himself was found dead upon the field of battle.

A.D. 724. Flaithbheartach succeeded in the throne. He was the son of Loingseach, son of Aongus, son of Daniel, son of Hugh, son of Ainmereach, a descendant from the royal line of Heremon, and enjoyed the crown seven years. The mother of this prince was Murion, the daughter of Ceallach. The venerable Bede, in his English history, relates, that the dreadful battle of Drom Dearg was fought in Scotland, in the reign of this Irish monarch, between Drust and Aongus, two brothers, and sons of Aongus, king of the Picts. The succession to the kingdom of Scotland was determined in this engagement, where Drust, and the army that asserted his right, was subdued, and himself slain. The battle of Murbuilg was fought soon afterwards, in the same kingdom, between the noble tribe of the Dailriadas and the Picts, where the Picts were defeated with great slaughter, and drove out of the field. About the same time was fought the battle of Fotharta, in Muirtheimne, between the forces of Aodha Allain, the noble Clanna Neill, and the inhabitants of Ulster, in which sharp engagement Aodha Roin, who had been king of that province for thirty years, and Concha, son of Cuanach, king of Cobha, were unfortunately slain. Not long after this action, Loingseach, the monarch of Ireland, died a natural death at Ardmach.

731. Aodha or Hugh Ollan got possession of the sovereignty. He was the son of Feargaile, son of Maolduin, son of Maolfithrig, son of Aodha Uairiodhnach, descended from the royal family of Heremon, and governed the kingdom nine years. The mother of this Irish prince was Bridget, the daughter of Orca, son of Carrthon. In his reign the provinces of Munster and Leinster fought the bloody battle of Beallach Faile, where there was a dreadful slaughter on both sides, and in the conflict perished Ceallach, the son of Faobhuir, king of Ossery. In this dispute the victory was doubtful for some time but at last the fortune of the day fell to Cathall, the son of Fionguine, king of Munster.

In the government of this king, Aongus, the son of Feargus, king of the Picts, raised a considerable army and invaded the territories of the tribe of the Dailriada, in the kingdom of Scotland, and committed terrible devastations, having entered the country with fire and sword. Among other hostilities he plundered without mercy and distinction Dun Greidhe, and hen set the place on fire, and levelled it with the ground. This Pictish king was followed with victory in this attempt, his arms and cruelties were a terror to the inhabitants, and among his successes, the fortune of war delivered into his hands Dongall and Feargus, the sons of Sealbhaigh, who was at that time king of the Dailriada, whom he made prisoners, and confined closely under a strong guard.

About the same time there was an interview between Hugh Allan, king of Ireland, and Cathall, the son of Fionguine, king of Munster, at a place called Tirda Glass, in the county of Ormond, where, among other debates, it was consulted what methods should be used to advance the yearly revenue of St. Patrick throughout the kingdom, and they established a particular law for that purpose. The battle of Athseanuigh was soon afterwards fought between Hugh Allan, king of Ireland, and Hugh, the son of Colgan, king of Leinster. This engagement was fought with desperate courage on both sides, and many persons of distinction lost their lives. The king of Ireland received a dangerous wound, and Hugh, son of the king of Leinster, was slain ; the provincial troops fought with great bravery, but the principal nobility of the province perished in the action, and it is said that 9000 of the forces of Leinster remained dead upon the field of battle. The army of the kingdom of Ireland suffered great difficulties and loss of men ; and among the commanders, Hugh, the son of Mortough, a brave and experienced soldier, who shared the sovereignty of the island with Hugh, was wounded mortally, and did not survive the action of the day. The reign of this prince was distinguished by the death of these eminent persons, Flann, the son of Cronmaol, the pious and charitable bishop of Rotheruine ; Cahall, the son of Fionguinne, who governed the province of Munster ; and the martial prince Hugh Balve, the son of Ionrachta, who had been king of Conacht seven years. Hugh Allan, king of Ireland, fell under the victorious sword of Daniel, the son of Morrough, in the noted battle of Seiridhmidh, known otherwise by the name of the battle of Ceananus.

A.D. 740. Daniel succeeded to the crown of Ireland. He was the son of Morrough, son of Diarmuid, son of Airmeadh Caoch, son of Conull Guthbhin, son of Suibhne, son of

Colman More, son of Feargus Ceirbheoil, son of Conall Creamthuine, son of Niall, the martial hero of the nine hostages, a
lineal descendant from the renowned line of Heremon, and was
monarch of the island forty-two years. The mother of this
prince was Ailpin, the daughter of Congall of Dealbhna Mora.
In the reign of this Irish king, Colman, the bishop of Laosan,
was killed by the hands of O'Durraire ; and Cormac, the bishop
of Ath Trim, left the present life for a better. About this time,
as the chronicle relates, a prodigy was observed, for the appearance of a monstrous serpent was seen moving in the air : this
apparition was followed by the death of Seachnusach, the son
of Colgan, king of Cinsalach ; and soon afterwards Cathasach,
the son of Oiliolla, king of the Picts, was killed at Rath Beathach, by the inhabitants of the province of Leinster. Under the
government of Daniel two eminent prelates, whose names were
Suarleach, bishop of Fabhair, and Osbran, the bishop of Cluain
Creamha, were translated into another life. The memorable
battle of Beallach Cro was fought about this time by Criomhthan, the son of Eana, in which engagement Fionn, the son of
Airb, king of Dealbhna, was slain, and great numbers of his
army followed him into another world. This terrible fight happened at a place called Tiobraid Fionn, and from the dreadful
slaughter and bloodshed of that action, the adjoining lake that
is near the place has been ever since distinguished by the name
of Loch Beallin Cro ; for the word Cro in the Irish language,
signifies blood in the English, and the spring that gives rise to
that lake is called Tobur Fionn. In the same reign died these
remarkably great men : Comusgach, the king of O'Faly, who
was killed by the hands of Maolduin, the son of Hugh Beanain,
king of Munster ; and Aongus, the king of Scotland, who resigned his crown and his life. About the same time the battle
of Beallach Gabhrah was fought, by Maconceara and the inhabitants of Ossery, who, with their joint forces, engaged Dungall,
the son of Laidhgin, son of O'Cinnseallach, in which action
Dungall with the principal gentry of Leinster lost their lives ;
and soon afterwards died Mortough, the son of Murchadh, king
of Leinster ; and after a long reign followed Daniel, the son of
Morrough, king of Ireland. This prince descended from Clan
Colman, and died it is supposed naturally and without violence.

    Niall Freasach was the next successor. He was the
A.D. son of Feargall, son of Maolduing, son of Maolfithreach,
782. son of Aodh Uairiodhnach, derived from the royal posterity of Heremon ; he enjoyed the crown four years. The

mother of this prince was Aithiochta, the daughter of Cein
O'Connor, king of Cianachta. The reason why he was distinguished by the name of Niall Freasach was, because there fell
three preternatural showers in the kingdom of Ireland the time
he was born ; a shower of honey, a shower of silver, and a
shower of blood ; for the word Fras in the Irish language, signifies a shower in the English. Under the government of this
prince died Dubhionrachtach, the son of Cahal, son of Muireadhach Muilleathan, after he had governed the province of
Conacht five years. The reign of this Irish king was afflicted
with many dreadful calamities ; for many terrible earthquakes
happened in several parts of the island, and a most miserable
famine raged throughout the kingdom, and destroyed multitudes
of people. Dungall, the son of Ceallach, king of Ossery, died
about this time ; likewise Cronmaol, the pious bishop of Cill
More, and Ailpin, king of the Picts, and Colgnait, the charitable
bishop of Ardbreacan, who were removed into another world.
The battle of Acha Liag was fought in the reign of Niall, between Jobh Bruin and Jobh Maine ; the action was sharp, and
concluded with great slaughter on both sides. Soon after this
engagement Artgoile, the son of Cathal, undertook a pilgrimage,
and went to Aoii Collum Cill, in the dominions of Scotland ;
about the same time, Feargus, the bishop of Damhliag, was
translated into a better state, and the bloody engagement of
Corann was fought between Cineal Connuill and Siol Eogain, in
which action Hugh Allain, the king of Fochla, came off with
complete victory, and Daniel, the son of Hugh Mundeirg, was
defeated with exceeding loss, and a general rout of his whole
army. Niall Freasach, the king of Ireland, did not long survive this fight, but died in Aoii Collum Cill, in the kingdom of
Scotland.

A.D. 786. Donchadha obtained the government. He was the
son of Daniel, son of Murchadha, son of Diarmuid, son
of Airmeadh Caoch, son of Conull Guthbhin, son of
Suibhne, son of Colman More, son of Feargus Ceirbheoil, son of
Conall Creamhthuine, son of Niall, the celebrated hero of the
nine hostages, descended from the royal stock of Heremon, and
enjoyed the sovereignty twenty-seven years. He escaped the
sword by which most of his predecessors fell, and died in his bed
in his own royal palace.

813. Hugh, who was otherwise called Aodha Dorndighe,
succeeded in the throne of Ireland. He was the son of

Niall Freasach, and derived from the illustrious line of Heremon, and was monarch of the island twenty-four years. The
mother of this prince was Dunflaith, the daughter of Flaithbheartach, son of Loingseach, king of Cineall Conuill; and he
was distinguished by the appellation of Aodha Dorndighe, or
Oirndighe, because when weaned from the breast of his nurse,
he used himself to that unbecoming practice of sucking his fingers; for the words Aodha Dorndighe, in the Irish language,
signify in the English, Hugh, the fist or finger sucker. The
reign of this prince was signally remarkable for the invasion of
the Danes, who were hitherto strangers to the island, and landed
in a hostile manner in the west of Munster, with a numerous
army transported in fifty sail. Airtre, a descendant from the
race of Heber Fionn, governed the province of Munster at that
time; and, upon the first notice of the attempt, he marched
with a strong body of his provincial troops, resolved to repel the
invaders. A most desperate and bloody action followed, where
the Danes were defeated, and fled in confusion to their shipping,
leaving 416 of their countrymen dead upon the spot. The
darkness of the night favoured their retreat, and hindered the
pursuit, which otherwise would have been attended with much
greater slaughter. After this trial of Irish courage the Danes
gave over the attempt for that time, and were obliged to return
into their own country.

Six years after this expulsion of the Danes, when Feidhlime,
the son of Criomhthan, was king of Munster, another fleet set
sail from Norway, and landed upon the coast of that province,
where they plundered and ravaged with the utmost barbarity,
and reduced the inhabitants to great extremities; but an army
being raised with all possible expedition, to oppose the dreadful
progress of the invaders, the provincial troops gave them battle,
Irish bravery prevailed, and the Danes, repulsed with great
slaughter, were obliged to quit the island. In the seventeenth
year of the reign of this monarch, that bloody tyrant, Turgesius, made an attempt upon Ireland; at which time Olchabhair,
son of Cionnfhaoith, son of Congall, son of Maolduin, son of
Hugh Beanain, was king over the province of Munster. This
account is confirmed by the authority of some Irish chronicles,
though the Polychronicon, speaking of the affairs of Ireland,
expressly asserts, that the Danes made their invasion upon the
island when Feidhlime, the son of Croimhthan, was the king of
Munster. His expression upon this subject it may not be im-

proper to transcribe :* "From the coming of St. Patrick down
to the time of Feidhlime, thirty-three kings reigned in Ireland
for the space of 400 years ; but in the time of Feidhlime, the
Norwegians, under the conduct of Turgesius, got possession of
the country." There are other authors which say, that the
Danes made their first attempt upon the kingdom of Ireland,
at the time when Artry, the son of Conall, was king of Munster, and this is affirmed with great truth ; but it must be observed they were not able to obtain footing in the country, but
were obliged to desist and return with loss, after they had plundered the people, and done incredible damage wherever they
came. The writer of the Polychronicon likewise is to be credited in what he asserts, for he observes that Feidhlime was
king of Munster when that cruel tyrant Turgesius with his followers landed upon the coasts, and with dreadful hostilities
harassed the inhabitants, who were miserably pillaged and enslaved under the oppression of these barbarous foreigners.
Neither are we to reject the testimony of those writers, who
affirm that the Danes landed in the country when Olchobhair
was in possession of the throne of Munster ; for those foreigners, who made an attempt upon the island at that time, were
natives of the kingdom of Dania or Denmark and these people
are called in the old Irish records by the name of Dubhgeinte or
Dubh Lochlannaig ; the Norwegians, who came originally from
Norway, are styled in the chronicles Finngeinte or Fionn Lochlannaig. It is to be observed in this place, that the word Lochlan-
nach, does not signify in the Irish language any particular tribe
or nation, but it implies strong or powerful at sea ; for the word
Lonn signifies strong in the English, and Loch is the Irish word
from the sea : for the people of Norway and Denmark were
skilful in navigation, and expert seamen, and by their shipping
transported powerful armies into Ireland, when they attempted
to make a conquest of the country. The particular exploits
and invasions of these foreigners will be related at large in the
following part of this history, extracted from that valuable record, known in the Irish language by the name of Cogadh Gall
ra Gaoidhealuibh, or An account of the wars of the Gauls
against the Irish.

In the reign of Hugh Oirndighe, king of Ireland, and Artry,

* Ab adventu Sancti Patricii usque ad Feidhlimidii regis tempora, triginta
tres reges per quadringentos annos in Hibernia regnaverunt, tempore autem
Feidhlimidii, Norvogesenses duce Turgesio, terram hanc occuparunt.

the son of Cohall, king of Munster, the Gauls made an attempt upon the island, and landed at Caomh Inis Obhrathadh, with a fleet of 60 ships; these transports brought over a numerous body of troops, who, upon their arrival, plundered the coasts with dreadful cruelty, and then set the country on fire. In their fury Inis Labhraine, after it had been pillaged, was consumed, and Dairinis suffered the same calamity, and was burned to the ground. The inhabitants of Eoganacht and of Loch Lein resolved to repel the invaders, and raising what forces they were able, they resolutely gave them battle; the action was short but violent, and the natives obtained a complete victory, and 416 of the Gauls were slain. This defeat so discouraged the foreigners, that they retired with great precipitancy to their ships, they weighed anchor, and made homewards with all their sail.

But the kingdom of Ireland was so preferable in its wealth and fertility to the barren country of Norway, that those northern people soon prepared for another descent upon the island, and in the second year of the reign of Feidhlime, king of Munster, they landed and practised their usual barbarities upon the natives. Among other ravages they burned Inis Eibhin, Beannchuir, Cluain Umhadh, Ross Maoiladh, and Sgeilg Michael. Another fleet of these foreigners arrived about the same time, and landed in the east part of the island: they carried with them the utmost miseries of fire and sword; they plundered Beannchuir, and killed the bishop and the religious of that place, and added sacrilege to their cruelty by breaking open the rich shrine of Combgoll. These invaders were reinforced with another fleet of Norwegians, who, hearing of the success of their countrymen, resolved to try their fortune, and landed at Jobh Cinnseallach. Their arrival struck fresh terror into the inhabitants, who fled for the security of their lives, and left the country to the mercy of the invaders. In this attempt were plundered Teach Munna, Teach Moling, and Inis Tiog. The hopes of booty encouraged them to proceed in their hostilities, and coming to Ossery, they began to spoil and pillage without opposition; but the people of that country rose upon them, and with great bravery attacked the foreigners, who were unprepared for an assault, and intent upon carrying off their booty, and after a desperate and bloody conflict gave them an entire defeat, and slew 707 of them upon the spot. The Danes, nothing dispirited by this misfortune, distressed the country, and practised their usual devastations, plundering Dundergmuighe, Inis Eogan, Diosiort, Tiobruid, and Lismore; and they ransacked and burned to the ground Cillmolaisy, Glindaloch, Cluainard, Mobeodhg, Suirn Collum Cill, Diamhliag Ciaran, Slaine, Cealla Saile, and Cluain Uadhme Mungairid. The churches felt the common calamity, and after they had been stripped of their ornaments and sacred vessels they were set on fire ; and most of the monasteries and religious houses in the kingdom were consumed by these savage and wicked invaders, without remorse or distinction.

Another fleet of these freebooters followed the former, and landed in the harbour of Limerick. The coasts were immediately plundered with military execution, and Corcabaisgian Tradruighe and Jobh Conuill Gabhra were set on fire and consumed to ashes. But the Danes were not suffered to carry off their prey without opposition ; for Jobh Conuill, with a stout body of native Irish, gave them battle at Seanuid, and putting them to rout with considerable slaughter, recovered the spoil out of their hands. But the most dreadful attempt upon the island was by the cruel tyrant Turgesius, supported by a number of his countrymen, and a great fleet of ships, who, with great terror to the inhabitants, landed upon the northern coasts of Ireland. The historians of this time differ in their account of this Turgesius, some asserting that he was the king of Norway, others that he was the king's son ; but of whatever quality he was, it is certain that he was a man of great personal courage, but of a savage and inhuman disposition. The Danes, whom he found in the kingdom, received him with universal joy and loud acclamations ; and being before divided into several bodies, under many commanders, they united under him, and with one consent chose him for their general. Under the conduct of this leader they renewed their hostilities, and proceeded in their ravages with that success that they determined to conquer the whole island ; he fortified himself in the possession of what he had got, and dispatched a considerable part of his army to seize upon the northern half of the country, called for distinction Leath Coinn. He divided his fleet likewise, and setting a sufficient number of his men on board, he sent some of his ships to Loch Meabhach, others had orders to sail to Lughmiagh, and others were commanded to Loch Ribh, with positive commissions to ravage with fire and sword, to spare neither age nor sex, but by their cruelties and terror of their arms to dispirit the people, and fix themselves without fear of being dispossessed. And these incursions were successfully executed ; and among other instances of barbarity, Ardmach was miserably plundered three times within the space of a month, and Turgesius, without any regard to his character, seized upon the abbot of Ardmach, and made him his prisoner. The Irish apostle, St. Collum Cill, foretold the captivity of this abbot, as it is recorded in the following lines:

> The most religious abbot of Ardmach,
> Shall, by the force of the Norwegian arms,
> Be seized, and made a prisoner of war.

There were many of the clergy of several orders within the kingdom of Ireland, who, by a prophetic spirit, foresaw the sore calamities that were coming upon their country long before they happened; for the inhabitants were become very profligate and corrupt in their manners, and a torrent of vice and profaneness had overspread the nation, but prevailed chiefly among the nobility and gentry, whose pride, injustice, and ambition, deserved the severest inflictions from the hand of Providence; so that the cruel Danes were used as instruments by Divine vengeance to scourge and correct a wicked and debauched nobility, and an immoral and licentious populace: it was therefore predicted by some of the ecclesiastics of the kingdom, that the sins of the inhabitants would be punished by very terrible visitations, which should overrun the land in the reign of Aodha Dorndighe, king of Ireland, and Artry, the son of Cohall, king of Munster.

The province of Munster, it has been before observed, was under the government of Feidhlime, son of Criomhthan, when Turgesius, the cruel Dane, invaded the island and spoiled the country. Among other ravages he plundered the churches and monasteries, sacrilegiously seized upon the ecclesiastical revenues and expelled the primate of Ardmach and his college of clergy out of their benefices, and fixed himself in possession of that church and the estates belonging, which he kept till he was taken by Maolseachluin, and afterwards drowned by him in Loch Aiunin, as will be particularly related in its proper place. In the reign of Hugh Dorndighe, Inis Patrick suffered in the common calamity, and was plundered by the merciless Danes, who by the benefit of their shipping spoiled most of the islands between Ireland and Scotland, and returned loaden with booty.

About this time the revenue of St. Patrick was established upon the province of Conacht, by the authority of Gormgall, the son of Diondaithbaigh; soon after Hugh Dorndighe divided the country of Meath between the two sons of Donough, son of Daniel; the names of these two brothers were Connor and

Oilioll. The monastery of Aoii Collum Cill, about this time fell a sacrifice to the cruelty of the savage Danes, who had made an invasion upon Scotland; and their countrymen, inspired with the same barbarity, were not behind in their executions upon the Irish.

The kingdom of Ireland, notwithstanding the oppression o. these victorious foreigners, was rent asunder by civil discord; for the king and petty princes of the country, instead of opposing the common enemy with their united strength, quarrelled among themselves, and laid themselves open with great disadvantage to the invaders. Hugh Dorndighe, the monarch of the kingdom, was provoked by the people of Leinster, and entering the province in a hostile manner, he slew the inhabitants that fell in his way; and within the space of a month he plundered and reduced the country to the last extremities. About a year after these calamities, in the latter end of the month of March, there were such terrible shocks of thunder, and the lightning did such execution, that 1010 persons, men and women, were destroyed by it, between Corcabaisginn and the seaside; at the same time the sea broke through its banks in a violent and dreadful manner, and overflowed a tract of land that would every year afford sufficient pasture for twelve head of cattle; it was added to the channel and could never be recovered. The tempest raged with exceeding terror, and the current of the waters was so violent, that the island, called Inis Fidhe, was forced asunder, and divided into three parts.

Hugh Dorndighe, king of Ireland, in his expedition against the people of Leinster, pierced as far into the province as Dun Cuair; and having subdued the country as he went, he divided it in equal parts between Muireadhach, the son of Ruarach, and Muireadhach, the son of Bruin. Some time after this division Muireadhaig was set on fire and consumed by the Danes, after it had been plundered; and these ravagers, emboldened by success, made incursions upon the people of Omhaill, overran the country, and carried off the spoil. In the reign of this Irish monarch died the venerable Eochaidh, bishop of Tamhlachta, and likewise Eidersgeoil, the son of Ceallaig, the pious prelate of Glindaloch, and Siadhuall, the good bishop of Roscommon, did not long survive the miseries of his country, but was translated to a better life. Hugh Dorndighe, after a troublesome reign, was killed at Moigh Conuille, by the sword of Muolcanaugh, in the battle of Da Fearta.

2 D

Conchabhar, otherwise called Connor, sat next upon the throne. He was the son of Donough, son of Daniel, son of Murchada, son of Diarmuid, son of Airmeadh Caoch, descended from the royal line of Heremon, and was possessed of the sovereignty fourteen years. In the reign of this Irish prince, the most exemplary Cionfhaola, bishop of Athtrym, left the world; Eochaidh O'Tuathail, the bishop of Luigh Moigh, soon followed into another life. The reign of this king was miserably harassed by the Danes, who began to settle in the island, and among other devastations Inis Damhly and Cork were plundered and burned.

About this time the revenue of St. Patrick was established upon the province of Munster by Feidhlime, the son of Criomhthan; and Artry, the son of Connor, enjoined the same tax upon the province of Conacht. Beannchuir and Dundaleth Glas were attacked and plundered by the Danes, and not content to set fire to Moigh Bille, they enclosed the hermits that belonged to the place, and consumed them to ashes. Mortough, the son of Eogan, was king of Ulster at this time; and Connor, the king of Ireland, attempted to chastise the Gailiongachs, who had provoked him by their insolence; and for that purpose he raised a gallant army, marched against them, and offered them battle. They accepted the challenge, and engaged in the plain of Tailtion, where the king's troops slew multitudes of the enemy, and won the day. The inhabitants of Leinster resolved to oppose the progress of the Danes with all the forces of the province; they met the army of the foreigners at Druim Conla, and a bloody action followed: fortune remained doubtful for some time, and in suspense between both parties, but the provincial troops gave way and fled, which occasioned a terrible slaughter in the pursuit; among the slain was the valiant Conuing, son of Conchoingiolt, chief of the tribe of the Fothartuarths. Soon after this defeat Ardmach was plundered with great barbarity by the victorious Danes, who, in the month following, spoiled with their accustomed cruelty Lughmagh, Finne Cianachta, and Lismore, with all the churches and religious houses that fell in their way, which they violently broke into, killed or expelled the members, and seized upon the consecrated vessels and whatever they found, as lawful booty. Before these ravages of the Danes, there were four flourishing universities of principal note in the kingdom of Ireland: one at Ardmach, which was filled with 7000 students, as appears expressly by an old roll discovered lately in the library of Oxford; the university of Dunda Leath Glass: the university of Lismore, and the university of Cashel, with many academies and colleges of smaller account; but they felt the destroying sword of these barbarians, who had no regard for learning or learned men; nothing sacred or civil escaped their rage, but they swept all they could lay hold on with a cruel and undistinguishing fury. Connor, king of Ireland, unable to bear or redress the misfortunes of his country, it is supposed died of grief.

A.D. 851.
Niall Caille was the succeeding monarch. He was the son of Hugh Dorndighe, son of Niall Frasach, a descendant from the posterity of Heremon, and he ruled the island fifteen years. The mother of this prince was Meidhbh, the daughter of Jonrachtach, son of Muireadhach, king of Durlus. He was particularly known by the name of Niall Caille for this reason: upon a time he came attended with a great retinue of horse to the bank of the river Callain, with a design to ford the stream, but it happened that the river was swollen to a great height by the violence of the rains, which occasioned him to halt, and sound the depth before he attempted to enter the water. For this purpose he commanded a gentleman who rode in his train to try the ford, who, before he had gone far, was carried down by the current, and washed off his horse. The king, willing to preserve him, gave orders for those about him, who had the ablest horses, to plunge into the water and lay hold of the gentleman; but they were all afraid and astonished at the fury and rapid course of the river, and refused to venture, which made the king, concerned for the misfortune of the guide, who by this time was almost drowned, resolve to hazard his own person, and, if possible, to save his life. With this design he advanced to the very brink of the water, and preparing to jump in, the ground, undermined by the stream, broke under the horse's feet, and the current being exceeding violent, rolled man and horse headlong, and the king perished in the attempt. This unfortunate prince had some warning to avoid the river Callain, for it was predicted some time before, that he should be drowned in that stream, which was the sad occasion of his name, and he was always mentioned afterwards by the name of Niall Caille. In the reign of this prince died Diarmuid, the son of Tumaltach, who governed the province of Conacht. The Danes still continued spoiling the country; they plundered Loch Bricirne, and killed Congallach the son of Neachach.

Niall, whose life we are writing, invaded the province of

Leinster at the head of a numerous army, designing by this expedition to place upon the throne of that country a prince whose name was Bryen, the son of Faolan. The cruel Danes carried on their depredations in a very dreadful manner; they plundered Fearna Maoidog, Mungairid, and Jollar Ceall, in the county of Ormond; the churches and monasteries were rifled and demolished, the religious expelled with unheard-of violence, and in their sacrilegious fury the magnificent church of Kildare was wholly destroyed.

The success of the Danish invasion, promoted by the most savage barbarities, that spared neither sex nor age, encouraged the Normans to try their fortune; who having fitted out a number of transports, set sail from their own country, and arrived in the mouth of the Boyne, and another fleet of forty sail came into the mouth of the river Liffy. These invaders, if possible, exceeded the bloody Norwegians in their hostilities and military executions; they pillaged the coasts, and devoured what the Danish locusts had left; they carried with them the terror of fire and sword in their incursions, they plundered Magh Liffy, in the county of Dublin, Magh Breagh, and Fingal. The progress of these foreigners alarmed the Danes, who, fearing the Normans would deprive them of their conquests, and drive them out of the kingdom, either by their own power or joining with the natives, collected their scattered forces, that were divided into several bodies for the convenience of plunder, came to Jobh Neill, and offered battle to the Normans. The fight began briskly, and a dreadful slaughter followed on both sides, but the victory inclined to the Danes, who, after a terrible impression upon the enemy, turned the fortune of the day, and pursued them from Inbher Nambark, where the battle was fought, along the banks of the Shannon, to the sea side. This success animated the Danes, who, finding the country open and unguarded, renewed their hostilities, and ransacked and burned Inis Cealtrach Cluain Mac Nois, and all the churches of Loch Eirne were consumed to ashes.

In the time of these public calamities, Feidhlime, the son of Criomhthan, governed the province of Munster; and having entered into holy orders, presided in the archiepiscopal chair of Leath Modha, as the south half of Ireland was generally called. This prince received provocations from the northern half of the island, known by the name of Leath Cuin, and carrying his arms into that part of the country, he sorely distressed the inhabitants, and plundered without distinction from Birr to

Teamhair Breag; but he met with opposition at Tara, which he overcame with some difficulty, and in a conflict, wherein his forces engaged Jonrachtach, the son of Maolduin, lost his life. This ecclesiastical prince did not long survive to enjoy the benefit of his victories, being cut off by death, after he had filled the throne of Munster for twenty-seven years. There is a valuable treatise extant, which gives a great character of this Feidhlime, the son of Criomhthan; and, speaking of his disease, says :* " The most excellent and wise anchoret of the Scots departed this life ;" which is authority sufficient to believe that this prince was a person of great learning and accomplishments, and, by reason of his piety and the holiness of his life, a bright ornament of the Christian profession.

In the same year with the death of Feidhlime, Olchobhair, abbot of Imly, a man ambitious and fond of power, had interest sufficient to have himself elected king of Cashel. Maolseach-luin, king of Meath, about the same time engaged the Danes at Casan Linge, and gave them a signal overthrow, which concluded with the slaughter of 700 of them upon the spot. The Danish general, whose name was Saxolb, was killed by Cianach-taibh, in an encounter wherein the foreigners were defeated with great loss. The fortune of the Danes began now to abate, for they were generally routed by the natives, who struggled hard for their liberties, and particularly destroyed numbers of them in the battle of Easruaidh ; but after this bad success the invaders recovered their strength, and with the choicest of their forces, laying siege to the city of Dublin, took it sword in hand. The famous Cormac Mac Cuillenan, who was archbishop of Cashel, and governed the province of Munster for seven years, was born about this time ; soon after the pious bishop of Teilge, whose name was Exnich, was unfortunately killed. The inhabitants of Conacht attempted to oppose the incursions of the Danes, and gave them battle, but with ill success ; for the provincial troops were cut off in great numbers, and Maolduin, the son of Muirguisa, was slain. Near this time died Bryen, the son of Faolan, king of Leix.

The Danes were continually reinforced with fresh recruits from their own country, and a fleet of many sail, with a body of troops on board, arrived upon the coasts, and landed at Loch Neachach. They committed their usual hostilities, and plundered the country in an inhuman manner ; they broke

* Optimus et sapiens anachorta Scotorum quievit.

through the law of nations, and contrary to the practice of declared enemies, they ravaged with all the terror and calamities of fire and sword. The churches in the northern part of the island fell a prey to these barbarians, who had no regard to religion and the Christian worship, but with a savage brutality they destroyed every thing civil and sacred; and among other acts of violence, Fearna and Corke were spoiled and pillaged, and then set on fire and consumed to ashes.

Niall Caille, king of Ireland, about this time, at the head of a numerous army, plundered and destroyed Fearceall and Deabhna Eathra; and soon after Morrough, the son of Hugh, king of Conacht left the world; the celebrated bishop of Cluain Heois followed, and was delivered from a troublesome life. The Danes, encouraged by their success. and to secure what they had conquered, erected a fort at Linn Duachaill, which they filled with their choicest troops; this garrison was a terror to the natives, and by their continued excursions plundered and destroyed the country called Tuatha Teabhtha. They also built another castle at Dublin, from whence they had an opportunity of ruining the province of Leinster and Jobh Neill; the churches were levelled with the ground, and the country was miserably distressed, from the city of Dublin to Sliabh Bladhma. They ransacked Cluain Aidhnach, Cluain Joraird, and Cluain Mac Naois; the whole land around became desert, and was like an uninhabited wilderness. About this time Feargus, the son of Fothig, who governed the province of Conacht, departed this life; and the cruel Dane, Turgesius, erected a fort at Loch Ribh, which commanded the country about, and infested Cluain Mac Naois, Cluain Fearta Breanuin, Tirdaglass, Lothra, and many other adjacent places and cities, which were plundered and destroyed, and fell a miserable sacrifice to the fury of these invaders. Not long afterwards the venerable Muireadhach, bishop of Laine Leire, was translated to a better life; and about the same time Niall Caille, king of Ireland, engaged the Danes in a pitched battle, and gave them a signal overthrow, which was attended with the loss of numbers left dead upon the spot; but this prince did not survive long enough to enjoy the fruits of his victory, for he was unfortunately drowned in the river Callain, in the manner before related.

▲ D.
866.

Turgesius, the Dane, usurped the sovereignty of Ireland. This foreigner was the king of Norway, as some writers affirm, or as others, the king's son. His countrymen, the Norwegians and other easterlings who sided against the natives, proclaimed him king of Ireland, and invested him with the government of the island, which he ruled thirteen years. Before he came to the throne he had been seventeen years in the country, plundering and destroying the inhabitants with inexpressible calamities. He was a scourge in the hands of divine Providence, to punish the Irish nation, which was reduced to the last extremities, and at last compelled to submit under the yoke of this usurper. The island had been for many years harassed with wars and intestine divisions, as well as continual struggles to preserve their oppressed liberties, and repel the insolence and cruel hostilities of the invaders ; but the foreigners being constantly supported with recruits from Norway, and all the eastern countries adjacent, poured in such numbers upon the natives, that they were forced to give up the defence of their country, and submit to the tyranny of this usurper, who reduced them to the lowest servitude, imposed insufferable taxes, and by other acts of cruelty and oppression established himself in the government, and as it were, made a conquest of the island. This foreigner had no sooner seized upon the crown, but he dispatched messengers into Norway, who were commissioned to give notice of his accession to the throne, and to desire a supply of forces sufficient to support his pretensions against any attempts of the natives, who were a people jealous of their liberties, and if not kept under by the terror of a standing army, would occasion him an uneasy reign. Accordingly a fleet of many sail, and a number of transports filled with regular troops, were dispatched, and landed upon the western coast. The country was immediately laid waste, the inhabitants were forced by droves like sheep into captivity, and such as escaped were obliged to retire into woods and wildernesses with their families, and lie exposed to the miseries of famine, to preserve themselves from slavery. These foreigners manned out several boats that were ordered upon Loch Neachach and Loch Ribh, from whence they ravaged and committed hostilities savage and terrible beyond expression. St. Collum Cill, many years before the invasion of the Danes, foretold the calamities that should fall upon his country ; and Bearchan the prophet predicted particularly, that the Norwegians should arrive and bring the country into servitude. The verses of this ancient poet may be thus translated :

The bold Norwegians, with a numerous sail,
Shall try the Irish ocean, and arrive
Upon the coasts. The isle shall be enslav'd

By these victorious foreigners, who shall place
In every church an abbot of their own,
And shall proclaim, to fill the throne of Ireland,
A king of the Norwegian race.

AN ACCOUNT OF THE MANY BATTLES FOUGHT BY TURGESIUS,

Turgesius, having reduced the island under his subjection, and by usurpation broke in upon the succession of the royal line of the Irish monarchs, exercised his government with great tyranny, establishing himself upon the ruins of the national liberties, and made his arbitrary and unbounded will the rule of his administration. The natives were miserably galled with the heavy yoke of this foreigner, and, resolving to attempt a recovery of their freedom, a conspiracy was formed by the principal nobility and gentry of the kingdom, to dethrone the tyrant, and fix the state upon its ancient foundation. They reflected upon the bravery of their ancestors, how prodigal they were of their blood in defence of their country, and what noble efforts they made to secure their rights and privileges, and deliver them down unoppressed to posterity. Inspired with these reflections, the revolt became universal, the Irish unanimously armed, and assembled in bodies over the whole kingdom. They engaged the Danes in several desperate battles, and fought with success in many encounters. A spirit of freedom and liberty prevailed throughout the island, and was attended with victory, insomuch that the foreigners began to be weary of their conquests. They were so harassed and borne down by the old Irish courage, that they were overthrown and defeated with incredible loss, and at last obliged to retire to their shipping, and bid adieu to the island.

It may not be improper in this place to relate particularly some of the most memorable battles that were fought between the natives and the invaders, and express some of the most remarkable circumstances that attended them; in order to give posterity a just idea of the courage and bravery of the ancient Irish, who were a nation fond of their liberties, and of the royal family of their kings, whose throne they could not endure should be filled by foreigners, but exposed themselves to preserve their country, and put an end to those calamities that closely followed a foreign yoke, and are the necessary effects of tyranny and usurpation.

The Irish, led on by the principal nobility of the country,

particularly the tribe of the Dailgais, engaged the Danes, and gave them a signal overthrow at Ardbreacan. The foreigners were again attacked by the people of Colgain, and routed with the loss of all their forces; in which action Saxolb, a commander of great courage and experience among the Danes, was slain. Olchobhair, the son of Cionnfaoith, who governed the province of Munster, and Lorcain, the son of Ceallach, king of Leinster, joined their provincial forces, and fell upon the army of the invaders with irresistible bravery; the dispute was hot and bloody, but the impetuosity of the Irish broke the ranks of the enemy, and a general rout followed. In this engagement the earl of Tomair, heir apparent to the crown of Denmark, was slain, and 1200 of the best soldiers of the Danish army followed him to the other world. The king of Munster before mentioned, and the inhabitants of Eoganacht Cashel, defeated the Danes in a pitched battle near Cashel, where 500 of them were killed, and the rest fled for their lives. The people of Tyrconnel armed to recover their liberties, and attacked the invaders near Easruaidh, and fought them with success; for the choicest of their forces perished in the engagement, and few escaped the slaughter of the day. The men of Jobh Figinty resolved to be no longer slaves, and, observing an opportunity, fell upon the Danes, and killed 360 of them. Two hundred of these foreigners were destroyed by the people of Cianachta; and 240 at Druin da Chonn, were slain by Tighernach, king of Loch Gabhair. Maolseach luin, king of Meath, attempted to shake off the yoke, and engaged the Danes with such success at a place called Glasglean, that 1700 of them were cut off. Yet, notwithstanding these victories, the foreigners were far from being suppressed; for they were constantly supplied with fresh recruits from their own country, which inspired them with courage under the greatest slaughter of their troops; their broken armies were soon completed, and the natives were so harassed with continual skirmishes and attacks, that they lost their choicest soldiers without any prospect of filling their places; and therefore being dispirited and worn out, they were obliged to confess themselves a vanquished people, and submit to the cruel tyranny of Turgesius and his Danish soldiery, who ruled them with a rod of iron, and forced them to taste of the very dregs of servitude. The whole kingdom was reduced, the usurper seized upon the crown, and by his followers was proclaimed monarch of Ireland.

A PARTICULAR ACCOUNT OF THE SLAVERY IMPOSED UPON THE ANCIENT
IRISH, BY TURGESIUS, THE DANISH TYRANT.

The native Irish could neither bear nor shake off the oppressive yoke of these foreigners ; and Turgesius, who had possession of the government, thought no method more expedient to
secure his new power than to new model the state, to overturn
the old constitution, and to place his countrymen in the posts
of trust and authority.   Accordingly he appointed a Danish king
in every cantred of land throughout the island, and a captain
was settled in every territory.   He nominated an abbot in every
church and monastery, and a sergeant of the Danes was fixed
as the commanding officer in every village ; and to complete the
miseries of the natives, a soldier was billeted by authority upon
every house and cottage through the whole kingdom.   The insolence and rapines of these common soldiers were insupportable, for the master of a family had no power in his own house;
he could not command the use of a hen or a chicken of his
own, for fear of giving offence to this rascally foreigner, whose
vengeance he dreaded, and whose resentment perhaps would dispossess him of all he had.   If a poor man had but one cow to
afford milk for the support of his family, the soldier quartered
upon him would consume the whole, not regarding the cries
and wants of the young children, who were ready to die of hunger ; and if a person in the house chanced to be sick, and the
weakness of his stomach would admit of no other food but milk,
this barbarous Dane would not allow him a drop to save him
from death, but suffer him to perish.   And when the soldier
had a mind for a piece of beef, he would oblige the man of the
house to kill this cow, whose milk was the greatest part of his
sustenance, and when that beast was the whole stock he was
possessed of.   These barbarities and oppressions distracted the
unhappy Irish, who were obliged to conform to the sordid and
cruel temper of these soldiers, and supply them with what provision they required, how expensive soever ; otherwise they
would be dragged by violence to the general rendezvous of the
army, and committed to the guard-room, and kept under close
confinement till the prisoner had made satisfaction to his insolent guest, who often would be so unconscionable as not to be
content with less than the ruin of his family and fortune.
   The arbitrary Danes imposed likewise a heavy tribute on the
vanquished Irish ; for every master of a family throughout the

whole island was obliged, under the severest penalties, to pay, as a yearly tribute, an ounce of gold ; and if through misfortune or poverty he was incapable to furnish out his contribution, he was punished with the loss of his nose. No lord or lady was permitted to wear any clothes but what had been left off by the Danes ; for if their habit was of any value, it was torn off their backs, and ragged cast-off garments were given them in the place. These savage invaders were professed enemies to learning and learned men, and therefore the sovereignty of the kingdom being in their own hands, they determined to extirpate all schools and seminaries of education ; the Irish were not suffered to have their children taught to read ; the churches and holy places for divine service were likewise shut up or destroyed to the ground ; all the books they could find they burned or tore to pieces ; the poets, historians, musicians, and the professors of other liberal arts and sciences were banished, or imprisoned, or forced to abscond in woods and solitudes to preserve their lives. No young lady, of whatsoever quality, though she were the daughter of a lord or of a king, was allowed to work with her needle, or embroider in gold, silver, or silk ; and the sons of noblemen were forbidden to learn the use of arms, or exercise themselves in feats of activity or martial sports, lest they should one time or other reflect upon the bravery of their ancestors, and grow uneasy under the yoke of slavery. The Irish were discouraged, under the penalty of fines and imprisonment, to make feasts or public entertainments, or to use hospitality among one another, but were forced to be content with the scraps and offals that were left at the tables of the riotous and luxurious Danes, who prodigally consumed at once the support of many families, and spent the revenue of whole countries to indulge their palates, and to please themselves in the most scandalous and unnatural debaucheries.

Such was the miserable state of the island, under the oppression and cruel yoke of these domineering foreigners ; the natives were broken-hearted, and despaired of recovering their liberties; the clergy were forced to fly into woods and the most desolate places, for the security of their lives; for the Danes were a wicked and abandoned race of men, and so covetous of wealth and plunder, that churches and monasteries were rifled, their consecrated plate carried off, and the religious turned out of doors. But the cries and prayers of the pious clergy, who hid themselves in caves and deserts, and incessantly addressed themselves to heaven for the deliverance of their country, prevailed

at last with the divine mercy to find a way for their redemption
as unexpected as it was acceptable to the natives, who were in
despair, and gave themselves up for lost ; for it must be observed that the clergy, notwithstanding the inconveniences they
suffered, strictly performed the divine offices of the church in
the best manner they were able ; they fasted and prayed, and
obliged the laity to be regular in their devotions, and to entreat,
without intermission, that God would destroy the power of those
profane invaders, professed enemies to mankind and to his church,
and restore the kingdom to its ancient liberty.   And heaven
rewarded their piety with success, so far as to deliver the tyrant
Turgesius himself into the hands of the Irish.

For when this bloody usurper was in the height of his unjust
authority, among other methods to confirm himself in his new
power, and to prevent the natives from giving disturbance to
his reign, he erected a castle as a royal palace, where he designed
to reside, near the seat of Maolseachluin, who governed the
country of Meath.   This haughty Dane would sometimes condescend to make a visit to this neighbouring prince, who had a
daughter of excellent beauty, that had the finest shape and complexion, and was one of the most celebrated ladies in the island.
Turgesius, who by this time began to be aged, was at an entertainment in the palace of Meath, where this princess sat at the
table, and by her charms so captivated this royal lecher, that
the blood grew warm in its old channels, and he conceived so
strong a passion, that he desired Maolseachluin to resign his
daughter to his arms, and promised she should be the favourite
mistress in his seraglio.   The king of Meath, not daring to incense the tyrant by a denial, who he knew would gratify his
lust by violence, with great submission requested, that since his
majesty was pleased to make choice of his daughter for a mistress, he would not make it known in a public manner, out of
respect to the character of the young lady, whose reputation
would suffer, and her honour be so blemished, that it would be
difficult afterwards to dispose of her in marriage, and provide a
husband for her suitable to her quality ; and therefore he desired, that since his royal palace was at no great distance, he
might be permitted to send the princess to him privately, to
conceal it from the knowledge of the world.   And, continued
he, I will convey to your majesty fifteen of the most celebrated
beauties that my small territories produce, who, I am confident,
will so far eclipse the charms you are pleased to commend in
my daughter, that she will scarce receive the honour of being

admitted to your embraces, when you are convinced she is excelled by so many of a superior beauty. Turgesius was transported with the expectation of receiving the young lady, and a night was appointed to crown his hopes and give him posses sion ; she was to be conducted with all possible privacy into one of his royal apartments, and the young ladies were to be disposed of as the lusts and humour of the tyrant directed.

It happened that at this time there was a convention of the principal Danes throughout the kingdom summoned by Turgesius, to assemble at Dublin, in order to settle his infant government upon lasting foundations ; to defeat the prospects of the natives, who were inclined to a revolt ; to defend the country from other invaders, and to perpetuate the succession to his posterity. These matters, and whatever seemed to contribute to the establishment of the usurpation, being adjusted, the king appointed an entertainment for some of his prime ministers and favourites ; and being well warmed with wine, he communicated to fifteen of them his intrigue with the young princess, the daughter of the king of Meath, and promised to bestow upon each of them a young lady of consummate beauty, if they were disposed for an act of gallantry, and thought proper to follow him to court. These lascivious Danes, conforming to the practice of the tyrant, expressed their gratitude for his royal bounty, and fired with the prospect before them, desired the honour of waiting upon him ; and accordingly Turgesius, attended with fifteen of his debauched nobles and officers, set out from Dublin, where the assembly sat, and arrived at the palace where he usually kept his residence.

But Maolseachluin, the king of Meath, designed nothing less than to contribute to the prostitution of his daughter, and resolving to vindicate the honour of the young lady, he entered upon a desperate attempt to dethrone and destroy the tyrant, and sacrifice him to the fury of his own lust. Accordingly he selected fifteen of the stoutest and most beautiful youths in his dominions, who were of a fair fresh complexion, and had no beards upon their faces ; he ordered them to be apparelled in the habit of young ladies, and to conceal under their gowns a short sharp sword, which they were to make use of according to his directions. Thus fitted out, the princess, attended with her retinue, upon the night appointed left her father's court ; and when she arrived near the castle, where Turgesius had his royal seat, she sent privately to acquaint him of her approach, which he received with inexpressible joy : he gave notice to his officers

that the ladies were coming, and having ordered them to retire
to their chambers, he sent one of his favourites to meet the
princess, and conduct her to his court. The Danish nobles severally repaired to their apartments, that were made proper for
their reception, and impatiently expected their Irish mistresses;
while the king, with the same fury of passion, was waiting in
his bedchamber, transported with the prospect of satisfying his
brutish desires upon a princess of the greatest beauty and quality throughout the island.

But providence determined to put a final end to the tyranny
of this usurper; for Maolseachluin, king of Meath, the better
to accomplish his design, so glorious in the event as to subvert
the oppressive yoke of these foreigners, under cover of the night
marched with a resolute body of hardy Irish, and advancing
towards the castle of Turgesius, he drew up his men silently
under the walls, in order, when he received the signal from those
within, to break into the fort, and to put the tyrant and all his
retinue to the sword.

The princess with her followers were by this time admitted
into the palace, and the gentlemen who attended her had
orders from the king to preserve the honour of his daughter
at all hazards, and to fall upon the tyrant, unguarded as he
was, before he had perpetrated his design; and inspiring them
with a love of liberty, and of redeeming their country from a
cruel slavery, he had raised their indignation to that height,
that they engaged to a man to expose their lives in this great
adventure, and they did not doubt of success. Their commission was to seize upon the usurper and take him alive, but to
bind him with strong cords that he could not possibly escape:
then they were to secure his nobles and officers, who expected
other sort of embraces, and not to leave a man of them alive:
and there seemed no difficulty to bring to pass this surprising
event; for the tyrant thought he had established his power, and
broken the spirit of the natives, and therefore there was no occasion to keep a strict guard about his person; and his officers
were so infatuated by their lusts, that they left their arms behind
them, lest they should frighten the ladies, and discompose them
for softer encounters. There was a proper signal agreed upon, to
give notice to the king under the walls, when he should rush
into the fort, and assist with his troops to fall upon the Danes,
who perhaps might be so numerous as not easily to be dispatched.

The circumstances of this secret adventure being thus adjusted, the princess with all her retinue were introduced into the king's apartment, who received her with open arms, and though of a very advanced age, proposed wonderful delights to himself in the possession of her. He examined into the beauty of her attendants, who, though very handsome and genteel youths, yet made but an awkward appearance in their unaccustomed dress, and therefore the princess was sure to find no rival among them, and was made choice of to sleep in the arms of this lascivious Dane, who embraced her tenderly, and was conducting her into his private chamber. The Irish youths thought now was the time to discover and exert themselves in defence of the honour of their mistress and of their enslaved country; and throwing aside their loose gowns, laid hold of the tyrant, and pointing one of their short swords to his throat, threatened him with instant death if he cried out, which so terrified him that he submitted, and they instantly bound him; then destroying all they met, they forced into the apartments of the nobles and officers, who were unarmed and prepared for other engagements, and put them all to the sword. The palace was filled with cries and slaughter, and to add to the terror, the signal was given to the king under the walls, who broke into the castle with dreadful shouts, and finished what was left undone; the guards were killed, no quarter was given, the darkness of the night increased the fears of the Danes, officers and soldiers fell promiscuously in the carnage, and not a man of them escaped. When the fury of the Irish was abated, and there was no enemy left in the castle, the king of Meath entered the room where Turgesius lay bound, and upbraiding him with his excessive cruelties, the many rapes and violences he had committed upon the Irish ladies, and his repeated murders; he commanded him to be loaded with irons, and to be carried before him in triumph. The soldiers were allowed to plunder the castle, where they found an incredible booty, and the king with the princess and his brave hardy troops returned to Meath.

This transaction was soon spread over the whole kingdom; and the Irish, animated with the success of the king of Meath, unanimously revolted, and resolved to throw off the Danish yoke. The foreigners were quite dispirited and abandoned to their fears, when they heard that their king Turgesius was taken prisoner, and his principal nobility and commanding officers put to the sword; and considering that the natives were up in arms, and themselves without a leader, they thought it safest to fly to their ships, and with all possible expedition to quit the island.

Those invaders, who lived near the sea coasts, got on board without much difficulty; but those who had possessed themselves of the inland country, at a great distance from the sea, were obliged to retire into cities and fortified places for their security; but the desperate Irish resolved to rid themselves of these foreigners, which now they had an opportunity to do, and fell upon them in all places without distinction : they hunted them out of the woods and wildernesses, where they had taken shelter ; they stormed their towns and forts, and engaging them with irresistible fury, slew infinite numbers of the Danes before they could reach their ships : no solitude or flight could protect them from the enraged Irish, who fought for their lives, and laws and liberties, and determined to bring about a complete revolution, and establish the government upon its ancient foundation. Some of those wretched foreigners escaped to the sea under favour of the night ; and others who were surrounded by their enemies, and found it impossible to fly, most submissively petitioned for quarter, and promised to become servants to the Irish ; and to save their lives, to comply with whatever tax or imposition should be laid upon them. The king of Meath, when the first fury of the Irish had in some measure subsided, perceiving that those few Danes that remained, might be so disposed of as to be incapable of giving any disturbance to the state, received them into mercy, and having disarmed them spared their lives. The tyrant, after he had been for some time kept in fetters, and been a witness to the miseries of his countrymen, had an end put to his unfortunate life, being thrown, by the command of the king, bound as he was, into Loch Annin, where he perished.

This wonderful revolution being accomplished by the death of the usurper, and the expulsion of the Danes, the nobility and gentry of Ireland, willing to settle the constitution of the government, and reduce the affairs of state into some order, assembled in a general convention, and reflecting upon the means by which they received their freedom and redemption, unanimously came to a resolution to place the crown upon the head of their great deliverer Maolseachluin, king of Meath.

It must be observed here, that Buchanan, the Scottish historian, asserts that Gregory, king of Scotland, invaded the kingdom of Ireland with a numerous army, and having plundered the inhabitants, and miserably harassed the country with their hostilities, they had the success to kill Bryen and Connor, who were appointed guardians to the king of Ireland, who was a minor. But this writer is miserably mistaken in this fact, because, as the authentic chronicles of the island expressly testify, the crown never descended to an infant, who was a minor, from the reign of Slainge, who was the first Irish king of the line of the Firbolgs, till the time of Henry II., king of England; for the succession, though it often descended to the next heir, yet he was always of man's estate; and when the hereditary right, by the iniquity of the times and the violence of parties, was laid aside, the nobility and gentry commonly made choice of the most accomplished person in the island, and placed him in possession of the government. This historian therefore is not to be credited; for it is beyond dispute that Turgesius, the Danish tyrant, was the king of Ireland at that time.

A.D.
879.
Maolseachluin, by the suffrage of the nobility and gentry, was placed upon the throne of Ireland. He was the son of Maolruanadh, son of Donough, son of Daniel, son of Murchadha, son of Diarmuid, son of Airmeadh Caoch, son of Conall Guthbhin, son of Suïbhne Meain, son of Colman More, son of Diarmuid, son of Feargus Ceirbheoil, descended from the royal stock of Heremon, and held the government sixteen years. The mother of this monarch was Arog, the daughter of Cahall, son of Fiachrad, king of Bearcuil.

The Danes, being driven out of the kingdom by the prevailing power of the natives, under the conduct of this prince, began to form designs of regaining their settlements in the island; for they had experienced so much of the fertility and richness of the country, that their native possessions were incapable of supporting them in that riotous and expensive way of life which they had used themselves to, when they had the command of the labours and the wealth of the industrious and frugal Irish. In order to concert measures for another descent, the principal of the Norwegians and Danes assembled, and, after many debates, came to a resolution to send three of their most experienced generals, and a well appointed fleet, with a commission to land upon the coasts of Ireland in a peaceable manner, to avoid the committing of hostilities, and by that means gradually insinuate themselves into the affections of the inhabitants, till they found themselves of ability to contend with them, and then violence was to be used. And the better to disguise their designs, these three commanding officers were to pass under the notion of mercantile men, and their fleet was to be called a sail of merchantmen, which was to be furnished with jewels and gaudy wares, to be sold or to be presented to the Irish as occasion offered; but a number of arms and military preparations were to be secretly

2 E

stowed in the ships, to be used when matters were well concerted, and ripe for execution. The people of the island were thus to be corrupted and softened into effeminacy by this stratagem of these subtle foreigners, in order that they might be subdued with the less difficulty, and in some measure be the instruments of their own misfortunes and destruction.

The author of the Polichronicon gives this account of this expedition :* "After the death of Turgesius, three brothers, Amelanus, Cyracus, and Imorus, came from the parts of Norway in a peaceable manner, and under pretence of merchandising arrived with their followers in this island ; and getting possession of places that lay upon the coasts, by the consent of the Irish, who were an idle and inactive people, they built three cities, Waterford, Dublin, and Limerick, and their numbers daily increasing, they often insulted and disturbed the natives." From the testimony of this writer it appears, that the Norwegians, by this political device, and under the conduct of those officers, in the disguise of merchants, obtained settlements in the island, which they gradually improved by new acquisitions, till they became able to oppress the natives, and bring the whole kingdom into subjection. And it is not to be wondered that these foreigners carried on their conquests with success, and after their expulsion regained what they had lost, and often enslaved the people ; for it must be observed, that the invaders were constantly supplied with fresh recruits, their own country was an inexhaustible store of men and shipping, which encouraged them to bear up against all misfortunes or defeats that might happen, and to prosecute their designs at all hazards. But the greatest advantages were given them by the natives, occasioned by the contests and civil discords among themselves. Nothing promoted the common ruin more than their animosities within themselves ; and their unnatural and irreconcilable quarrels were attended with more dreadful effects, than could follow from all the force of the enemy ; to add to the calamity, the contending parties would receive these Danes into pay, as auxiliary troops, who when opportunity offered turned their arms against those that hired them ; and thus, while the petty

* Post obitum Turgesii, de Norvegiæ partibus quasi sub pacis intuitu et Mercaturæ exercendæ prætextu, tres fratres, Amelanus, Cyracus, et Imorus, cum sua sequela in hanc insulam appulerunt et de consensu Hibernorum, otio deditorum, maritima loca occupantes, tres civitates, viz., Waterfordiam, Dubliniam, et Lumericum construxerunt, qui tamen numero succrescentes contra indigenas frequenter insultabant.

princes were striving and tearing each other to pieces for trifles, the Danes, when they found them sufficiently weakened, subdued the victor and the vanquished, and forced them both to confess their superior power, and own them for their masters. Thus were the unfortunate Irish, by a concurrence of unhappy circumstances, again obliged to pass under the yoke, which galled them with inexpressible misery, and could never be shaken off till the death of that illustrious hero, the brave Bryen Boiroimhe, king of Ireland.

The annals of Ireland assert, that when the Norwegians had subdued the inhabitants, not only by their arms, but by the effects of their own intestine divisions, the Danes, in hopes of plunder and conquest, fitted out a considerable fleet, and made a descent upon the island. They met with some opposition, but it was fruitless and without success, for they destroyed the country and the people, and plundered the city of Dublin, and terribly ravaged all the adjacent territories; but the Norwegians fearing to be driven out of their possessions by the Danes, determined to make head against them before they grew too powerful, and advancing towards them with a select body of troops, offered them battle. They accepted the challenge, and a desperate fight commenced at a place called Linnduachaill, wherein the Danes obtained a complete victory, the Norwegians were defeated with the loss of their best forces, and 1000 of them left dead upon the spot. Encouraged by this success, the victors seized upon the greatest part of the island, and still improving their authority, and plundering the natives, they became the most formidable power, and acquired the most considerable settlements in the country.

Not long after this victory of the Danes, Amhlaoibh, otherwise called Amelanus by some authors, son to the king of Denmark, arrived in Ireland, with a design to take upon himself the command of the Danes that were dispersed throughout the island; and putting himself at the head of his countrymen, he fought the natives in several engagements with great advantage, imposed heavy contributions upon them, and reduced them to a state of servitude. About this time died Olchabhair, the son of Cionnaoth, who governed the province of Munster, and Flaithnia, the pious bishop of Biorra, and Cormac, the devout prelate of Lathraigh Broin, soon followed that prince into the other world.

The unfortunate state of the island, under the oppression of these foreigners, was the reason that about this time Maolseach-luin summoned, by his royal writs, a convention of the principal nobility and gentry of the kingdom, to meet at a place called Rath Aoda Mac Bric, who unanimously assembled according to the summons; for the natives consulting their common safety, had laid aside their private contests and quarrels; but it was with some difficulty they united, and were reconciled by the unwearied diligence and importunity of that holy person Eatgna, a convert of St. Patrick, who had entered himself into some religious order. In this convention, among other acts that promoted the public good, it was determined, that Maolguala, the son of Dungaile, king of Munster, and Carról, king of Ossery, should conclude a peace with the inhabitants of Leath Cuinn; and in the assembly it was agreed, that the king of Ossery aforesaid should make his submission to Eatgna above-named, who was a saint of excellent holiness and devotion.

Some time after this the Normans fell in a desperate fury upon Maolguala, who governed the province of Munster, and slew him with stones; and not long after this unfortunate accident, Maolseachluin, king of Ireland, engaged the Danes, and fought the remarkable battle of Drom da Moighe, wherein great numbers of the foreign troops were destroyed, especially such as were quartered in the city of Dublin. After this victory obtained by the Irish, Daniel, the son of Ailpin, king of the Picts, left the world; and the king of Ireland did not long enjoy the fruits of his success, but died of a natural death after a very troublesome and distracted reign.

Hugh Fionnliath was the succeeding monarch. He was the son of Niall Caille, son of Hugh Dorndighe, son of Niall Freasach, descended from the royal line of Heremon, and possessed the throne eighteen years. The mother of this Irish prince was Gormfhlaith, the daughter of Dinnis, the son of Daniel. He took to wife Maolmuire, the daughter of Cionaoith, son of Ailpin, king of Scotland, by whom he had a son called Niall Glandubh. During the reign of this king several actions of importance happened; among the rest, Connor, the son of Donnogh, who had the government of half the country of Meath, was unfortunately slain by the sword of Humphry, son to the king of Denmark, at a place called Cluain Joraird. This Danish prince, known in the Irish language by the name of Amhlaoibh, after this victory, transported a sufficient number of his countrymen into Scotland, and falling upon

A.D.
897.

the Picts, he slew multitudes of them, and made many of them prisoners, whom he carried away with him and made them slaves.

Near this time it was that Hugh Fionnliath, monarch of Ireland, fell upon the Danes at a place called Loch Feabhail, and gave them a general defeat. In this action the foreign troops suffered exceedingly, and most of the officers were cut off; for the victor brought away with him the heads of forty of the principal commanders, and the fight concluded with the loss of 1200 of the Danes, who perished in this engagement. The Irish army, encouraged with this success, attacked the fortifications and garrisons of the enemy, and beat them out of their fastnesses, and recovered all the booty and plunder they had taken. Conall, the religious bishop of Cill Sgire, died soon after this victory; about which time the palace of Humphry, son to the king of Denmark, which he had built at Cluain Dalchain, was clandestinely set on fire by Gaoithin, and Mac Ciaran, the son of Roannan, and consumed to the ground. This accident occasioned great confusion of those within, and the Irish taking advantage of the fears of the Danes, fell upon them, and slew 100 of their principal commanders. Humphry, to revenge himself upon the Irish, laid an ambuscade, and surprised 2000 of them, who were either killed, wounded, or taken prisoners; and this victory inspired him with fresh courage, for he plundered Ardmach and the adjacent country; and when he had raged with all the fury of an incensed enemy, he carried off very valuable spoils, with which he paid and rewarded his army.

The death of Cionfhaola, the son of Mochtighern, who had filled the throne of Munster for thirteen years, happened about this time; and he was succeeded in the government of that province by Donnogh Mac Dubhdabhoirionn, who seized upon the crown and proclaimed himself king.

The Danes by this time were become a terror not only to the Irish, but the success of their arms gave them power to improve their conquests among the Picts in Scotland and the Welsh; the first of these they overcame in a battle, and slew great numbers of them, and Roger, the son of Moirmin, king of Wales, being terrified with the fame of their victories, left his own country, and fled into Ireland for refuge and protection, where he met with an honourable reception suitable to his quality. These foreigners, it has been observed, broke open churches and shrines, and plundered the dead as well as the living, which was the reason that the relics of St. Collum Cill were removed to Ire-

land, to preserve them from injury and the sacrilegious hands
of these impious barbarians. Lorcan Mac Lachtna about this
time was fixed in the possession of the crown of Thumond. The
tribe of the Dalgais inhabited this country, and their territories
extended to the gates and walls of Cashel : they had twelve
cantreds in their divisions, which reached from Leim Congculion
to Bealach Mor, in the county of Ossery, and from Mount Eachtighe to Mount Eibhlinne. This was a brave and martial clan,
and it was observed particularly of them, that they always chose
to be in the front of the Momonian forces when they entered
an enemy's country, where they distinguished themselves with
signal courage ; and when they were marching homewards, and
leaving the country of the enemy, their place was in the rear ;
so that they were exposed to the greatest dangers, and were a
shield to the rest of the army, whom they always led on to action, and covered in their retreat. The old poet, Cormac Mac
Cuillenan, gives an express account of the bravery of this tribe
in the following lines :

> The martial clan of the Dalgais appear
> In front, and make the foremost ranks, exposed
> To the first fury of the enemy ;
> And when the military instruments
> Sound a retreat, they last forsake the field
> And cover all the rear ; these martial chiefs,
> Strangers to fear and flight, with victory
> Were ever crown'd, their all-subduing arms
> With never-failing force their javelins threw,
> And scattered certain death.

Hugh Fionnliath, monarch of Ireland, died without violence
at Druim Jonasglan, in Crioch Conuill ; and the pious Tighernach, the son of Muireadhaidh, bishop of the same Druim Jonasglan, was about the same time translated to a better life.

Flan Sionna was the succeeding king. He was the
A.D. son of Maolseachluin, son of Maolruadhna, descended
913. from the royal line of Heremon, and governed the kingdom 38 years. The mother of this prince was Lan, the daughter of Dungoil, son of Feargoil, king of Ossery. This Irish
king met with many disturbances in his reign ; for he was no
sooner fixed in the throne but he found it necessary to raise an
army and invade the province of Munster. This attempt was
successfully prosecuted, for the provincial troops were unable to
oppose him, so that the whole country lay exposed to the fury
of the royal army, who miserably distressed the inhabitants,

and carried them away after they were cruelly plundered, into a wretched captivity. In the reign of this prince, Daniel, the son of Muireagein, was treacherously slain by his own followers; and Fiachna, the son of Ainbroith, son of Hugh Roin, who had governed the province of Ulster the space of one year, left the world; and about the same time died Donnogh Mac Dubhaob-virunn, king of Munster.

The Danes still carried on their hostilities, and behaved more like robbers than enemies, for they plundered Cluain Joraird, and Kildare suffered the same devastations. The celebrated fair of Tailton was proclaimed about this time by the king of Ireland; which was no sooner ended but Maolguala, who had governed the province of Munster seven years, departed the present life. The Normans were now in possession of some part of the island; and these foreigners fell upon Sitrick Mac Jobhair, and slew him. Aidhet, king of Ulster, was inhumanly murdered by his own subjects, which occasioned such disturbances in the province, that the Danes took advantage of their civil discords, and such of them as lived at Loch Feabhail entered Ardmach, and plundered the country. In this expedition they surprised Cumasgach, king of Ulster, and his son Hugh, and made them prisoners. About this time died Daniel, a prince of great hopes, the son of Constantine, king of Scotland.

Cormac Mac Cuillenan had now fixed himself in the government of Munster, and reigned with great conduct and moderation for seven years. During the reign of this prince the kingdom of Ireland enjoyed settled peace and tranquillity; the island began to recover breath, after the calamities of intestine wars and foreign invasions; the lands were manured and cultivated, and afforded plentiful crops; and so remarkable was the happiness of the island at this time, that not a shepherd or herdsman was wanting through the whole country. The churches, and abbeys, and religious houses, began to be repaired and new built; for these structures were reduced to ruins by the sacrilegious Danes, who ravaged without distinction of places, so that nothing however solemn or sacred could escape their fury. Learning now revived, and many free schools and academies were erected, for the education of youth in arts and in the liberal sciences. Their former miseries were forgotten by the inhabitants, a new scene appeared, and opened a delightful prospect of peace, happiness, and prosperity.

Such was the flourishing state of the kingdom when Cormac

Mac Cuillenan wore the crown of Munster, that the contests and animosities between the petty princes were happily concluded; insomuch, that the Danes, fearing the effects of this reconciliation, desisted from their usual hostilities; and, though the desire of plunder remained, and nothing of their savage disposition abated, yet they apprehended their lives were in continual danger from the natives, who by their common union and friendship were able to drive them out of the kingdom; and therefore a great number of these foreigners retired to their ships of their own accord, and bid adieu to the island.

Cormac proposed, in one year of his reign, to celebrate the festival of Easter with great state and magnificence at Cashel; and a short time before the holydays he sent a messenger to the country called Eoganacht, that lay near Cashel, to demand of the inhabitants a quantity of provision, that would be sufficient for himself and his attendants during his stay at that place. But the messenger was dismissed with a refusal; and an account of this rude denial being brought to the generous tribe of the Dailgais, they prepared with all possible speed what provisions were necessary for the king of Munster, and supplied his wants. This relief was very seasonable, and was received by Cormac with the most grateful acknowledgments. The king resolved once more to try the spirit of the people of Eoganacht, and for that purpose sent to them, to desire that they would assist him with some of their best arms and horses, to bestow upon those strangers who should come to his court, according to their deserts and merits: and the messenger was to notify that his master did not doubt of their compliance, since they were sensible of the obligations they lay under, and had not yet paid him the usual compliments, or convinced him of their good affections by one single testimony of their respect. The inhabitants of Eoganacht did not absolutely refuse to answer his demand, but their manner of complying was a notorious affront to the king, for they mustered together all their old battered arms, and picked out the most useless and disabled horses they could find, and sent them to Cashel to the court of Cormac. The clan of the Dailgais was soon acquainted with this insolent behaviour, and chose a number of strong able horses, with suitable equipage and furniture, and presented them to the king; the best of their arms likewise, and a collection of valuable jewels, were generously offered to his acceptance. Cormac received their favours with sincere expressions of gratitude, and upon the occasion composed the following lines; for he was a prince of great learning, but his genius chiefly inclined to poetry.

> May heaven protect the most illustrious tribe
> Of Dailgais, and convey its choicest blessings
> On their posterity. This renowned clan,
> Though meek and merciful as are the saints,
> Yet are of courage not to be subdued.
> Long may they live in glory and renown,
> And raise a stock of heroes for the world.

The authentic records of Ireland expressly assert, that from the reign of Aongus, the son of Nadfraoch, king of Munster, to the time of Matthew, the son of Kennedy, who likewise governed that province, there had reigned forty-four princes lineally descended from Eogan More, the son of Oilioll Ollum; and during this space of time it is observed, that the tribe of Dailgais had the possession of no more lands than the kingdom of Thumond; but after the decease of Cormac Mac Cuillenan, the succession to the crown of Munster devolved upon Lorcan, who was of the line of Dailgais, and governed that province till his death. The country of Thumond had a king of its own, and consisted of all the lands from Slighe Dala, known otherwise by the name of Bealach Mor, in Ossery, to Leim Congculion, in the west of Corca Baisain. This tribe of the Dailgais always took up arms in defence of the kings of Cashel, against the provincial troops of Leinster, and the army of Leath Cuinn. This account we find recorded in a poem composed by O'Dugan, who has related the particulars in the verses following:

> The Dailgaisian troops with glory fir'd,
> Fought for the honour of the kings of Cashel,
> And carried into other provinces
> The terror of their arms.

Cormac Mac Cuillenan governed the province of Munster for the space of seven years, and acquired the character of a learned and just prince. Fortune favoured him in all his attempts, his enemies dreaded his power, and his subjects almost adored him for his virtues; and his reign might have continued for many years longer, attended with the same glory and prosperity, had he not been misled and overruled by the advice of his counsellors, who put him upon destructive measures, which robbed him of his life and crown. The principal nobility and gentry of his province urged him forward to invade the territories of Leinster, and demand a tribute or chief-rent from the inhabitants; and if they refused to pay their acknowledgments of subjection, they persuaded him to use violence, and immediately enter into hostilities. This enterprise was not agreeable to the king, but upon the advice of his council, and particularly of Flathbhertach Mac Jonmuinein, abbot of Inis Catha, and of the blood royal, who insisted that the king had a just demand upon that province, as it was a part of Leath Modha, he raised a numerous army, consisting of the flower of his provincial troops, and prepared for the undertaking. His forces assembled at a place appointed, and the gentry of Munster were resolved to prosecute the right of their king with their lives and fortunes; for they supposed he had a just title to this tribute, upon account of the division that was formerly made between Modha Nuagatt and Conn. But the king of Munster opposed this expedition, and would have disbanded his troops; for he was endowed with a prophetic spirit, and foreknew that the attempt would be attended with an unfortunate issue, and he should lose his life in the action. Under these apprehensions he delayed his march, till overcome by the importunity of his friends, he advanced towards the borders of Leinster; but before he had entered that province, he determined to make his will and testament, being sensible he should never return; and having prepared himself by devotion for that solemn act, he left considerable legacies to uses of charity, and particularly expressed his bounty to the principal abbeys and religious houses throughout the kingdom: he left an ounce of gold and an ounce of silver, a horse and arms, to Druimabhradh, now known by the name of Ard Fionane. A golden and a silver chalice, and a vestment of silk, he bestowed upon Lismore. A golden and a silver chalice, four ounces of gold and five of silver, he bequeathed to Cashel. He gave to Imleach Jubhair three ounces of gold and a mass book; this place at present is called Imly. To Glean da Loch he demised an ounce of gold and another of silver. A horse and arms, an ounce of gold, and a silk vestment, he bequeathed to Kildare. Twenty-four ounces of gold and silver he left to Ardmach; three ounces of gold he gave to Inis Catha; three ounces of gold and a silk vestment, with his royal benediction, he bestowed upon the successor of Mungairid, with several other noble and charitable benefactions.

This excellent prince being poetically inclined, composed his last will and testament in verse, which may not improperly be thus translated:

Summon'd away by death, which I perceive
Approaches, (for by my prophetic skill
I find that short will be my life and reign,)
I solemnly appoint, that my affairs
Shall thus be settled after I am dead;
And this I constitute my latest will.
   My golden vestment, for most sacred use
Ordain'd, and for the service of my God,
I give to the religious St. Shanon
Of Inis Catha, a most holy man.
My clock, which gave me notice of the time,
And warn'd me when to offer my devotion,
I leave, nor is my will to be revok'd,
To Conuil of Feargus, a true friend,
And follower of my fortune, good or bad.
My royal robe, embroider'd o'er with gold,
And sparkling with the rays of costly jewels,
Well suited to a state of majesty,
I do bequeath to Roscre to be kept
By Cronane with the strictest care. My armour,
And coat of mail of bright and polished steel,
Will well become the martial king of Ulster,
To whom I give it; and my golden chain
Shall the most pious Machuda enjoy,
As a reward for all his worthy labours.
My royal wardrobe I resolve to give
To Mac Gleinin at Cluain by Colman.
My Psalter, which preserves the ancient records
And monuments of this my native country,
Which are transcrib'd with great fidelity,
I leave to Ronal Cashel, to be preserv'd
To after times, and ages yet to come.
My soul for mercy I commit to heaven,
My body leave to dust and rottenness.
May God his choicest store of blessings send
Upon the poor, and propagate the faith
Of Christ throughout the world.

This Cormac, king of Munster, gives in his writings an exact account of the convention of Mungairide; as appears expressly in that part of his poetical composition which begins with these words, A ghille, ceangaill ar loin, where he expressly mentions the number of monks that were members of the six churches that stood in that place. There were five hundred, who were men of approved learning, and were appointed to attend the office of preaching, six hundred presbyters served in the choir, and four hundred ancient men of exemplary piety spent their whole time in prayers and contemplation.

But to return to the design of Cormac upon the province of Leinster. When he had concerted measures, and made the necessary preparations for this expedition, he thought it not suffi-

cient to make his will, and settle his private affairs, but that it
was his duty to provide for his people, and regulate the point of
succession before his decease ; for this purpose he dispatched a
messenger to Lorcan, the son of Lachtna, king of Thumond, to
desire the favour of a visit from him in his camp before he passed the frontiers and entered upon action.   This neighbouring
prince came upon the message, and was received by Cormac with
great tenderness and affection.   Soon after his arrival the king
of Munster called a council of the principal nobility and gentry,
and commanding officers, and leading his royal guest by the hand
into the assembly, he told them, that he apprehended the expedition he had undertaken would be fatal to himself; and therefore to prevent all tumults, and defeat the pretensions of contending factions, he thought himself obliged to settle the succession before his decease ; and for that purpose he declared,
before the nobility of Siol Eogain, who were chiefly concerned,
that he demised the crown of Munster to Lorcan, king of Thumond, whose indisputable right it was, and persuaded them to
ratify his nomination, and accept him for their king.   He did
not think proper to bind them to this convention by oath not
to withdraw their allegiance from the king of Thumond ; which
was the reason, it is supposed, that after the death of Cormac
his designation was rejected by the nobility and gentry, who by
election placed another prince upon the throne of Munster ;
though it is evident, that Lorcan, king of Thumond, was the
apparent successor in the government of that province, in con-
formity to the last will and testament of Oilioll Ollum, who
ordained that the crown of Munster should descend alternately
to the posterity of Fiachadh Muilleathan and the royal family
of Cormac Cas.

The provincial troops of Munster being assembled, Cormac,
attended by Flathbhertach Mac Jonmuinein, abbot of Inis Catha, who was the principal promoter of this war, advanced at
the head of the army towards the borders of Leinster ; but,
before he passed the boundaries, he sent a herald to the king of
Leinster, to demand a yearly tribute as a testimony of subjection, which he insisted upon as his right, as that province was a
part of Leath Modha.   If the king of Leinster was not prepared to answer his chief-rent in ready money, the messenger
was to require hostages for the security of the payment, and
upon refusal to denounce war.   The king of Munster halted in
the expectation of the return of the herald, and in that interval an unfortunate accident happened, that was of fatal conse-

quence to the army of Munster ; for Flathbhertach Mac Jonmuinein, abbot of Inis Catha, who, though in orders, was a person of courage and warlike disposition, mounted his horse, with
a design to ride through the ranks and take a view of the camp ;
but the horse being frighted, fell into a deep ditch with the rider upon the back of him, which was understood by the soldiers
to be an unfortunate omen, and filled their minds with such impressions of fear, that many of them, despairing of success, resolved not to wait for the event, but withdrew from the camp
and returned home.

The herald returned to the king of Munster, and brought
with him ambassadors, who were commissioned by Carrol, the
son of Muireagain, and the nobility of Leinster, to propose a
treaty and cessation of arms till it took effect. They were to
insist, that hostilites should cease on both sides, and that the
country should be freed from the apprehensions of war till the
month of May following. To induce the king of Munster to
attend to these conditions, and accept them, they brought with
them a large sum of money, and a quantity of choice jewels,
and other presents of value, to offer him and soften him into
compliance. This treaty began in the first fortnight of harvest ;
and to convince the king of Munster, that the king of Leinster
was sincerely inclined to peace, he ordered his ambassadors to
promise, that hostages should be placed in the hands of the abbot of Diseart Diarmuida, until matters were brought to a con-
clusion. Nor did the king of Leinster forget to send a noble
present to Flathbhertach, being sensible what interest he
had with the king of Munster, who would enter into any measures upon his recommendation. But this abbot, who ought to
have been the minister of peace, was the great incendiary, and
was not to be mollified into other sentiments. For when the
ambassadors of Leinster were admitted to audience, and had
made proposals, notwithstanding the king of Munster, who
dreaded the consequences of the war, was disposed to accept of
the conditions, and to prevent bloodshed, and with great condescension desired the concurrence of Flathbhertach in his opinion,
yet the passionate and implacable abbot could not be brought
into any pacific measures, but resolved to push on the war at
all hazards ; and proceeded so far in his resentment against the
ambassadors, that he insolently upbraided the king of Munster
with cowardice, and told him to his face, that the paleness of
his complexion evidently betrayed his want of courage ; and
used many other aggravating expressions, reflecting upon the

conduct and personal bravery of the king.   But Cormac thought
fit to overlook the affront, and replied mildly, with great sedate-
ness, that his aversion to the war was not the effect of fear, but
proceeded from the sense he had of the consequences that would
inevitably attend the expedition, which he was convinced would
be fatal to his own life ; for, says he, I am assured that I shall
not survive the first battle, and perhaps your rashness and precipitancy will likewise prove your destruction.

After this conversation with the abbot, the king retired to his
tent, with very disconsolate and melancholy impressions upon
his mind, and admitting none but his chief favourites into his
presence, they persuaded him not to oppress himself with grief,
but to support his spirits, and refresh himself with what the
circumstances of the place would afford.   Accordingly a basket
of apples was brought before him, which he distributed among
those that were present, but with this afflicting prediction, that
his death was at no great distance, and that he should not have
an opportunity of dividing his favours of this kind among them
more.   The company, surprised and dejected at this expression
of the king, were overcome with sorrow, and dreaded the event
of the war ; for they were sensible that Cormac had an insight
into futurity, particularly when himself was immediately concerned ; and that no unfortunate accident happened to him,
through his whole life, but what he particularly foretold before
it fell out, though it was not in his power to prevent it.

Cormac ordered every one out of his presence, and resolved
to spend what time he had to spare from public affairs in piety
and exercises of devotion ; and the better to prepare himself
for his dissolution, which he foresaw was approaching, he sent
for his confessor, whose name was Comhgoll, a person of great
judgment and exemplary holiness, with a design to confess his
sins and receive the absolution of the church.   He likewise
made some altérations in his will, and particularly added a
codicil, that related to his funeral and the place of his interment.   But though he was certain that he should be slain in
the engagement with the king of Leinster, yet he had that regard for the happiness of his people, that he commanded those
to whom he had communicated the secret, not to divulge it
among the army, lest the soldiers should be intimidated ; for he
designed to sell his life at a dear rate, and if possible to secure
a victory to his subjects.   His body, if it could be recovered
from the enemy, he ordered to be buried at Cluain Umha ; or if
that could not be obtained, he would be interred at Diseart

Diarmuda, for which place he had a great respect, because he resided there for some years in his youth, and received his education : but Cluain Umha he designed for the repository of his bones, if his people could convey him thither, because Mac Leimhnin was buried there. Yet this part of the king's will was disagreeable to a holy and religious person, whose name was Maonach, who had a particular veneration for Diseart Diarmuda, and endeavoured to honour it with the interment of the king's body ; because there was a convent of monks under the government of Comhgoll, and Maonach likewise exercised some share of authority in the monastery, being the confessor of Comhgoll at this time.

This Maonach was a person of distinguished piety, and of a merciful and compassionate disposition, that inclined him to peace, and preventing the shedding of Christian blood ; and therefore he used all possible endeavours to heal the breach, and prevail with the king of Munster to desist from the prosecution of the war, and accept of the conditions offered by the nobility of Leinster ; and as an argument to dissuade the king from his expedition, he assured him that Flann, the son of Maolseachluin, king of Ireland, was followed by a number of brave troops, and was now at the royal palace of Leinster, with a design to defend and vindicate the cause of that province ; and therefore it would be prudence and policy to admit of the honourable terms proposed, to receive the hostages as preliminaries of a treaty, and not to enter upon hostilities on either side, rather than to persist and refer the matter to the decision of the sword and the uncertain issue of a battle. This representation was well received by the king and many of his Momonian forces ; and had that effect upon some of the soldiery, who dreaded the united power of the king of Ireland and the people of Leinster, that they left the camp out of fear and discontent, and returned home. Those who remained declared in favour of peace, and thought the terms that were offered ought not to be denied, especially considering the quality of the hostages, who were persons of no less rank than two young princes, the son of the king of Leinster, and a son of the king of Ossery : and to show with what unwillingness the army followed the king in this undertaking, they murmured in a mutinous manner against Flathbhertach Mac Jonmuinein ; and charged him with being the fomenter of the difference between the two provinces, and exclaimed against him as the author of all the miseries that might be the consequence of the war.

But the abbot of Inis Catha had that commanding influence over the king's counsels, that he determined to prosecute the war with vigour, and accordingly gave orders to the army to march. He directed his course eastwards to mount Mairge, and came to the bridge of Leithglin, called otherwise by the name of Loghlin. The baggage and the spare horses of the army were sent before, and Tiobruide, the religious successor of Aoilbhe, with a number of clergy, halted at this bridge till the king with his Momonians arrived and joined them. From hence the army advanced, with trumpets sounding and colours flying, and came to a place called Magh Ailbhe, where he marked out a camp and fortified himself by the side of a wood, expecting the enemy. Here he drew up his men in order of battle, and divided them into three parts under three several commanders. The abbot Flathbhertach Mac Jonmuinein, and the king of Ossery, commanded the first battalion; Cormac Mac Cuillenan commanded the second; and the third was under the conduct of an experienced general Cormac Mac Mothly, king of the Deisies. The battle was agreed to be fought in the plains of Magh Ailbhe, where the army of Munster stood prepared to receive the enemy; but their courage began to fail them before the engagement, for they were terrified with the account they heard of the numbers they were to fight with, which, as some authors assert, were at least five to one, and consisted of the choicest and best disciplined troops in the kingdom.

The Lagonians, or the army of Leinster, advanced with assurance of victory, and began the fight; they relied upon their numbers, and their personal bravery, and fell on with such irresistible fury, that the forces of Munster could not stand the first charge, or resist the impression of the enemy, but fled out of the field, which was covered with dead bodies; for the defeat was attended with dreadful slaughter, and great numbers were killed in the pursuit.

This general rout was in a great measure owing to two unfortunate accidents in the beginning of the battle. The one was, a treacherous and cowardly action of Ceilliochair, the brother of Ceangeagan, a former king of Munster, who rode through the Momonian ranks, and being averse from the beginning to the prosecution of this war, addressed himself aloud to the soldiers, persuading them to save themselves by flight, for they were certain to be all cut to pieces; and fixing the odium of this undertaking upon the rashness of the abbot of Inis Catha, he advised them to secure their own lives, and leave those who occasioned

The war to stand the issue of it, and fight it out by themselves. After this harangue he clapt spurs to his horse, and galloped out of the field; and the soldiers were so dispirited with what he had offered, that they threw down their arms, and at the first charge quitted their posts and shifted for themselves. The other misfortune that occasioned the defeat was, the cowardice of Ceallach Mac Carrol, who had a principal command in the army of Munster; this officer, amazed and shocked at the dreadful slaughter of his men, rode out of the field with full speed, ordering his men to provide for themselves, and follow his example before it was too late, and the enemy prevented their retreat. They complied with this advice, and instantly fled, which so discouraged the rest of the army, that the defeat became universal, and more were slain in the pursuit than fell in the engagement, which was but of a short continuance, for the Momonian troops were not able to stand against the first impression of the enemy, so that the bloodshed was dreadful, and the officers and the clergy were cut off in great numbers, without quarter or distinction; and if any person of rank escaped after the first fury of the soldiers was abated, he was saved, not from a principle of humanity and compassion, but for the sake of a large sum of money expected for his ransom.

Cormac Mac Cuillenan, though convinced of the certainty of his death, behaved with signal bravery at the head of his troops, and exposed himself, not out of despair, but from a principle of true courage, in the front of the battle; but in the disorder of the fight his horse fell into a pit, and threw him. He was much bruised with the fall, and being unable to rise, it was his fortune to be seen by some of his own troops, that were precipitately flying out of the field, who remounted him upon a fresh horse with some difficulty, and left him to provide for his life. The king by chance espied one of his favourites, whom he much esteemed for his learning and other accomplishments, making towards him; and understanding by him that his army was broken in pieces, and the slaughter of his troops almost incredible, he commanded this loyal person whose name was Hugh, and who promised never to abandon him, but to share with him in all his misfortunes, to take care of his own safety, and not to venture himself in his company, which would be his inevitable destruction; for his enemies, he was sensible, would give no quarter, and he had but a few moments to live. It was with great regret that his orders were obeyed by this gentleman, who no sooner left the king, but his horse, attempting to climb

2 F

a steep ascent, that was exceeding slippery with the blood of the slain, made a false step, and tumbled with the rider down the hill; and by that accident broke the king's neck and his backbone, so that he died upon the spot. Thus was his prediction accomplished, and he did not survive the action of the day His body being found among the dead, by some soldiers of the enemy, they had no regard to the dignity of his person, but inhumanly mangled and thrust it through with their lances, and then cut off the head, which they carried away with them in triumph. This unfortunate prince, if providence had thought fit, seemed to have deserved a better fate; for he was a person of exemplary life, and consummate piety, as may be concluded by his behaviour in the last moment of his life, which ended with this devout ejaculation: " Into thy hands, O God, I commit my spirit."

Hanmer the historian in his chronicle attempts to impose upon the world with a falsehood, for he asserts that Cormac Mac Cuillenan, and Carrol, king of Leinster, were killed in an engagement with the Danes, in the year of our redemption 905 ; but this writer has notoriously mistaken the fact, for Cormac neither lost his life in that manner, nor were the Danes any way concerned in that action ; but the battle was fought, and the victory obtained by Flann Sionna, monarch of Ireland, who assisted the forces of Leinster, as appears expressly by the history known by the name of Beallach Mugna, which relates that Cormac Mac Cuillenan fought bravely among the thickest of the enemy, and lost his life by a fall from his horse ; and gives a particular account of the principal persons on both sides, that fell in the action of that day. Among the slain was Ceallach Mac Carrol, the valiant king of Ossery, and his son, a prince of promising hopes ; many of the nobility of Ireland lost their lives, and numbers of superior officers and eminent clergy perished. Fogartach Mac Suibhne, king of Kerry, Oilioll Mac Eogain, a gentleman of unblemished reputation, and Colman, the religious abbot of Cinneity, left their bodies among the dead. This holy person was lord chief justice of Ireland, and sat upon the bench, and administered the laws with great honour to himself and advantage to his country. It is impossible to relate the particular names of all who fell in this battle, but these following personages are transmitted to us ; Cormac, king of Deisies, Dubhagan, king of Fearmuigh, Cionnfaola, king of Jobh Connell, Aidhin, king of Aidhne, who was an exile in the province of Munster, Hugh, king of O'Liathan, Daniel, king of Dun Cearmna.

Conna Hadair of Aineislis in Uidirreadh Maolmuadh, Madcgan Dubhdabhuirrionn, Connal Fearadhach, and many others, who are not delivered to the notice of posterity. The most eminent commanders in the army of the king of Ireland, and of the provincial troops, to whose courage was owing the slaughter and the defeat of the Momonians, were Flann Sionna, monarch of Ireland, Carrol Mac Muireagain, king of Leinster, Teige Mac Faolain, king of Cinnseallach, Teimeinean, king of Deagadh, Ceallach and Lorcan, the two kings of Cinneal, Inneirge, the son of Dubhgiolla, king of O'Drona Fallomhar, the son of Oiliolla, king of Fothartafea, Tuathal, the son of Ughoire, king of O'Muireadhaig, Odhran Mac Kennedy, king of Leix, Maolcalann, son of Fearghoile, king of Fortuath, and Cleircin, king of O'Bairce, and many other princes and noble personages who distinguished themselves in the action of that day.

Flann Sionna, king of Ireland, when he had refreshed his troops after this victory, marched into Ossery, with a numerous and princely retinue, to place Diarmuid Mac Carrol upon the throne of that petty kingdom, which became vacant by the decease of Ceallach Mac Carroll, his brother, who was slain in the battle above-mentioned, and was a tributary prince to Cormac Mac Cuillenan, king of Munster and of Leath Modha. Here the soldiers brought the head of Cormac to the king, and laid it at his feet, expecting a great reward for the service they had done; but Flann Sionna was a generous enemy, and instead of applauding and giving them a gratuity for the action, he upbraided them with cruelty and inhumanity for violating the law of nations, which forbids mangling and stabbing of the dead, and commanded them from his presence as barbarous ruffians, who had no more veneration for the dignity and majesty of a king than for a common enemy. The head was left, and the king of Ireland, with difficulty refraining from tears, took it up in his hand, and kissed it, lamenting the instability of human greatness, and the untimely fate of so religious a prince and so venerable a prelate. He then gave strict orders for the body to be searched after, and to be interred as his will appointed. Maonach, the confessor of Comhgall, had the royal relics committed to his care, who removed them with great solemnity to Diseart Diarmuda, where they were interred as became his character.

The king of Ireland having fixed Diarmuid Mac Carrol in the throne of Ossery without opposition, after he was proclaimed and crowned with the usual ceremonies, and reconciled some small disputes that arose between that prince and his brothers, returned with his army to his own royal palace. He received the most grateful acknowledgments from the king of Leinster, for his assistance in the war; who likewise returned with his forces into his own province, laden with spoils, and followed by a number of prisoners of the first quality.

Carrol, the son of Muireagein, king of Leinster, directed his march towards Kildare, where he arrived with many prisoners of note of the Momonians; and among the rest, the author of this rash and unnecessary war, Flathbhertach Mac Jonmuinein, abbot of Inis Catha, was led in triumph among the captives. The clergy of Leinster were so enraged at his conduct, that they upbraided him with being the fomenter of the divisions between the two provinces, and the cause of all the bloodshed on both sides; and they prosecuted their resentment with that violence, that the unfortunate abbot was closely imprisoned and severely used, so long as Carrol, king of Leinster, lived; after whose decease he was discharged, and obtained his liberty.

About a year after the decease of this provincial prince, Muirionn, the pious abbess of St. Bridget, was so concerned about the safety of this abbot, that though he was released from his imprisonment and received his pardon, yet she apprehended he might be set upon by the enraged populace and his life endangered, and therefore, for his security, she prevailed with a number of the most religious clergy, to procure a guard for him till he arrived at a place called Magh Nairb; from thence he came to Munster, and retiring to his monastery of Inis Catha, he spent some time there in great devotion and exemplary practice of holiness, till the death of Dubhlachtna, the son of Maolguala, who governed the province of Munster for seven years after the decease of Cormac Mac Cuillenan. By the death of this king the throne of Munster became vacant, and this abbot was removed from his retirement at Inis Catha, to administer the government of that province, which he held for many years with great applause; and notwithstanding his want of policy with regard to the invasion of Leinster, he proved a sober and discreet prince, and was possessed not only of the command but of the affections of his people. The transactions abovementioned stand upon record in a very ancient treatise of Cluain Aidhnach Fiontan, in Leix, where the particulars of the battle of Beallach Mugna are related at large. It is a poetical composition of a learned person called Dallan, who was retained as principal historiographer to Cearbhal, king of Leinster. This writer gives an express account of the number of the slain, as well officers as soldiers, who perished in that engagement ; the beginning only of the poem shall be inserted in this place, because it would be too prolix to translate the whole, especially considering that the names of the most eminent nobility have been already taken notice of. The lines carry this sense :

> The valiant Cormac, Feimhin, and Fogartach,
> And the renowned Colman Ceallach
> With six thousand of the best provincial troops,
> Were slain, engaging in the bloody fields
> Of Mugna.

A.D. 913. Niall Glundubh succeeded in the throne of Ireland. He was the son of Hugh Fionnliath, son of Niall Caille, descended from the royal line of Heremon, and reigned monarch of the island three years. This prince re-established the celebrated fair of Tailton, which had been omitted for some time; and the Danes attempting to disturb the state, were overthrown by him, in a pitched battle, at Loch da Chaoch, in the province of Ulster. In this engagement a great number of foreigners were slain ; but they did not fall unrevenged, for the Irish, though victorious, suffered great loss, and some of their best troops perished in the action. In the reign of this monarch the Lagonians, or the inhabitants of Leinster, encountered the Danes with their provincial forces, but they were totally routed by the bravery and conduct of Jomhair an experienced commander of the enemy, at Ceannfuaid, and left 600 of their best soldiers dead upon the spot. In this bloody action Mac Muireagin, king of East Liffy, was slain ; and with him fell the valiant Ughaire, the son of Oiliolla, and Mogroin, the son of Kennedy, king of the Comanns and Leix, and many renowned generals, whose names are now lost to posterity.

About this time it was that Oittir, a very able and accomplished general of the Danes, attempted an invasion upon the kingdom of Scotland ; for that purpose he transported a body of choice troops from Loch da Chaoch, and landed in that country ; but upon his arrival he met with a warm reception from Cuas, the son of Hugh, who fell upon him with a fury not to be resisted, forced the Danes to retire to their ships, after a terrible slaughter, and obliged them to return without their captain, who met his fate in the first heat of the action.

But Niall Glundubh, the king of Ireland, was not so successful in repelling an invasion of these foreigners, who landed a numerous army upon the island, under the conduct of Sitrien and the sons of Jomhair. Upon their arrival they plundered and distressed the people with incredible oppressions, and among other successes, they made an attempt upon the city of Dublin and took it sword in hand. Niall, alarmed at these hostilities, resolved to oppose the progress of the proud Danes, and collecting with the utmost expedition all the forces of Leath Cuin, gave them battle; but the foreign army, emboldened by their conquests, received the charge with great courage, and falling on with terrible fury, broke through the Irish troops, and gave them a general defeat; the pursuit was hot and bloody, and in the flight great numbers were cut off, for the victors resolved to give no quarter. In the engagement fell Niall Glundubh, king of Ireland, and Connor Mac Maolseachluin, prince of Ireland; and there followed them into the other world, Hugh Mac Eochagain, king of Ulster, Maolmithig, son of Flanagan, king of Breag, Maolcraoibhe O'Dubsionna, Riogh Oirgial, with many more illustrious personages, who had the principal command in the Irish army, and chose rather to die in the field of honour than survive the liberty and freedom of their country.

A.D.
954.
Donough was the succeeding monarch. He was the son of Flann Sionna, descended from the royal stock f Heremon, and governed the kingdom thirty years. The mother of this prince was Gormflath, the daughter of Flann, son of Conuing, and his reign was made memorable by many signal transactions.

This king sat upon the throne of Ireland when Ceallachan, the son of Buadhachain, but more commonly known by the name of Ceallachan Cashel, began his government over the two provinces of Munster, and wore that provincial crown for ten years. But he met with opposition with regard to his succession in that throne, which was like to be attended with fatal consequences: but was at length happily overcome; for Kennedy Mac Lorcan, a prince of formidable interest in that country, designed to lay claim to that province, and for that purpose came as far as Gleanamhuin with a numerous retinue, to treat with the nobility and gentry of Munster about the point of succession. The throne of that province was vacant at this time, and the proposals of Kennedy were near taking effect; but the mother of Ceallachan, a lady of great prudence, and much esteemed by the people, fearing that her son should be excluded and Kennedy proclaimed king, resolved to use her utmost efforts to secure the succession in her family, which had a just claim.

but were unable to support their pretensions with a military
force ; and therefore boldly addressing herself to Kennedy, and
expostulating with him about the injustice of his design, she
told him, that he was bound by the agreement made many years
before between Fiachadh Muilleathan and Cormac Cas, wherein
it was stipulated, that the government of Munster should descend alternately to their respective families ; and the right
being in her son, she desired that he would not violate the contract of his ancestors, and seize upon a crown by usurpation,
which he could have no just pretence to. This transaction is
recorded in an ancient poem, and the lines may not improperly
be rendered thus :

> Most noble Kennedy, let no injustice
> Derive a blemish on your princely name.
> Consider the most solemn contract made
> By the brave Fiachadh and Cormac Cas,
> That Munster should alternately be ruled
> By the successive heirs of both their families.

The representation of this princess had its desired effect; for
Kennedy, overcome by the justice of it, and conscious of the defect in his own title, relinquished his pretensions peaceably, and
Ceallachan was acknowledged and proclaimed king of Munster.
But notwithstanding he had possession of the government, the
Danes disturbed his reign with frequent incursions ; and when
these foreigners perceived that they could not carry on their
designs by force, they had recourse to treachery, and were so
successful, as by a stratagem to seize upon Ceallachan and take
him prisoner ; but his captivity was of no long continuance,
for he soon obtained his freedom by the victorious arms of the
Eugenians and Dailgaisians, who were resolved to recover him
out of the hands of the Danes or perish in the attempt.

This provincial prince and his hardy Momonians, inspired
with revenge, engaged these foreigners in many battles, and
fought them with that success, that they found it proper to
abandon the province of Munster, and look out for new settlements. But the Danes still retained an affection for their old
possessions, and finding themselves too weak to be reinstated by
force of arms, they betook themselves to their usual arts, and
formed a design so base and treacherous in itself, that history
can hardly parallel it, and deserves from us a particular relation.

At this time the Danes were under the command of Sitric,
the son of Turgesius, that cruel usurper, whose name alone was

a terror to the Irish.   This general, the son of that tyrant, having first taken the advice of his council, sent a messenger to Ceallachan, king of Munster, to notify to him his sincere inclinations to peace and a good understanding and correspondence between them ; and as a testimony of his integrity and respect he offered him his sister, the princess-royal of Denmark, in marriage, who was a lady of consummate virtue and unexceptionable beauty.   He would oblige himself likewise, never to invade or disturb his government in Munster, and promised that he would withdraw his forces, put an end to his hostilities, and for the future not only make no attempt upon his crown, but enter into a league offensive and defensive, mutually to assist each other against their enemies; and to give a sanction to these proposals, he engaged to send him suitable hostages, whose safety and quality would oblige him to the execution of them.   But Sitric intended nothing less than to contract his sister to the king of Munster ; his design was, to murder him and his retinue upon the night the marriage was to be solemnized, and then seize upon his crown.   To support his interest after the commission of this execrable fact, and the better to establish himself in that province, he communicated this cruel resolution to Donnogh, the son of Flann Sionna, king of Ireland ; who, instead of starting at the attempt, encouraged it, and applauded the treacherous Dane, and promised him his friendship and alliance after the execution ; for it must be observed, that the king of Ireland was at that time an enemy to the king of Munster, because he refused to pay his contributions and chief rents ; and by this means he thought he should get rid of a troublesome neighbour, who disputed his authority, and denied him the homage and testimonies of subjection which his predecessors laid claim to.

The messenger of Sitric being introduced to Ceallachan, delivered the proposals, and that unfortunate prince fell into the snare that was laid for him by one of his most inveterate enemies ; for when he was told of the contract with the young princess, he was transported with the news ; the fame of this young lady's beauty, her virtue and other accomplishments having reached his ears long before, and he had conceived a passion before he had seen her.   He suspected nothing of the design, and being of an amorous disposition, returned his compliments to Sitric, and promised he would make him a visit with all possible expedition. Accordingly very noble and expensive preparations were made for this journey ; he was to be attended with a splendid retinue, and a princely equipage, to be followed by his body guards and the choicest of his troops, in order to conduct the princess into his province with the state and magnificence that became her birth and quality.

But Kennedy, the prince of North Munster, hearing of the design of Ceallachan, and that he intended to take with him his choicest forces, and to leave the province of Munster unguarded, and open to the incursions of any one who would attempt to invade it, represented the imprudence of this resolution, and how dangerous it was to leave the country without defence ; and by his advice, and the strength of his reasons, dissuaded the king from his purpose, who altered his measures, and appointing a sufficient force to secure the province, began his journey, attended by the young prince Dunchuan, the son of Kennedy, and followed only by his body guards. He continued his journey with quick marches, and soon arrived within sight of Dublin.

It happened that Sitric, the Danish general, had married an Irish lady, whose name was Morling, and daughter of Hugh Mac Eochaidh. This princess, hearing that Ceallachan, king of Munster, was upon his journey to accomplish the marriage rites with the princess-royal of Denmark, and arrived almost as far as Kilmainham, near Dublin, was somewhat surprised at it ; and for satisfaction freely expostulated with Sitric, her husband, what could induce him to bestow his sister in marriage upon the provincial prince, who was a professed enemy to the Danish race, and had destroyed so many of the principal nobility and gentry of his country. Sitric, with great freedom, discovered his design, and replied, that he was urged on by revenge to invite the king of Munster to Dublin ; for he would disappoint him of his nuptial pleasures with his sister, and, when he had him in his power, he was resolved to sacrifice him to the ghosts of those renowned Danes he had destroyed. His wife was astonished at the barbarity of this action, especially since Ceallachan was appointed to be the victim ; for she had entertained a very tender esteem for that prince, and was perfectly in love with him from the time she by chance saw him at Waterford, but had the prudence not to discover her concern, and appeared before her husband to approve of his design, and outwardly encouraged him in the execution of it.

But the next morning she rose much earlier than usual, and being sensible that Ceallachan was upon the road to Dublin, she conveyed herself with great privacy out of the town, and took up her standing in a convenient place by which the king of Munster was to pass.   Here she discovered herself to him, and, declaring the particulars of the conspiracy that was formed against his life, advised him to retire with the utmost speed, and provide for his own safety and that of his followers.   He was amazed and confounded with the intelligence, and expressing himself in a grateful manner to the lady for her information, he took leave of her, and turning about made the best of his way to Munster.   But Sitric had taken care to prevent his retreat; for he had lined the hedges with armed Danes, and laid so many ambushes in his way, that it was impossible for him to escape.   Ceallachan and his retinue found themselves surrounded with enemies, who galled them on all sides, and did great execution.   The king of Munster ordered his men to fall on, and defend themselves against the treacherous Danes; and a desperate conflict began, in which many of the principal of the Momonians were slain. The Danes likewise suffered exceedingly in the action, and must have given way to the superior courage of the king's guards, had they not been supported by fresh supplies from the city, which renewed the fight, and at length, after a terrible slaughter, obtained a complete victory. In this engagement Ceallachan, king of Munster, and Dunchuan, son of Kennedy, were taken prisoners, after a long and resolute resistance; and the Danes, after they had stripped and plundered the dead, returned with their royal captives in triumph to the city of Dublin.   Here they were confined but a short time, and were removed under a strong guard to Ardmach, where they were imprisoned with great strictness and severity; and nine Danish noblemen, of the quality of earls were appointed to command a strong body of troops, whose business was to secure these prisoners, so that it was impossible for them to escape.

The forces of Munster, that had the good fortune to save themselves by flight, returned home, where they related the treachery of the Danes, and brought the intelligence of the captivity of their king, and the death of many of his followers, who perished by the ambuscade.   This account alarmed the whole province, but more particularly affected Kennedy, prince of Munster, who was deputed regent of the country, and had the sole management of public affairs in the absence of the king.   He was so incensed at the baseness of the act, and concerned at the captivity of his son, that he resolved to take ample satisfaction of those treacherous foreigners, and rescue the prisoners at all events; for this purpose he summoned together the provincial troops, and making the battalions complete by fresh recruits, he provided a formidable army by land; and to accomplish his design with greater certainty, he fitted out a fleet of ships, and manned it with able seamen, that he might make sure of his revenge, and attack the enemy at once by sea and land. The command of the army was committed to the conduct of a brave and experienced general, Donnogh Mac Keeffe, king of Fearmoighe. To raise the courage of this general, and to inspire him with proper sentiments of indignation, he reminded him of the nobility of his blood, and of the magnanimity of his ancestors, who were kings of Munster; and having repeated their names, and mentioned them with honour and due applause, he related their particular exploits, how they exposed their lives for the good of their country, and repelled the insolence of foreign invaders; and concluded with informing him of the prospect he had of success, under his conduct and bravery, which he was certain would chastise those insolent Danes, for violating the law of nations, and the established rights of hospitality, and by that means procure deliverance to the island and glory to himself. To support the provincial troops, if there should be occasion, Kennedy ordered 1000 choice soldiers of the martial tribe of the Dailgais upon this expedition, and disposed them under the command of three captains of confessed courage and experience, who were his own brothers, and were distinguished by the names of Cosgrach, Lonargan, and Congallach. This transaction is upon record in an ancient composition, wherein are these verses :

Go, my renowned brothers, and command
This warlike tribe; your names shall not be lost,
But the brave Cosgrach, and the stout Lonargan,
And Congallach invincible in war,
Shall stand immortal in the lists of fame.

Kennedy resolved to prosecute this design with the utmost vigour, and therefore he raised 500 more of the clan of the Dailgais, and appointed for their general the heroic Sioda, the son of Clan Cuilleain; and another 500 of the same tribe he placed under the conduct of Deagadh, the son of Daniel, a captain of distinguished bravery and experience, who likewise had the command of numbers of the nobility and gentry of the Dailgais, who came from the country of Thumond, and voluntarily offered their service in this expedition. The fleet was now ready to sail, and the command of it was conferred upon an admiral perfectly skilled in maritime affairs, Failbhe Fionn, king of Desmond.

These military preparations being adjusted, the army began to march from Munster, and took their route through the province of Conacht, where they halted; and a council of war being called, it was agreed to send out considerable parties, to forage and fetch in provisions from Jerny and Umhall. In these places they found a good booty of cattle and other necessaries, and designed to carry them off to the camp. They thought themselves secure of their prey, but their scouts surprised them with the intelligence that they had discovered a body of troops marching towards them in regular order, with their commander at the head of them. This information obliged the foragers to retire without the plunder to the main body, who were immediately ordered to stand to their arms and expect the event. By this time the strange troops approached near the outlines of the camp, but advanced without beginning hostilities, or discovering that they had any design to attack it. The general of Munster resolved to be satisfied of their intention, and for that purpose the brave Donnogh Mac Keeffe called to the commanding officer, and demanded from whence he came, and whether he was a friend or an enemy. The captain answered, that he came out of Munster, and that his followers belonged to that province, and were raised out of two particular places, called Gaileangaidh and Luignig. He replied farther, that most of them were the posterity of Teige, the son of Cein, the son of the great Oilioll Ollum; and the rest were the men of Dealbna, descended from the renowned Dealbhaoith, the son of Cas, son of Conal Each-luath, and were resolved to expose their lives against those barbarous Danes, who by the basest treachery had surprised their king, and kept him in an unjust captivity. He moreover informed Donnogh Mac Keeffe, that he had with him three officers of signal courage and abilities, who had a principal command over three clans. The tribe of the Gaileangaidhs were under the conduct of Hugh, the son of Dualgaia, Diarmuid Mac Fianach-taig was the superior officer over the Luignigs, and Dinis Mac Maoldomhnaig was captain of the Dealbhnas. This account is recorded in a poem of good authority, which begins with these verses subjoined :

The most courageous tribes of Clanna Cein,
And the invincible Dealbhaoith,
United all their forces to redeem
Their king, and free him from imprisonment.

This unexpected supply consisted of 500 expert archers, and 500 completely armed with swords and shields, and was a seasonable recruit, and of eminent service in this expedition.

The army of Munster was formidable, and began their hostilties by plundering the adjacent country, and destroying the inhabitants. Mortough, the son of Arnalaig, applied to the general, Donnogh Mac Keeffe, and desired that he would return the booty that was carried away by the Momonian soldiers; for he insisted upon the injustice of the action, and pleaded that it was barbarous to oppress a people who were unconcerned in the quarrel, and who deserved protection rather than to fall a sacrifice to the greedy soldiers; but his request was denied, though not absolutely; for Donnogh was content, that if there remained any of the booty over and above what would satisfy the necessities of the army, it should be returned. But this answer was unsatisfactory, and Mortough, resolved to revenge himself upon the troops of Munster, dispatched messengers privately to Ardmach, to inform the Danes that the provincial troops were upon their march, and determined at all hazards to recover their king from imprisonment, and to do themselves justice upon those perfidious foreigners, who broke through the received laws of mankind to make him their prisoner.

The nine Danish earls, who were the sons of Turgesius the tyrant, and were appointed to guard the castle where Ceallachan, the king of Munster, and Dunchuain, the son of Kennedy, were confined, were alarmed with this intelligence of Mortough; and leaving a small number of their forces to secure the prisoners, whom they resolved to remove, drew out their troops, and marched out of Ardmach, with a full resolution to offer battle to the army of Munster. The provincial army directed their course towards Ardmach, but when they arrived they understood that the prisoners were conveyed out of the castle, and carried to Sitric, who had put them on shipboard. Donnogh, enraged at this disappointment, gave no quarter to the Danes that fell in his way, but cut them off to a man, and next morning marched towards Dundalk, where they had intelligence that their king and the young prince were confined under deck by Sitric; who being informed of the number of the provincial forces, and sensible of his own incapacity to oppose them, had ordered all his men on board, and resolved to try his fortune by sea, for by land he was much inferior to his enemies; and his shipping lying conveniently in the bay of Dundalk, were of infinite service, and for the present put him in expectation of getting clear of the enemy.

The army of Munster pursued him to the shore, and expected the Danes were shut in by the sea which would prevent their retreat; but were surprised to find them on shipboard, for they had no notice that their fleet lay at anchor in that bay. The Irish were enraged at this disappointment, and while they were consulting what they should do in this juncture, they espied a sail of ships, in regular order, steering with a brisk gale towards the Danish fleet, which they supposed to be the fleet of Munster under the conduct of that brave admiral, Failbhe Fionn; and so it fortunately proved, for they perceived them draw up in line of battle, and attack the Danes, who expected no such treatment, for they thought themselves secure, and that no enemy could possibly disturb them in those seas. The admiral of Munster, observing the disorder of the enemy, fell upon the ship where Sitric and his two brothers, Tor and Magnus, were, and with irresistible force boarded her. He no sooner found himself upon deck but he saw Ceallachan tied with cords to the main-mast. This spectacle inspired him with a fresh supply of courage, and he resolved to deliver the prince at all hazards; he laid about him with incredible fury, and after having slain several of the Danes, he cut the cords, and set the prince at liberty. He then put a sword in his hand, and advised him to take upon himself the charge of the ship from whence he came, which was now left without a com- mander, and leave him to engage the Danish admiral, whom he made no question to give a good account of.

Ceallachan complied with this proposal, and Failbhe Fionn continued on board the Dane, and behaved himself with sig- nal courage, but was at length overborne by numbers, when fainting with loss of blood, he was slain; and to discourage the Irish, some of whom followed their admiral into the enemy's ship, the Danes hacked and mangled his body, and at last cut off his head. Thus fell the brave Failbhe Fionn, who was obliged to give way to multitudes that pressed upon him, after he had dispatched many of them to the other world; and Sitric and his brothers, being sensible that the loss of that ship would occasion the ruin of the fleet, showed themselves able seamen and experienced commanders, and appeared with that intre- pidity at the head of their body guards, whom they had on board, that for some time the fortune of the day seemed to be on their side, and they began to have a distant prospect of victory.

But Fiongall, a valiant and expert commander among the Irish, resolved to revenge the death of the admiral, whom he followed on board, and maintaining his post with incredible bravery, he slew the foremost of the Danes that opposed him, and the decks of the ship were covered with blood. But the number of the enemy was much superior to the Irish, and they continued the fight, and supplied the place of the slain. Fiongall found himself unable at length to keep possession of the Danish ship, and ashamed to retire to his own, he recollected himself, and seizing upon Sitric by the collar, grasped him close, and threw himself with him in his arms into the sea, where in the disorder of the fight they both perished.

Seagda and Conall, two undaunted captains among the Irish, fired with the glory of this action, fell upon the Danes with redoubled fury, and resolving to put an end to the dispute by one instance of courage, they made their way through the enemy to Tor and Magnus, the two brothers of Sitric, and rushing violently upon them, they caught them both up in their arms, and jumped with them overboard, where in the confusion they were all lost.

The Danes, astonished at these desperate exploits of the Irish, began to abate of their courage, and the Momonians perceiving they gave way, pursued their advantage with that success, that they boarded most of the Danish fleet, killing and destroying without distinction, till victory finally declared for the Irish ; but it was bought at the expense of much blood, for many brave officers and soldiers perished in the engagement. Nor is this to be wondered at, if it be considered, that the Danes were good seamen, that they were perfectly skilled in maritime affairs, and were likewise resolute and fierce, and resolved to sell their lives at a dear rate ; for on the success of this action depended not only their present security, but likewise their future peace and establishment in the island.

The historians, who have delivered down to us an account of this action, relate that this fight between the Irish and the Danes was the most dreadful and terrible of any that happened upon those coasts for many ages ; for the officers eminently distinguished themselves on both sides, nor were the seamen wanting in their duty, so that the slaughter was surprisingly great, no less than dominion and liberty being the prize of victory. The army of Munster, that stood upon the shore in sight of the engagement, were distracted, and ran up and down the coasts with fury and distraction, because it was out of their power to assist their countrymen, who engaged with great disadvantage, so that the event remained doubtful for some time ; for the Danes had all their land forces on board, which yet were not a match for the Irish seamen, who behaved with wonderful conduct and bravery, and would have entirely destroyed the Danish fleet, had not some of the enemy escaped in their light galleys, which were chased briskly by the victorious Irish, but they could not overtake them.

The Irish fleet, having cleared the coast of those foreigners, made to the shore, where they found their land army, who received them with open arms and joyful acclamations, and were transported at the sight of their king, who had obtained his liberty by this victory. Nor was Ceallachan, who was under constant apprehension of death, so long as he was in the custody of the enemy, less pleased with his deliverance ; for Sitric was a cruel tyrant, of a savage and unmerciful disposition, and had no regard to the majesty of a king, or the law of nations, by which his person was sacred and inviolable ; and therefore the king of Munster retained a grateful sense of the loyalty of his people, and applauded the bravery of his sea forces, who had actually procured his freedom ; and the fidelity of his land army, who had discovered so great an affection to his person, and zeal for his safety, as to pursue the Danes, and if they would have accepted of a battle, to expose their lives in his service. He ordered provisions for his fleet, and, when he had given instructions for the care of the wounded, he put himself at the head of his army, and by long marches arrived in Munster, where he resumed the management of affairs, and fixed himself in the government of that province.

But he met with opposition in his march that was near being attended with fatal consequences ; for Mortough Mac Flann, king of Leinster, attempted to obstruct his passage, and hinder him from conducting his troops through that province. This prince was of a mean servile disposition, and consulted more the interests of the Danes than the prosperity of his native country ; upon which account he determined to take revenge upon the army of Munster, and vindicate the cause of those foreigners upon the brave Irish, by cutting off their retreat, and harassing them in their marches ; for this purpose he summoned all the forces under his command, and resolved to lay ambushes in their way, and fall upon them when unprovided for defence. But Ceallachan, king of Munster, having timely intelligence of the treachery of this apostate prince, who had renounced the love of his country, and wanted to betray it under a foreign yoke, prepared to receive him ; and was so incensed at the baseness of the attempt, that he commanded his men to give no quarter, but to make examples of those perfidious Irishmen, who had no title to mercy, and were not to be treated as open and honourable enemies ; and to raise their indignation the more, he declared that the Danes, being of another country, were to be used as the laws of nations direct ; but the enemies they were to encounter had forfeited the common and established rights of mankind, and therefore they were to be hunted down as robbers and beasts of prey, and not a man of them was to be spared. These severe injunctions, and the resolution of Ceallachan, was carried by deserters to the king of Leinster, who, dreading the resentment of the Momonians flushed with victory, desisted from his enterprise, and withdrawing the forces of his province, he retired to a considerable distance, and left the army of Munster to prosecute their journey without hinderance or molestation.

Ceallachan having settled himself in the command of Munster, began to reflect upon the servitude his subjects had endured under the oppression of the Danes ; and urged on by the treachery of those foreigners, which he had sufficiently experienced, he entered upon a resolution to fall upon them in every division of the province, and to unite his whole forces in order to expel them the country. For this purpose he recruited his troops and completed his battalions, and first assaulted, with unexpected fury, the Danes that inhabited about Limerick, and without much opposition he obtained a signal victory ; 500 of the enemy he killed, and took the rest prisoners. This success gave new life to the prospects of the Irish; they plundered the country of Cashel, where they found a body of 500 Danes, whom they put to the sword. Sitric, the general of the foreigners, attempted to recover the booty from the victors, but was obliged to retire after 500 of his soldiers were slain ; neither had the general himself escaped the slaughter, if he had not fled to his shipping, and by that means put a stop to the pursuit.

After this uninterrupted success, Ceallachan marched with his victorious army to pay a visit to Daniel O'Faolan, king of the Deisies, with whom he entered into strict friendship ; and he admitted him into his alliance, by bestowing upon him in marriage his sister, whose name was Gromflath, who was a prin-

2 G

cess of great beauty and exemplary virtue. The king of Munster soon after left the world, and after a troublesome and hazardous reign descended peaceably to his grave, and without violence.

His successor in the throne of that province was Feargna, the son of Ailgeanan, son of Dungala, and he enjoyed the government of that country but two years, his life and reign being ended by treachery; for he was murdered by a set of conspirators who were near relations to him.

The crown was then seized by Mahon, the son of Kennedy. His reign was much longer than that of his predecessor, for it continued twelve years; his brother Eichiaruinn possessed the government of Thumond at this time. This prince had another brother, whose name was Bryen, that had a principal command in the army of Munster when Mahon fell upon the Danes, and fought the battle of Sulchoid. In this engagement the foreigners received a memorable defeat, and many of their most experienced officers perished in the action. Teitill, a person of great strength, and a distinguished champion of the enemy, lost his life, and his government of Waterford; Ruanon, governor of Cork; Muiris, governor o Limerick; with Bernard and Toroil, two office s of the first rank for courage and conduct, did not survive the action of that day. The slaughter among the soldiery was exceedingly bloody and terrible, for 2000 of the Danes, remained dead upon the field of battle. The victors pursued the flying enemy into the city of Limerick, and chased them through the streets and into their houses, where they were slain without mercy or quarter. The plunder of that city was bestowed upon the soldiers of Mahon, where they found an immense booty of jewels, gold, silver, and rich furniture, to a surprising value. After they had rifled the houses they set them on fire, they burned the fortifications, demolished the walls, and perfectly dismantled the town, and made it incapable of defence. After this victory, Mahon, the king of Munster, a fortunate and a worthy prince, was betrayed and seized by his traitorous subjects in his own palace, and conducted as a prisoner, under a strong guard, to Mac Broin, where he was barbarously put to death by the people of that place; nor would the importunate intercession of the blessed St. Collum Mac Ciaragain, the confessor of St. Bairre, prevail to save his life.

In the reign of Donough, the son of Flann Sionna, king of Ireland, before mentioned, several important occurrences happened, which must not be omitted in the course of this history.

Inder the government of this prince died the pious bishop of
uileim; near the time of whose decease Donnogh invaded the
erritories of Conacht, but the attempt was unfortunate, for
many of his subjects perished at Dubhtir near Athlone; at
which place Cionaoth, son of Connor, king of Falie, was slain.
oon after this defeat Cluain Mac Nois was entered by the
Danes, and plundered; and this success encouraged the foreign-
rs to proceed to Loch Ribh, where they committed dreadful
avages, and spoiled the adjacent country on both sides. They
kewise carried on their conquests to Ein Inis, which they
poiled, and after a sharp engagement cut off 1200 of the Irish,
who opposed them and gave them battle; but the foreigners
within a short time lost the same number of their men, for
200 of them perished in Loch Rughruidh. The Danes about
his time succeeded in most of their attempts, for when they
ould not accomplish their designs by force they prevailed by
reachery; and by stratagem the Danes of Dublin surprised
aolan, the king of Leinster, and his children, and made them
risoners. They likewise continued their hostilities with great
ruelty, and Dun Sobhairce was spoiled by the Danes of Loch
uain; and the country of Kildare suffered great oppressions,
nd was plundered by the foreigners of Waterford.

The inhabitants of the province of Ulster, a brave and war-
ke people, by this time grown jealous of their liberty, were
larmed at the progress of the Danes, and therefore resolved to
ppose their conquests; they summoned their provincial troops
ogether, and fell upon the Danes with such fury and success,
hat victory appeared for them at the first charge; for the
Danish forces were unable to bear up against the impression of
he Irish, and a general defeat and a dreadful slaughter followed.
n the action of that day fell 800 of the foreign forces, which
ass was the more considerable by the death of three of their
ravest commanders, whose names were Albdan, Aufear, and
toilt, who likewise fell among the slain. This victory was
niefly owing to the courage and experience of Mortough Mac
eil, the Irish general; and the success of the engagement was
tended with such happy consequences, that the effect of it was
nsibly perceived through the whole kingdom. The Danes
are dispirited, and ceased from their former oppressions, and
e natives enjoyed a taste of tranquillity and freedom, which
d been banished the island for many years before, and trad-
g and a state of prosperity succeeded in the room of a long
ene of misery and slaughter.

But this sunshine was in danger of being dismally obscured, by an unexpected attack from the Danes, who had been encouraged by their countrymen to new attempts, and came with a numerous and well-disciplined army from Limerick and Conacht, under the command of an enterprising general, whose name was Olfinn, who designed by this expedition to surprise the natives, who were at that time assembled from all parts of the country at the celebrated fair of Roscrea, which was annually kept upon the festival of St. Peter and St. Paul. But the Irish were so well acquainted with the Danish treachery, that they thought proper to bring their arms with them; and when they had intelligence that the foreigners were marching against them, they immediately left their trade, their shops, and their merchandise, which they esteemed of small importance to the concern of their country, and made head against the Danes; and notwithstanding the disadvantages they lay under from the surprise, which gave them no time to draw up in regular order, they supplied this defect by their unanimity and courage, and so shocked the foreign troops at the first charge, that they felt the impression through all their ranks, and a terrible slaughter and an universal rout followed, and fortune and victory declared for the Irish; 4000 of the enemy were left dead in this engagement, and Olfinn, a Danish earl, and general of the army, was slain. This memorable instance of success, obtained by merchants, shopkeepers and traders, met together without order and discipline in a public fair, is expressly recorded by a reputable author, called Florence Mac Carty, who has delivered down the transactions of Ireland for many ages.

About this time died Teige, the son of Cahill, who enjoyed the government of Conacht for 20 years; as did likewise Sitric, the son Jomhair, who was the king over the Danes and Norwegians, wherever dispersed throughout the island. The inhabitants of the province of Conacht, being concerned for the public liberty, attempted to dispossess the foreigners, particularly such as resided about Loch Oirbhsionn, whom they engaged and defeated; which success was followed by another victory, for soon after Conuing Mac Neil observing his opportunity fell upon the Danes, and slew 1200 of them at Loch Neachach. But this misfortune was recovered by the foreigners, who came to Loch Eirne, and plundered the adjacent country with incredible barbarity, Nothing however sacred or devoted to divine use escaped their fury, but the churches and religious houses were spoiled and rifled, and the clergy dispossessed without mercy. The

province of Ardmach was likewise invaded and harassed by
Godfrey, who was the principal commander of Loch Cuain ;
and Cilcuillen about the same time was spoiled by Ambrose, the
son of Godfrey, who destroyed the country with fire and sword
and carried away 1000 prisoners. Oilioch Neid likewise felt
the fury of these foreigners, who plundered it, and seized upon
Mortough Mac Neill, who they closely imprisoned, but by a
stratagem he freed himself from confinement and escaped their
hands.

But the Irish, resolving to shake off the oppression of the
Danes, encountered them ; particularly the people of Conacht
exerted themselves, and in the assault killed Arolt Mac Jomhair,
who held the government of Limerick for the enemy. About
the same time Ambrose, the son of Godfrey, king of the Danes
and Norwegians, who had possessions in the island, was slain by
the Normans, who had landed upon the coasts and attempted a
conquest of the country.

There was a prince of Wales about this time, whose name was
Rodericus, a brave and experienced commander, that transported
a numerous army of Welsh, with a design to plunder and spoil
the country, and if possible to obtain possession of it. But the
Irish repelled his attempt with great resolution and success, for
this prince lost his life in the first engagement, and the greatest
part of his army were destroyed. Hanmer, the historian, expressly relates, that in the year of our redemption 966, Congallach, the son of Maolmithig, took the city of Dublin, then inhabited by the Danes, and gave it up to be plundered by his
soldiers, after 740 of the enemy were put to the sword. Donnogh, the son of Flann Sionna, king of Ireland, did not long
survive this success, but gave up his life and his government by
a natural death.

Congall was the succeeding monarch. He was the son
A.D.
974.
of Maolmithig, son of Flanagan, son of Ceallaig, son of
Conuing, son of Congalla, son of Hugh Slaine, descended
lineally from the royal house of Heremon, and possessed the throne
ten years. The mother of this Irish prince was Mary, the daughter of Cionaoth, son of Ailpin, and his reign was remarkable by
the death of two neighbouring kings, Eitimont, king of England,
and Blathchuire Mac Jomhair, kind of Normandy. The Danes
raised great disturbances under the government of this prince,
but they were severely chastised by the Irish forces, who killed
7000 of them in the memorable battle of Muine Breogain ; but

though the victory declared for the natives, yet they suffered great loss, and many of their best troops were slain.

In the fourth year of the reign of Congall, king of Ireland, that renowned hero, Bryen Boiroimhe, entered upon the government of the two provinces of Munster; and this prince had not possessed the crown of that province above two years, before he dispatched one of his heralds at arms to challenge Meills Mac Broin, the king of Oneachach, to a pitched battle in the plains of Beallach Leachta, in order to revenge upon him and his army the barbarous death of Mahon, his brother, who was treacherously murdered by some of the subjects of that prince. The king of Oneachach received the challenge, and promised to meet him at the place appointed; and for that purpose he raised a formidable army, consisting of Irish and foreigners, for he depended in a great measure upon the courage of the Danes, whom he enlisted among his forces to the number of 1500. Bryen, king of Munster, marched at the head of his provincial troops, and being followed by the illustrious tribe of the Dailgais, offered battle to the enemy. The fight began furiously on both sides; and the slaughter was terrible, but the Momonian forces broke through the opposite army, and a general rout followed; the mercenary Danes fled, but were pursued, and great numbers of them were slain, and those who had the fortune to escape the sword were made prisoners.

This success of Bryen against the king of Oneachach, was very unacceptable to Daniel O'Faolan, king of the Deisies, who resolved to revenge the slaughter of the Danes, and take ample satisfaction of the king of Munster; for that purpose he raised a numerous and well disciplined army of his own people, and being supported by a formidable body of Danes, he determined to invade the territories of that province. He no sooner entered the country but he behaved with all the cruelty of an enraged enemy, and committed inexpressible barbarities upon the inhabitants. Bryen Boiroimhe soon received intelligence of these hostilities, and the progress of the enemy; he immediately led his army to oppose their incursions, and overtook them plundering the country at Fan Conrach, where he set upon them with incredible bravery, and impressed such a terror upon the auxiliary Danes, that they were totally routed; the king of the Deisies with his forces was unable to maintain the fight, and quitting the field, was obliged to fly for his life; the pursuit was hot and bloody, and the king of Munster with his invincible

Dailgais chased the Danes and the vanquished Irish into the town of Waterford, which they entered, and put all to the sword, and among the rest Daniel O'Faolan perished in the confusion of the slaughter. The town was sacked and plundered by the victors, who, after they had secured the booty, set it on fire, which raged dreadfully, and consumed it to the ground.

This great hero, Bryen Boiroimhe, had enjoyed the crown of Munster about eight years, when he by force of arms obliged the country of Leath Modha to become tributary and pay him obedience. But after the death of Daniel Claon, the son of Daniel, king of Leinster, the subjects of that province, both Irish and Danes refused to confess the authority of Bryen, and denied him their subjection. The king of Munster resolved to chastise them into their duty, and for that design he mustered his Momonian forces, that were become invincible under his conduct, and invaded the territories of Leinster. The Lagonian army, consisting of Irish and Danes, offered them battle, which began with great fury on both sides; but the army of Munster soon broke into the ranks of the enemy, and pursued their advantage with a dreadful slaughter, which ended in a general and bloody defeat, for in this battle of Gleann Mama 5000 of the Lagonians and Danes remained dead upon the spot. This martial and renowned prince, Bryen Boiroimhe, king of Munster, was an instrument in the hand of providence, to scourge the insolence and cruelty of those foreigners, which he did successfully, for he routed them in twenty-five battles, from the first time he entered the field against them, to the last conflict he had with them, which was the battle of Cluaintari, where he was slain, being then possessed of the government of the island.

It was not long after the battle of Gleann Mama, fought by that great commander Bryen Boiroimhe, that Congall, son of Maolmithig, king of Ireland, entered the province of Munster in a hostile manner, and plundered the country about him, and put the two sons of Kennedy Mac Lorcan, whose names were Eichiaruin and Dunchuan, to the sword. The Danes likewise made frequent incursions upon the neighbouring Irish, whose possessions they destroyed; and, under the command of Godfrey Mac Sitric, they spoiled Ceananus Domhnach, Patrick Ard Breacain, Cill Sgirre, and many other places dedicated to divine use, which never escaped their fury. The number of prisoners they carried away in this expedition amounted to 3000; besides great quantities of gold, silver, and other spoils, which were prized at an immense value.

The royal consort of Congall, king of Ireland, died about this time; the name of this lady was Eithne, and she was the daughter of Feargoll who had been queen of Ireland. The death of these illustrious personages happened soon after; Maolcullum Mac Daniel, king of Scotland, the most religious Gaoithne, bishop of Dun da Leathglass, and Teighe, the son of Cahil, king of Conacht. Nor did Congall, king of Ireland, long survive, for he fell into the hands of the Danes that served in the provincial army of Leinster, who killed him at Ardmach.

A.D. 984. Daniel succeeded in the Irish throne. He was the son of Mortough, son of Niall Glandubh, descended from the posterity of Heremon; and he administered the government for ten years. The reign of this prince was disturbed by the hostilities of the Danes; for in his time the foreigners, who inhabited the city of Dublin, plundered the country of Kildare, under the command of Humphry, or Amhlaoimh, the son of Sitric. This Irish monarch upon some provocation invaded the territories of Conacht, and spoiled that province without mercy, where he found a valuable booty, which he carried off, with a great number of prisoners; and the king of Conacht, whose name was Feargal O'Rourke, was obliged to let these hostilities pass unrevenged, the forces of his province being too weak to engage in the defence of the country.

In the reign of Daniel, the son of Mortough, king of Ireland, that noble fabric, the great church of Tuam, was erected by the pious prelate, Cormac O'Cilline, bishop of Tuam Greine; and Feargal O'Rourke was killed by Daniel, the son of Congall, son of Maolmithig. Bryen, the son of Kennedy, king of Munster, about this time assaulted the Danes who inhabited the city of Limerick, and set it on fire. Daniel O'Neill, who governed the province of Ulster, raised a formidable army of his subjects, and entering the territories of Leinster, he miserably distressed the people, and plundered all the country from the Bearow eastwards to the sea. He encamped in the heart of this province for the space of two months, notwithstanding the united strength of the Lagonians and Danes used their utmost endeavours to dislodge him and force him to retire. Near this time died Maolfinnin, the son of Uchtain, the pious bishop of Ceananus, and the venerable confessor of Ultan was translated to a better state.

The Danes, notwithstanding the many discomfitures they met with from the natives, continued their hostilities, and were supported in their incursions by the army of Leinster. These foreigners, under the command of Humphrey Cuarain, and the

Lagonians, conducted by a general of their own province, plundered Ceananus, where they found spoils of great value, which they carried off, and by that means impoverished the people, and reduced them to miserable extremities. The battle of Cillmona was fought about this time between Daniel, the son of Congall, who was assisted by the Danes that inhabited the city of Dublin, and Daniel, the son of Mortough, king of Ireland. The action concluded with great slaughter on both sides; and among the slain fell Ardgall, the son of Madagan, who had governed the province of Ulster for seventeen years, and Donnagan, the son of Maolmuirre, king of Oirgiallach, and many other noble personages of the first quality and distinction. The most religious Beacan, the bishop of Finne, did not long survive the engagement of that day.

It was the misfortune of the Irish that they were never free from intestine divisions, which contributed to their ruin; and so implacable was the spirit of discord among them, that they would often join with the forces of the Danes to bring slavery upon the country; for about this time Cionaoth O'Hartagan, the primate of Ardmach, assisted the foreigners, who lived in Dublin, and by that means Ugaire, the son of Tuathal, king of Leinster, was surprised and taken prisoner; but this enterprise was revenged by Bryen, the son of Kennedy, who engaged the Danes of Inis Catha, and gave them a general defeat, with the loss of 800 of them upon the spot. In this action three of their principal commanders were taken, and made prisoners of war, and the names of these captive officers were Jomhair, Humphry, and Dubhgeann. We receive an account of this transaction from the testimony of a poet of reputation in the following lines:

> The memorable fight of Inis Catha
> Was fatal to the Danes, whose slaughter'd bodies
> Lay scatter'd o'er the plain; these foreigners
> Lost three of their renowned generals,
> Jomhair, Humphry, and Dubhgeann.

About this time the Danes, who inhabited the city of Dublin committed hostilities in Leinster, and engaged the provincial troops of that country in the battle of Boithlione; and in the action Ugaire, the son of Tuathal, king of Leinster, was slain. Soon after this victory obtained by the Danes, Daniel Mac Mortough, king of Ireland, left the world by a natural death, and expired at Ardmach

Maolseachluin was the succeeding monarch. He was the son of Flann Sionna, a lineal descendant from the posterity of Heremon, and filled the throne twenty-three years. The mother of this monarch was Dunflath, the daughter of Mortough Mac Neill, who likewise was the mother of Glunioruin, that was king of the Danes dispersed throughout the whole kingdom. Many transactions of importance happened during the reign of this monarch; particularly the memorable battle of Tara, which he fought against the Danes of Dublin and the sons of Humphry, and gave them a total defeat, after 5000 of those foreigners were slain. In this engagement Randle, the son of Humphry, a prince of distinguished courage, who had the principal command over the whole settlement of the Danes throughout the island, lost his life. Encouraged by this victory, Maolseachluin, king of Ireland, and Eochaidh, son of Ardgail, who had governed the province of Ulster for thirty-five years, joined their forces, and resolved to attack the city of Dublin, the place of refuge to which the Danes retired, and drive them out of the country; for that purpose they made all necessary preparations for a siege, and with a numerous and well disciplined army sat down before the walls. Three days after their first encampment they resolved to make a general assault, and try the courage of the besieged. The attack was most violent, and attended with great slaughter, but the superior bravery of the Irish prevailed, and having fixed their standard upon the walls, so intimidated the Danes, that they surrendered. The victors avoided such dreadful cruelties as usually follow the taking of towns, and behaved with humanity and moderation. They set at liberty many of the principal gentry of the Irish, who had been taken captive by the Danes, and suffered a severe and long confinement; particularly Daniel of Claon, king of Leinster, and the hostages of O'Neill, were relieved and discharged. The affairs of the Danes were reduced to great extremities by this success of the Irish, and the vanquished were obliged to accept of hard conditions, and were glad to be admitted to mercy upon the terms of quitting all their conquests from the river Shannon eastwards to the sea; to forbear hostilities under the penalty of death; and to submit to whatever tribute it should be thought proper to lay upon them.

About this time it was, that Humphry, the son of Sitric, was forced to fly for security to Aoii Collum Cill, in the kingdom of Scotland, being banished the island by the victorious Irish. Near the same time Maolseachluin, king of Ireland, had a quar-

rel with the famous tribe of the Dailgais, and destroyed Bile
Moigh Hadair; but this action was afterwards revenged by
Bryen. Glen da Loch was taken and plundered by three sons
of Carrol, the son of Lorcan; but these three brothers were
pursued by divine vengeance for this execrable act, and were
found dead the night afterwards, by the influence of the importunate prayers of the pious Caomhgin, who consecrated that
place for divine uses.

The death of those two eminent persons happened about this
time, Morling, the daughter of Donnogh Mac Cealla, queen of
Ireland, and Joraird Mac Coisie, primate of Ardmach. The
Danes, notwithstanding the stipulations they had made, having
in some measure recovered their former losses, prepared for new
attempts. The foreigners of Dublin, under the command of
Mortough O'Congallach, plundered Dounach Patrick with great
cruelty; but Providence soon corrected them for their breach of
faith, for a visitation fell among them, by which infinite numbers
were destroyed. This affliction was followed by another, for
Maolseachluin, king of Ireland, engaged the foreigners with success, and encountering hand to hand with one of their professed champions, whose name was Tomor, he foiled him, and took
from him a collar of gold, which he wore about his neck, as a
trophy of victory. He fought Carolus, another of their chief
commanders, with the same success, and carried off his sword.

But the foreigners receiving constant supplies from Denmark
and Norway, began to raise new commotions, and in a short
time were attended with that success in their attempts, that the
natives were in great danger of being subdued and forced into
slavery; nor was there any prince in the island who opposed
these insults of the Danes but the brave Bryen Boiroimhe, king
of Munster. This renowned hero, with his stout Momonians,
was always in arms, harassing the foreigners, which humbled
their insolence, and made them less frequent in their incursions.
The success and industry of the king of Munster had so fixed
him in the esteem of the natives, who owed their lives and
liberties to his protection, that they made an attempt to dethrone the king of Ireland, and give him possession of the government in his room; and they were the more encouraged in
this design, because Maolseachluin was an indolent inactive
prince, addicted to pleasure and a love of ease, and sacrificed
the happiness of his country to his own private diversions; and
the people, who were immediately under his authority had contracted a servile habit of idleness from the example of the

court, and never disturbed themselves with opposing the inroads of the Danes, or calling them to an account for their cruelties and oppressions.

The nobility of Munster, and the principal inhabitants of the province of Conacht, reflecting upon the distressed and melancholy state of their country, applied themselves to Bryen Boiroimhe, as a deliverer ; and it was unanimously agreed in council that ambassadors should be sent to Maolseachluin, to signify to him in express terms, that he was unworthy of the government, and unfit for the management of public affairs, since he neglected the protection of his subjects, and unconcernedly permitted them to be oppressed by the merciless Danes, who took advantage of his indolent disposition, to destroy the country and bring it into slavery.   They farther expostulated with him, and used the freedom to inform him, that a king of Ireland, who had at heart the happiness of his people, would never suffer the insolent attacks of those foreigners to pass unrevenged as he did ; that the brave Bryen Boiroimhe had undertaken the cause of public liberty, and to repel the incursions of the haughty Danes, and therefore that he deserved to wear the crown of Ireland, who knew how to defend it with honour to himself, and happiness to his subjects ; in the end these ambassadors declared they were commissioned to acquaint him, that the nobility and gentry designed to dethrone him ; and therefore to prevent bloodshed and disturbances they advised him to resign of his own accord, and to retire to a private life.   This representation was received with the utmost scorn and indignation by the king, who absolutely refused to comply, and knew the value of a crown too well to deliver it up only for asking.   He likewise resolved to enter into no treaty with the nobility of Munster, who desired to meet him on the plain of Magh da Caomhog, but insisted upon his right of possession, which he determined to maintain to the last extremity.

The king of Munster being informed by his messengers of the resolution of the king of Ireland, resolved to make use of the affection of the natives to seize upon the crown, and to dispossess him by force ; for this purpose he raised a numerous army, consisting of the standing forces of his own province, and the auxiliary troops of the Danes, whom he received into pay, particularly those who had possessions in Leath Modha, and for that reason owed homage and subjection to the king of Munster. He set himself at the head of his Momonian battalions, and directed his march towards Tara ; but before he began hostilities he dispatched a herald to the king of Ireland, who had orders to summon him to resign the throne, and to send him hostages of the first quality for his future obedience ; and if he refused, he was to challenge him to a decisive battle, and to submit the dispute to the longest sword. The king of Ireland, somewhat surprised at this message, answered, that he was in no condition to give him battle immediately, because his army was disbanded, and it would require some time to collect them together ; but as a testimony that it was not out of cowardice that he refused to meet the army of Munster in the field, if Bryen would suspend hostilities, and allow him the respite of a month, to muster his forces, particularly the troops of Leath Cuinn, he would accept his challenge ; or if his subjects refused to support him with men or money for this expedition, he promised to send proper hostages as a security for his obedience. He likewise desired the commissioners of Munster to use their interest with Bryen, that he would not permit his army to plunder the country of Meath, but that he would restrain the excursions, and continue at Tara till the time of the cessation was expired.

The ambassadors returned with this answer to the king of Munster, who accepted of the conditions proposed, and commanded his officers to continue the soldiers peaceably in their quarters till farther orders. In the meantime Maolseachluin convened the principal nobility of Leath Cuinn, and advised with them upon this important subject. He likewise dispatched messengers to most of the petty princes of the kingdom, to demand their assistance ; particularly he sent Giolla Comhgall, whom he retained as his antiquary, to the great O'Neill, to require his proportion of troops upon this occasion, upon which his crown and the security of his person depended, and to enjoin him, if he refused to supply him with his quota, to provide hostages and send them to Bryen Boiroimhe, king of Munster, as an evidence of his subjection and obedience ; for these were the terms he was bound to accept, which, though severe in themselves, yet the necessity of his affairs would oblige him to comply with. This antiquary had a commission to deliver the same message to Eochaidh, the son of Ardgail, king of Ulster, and to Cathal O'Connor, king of Conacht, and require their immediate assistance ; and if they were unwilling to support him against the army of Munster, he had orders to represent to them, that if the king of Ireland was forced to resign his crown, and give up the royal seat of Tara, where the monarchs of the island had resided for many ages, it could be no reproach to him, because he was denied the assistance of his subjects, but the dishonour would more immediately affect the O'Neills, and the principal nobility of Leath Cuinn, whose ancestors had been in possession of the Irish throne for many successive generations.

The messenger was very faithful in the execution of his orders ; and when he represented the circumstances, and the necessity of the king's affairs, to the nobility of Leath Cuinn, the answer he received from Hugh O'Neill was, that when the oyal seat of Tara was possessed by the posterity of Eogan, his great ancestor, they defended it against all attempts, and therefore it was reasonable that those who were masters of it should secure themselves in the possession, or deliver it up ; but with regard to himself, he absolutely denied to assist the king of Ireland, who had lost the affections of his people, or to draw upon himself the displeasure and resentment of the noble tribe of the Dailgais, whose friendship he esteemed, and therefore he determined to be neuter in the dispute. Giolla Comhgaill returned with this unwelcome answer to the king of Ireland ; who, finding himself abandoned by the petty princes, and reflecting that the non-compliance of Hugh O'Neill might be attended with bad consequences, and by the influence of his example prevail upon others to withdraw their supplies, he resolved to pay a visit to Hugh O'Neill in person, and persuade him, if possible, to interest himself in his cause ; and as an argument, which he thought was irresistible, he offered, that rather than the royal seat of Tara should fall into the power of Bryen Boiroimhe, he would resign his right, and if he would use his utmost efforts to defend it against the enemy, he would confirm him in the possession of that ancient palace and the lands belonging to it, and engage for him and his successors, that no claim should be revived, and that it should descend without opposition to his posterity ; so violent was the resentment of the king of Ireland against Bryen Boiroimhe, that he resolved to disappoint him in his designs at any rate, particularly that the seat of Tara, which was the court of the Irish monarchs, should not fall into his hands.

Hugh O'Neill desired to be excused from giving an immediate answer, and insisted upon time to convene the principal nobility of Siol Eogain, in order to receive their sentiments upon a matter of such importance. Accordingly when the assembly met, he communicated to them the cause of the king of Ireland's arrival, and the advantageous proposals that he offered, if they would support him with their assistance against the king of Munster, and the army that was raised against him by the tribe of the Dailgais. After some debates, the chiefs of Siol Eogain came to a resolution not to concern themselves with the king of Ireland, for they suspected the integrity of his of. fers, and that he did not design, after his business was accomplished, and he found himself established in the throne, to abide by his resignation of Tara ; and therefore their advice to Hugh O'Neill was, that he should return a civil answer to the king of Ireland, but refuse absolutely to act in a quarrel of that consequence, that possibly might draw upon him new enemies, whose resentment might prove his destruction.

But the convention, upon second thoughts, perceived that they might procure some advantages to themselves by the misfortunes and exigencies of the king of Ireland, and therefore they imagined that the answer agreed upon at their last meeting might be altered and mollified ; and though they seemed satisfied that if they joined the army of the king of Ireland against the forces of Munster, they might lose their lives, and scarce a man of them return home, especially since they were to engage against the martial and invincible tribe of the Dailgais, who never turned their back, and were the constant scourges of the Danes, yet they resolved to venture themselves, and assist the king of Ireland with a competent force, on condition that they might find a recompense equal to the hazard, and that he would deliver to them one half of the country of Meath, and the lands of Tara for a reward ; for they resolved, if they did not meet with success in the expedition, their wives and children should be sufficiently provided for ; and though they lost their lives, it was their duty, they judged, to take a proper care of the interest of their posterity.

These proposals were offered to Maolseachluin, who received them with indignation, apprehending them to be exorbitant and unjust ; he therefore left O'Neill, and with his retinue returned to his own court. Under these disappointments he was undetermined what course to follow, and therefore he summoned the principal of Clan Colman to repair to him, and assist him with their advice. He represented to the nobility of that tribe the deplorable state of his affairs, and particularly informed them of the insolence and haughty demands of Hugh O'Neill and the chiefs of Siol Eogain, requesting withal that they would not leave him in his extremities, but continue their fidelity to him at this time when he had most occasion for their counsel and assistance.

The clan assembled upon this occasion, and weighing even the minutest circumstance of the case, came to this resolution, that the king being unable to meet the king of Munster in the field, and decide the dispute by force of arms, should make his submission to Bryen Boiroimhe, and immediately go to his camp at Tara, where he had lain for a month, and offer him his future obedience. This advice was complied with by the king, who taking with him 1200 horse, arrived at the king of Munster's camp; he was soon admitted into the presence of Bryen Boiroimhe, who received him with great courtesy, and accepted his submission.

But Maolseachluin so resented the treatment he received from Hugh O'Neill, that he informed Bryen of what had passed; and notwithstanding his unfortunate circumstances obliged him to submit, yet he still retained so much of the spirit of a king, that he told the king of Munster that his submission was no reflection upon his personal courage, for he had fully determined to give him battle if his subjects would have allowed him a competent supply; and therefore his present tender of obedience was the effect of invincible necessity, which it was out of his power to overrule. This ingenuous declaration made such an impression upon the king of Munster, that he told him, he was sensibly affected with the posture of his affairs, and promised, that if he had any prospect of retrieving the difficulties he lay under, he would forego the advantages he had, and allow him a year's respite to repair his broken fortune, and then he would meet him in the field, and decide the controversy by the sword; and he further engaged, that he would rely upon his honour for the execution of the terms after the year was expired, and would not insist upon hostages as a security for its performance. In the mean time he proposed to march northwards with his army, to watch the motions of Hugh O'Neill, and Eochaidh, son of Ardgail, king of Ulster, whom if he found inclined to oppose him, he resolved to engage; and said, that he should not be surprised if Maolseachluin should join his northern confederates and fight against him, since he was willing to put the cause upon the issue of a battle, and that the victor should enjoy the crown of Ireland without disturbance. Maolseachluin, moved with the generosity of the Momonian king, assured him that he abhorred such ungrateful practices, and he also promised that he would not, were it in his power, assist them against him; but told him he was of opinion, that his northern progress was unseasonable at that time, and might be justly deferred to another opportunity, and therefore he dissuaded him from undertaking it. This advice

was accepted by Bryen, and was suitable to the condition of his
army, for the greatest part of his provision was exhausted, and
he was in no capacity to attempt such a journey, or to execute
such a design.

Bryen therefore decamped from Tara, and directed his march
homewards; but first he made a present of 240 fine horses to the
Irish monarch, and bestowed very munificent gifts of gold and
silver upon his retinue, and the two kings parted with great
friendship, and with all the outward testimonies of affection and
respect. Bryen Boiroimhe returned to his court in Munster,
and Maolseachluin took upon him the care of his government,
and the administration of the public affairs as before.

After the expiration of the year, for which time a cessation
of arms was concluded between the two kings, Bryen Boiroimhe
began his military preparations with great vigour; he ordered
his army, after he had completed his regiments, to a general
rendezvous, and summoned not only the natives of his own
province, but the Danes, to enter into the service; there offered
themselves, as auxiliaries, the Irish and Danes of Waterford, of
Wexford, of O'Neachachs in the province of Munster, of Cor-
coluigheach, and of Jobh Cinsealach. These, when they were
united, made a formidable body, and the king of Munster at
the head of them marched to Athlone, where he was met by
the principal nobility of the province of Conacht, who had prepared hostages of the first quality, and delivered them up as a
security for their future submission and obedience to him as
king of Ireland. Here likewise he received hostages from
Maolseachluin, king of Ireland, who was not capable of meeting him in the field, and therefore was obliged to confess himself a tributary prince, and pay homage to the king of Munster. Bryen Boiroimhe, attended by the confederate forces of
Munster, Leinster, Conacht, and Meath, directed his march
towards Dundalk, where he met with some opposition from the
people of Ulster, but they were subdued with small difficulty,
and the principal nobility of the province were taken prisoners.
A continued course of victory and success followed the arms of
this renowned prince, who having extended his conquests over
the most considerable part of the island, what remained voluntarily submitted; and thus he seized upon the crown, and was
proclaimed monarch of Ireland.

And worthy he was to command a kingdom of much larger
extent, for he was a prince invincible in arms, of great experience in military discipline, munificent to his friends, and mer-

2 H

ciful to his enemies. He had a great share in the affections of
the people, upon account of his many heroic victories and accomplishments; nor was it unjust or inglorious in him to make
an attempt upon the crown of Ireland, for it appears in this
history that the course of succession was often interrupted, and
hereditary rights laid aside; the monarchy was in some measure
elective, and generally fell into the hands of the most valiant
and beloved by the people; so that the aspersions that are fixed
by some authors upon the character of this Momonian prince,
for thrusting himself by violence into the throne of Munster,
are ill supported; nor did he violate any of the established
laws, or act contrary to the constitution of the kingdom. The
greatest part of the island he subdued by his arms, for he forced
under his obedience all who refused to confess his authority;
but the justice and natural clemency of his temper soon procured him the affections of the people of all ranks and conditions, so that he was proclaimed by universal consent, an I
Maolseachluin was obliged to resign the sceptre, and retire
peaceably to the state of a subject.

Bryen Boiroimhe was now in possession of the throne. He
was the son of Kennedy, son of Lorcan, son of Lachtna, son of
Cathal, son of Corc, son of Anluan, son of Mahon, son of Tur-
lagh, son of Cathol, son of Hugh Caomh, son of Eochaidh Bal-
dearg, son of Carthan Fionn, son of Bloin, son of Cais, son of
Couall Eachluath, son of Luighdheach Meann, son of Aongus
Tireach, son of Fearchorb, son of Modhchorb, son of Cormac
Cas, son of Oilioll Ollum, descended from the royal line of Heber
Fionn, and governed the kingdom twelve years. The mother
of this warlike prince was Beibhionn Cianog, the daughter of
Archadb, king of the western part of the province of Conacht.
There were many memorable transactions happened during the
reign of this prince, particularly an attempt of Sitric, the son
of Humphry, general of the Danes. This foreigner, with a
number of his countrymen, fitted out a fleet, and plundered the
coasts of Ulster with great cruelty; he likewise destroyed an I
ransacked Cill Cleithe, and Ines Comeasgraidh, and carried off
very valuable spoils and many prisoners.

After these outrages of the Danes, the pious Naomhan, son
of Maolciarain, primate of Ireland, was translated to a better
life; and about the same time died Randle, the son of Goffra,
king of the isle of the Danes. Bryen Boiroimhe, king of Ireland, with a strong body of troops, marched to Cineal Eogain,
in the province of Ulster, and from thence he directed his

course to Meath, where he continued for the space of a week; and being a prince of singular piety, he laid twenty ounces of gold upon the altar of Ardmach as an oblation. He proceeded from thence with his army to Dalnaruidhe, where the principal nobility of Ulster met him with their hostages, whom they delivered to him as security for their future obedience. Soon after this he removed to Tyrconnel, where he likewise received hostages from the principal nobility of that country, who confessed his authority, and paid him homage as a prince in actual possession of the throne, and therefore as the lawful monarch of the kingdom.

About this time Maolruana, the son of Ardgail, king of Ulster, died; as did likewise the learned Clothna, son of Aongus, the principal poet of Ireland, and Cathall O'Connor, who governed the province of Conacht for twenty years, and expired at Inis Domhnain.

The provincial troops of Munster and Leinster, under the conduct of Mortough, the son of Bryen Boiroimhe, made incursions and plundered Cineal Luigheach. There attended him in this expedition Flathbhertach, the son of Muireadhach, who raised a resolute body of the martial tribe of the O'Neills, and did great execution upon the enemy. In this attempt the spoils that were carried off amounted to a great value, and the number of prisoners was 300. The king of Ireland likewise, at the head of a formidable army, marched to Magh Coruinn, and surprised Maolruadhna O'Doraidh, king of Cineal Conuill, and carried him prisoner to Cean Coradh. Mortough, the son of the king of Ireland, a valiant and warlike prince, entered the province of Leinster with fire and sword, and raged over the country in a terrible manner, as far as Glean da Loch, and from thence he led his victorious army to Kilmainham. The Danes about this time set to sea and landed upon the coasts of Munster, where they committed dreadful ravages, and plundered Cork and then set it on fire. But the divine vengeance pursued these savage barbarians; for soon after these hostilities, Humphry, the son of Sitric, king of the Danes, and Mathghamhuin, the son of Dubhgoil, son of Humphry, were seized by stratagem and murdered by Daniel Dubhdabhoireann. About this time the Lagenians, in conjunction with the Danes of Leinster, entered the country of Meath, and plundered Tarmuin Feicinn with great cruelty, and carried away a multitude of prisoners. But the hand of God was distinguished in the punishment of these ravagers, for they perished soon after by exemplary inflictions from heaven.

Bryen Boiroimhe, having fixed himself in the absolute possession of the throne of Ireland, and suppressed by force of arms the unruly Danes, and others who opposed him, resolved to settle the disordered state of his dominions, and repair what the fury of the civil wars had destroyed. In the first place he judged it would contribute to his future security, to bestow some popular favours upon the principal nobility and gentry of the kingdom, whom by degrees he so obliged, by conferring very valuable rights and privileges upon them, that instead of disturbing his reign with new commotions, they were overcome by his clemency and indulgence, and approved themselves a loyal and obedient people. This generous and princely conduct fixed him in the affections of his subjects, and obtained him the character of a worthy and munificent prince. By this time a general peace and tranquillity prevailed throughout the island, which afforded a proper opportunity to the king of Ireland to rebuild and repair the churches and religious houses which the wicked Danes had destroyed. He summoned together all the clergy of whatever order, who had been ejected by these cruel sequestrators during the time of the public troubles, and inquiring strictly into the rights and pretensions of every one, he restored them all to their several rights, and filled the cathedrals and abbeys with the members that belonged to them. The revenues likewise of the church, which had been seized by the sacrilegious Danes, and perverted to abominable purposes, he recovered and established them upon their original foundations.

The face of religion being thus cleared up, his next care was to provide for the education of youth; and for that end he repaired the public schools, that had been destroyed by the Danes, who were professed enemies to learning, and erected new academies where they were wanting in several parts of the kingdom. In these nurseries the liberal sciences and all the branches of human learning were taught; public libraries were built for poor students, and a provision made for youth of promising hopes, who were unable to support themselves. And thus were the universities enriched and governed by regular discipline, which had that effect as to train up persons of excellent abilities in all professions, who revived the decayed state of learning, and not only concerned themselves in instructing the youth of their own kingdom, but were of excellent use in polishing the rugged and illiterate disposition of the neighbouring nations.

The commons likewise of the king lom, who were lords of lands, the farmers, and the lowest degree of the people, were endowed with large immunities by the munificence of this prince, who bestowed upon the native Irish whatever territories he conquered from the Danes; and if those who were the original proprietors were alive, and could give evidence of their right, they were settled in their former possessions and confirmed in them. This prince kept his court free from sycophants and favourites; nor would he enrich his nearest relations by oppressing the meanest subject in the island. He it was that appointed sirnames of distinction to all the several branches of the Milesian race, and to other principal families in Ireland, in order to avoid confusion, and that the genealogies might be preserved with more regularity. Among other public structures this prince erected the great church of Killaloe, and the church of Inis Cealtrach, and repaired the steeple of Tuam Greine, that was ruinous and decayed. He likewise laid causeways throughout the kingdom, and mended the high roads for the ease of travellers, which was an act very popular to his subjects. He built garrisons, and raised fortifications in proper places, where he kept a standing force, to be ready upon all exigencies and necessities of the state. He also fortified the royal palaces of Cashel, of Cean Feabradh, of Inis Locha Cea, of Inis Locha Guir, of Dun Eochair Maighe, of Dun Jasg, of Dun Trilliag, of Dun Gerott, of Dun Cliach Insi an Gaill Ducbh, of Inis Locha Saighlean, of Rosna Riogh, of Ceann Coradh, of Boiroimhe, and of all the royal forts in the province of Munster. He built bridges over rivers and deep waters that were impassable before; and repaired and purged the corruptions that had crept into the established laws; and inspired his subjects with such a spirit of honour, integrity, and virtue, that a young lady of excellent beauty undertook a journey from the north of Ireland, adorned with jewels and a most costly dress; and as a testimony of the security there was in travelling, she carried a wand in her hand, with a gold ring of great value fixed on the top of it, and arrived at a place called Tonn Cliodhna, which lay in the southern part of the island, and was at the utmost distance from the place she set out; yet such impressions had the good laws of Bryen fixed upon the minds of the people, that no person attempted to injure her honour, or to rob her of the ring that she carried openly upon a stick, or strip her of her clothes, which would have been a valuable booty. This transaction is delivered to posterity in a poetical composition of good authority, wherein are the lines following:

> The institutes of Bryen Boiroimhe,
> So wholesome for the support of virtue,
> Were kept with so much reverence and regard,
> That a young lady of consummate beauty,
> Adorn'd with jewels and a ring of gold,
> Travell'd alone on foot from north to south,
> And no attempt was made upon her honour,
> Or to divest her of the clothes she wore.

The kingdom of Ireland recovered from intestine and foreign wars, under the kind influence of the administration of this prince, who opened a scene of plenty and tranquillity to the inhabitants, which continued without interruption for the space of twelve years, which was the whole time of his reign. The state of happiness which prevailed throughout the island is recorded in the verses subjoined:

> The most renowned Bryen Boiroimhe
> Govern'd the isle in peace; and through his reign
> The Irish were a brave and wealthy people,
> And wars and discords ceased.

The historians of those times reckon this excellent prince in the number of the heroic and munificent kings that sat upon the throne of this kingdom. They always mention him as the third whose conduct and heroic virtues raised the reputation of the Irish, and made them formidable to their enemies. The first of these excellent monarchs they esteem to be Conaire the great, the son of Eidirsgeoil; the second was Cormac, the son of Art, son of Conn, the renowned hero of the hundred battles; and the third was the most illustrious Brien Boiroimhe, king of Ireland. This magnificent prince supported his royal grandeur by a splendid court, and kept a most sumptuous and hospitable table suited to his dignity. The quantity of provisions that were daily consumed is scarce credible. The place of his residence was Ceann Coradh, where his retinue was becoming the majesty of an Irish monarch, and whither the three provinces of the island brought their subsidies and contributions, which were very large, to defray the expenses of his royal court, beside the constant revenue which arose from the two provinces of Munster. and was paid yearly into his exchequer. An account of these particulars is transmitted to us by a celebrated poet and antiquary, in a poem which begins in these words, Boiroimhe baile na Riogh. This writer expressly relates the constant tribute both of provisions and other necessaries that was paid, not only by the two provinces of Munster, but by the other three provinces of the island. The particulars are specified in the following order : 2670 beeves, 1370 hogs, 180 loads or tons of iron, 325 hogsheads or pipes of red wine, and 150 pipes of other wines of various sorts, and 500 mantles. These annual tributes,* appointed for the use and service of the crown, were laid by public laws upon the several countries of the island, and in the following proportion : 800 cows and 800 hogs were fixed upon the province of Conacht, and appointed to be sent in annually upon the first day of November ; 500 cloaks or mantles, and 500 cows, were to be supplied from the country of Tyrconnel ; 60 hogs, and 60 loads or tons of iron, was the yearly tribute of the inhabitants of Tir Eogain ; 150 cows, and 150 hogs, were to be paid by the Clana Rughraidhe, in the province of Ulster ; 160 cows was the contribution of the Oirgiallachs ; 300 beeves, 300 hogs, and 300 loads or tons of iron, were to be paid by the province of Leinster ; 60 beeves, 60 hogs, and 60 loads or tons of iron, were provided by the people of Ossery ; 150 pipes or hogsheads of wine was the proportion of

* Let 'l of e Public Rights, regarding both the king of Munster and the subordinate princes and states of the same province: extracted from Gen. Vallancey's Collect. de Rebus Hibernicis, Vol. I. No. III. p. 874, &c.

I. The king of Munster, (who was also called the king of Cashel, from his residing at that place,) presented by way of subsidy every year, ten golden cups, thirty golden-hilted swords, and thirty horses in rich furniture, to the Dal-Cassian king, whenever he was not the sovereign of all Munster, to which he had an alternate right by the will of Olliol Olum. In some copies of the book of rights, I find added to the above presents, ten coats of mail, two cloaks richly adorned, and two pair of chess-boards of curious workmanship.

II. To the king of Eoganact Caisil, when the Dal-Cassian chief became king of Munster according to his alternative, ten men slaves, ten women slaves, ten golden cups, and ten horses in full furniture.

III. To the king of Ossery, otherwise called the king of Gabhran, ten shields, ten swords, and two cloaks with gold clasps and rich embroidery. The prose mentions ten horses, ten shields, ten cloaks, and two suits of military array.

IV. To the king of Ara, six swords, six shields of curious workmanship, and six scarlet cloaks. The prose adds, seven shields, seven swords, and seven horses.

V. To the king of Eile, six men slaves and six women slaves, six shields, and six swords; according to the prose, eight coats of mail, eight shields, eight swords, eight horses, and eight cups.

VI. To the king of Uaithne, six shields, six swords richly mounted, and six horses magnificently accoutred, and particularly with golden-bitted bridles: according to the prose, seven horses, eight swords and eight cups, together with particular marks of honour and distinction shown him at the court of Cashel.

the Danes who inhabited the city of Dublin, and 365 pipes or hogsheads of red wine was the yearly tribute demanded from the Danes of Limerick.

The great revenues that were paid annually into the exchequer of this prince, by the several counties throughout the island, are an evident testimony of the pomp and grandeur of his royal court at Ceann Coradh, with what liberality and magnificence he supported his princely character, and how he exceeded the munificence and state of most of his predecessors. It would be inconsistent with the brevity of this chronicle, to take particular notice of all the virtues and accomplishments of this Irish monarch, and of the several laws which he ordained for the government of his kingdom. Among the rest, what injunctions he established for regulating the precedency of the nobility, when they took their places in the public assemblies convened by his summons; of which the curious may be thoroughly informed by having recourse to the poetical composition above mentioned, where the several orders are at large expressed; but it may not be improper to observe in this place, that none, of whatever quality, were permitted to wear arms in the court of this prince, but the noble tribe of the Dailgais, as the following verses testify:

VII. To the king of Deisies, a ship well rigged, a gold-hilted sword, and a horse in rich furniture: by the prose, eight ships, eight men slaves, eight women slaves, eight coats of mail, eight shields, eight swords, and eight horses.

VIII. To the king of Cairbre Aodhbha, whose principal seat was Brughrigh, ten slaves made captive in a foreign country, as appears from the plain text of the verse, viz., Deith Gaill gan Gaedhilga: the prose has seven bondslaves, seven freeservants, seven swords, and seven cups.

IX. To the king of Conall Gabhra, the following privileges and presents, viz., while the king of Conal Gabhra remained at the court of Cashel, he had the honour to sit near the king at table, and at his departure from court was presented with a horse in rich furniture, and a military suit of array, and all his attendants received the like presents proportioned to their respective ranks: according to the prose, the whole was only ten shields, ten swords, ten horses, and ten cups.

X. To the king of Aine Cliach, a sword and shield of the king's own wearing, and thirty cloaks, which were given him in the month of May, precisely according to the verse, Is triocad brat gach Beiltine; the prose has eight swords, eight horses, eight cups, two coats of mail, and two cloaks.

XI. To the king of Fearmuighe or Gleanamhain, one horse richly accoutred, one shield curiously wrought, and one sword: by the prose, seven horses, seven shields, and seven cups.

XII. To the king of Aiobh Liathain, a sword and shield of the king's own wearing, one horse richly accoutred, and one embroidered cloak: according to the prose, five horses, five swords, five cloaks, and five cups.

XIII. To the king of Musgruidhe, one of the king's own swords, one of his horses, and one of his hounds: the prose allows seven horses, seven coats of mail, and seven suits of complete armour.

The most illustrious tribe of Dailgais
Alone were honour'd with the privilege
Of wearing arms when they appear'd at court.

Bryen Boiroimhe having thus established his revenues, and by his munificence and other virtues recovered the ancient character of the Irish, that had been declining for some ages, resolved to build some shipping and become formidable at sea. For this purpose he sent to Maolmordha Mac Murchuda, desiring that three of the longest and largest masts that could be found in his territories should be sent to him. The request was immediately granted by the provincial prince, who ordered his woods to be surveyed, and the fairest trees to be cut down and hewed by shipwrights, and sent to the court of Ceann Coradh, and came himself to present them to the king of Ireland. The first of these masts was carried by the inhabitants of Jobh Failge, the second by the people of Jobh Faolain, and the third by those of Jobh Muireadhuig. In their way, as they came through Sliabh and Bhoguig, or as other authors assert, at a remarkable bog near the wood where the trees grew, there arose a violent contest between the three tribes, that were appointed to carry the masts, about the point of precedence; and the

XIV. To the king of Raithleann, ten swords, ten scarlet and ten blue cloaks, and ten cups: according to the prose, ten horses, ten coats of mail, and ten shields.

XV. To the king of Dairinne, seven ships, seven coats of mail, and seven swords: by the prose, seven ships, seven coats of mail, seven horses, seven swords, and seven cups.

XVI. To the king of Leim-con, a ship in full rigging, one horse in rich furniture, one cup curiously wrought, and one sword: in the prose, seven ships, seven horses, seven coats of mail, seven shields, and seven swords.

XVII. To the king of Loch-lein, ten ships, ten dun horses, and ten coats of mail: by the prose, seven ships, seven horses, seven coats of mail, seven shields, and seven swords.

XVIII. To the king of Ciaruidhe, ten horses well accoutred, and a silk cloak according to the prose, seven cloaks with gold clasps, seven horses, and seven cups.

XIX. To the king of Dairbre, three ships well rigged, and three swords: according to the prose, seven horses, seven hounds, and seven cups: and so on to other petty kings and states, too tedious to be mentioned; every one of which he complimented with a proportionable present, by way of an annual subsidy."

"The Fiscal Tributes, the manner of paying them, agreeably to the primitive times, will be sufficiently exemplified by the following entries, faithfully translated word for word, out of the ancient record, called Leabhar na gcort, or The book of Irish rights.

i. The king of Cashel or Munster received a yearly tribute of 1000 bullocks, 1000 cows, 1000 wethers, and 1000 cloaks, from the inhabitants of Burren,

dispute was, which of those tribes should go foremost with their
burden, and be first admitted into the presence of the king of
Ireland. This controversy was carried on with great heat and
animosity on all sides, and at length came to the ears of Maolmordha, king of Leinster, who, instead of behaving as a neuter
in the quarrel, immediately got from his horse and declared himself
in favour of the tribe of Jobh Faolain. He rushed into the midst
of the throng, and by force coming to the mast that belonged to
that tribe, he clapped his shoulders under it as a common
bearer, and took his share of the burden with the rest. But
in the struggle he made to distinguish himself upon this occasion, the silver button that kept together his rich mantle flew
off and was lost. This mantle, worn by the king of Leinster,
was made of the richest silks, embroidered in a splendid manner with gold and silver; the bottom of it was fringed about
with a lace of inestimable value, and had some time ago been
presented to this prince by Bryen Boiroimhe, king of Ireland.

The king of Leinster interposing by his authority in this dispute, the tribes proceeded leisurely in their journey, and by
slow marches arrived at Ceann Coradh, where they were courteously received, and were honourably rewarded by the king.
The king of Leinster was admitted into the court, where he was

II. From the inhabitants of Corcamruadh, 1000 bullocks, 1000 cows, 1000
sheep, and 1000 cloaks.

III. From the people of Corcabhaiscin, 1000 bullocks, 1000 wethers, 1000
hogs, and 1000 cloaks.

IV. From the inhabitants of Corcaduibhne, 1000 bullocks and 1000 cows; but
according to the poem beginning with the words, "Cios Casil Accualabhair,"
it is added, 30 scarlet cloaks, 30 bullocks, and 30 milch cows.

V. From those of Ciaruidhe, 1000 bullocks, 1000 cows, and 1000 hogs.

VI. From the people of Seactmadh, 100 bullocks, 100 cows, and 100 hogs:
according to the poem, they were to pay only 60 bullocks, 60 cows, and 60 black
wethers.

VII. From the inhabitants of Corcaluighe, 100 bullocks, 100 cows, and 100
hogs.

VIII. From the people of Musgruidhe, 1000 cows and 1000 hogs; though
other accounts add 300 beeves, 300 hogs, 100 milch cows, and 100 cloaks.

IX. From the inhabitants of that part of Fearmuighe which belonged to
O Dugain, of the race of Ir, son of Mileadh, 40 bullocks, 40 beeves, and 40
milch cows.

X. From the people of the Desies, 1000 bullocks, 1000 milch cows, 2000
hogs, 1000 sheep, and 1000 cloaks.

XI. From those of Uaithne, 300 milch cows, 300 hogs, 100 bullocks, and 300
cloaks.

XII. From the inhabitants of Ara, 100 cows, 100 hogs, 200 wethers, and
100 green cloaks.

XIII. From the people of Ossory, 700 cows and 700 cloaks; beside the obli-

welcomed by his sister, whose name was Gormfhlath, and who, by her marriage with Bryen Boiroimhe, was acknowledged queen of Ireland. After the usual ceremonies were past between the brother and sister, the king of Leinster desired the queen that she would be pleased to fix a button upon his mantle, in the place of one he had lost, in a dispute that arose between the tribes that were appointed to carry the masts, which he was proud of the honour of bearing upon his shoulders, as a testimony of his subjection and obedience to her husband, the king of Ireland. The queen, reflecting upon the glory of her ancestors, who never paid homage to any prince in the world, was so incensed at this servile disposition of her brother, that she upbraided him severely for his cowardice and meanness of spirit, degenerating from the courage and bravery of his family, and submitting to a yoke that was never worn by any of her illustrious house, and by that means entailing bondage and slavery upon all his posterity; and pulling the mantle from his shoulders with indignation, she threw it into the fire.

The king of Leinster was moved with this violent and bold

---

gation incumbent on the king of Ossery of supplying the king of Munster with his contingent of armed men, when demanded upon any necessary occasion and so on from different other countries and petty states: all which supplies were to be paid in by those different people at stated times and certain seasons of the year.

N.B.—The Dailgais, and the following tribes and principalities, were exempted from paying this kind of fiscal tribute to the king of Munster, as is set forth in The book of rights, but more at large in the Irish poem beginning with the words, A eolcha mumhan moire, viz.:—

1. Eoganact Cashel. 2. Eoganact Aine; 3. Eoganact Gleannamhain; 4 Eogonact Raithlean; 5. Eoganact Locha Lein; 6. Eoganact Graffan; 7. Aoibh Liathain; 8. Ua Cconuill Gabhra; 9. Aoibh Cairbre Aodhbha; 10. Eile y Fhogurtha. In a word, all the tribes descended from Olliol Olum, by his three sons, Eogan More, Cormac Cass, and Cian, were considered as free states exempted from the payment of this sort of annual tribute for the support of the king's household."

"Subsidiary Presents made by the king of Munster to the different pentarchs or provincial kings, and other princes of Ireland, in his royal tour to those princes, as the same is described in The book of rights.

1. The king of Munster, attended by the chief princes of his kingdom, began his visits with the king of Connaught, and presented to him 100 steeds, 100 suits of military array, 100 swords, and 100 cups; in return for which, he was to entertain him for two months at his royal palace of Cruachan, and then escort him to the territories of Tyrconnell.

II. He presented to the king of Tyrconnell, 20 steeds, 20 complete armours, and 20 cloaks, for which the said king supported him and the nobility of Munster, for one month, at his palace of Boisruadh, and afterwards escorted him to the principality of Tyrone.

remonstrance from his sister, but suppressed his passion at that time, and made no reply; but the next day it happened that Morrough, the son of Bryen, and Conuing, the son of Dunchuain, were playing at tables, (though other writers assert that the confessor of St. Caomhgin of Glindaloch was engaged in the game with Morrough,) and the king of Leinster stood by, that as an unfair spectator he advised Conuing to make a point on his tables, which had that effect, that Morrough lost the game. This ungenerous behaviour was so resented by the prince of Ireland, that, among other things delivered in passion, he told the king of Leinster that it was by his advice that the Danes lost the battle of Gleann Madhma; which charge occasioned the king of Leinster to reply, that if the Danes were defeated by his advice, he would soon put them in a way to retrieve their loss, and have full revenge upon himself and his father, the king of Ireland. The prince made answer, that those foreigners had been so often chastised by the Irish army, that he stood in no fear from any attempt they could make, though the king of Leinster was at the head of them. Maol-

III. He presented to the king of Tyrone, 50 steeds, 50 swords, and 50 cups; for which this king entertained him and his court for a month at his palace of Oiligh, and then conveyed him to Tulach-og.

IV. He gave the king of Tulach-og 30 sorrel steeds, 30 swords, and 30 cups; in return for which this dynast treated him and his suit for twelve days at Drumchla, and thence escorted him to the principality of Orgialla.

V. He presented the king of Orgialla with 70 steeds, 70 suits of military apparel, and eight corslets; in gratitude of which the said prince was to entertain him and his nobility for one month at his palace of Eamhain, and afterwards to escort him to the kingdom of Ulster.

VI. To the king of Ulster he presented 100 steeds, 100 swords, 100 cloaks, 100 cups, and 100 bed-covers or counterpoints curiously wrought; in consideration of which royal present, this king regaled him and his retinue for two months at his palace of Boirce, and then waited upon him with the princes and noble of his court to the kingdom of Meath.

VII. He presented to the king of Meath 100 steeds, 30 complete armours, 30 corslets, and 30 cloaks; for which the said king treated him and his court for one month in his palace of Teamhair or Tara, and afterwards escorted him with 100 of his own chiefs to the kingdom of Leinster.

VIII. He presented the king of Leinster with 30 bond-women, 30 steeds, 30 cups, and 30 rich bed-covers; in return of which he was entertained for two months by the two kings of the north and south parts of Leinster; and then the said kings, together with their nobles, were to accompany him to the principality of Ossery.

IX. He presented the king of Ossery with 30 horses, 30 corslets or coats of mail, and 30 swords: for which this king was to entertain him at his palace of Gowran for one month, and then to escort him to the territories of his own kingdom."

mordha immediately retired to his chamber, and overcome with reflecting upon the indignity he had received, he refused to eat or drink publicly, as his custom was ; and lest the prince of Ireland should find means to seize upon his person, and prevent ais return, he rose early the next morning, and left the court, full of indignation and desire of revenge, which he resolved to put in execution the first opportunity.

The king of Leinster was soon missing, and Bryen Boiroimhe, considering that he was gone without the ceremony of taking leave, was resolved if possible by fair means to induce him to return ; and for that purpose he dispatched a messenger after him, to desire he would come back to Ceann Coradh, and receive a present from the king of Ireland, which he had provided as an acknowledgment for his past services. The messenger overtook the king upon the east side of the river Shannon, near Killaloe ; and having delivered his message from his master, Maolmordha in his passion struck him violently thrice upon the head, with a cane which he held in his hand, by which means he fractured his skull. The name of this messenger was Cogaran, who by reason of his wound was obliged to be carried back to Ceann Coradh in a litter : from this unfortunate person, Jobh Cogaran, in the province of Munster, received its name. Upon his return, relating the cruel circumstances of his usage, the household troops desired leave to pursue the king of Leinster, and bring him to answer for this barbarous treatment of the king's messenger, who represented the king ; and therefore it reflected upon his majesty's honour, to permit an indignity of this nature to pass unpunished. But the king of Ireland, considering that Maolmordha had received an affront in his palace, against the laws of hospitality, appeased the fury of his guards, and told them he would chastise the insolence of the king of Leinster at his own doors ; and so permitted him to make his escape, and to return with safety into his own province.

Immediately upon his arrival the king of Leinster summoned a convention of the principal nobility and estates of his country ; and representing the usage he received at the court of Ceann Coradh, and relating the indignity of the action in the most aggravating circumstances, the whole assembly came instantly into a resolution to join the power of the Danes, and to fall upon the king of Ireland ; which design was soon after executed in the battle of Clountarffe, as will be particularly mentioned in the course of this history.

It must be observed in this place, that Bryen Boiroimhe, king of Ireland, had the honour of his country so much at heart, that by his authority he expelled all the Danes throughout the island, except such as inhabited the cities of Dublin, Wexford, Waterford, Cork, and Limerick, whom he permitted to remain in the country for the benefit of trade ; for these foreigners were a mercantile people, and by importation supplied the kingdom with commodities that served both for pleasure and use, and by this means were a public advantage to the whole nation ; the king of Leinster determined to prosecute his design, and for that purpose he dispatched his messengers to the king of Denmark, to desire the assistance of auxiliary forces against the king of Ireland, who had erected a tyranny in the island, and used the Danes with great barbarity, and forced them to abandon their possessions in the country. The Danish king complied with his solicitations, and selecting a choice body of his army, consisting of 12,000 men, he placed them under the command of two of his sons, Carolus Cnutus and Andrew, who safely arrived with them at the port of Dublin.

The king of Leinster having received this foreign aid, sent a herald to Bryen Boiroimhe, to challenge him to fight him at Clountarffe ;[*] by this time the king of Ireland had intelligence

---

[*] The following beautiful description of the memorable battle of Clontarf, from the annals of Innisfallen, extracted from Gen. Vallencey's Coll. de Rebus Hib. Vol. I. No. IV. p. 525, &c., may not be unacceptable to the reader.

" Brien, hearing of the immense preparations of the Danes and Lagenians, and of the landing of very considerable Danish auxiliaries from Denmark, Norway, Sweden, the Orkney Islands, the Islands of Shetland, the Hebrides, the Isle of Man, the Island of Lewis, the Isle of Sky, Cantire and Cathness, both at and near the city of Dublin, marched at the head of his Momonian forces, joined by the troops of Meath and Connaught, under the command of their respective kings, Malachy and Teige, son of Cathal, son of Connor, and encamped, as he had done the year before, at Kilmainham, within full view of his enemies. Soon after the encampment of his army, he detached into Leinster a select body of troops consisting of the flower of his Dal-Cassians and the third part of the Eugenians, under the command of his son Donogh, unperceived by the enemies, charging them to return in two days' time, after they had annoyed the Lagenians, and destroyed their country. This expedition, which was designed for causing a diversion, had been approved of by Malachy and all the other princes of Brien's council: but in the mean time the treacherous and ungrateful king of Tara lost no time to send a trusty emissary to the Danish camp, to inform those foreigners of what had happened, entreating them in the most pressing manner to attack Brien the following day, and as an additional encouragement to them, he promised to desert from the monarch in the beginning of the action.

These advantageous offers of the king of Tara were soon accepted of by the Danes and Lagenians, insomuch that they spent the night in preparing for a

of the landing of the Danes, which news not only surprised the court of Ceann Coradh, but the whole kingdom was alarmed, as dreading the consequences of a war, which had so terrible an aspect, and might be attended with an issue fatal to the peace and liberty of the island. But the heart of Bryen was a stranger to fear, and therefore he accepted of the challenge, and collected all the force he was able, to repel this formidable conspiracy of natives and foreigners, and reduce the state to its former tranquillity; for this purpose he mustered the provincial troops of Munster and Conacht, which consisted of a number of martial clans, among whom were the posterity of Fiachadh Muilleathan with all their dependants. The posterity of Cormac Cas rose in defence of their country, which were branched out into several families, Jobh Bloid, Jobh Caisin, Clann Aongusa Cinnathrach, Cineal Baoth, Cineal Cuallachta, Cineal Failbhe, and Clan Eachach, with Ceallach, son of Dubhgin, Clan Cuilleain, Meanmain, the son of Assiodha, son of Sioda, son of Maolcluithe, Cineal Fearmach, with Maolmeadha, son of Baodan. There came likewise to the support of public liberty the sons of Kennedy, son of Lorcan, whose names were Dunchuain, Eichiarainn, Anluan, Lachtna, Cosgrach, Lorcan Seanachan, Ogan, Maolruadhna, and Aingidh; Morrough, the prince of Ireland, was

general action, and presented themselves at the first appearance of daylight before Brien's army on the plain of Clontarf, with colours displayed, and formed into three separate corps or divisions. The first was composed of the Danes of Dublin, under the command of their king Sitricus, assisted by the auxiliaries sent from Sweden, Norway, and Denmark, who were commanded by their generals Carrol and Anrud, the two sons of Euricus, king of Norway, Dolanus and Conmaolus, two famous officers, and Brodar, general of the troops of Denmark; and what was remarkable in those days, 1000 of these auxiliaries had their bodies covered with entire coats of brass. The second division consisted of the insular Danish auxiliaries, under the command of Sitricus, son of Lodar, earl of the Orkney Islands, who was an officer of distinguished experience and merit; and the last consisted of the forces of Leinster, under the command of Maolmordha Mac Murchada, principal king of that province, Baodan, son of Duluing, petty king of the western parts of Leinster, Mac Tuathil, king of Liffe, Mac Brogarvan, king of Ive Failge, and 1000 Danish troops to support them in the engagement.

Brien had no sooner reconnoitred the order of his enemy's battles, than he divided his own troops into three separate columns. The first was composed of the tribe of Dal-Cas, under the particular command of Brien in person, and of his son Morrogh. His four other sons, by name Connor, Flan, Teige, and Donnal, had also a particular share in the command of this corps. The other officers of distinction were Conuing, son of Donnchuan, son of Kennedy; as also Lonargan, Ceillochar, Fingalach, and Jonnrachtach. Beside the Dal-Casians, Malachy, king of Tara, with the forces of Meath, formed a part of this

resolved to distinguish himself in this expedition, and took with him his son Turlough and his five brothers, Teige, Donough, Daniel, Connor, and Flann. The sons of Dunchuain, the son of Kennedy, voluntarily offered their service to the king of Ireland; their names were Lonargan, Ceilliochair, Kennedy, Fiangolach, and Jonnrachtach. Eochaidh, son of Jonnrachtach, and Dubhgin, son of Eochaidh and Beolan, appeared at the head of their friends, relations, and dependants, to fight for the common cause against the king of Leinster who conspired with a foreign power to bring slavery upon his country. The king of Ireland was supported likewise by the assistance of Teige, the son of Morrough O'Kelly, king of O'Maine, who had raised a strong body of men out of the province of Conacht, and appeared at the head of them; and this gave encouragement to Maolruadhna na Paidre O'Heon, the prince of Aidhne, with many others of the first quality and interest in their country, to gather what strength they were able, which amounted to a considerable number, because of their near relation to Bryen Boiroimhe whose mother was a princess of that province. Maolseaohluin, the deposed king of Ireland, mustered all his forces in the country of Meath, and joined the whole body of the Irish army; with these auxiliaries Bryen Boiroimhe began to march, and di-

division, and was to supply instead of Donogh O'Brien and his party; and the whole corps was to attack the first division of the enemies.

The second division of Brien's forces consisted of the Conatians under the command of Teige, son of Cathal, son of Connor, principal king of Connaught, Maolruana, son of Heidhne, king of Fiachrach-Aidhne, Kelly, king of Ive-Maine. Flaherty, king of the west of Connaught, and Connor, son of Maolruana, king of Magh-Luirg. And these troops were supported by a strong body of Munstermen, under the command of Mortagh son of Corc king of Musgry-Cuire, Aodh son of Lochlin king of Conuagh, Donogh son of Cathal king of Musgry-Aodha, Donal son of Dermod, king of Corcobhaisgin, and Eichiaran son of Donagan, king of Ara. This whole corps was to engage the second division of the enemies, consisting of the insular Danish auxiliaries.

The last division of the king of Ireland's army was composed of the Eugenians and Desians, under the command of Cian son of Maolmuadh Mac Brain, and Donal son of Dubhdabhoirean, the two chief kings of Ive-Eachach; the other chief officers of note, who fought under them, were Mothla son of Felan king of the Desies, Mortogh son of Anamchada king of Ive-Liathain, Scanlan son of Cathal king of Loch-Leane, Loingsioch son of Duloing king of Connallgabhra, Cathal son of Donovan, king of Cairbre-Aodhbha, Mac Beathach king of Kerry-Luachra, Geibhionach son of Dubhgan king of Fermoy, Carrol king of Eile, with some others. This entire corps was supported by a considerable reinforcement of Ultonian troops, under the command of Carrol, principal king of Uirgiall, and Mac Guibhir king of Fearmanach, who were to supply the place of the absent Eugenians; and they were jointly to attack the third division of the enemy's army, consisting of the forces of Leinster.

rected his course to the plains of Magh Nealta, where he found the king of Leinster and the Danish forces expecting his arrival. Morrough O'Bryen was appointed general of the Momonians and the troops of Conacht ; but Maolseachluin, king of Meath, drew off his men from the Irish army, and refused to be concerned in the engagement ; for he thought to be revenged upon Bryen, who had robbed him of the crown of Ireland, and supposed that by his desertion at so nice a conjuncture, he should infuse a terror into the rest of the troops, and occasion the defeat of the whole army ; he therefore drew off with the forces of his country, and planted himself at a convenient distance in expectation of the event.

And now both armies being drawn up in order of battle, the sign was given, and the charge began dreadfully on both sides. The conduct of the officers, and the bravery of the soldiers, at first seemed equal ; there was no breaking of ranks, for every man stood immoveable in his post till he fell, and was supported with the same courage by those behind him. In this manner the fight continued doubtful and terrible, and victory for some time hovered in suspense over both armies, but at last, after great slaughter, and a most bloody contest, declared in favour of the king of Ireland ; for the Danes could not stand the

While Brien was employed in ranging his army in order of battle, he represented to his troops the indispensable necessity of distinguishing themselves in that action against a foreign enemy, who had been for some ages past the perpetual oppressors and murderers of their kings, dynasts, and clergy, without showing the least mercy to sex, character, or age, had so often spoiled and burned or pillaged their churches, and trampled under foot the most sacred relics of their saints. And, "I am convinced," says he, "that your valour and conduct will this day put an end to all the sufferings of your dear country, by a total defeat of those sacrilegious and merciless tyrants And what proves providential in our favour is, that we shall take full revenge of them for their constant acts of treachery, and for the profanation of so many churches this Friday in Holyweek, on which Jesus Christ had suffered an ignominious death for our redemption, who will undoubtedly be present with us, as a just avenger of his holy religion and laws." Saying these last words, he showed them the crucifix, which he held in his left hand, and his sword in his right, intimating thereby that he was willing to sacrifice his own life in the assertion of so just, so honourable a cause

After these words, he ordered the different corps of his army to fall upon the enemies with sword in hand, when to his great surprise, Malachy and the forces of Meath deserted their post, and retired with precipitation from the field of battle. This act of treachery and ingratitude, in so considerable an ally as Malachy, at the first setting out of the action, animated the Danes of the first division to such a degree, that the first attacks of their cuirassiers were almost insupportable; yet Brien and his corps, far from being daunted, maintained their ground with great firmness and intrepidity, redoubling their courage upon see-

shock, but were disordered, and a general rout soon followed ;
the forces of Leinster were so terrified by the flight of their
auxiliaries, that the defeat became universal, and the Irish following their blow, and animated with a prospect of victory,
drove the enemy out of the field.   In this engagement, which
concluded with the loss of many brave persons, fell the generals
of the Danes, Carolus Cnutus and Andrew, the sons of the king
of Denmark, whose death was attended by the chiefest foreigners who inhabited the city of Dublin, of whom 4000 were slain
in the first charge.   The unfortunate king of Leinster, whose
passion and inadvertency was the first occasion of the war, did
not survive the action of that day, and the principal nobility
and gentry of his province accompanied him as a retinue into
the other world ; the number of the Leinster forces that were
slain amounted to 3700.   Nor was the success of the victors
obtained without great slaughter of persons of the first quality
and distinction, among whom fell Murrough O'Bryen, and the
greatest part of the nobility of the two provinces of Munster
and Conacht, whose loss was followed by 4000 of the Irish army
who perished in the action.   The Danes were the greatest sufferers in this battle, but their loss was in some measure recom-
pensed by the death of Bryen Boiroimhe, whom they slew in

ing their tribe of Dal-Cas all alone, and without the mixture of any other troops
to share in the glory of their exploits : now it was, that a general and obstinate
fight began between the different corps of both armies, which lasted from soon
after the rising of the sun till late in the evening, at the expense of much blood
on both sides.   The Danes and Lagenians, after the loss of most of their commanders and troops, gave ground and fled for shelter to Dublin and to their
ships, but were so closely pursued by the victors, that very few of them arrived
at their places of refuge.   The Irish in this deroute of the Danes had the woe-
ful misfortune to lose their famous monarch Brien, who, after having shown pro-
digies of valour as well as of military skill in the general command of his army
during the whole action, pursued the enemies at the head of his corps, where he
was slain by Brodar, general of the auxiliaries from Denmark, by a stroke of a
battle-ax; but Brien at the same time gave him a thrust of his sword, of which
that Dane immediately expired.
    Brien's eldest son Morrogh, at the age of 63 years, did wonders in this action,
and slew several Danish officers of distinction, among whom were Carrol and
Anrud, the two sons of the king of Norway, as also Conmaol another famous
commander.   He in like manner slew Sitricus, son of Lodar or Lotharius, earl
of the Orkney Islands, and chief commander of the insular Danes, by dividing
him into two equal parts through his coat of brass from his head to his rump
with a single blow of his military axe.   For when his father had observed that
Danish commander make a great carnage of the Eugenians in the heat of the
battle, he commanded his son Morrogh to hasten and go to meet him, charging
him to check his proceedings if possible.   Morrogh soon obeyed this order, and
dispatched the Dane in the now described manner, and then returned without

their retreat, for a body of these foreigners in their flight chanced
to pass by the royal pavilion of the king, which when they
understood, they entered under the leading of Bruadar, who was
captain of those runaways, and finding the king of Ireland, they
drew upon him and slew him ; but the death of this monarch
was soon revenged by the Irish guards, who coming into the tent,
and seeing the king dead upon the ground, fell upon Bruadar
and his cowardly Danes and cut them all to pieces.

It may not be improper in this place to insert a list of the
principal of the Irish army who were slain in this engagement,
which upon the best survey stands as follows : Turlough, the
son of Morrough, son of Bryen, king of Ireland ; Conuing, the
son of Dunchuain, son of Kennedy ; Mothla, the son of Daniel,
son of Faolan, king of Deisie, in the province of Munster ; Eochaidh, the son of Dunadhaig, king of Clan Sganlan ; Niall
O'Cuin, and Cudoilaig, the son of Kennedy ; Teige, the son of
Morrough O'Kelly, king of O'Maine ; Geibhionach, the son of
Dubhagin, king of Fearmioys ; Maolruadhna na Paidre O'Heyn,
king of Aidhne ; Mac Beathaig, the son of Muireadhach, heir
apparent in the succession to the kingdom of Kerry Luachra ;
Daniel Mac Dermott, king of Corca Baisgin ; Scanlan, the son
of Cathall, king of Eoganacht Locha Lein ; Daniel, the son of

---

delay to his father's corps, at the head of which he performed great exploits, and
continued to press the enemies with such irresistible fury and strength, that his
right hand was entirely mangled from the repetition of his blows. After this
disability of his hand, the Norwegian prince Anrud above mentioned made towards him with sword in hand ; Morrogh endeavoured to parry his passes, and
then taking fast hold of him with his left hand, he lifted him above ground,
and shook him quite out of his coat of brass ; then prostrating him he leaned
upon his sword with his breast, and pierced it through Anrud's body. The Norwegian in the meantime drew Morrogh's knife or scimetar from his belt, and
gave him a mortal wound, of which he soon expired, after having made his
confession and received the holy communion of the body of Christ. Such was
the point of honour and way of fighting between the princes and chief commanders of all engaged armies in those days, as well as in the heroic ages of the
Romans and Greeks, witness the personal engagements of Æneas and Turnus ·
they generally encountered each other of both sides hand to hand during the
heat of the action. An ill-judged practice, unless it was their established discipline and maxim at the same time to have appointed lieutenants, who should
supply their place in the general command and direction of the action during
those personal engagements with each other.

Besides the Danish commanders slain by Morrogh, there also fell in the first
division of the enemy, Dolatus, an officer of note, Dubhgall, son of Aulavius,
and Giolla Curain, son of Gluniaran, two of the principal Danes of Dublin,
together with the greatest part of their troops. The Eugenians made a great
carnage upon the auxiliaries of the islands, and slew almost all their officers and
men. Maolmurdha, principal king of Leinster, Mac Tuathail, son of Gaire, a

Eimhin, son of Cainaig; Mormor Muireadhach sirnamed the Great, of the kingdom of Scotland, with many more of the gentry of the island, whose names are not transmitted, who fell in this memorable battle. This action happened in the year of our redemption 1034, upon Good Friday, as the lines of a poem particularly mention in this manner :

> The most renowned Bryen Boiroimhe,
> Was slain one thousand four-and-thirty years
> After the birth of Christ.

This monarch lived to a venerable old age, and lost his life in this engagement, after he had lived eighty-eight years. This computation is recorded in the same poem in the verses subjoined :

> In the most dreadful fight of Clontarffe
> Was slain the valiant monarch of the island,
> After a life of eighty and eight years.

The Irish army having obtained this signal victory, though with the loss of the most eminent officers and the principal nobility of the island, determined to break up and return home Accordingly they began their march, and the tribe of Dailgais,

Lagenian prince of great valour, Mac Brogarbhan, king of Ive-Failge, and most of the nobility of Leinster lay stretched on the plain. And the attention to slaughter alone was so great, that the victors, pursuant to the orders of Brien, did not lose time in making prisoners of war, but put all enemies to the sword without distinction. This account of the battle of Clontarf, which is inserted in my copy of the annals of Innisfallen, makes the number of the slain on the part of the Danes and Lagenians to amount to 13,800 men ; that is to say 4000 of the Danes of Dublin and Ireland, 6700 of the auxiliary Danes, and 3100 of the forces of Leinster. The Chronicon Scotorum, which gives but a very short sketch of this battle, still gives us a very good idea of the obstinacy with which it was fought, by saying, "that the like battle, or any equal to it, had not been fought in Ireland for many ages." But the account that chronicle gives of the number of Danes slain in this battle, falls short of the above computation, as it positively mentions, "that there were in all but 4000 Danes killed, among whom were 1000 brass-coated combatants," and is quite silent concerning the loss of the Lagenians. According to the account inserted in the Innisfallen annals, there were 4000 of Brien's forces killed during the engagement, and many wounded; but the Chronicon Scotorum gives no further account of it than that the loss of Brien was very considerable.

Besides our renowned monarch Brien Boiroimhe, and his illustrious son Morrough, with his son Turlough, a youth of fifteen years, there were several other Irish commanders of distinction killed by the enemy, of whom the most remarkable were Conuing, son of Donnchuan, Brien's brother's son, Mothla, son of Donal, son of Felan, king of Deisies, Eocha, son of Dunuidhe, Nial, son of Cuinn, and Cadula, son of Cinidhe, who were all three Brien's most intimate

and the posterity of Fiachadh Muilleathan happened to take the same rout, and came together as far as Mullach Maistean. Here the family of Fiachadh Muilleathan resolved to separate from the other tribe, who were under the conduct of Donough, the son of Bryen ; but before they parted they agreed to send a messenger to Donough, to demand his submission, and that he would relinquish his pretensions to the crown of Munster, which by ancient contract was to be alternately governed by both tribes ; they insisted farther that he should send hostages as a security for his obedience, for his father and uncle received hostages from them ; and now they resolved to vindicate their right, and to settle the succession in the ancient channel, as formerly stipulated between the two families. Donough was surprised at this message, and returned for an answer, that the submission they paid to his father and uncle was involuntary, and extorted from them by force, for the whole nation was compelled by arms into subjection and to deliver hostages ; and replied farther that they durst not be so insolent in their demands, if they had not taken the advantage of his misfortunes ; and that if the brave tribe of the Dailgais had not suffered so deeply in the last battle, he would, instead of giving up hostages, chastise them into their obedience, and oblige them to give sufficient security for their future conduct and submission. The forces of Desmond receiving this answer, determined to fall

favourites and his aids-de-camp in the battle, Tiege, son of Kelly, king of Ive-Maine, Maolruana, son of Heidhin, king of Aidhne, Geibhionach, son of Dubhgan, king of Farmoy-Feine, Mac Beothach, son of Muireadhach Claon, king of Kerry-Luachra, Donal, son of Dermod, king of Corcabhasgin, Scanlan, son of Cathal, king of Lough-Leane, Donal, son of Eimhin, son of Caine, with many other princes and heads of tribes, who are too tedious to be enumerated.

After the victory had been thus gloriously obtained by the Momonian and Conatian forces, Teige, son of Brien, and Cian, son of Maolmuadh, conveyed such of the wounded as were not judged incurable to the camp at Kilmainham, and applied medicaments and remedies to their wounds. As soon as the monks of Sord had heard of Brien's death, they came directly to the camp, and took the bodies of Brien and his son to Sord, and afterwards bore them to the religious house of St. Kiaran at Duleek, and those conveyed them to Louth, to which place Maolmuire, or Marianus, son of Eochadh, archbishop of Armagh, accompanied by his clergy, came for the bodies, and conveyed them in great solemnity to the cathedral church, where they offered masses for the repose of their souls, and continued their sacrifices, prayers, and watchings over the bodies for twelve days and nights without intermission. After which the body of Brien was solemnly interred in a monument of hewn marble, at the north side of the cathedral church, and the bodies of Morrough and his son Turlough, and of Conuing, son of Donnchuan, were interred in another tomb at the south side of the same church."

upon Donough unprepared as he was, and immediately stood to
their arms.   The tribe of the Dailgais, perceiving that they
were in instant danger of being set upon, commanded that their
sick and wounded, who were unfit for action, should be disposed
of in a strong garrison that was on the top of Mullach Maistean, and that the third part of the sound forces should be left
to guard and secure them from any attempts of the enemy, and
the remaining body should engage the Desmonian army, though
superior in number ; for the tribe of the Dailgais, after this de-
duction, amounted to no more than 1000 complete men, and the
enemy were full 3000.

But the wounded and sick resolved not to be separated from
their companions, and charmed with the bravery of their general, agreed, notwithstanding the anguish of their wounds, to
share in the common event and abide the issue of a battle.
Accordingly they refused to be put into garrison, and seizing
their weapons, and stopping their wounds with moss, they prepared for the fight.   This surprising courage of the Dailgais so
astonished the Desmonian army, that they desisted from their
pretensions, withdrew their forces, and continued their march
homewards ; the Dailgais likewise directed their course towards
Athy, which stands upon the bank of the river Barrow, and refreshed themselves with drinking of that stream.

But this illustrious tribe met with new difficulties in their
return, for Donough Mac Giolla Patrick, king of Ossery, having
raised a considerable army of his own subjects and the people
of Leinster, resolved to hinder the march of the Dailgais, and
oppose their journey through any part of his territories ; for
this purpose he sent out scouts and spies to attend the motions
of this tribe, and to bring him intelligence of every day's
march, since they began their journey from the battle of Clountarffe.   The king of Ossery had conceived an invincible hatred
against the Dailgais, because Bryen Boiroimhe had made his
father prisoner, and killed many of his subjects ; and therefore
he thought that it was seasonable for him at this time to take
revenge for the indignities his father had received, which he
proposed to accomplish by harassing the Dailgais, and cutting
them off in their return ; but before he begun hostilities he sent
a messenger to Donough, the general of that tribe, to Athy,
where he was encamped, to demand hostages from him, as security that he would not commit any outrages in passing
through his country, or if he refused, the king of Ossery would
oppose his march and prevent his return ; Donough received

his insolent demand with scorn and indignation, and instead
of complying returned for an answer, that he was amazed at
the baseness of the king of Ossery, for taking advantage of
the distress of his army; but notwithstanding his men were
fatigued by their long journey, he would decide the dispute with
him in a pitched battle, and give him ample satisfaction; and told
the messenger withal, that it was the greatest misfortune of his
whole life to be insulted by Mac Giolla Patrick, whom he ever
despised as below his notice; but now his circumstances were
so changed, as to put him under the contempt of a cowardly
prince, who had the insolence to demand hostages, or to challenge him into the field, where he did not doubt to make him
feel the force of his arms, and of his courageous followers, who
were justly esteemed invincible. The messenger, instead of returning the answer, presumed to dissuade Donough from his
design of fighting; and insisted that his men were in no capacity to engage with the forces of his master, whose army was
fresh and in good heart, and seemed impatient to enter into the
field. But Donough replied with his usual majesty, that if the
law of nations had not secured him from ill treatment, he
would instantly cut his tongue out for his insolence, and ordered
him out of his presence with this injunction, to tell his master
that he would meet him and his subjects of Ossery in the field
if he had but one man to stand by him.

With this answer the messenger returned, and Donough drew
up his men in order of battle. His sick and wounded he designed to commit to the charge of one third part of his army,
and with the rest he resolved to engage the enemy; but the
wounded soldiers, who were lying upon the ground, immediately
started up, and by the violence of the motion bursting open
their wounds, they desired their general not to leave them behind, but suffer them to have a part in the action; and stopping their wounds a second time with moss, they laid hold of
their weapons, and took their places in the ranks, resolved to
assist their companions, and come off with victory or bravely
die in the attempt. But most of them were so much reduced
by loss of blood, that they could not stand upon their legs;
and to remedy this misfortune, they desired the general that a
number of stakes should be cut in the neighbouring wood and
driven into the ground. Every wounded soldier was to be tied
fast to one of these piles, and then to be placed regularly between two sound men, which would have that effect, that their
sound companions would be ashamed to fly, and abandon them

in that helpless condition to the fury of the enemy; and therefore it would sharpen their courage to reflect that nothing but
victory could secure the lives of their distressed friends, who
would be cut off to a man, if they were not relieved by the
bravery of their fellow-soldiers. This proposal was put in execution, to the great surprise of the enemy, who judged that
they had nothing to expect but death or victory.

The army of Leinster and Ossery, under the command of
Mac Giolla Patrick, were astonished at the resolution of that
martial tribe, who were under arms expecting the sign of battle.
They positively refused to fight, and told the king in a mutinous manner, that nothing but a defeat was to be expected from
the bravery of the Dailgais; that the wounded were as eager
to engage as the sound, and therefore they would not r i wil-
fully into the jaws of lions, who would inevitably tear them to
pieces. Mac Giolla Patrick was ashamed, after he had given
the challenge, to retire without fighting, and upbraiding his
army with fear and cowardice, insisted that they had the advantage of numbers, that the enemy had but a handful of men,
worn out with grievous wounds and long marches, and that the
first charge must give them victory. But the courage of the
Dailgais, and their unexpected resolution, had impressed such
a terror upon the army of Leinster, that they absolutely refused
to engage with such desperate enemies; and the king fearing a
general mutiny and defection, was obliged to give over his design, and content himself with falling upon the Dailgais, and
by constant skirmishes and stratagems of war, to cut them off
in their retreat; and this method was so successfully executed,
that he annoyed the Dailgais, and destroyed more of their men
than he could possibly have done in a pitched battle. The conduct and experience of Donough was remarkable in making
good his retreat, and securing his men against the sudden attacks of the enemy; but notwithstanding all his diligence and
caution, he brought back into their own country no more of
that valiant tribe than 850; for a great number perished in
the battle of Clountarffe, and 150 were cut off in their return
by Mac Giolla Patrick, king of Ossery.

The memorable battle of Clountarffe makes such a figure in
the Irish history, that it may not be improper, over and above
what has been said, to take notice of a particular description of
that fight that was sent to Clan Colman, by Maolseachluin, the
son of Daniel, king of Meath, a month after the engagement.
"I never," says he, "beheld with my eyes nor read in history

ın account of a sharper and bloodier fight than this memorable
ıotion ; nor if an angel from heaven would descend and relate
:he circumstances of it, could you without difficulty be induced to
ʒive credit to it : I withdrew with the troops under my command, and was no otherwise concerned than as a spectator, and
ıtood at no greater distance than the breadth of a fallow field
ınd a ditch. When both the powerful armies engaged, and
ʒrappled in close fight, it was dreadful to behold how the swords
ʒlittered over their heads, being struck by the rays of the sun,
which gave them an appearance of a numerous flock of white
ıea gulls flying in the air ; the strokes were so mighty, and the
fury of the combatants so terrible, that great quantities of hair
torn or cut off from their heads by their sharp weapons, was
ıriven far off by the wind, and their spears and battle-axes were
ıo encumbered with hair cemented together with clotted blood,
:hat it was scarce possible to clear or bring them to their former
ırightness."

It was observed before that Maolseachluin, with his forces
:aised out of the country of Meath, though he joined the army
ıt Bryen Boiroimhe, as if he designed to fight in defence of his
:ause, yet when he came to the field of battle was so influenced
ıy the Danes that he withdrew, and at a distance was a spec-
:ator of the fight. Nor did Cineal Eogain, though he offered his
ıssistance to the king of Ireland, bear a part in the action of that
day ; for that monarch had such confidence in his own personal
:ourage, and the bravery of his army, that he told them, since
he had fought so many battles, and obtained so many victories,
without their auxiliary troops, he would not lay himself under
ın obligation at present, but would take the success or the defeat
ıf that day wholly upon himself.

A.D.
1039.
Maolseachluin again recovered the crown of Ireland,
and was the succeeding monarch after the death of Bryen
Boiroimhe, who was slain in the battle of Clountarffe,
and governed the island nine years, though some authors place
ten years to his second reign. This prince, in conjunction with
O'Neill and O'Maoldoruig, led a formidable army to the city of
Dublin, which he surprised, and after it was plundered by the
soldiers he set it on fire. The Danish inhabitants of that city,
who escaped the battle of Clountarffe, and were dispossessed of
their houses, united in a body and marched to Jobh Cinnseallach,
which they rifled and burned to the ground ; in this expedition
they ravaged the country with fire and sword, killed multitudes
of people, and carried off many prisoners. Soon after Maol-

seachluin entered the province of Ulster in a hostile manner, and when he had plundered the country he made slaves of the inhabitants. Near the same time Donagan, king of Leinster, with many of his principal nobility, were barbarously murdered in the palace of Teighe O'Ryan, king of Ondroua, by Donough Mac Giolla Patrick. About this time died the celebrated Mac Liag, who was the most eminent poet in the whole island. Maolseachluin not long after led his army into the country of Ussery, and killed Dungal Mac Giolla Patrick Mac Donough, and a great number of his subjects, and such as escaped the slaughter were made prisoners. There is a tradition, but upon what authority is uncertain, that this Irish monarch laid the foundation of St. Mary's abbey, in the city of Dublin, in the year of our redemption 1045; but of this we are assured, that in his last reign he followed the example of his predecessor, the great Bryen Boiroimhe, and he was a prince of exemplary goodness and devotion in the latter part of his life. He repaired decayed churches and monasteries, and re-established the public schools that were destroyed by the civil wars and brought to ruin; and it is asserted with great truth, in the annals of his reign, that he maintained 300 poor scholars at his own expense.

In the reign of Maolseachluin it was, that Sitric, the son of Humphry, struck out the eyes of Bran, the son of Maolmordha, son of Murchada, in the city of Dublin, after he had governed the province of Leinster for two years. The Danes who inhabited Dublin, under the conduct of Sitric, plundered Ceananus in a cruel manner, killed multitudes of people, and forced many more into slavery. About this time Ugaire, the son of Dunlaing, who was king of Leinster for three years, encountered the Danes of Dublin, and overthrew them in a pitched battle. Soon after this defeat Sitric, the son of Jomhair, who was governor of the Danes of Waterford, was killed by the king of Ossery; nor did Maolseachluin long survive, for he died at Cro Inis Locha Hainninn. After the decease of this prince, some of the chronicles of the island give an account of many monarchs in succession to the throne of Ireland; but it is a more probable opinion, that from the death of this king till the English arrived, there was no absolute monarch of the country, though there were several who assumed to themselves the names of kings. The island was governed afterwards by petty princes, as may be collected from the testimony of a poet, who has these lines:

> After the death of Maolseachluin,
> The famous son of Daniel, son of Donough,
> There was no monarch in the Irish throne.

A..D.
1048.

Donough, the son of Bryen Boiroìmho, succeeded Maolseachluin in the government of Leath Modha, and had likewise under his command the greatest part of the Irish dominions. This prince enjoyed a long reign of fifty years, as Florence Mac Carty asserts in his general history of Ireland, which computation is supported by the authority of other chronicles, which allow him the same time. Some writers contradict this opinion, and place the reign of this prince to no more than twelve years ; but the account of Florence Mac Carty deserves the preference, for he agrees with the number of years which passed from the death of Bryen Boiroimhe to the first arrival of the English, and therefore the last computation dissenting from that number is not to be believed or allowed of.

About this time it was that Harolt Conan, by others called Harott Coran, fled for refuge into Ireland, where he received honourable support and protection, becoming his grandeur and high quality. Many memorable transactions happened in the reign of Donough king of Ireland. In his time Humphry, the son of Sitric, who was commander of the Danes throughout the island, was taken prisoner by Mahon O'Riagan, king of Breag, and was obliged to purchase his freedom at no less an expense than 200 cows and twenty horses. In the year of our redemption 1073, Flathbheartach or Flaharty O'Neill, undertook a pilgrimage to Rome, which he accomplished : soon after Teigo O'Lorcain, king of Cinsealach, departed the present life, at Glen da Loch ; and about the same time died Gormflaith, the daughter of Morrough Mac Flinn, king of Leinster, who was mother to Sitric, the son of Humphry, commander of the Danes in Ireland. This lady was likewise the mother of Donough, the son of Bryen Boiroimhe. Near this time Arthurcileach O'Rourke, king of Breifne, committed great ravages, and plundered the church of Cluain Fearta Breanon, but was chastised the same day for this sacrilegious action by Donough, king of Ireland, who slew him, and destroyed most of his army. The city of Waterford was pillaged and ruined by Diarmuid Mac Maol Nambo, who, after he had secured the plunder set the town on fire, and burned it to the ground. This Diarmuid was at the same time king of Leinster. Cluain Mac Nois was soon after miserably spoiled, and afterwards burned by the people of Conmacine ; but their barbarity was sorely punished by the hand of God, who sent a pestilential distemper among them, which occasioned a great mortality, and the infection reached their cattle and carried off whole droves.

In the reign of this Irish prince, Carthach, the son of Justin, king of Eoganacht Cashel, was burned to death, with many persons of the first quality, in a house that was set on fire by Mac Lonargain, the son of Dunchuain. Soon after this accident, Donough, the son of Bryen Boiroimhe, was deposed from his government by the states of the kingdom, because he was concerned in the murder of Teige, a prince of great hopes, who was his elder brother. After his expulsion from the throne he was contented to lead a private life, and resolved to spend the remaining part of his days in piety and exercises of devotion ; and for that purpose he undertook a religious pilgrimage to Rome, where he died, and was buried in St. Stephen's abbey.

There are some at this day, who assert that the families of the Powers, the Plunkets, and Eustaces, are descended lineally from the posterity of this Donough, son of Bryen Boiroimhe ; but I could never find any authority to justify this opinion, either in prose or verse, excepting the composition of a modern poet of a late age, called Maolin Mac Bruadeadha, in a poem which begins with these words, Cuirfiod cumaoin ar chlointail. It must be observed in this place, that the foundation of this opinion depends upon an idle fictitious story, of no truth or probability, concerning what happened to this Donough atter he arrived at Rome. The legend says, that this prince, when he came to that city, got access to a lady, who was the daughter of an emperor, whom he enjoyed, and became the father of a son ; and from this son, it seems, descended the three families abovementioned. But in opposition to this story it must be considered, that Donough was fourscore and eight years of age before he undertook that pilgrimage ; and it is perfectly incredible, that a young princess could be disposed to receive into her arms a pilgrim of so advanced years ; neither is it to be supposed that if the lady were inclined, Donough, who came thither for devotion, would commit such wickedness, or gratify her desires upon the most importunate solicitations ; and these reasons, I presume, are sufficient to destroy the pretensions of these three families, since it is morally impossible that Donough should have a son at Rome by an emperor's daughter, from whom they value themselves for being descended. And as an unanswerable testimony upon this occasion, it must be observed that the book called Leabhar Andala, that was transcribed out of the book of Mac Eogan, about 400 years ago, as near as can be computed, asserts positively that Donough, the son of Bryen Boiroimhe, after he had finished his pilgrimage at Rome, took the religious habit in Saint Stephen's abbey, where he spent the remaining part of his life in piety and exercises of devotion. Besides it appears evidently to any one who peruses the chronicles of Ireland which are written by English authors, that upon the first arrival of the English in that country, Robert la Poer was among the first that landed in the island, from whom the families of the Powers and Eustaces originally sprung; as for the family of the Plunkets the same writers assert, that they are originally of foreign extraction, and descended from the Danes, and therefore have no claim to a descent from the ancient Irish, and by consequence not from Donough, the son of Bryen Boiroimhe, king of Ireland. .

A.D. 1098. Turlough was the succeeding monarch. He was the son of Teige, son of Bryen Boiroimhe, and governed the province of Munster, and the greatest part of the island, for the space of twelve years. The mother of this prince was Morling, the daughter of Giolla Bride, king of Cineal Fiachadh and Fear Ceall. Many transactions of importance happened in the reign of this king; Connor, the son of Maolseachluin, son of Floin, was inhumanly murdered by his own brother, whose name was Morough; Connor was at that time king of Meath, and his head was seized by force by Turlough, and removed from Cluain Mac Nois to Ceann Coradh, in order to be interred upon the Friday before Easter: but the day after the head was miraculously conveyed back to Cluain Mac Nois, (which is scarce credible,) by the prayers of the pious Ciaran.

In the reign of Turlough, William Rufus, king of England, had occasion for timber to build the roof of Westminster-hall; this was about the year of our redemption 1099; and not contented with the wood that grew in his own dominions, he sent a messenger to the king of Ireland, to desire leave to be furnished out of his country with a quantity sufficient for the work. In the preceding year a bishop, whose name was Malchus, was consecrated by Anselm, archbishop of Canterbury. About this time died Dearbhforguill, the daughter of Teige Mac Giolla Patrick, that was married to Torlough, king of Ireland; and he did not long survive, but was soon after removed to another life.

1110. Mortough may be properly said to succeed to the crown of Ireland. He was the son of Teige, the son of

Bryen Boiroimhe, and was king of Leath Modha and the principal part of the island, and sat upon the throne for twenty years. The mother of this prince was Ceallrach, the daughter of Ui Eine, who also had another son called Roger O'Connor. Mortough was a prince of great virtue and exemplary piety ; it was he who bestowed Cashel upon the clergy, as a testimony of his munificence and divine charity, in the first year of his reign, and confirmed it to them in the year of our redemption 1111.

This monarch summoned a general assembly of all the nobility and clergy of his kingdom, and ordered them by his royal summons to meet him at a place called Fiadh Mac Naongusa. The clergy of the island, who appeared in that convention, consisted of the persons following : Maolmuire O'Dunain, archbishop of the province of Munster, Cealach Mac Hugh, the comverb of St. Patrick, and vicar-general to the primate of Ardmach, eight other bishops of inferior diocese, 360 priests and priors, 140 deacons, and many other religious persons of all orders. In this convention were many wholesome laws and regulations established, not only for the government of the clergy, but of the laity likewise, throughout the kingdom ; soon after Maolmuire O'Dunain, archbishop of the province of Munster, was translated to a better life.

Another general convention was summoned in the reign of Mortough, in the year of our redemption 1115, by Giolla Easbuig, bishop of Limerick, who was then legate of Ireland, and the first person in authority over the whole assembly. The old book of Cluain Aidnach, in Leix, gives a particular account of this synodical meeting, and records the principal transactions that were debated and agreed upon in that assembly. This treatise relates, that in that convocation it was ordained that there should be twelve episcopal sees fixed in Leath Modha, which contained the southern half of the island ; and that the same number of bishops should be appointed in Leath Cuinn, which included the northern half: it was agreed likewise that two bishops should be settled in the country of Meath. In this convention the revenue of the clergy and the church lands were confirmed to the several bishops of the island, for their maintenance and support of the episcopal character, which lands were to be exempted from tribute and chief-rents and other public contributions, and so remain in that state of freedom and independency for ever. At this time the boundaries of all the dioceses in the island were distinctly laid out ; and it was established, that in the division of Leath Cuinn there should be twelve bishops beside the primate ; five being fixed in the province of Ulster, five in the province of Conacht, and two in the country of Meath, which make up the whole number. The primate had the government of Ardmach, and exercised a spiritual jurisdiction over the whole kingdom, over Clochar, Ardsratha, Derry, Coinire, and Dun da Leath Glass.

The seats of residence for the bishops of Meath were Damhliag and Cluain Joraird. The bishops in the province of Conacht resided at Tuam da Gualann, Cluain Frearta, Brenoian, Conga, Killala, and Ard Carna. The palaces of the bishops in Munster were, Cashel, where the archbishop of Leath Modha resided, Lismore or Waterford, Cork, Rathmoigh, Deisgirt, Limerick, Killaloe, and Emlioch Jobhair ; these seven seats were appointed for the bishops of Munster in that convention. In the province of Leinster were ordained five sees, viz., Killcuillin, Laghlin, Kildare, Glean da Loch, and Wexford, otherwise called Fearna ; which five sees being added to the seven in the province of Munster above-mentioned, make up the number of twelve, ordained in the division of the island distinguished by the name of Leath Modha. The reason why the see of Dublin is not taken notice of in this place is, because the bishop of that diocess generally received his consecration from the hands of the archbishop of Canterbury in England. Hanmer, the historian, very unjustly asserts in his chronicle, that the clergy of Ireland were under the spiritual jurisdiction of the archbishop of Canterbury, from the time of Augustine the monk to the reign of king Henry II. ; but he brings no evidence to confirm this opinion, nor is it possible for him to prove that the Irish clergy in general throughout the kingdom paid obedience to any of the prelates of Canterbury, except Lanfranc, Randulph, and Anselm ; nor at that time did the clergy in general throughout the kingdom pay obedience to these archbishops, but only such as lived in Dublin, Waterford, and Limerick, that originally descended from the Danes, or else were of the Norman race, who were derived from the same extraction. And as a testimony not to be denied upon this occasion, I appeal to the writings of that prodigy of learning and industry, archbishop Usher, who asserts the same upon good authority, and confutes this English historian beyond a possibility of reply. It appears therefore evidently, that the number of bishops in the province of Munster were six, and that six likewise were appointed over the province of Leinster, and all of them were under the spiritual power of the archbishop of Cashel, as arch-prelate of Leath Medha, in imitation of the form of government established in the state, which who-ever pleases may be fully informed of by turning back to the reign of Laogaire, king of Ireland.

The Irish synod, called the convocation of Rath Breasail, determined the boundaries of several dioceses, and fixed them in the manner following : the diocess of the bishop of Ardmach extended from Sliabh or Mount Breag to Cuill Cianachta, and from Biorr to Abhainmore. The diocess of the bishop of Clo-chair extended from Abhainmore to Gabhail Liuin, and from Sliabh or Mount Biatha to Mount Larga. The diocess of Ard Sreatha extended from Mount Larga to Carn Glas, and from Loch Craoi to Binn Fiobhne. The diocess of the bishop of Derry extended from Easruadh to Srubh Broinn, and from thence to Carn Glass. The diocess of the bishop of Cuinire extended from Binn Fiobhne to Torbuirg, and from port Mur-builg to Hollorba, and to Cuan Snamha Haighne, and from Gloin Riogh to Colbha Gearmann. The diocess of the bishop of Dun da Leath Glas is not laid out in the journal of this convention. The diocess of the bishop of Damhliag extended from Mount Breag to Carn Dun Cuair, and from Lochan na Hinrime eastwards to the sea. The diocess of Cluain Hioraird extended from Clochan eastwards to the Shannon, and from Vir Coilte to Cluain Conaire. The diocess of Cluain Fearta ex-tended from the Shannon to Buirinn, and from Eachtighe to Suca. The diocess of Tuam extended from Suca to Ard Carna, and from Athan Tearmon to the Shannon. The diocess of Conga extended from Abhain O'Broin in the north to Neamh-thain, and from Athan Tearmon westwards to Killala. The dioces s of Killala extended from Neimhthin to Easruadh, and from Cill Ard Bille to Srathan Fearainn. The diocess of Ard Carna extended from Ard Carna to Sliabh an Jaruinn, and from Ceis Corainn to Huircuilten. If the clergy of the province of Conacht will allow of these boundaries it will be a satisfaction to me, but it must be granted that there were but five biscop-rics in that province.

The diocess of the archbishop of Cashel extended from Mount Eibhlinne to the river Suir, and from Cnamh Coill by Tipperary to Grein Airbha, that is to Cross Greine westwards. The diocess of Lismore or Waterford extended from Mileadhach upon the bank of the river Barrow to the meeting of the three streams of Cork, and from the river Suir southwards to the sea. The diocess of Cork extended from Cork to Carn Ui Neid, and from the

Blackwater southwards to the sea. The diocess of Rath Maighe Deisgirt extended from Baoi Bearra to Ceau Meara, and from Feil to Dairbhre. The diocess oi Killaloe extended from Slighe Dhala to Leim Congoulion, and from Mount Eachtighe to Mount Uidhe an Riogh, and from thence to Mount or Glean Caoin. The diocess of Limerick extended from Maolcearn westwards to Ath an Coinne Lodain, and to Laoh Guir, and to Lathach More, and from Aidhne westwards, and Ard Patrick southwards, and Beallach Feabhrat and Tullach inclusive ; Feil and Tairbeart westwards, and Ouinche in Thumond Cross in Mount Uidhe an Riogh, and Dubh Abhain. The journal of that convention adds this sanction in this place, " whoever exceeds these boundaries acts contrary to the will of God and the intention of St. Peter and St. Patrick, and all the Christian churches." The cathedral of this diocess is St. Mary's church in Limerick. The diocess of Emly Jobhair extended from Cluain Caoin to the Blackwater, and from Cnamh Coill by Tipperary to Abhaid Alla. The diocess of Kilkenny extended from Mount Bladhma to Mileadhach, and from Greine Airb to Mount Mairge. The diocess of Leith Glin extended from Mount Bladhma to Mount Uidhe in the province of Leinster, and from Mount Mairge to Beallach Carcrach, and from Beallach Mugna to Teach Moling and to Natearmann. The diocess of Kildare extended from Ross Fionglaise to the Naas in Leinster, and from thence to Cumar Cluana Hioraid, and to the Mounts Glin da Loch. The diocess of Glin da Loch extended from Grianog to Breigeirinn, to the Naas, and to Reachroinn. The diocess oi Fearns or Wexford extended from Beigeirn to Mileadhach, on the west of the river Barrow, and from Mount Uidhe in the province of Leinster southwards to the sea. The clergy of the province of Leinster, I presume, will allow of this method of laying out the boundaries of the several dioceses ; nor is it to be disputed that there were any more than five bishoprics in that province. The famous convocation of Rath Breasal, and the 25 bishops who sat in that assembly, left the blessing of God, and their own likewise, upon the succeeding bishops, in the 25 dioceses above mentioned, who should support and vindicate the orders and laws that were ordained in that synod, with regard to the limits of their several bishoprics, and invoked dreadful imprecations upon such as presumed to violate those injunctions, or disputed the authority of that venerable synod.

It is observed by Hacluit in his chronicle, that when Mortough O'Bryen was possessed of the government of Ireland, the inhabitants of the neighbouring islands sent a messenger to that prince, that he would send them a person of the royal blood to command those isles, during the minority of Olanus or Humphry, the son of Godfrey, who was heir apparent to the crown of those countries. Mortough complied with their request, and sent a cousin of his own, whose name was Daniel, the son of Teige O'Bryen, who administered the government for the space of three years; but notwithstanding he was no more than a viceroy over the people, he ruled with such tyranny and despotic power, that the inhabitants began to suspect his designs, and grew jealous of their rights and privileges, which he attempted to invade, and therefore the principal persons of the island deposed him from his authority, and ignominiously sent him back into Ireland.

We have an account likewise in the same historian, that Magnus, the son of Olanus, son of Arailt, king of Norway, dispatched messengers to Mortough O'Bryen, to demand his homage and submission; and likewise sent a pair of his shoes, which he commanded him to carry upon his shoulders, as an evident testimony of his subjection. Mortough dreading an invasion from these foreigners, we are informed, obeyed, which servile compliance of his was so resented by the nobility and chief persons of his dominions, that they upbraided him with cowardice and a meanness of spirit, for degenerating from the courage of his ancestors, who abhorred such abject behaviour, and would have chastised with the sword the haughty Dane for the insolence of his demands. But Mortough was not the least incensed by this remonstrance, and he replied with great mildness, that he would rather advance the happiness and security of his country by his submission, than to expose to ruin and desolation the least province in his dominions.

But Magnus, not satisfied with this servile homage from Mortough, fitted out a numerous fleet, which he manned with Danes and Norwegians, and set sail for the Irish coasts. His design was to plunder and destroy the country, and to harass it in a dreadful manner; the people he determined to put to the sword without mercy, and to take ample revenge upon the Irish for all the victories they had obtained over the Danes, and for driving them out of the island. And so impatient was this cruel Dane to put his design into execution, that he landed, with his wife, a few of his nobility, and a small number of soldiers, before the body of his fleet approached the shore, and set the country about him on fire. But the Irish were prepared to receive him, for they had laid ambushes to cut him off before the rest of his forces arrived, and surprised him with such success, that Magnus and all his men were destroyed. When the rest of the fleet arrived, they were so astonished with the misfortune of their captain and companions, that they made all the sail they could homewards, and bid a final adieu to the island.

Mortough O'Bryen, king of Ireland, fell sick of a languishing disease, which attended him for five years, and then concluded his life and reign. He died at Ardmach, and made a most religious exit: his body was buried in the great church at Killaloe, in the year of our redemption 1130.

A.D. 1130.   Turlough, the son of Roger O'Connor, succeeded to the government of the greatest part of the island, and sat upon the throne for twenty years. This prince distinguished his reign by many memorable actions; among the rest he erected three remarkable bridges in the province of Conacht, the bridge of Athlone and the bridge of Ath Chrochta, both which stood over the Shannon, and the bridge of Dun Leogha over the Suca. This monarch entered the territories of Munster in a hostile manner, and among other devastations he plundered Cashel and Ard Fianan; but the provincial troops falling successfully upon his rear, did great execution, and slew Hugh O'Heyn, king of Fiachrach Aidhne, and Muireadhach O'Flatherty, king of West Conacht, and many other persons of the first distinction. But this misfortune did not discourage Turlough in his designs upon that province, for he soon repaired the loss he had suffered, by recruiting his forces and completing his battalions, and entered the country with all the fury of an enraged enemy, where he used great cruelties, and committed inexpressible barbarities upon the people. He reduced the province under his obedience, and as his own by right of conquest, he divided it into two parts; the south division he gave to Donough Mac Carty, and the north he bestowed upon Connor O'Bryen; but acting with great policy before he fixed them in possession, he obliged them to deliver hostages as a security for their future homage and subjection.

About this time the church of Cormac, at Cashel, was consecrated, at the performance of which solemnity the principal clergy and nobility of that kingdom were present, in the year of our redemption 1134. Soon after Cormac Mac Carty was barbarously murdered by Connor O'Bryen, who was his near relation; and about the same time the pious Muolmavodhog or

Malichias, who was archbishop of Ireland and Scotland, was removed to another life.

Turlough O'Connor made an attempt upon the whole province of Munster, and for that purpose he collected all the forces of Conacht and Leinster, of Meath Teasa and O'Rourk, and directed his march to Gleann Maghair; but there he was met by Turlough O'Bryen and the son of Connor O'Bryen, attended with the provincial troops, which consisted of three battalions. Both armies prepared for battle, and began the fight with great fury and slaughter; for some time the success was doubtful, but at last favoured Turlough O'Connor, and the Momonian troops and the martial tribe of the Dailgais received a terrible defeat at Moin More, and suffered inexpressible loss in the engagement. After this victory Turlough O'Bryen was banished to Tir Eogain, and Turlough O'Connor made another division of the province of Munster, between Teige O'Bryen and Diarmuid, the son of Cormac Mac Carty.

Turlough O'Connor, king of Ireland, did not long survive this memorable battle; he died in the sixty-eighth year of his age, and was interred with great solemnity near the great altar of Ciaran at Cluain Mac Nois. This prince left to the clergy of the kingdom the greatest part of his personal estate, which consisted of 540 ounces of gold, forty marks of silver, all his jewels, plate, horses, arms, bows, quivers, arrows, and all his military equipage, and ordained that this legacy of his should be divided into just proportions, and given to the clergy according to their several degrees and the orders they professed. The decease of this prince was accompanied by the death of the most religious Teige O'Lonargain, bishop of Killaloe, who expired in the year of the Christian era 1150.

A.D. 1150.   Mortough Mac Neill Mac Lachluin succeeded in the government of Ireland. This prince was descended from the posterity of Heremon, and commanded the greatest part of the island for eighteen years. In the seventh year of his reign was convened a national synod of the clergy, which assembled at Ceananus, in the country of Meath, and in the year of our Lord 1157. The design of this convocation was to consult proper measures for the better propagation of the Christian faith; for the more effectual edification of the people, and to ordain two more archbishops in the island; for before there were no more than the archbishops of Ardmach and Cashel. The principal persons who were appointed by the Pope to preside in this convention were, Giolla Criost O'Conaire, bishop of Lismore, superior of all the monks in Ireland, and the Pope's legate, and Johannes Papiron, one of the Roman cardinals. They regulated the dioceses throughout the kingdom, and bestowed four copes upon the four archbishops, which was very ungrateful to the Irish ; for they would have been better satisfied with the old form, without the addition of any more archbishoprics. One of these copes, called Pallium in the journal of that synod, was bestowed upon Ardmach, and another upon Cashel, which was contrary to the will of the clergy of Ardmach and Dun da Leath Glas ; the other two were presented to the new archbishops, as appears expressly by an old book of the clergy of Cluain Aidnach, where the determinations of that council are particularly recorded ; the same treatise mentions, that the synod assembled in the year of Christ 1157, and gives the following account of the injunctions that were established, and the delivery of the four copes, in the manner following : * "In the year 1157 from the Incarnation of our Lord Jesus Christ, being bissextile, was celebrated in the spring a noble council at Ceananus ; in which synod presided Cardinal John, a presbyter of the blessed St. Laurence, and the assembly consisted of twenty-two bishops, and five bishops elect, and of so many abbots and priors, belonging to the blessed apostles Peter and Paul, and our apostolic father Eugenius. This cardinal condemned, and by all proper methods extirpated, the practice of simony and usury, and commanded tithes to be paid by apostolical authority. He delivered four copes to the four archbishops of Ireland, to the archbishop of Dublin, of Tuam, of Cashel, and of Ardmach : moreover he constituted, as it became him, the archbishop of Ardmach primate over the rest, and as soon as the council was ended he began his journey, and passed the seas upon the ninth day of the calends of April."

The names of the bishops that were present in this synodical meeting, are delivered down to us in the manner following :

MCLVII. anno ab Incarnatione Domini nostri Jesu Christi bissextili, nobile concilium in vernali tempore apud Ceananus celebratum fuit; in quo presidens dominus Joannes cardinalis, presbyter beati Laurentii, inter viginti duos episcopos, et quinque electos, et inter tot abbates et priores ex parte beatorum apostolorum Petri et Pauli et domini apostolici Eugenii. Simoniam et usuras omnibus modis extirpavit, et damnavit, et decimas dandas apostolica authoritate praecepit. Quatuor pallia quatuor archiepiscopos Hiberniae, Dubliniensi, Tuaimensi, Caiselensi, et Ardmachano tradidit. Insuper Ardmachanum episcopum in primatem super alios pro ut decuit ordinavit; qui etiam cardinalis Joannes protinus post per actum concilium iter arripuit et nono calendas Aprilis transfretavit.

Giolla Criost O'Conaire, bishop of Lismore, and the Pope's legate; Giolla Mac Liag, primate of Ireland; Daniel O'Lougargan, archbishop of Munster, that is, Cashel; Hugh O'Heyn, archbishop of Conacht, that is, Tuam Greine; Gregory, bishop of Dublin; Giolla na Naomh, bishop of Glean da Loch; Dungal O'Caollaighe, bishop of Leithglinn; Tuistius, bishop of Waterford; Daniel O'Fogartaigh, vicar-general bishop of Ossery; Fionn Mac Tiagurnain, bishop of Kildare; Giolla an Choimde, or Deicola, a worshipper of God; O'Hardmhaoil, bishop of Imleach or Emly; Giolla Aodh O'Heyn, bishop of Cork; Maolbreanuin O'Ruanain, bishop of Kerry, that is, Ard Fearta; Turgesius, bishop of Limerick; Mortough O'Maolidhir, bishop of Cluain Mac Naois; Maoiliosa O'Conachtain, bishop of Oirthior Conacht; Ua Ruadhain, bishop of Luighne, that is, Achad or Achonry; Macraith O'Morain, bishop of Conmaicne or Ardacha; Eathruadh O'Miadhachain, bishop of Cluain Joraird; Tuathal O'Connachtaig, bishop of Jobh Bruinn, that is Enachduin; Muireadhach O'Cobhthaig, bishop of Cineal Eogain, that is, Derry; Maolpadruic O'Beanain, bishop of Dailnaruigh, that is, of Connor; Maoiliose Mac an Chleirighchuirr, bishop of Down.

The archbishop of Ardmach had under his jurisdiction the following sees: Connor, Down, Louth, Clonard, Kells, Ardachadh, Raphoe, Rathlury, Duleek, and Derry; but some of these have been since united into one bishopric. The archbishop of Cashel presided over the diocesses of Killaloe, Limerick, Inis Catha, Kilfenora, Emly, Roscrea, Waterford, Lismore, Cloin, Cork, Ross, and Ardfearta; but the number is not so many at present, because some of them have been likewise united. Under the authority of the archbishop of Dublin are these sees, Gleandaloch, Ferns, Ossery, Leithglin, and Kildare. The jurisdiction of the archbishop of Tuam extends over the diocesses of Mayo, Killala, Roscommon, Cluainfeart, Achonry, Cluain Mac Nois, and Kilmacogh, in Irish Cill mhic Duach; but those sees are now fewer, and some of them at this time are utterly unknown.

Not long after this national convention broke up, Daniel O'Longargan, bishop of Munster, left the world; nor did Mortough Mac Neill long survive, who was king over the principal part of the kingdom of Ireland.

A.D. 1168.   Roderick, otherwise called Roger, fixed himself in the throne of his predecessor. He was the son of Turlough O'Connor, sirnamed the Great, and descended from the royal line of Heremon. This prince, by the historians of those times, was always placed in the table of the Irish monarchs, and called king of Ireland; and not improperly, for the kings of Oirgiallach, of Meath, and Breifne, submitted to him, though many of the nobility and gentry of the island stood out and opposed his government. He is said to wear the crown eight years.

In the reign of Roderick, king of Ireland, Teighernan O'Rourke, king of Breifne, had married a lady of a very lascivious disposition, who had banished the conjugal esteem of her husband, and resolved when opportunity offered, to fly away from his court. The name of this lady was Dearbhfhorguill, the daughter of Mortough Mac Floinn, king of Meath, and not the wife of that prince, as Giraldus Cambrensis falsely asserts. In order to accomplish her designs she sent a private message to Diarmuid Mac Morrough, king of Leinster, with whom she was in love, and entreated him that he would rescue her from the embraces of a husband she hated, and use any methods, either of stratagem or force, to carry her away: and to favour her escape, the messenger was to acquaint the king of Leinster, that he might safely remove to Conacht, and continue there till her husband set out upon his pilgrimage to St. Patrick's Purgatory, which he proposed to undertake in a short time; so that if he complied with this opportunity he might easily convey her to Leinster, where they might both gratify those desires with security, which her forced marriage with the king of Breifne would not suffer her to improve.

Diarmuid received this message with all the joy of a transported lover; and immediately prepared to accomplish an amour that had been long carried on, but by some unfortunate accidents had been always perplexed and disappointed. He ordered a party of horse to attend him, and arriving at the place where the lady was, he found her ready to receive him. He caught her in his arms, and mounted her on horseback behind one of his superior officers, who soon arrived with her at his palace in Leinster. But the lady did not seem outwardly to be concerned in this design, for when she was seized she cried out for help, as if she had been carried away by violence, the better to put a colour upon her escape.

The king of Breifne was at this time upon his pilgrimage; but when he returned he soon missed his wife, and understanding she was seized by force by the king of Leinster, for the lady by her outcries had deceived her attendants, he instantly meditated revenge, and applied himself to Roderick, the king of Ireland, for assistance; he likewise instigated the nobility and gentry of his own country to undertake his quarrel, and to chastise the ravisher for this outrageous indignity, which so sensibly affected the honour of himself, his wife, and his family. The king of Ireland immediately mustered all the provincial troops of Conacht, the forces of Breifne, of Oirgiallach, and the country of Meath, with a full resolution to enter the province of Leinster with fire and sword, and take ample satisfaction of that prince for the base and unworthy act he had committed. Diarmuid soon had intelligence of these military preparations against him, and summoning his nobility about him, he laid before them the formidable strength of the confederate army, and with great condescension implored their help to scatter the impending storm, that would not only overwhelm himself but involve them in the common ruin, and bring destruction upon the whole country. But this application had not the desired effect, for the nobility had conceived such a violent resentment against their prince, for the abominable injury he had committed, that they absolutely refused to support him in so wicked a cause, which no excuse could palliate, and nothing but repentance and restitution could atone for; and to secure themselves from any violence that Diarmuid might propose to execute, the nobility renounced his authority, and put themselves under the protection of Roderick O'Connor, king of Ireland; for the king of Leinster had incensed his subjects by many former provocations, and by his impolitic and tyrannical government had so lost their affections, that they left him in his distress, and abandoned him to the power of his enemies. The king of Ireland, encouraged by this defection of the nobility of Leinster, marched his army into the territories of that province, and plundered the country that had continued firm in their allegiance to Diarmuid; for he met with no opposition, the king of Leinster being obliged to fly with a few followers, and leave the province without defence. The confederate army raged with all the terrors of fire and sword, and among other dreadful devastations they marched to Fearna, plundered and demolished the royal palace of Diarmuid, and drove that unfortunate prince out of the island.

This exiled king, thus forced from his dominions, was bent upon revenge, and giving a full loose to his passions, determined to punish his rebellious nobility at all hazards, though the happiness of his country was to be sacrificed in the attempt. For this purpose he fled into France, and implored the protection of Henry II., king of England, who was carrying on his conquests in that country. The English monarch was not then in a capacity to lend him any troops to assist him in the recovery of his crown, but wrote letters by him to some of his ministers in England, which gave him authority to raise what men were willing to enlist themselves in his service, and transport them into Ireland. Diarmuid gratefully received and acknowledged the civility he found from King Henry, and taking his leave of that prince, he left France and landed safely in the port of Bristol. Upon his arrival he delivered his commission to the magistrates of that city, where the letters were publicly read; and to encourage men to engage in his service, he made ample promises of lands and estates to such as offered themselves, and would assist him in the expedition against his enemies, who had invaded his province and robbed him of his crown. In this city he met Richard Mac Gilbert, son to the Earl of Strangwell, to whom he engaged, that if he would appear in his cause, and raise a body of men for his service, he would bestow upon him his daughter Aoiffe, who was heir apparent to his dominions, and as a dowry would confirm to him and his heirs the crown of Leinster after his decease. The English nobleman joyfully accepted of the terms, and promised that he would instantly beat up for volunteers, and when he had completed his number he would transport them into Ireland.

Diarmuid having met with this encouragement from the English, went into Wales, the prince of which country was Ralph Griffin, who was deputed to that government by Henry II. of England. To him he notified the cause of his arrival and the circumstances of his distressed affairs, and desired that he would favour the cause of an exiled prince, driven from his dominions by a seditious nobility and the rebellion of his own subjects. Here he was informed that a nobleman of signal courage and an experienced commander, whose name was Robert Fitz Stephen, was detained a prisoner by the viceroy of Wales, for some traitorous practices against the king of England. This person he thought would be of great importance to carry on his designs, and therefore he solicited his enlargement with all his interest, and promised, if Ralph Griffin would release him from his confinement, and oblige him to engage in the Irish expedition, Fitz Stephen should never be under a temptation to raise disturbances in England; for he would provide for him to his satisfaction, and bestow estates upon him that should support him in a princely grandeur, and satisfy the utmost extent of his ambition. Robert Fitz Stephen had a brother-in-law in that country, whose name was Maurice Fitz Gerald, who was in great favour with Ralph Griffin ; and he, with the bishop of St. David's, interceded for the releasement of Fitz Stephen, and with much importunity prevailed for his discharge, but upon condition that he should transport himself into Ireland between that time and the summer following, and contribute his utmost to the restoration of the king of Leinster. Diarmuid likewise obliged himself to confirm to this English nobleman the town of Wexford, and the two canthreds of the lands adjacent, to his heirs for ever, as a reward for his service, in assisting him to recover his right, and to re-establish him in his dominions.

The king of Leinster having thus successfully managed his solicitation among the English and the Welsh, conveyed himself with great privacy, and with a very small retinue, into Ireland, in order to be ready to receive the succours he expected. He came to Fearna in a disguise, and discovering himself to the clergy of that place, they promised to protect him till his designs were ripe for execution. Here he lay concealed in his retirement till the summer following, at which time Robert Fitz Stephen, having finished his preparations, and raised what forces he was able, landed upon the coasts. The number he brought over with him seemed unequal to the attempt ; for it consisted of no more than 30 knights, 60 esquires, and 300 foot soldiers, who were set on shore at a place called Cuan an Bhaimbh, which lies upon the border of the country of Wexford upon the south by Beg Abhain. These English auxiliaries landed in Ireland in the seventh year of the reign of Roderick O'Connor, and in the year of our redemption 1175. There came over likewise in this expedition a valiant knight, whose name was Hermon Morty, who belonged to the Earl of Strangwell, and was sent by him to inspect into the manners and disposition of the Irish, and to make discoveries of the produce and the extent of the island.

Upon the arrival of the English, Robert Fitz Stephen dispatched a messenger to the king of Leinster, with whom he kept correspondence. This news was very acceptable to Diarmuid, who immediately left his obscurity, and putting himself at the head of 500 horse, whom he always had in readiness in the country adjacent, he made all possible haste to join the English, and enter upon action, before his enemies were apprised of his design, or were in any capacity to oppose him. A council of war was immediately called, and it was resolved that Wexford should be closely besieged, and accordingly the army was drawn up before the walls ; but the inhabitants were so terrified at the approach of the king of Leinster, that, in a meeting of the principal burghers, it was unanimously agreed to open the gates before any assault was made, and by that means recommend themselves to the favour of the victors, and prevent the sacking of the town. It was likewise concluded, that a number of select hostages should be sent to Diarmuid ; as a security for their future obedience and submission, and as pledges for an annual tribute they would oblige themselves to pay, as the most effectual method that could be thought in that exigency to save their lives and preserve their houses from plunder. These proposals were no sooner offered but they were accepted by the king of Leinster, who, to fulfil his engagement, upon the surrender bestowed the town of Wexford, and two canthreds of the lands, upon Robert Fitz Stephen ; and likewise conferred the two next canthreds upon Hermon Morty, as he had formerly promised, when he was soliciting assistance in Wales against the prevailing power of his enemies.

Diarmuid having thus rewarded his auxiliaries, made a general muster of his forces, and found upon a review that his force consisted of a complete body of 3000 men. He gave orders to decamp, and marched towards the territories of Ossery, with a design to plunder the country, and reduce it to obedience. The king of Ossery at this time was Donough, the son of Daniel Ramhar, who was a professed enemy to the king of Leinster But when the confederate army had passed the boundaries, and began to commit hostilities upon the inhabitants, the king of Ossery, finding himself in no capacity to oppose the invaders, summoned a council of his principal nobility and gentry, who, after mature consideration, were obliged to resolve to send hostages to the king of Leinster, as a testimony of their submission, and to pay him an annual tax and acknowledge themselves tributaries ; accordingly a messenger was dispatched express with these conditions, which the king of Leinster complied with, and by this means the fury of the soldiers was restrained, and the country secured from further depredations.

By this time the whole kingdom was alarmed with the success of Diarmuid and his auxiliary English ; and to prevent the dreadful calamities of a civil war, the chiefs of the island both nobles and gentry, applied to Roderick O'Connor, king of Ireland, to consult upon proper methods to put a stop to the ambitious designs of the king of Leinster, and scatter the impending storm before it grew formidable, and in a capacity of overwhelming the island in blood and confusion. A convention of the estates therefore was assembled, and after many debates it was agreed, that every province in the island should be obliged to supply the king of Ireland with an appointed number of forces, in order to confine the king of Leinster within the bounds of his province, and drive the English out of the country. This resolution was punctually executed, and every province raised their quota of men, who were sent to the place of rendezvous with the utmost expedition. When Roderick found his army complete, he began his march, and directed his course towards Jobh Cinsealach, with a full design to give battle to the king of Leinster, and fight him at all adventures. But Diarmuid being much inferior in the number of men, determined not to stand the shock of this formidable army; but as Roderick approached he retired, and withdrew with his troops into the woods and wildernesses, which at that time stood near Fearna and afforded him a secure retreat. The king of Ireland, perceiving that the enemy would not abide the issue of a decisive battle, but lurked in the woods, where they could not be attacked, sent to Robert Fitz Stephen, the commander of the English, with orders that he should instantly leave the country with all his foreigners; for the cause he was engaged in was unjust and dishonourable, and he had no right to a foot of land throughout the island. But Robert despised this proud command, and returned for answer, that he had no inclination to quit the country, and would never forsake the king of Leinster, but prosecute his right as long as he had a man left. Roderick, enraged with this reply, divided his army into small bodies, and gave orders to his officers to enter the woods and attack the king of Leinster in his fastnesses, and he commanded them to give no quarter to native or foreigner, but to put them all to the sword, and by that means at once to bring the war to a final end.

But the clergy of the province of Leinster, foreseeing that these commotions would be of fatal consequence to their country, and that these intestine broils were destructive to the peace and the established revenues of the church, resolved to use their utmost efforts in reconciling the two kings, and securing the kingdom from bloodshed and other miseries, that the continuation of the war made unavoidable. For that purpose they assembled in a body, and marched towards the army of the king of Ireland. When they arrived they were admitted into the king's presence, and prostrating themselves before him as humble supplicants, they besought him to commiserate the distressed state of his native country, and prevent the effusion of Christian blood, by ceasing hostilities, and entering into a treaty with the king of Leinster. Roderick, who was a prince of a merciful disposition, relented at this representation of the clergy, and was contented to withdraw his army and come into pacific measures with the king of Leinster. The conditions of peace were agreed upon, which established that Diarmuid should enjoy the government of Leinster in as full extent as any of his predecessors did before him; but he was obliged to send hostages of the first quality to the king of Ireland, as a security for his future obedience, and that he would not embroil the kingdom in new troubles; he was likewise bound to promise fealty and homage to the crown of Ireland, as the kings of Leinster had ever done to the Irish monarchs, and engage that he would give no encouragement to foreigners to invade the island, particularly that the English should find no protection from him, but be compelled to quit the country. These conditions were accepted by Diarmuid, who, as an evidence of his integrity, delivered to Roderick, as a hostage, his son, whose name was Art na Ngiall, and the king of Ireland stipulated that he would bestow his sister in marriage upon the king of Leinster; by which alliance it was hoped that a solid and lasting peace would be established between the two families, and the island restored to its former tranquillity.

But this happy prospect was soon obscured; for the summer following Maurice Fitz Gerald, remembering the promise he had made to the king of Leinster, landed in Ireland. Nor was he without hopes that by assisting that prince to recover his right, he should be entitled to a great reward, and obtain large possessions in the country. The number of men that he brought over in this expedition, consisted of no more than 10 knights, 30 esquires, and 100 foot, whom he set on shore in the port of Wexford.

He soon notified his arrival to the king of Leinster, and Robert Fitz Stephen, the English general; and Diarmuid, urged on by his ambitious designs, resolved to break the peace, and with his auxiliary English again try his fortune and take the field; accordingly he marched at the head of his forces to Wexford, to congratulate the arrival of Maurice Fitz Gerald, and to assign him a post in the army suitable to his experience and his quality. With this additional aid he resolved to begin the campaign, and laid close siege to the city of Dublin; for the inhabitants of that place had always professed themselves enemies to his father and himself, and therefore he proposed to take revenge for the indignities which his family had received, and chastise the pride and insolence of those haughty citizens. But Robert Fitz Stephen did not attend him in this expedition, but stayed behind to erect a fort at a place called Carraick, within two miles of the town of Wexford. Diarmuid, with his auxiliaries under the command of Maurice Fitz Gerald, directed his march to Fingall, and set all the adjacent country on fire. These hostilities alarmed the magistrates of Dublin, who immediately summoned a council, and resolved to make their peace with the king of Leinster upon any terms, and save the city from plunder. They sent to him in his camp a large quantity of gold, silver, jewels, silks, and other valuable presents, and surrendered themselves to his mercy, imploring him to spare a deluded and unfortunate people, and accept of hostages, whom he should receive as an evidence of their loyalty, and a security for their future obedience; they promised likewise that they would cheerfully pay whatever tribute was laid upon them, and atone for their former miscarriages by a double share of duty and fidelity. These articles were accepted by Diarmuid, and the citizens delivered from their fears.

This continued course of success animated the king of Leinster to more ambitious designs; and reflecting that many of his ancestors had worn the crown of Ireland, he entertained hopes of being monarch of the island, and resolved to make an attempt upon the throne. The kings who swayed the sceptre from whom he descended were, Cathaoir More, Connor Abhraruadh, Labhra Loingseach, Laogaire Lorc, and Ugaine More. Diarmuid communicated his resolution to Robert Fitz Stephen and Maurice Fitz Gerald, who approved of his design, and told him that he was now become formidable, and might with small difficulty fix the crown upon his head; but withal, politically advised him to proceed with great caution and secrecy, and not to enter upon execution before his army was reinforced with fresh supplies, which would soon be transported from England, and put him into a capacity of carrying on his designs beyond a possibility of disappointment. This approbation of the English generals added fuel to the fire of ambition already kindled in the breast of the king of Leinster, who, transported with the friendship and sincerity of his auxiliaries, offered his daughter to either of them, as a reward for their zeal and faithful services; but they both had too much honour to accept of the lady, because she had been formerly contracted to the Earl of Strangwell, when Diarmuid was soliciting assistance from the crown of England. They advised him to apply to this nobleman immediately; to write him an obliging letter, requesting him to come over to his assistance with the forces he promised him, and engaging that the conditions on his part should be fulfilled, the marriage to his daughter should be contracted, and that he was ready to settle the crown of Leinster upon him and his heirs after his decease. He was to signify likewise, that his affairs went on prosperously, that his province of Leinster was recovered, and he had a fair prospect of reducing the other four provinces under his government, and fixing himself in the monarchy of the whole island.

This letter was sent and received by the Earl of Strangwell, who perused it with great deliberation, and reflecting upon the good fortune of the king of Leinster, and the success of his countrymen, Maurice Fitzgerald and Robert Fitz Stephen, determined to accept of the invitation, and transport himself with all possible speed into Ireland; but first he applied to his sovereign, the king of England, and desired leave to go out of the kingdom and seek his fortune abroad, for he was weary of an inactive life, and requested his permission to travel and try the mettle of his sword in foreign countries. The king, not willing to discourage the enterprising genius of this noble earl, nor yet willing to be reflected upon if he miscarried, neither gave his actual licence, nor repulsed him with a positive denial, but left him to pursue the bent of his inclination; which silence of the king was understood by the earl as an evidence of his permission, and taking leave of his majesty, he prosecuted his design with vigour, raised a small party of men, and made all necessary preparations for his Irish expedition. But before he came over himself in person, he thought it proper to send before him two of his superior officers, Redmond de la Grose, and William Fitz Gerald, (the elder brother of Maurice Fitz Gerald above mentioned,) with a small body of forces, to inquire into the posture of affairs, and signify to the king of Leinster, and his countrymen, that he would soon follow with large supplies, and fulfil his promise. These officers set to sea, and landed at Dun Domhnail, four miles south of Waterford; and according to Stanihurst, in his chronicle, the number who were sent over at this time, consisted of no more than ten knights, ten esquires.

and sixty foot soldiers; and when they came upon the coasts they erected a strong fort of sods and stones, to defend them from the attempts of the inhabitants.

When the inhabitants of Waterford, and Maolseachluin O'Faolain, king of the Deisies, received intelligence that the English had fortified themselves in their neighbourhood, they apprehended themselves to be in imminent danger; and summoning a council, it was unanimously agreed to attack the fort, which was defended but by a handful of men, and put them all to the sword, before they were relieved by fresh supplies. Accordingly a select party of 200 men, under the conduct of an experienced officer, was ordered to dislodge these foreigners, and not suffer a man of them to escape.

Redmond de la Grose, who had the command of the fort, observing the Irish advancing towards him, resolved to oppose them before they came near the walls, and drawing out his small number of men, he led them on, and with great indiscretion began the charge. But the Irish received him smartly, which soon convinced him of his mistake, and finding the enemy to be more numerous than he expected, he sounded a retreat, and thought to recover the fort with small loss. But the Irish fell upon his rear and pursued him so hotly, that he was obliged to face about, and fighting with desperate courage at the head of his company, he so astonished the Irish troops, that they were not able to stand the shock, but gave way and fled for their lives. The slaughter in this action was terrible; for the English were a handful of brave well disciplined troops, and notwithstanding the disproportion of numbers, they broke the ranks of the raw disordered Irish, and gave them a general defeat.

The year following, upon St. Bartholomew's day, in the time of harvest, the Earl of Strangwell landed in Ireland, and brought over a strong body of forces, consisting of 200 valiant knights, and 1000 esquires that were bowmen, whom he set on shore in the port of Waterford. Upon his arrival he sent intelligence to the king of Leinster, and to his countrymen Robert Fitz Stephen and Redmond de la Grose, and likewise notified how well provided he came, and what forces he had to support him. Diarmuid received this news with great joy, and with his auxiliary English immediately directed his march to welcome the Earl of Strangwell, and pay him his compliments. After a small time was spent in ceremonies and mutual civilities, a general council of war was called, wherein it was agreed that the army should instantly enter upon action, and open their designs by laying close siege to the town of Waterford. Accordingly they decamped the next day, and presented themselves before the walls. The inhabitants within made a vigorous defence, but the valiant Earl of Strangwell was not to be repelled; his troops signally distinguished themselves in this action, and making a general assault, entered the town. The soldiers in their first fury destroyed all they met, and gave no quarter. Maolseachluin O'Faolain, king of the Deisies, was taken prisoner, and hardly escaped with his life, which would certainly have fallen a sacrifice to the enraged victors, if the king of Leinster had not interceded, and with great generosity rescued him out of their hands.

It was observed before, that Diarmuid, king of Leinster, had a young lady to his daughter, whose name was Aoiffe, whom he promised in England to the Earl of Strangwell. This princess, after the taking of Waterford, was sent for by her father, and was married there with great solemnity to that noble earl, upon the conditions formerly stipulated between them. After the accomplishment of the nuptial rites, the earl left his lady, and the town of Waterford, under the care of a strong guard, and at the head of his troops directed his march towards the city of Dublin. Never did the approach of an enemy make a more terrible impression upon a distressed city, than the advancing of the Irish and English upon the inhabitants of Dublin, nor could a victorious general lay siege to a town with more fury and resentment about him, than raged at that time in the breast of the king of Leinster against the people of that city, who had killed his father, and used him in an ignominious manner after his death; for they buried a dog in the same grave with him, as a testimony of their hatred, and offered such indignities to him as history can scarce parallel. These affronts were fresh in the memory of the king of Leinster, who resolved to take ample revenge of these vile citizens; and they were so convinced of what usage they had to expect from him, that they immediately met in council, to debate upon the necessity of their affairs, and avert the impending storm before they were overwhelmed by it. In this assembly it was unanimously agreed to send Laurence O'Tuathail, in the English language O'Toole, archbishop of Dublin, with a commission to treat in the most submissive manner with the king of Leinster, and to prevail with him, upon any terms, to spare a distressed city, that was now too sensible of the indignities she had offered him; and promised by way of atonement, to purchase his friendship at the

2 L

expense of all the gold and silver they could raise, and deliver
him hostages to secure their future submission, if he would
raise the siege and withdraw his army.

But while the archbishop was interceding for the acceptance
of these conditions, and adjusting the capitulation, it happened
that Meills Cogan and Redmond de la Grose, with a strong
body of his English knights, were posted on the other side of
the town, and carried on the attack with such vigour and success, that they made a considerable breach in the walls, and
forcibly entered the city. The citizens and whomsoever the
soldiers met, in their first fury, they put to the sword without
distinction ; the gates were seized, and the city secured for the
king of Leinster, who, after, he had left a strong garrison to
defend it, drew out his men, and led them in pursuit of farther
conquests. The king of Breifne at this time was O'Rourk, who
had always professed himself an enemy to the king of Leinster ;
Diarmuid therefore, attended by his confederate English, entered
the country of Breifne with fire and sword, and committed
incredible barbarities upon the inhabitants. O'Rourk was
reduced to great extremities by this invasion ; and the king of.
Leinster was so elevated by a constant course of success, that
he made no question of gratifying his ambition with the monarchy of the island, for his very name was a terror throughout
the kingdom, and victory followed him in all his undertakings.

Roderick O'Connor, king of Ireland, was alarmed at the progress of the king of Leinster, and was now convinced that no
treaties or obligations could bind a prince, who resolved to stand
to no engagements which shortened his prospects and opposed
his designs, for he had broken the peace in a most outrageous
manner, not considering that his son was a hostage, and that
he had sworn allegiance to the king of Ireland. But before
Roderick took the field to chastise his insolence, he thought
proper to send a messenger, to expostulate with him upon his
breach of faith, to upbraid him for his perjury and perfidious-
ness, and to assure him that if he would not return to his duty,
and send back the English into their own country, he would
send him his son's head, and lay him under a public interdict,
and again oblige him to quit the island. This message was
delivered, but made no impression upon the king of Leinster,
who knew himself to be too well supported to be terrified by
words, and returned an answer, that he would not send back
the English, but soon transport more of them into the country ;
and that he would not lay down his arms until he had reduced

the whole kingdom under his authority; and withal, that if the king of Ireland offered to take away the life of his son, he would revenge his death by hostilities yet unheard of, and not give up his resentment without a complete destruction of himself and his family. Roderick O'Connor was astonished at the insolence of this petty prince, and resolved in his passion to execute his purpose upon the royal hostage he had in his hands; but upon mature reflection he desisted, and wisely considered that his enemy was in possession of a great part of the kingdom, and a terror to what remained unsubdued; that the event of war was uncertain, and that such a barbarous act would render him odious to his people, whose affections were his only support against the prevailing power of a successful and haughty enemy.

The king of England had received intelligence of the proceedings of his subjects in Ireland, under the conduct of the Earl of Strangwell, and other valiant commanders; and, not approving of their designs, he published a proclamation, that no ship or bark should sail for Ireland out of any of the English ports; and that no trade or correspondence should be maintained with that island, under the severest penalties; and that all the English in that kingdom should immediately return home, upon pain of losing their estates, and of being declared rebels and traitors. This proclamation soon came to the hands of the Earl of Strangwell, who immediately called a council of the English officers, and it was agreed not to return instantly and quit that country, but to send Redmond de la Grose to the king of England, with a commission to represent to his majesty, that it was by his own royal permission that the Earl of Strangwell espoused the cause of Diarmuid Mac Morrough, king of Leinster; and that the English had no design to withdraw their allegiance from their natural sovereign, but intended to conquer the country in his name, and submit the territories they should subdue to his authority and disposal.

With this message Redmond de la Grose sailed into France, and found the king of England in Gascoign. This was the year in which that famous prelate, Thomas Becket, archbishop of Canterbury, was murdered; which barbarous act was committed upon the first day of Christmas, in the year of our redemption 1171. In the month of May following Diarmuid Mac Morrough, king of Leinster, died, and was buried at Fearna.

Henry II., soon after he had received this message from his

subjects in Ireland, returned into England, and sent one of his
knights, whose name was Hermon Morty, with letters to the
Earl of Strangwell; Redmond de la Grose was likewise sent
back to the earl, who, receiving the letters, found that he was
obliged instantly to repair to England, and give an account of
his conduct to his majesty. When he came to court he was
admitted into the king's presence; and, after he had faithfully
informed him of the posture of the Irish affairs, he offered to
deliver up the possession of Dublin, Waterford, and other principal towns in the province of Leinster, into his Majesty's hands,
if he pleased by his royal grant to confirm to him and his heirs
the enjoyment of the remaining parts of that province. The
king condescended to accept of these terms, and in a short time
followed the earl with a numerous army into Ireland; he landed
in the port of Waterford, and was attended in this expedition
by 500 knights, besides a select army of horse and foot, who
were all set on shore in the year of Christ 1172.

The king continued at Waterford for some time: this was
his head quarters, and here the burghers of Wexford, and the
English throughout the kingdom, who had notice of his arrival,
came and paid him homage, and submitted to his authority.
Diarmuid More Mac Carty, king of Cork, likewise made a
tender of his submission to King Henry, which he accepted.
From Waterford the king removed to Cashel, where he was
met by Daniel O'Bryen, king of Limerick, who submitted himself, and promised to continue faithful in his obedience, in the
same manner as Diarmuid, king of Cork had done before him.
The king of England was pleased with this success, and sent a
party of horse and foot to secure Cork and Limerick for his
service. At Cashel, the principal nobility of Munster waited
upon him, and promised him obedience; from thence he returned to Waterford, where he received homage from the king
of Ossery, and assurances of his future fidelity. From Waterford the king of England removed to Dublin, where he was met
by the nobility of the province of Leinster, whose submission
he removed, and promised to continue them in the possession of
their lawful privileges.

This general defection was very unacceptable to Roderick
O'Connor, king of Conacht, and of the greatest part of the
island, who, finding himself abandoned by his countrymen, who
rather chose to submit to a foreign yoke than attempt to repel
these foreigners, thought it prudential in him to make a virtue
of necessity, and submit likewise to the king of England; for

he was forsaken by most of the princes of the island, and was in no circumstances to oppose the progress of the English arms; and therefore he thought that the condition of his affairs required that he should rather confess an authority, however unjust, than oppose it to his own destruction. Under these reflections he received a message from the king of England, by two principal noblemen, whose names were Hugo de Lacy and William de Adelmel, with a kind invitation to wait upon their master, who lay with his army upon the bank of the river Shannon. The king of Ireland was obliged to comply, and accordingly he met the English monarch at the place appointed, who received him with great generosity and friendship, and after mutual compliments a peace was concluded before the nobility of both kingdoms. Morrough Mac Floinn was at that time king of Meath; and he likewise confessed the authority of the king of England, so that there was an universal submission, nor was there any king, prince, or nobleman throughout the island, who refused to receive this invitation, or did not pay homage to the English crown.

The following winter proved stormy and tempestuous, so that navigation was dangerous, nor would any ship venture to sail in the Irish sea; by this means the king of England could receive no intelligence from his own country till the month of March, at which time he had letters brought him from England and France, which were very unacceptable, and gave him great uneasiness; among other articles of news, he had an account that the Pope of Rome sent cardinals into England to make particular inquiry into the death of the archbishop of Canterbury, and if the king in person refused to give them satisfaction upon that head, they had commission to excommunicate him, and all his subjects who should afterwards submit to his authority, or acknowledge him for their sovereign. This intelligence was very unwelcome to the king, as the circumstances of his affairs then stood; but he was equally surprised to hear that his eldest son had, in his absence, seized upon the crown of England, and resolved to defend it against his father by force of arms. Under this difficulty of affairs he called a council of his superior officers, wherein it was agreed that a select body of forces should be transported into England with all expedition, and the king himself should soon follow them. This advice was immediately executed; a strong body was detached, who landed in England, and the king, after he had settled his Irish affairs, set to sea, and arrived safely in his own dominions. He disposed of the.

forces he left in Ireland in proper garrisons, for the defence of
the country, and to suppress all attempts that should be made
by the natives, in case they should be any ways troublesome
under his government.   Hugo de Lacy he left with twenty
knights in Meath, and bestowed upon him that country, and
confirmed it by his royal grant to his posterity.   The command
of the city of Dublin he committed to Robert Fitz Stephen
and Maurice Fitz Gerald, and allowed them twenty knights for
guard.   He left William de Adelmel in the government of Wexford, and joined with him in commission Philip de Hastings and
Philip de Bruss, who likewise had twenty knights in their service.   The command of Waterford he appointed to Humphry
Bolum, Hugo Gundavil, and Robert Mac Bernard, who were
attended by twenty knights.   When King Henry arrived in
England, he found that the necessity of his affairs obliged him
to submit to the Roman cardinals, and to comply with whatever
they required, in relation to the death of the archbishop of
Canterbury.   These missionaries likewise adjusted the difference
between Henry and the crown of France, and established a
peace between the two kingdoms.

If it should be inquired in this place upon what account
Diarmuid, king of Leinster, chose to commit himself and his
affairs under the protection of the king of England, rather than
to the king of France, or any other monarch of Christendom,
it must be understood, that Donough, the son of Bryen Boiroimhe, was a prince very unacceptable to the principal nobility
of Ireland, who, rather than pay him obedience, unanimously
came to a resolution to make a present of the whole island to
Urbanus II., Pope of Rome, which was done in the year of our
redemption 1092; so that by this donation the Popes laid claim
to the sovereignty of Ireland, which they executed so far, as to
govern the nobility and clergy by wholesome laws, and to establish a regular discipline in the church.   And the Popes maintained this authority till Adrian, the fourth of that name, sat
in St. Peter's chair, which was in the year of our Lord 1154.
This Pope was an Englishman by descent, and his original
name was Nicholas Brusber.

Stowe, the English annalist, asserts, in his chronicle, that
this pope bestowed the kingdom of Ireland upon Henry II. in
the first year of his reign, and in the year of our redemption
1154.   This author likewise relates, that this donation was conferred upon the king of England, on condition that he would
revive the profession of the Christian faith, which was dead

throughout the island; that he should polish the rude manners of the inhabitants, defend and restore the rights and revenues of the church and clergy, and take especial care that every inhabited house in the kingdom should pay annually one penny to the Pope, under the name of St. Peter's penny.

This grant of the kingdom of Ireland to King Henry was drawn up in writing, which when he received, he sent John, bishop of Salisbury, with this instrument of the Pope's donation into Ireland. Upon his landing at Waterford he sent to the bishops and the principal clergy of the island, and gave them an account of his commission. They attended upon him at Waterford, where he published the Pope's grant of the kingdom of Ireland to Henry II., king of England, with the conditions to be performed on his part, and by all who succeeded him in that crown. The clergy took the matter into consideration and after some debates an instrument was drawn up, which contained their absolute submission to this donation of the Pope, and to this they all unanimously subscribed. The bishop returned with this confirmation of the Pope's grant by the clergy of Ireland, and the king of England sent the same prelate with the instrument to the Pope, who was well pleased with the submission of the Irish clergy, and sent a ring to King Henry, as a confirmation of his former grant, by which he was established in the possession of the Irish crown.

Bellarmine, an eminent cardinal, agrees with this account in a part of his works, where are these words :* "Adrian IV., Pope

---

* Adrianus Papa quartus, natione Anglus, vir sapiens et pius, Hiberniam insulam Henrico secundo regi Anglorum concessit ea conditione, ut in ea insula virtutes plantaret et vitia eradicaret, ut a singulis domibus quotannis denarium Sancto Petro pendi curaret, et ut jura ecclesiastica illibata servaret.'. Extat diploma T. XII. Cardanolis Baronius.

Although to Diarmuid Mac Morrough is to be attributed the introduction of the English, yet it is apparent, that the ambitious Henry merely waited an opportunity to carry the designs he had formed upon the Irish crown into execution. His application to the court of Rome evinces the determination of a monarch, who, to further his ambitious views, made the pretext of propagating true religion, in a country already Christian, and so remarkable for the piety and sanctity of the natives, as to be styled the Island of Saints, the means of obtaining a colourable sanction for the aggression he meditated upon a weak and unoffending nation. This sanction, the Bull of Pope Adrian IV., not being given complete by our author, for the gratification of the curious reader, is here annexed.

"Adrian the bishop, the servant of the servants of God, to his most dear son in Christ, the noble king of England, sendeth greeting and apostolic benediction. Your magnificence hath been very careful and studious how you might enlarge the church of God here on earth, and increase the number of saints and elect in

of Rome, by birth an Englishman, a wise and pious man, hath granted the island of Ireland to Henry II., king of England, upon condition that he propagates virtue in that island and extirpates vice; that he takes care that one penny be paid yearly to St. Peter by every house, and that he preserves the rights of the church inviolable; the diploma is extant in the 12th volume of Cardinal Baronius."

Stanihurst, in his chronicle, asserts the same thing, where he gives the account that Henry II., king of England, procured a bull from Adrian, the Pope of Rome, which enjoined the clergy of Ireland, and likewise the nobility of the kingdom, to pay obedience to Henry II. upon the conditions and under the restrictions therein contained. The same author likewise relates, that Alexander, the third Pope of that name, sent a cardinal (whose name was Vivianus) into Ireland, to inform the subjects of that kingdom of the grant that he and the precedent Pope made of that kingdom to Henry II., king of England; by the tenor of which that crown was confirmed to Henry and his successors, upon condition of paying to himself and his successors in Saint Peter's chair, a yearly tribute of a penny from every inhabited house throughout the island.

It appears therefore, that the reason why Diarmuid, king of Leinster, applied to the king of England rather than any other prince, was, because the king of England laid claim to the kingdom of Ireland, by virtue of the donation from the two Popes above-mentioned; and therefore that king had power,

heaven, in that as a good Catholic king, you have and do by all means labour and travel to enlarge and increase God's church, by teaching the ignorant people the true and Christian religion, and in abolishing and rooting up the weeds of sin and wickedness. And wherein you have, and do crave, for your better furtherance, the help of the apostolic see (wherein more speedily and discreetly you proceed) the better success, we hope, God will send; for all they, which of a fervent zeal and love in religion, do begin and enterprise any such thing, shall no doubt in the end have a good and prosperous success. And as for Ireland and all other islands where Christ is known and the Christian religion received, it is out of all doubt, and your excellency well knoweth, they do all appertain and belong to the right of St. Peter, and of the church of Rome; and we are so much the more ready, desirous and willing, to sow the acceptable seed of God's word, because we know the same in the latter day will be most severely required at your hands. You have (our well beloved son in Christ) advertised and signified unto us, that you will enter into the land and realm of Ireland, to the end to bring them to obedience unto law, and under your subjection, and to root out from among them their foul sins and wickedness; as also to yield and pay yearly out of every house, a yearly pension of one penny to St. Peter, and besides also will defend and keep the rights of those churches whole and inviolate. We therefore, well allowing and favouring this your godly disposi-

by his superior authority, to adjust the pretences of the princes in Ireland, and to engage in their disputes, and consequently to interpose in the quarrel of the king of Leinster, and settle him in the possession of that province.

It must be surprising to every one, who makes himself acquainted with Irish history, to find such an expression in the bull of Pope Adrian, as that the king of England was to enjoy the crown of Ireland, upon condition that he would revive the Christian faith, and restore it to its former lustre ; as if Christianity had been expelled, and the people had returned to a state of paganism and idolatry. Whoever gave this account to the Pope was as great an enemy to truth, as he was to the glory of the Irish nation ; since it is evident beyond contradiction, that the religion that was propagated in the island by St. Patrick was never totally suppressed, though by frequent confusions in the state it might sometimes be a little obscured. And this is confirmed, not only by writers among the Irish, but by many authors of other nations ; for notwithstanding, as the venerable Bede relates in his history of England, there was a difference between the Irish and the English clergy, and some of the former were infected with the heresy of Pelagius, yet the principal and the more learned part of the clergy of Ireland were free from the contagion of those pestilential doctrines ; and not only kept the Christian faith alive, but by their preaching and example occasioned it to flourish through the greatest part of the island, especially from the reign of the illustrious Bryen Boiroimhe till Henry II. landed upon the coasts.

tion and commendable affection, do accept, ratify, and assent unto this your petition, and do grant that you (for the dilating of God's church, the punishment of sin, the reforming of manners, the planting of virtue, and the increasing of Christian religion) do enter to possess that land, and there to execute, according to your wisdom, whatsoever shall be for the honour of God and the saiety of the realm. And further also we do strictly charge and require, that all the people of that land do with all humbleness dutifulness, and honour, receive and accept you as their liege lord and sovereign, reserving and excepting the right of Holy Church to be inviolably preserved, as also the yearly pension of Peter pence out of every house, which we require to be truly answered to St. Peter and to the Church of Rome. If therefore you do mind to bring your godly purpose to effect, endeavour to travail to reform the people to some better order and trade of life, and that also by yourself and by such others as you shall think meet, true and honest in their life, manners, and conversation, to the end the church of God may be beautified, the true Christian religion sowed and planted, and all other things done, that by any means shall or may be to God's honour and salvation of men's souls, whereby you may in the end receive of God's hands the reward of everlasting life, and also in the meantime, and in this life, carry a glorious fame and an honourable report among all nations."

And that the state of religion was not so languishing as the bull of the Pope would represent, among other testimonies that might be produced, it will be sufficient to insist upon the number among the principal nobility and gentry of the kingdom, that, in the latter part of their life, entered into religious houses, as retirements wherein to spend their remaining days in piety and exercises of devotion.   Among the illustrious personages, who secluded themselves from the pleasures of the world for the sake of devotion, was the pious Flathbheartach an Torsdan O'Neill, who was the first professed penitent in Ireland, and afterwards undertook, according to the custom of those times, a pilgrimage to Rome, in the year of our Lord 1073. Donough, the son of Bryen Boiroimhe, as appears by this history, finished a pilgrimage to the same place ; and devoted himself to a holy life in the abbey of St. Stephen, where he ended his days.   Teige Mac Lorcan, king of Cinseallach, spent the latter part of his life in Glean da Loch, in a most penitent and religious manner.   Cathal, the son of Roger O'Connor, king of the east part of the province of Conacht, ended his life with great devotion in Ardmach ; and Mortough O'Bryen, king of Leath Modha and of the greatest part of Ireland, retired to the same place for his five last years, and died a severe penitent.

Many more instances might be produced of the principal nobility of the kingdom, who ended their days in religious sorrow and the strictest piety, from the reign of the great Bryen Boiroimhe to the arrival of the English upon the coasts ; from whence it is evident, that whoever gave intelligence to Pope Adrian, that the Christian faith was suppressed and abolished throughout the kingdom of Ireland, was as great an enemy to truth and integrity, as he professed himself to be to the piety and character of the Irish nation.

A second evidence, to prove that the doctrines of Christianity were received and established in the island long before the coming of the English, may be deduced, by taking a survey of the many churches, monasteries, and abbeys erected throughout the island by the charity of pious persons, for the benefit of devotion and the service of divine worship, before the English drew breath in the country.   Maolseachluin, king of Meath, and monarch of the island, built St. Mary's abbey, in the city of Dublin, in the year of our redemption 1139.   Donough O'Carrol, king of Oirgiallach, erected the abbey of Mellifont, in the county of Louth ; this pious work was begun at the solicitation of St. Malachias, and completed in the year 1142   St.

Malachias, the bishop of Each Dun, built the abbey of Jobhair
Cintragha, in the year 1144. Diarmuid Mac Morrough, king
of Leinster, laid the foundation of the abbey of Bealtinglass,
in the year of our Lord 1151. The abbey of Beiotif, otherwise
called de Beatudine, in the county of Meath; the abbey
O'Dorna, in the county of Kerry; and the abbey of Boyle, were
erected in the year of our redemption 1161. Daniel O'Bryen,
king of Limerick, built the abbey of the Holy Cross, in the
county of Tipperary, in the year of Christ 1169. The abbey of
Fearmoy, in the county of Cork, was finished in the year 1170.
Many more instances might be produced of churches, abbeys,
monasteries, and other religious foundations, erected in those
pious times, before the English came upon the Irish coasts;
and consequently it follows, that those foreigners did not plant
the Catholic faith in the island, but found it as it was believed
and established for many preceding ages.

A third testimony, in confirmation that Christianity was not
extinguished in the island before the arrival of the English,
may be drawn from the ancient annals of the kingdom, which
give an account of many synods and ecclesiastical conventions,
consisting of the clergy and nobility, that were held with a
design to regulate the discipline of the church, and likewise
matters of secular concern; and it is certain that the affairs of
religion were settled by those assemblies, and canons and injunctions established, from the reign of Donough, the son of
Bryen Boiroimhe, till the English obtained possessions in the
island.

The first convocation of note in Ireland, was assembled at
Fiadh Mac Naonguasa, in the first year of the reign of Mortough O'Bryen, and in the year of Christ 1110. In this synod
the old laws and canons, both ecclesiastical and civil, were revised and corrected; and whatever errors or heretical doctrines
had, through the indolence of the church discipline, crept into
the church, were censured and condemned, and the fomenters
of schism and division brought to punishment.

Another ecclesiastical convention was summoned in the fifth
year of the reign of Mortough above-mentioned, and the whole
body of the clergy and nobility assembled at Rath Breasail, in
the year of our redemption 1115. In this synod the dioceses
were laid out, their several boundaries fixed, and bishops ordained throughout the kingdom.

A third convocation of the clergy and nobility of Ireland
was held at Ceanauus, in the country of Meath, in which

Christianus O'Conaire, bishop of Lismore, presided, and was commissioned with a legatine power from the Pope. In this synod also sat a Roman cardinal, called Johannes Papiron. He was sent from the holy father, to present four copes to the four archbishops in Ireland, to ordain ecclesiastical canons, and to regulate the discipline of the church. In this convention, among other excellent injunctions, the wicked practice of simony was suppressed, usury was censured and forbidden, tithes were ordered to be paid by divine right, rapes, incontinence, profaneness, and immorality, were interdicted and restrained. It would be a repetition to insist upon the particular matters debated and confirmed in this synod, since they have been related before in their proper place. These are arguments of force sufficient to overthrow the aspersions of those writers, who confidently assert that Christianity was extinguished in the island when the English first made an attempt and landed upon the coasts.

The English historians have likewise abused the ancient Irish in another instance, by charging them with barbarities and unheard-of cruelties, and with a peculiar savageness in their nature, that inclined them to the most uncivilised and brutish practices; but to qualify the severity of this censure, it will appear unquestionably true, that five of the superior officers, who came over with the English, were guilty of more vile and inhuman actions than had been committed in the island from the reign of Bryen Boiroimhe till those foreigners arrived. Nothing civil or sacred escaped the fury of these commanders; churches and religious houses were plundered and destroyed without mercy and distinction; murders, rapes, tyranny, and the most unconscionable oppressions, were the recreation of these foreigners, who, without remorse or regret, confounded every thing human and divine, and made the island a most deplorable scene of bloodshed and misery. The Earl of Strangwell, Robert Fitz Stephen, Hugo de Lacy, John de Courcy, and William Aldelmel, were severe instruments in the hands of Providence to chastise the divided natives; as will appear from some instances of their barbarity, but more particularly from the chronicle of Stanihurst and other writers. But divine vengeance, notwithstanding they raged with impunity, fixed a mark of infamy upon the families of these plunderers, for scarce a man of them left a son behind him to enjoy the effects of their father's oppressions; as Stanihurst expressly testifies of the Earl of Strangwell, who, after he had committed inexpressible outrages upon the natives, ravaged and destroyed churches and monasteries, and expelled the clergy, regular and secular, without distinction, died miserably at Dublin, in the year of Christ 1177, after a tyranny of seven years from his first landing in the country. It was observed before, that this English nobleman was married to Aoiffe, the daughter of the king of Leinster ; by this princess he left issue but one daughter, whose name was Isabella ; this lady was contracted to William Marshal, an Englishman, by whom she had five sons and five daughters ; all the sons died childless ; the daughters were married to English noblemen, among whom was divided the country of Leinster, in the year 1230, which brought great and lasting calamities upon that province. Thus were misfortunes entailed upon the posterity of the Earl of Strangwell ; from whom, by his grand-daughters, were derived the Mortimers, the Bruces, and other families of good quality.

Hugo de Lacy, when he had fixed himself in the government of Meath, by a grant from King Henry II. most injuriously treated Clan Colman, and the nobility and gentry of that country : he put as many to the sword as were persons of any distinction, and reduced the inhabitants to the utmost distress. These barbarities procured him the hatred of the people, insomuch that a young gentleman of Meath resolved to destroy the tyrant ; and the better to execute his purpose, he came to a fort which Hugo was raising at Diarmuigh, and disguising himself in the habit of a common labourer, he found an opportunity to accomplish his design. Stanihurst bestows an infamous character upon this English nobleman, and particularly charges him with ungovernable lust, which he brutishly gratified at all adventures. But as the same historian observes, his death was severely prosecuted and revenged by a son of his own name, upon the people of Meath ; for the young Hugo de Lacy, supported by the assistance of John de Courcy, fell upon the inhabitants, plundered the country, and committed the most cruel outrages, that fire and sword in the hands of an enraged enemy could attempt and execute.

The chronicle above cited gives an account that William Adelmel was of a malicious and cruel disposition, was miserably covetous, and the most fickle, false-hearted, and inconstant of men. Among other acts of oppression, he violently seized upon a manor of land, that was possessed by the children of Maurice Fitz Gerald, which was their lawful right and inheritance, and to whom this William bore an irreconcileable hatred.

The old annals of Ireland expressly mention, that when Wil-

ham Adelmel held the command of Limerick by commission
from the king of England, there arose a violent contest between
two princes of the line of the O'Connors, who were brothers,
concerning the government of the province of Conacht.   The
names of these rivals were Cathall Carrach and Cathall Crobhdearg ; and the historian relates, that William Adelmel espoused
the cause of Cathall Carrach, and John de Courcy professed himself on the other side, and declared in favour of Cathall Crobhdearg.   Forces were raised, and many encounters happened, and
the province was miserably plundered by both parties : in this
dispute the principal nobility of Conacht were destroyed, but at
last the controversy was ended by a decisive battle, that was
fought courageously by the Irish and English on both sides,
and victory was for some time in suspense, but the forces of
Cathall Carrach in the end received a general defeat, and he
himself was slain.   After this battle William Aldelmel built a
strong castle for his security at Mileach O'Madden, which he fortified with a good guard, and then returned to Limerick.

Cathall Crobhdearg laid close siege to this garrison, and continued his attack with vigour, that the party within were apprehensive the castle would be taken, and every man of them put
to the sword.   To avoid this military execution they stole away
by night and fled for protection to William Aldelmel at Limerick.   Cathall, in the morning finding the fort without defence
set it on fire, and razed it to the ground.   Aldelmel, after this
misfortune, raised fresh troops, and when he had completed his
numbers, he led them into the province of Conacht, where he
raged in a most hostile manner, and plundering the country, he
found booty of immense value.   But cruelty was the predomi-
nant passion which this nobleman resolved to gratify ; he therefore put all that he found to the sword, without distinction of
clergy or laity, and demolished all the consecrated places, and
destroyed most of the religious houses throughout the province.
For these impious and inhuman practices he was prosecuted by
the discipline of the church, and solemnly excommunicated by
the clergy of Conacht.   This transaction stands upon record in
a book of the annals of Ireland, written about 300 years ago ;
this chronicle is of undisputed authority, and is commonly
known by the name of the Speckled book of Mac Eogain, and
in the Irish language called Leabhar Breac.   The same author
observes likewise, that the vengeance of heaven pursued this
oppressor, William Aldelmel, in a wonderful manner, and fixed
such distortions and strange diseases upon his body, that were

utterly incurable, so that he died in a most deplorable manner, without any symptoms of remorse or repentance, and was deprived of the decent rites of Christian burial; for his body was carried to a village, whose inhabitants he had murdered, and thrown into a pit in unhallowed ground, from whence it was never removed.

Near the same time there arose a violent difference between John de Courcy and Hugo de Lacy the younger, which was carried on with great passion and animosity on both sides. In this contest most of the principal nobility and gentry of Ulster, and the country of Meath, lost their lives, and the people were dreadfully plundered; but in the end John de Courcy was taken prisoner by Hugo, who charged him with treasonable practices against the crown of England, and therefore he delivered him into the hands of the English, who undertook to support their allegations and prove the accusation against him. De Courcy was accordingly sent into England to answer the treason he was charged with, and as soon as he arrived the king commanded him to be laid in irons; but he was soon delivered from his imprisonment, and not only fully pardoned, but received a licence if he pleased to return to try his fortune again in Ireland. For this purpose he set to sea, but was driven back to England fourteen times by storms and bad weather; but nothing discouraged, as Stanihurst relates in his chronicle, he again weighed anchor, but was encountered by a violent tempest and driven upon the coasts of France, where he landed, and in that country he ended his life.

The above cited annalist gives an account, that an English gentleman of the family of the Courcy's had fixed himself in Ireland, and was treacherously slain by Hugo de Lacy and his brother Walter, who conspired his death. To revenge this action, the relations of the deceased took up arms, and many misfortunes arose from this difference, and such heart-burnings between the two families, that they could never be reconciled. Their mutual animosities were at length carried to that height, that they affected the peace of the whole kingdom, insomuch that King John of England was obliged to transport a numerous army, which being joined with several bodies of the Irish, entered the country of Meath, in order to suppress the quarrel, and punish the family of Hugo de Lacy, who had been the aggressor. Hugo had quick intelligence of the march of the king's forces, and fled with his followers to Carrick Feargus. He was pursued close, and being in immediate dangers, the two brothers went on shipboard and sailed to France. In that country it was necessary they should conceal their quality, and for that purpose they disguised themselves in a mean dress, and hired themselves as labourers to work in the garden of an abbot, in the country of Normandy. In this obscurity they remained for some time, but weary of their hard service, and desirous to return to their own country, they at length found an opportunity to discover themselves to their master; when they had made known to him the circumstances of their misfortunes, they entreated him that he would intercede for them to the king of England, and endeavour to obtain their pardon. The abbot immediately undertook the good office, and not only prevailed that they should be forgiven, but that they should be restored to their estates. The brothers under this security returned to Ireland, and John, king of England, died soon after, in the year of Christ 1216.

In the reign of Henry, king of England, very violent wars were carried on between Hugo de Lacy and William Marshall, insomuch that by the hostilities on both sides the country of Meath was almost destroyed, and many of the Irish nobility, who engaged in this dispute, lost their lives. The same William Marshall fought Meills Fitz Henry in many battles with various success, and by these intestine broils, the two provinces of Munster and Leinster were plundered, and the inhabitants reduced to the utmost misery.

Hanmer observes, in his chronicle, that William Marshall was publicly excommunicated by the bishop of Fearns, because he had seized upon a manor of land that was his, and refused to restore it. Under this sentence that cruel Englishman died in his own country, and the divine vengeance severely chastised him for his sacrilege and other impieties, for out of five sons, not one survived to enjoy the cursed acquisitions of the father, who died childless, with a brand upon his memory that will never be worn out.

The abovesaid Meills was of a cruel and merciless disposition, and committed great outrages upon the natives. Among other hostilities, he led his troops to Cluain Mac Nois, and laying close siege to it for twelve days, he took it by storm, and put all he met with to the sword. The houses were plundered, and the provisions and cattle which they found were carried off: nothing, however sacred, escaped the fury of the soldiers; churches and religious houses were pillaged, and all their ornaments and consecrated plate they esteemed as lawful booty.

These barbarous and wicked hostilities were practised by the English wherever they came, and the whole island was almost destroyed by their continual devastations. Lismore and the liberties of it were plundered, as the chronicles of Stanihurst expressly testify, by Hermon Morty and Redmond de la Grose; though it must be confessed that Hermon, before he died, was struck with remorse for all the cruelties he had acted, and as atonement he assumed the habit of a monk, and built the abbey of Dun Broith, in the country of Wexford, in the year of Christ 1279. This nobleman had been very active in reducing the Irish, and was concerned in many wicked and unwarrantable practices; but what made the deepest impression upon his mind was, his being concerned with William Aldelmel in plundering and ravaging the church of Inis Catha, and alienating the revenues belonging to it to their own use.

The Irish were at length enraged by these insupportable oppressions, for when they observed that the English, instead of propagating the religion of Christ, and reforming the rugged manners of the people, had nothing in view but plunder and booty, and that churches and monasteries were not exempt from their covetous and sacrilegious attempts, they formed a design to free themselves from such merciless auxiliaries, and to drive them out of the island. For this purpose the principal of the Irish nobility applied themselves to O'Connor Maonmuighe, king of Conacht, and offered to raise him to the sovereignty of the island, if he would but assist to expel these foreigners, and restore liberty to his country. The first who made these proposals to the king of Conacht was Daniel O'Bryen, king of Limerick, who was followed in the same generous design by Roger, son of Dunsleibhe, king of Ulster, Daniel Mac Carty, king of Desmond, Maolseachluin Beag, king of Meath, and by O'Rourke, king of O'Broin and O'Conmaine. But before any resolutions were formed upon this scheme, O'Connor, king of Conacht, was unfortunately killed by an accident, at Dun Leoga, in Jobh Maine, where he kept his court.

It is evident, from what has been hitherto observed, that the tyranny, the oppression, and many cruelties perpetrated by the English upon the native Irish, was the cause of that disaffection which appeared in general throughout the island. The inhabitants were made a sacrifice of upon all occasions, and when the English quarrelled among themselves, whatever party succeeded, the natives were sure to be the sufferers. The pride, ambition, and covetousness of those foreigners was perfectly insupportable, they offered outrageous violence to the law of nations and the received usages of mankind ; and therefore it is no wonder that the Irish made frequent attempts to depose their lordly masters, and shake off a yoke that they were unable to bear. The English government in Ireland, had it been administered with discretion and good policy, would have been well received by the inhabitants, who naturally are a submissive and obedient people, and esteem the authority of the laws as sacred, when they are executed with moderation and prudence.   And this character is consistent with what John Davies observes, in the last leaf of his Irish history : " There is no nation of people under the sun that doth love equal and indifferent justice better than the Irish, in case it would proceed against themselves in justice, so as they may have the proportion and benefit of the law, when upon any just occasion they require it."   It was the opinion, we perceive, of this author, that the seeds of disobedience were not naturally planted in the people of Ireland ; but the oppressions they suffered, by the tyranny of the English commanders, made them desperate, and urged them on to attempts which they would never have thought of, had they been well used, and treated with that tenderness and humanity which the circumstances of their case so justly deserved.

Notwithstanding what has been said of the cruelties and sacrilegious acts of some of the English, it must be observed, that many of those foreigners, who came into Ireland, were persons of different qualities from those five superior officers above mentioned.   Many of them were men of virtue and strict piety, who promoted the service of God and the cause of religion by erecting churches and monasteries, and bestowing large revenues upon them for their support : and God rewarded their charity and acts of mercy with particular marks of his favour, and not only blessed them in their own persons, but in a noble and worthy posterity.

INDEX.

THE END.

119